Journal of Pentecostal Theology
Supplement Series
9

Editors
John Christopher Thomas
Rickie D. Moore
Steven J. Land

Sheffield Academic Press
Sheffield

Power from on High

The Spirit in Israel's

Restoration and Witness

in Luke–Acts

Max Turner

Sheffield Academic Press

To Lucy,
my beloved

Copyright © 1996 Sheffield Academic Press

Published by
Sheffield Academic Press Ltd
Mansion House
19 Kingfield Road
Sheffield, S11 9AS
England

Typeset by Sheffield Academic Press
and
Printed on acid-free paper in Great Britain
by Cromwell Press
Melksham, Wiltshire

British Library Cataloguing in Publication Data

A catalogue record for this book is available
from the British Library

ISBN 1-85075-756-9

CONTENTS

It was as a young and enthusiastically Pentecostal theological student that I first came to grapple with the issues in this book. James Dunn's *Baptism in the Holy Spirit* had only just been published, and it seemed to mount a formidable attack on the classical two-stage view of conversion and subsequent Spirit-reception to which I was fully committed. Sensing that the evidence did not go Dunn's way in Luke–Acts, I embarked on a thesis on Luke's understanding of the Spirit. The resulting dissertation (submitted in 1980, some years before the contributions afforded by Roger Stronstad's and Howard Ervin's responses to Dunn) maintained there was substantial unexplored middle ground: the Pentecostal gift of the Spirit in Acts was a Christianized version of the Jewish 'Spirit of prophecy', both broader in scope than that envisaged by E. Schweizer and more closely related to conversion–initiation than that envisaged by Haya-Prats (so not simply a *donum superadditum*), while nevertheless technically 'subsequent' to conversion. Essentially I concluded that the Lukan 'Spirit of prophecy' was the source of the whole charismatic dimension of Christian life, bringing wisdom, guidance, revelation, prophecy and doxological speech (including tongues) which both fuelled the Church's witness to outsiders and vigorously shaped its own dynamic life of worship and discipleship. Some of the fruits of that study were published in a series of articles between 1980 and 1985.

I might not have pursued the matter further had it not been for the pleasure of engaging at Aberdeen University with the original and tough-minded young Pentecostal scholar, Robert Menzies. Bob took up significant aspects of my thesis, but pressed them in the direction of classical Pentecostalism (at the very time when further deliberation was moving me towards a more broadly Charismatic position). For him, to say the Spirit in Luke is the Jewish 'Spirit of prophecy' is to say it is empowering for mission: that is, that (for Luke) the focus of the Spirit's activity in a person is not his or her own personal Christian development at all, but rather through him or her to address others. His rigorous and perceptive case caused me to reconsider the evidence, and some of the preliminary results of my rethinking of the (predominantly background) issues were published in a further series of articles in 1991–94. This volume thus represents a second attempt to interpret Luke's understanding of the Spirit (and as it includes revised forms of works I have already published, this book has an unusually high number of references to the author).

The production of yet another work on Luke's theology of the Spirit requires, nevertheless, some justification; for there has recently been something of a spate of them, in English, French and German. I venture the following brief justification of this addition to literature.

1. Despite the many monographs and articles on Luke's view of the Spirit, there has as yet been no critical survey of scholarship on the subject. Writers on the Spirit in Luke–Acts rather rarely make it clear what agenda of questions has dominated their inquiry. There is room, therefore, for a work which endeavours to outline something of the sequence of questions and answers which has built up to the present 'position'. The only attempts that have been made at this to date, in monographs, have been fragmentary, and largely thematic. Part I of this work will attempt a sketch—mainly chronological, but partly thematic—of the issues which dominate modern NT scholarship on the Spirit in Luke–Acts. We believe such a study both highlights the central questions and gives a fair indication of the strengths and weaknesses of the solutions proposed to date.

2. It will be clear from our survey in Part I that there is at present no consensus: the published works on Luke's view of the Spirit offer quite disparate and competing theories of Luke's meaning. We need criteria for assessing rival theories, and so for arriving at Luke's meaning.

3. An important criterion is continuity with Luke's 'background': Luke will inevitably have inherited and built on (and modified) earlier understandings of the Spirit. These have often (rightly in our view) been designated as 'Jewish' in character. But there has not been agreement about the sort of 'Jewish' views he drew upon, what the various Jewish views were, and to what extent the views Luke inherited were already modified by Christian perceptions. At least two notable scholars (Schweizer and Menzies) argue Luke turned back from the earlier Christian understandings (in Matthew and Mark) to a more strictly Jewish view of the Spirit as 'the Spirit of Prophecy'. Without doubting Luke thought of the Spirit as the latter, we shall question whether such scholars have not (at least partly) misunderstood both the Jewish view of 'the Spirit of prophecy' (on which see Part II) and its relation to both early Christian perceptions and to Luke's pneumatology.

4. A second significant criterion relates to how the proposed Lukan pneumatology fits with other Lukan theology (of God's people, and of their salvation). Too often monographs on Luke–Acts attempt to provide a Lukan pneumatology without relating it credibly to other aspects of Luke's theology. While a satisfyingly full account would require more space than

this volume affords, we shall nevertheless attempt to show how our findings mesh with Luke's fuller picture, and with his central concerns.

5. A third important criterion concerns Luke's place in the development of more general New Testament thinking about the Spirit. Most attempts at describing Luke's pneumatology have made little if any attempt to locate his views within a more general history of the development of understanding(s) of the Spirit from Jewish views through to the second century. The only work that has seriously dealt with the question of development (that by Menzies) has, in my view, quite seriously misunderstood it. Menzies has thereby (I think) created a quite implausible antithesis between Luke's reversion to the allegedly 'Jewish' view of the 'Spirit of prophecy' and what he regards as the later and quite distinctively Christian 'soteriological Spirit' in Paul and John. In another volume I argue that Paul's theology, and John's, is merely a logical extension of the 'Spirit of prophecy', but here I attempt to show that Luke's 'Spirit of prophecy' is much more strongly soteriologically orientated than has hitherto been supposed.

6. I hope within the exegesis of Luke–Acts to provide some fresh light on specific Lukan concepts and favoured terms (including e.g. such phrases as 'fill with/ full of the Holy Spirit', 'baptize with the Holy Spirit [and fire]', etc.) which have been of significance not merely for the discipline of New Testament studies but also for the confessional theologies of major streams of Christianity today (whether traditional evangelical, or more distinctively Pentecostal or Charismatic). More importantly, however, I shall seek to advance a more coherent understanding of the general shape of Luke's pneumatology than has hitherto been offered.

9. While this book is primarily intended as a contribution within the discipline of New Testament studies, I shall follow the example of my friend Robert Menzies in offering (in the final chapter) some more theological reflections on the implications of my description of Luke's pneumatology for the church today. Inevitably I must leave most of this kind of discussion to a forthcoming companion volume, but this series quite rightly invites at least some reflection on the implication of exegesis for the contemporary church.

The nature of this work as a contribution within New Testament research has required me to use the full range of scholarly critical tools normally associated with Synoptic research, including tradition criticism and redaction criticism, etc. In some sectors of the anticipated readership, the use of such methods may be questionable; but I shall try at each stage to explain their relevance to the task of interpreting Luke's text as it would be understood by his first-century readers.

Finally, may I say how grateful I am to the editors for the invitation to contribute this volume to the Journal of Pentecostal Theology Monograph

Series. I recognize that I do not stand fully within the Classical Pentecostal tradition, and that my views at many points are not in agreement with those of the very patient editors of this series. I hope, nevertheless, to make a contribution that will stimulate further discussion and bring refinement of understanding. Above all I hope to be able to bring Pentecostal, Charismatic and traditional Evangelicalism closer to agreement.

ACKNOWLEDGMENTS

This work owes a great deal to too many people and institutions for me to name. But special mention must be made of the following:

(1) Professors John O'Neill and Charlie Moule, who at different stages supervised my original doctoral studies with a rigour suitably tempered with patience and Christian friendship. To these, in particular, I owe an inestimable debt.

(2) Professors Don Carson, Howard Marshall, Charlie Moule, Max Wilcox and Dr Peter O'Brien (*inter alios*), who at various points read a number of my articles and encouraged me to write them up as a monograph. In this connection, special mention must be made of Dr Christopher Thomas, the editor of this series, who kindly offered to publish the work, and has been warmly supportive of it throughout, even when in disagreement with some of its thrust and arguments. His advice and comments have been of enormous value.

(3) The University of Aberdeen and London Bible College, who provided the two sabbatical terms which enabled me to complete the task, and especially my immediate colleagues in the respective New Testament departments (Howard Marshall, Ruth Edwards, Conrad Gempf and Stephen Motyer), who cheerfully bore the brunt of the work from which I was released, while also offering unstinting encouragement. For Professor Marshall's example of scholarship and friendship, I shall forever be grateful

(4) Dr Robert Menzies, who has been a constant source of stimulation through his writing and correspondence, and, along with him, the whole community of research students in Aberdeen and London Bible College (especially those of my own research students, who were working in closely related areas—Archie Hui, Mark Strauss and Jon Weatherly. I hope I have not inadvertently stolen too many of their ideas!)

(5) The editors of *Evangelical Quarterly*, *New Testament Studies*, *Novum Testamentum*, *Tyndale Bulletin*, *Trinity Journal* and *Vox Evangelica*, as well as of Inter-Varsity Press and Paternoster Press, for permission to revise and incorporate material from articles earlier published with them.

(6) Jenny Davies, who proof-read this work and Volker Rabens and Gabriele Braun who also read chapters and to the editorial team at Sheffield Academic Press.

(7) My family, who have been the ones to suffer most of the burdens of this project; especially my wife, Lucy, our son, Duncan, and daughter, Abbie. What I owe them for their patient love and support is incalculable.

Max Turner, August 1995

ABBREVIATIONS

ATR	*Anglican Theological Review*
BAGD	W. Bauer, W.F. Arndt, F.W. Gingrich and F.W. Danker, *Greek–English Lexicon of the New Testament*
BBR	*Bulletin of Biblical Research*
BDF	F. Blass, A. Debrunner and R.W. Funk, *A Greek Grammar of the New Testament*
Bib	*Biblica*
BibLeb	*Bibel und Leben*
BJRL	*Bulletin of the John Rylands Library*
BSac	*Bibliotheca Sacra*
BTB	*Biblical Theology Bulletin*
BVC	*Bible et vie chretienne*
BZ	*Biblische Zeitschrift*
CBQ	*Catholic Biblical Quarterly*
CJT	*Canadian Journal of Theology*
CTM	*Concordia Theological Monthly*
DSD	*Dead Sea Discoveries*
EKKNT	Evangelisch-Katholischer Kommentar zum Neuen Testament
ErJb	*Eranos Jahrbuch*
EtB	*Etudes Bibliques*
ExpTim	*Expository Times*
ETL	*Ephemerides Theologicae Lovanienses*
EvQ	*Evangelical Quarterly*
EvT	*Evangelische Theologie*
HeyJ	*Heythrop Journal*
HTR	*Harvard Theological Review*
IB	*Interpreter's Bible*
IBS	*Irish Biblical Studies*
IEJ	*Israel Exploration Journal*
Int	*Interpretation*
ITQ	*Irish Theological Quarterly*
JANES	*Journal for Ancient Near Eastern Studies*
JBL	*Journal of Biblical Literature*
JETS	*Journal of the Evangelical Theological Society*
JJS	*Journal of Jewish Studies*
JPT	*Journal of Pentecostal Theology*
JSNT	*Journal for the Study of the New Testament*
JSS	*Journal of Semitic Studies*
JTS	*Journal of Theological Studies*

KD	*Kerygma und Dogma*
Neot	*Neotestamentica*
NRT	*La Nouvelle Revue théologique*
NTA	*New Testament Abstracts*
NovT	*Novum Testamentum*
NTS	*New Testament Studies*
RB	*Review Biblique*
RefR	*The Reformed Review*
ResQ	*Restoration Quarterly*
RevQ	*Revue de Qumran*
RevRel	*Review for Religions*
RSR	*Revue des Science religieuses*
RHPR	*Revue d'Histoire et de philosophie religieuses*
RSPT	*Revue de Sciences philosophiques et théologiques*
RSR	*Rescherches de Science Religieuse*
RTP	*Revue de Théologie et de philosophie*
SE	*Studia Evangelica*
Sem	*Semitica*
SJT	*Scottish Journal of Theology*
ST	*Studia Theologica*
TD	*Theological Digest*
TDNT	G. Kittel and G. Friedrich (eds.), *Theological Dictionary of the New Testament*
Theol	*Theology*
TLZ	*Theologische Literaturzeitung*
TrinJ	*Trinity Journal*
TRu	*Theologische Rundschau*
TS	*Theological Studies*
TTZ	*Trierer theologische Zeitschrift*
TynB	*Tyndale Bulletin*
TWNT	*Theologisches Wörterbuch zum Neuen Testament*
TZ	*Theogische Zeitschrift*
VoxEv	*Vox Evangelica*
WTJ	*Westminster Theological Journal*
VT	*Vetus Testamentum*
ZNW	*Zeitschrift für neutestamentliche Wissenschaft*
ZTK	*Zeitschrift für Theologie und Kirche*

In the interests of economy of space, all references to standard commentaries are given without a title or short title, and with no following p. or pp.: e.g. Haenchen, 135 = E. Haenchen, *Acts of the Apostles* (Oxford: Basil Blackwell, 1971), p. 135.

Part I

LUKE AND THE SPIRIT IN CONTEMPORARY SCHOLARSHIP

Chapter 1

THE LAYING OF THE FOUNDATIONS: THE HISTORY OF RELIGIONS
SCHOOL AND THE RESPONSE TO ITS CHALLENGE

The agenda for most modern scholarly discussion[1] of the Spirit in Luke's
writings[2] was really set by the developments leading up to and including

1.   I am grateful to the publishers of *Trinity Journal* for permission to include
material here from my earlier study 'The Significance of Receiving the Spirit in Luke–
Acts: A Survey of Modern Scholarship', *TrinJ* 2 (1981), pp. 131-58. That article was
itself a mild revision of part of the first chapter of M.M.B. Turner, 'Luke and the Spirit:
Studies in the Significance of Receiving the Spirit in Luke–Acts' (unpublished PhD
dissertation, Cambridge, 1980). For other surveys of the literature see, e.g., J.D. Dubois,
'De Jean-Baptiste à Jésus: essai sur la conception lucanienne de l'Esprit à partir
des premiers chapitres de l'évangile' (unpublished doctoral dissertation, Strasbourg,
1977), pp. iii-xx; F. Bovon, *Luke the Theologian* (Allison Park: Pickwick, 1987), ch. 4;
R.P. Menzies, *The Development of Early Christian Pneumatology with Special
Reference to Luke–Acts* (Sheffield: JSOT Press, 1991), ch. 1; O. Mainville, *L'Esprit dans
l'oeuvre de Luc* (Montreal: Fides, 1991), pp. 19-47; H.S. Kim, *Die Geisttaufe des
Messias: einem kompositionsgeschichtliche Untersuchung zu einem Leitmotiv des
lukanischen Doppelwerks* (Berlin: Lang, 1993), pp. 18-26.
2.   The name 'Luke' will be used to designate the author both of the Third Gospel
and of Acts. A.C. Clark (*The Acts of the Apostles* [Oxford: Oxford University Press,
1933], pp. 393-408) and A.W. Argyle ('The Greek of Luke and Acts', *NTS* 20 [1974],
pp. 441-45) have argued on linguistic grounds that Luke and Acts do not come from
the same hand, but see the criticism of W.L. Knox (*The Acts of the Apostles*
[Cambridge: Cambridge University Press, 1948], pp. 1-15, 100-109), B.E. Beck ('The
Common Authorship of Luke and Acts', *NTS* 23 [1977], pp. 346-52), R. Maddox (*The
Purpose of Luke–Acts* [Edinburgh: Clark, 1982], pp. 6-9), C.J. Hemer (*The Book
of Acts in the Setting of Hellenistic History* [Tübingen: Mohr, 1989], pp. 30-33) and
I.H. Marshall, 'Acts and the "Former Treatise"', in B.W. Winter and A.D. Clarke
(eds.), *The Book of Acts in Its Ancient Literary Setting* (AICS, 1; Carlisle: Paternoster,
1993), pp. 163-82.
I incline towards the traditional view of the identity of the author, even if allowing
that Luke may only have been a young and occasional member of Paul's circle. Two
objections of weight have been made against the traditional view: (1) Luke's picture of
Paul corresponds too little with the real Paul for the writer of Acts to have been the
apostle's companion, and (2) his account of the church bears the hallmark of 'early
catholicism'. But the first of these objections has been very much overstated: see the

von Baer's magisterial study in 1926. Major works since then have largely posed different solutions to the problems highlighted during this period, and most of them have fallen roughly within the framework of von Baer's own proposed solutions. The Pentecostal Church, which was born and began to flourish within this initial but formative period of scholarship, left surprisingly little if any trace on the academic discussions of the day. At this stage New Testament scholarship and Pentecostal teaching passed like ships in the night, with different passengers and different ports of interest.

1. *The Challenge of the History of Religions School*

O. Pfleiderer's *Der Paulinismus*[3] gave a decisive impetus to truly modern study of New Testament pneumatology by sharply distinguishing Paul's concept of the Spirit from that of the pre-Pauline community.[4] The earliest community, he maintained, did not think of the Spirit as conveying salvation, but merely (as in the narrative portions of the Old Testament) as the power of miracle, ecstasy and revelation—and so a *donum superadditum* (a 'supplementary gift'); it was Paul who first came to expound the Spirit's work as the inner principle of new-creation life itself.[5] This antithesis between the understanding of the Spirit in the primitive community depicted in Acts (and reconstructed from the Pauline epistles, especially 1 Corinthians), and Paul's own teaching, became the subject of H. Gunkel's perceptive and influential monograph, *Die Wirkungen des heiligen Geistes*

rejoinders by, among others, F.F. Bruce, 'Is the Paul of Acts the Real Paul', *BJRL* 58 (1975–76), pp. 282-305; Ellis, 42-51; U. Wilckens, 'Interpreting Luke–Acts in a Period of Existentialist Theology', in L.E. Keck and J.L. Martyn (eds.), *Studies in Luke–Acts* (London: SPCK, 1968), pp. 60-83; J. Jervell, *The Unknown Paul: Essays on Luke–Acts and Early Christian History* (Minneapolis: Augsburg, 1984), pp. 52-76, and Hemer, *Book*, ch. 6. The second objection has been subjected to telling criticism by H. Conzelmann, 'Luke's Place in the Development of Early Christianity' in Keck and Martyn (eds.), *Studies*, pp. 298-316, and I.H. Marshall, ' "Early Catholicism" in the New Testament', in R.N. Longenecker and M.C. Tenney (eds.), *New Dimensions in New Testament Study* (Grand Rapids: Zondervan, 1974), pp. 217-31. Most recently the case for the traditional Lukan authorship has been considerably strengthened by the detailed study of Hemer, *Book*, ch. 8 and *passim*.

3. Leipzig: Hinrichs, 1873.

4. Though this distinction had already been anticipated by B. Weiss, *Lehrbuch der Biblischen Theologie des Neuen Testaments* (Berlin: Hertz, 2nd edn, 1873).

5. The monographs by H.H. Wendt (*Die Begriffe Fleisch und Geist im biblischen Sprachgebrauch* [Gotha 1878]) and J.E. Gloël (*Der heilige Geist in der Heilsverkündigung des Paulus* [Halle 1888]) were written in an attempt to correct Pfleiderer's antithesis.

nach der populären Anschauung der apostolischen Zeit und der Lehre des Apostels Paulus, first published in 1888.[6]

1.1. *Gunkel: The Spirit as Naked Supernatural Power*

Gunkel at times appears to come close to a classical Pentecostal[7] or Charismatic[8] exposition of the Spirit, but his work is really a *historian's* attack on the idealism of Liberal theology, which tended to reduce 'Spirit' to the rational development of ideas. Gunkel argued that for the earliest (pre-Pauline) community the Spirit was essentially not a matter of doctrine, but of experience.[9] And then only certain *types* of experience were traced to the Spirit; for the Spirit was not conceived of as the principle of Christian religious and ethical life.[10] It was given *to* faith, but was not the author of it (*Influence*, pp.16-21). If we ask what was the primary symptom by which earliest Christianity determined that a phenomenon was an activity of the

---

6.   ET: *The Influence of the Holy Spirit: the Popular View of the Apostolic Age and the Teaching of the Apostle Paul* (Philadelphia: Fortress Press, 1979). References are to the English translation except where otherwise indicated.

7.   I use the term 'Pentecostal' (a) in expressions referring to events at Pentecost (Acts 2), or (b) to denote churchmanship (i.e. belonging to Pentecostal denominations). 'Classical Pentecostal' I reserve for an interpretational position on the Spirit in Luke–Acts corresponding approximately to that taught in the main Pentecostal denominations (excluding Oneness Pentecostals), that is, that Spirit Baptism is subsequent to regeneration/salvation and is a special gifting and empowering for Christian service (especially for mission). I will use the phrase 'classical Pentecostal' for this position even if it is held by those in the charismatic renewal movements outside the mainline Pentecostal denominations, that is for those for whom Lederle would prefer to use the term 'neo-Pentecostal'. Otherwise my typology follows that of H.I. Lederle, *Treasures Old and New: Interpretations of 'Spirit-Baptism' in the Charismatic Renewal Movement* (Peabody: Hendrickson, 1988), chs. 1–2.

8.   I use the term 'Charismatic' of interpretational positions which (like the classical Pentecostal one) emphasize the importance of the whole charismatic dimension of Christian life (including e.g. glossolalia, healing and prophecy), but regard this theologically as part of the gift of the Spirit given in conversion. According to this usage G.D. Fee is thus a Pentecostal scholar who embraces a Charismatic rather than a classical Pentecostal interpretation of the Spirit. For a typology of Charismatic interpretations see Lederle, *Treasures*, chs. 3–5.

9.   *Influence*, p. 13. Gunkel recognized charismatic faith as produced by the Spirit, but then precisely because it was *charismatic*.

10. See Gunkel's criticism of Gloël: '(When) J.E. Gloël supposes that in Acts the total "religious and moral life of fellowship in the earliest community" is an effect of the Spirit, this can be proved neither from the Pentecost narrative, in which the Spirit directly works only glossolalia and prophecy, nor from Acts 2.42-47, in which there is not one syllable to indicate that the ideal state of the community described derives from the Spirit' (*Influence*, p. 16; and compare pp. 17-21).

Spirit, the answer would be the blatantly supernatural character of the event. According to Gunkel:

> an activity of the Spirit is ascertained not within the scheme of means and ends but rather within the scheme of cause and effect. Belief in the Spirit is not for the purpose of grasping God's plan for the world but for the purpose of explaining the presence of certain, above all inexplicable, phenomena by means of the transcendent...Accordingly, it is clear what the apostolic age had in mind by the term *Spirit*. It is the supernatural power of God which works miracles in and through the person (pp. 32, 35).

This is then qualified. At least some expressions of supernatural power were considered by the community to be demonic, rather than traced to the Spirit, and yet others could not be derived from the Spirit because they did not relate to the Christian community (pp. 36-48). In the final analysis,

> Activities of the Spirit are mysterious demonstrations of power in the sphere of human existence which enjoy some kind of connection with the life of the Christian community, which in any event do a person no harm, which often occur by naming the name of God or Christ, and which in all instances concern only such persons who are not unworthy of fellowship with God. The Spirit himself is the supernatural power sent from God through Christ to believers in whom he does great things (p. 58).

Glossolalia was not only the most striking gift of the Spirit in the earliest church but, according to its understanding of the Spirit, also the most characteristic.[11] All Christians were considered to be filled with this Spirit (albeit in varying degrees; 42-43), which was considered to be a heavenly substance which could be poured out (Acts 2.33), conveyed by laying on of hands, and seen (Lk. 3.22; Acts 2.3: *Influence*, pp. 42-43 and 59-66). Sometimes the Spirit was conceived of as an abiding power which lived with men and, on occasions, became more prominent; more often each act of the Spirit was traced to a repeated inspiration (pp. 42-43).

The *theological significance* of the Spirit for the primitive community lay (Gunkel claims) in part in the authoritative presence of God which the gift betokened but, primarily, in the eschatological dimension of which it was an index. The claim of the early church to have the Spirit must be read against a background of the Jewish doctrine that the Spirit had been withdrawn until the eschaton: 'what a powerful impression the πνεῦμα must have made when its fullness appeared to a Judaism bereft of the Spirit' (p. 70). The

---

11. *Influence*, pp. 31-33. Gunkel argues that in 1 Cor. 14.37 Paul uses traditional language according to which the *pneumatikos* is the man who speaks in tongues; it is the role of the 'prophet' to interpret them. But here Gunkel is reading through the spectacles of mantic phenomena: see T.M. Crone, *Early Christian Prophecy* (Baltimore: St Mary's University Press, 1973), pp. 15-38.

Spirit had come in Jesus as the power of the age to come, the presence of the kingdom. 'Where the Spirit of God is, there the kingdom of God is'.[12]

Paul's view of the Spirit too, Gunkel urged, should be traced fundamentally to his experience. If Paul came to view the Spirit as the power of Christian living, that is (arguing against H.H. Wendt[13]) not because he originally held to some alleged Old Testament/Jewish idea of the Spirit as the source of ethical renewal and new creation life (such a concept is altogether rare in Judaism), nor (arguing against J. Gloël) because he got such a concept from Jesus or from the early apostles. It was rather because he saw the *effect* the Spirit was having on the community, and the divine *purpose* which gave coherence to the Spirit's various activities, and eventually interpreted these in terms of the Old Testament passages. Essentially his was a projection of the earliest church view that the Spirit is the source of miracle: Paul simply saw the stamping of the life of Christ on men and women as the Spirit's most spectacular wonder!

Gunkel's achievement was remarkable, and his thesis was stated crisply and cleanly. In brief compass he had raised many of the questions which still face modern scholarship, and he had unquestionably established the importance of the supernatural and experiential dimension in the church's earliest pneumatology (against the prevailing immanentist views of the Spirit espoused by Gunkel's contemporaries[14]). That is not to say his views have commanded universal assent! His case that Judaism had no living hope for an ethical working of the Spirit has been widespreadly criticized with appeal to the rabbis and to Judaism more generally.[15]

There are also notable problems with Gunkel's view that for the earliest community the Spirit was intrinsically naked supernatural power. First, while all our available evidence indicates that, from the very beginning, the earliest church claimed the Spirit to be poured out universally on believers, it is not

12. 'Wo Geist Gottes, da Reich Gottes', *Wirkungen*, p. 59.

13. *Begriffe*. Gunkel could find such a view only in Isa. 11.1-2; 28.6; 32.15ff.; Ezek. 36.26-27; Ps. 51.13; 143.10, and perhaps Wis. 12.10, and did not regard it as a live hope in Judaism.

14. See Gunkel's opening remarks: *Influence*, pp. 1-2.

15. By F. Büchsel, *Der Geist Gottes im Neuen Testament* (Gütersloh: Bertelsmann, 1926, on whom see below) and W.D. Davies, *Paul and Rabbinic Judaism* (London: SPCK, 3rd edn, 1970), ch. 8, in the name of rabbinic Judaism; and by J. Vos, *Traditionsgeschichtliche Untersuchungen zur paulinischen Pneumatologie* (Assen: Van Gorcum, 1973), and J.-J. Suurmond, *The Ethical Influence of the Spirit of God: An Exegetical and Theological Study with Special Reference to 1 Corinthians, Romans 7.14–8.30, and the Johannine Literature* (PhD dissertation, Fuller Theological Seminary, 1983), in the name of the Old Testament and Judaism more generally. Menzies (*Development*, chs. 3–5 and 12–13) has attempted to reestablish Gunkel's view, though he appears to have overlooked Suurmond's thesis.

easy to see how the church could have come to the conviction (by observation) that all had received the gift of the Spirit in Gunkel's sense. Did all
really manifest naked supernatural power? Secondly, there is an inade-
quately explained tension between the theologically nuanced description of
the Spirit in Jesus' ministry (as the presence of the kingdom of God, etc.)
and the relatively crude concepts attributed to the earliest church's pneumatology. Was there then no connection between the pneumatology of the
traditions about Jesus, and that of the earliest community which used the
same tradition? Thirdly, the view of the Spirit Gunkel attributes to the earliest community is simply *not sufficiently christocentric* to be a complete
account of even the most primitive understanding of the Spirit: from the
beginning the Spirit was understood as the gift of the risen Lord, and
granted to enable the extension of his rule.[16] Fourthly, the gospel tradition
in the early church regarded the disciples of Jesus as partaking in his mission, and sharing his power *before* the cross (Mk 6.7 and pars.; Lk. 9.54;
10.1-12, 17-20): why, then (if Gunkel be right and the earliest community
regarded the Spirit as no more than naked power) did the same community
that used these traditions set the *terminus a quo* of its reception of the gift
of the Spirit *after* the cross and resurrection?[17] Fifthly, and most importantly,
Gunkel's whole starting point is fundamentally wrong: the earliest community was a Jewish community, and intertestamental Judaism did not use the
term Spirit as an explanation of all otherwise inexplicable manifestations of
supernatural power; only certain types of event were regularly attributed to
the Spirit—principally those that could be classed as manifestations of the
'Spirit of prophecy'; namely revelation, wisdom and charismatic speech.
Other types of miracles were usually (though not always) attributed to
angels, God's hand, 'power', etc. Once this is recognized, it is immediately
possible to see the connecting links between the conception of the Spirit in
Judaism, that in the Gospels and that in the earliest church described in Acts.
Gunkel's wrong starting point obscured this for several generations of
scholarship.

With respect to our own enquiry after a specifically Lukan theology of
the Spirit, and its relationship to the pneumatology of the early church,
we need to note the obvious further methodological problem in Gunkel's
work. Essentially he proceeded as though Acts was simply a quarry for the
earliest church's views on the Spirit, and did not make any serious attempt

16. See A.J. Hultgren, *Christ and his Benefits* (Philadelphia: Fortress Press, 1987),
pp. 31-36.

17. We might also note the problem that Jesus, the Pneumatic 'par excellence'
according to Gunkel (*Influence*, p. 71), did not demonstrate what Gunkel regarded as
the most characteristic expression of the Spirit's work—glossolalia.

to elucidate the Lukan interest. It is barely surprising that a later generation of scholars, less convinced that Acts represents historical tradition, was inclined simply to attribute the vivid portrayal of the experiential dimension in Acts as much, or more, to Luke's interest[18] as to the character of the Spirit in the primitive church.

In his exposition of the popular early church concept(s) of the Spirit, Gunkel had perhaps rightly emphasized the experiential dimension, and he had drawn from both Jewish and Greek (pagan) literature to illustrate his thesis. He had not, however, pressed the question of the *religions-geschichtlich* background of the experience he was describing. In 1919 and 1921 two books were to appear, both written by Hans Leisegang, but with essentially a single thesis: the majority of the Spirit-material reflects a thoroughly Hellenistic encounter with *pneuma*, not a Jewish one. To this hypothesis I now turn.

1.2. *Leisegang: The Spirit of Pagan Prophetism*

In 1910, W. Bousset developed Gunkel's thesis of Paul's indebtedness to Hellenistic motifs for his pneumatology;[19] and by 1913, R. Reitzenstein had pointed to the importance of mystical encounter with the divine, for Hellenistic religion, in his seminal work *Die hellenistischen Mysterien-religionen*. Leisegang's first monograph, *Der Heilige Geist: Das Wesen und Werden der Mystisch-Intuitiven Erkenntnis in der Philosophie und Religion der Griechen* (1919) analysed the part played by *pneuma* in such experiences. The book concentrated mainly on Philo, particularly on his concept of πνεῦμα προφητικόν ('Spirit of prophecy'). It was to be a test-case of the history-of-religions school hypothesis that Philo provides a bridge between ancient Greek concepts of the Spirit and those found in the church. The findings were to help decide the more general question, 'Is the teaching about the Holy Spirit of Greek or Semitic origin?'[20] Leisegang's conclusion with respect to Philo's position was that he had sold out to Hellenism. It is a tribute to the importance of this work—and to its thoroughness—that it is still in print.[21]

18. So (e.g.) Lampe, Schweizer, Parratt, Dunn, Kremer and Haya-Prats in the works cited below.

19. See especially *Kyrios Christos* (New York: Abingdon, 1970), pp. 181-99. Bousset found the closest analogies to Paul's doctrine of *pneuma* not in classical Greek thought, but in syncretistic Hellenism.

20. *Geist*, p. 4.

21. But see the criticisms of his understanding of *pneuma* in Philo made by H. von Baer, *Der Heilige Geist in den Lukasschriften* (Stuttgart: Kohlhammer, 1926), p. 27 n. 18; G. Verbeke, *L'Evolution de la doctrine du pneuma du stoicisme à S. Augustin* (Paris: Brower, 1945), pp. 236-60, and M.E. Isaacs, *The Concept of Spirit* (London:

More directly relevant to our enquiry, however, is Leisegang's second work, *Pneuma Hagion: Der Ursprung des Geistesbegriffs der synoptischen Evangelien aus der griechischen Mystik* (1922), which applies the insights of his earlier study to the origins of the Synoptists' Spirit material. Reacting against the one-sided claims of E. Norden and A. Harnack that the gospel traditions were purely Jewish (and that to find any trace of Hellenism in them 'ist...der Gipfel der ἀνιστορησία'[22]), Leisegang brought the counterclaim that all the material pertaining to the Spirit in the life and teaching of Jesus was late and derived from Hellenism,[23] more specifically, from the sphere of mysticism.

Four examples of his treatment of the Spirit in the Lukan writings will amply illustrate the eccentricity of his thesis (if also giving a hint of its genius).

1. Luke's account of the *virgin conception by the Spirit* (Lk. 1.32-35) derives essentially from Greek manticism, he claims (*Pneuma*, pp. 14-71). It is to be parallelled by (e.g.) the classic portraits of the Delphic prophetess receiving spirit by sitting on a tripod over the cleft whence πνεῦμα was supposed to rise.[24] Leisegang perceived that the Delphic prophetess received this 'spirit' in the *womb*, and he knew that in Luke's 'parallel' story such union gave birth to a *child*, rather than merely prophecy. He admits that this is unusual, but he tries to find a bridge between begetting of words and begetting of a child, partly in the myths concerning the birth of the prophet-gods (e.g. Dionysius and Branchus), and partly in a lay misunderstanding of mystical encounters and fructification of the soul by the Logos (such as Leisegang finds in Philo).[25]

Heythrop Monographs, 1976), pp. 28, 29, 54-8, 60-61, 141-42.

22. '[I]s...the acme of unhistoricity': so E. Norden, *Agnostos Theos* (Stuttgart: Teubner, 1956), p. 112.

23. *Pneuma*, p. 5 and *passim*. Since the fairly general recognition of M. Hengel's thesis (viz. that Hellenism had pervaded Judaism at all levels, in Palestine and outside it, even before the Christian era, see *Judaism and Hellenism* [London: SCM Press, 1974]), much of the discussion naturally sounds antiquated. Cf. also I.H. Marshall, 'Palestinian and Hellenistic Christianity: Some Critical Comments', *NTS* 19 (1973), pp. 271-87.

24. Cf. the descriptions given by Diodoros 16.26; Strabo, *Geography* 9.3.5; and Plutarch, *De Defectu Oraculorum* 432-35. But these are hardly close parallels: see Verbeke, *Evolution*, pp. 260-87; P. Amandry, *La Mantique Apollinienne à Delphes* (Paris: Boccard, 1950), pp. 215-30, and Crone, *Prophecy*, pp. 26-35.

25. The most careful criticism of Leisegang's view of the virgin conception is that given by J.G. Machen, *The Virgin Birth of Christ* (London: Marshall, 1930), pp. 360-79.

2.   The gospel tradition of *Jesus' Jordan experience*, Leisegang argues, is intrinsically parallel to Jesus' virginal conception: at some stage in its history it was an allegorical description of a mystical birth of the soul of Jesus, the dove representing the female principle or the spiritual Jesus produced by the fusion of the male and female principles in heaven.[26] Luke, by reference to Jesus as πλήρης πνεύματος ('full of the Spirit'), brings his account into line with the Hellenistic concept of the prophetic spirit as the spirit of 'enthusiasm' (p. 93).

3.   Luke has taken the saying about 'the *sin against the Spirit*' out of its original context in the Beelzebul controversy, and put it in a context of witnessing to Jesus in the face of persecution. By his placing of it in this context Luke has interpreted 'blasphemy against the Spirit' (12.10-11) as rejection of the prophetic Spirit given to aid the disciple's witness (12.12).[27] Such teaching is only plausible, Leisegang tells us, at a time, and within circles, where the Holy Spirit, and speaking in the Spirit, are amongst the most significant factors to the new religion—and that could only be in the Hellenistic community (p. 109).

4.   Central to the traditions concerning the *gift of the Spirit to the disciples* is a view of the Spirit as the power of miraculous speech, primarily prophecy and tongues (pp. 112-23). As there is no suitable Old Testament background to the phenomenon of glossolalia, it is to be derived from, e.g., the γλῶττα βακχεῖα ('Bacchic tongues') of Greek prophetism.[28] The Pentecost account that Luke offers is thus to be understood as a mixture of Jewish Sinai-tradition, Christian reflection (on Joel's promise of signs on earth, [fire in Acts 2.19] and on the tradition that the Baptist had promised a baptism of fire) and mantic prophetism (for the mention

26. See *Pneuma*, pp. 80-95. The former is alleged to be represented in the *Gospel according to the Hebrews*, and *Acts of Thomas*. But see the apposite comments made by C.K. Barrett, *The Holy Spirit and the Gospel Tradition* (London: SPCK, 2nd edn, 1966), p. 37.

27. *Pneuma*, pp. 96-111.

28. Cf. Aristophanes, *Ranae* 357; *Diodorus* 4.66; Plutarch, *De Pythiae Oraculis* 406. See also Leisegang, *Pneuma*, pp. 118ff. Leisegang regards glossolalia as incomprehensible utterance, such as was given by the oracle at Greek oracle-sites (and which it was the task of the 'prophets' to interpret; see e.g. Plato, *Phaedrus* 244-45) or was the result of Dionysiac *enthysiasmos*. But the phenomenon of glossolalia is more difficult to assess than Leisegang realizes; compare the cautious handling by J.D.G. Dunn, *Jesus and the Spirit* (London: SCM Press, 1975), pp. 148-52, 242-44 and 304-305. See also Turner, 'Luke and the Spirit', pp. 132-33, 256-57.

of tongues—the nature of which Luke is alleged to have changed[29]—and the advent of the Spirit with a sound of rushing wind[30]).

Leisegang's second monograph had relatively little of permanent value to offer. History may well claim its most vital contribution was to stimulate the works largely written to refute him. Nevertheless, this work focussed attention on the nature of the Spirit in the Lukan writings as πνεῦμα προφητικόν,[31] and it sharply posed (though it did not satisfactorily answer) the *religionsgeschichtlich* question of the vital background to this concept.

2. *The Response to the History of Religions School*

In 1926, two substantial works on the Spirit were published, both heavily criticizing Gunkel and Leisegang: Friedrich Büchsel's encyclopedic *Der Geist Gottes im Neuen Testament*,[32] and Hans von Baer's *Der Heilige Geist in den Lukasschriften*. The latter remains to this day one of the most significant monographs on the subject.

29. This follows from Leisegang's view of glossolalia as essentially *incomprehensible*, a view which provided the cornerstone for various attempts (including Leisegang's) to reconstruct the sources of the Pentecost story. For an early criticism of the premise that glossolalia was misunderstood by Luke see K.L. Schmidt, *Die Pfingsterzählung und das Pfingstereignis* (Leipzig: Hinrichs, 1919); for the very great difficulty of reconstructing the sources behind the Pentecost narrative see N. Adler, *Das Erste Christliche Pfingstfest* (Munster: Aschendorff, 1938), pp. 30-46: such theories shatter on the linguistic unity of the passage.

30. *Pneuma*, pp. 130ff; cf. *Geist*, pp. 51 and 227.

31. But it must be pointed out that the parallels Leisegang offered to Christian reception of the Spirit were quite inadequate. Mantic πνεῦμα as described by Strabo and Plutarch is material, restricted to special places and conditions, and can only act on those of special disposition. For Plutarch (*De Defectu Oraculorum* 40, 432) the effect of the spirit is purely physiological and is compared directly to the action of wine exciting the soul to an animal-like intuition about the future: the πνεῦμα does not impart the visions/oracles. Indeed Plutarch has to defend himself against the charge that his theory reduces inspiration to a merely psychological or physiological phenomenon. To do this he makes Lamprias, his mouthpiece, claim that while πνεῦμα is the divine plectrum, the efficient causes of inspirition are: (1) the earth which produces the divine outflow, (2) the divine sun which enables the earth to do so, and (3) the demons which control the proceedings (*De Defectu Oraculorum* 48, 436).

As Verbeke correctly summarizes the matter, 'la condition objective de cette divination...c'est la sympathie universelle du cosmos préconisée par les Stoiciens' (*Evolution*, p. 273). Plutarch merely fuses this with Platonism: cf. Amandry, *Mantique*, pp. 216-23. Gunkel (*Influence*, p. 47) had stressed the Jewish background to this central concept of πνεῦμα προφητικόν.

32. Gütersloh: Bertelsmann, 1926.

2.1. *F. Büchsel: The Spirit as Sonship to God*

Büchsel's main contribution to the *Forschung* lay in his attempt to bridge
the gulf between the religious experience of Jesus and that of the primitive
and Pauline churches: a rejection of the position taken by Pfleiderer, Gunkel
and Bousset. He set out first to show that John the Baptist's promise of
Spirit-baptism assumes that the Spirit is not merely the power to work
miracles, but the moral power of new life and communion with God
promised by the Old Testament. Jesus was the first man of the Spirit
(*Pneumatiker*), and he became this by virtue of his Jordan experience—
though Büchsel does not wish hereby to deny the virgin conception by the
Spirit.[33] Nevertheless, the Spirit now penetrates every aspect of Jesus'
ministry: it is this endowment which makes him the man he becomes.[34] He
owes to the Spirit both the power behind his miracles and the authority
behind his teaching;[35] but Jesus is to be sharply distinguished from the
magician and the θεῖος ἄνθρωπος ('divine man') by the fact that at the
heart of his experience of the Spirit is the awareness of unity in love with
the Father—in other words his 'sonship'.[36] His Spirit endowment is his sonship, his communion with the Father, his possession of God's love.[37] The
miracles, obedience in the temptation, the presence of the kingdom of God,
and willingness to face the cross all spring from this: he will rule as God's
son, not as his substitute (p. 214). The Jordan experience was a decisive
landmark in Jesus' awareness of his 'sonship': only when it reached the
level now attained could it become the mainspring of his ministry.[38] Here
then is the bridge between Jesus and Paul: the Spirit is the Spirit of sonship.
Yet Jesus was unique in receiving the Spirit directly from God, while his
disciples receive the Spirit only by virtue of their relationship to him
(p. 264).

When Büchsel comes to reconstruct the pneumatology of the earliest
post-resurrection community (mainly from Acts, but always testing it by
comparison with the epistles) his account is sometimes disappointingly thin

---

33. *Geist*, ch. 10, is mainly a criticism of Leisegang's views of the Hellenistic
origins of the virgin conception stories.

34. 'Für alle drei Evangelisten ist Jesus kraft seiner Begabung mit dem Geist in der
Taufe, was er in der Geschichte ist' (*Geist*, p. 150; cf. p. 223).

35. *Geist*, pp. 170-71, 177-78.

36. *Geist*, pp. 174, 226.

37. 'Jesu Geistbesitz ist Gottessohnschaft' (*Geist*, p. 165); 'Der Geist ist Gemein-
schaft mit Gott, Besitz der Leibe Gottes' (*Geist*, p. 168).

38. *Geist*, pp. 219ff. Büchsel insists that the baptismal experience was neither
merely a signal to commence the messianic ministry, nor simply the receiving of power
to exercise such a ministry: the essential transformation was in the new dynamic of
Jesus' consciousness of 'sonship' (*Geist*, pp. 223-24).

(pp. 228-66). Perhaps his most striking suggestion is that, historically speaking, 'Pentecost' (and especially the ecstatic phenomena associated with it) was a *spiritual reflex of resurrection joy, welling up in the disciples who already, in some sense, had received the Spirit*. Their experience then spread contagiously (pp. 236-38). For Büchsel, Pentecost was thus not, as Luke suggests, the irruption of the Spirit on those who had not previously received the Spirit. Büchsel's suggestion, however, is itself probably merely the reflex of his own view that the experience of the Spirit is the experience of sonship and communion with God, both of which he regards as experienced at least from the resurrection onwards, if not before, in the ministry of Jesus itself.

Büchsel goes on to assert that the early evidence of the Spirit was universal[39] and, while it was vigorous and included ecstatic elements (such as tongues), it was not primarily 'enthusiastic' in the derogatory sense. It follows from Büchsel's view of Pentecost that the tongues and prophecy that Luke describes were merely a sign of the Spirit at a deeper level. To take these phenomena as the essence of, or the characteristic of the Spirit is to confuse 'the mere froth of the Spirit for the flood' (262)! The Old Testament was expecting nothing less than religious renewal through the Spirit, and this is what Luke intends to depict in his summaries in Acts and by his description of (e.g.) Stephen as a man 'full of Spirit and wisdom' (6.10), or as 'full of faith and the Holy Spirit' (6.5).[40] Contra Leisegang, we need never step outside a Jewish-Christian milieu to explain the Spirit-motifs we discover in Luke (p. 253).

It is quite clear what Büchsel considers to have been the experience of Jesus, and that this relates directly to his understanding of *Paul's* theology. He also believes that the earliest community thought of the Spirit as the transforming power of fellowship with God as sons; though it is not entirely clear when he considers such 'sonship' to have commenced (probably within Jesus' ministry). By contrast he knows exactly when *Luke* believes the Spirit to have come on the disciples (Pentecost!), but as a result he seems to be rather unsure what Luke meant by that coming of the Spirit, even if he insists strongly that, for Luke, reception of the Spirit involves much more than is envisaged in the Joel prophecy quoted by Peter in Acts 2.17-21. The problem for Büchsel, and for all who followed him, is precisely how much more, and on what basis such a claim can be justified.

39. Especially *Geist*, pp. 228-29.
40. *Geist*, pp. 254-55.

2.2. *Hans von Baer: The Spirit as Eschatological Sonship and as Empowering for Mission*

Von Baer's monograph was more directly and explicitly concerned with the questions raised by Gunkel and Leisegang than Büchsel's had been. Methodologically his thesis was a remarkable and surefooted forerunner of modern redaction criticism,[41] both in his *intention* to elucidate the specifically *Lukan* pneumatology, and in his skillful execution of the task. But our interest must focus primarily on his findings and on their contribution to our understanding of what Luke meant by the gift of the Spirit.[42]

From the outset von Baer showed his awareness that the Spirit-material demonstrated considerable variation of nuance, but, he explained, we need never resort to explaining the various New Testament *pneuma* concepts in terms of influence from foreign cults. Despite all the diversity within it, the New Testament *pneuma* material stands together as a unity, separated by a deep gulf from the conceptions of 'spirit' in the pagan world (*Geist*, p. 4). To demonstrate this in Luke–Acts, against the thrust of Bousset and Gunkel, von Baer had to be able to show that the Spirit on the disciples after Pentecost is essentially the same Spirit (functionally) that was on Jesus (hence demonstrating the unity of the material), and that the Spirit in some sense *mediated the religious and ethical life of Jesus*. It was not sufficient for him merely to show that the Spirit was a power available both to Jesus and to his disciples, if he were to answer Gunkel.[43] To combat Leisegang effectively, he had also to show that the individual Spirit-motifs were derived from a Jewish background, and, if possible, that any bridge connecting the Spirit on Jesus with the Spirit on the disciples was erected of intrinsically Jewish materials, not Hellenistic ones.

To accomplish this task von Baer developed an observation made by E. Meyer, namely that *Luke had a special concern for salvation history* (p. 43). Von Baer set out to prove that Luke depicts the Spirit, first and foremost, as *the driving-force of redemptive history*. Here was a uniting theme to the *pneuma* material which was of indubitably Jewish extraction. Thus, according to von Baer, Luke envisaged three quite distinct epochs. In the first of these Luke (following sources) depicts a number of figures, including John the Baptist, as representatives of the epoch of Israel,

---

41. It is surprising that Hans Conzelmann (*The Theology of Saint Luke* [London: Faber, 1960]) does not note this especially in view of the closeness of their theories at major points. There are simply five footnotes to v. Baer (seven in the index; but two are actually to Bauer!), only two of which give any hint of the real parallel between their works: *Theology*, pp. 150 n. 1, 209 n. 1.

42. The outline below has already been published in briefer form in my 'Jesus and the Spirit in Lucan Perspective', *TynB* 32 (1981), pp. 3-42.

43. *Geist*, pp. 16-20, 184-92.

endowed with the Spirit of prophecy, preparing for the advent of the messiah. With the virginal conception and baptism of Jesus by the Spirit we have the dawn of a new epoch 'in which God's Spirit makes his appearance in this world in the nature of God's Son' ('als Wesen des Gottessohnes', p. 61). Von Baer thinks that Jesus' baptismal experience of the Spirit answers to John the Baptist's promise (3.16), and that Luke has thus deliberately accommodated the Jordan experience to Pentecost and to Christian baptism (which according to von Baer is a fulfilment of the same promise):[44] the dove of the new covenant comes upon him at the waters of Jordan and this transforms John's baptism into Christian baptism (pp. 157-67). Further, Jesus, like the disciples, receives the Spirit as empowering.[45] Lk. 4.18 refers to a governing power on him and ordination as messiah (p. 65), which, like the disciples (Lk. 11.13; Acts 1.14, etc.), he must pray to receive (Lk. 3.21).[46] The theme of the gospel is to display this Spirit working in the Son (empowering the preaching of good news, throwing back the powers of darkness and inaugurating the kingdom),[47] while in Acts the glorious march of the 'Pentecostal' Spirit to Rome is described.

But these are two completely separate epochs, and hence Luke must remove any hint (e.g. Lk. 10.19-20) that the disciples have already participated in the Spirit before Pentecost.[48] Luke further defines the two epochs in two ways: first, he makes sin against the Spirit, in Lk. 12.10-12, a possibility which assumes the (as yet) future gift of the Spirit, and contrasts this with blasphemy against the Son of Man in the epoch of the ministry.[49] Secondly, he creates 'an interregnum in the Spirit's activity', between Jesus' ascension and Pentecost (p. 179): in this period the Spirit is no longer present on earth, as is clear from the fact that the disciples must resort to lots in order to choose the successor to Judas (Acts 1.12-26).[50]

Pentecost was the decisive witness of Jesus' ascension, marking the beginning of a new era, inaugurated (according to Luke) by a special sort of glossolalia (p. 90). The third epoch, the 'Heilsepoche des Geistes' has commenced (p. 93): Jesus is attested by the gift of the Spirit as messiah, and the Spirit now continues Jesus' work. The Christian experiences the Spirit,[51]

44. *Geist*, pp. 65ff.
45. *Geist*, pp. 61ff, 164ff.
46. *Geist*, pp. 18, 34, 61.
47. *Geist*, especially pp. 69-73 and, on Lk. 11.20, pp. 132-36.
48. *Geist*, pp. 71-73, 132ff.
49. *Geist*, pp. 75ff, 137-44. Against this view see Marshall, 517-18; Fitzmyer, 962-66.
50. *Geist*, p. 83.
51. With Gunkel, von Baer insists that receiving the Spirit in Luke's writings is not a

not primarily as the power of moral renewal,[52] but as the inner certainty of Jesus' Lordship and as the driving force to witness and to preach.[53] Thus, as cause (*Ursache*) and effect (*Folge*) πνεῦμα and εὐαγγελίζεσθαι ('to preach the gospel') belong to the basic structure of Luke's theology and provide the *idée fixe* of his two works.[54]

Luke, then, is mainly concerned with salvation history (not with inner moral renewal) and with the establishing of God's reign (p. 108). The power which puts God's plan of salvation into effect, in each epoch, is the Holy Spirit (p. 109). While it is clear that in the interest of his thesis there was a tendency for von Baer to depict Jesus as the first Christian in an epoch before others could become Christians, he was, nevertheless, careful enough to point out that in each epoch the Spirit manifested himself in slightly different ways.[55] But he did not undertake to explore these differences in detail[56] and, indeed, played them down, as they ran counter to the substance of his thesis, the general outline of which has been widely accepted.

Despite the excellence of many of von Baer's insights, there arise some important questions about what he means by receiving the Spirit. If Jesus is the divine Son by virtue of the virginal conception by the Spirit, and if, as von Baer asserts, he therefore cannot grow in the Spirit as John the Baptist can (Lk. 1.80: *Geist*, p. 49), then the Jordan experience is nothing less than a messianic empowering (pp. 61-65). How, in that case, can we speak of the disciples receiving the *same* Spirit *functionally* as was on Jesus? On the one hand, consecration to messiahship is surely a *unique* experience of the Spirit. On the other hand, even if we allow the alleged parallel of the early church's experience with Jesus' empowering, this only leads to a second difficulty. It means, in accordance with the parallel of Jesus' case, that

matter of acquiescence in a dogma (*Geist*, p. 99), but of immediate and vigorous experience (pp. 4, 174, 179).

52. *Geist*, pp. 95-98: though the Spirit's presence does lead to a sense of unity with the risen Lord, to fearlessness, to joy and to the 'fear of the Lord' (pp. 187-90).

53. *Geist*, pp. 98ff.

54. *Geist*, p. 2, and *passim*.

55. 'Am Wesen Jesu... ist der Geist in anderer Weise beteiligt, wie das in dem Wesen des letzten Trägers des Prophetengeistes der Fall war, und der irdische Jesus hat diesen seinen Sohnesgeist nicht unmittelbar den Jüngern übermittelt, sondern als ganz neue Gabe von Himmel her ist der Pfingstgeist über die Apostel ausgegossen worden' (*Geist*, p. 111; compare pp. 4, 45, 103).

56. In practice the distinction von Baer made was between the Spirit in the *first* epoch and that in the *third*—and it lay in the fact that in the latter case the Spirit was the Spirit of Jesus; i.e. not merely the Spirit of the risen Christ, but the Spirit that was upon Jesus of Nazareth (*Geist*, pp. 42, 170ff.). It follows that in the very making of this distinction, Baer simultaneously identifies the Spirit in the second epoch (functionally) with that in the third.

receiving the Spirit in Acts is basically empowering to preach and to witness to Jesus. If this is so, von Baer should surely admit Gunkel's position to be correct: the Spirit in the communities depicted in Acts *has little to do with the inner life of the Christian's everyday experience*. And in that case we should wish to go on to ask why it is that Luke has linked reception of the Spirit so closely to conversion and baptism with which, *ex hypothesi*, it does not appear to have clear theological connections.

There is an important tension in von Baer's work here (or in Luke's) between two quite different concepts of the gift of the Spirit. Is the Spirit received as the source of eschatological 'life' and 'sonship' (accommodating Jesus' baptismal experience to what Paul would probably say of ordinary Christian conversion/initiation), or is the Spirit received as the empowering of the Christian mission (accommodating the apostles' experience at Pentecost, and that of all future Christians at their baptism, to Jesus' baptismal anointing with the Spirit)? It does not help to attempt to resolve the tension by affirming that the Spirit is simply the 'life' or 'vitality' of God (whatever activities that 'life' gives impulse to) and then to conclude that the 'same' gift of the Spirit is received by Jesus and the disciples *but in different manners*. Not only are there hidden difficulties in such a position (which will be explored in more detail below), but such an 'answer' to the problem misses von Baer's whole point against Gunkel, and is in danger of reducing his assertion to a banality. The tension in von Baer's work is a genuine one, and one that J.D.G. Dunn and G. Haya-Prats were later (in quite different ways) to attempt to resolve.

3. *The Legacy of the Phase of Research from Pfleiderer to Von Baer*

One has only to re-read Gunkel and von Baer to be impressed by their ongoing relevance. From Gunkel issues a stream of questions from which we can no longer hide: Did the primitive church have a *theology* of the Spirit (or was 'Spirit' just an 'explanation' offered for dramatic supernatural events or charismata)? Was there any link between Jesus' understanding of the Spirit and that of the earliest apostles? What (if indeed any) was the nature of the link between these and Paul's theology of the Spirit. What place (if any) did Old Testament concepts of the Spirit play in the developing understanding of the Spirit in the church, and did those concerning ethical renewal have any part in the earliest church's thinking? That Gunkel's proffered answers to the like questions were mainly negative only serves to sharpen them. And if he himself showed virtually no interest in a specifically Lukan theology of the Spirit, he has nevertheless provided the framework of thought in which such a study must be undertaken.

The reponse to the History of Religions School has also been fruitful.

Perhaps its single most enduring contribution has been to demonstrate
(*contra* Leisegang) that the Spirit motifs in Luke's writings are predominantly Jewish in origin, and owe little if anything to specifically Greek mysticism or Mantic prophecy. That conclusion is sufficiently certain for us to
leave the questions raised by Leisegang largely to one side; and that verdict
seems doubly justified in the light of C.K. Barrett's virtually independent
examination of the question.[57] A more obvious indication of the fecundity
of their work lies in the readily discernible influence of Büchsel and von Baer
on later studies. Von Baer's book especially is still acknowledged to be the
foundational study of Luke's pneumatology;[58] and much work since has
simply offered minor corrections and variations to his pioneering work.

But von Baer's writing also raised fundamental questions. Sharpest of
these is the question of the relation of the gift of the Spirit at Jordan to the
gift of the Spirit to the disciples at Pentecost, and the concomitant question,
'Is the gift of the Spirit *essentially* the power of eschatological sonship (and
ethical renewal?), or is it *essentially* the power to witness to the Gospel?

Let the interpreter emphasize the parallels between Jordan and Pentecost,
taking the former as Jesus' messianic anointing with power, and he pushes
Luke either towards the Confirmationist camp (so N. Adler) or, more probably, towards something like the classical Pentecostal one (so, differently,
H. Ervin, H.D. Hunter, R. Stronstad, G. Haya-Prats, E. Schweizer and
R.P. Menzies). But if Luke thought this way we may well ask (with Gunkel)
what he thinks the Spirit has to do with ordinary Christian living. And while
we can understand Jesus, the apostles, and men like Philip and Stephen,
receiving such a gift, it is puzzling why Luke thinks the gift should be
promised to *all*, and, what is more, *normally* given at conversion-initiation
(Acts 2.38-39).

The close connection between Spirit and conversion in Acts invites an
entirely different interpretation. It could imply Luke sees the gift of the
Spirit as the gift of new covenant 'life' and of that kind of discipleship we
might sum up in the term 'sonship' (as von Baer also asserted). This would
offer us a Luke who is indeed a much better friend of Paul, and a gift of the
Spirit far more immediately relevant to the everyday inner life of the
Christian; but at a cost. For if we now press the parallels between Pentecost
and Jordan, Jesus' experience of the Spirit becomes primarily prototypical
discipleship (so J.D.G. Dunn), and Luke's emphasis on the Spirit as empowering for mission (Lk. 24.49; Acts 1.4-5, 8) is easily marginalized, if not forgotten. And the tighter we make the connection between the gift of the
Spirit and entry into new covenant life, the more embarrassed we are liable

57. Barrett, *Spirit*, esp. pp. 3-4, 10-14, 36-41.
58. Cf. Haya-Prats, *L'Esprit*, p. 15.

to become by those passages where Luke seems to *dissociate* reception of the Spirit from conversion-initiation (notoriously in the case of the Samaritans in Acts 8).

Von Baer's analysis appears to have thrown those who follow onto the horns of a dilemma, and virtually all subsequent scholarship has had to try to extricate itself from that uncomfortable position. In the next chapter we shall examine some of the attempts to solve the problem (or simply to bypass it) and look at the difficulties they face.

Chapter 2

DIVERGING EXPLANATIONS OF LUKE'S CONCEPTION OF THE
ESSENTIAL CHARACTER OF THE GIFT OF THE SPIRIT

In the last chapter, we briefly surveyed the developments up to von Baer's thesis in 1926. The dilemma his work posed—whether the Spirit for Luke was essentially the power of eschatological sonship and new covenant life or whether, rather, it was essentially empowering for mission—led to diverging explanations of Luke's understanding of the Spirit in the years that followed. As we have reviewed the scholarly contributions to the subject in more-or-less chronological order, and in more detail, elsewhere,[1] we may here look rather at different types of solution (as presented by their chief exponents), and at some of the important questions they raise and the problems they face.

We shall begin (§1) by examining a traditional view which at first sight offers a way out of the dilemma: it is the view that at Pentecost the disciples received 'the Spirit himself', that is, the divine Giver whose gifts include both sonship and power. But we shall discover that this 'solution' is inherently problematic, and finds no secure purchase in Luke's presentation of his pneumatological material. We then (§2) turn to J.D.G. Dunn's notable attempt to show that the essence of the gift at Pentecost was of the Spirit as the source of eschatological sonship and new covenant life. Dunn, of course, did not overlook the fact that this gift of the Spirit often brought power too. But (against classical Pentecostalism) he insisted that the gift described in Acts 2 cannot be reduced to empowering for mission, and so made a second-stage grace. Rather, without this gift the disciples would not have been able to enter what we normally mean by 'Christian' existence at all. According to Dunn, then, the theological essence of the gift at Pentecost is that it brings new covenant 'life' to the recipient. The motif of 'empowering for mission' emphasised by von Baer, while often a significant feature of that 'life', nevertheless remains of secondary theological importance (even for Luke).

1. Turner, 'Receiving the Spirit in Luke–Acts', pp. 131-58; 'Luke and the Spirit', ch. 1.

By contrast with Dunn, the writers whose views we then consider in §§3–7 all see some kind of 'empowering' of people who are already Christians as the primary emphasis of Luke's pneumatology, though they offer markedly different interpretations of this. N. Adler (§3) argued the improbable thesis that Luke (especially in Acts 8) is consciously providing a model for the sacrament of confirmation. G.W.H. Lampe, at least in his earlier writings (§4), took up von Baer's insight that the Spirit in Luke is 'the Spirit of prophecy' and concluded from this that what Luke means by 'the gift of the Spirit' differs from other New Testament writers, and that he sees it primarily as an empowering for mission, and so separable from baptism. Other positions provide variations on Lampe's theme, and include some significant contributions by Pentecostal scholars. E. Schweizer and the Pentecostal scholars R. Stronstad and R.P. Menzies (§5) interpret 'the Spirit of prophecy' given at Pentecost largely if not exclusively as the power of prophetic speech, especially of missionary *preaching*, but with some associated gifts of wisdom and revelation. Others are less confident this is the whole story. J. Kremer, Lampe, J.B. Shelton, H.S. Kim and (revised) Dunn each (differently) argue there are at least traces in Acts of the more widespread Christian tradition that saw the gift of the Spirit as bringing salvation, sonship and new covenant life, and that these have a part in Luke's theology of the Spirit too (§6). By contrast G. Haya-Prats and others (§7) have argued that while (for Luke) the Spirit is always the Spirit of prophecy (rather than the soteriological Spirit) this nevertheless cannot be reduced to 'empowering for mission', but involves a variety of endowments that equip Christians for every manner of service, ministry, worship and witness.

We may now provide some detail and nuance to this oversimplified picture. Hurried readers may be advised to concentrate their attention on §2 and §§5–7.

1. *A Traditional Position: The Pentecostal Gift as 'the Spirit Himself'*

It is characteristic of the New Testament to speak of the Spirit being 'given' to and 'received' by Christians: Peter's promise that those who repent and are baptised will 'receive the gift of the Spirit' (Acts 2.38-39) is typical, at least at this point. A number of scholars have taken this language more or less literally, at least by analogy with the literal sense in which a man might be 'given' a wife and she might 'receive' a husband at their wedding. On this view, to talk of receiving the Spirit is to speak of the joining of persons: the Christian is united, as it were, to the Person of the Spirit, and the Spirit has come where He was not before. The Catholic exegete and theologian N. Adler has presented such a position in relation to the Spirit given at confirmation,[2] and something similar is frequently implied in the works of Protestant writers (e.g., *inter alios*, F.F. Bruce, F.D. Bruner, J.G. Davies, C.B. Kaiser and J.R.W. Stott) with respect to the Spirit received in conversion-initiation.[3] Common to both positions is the assertion that men and women had received a variety of gifts of the Spirit before Pentecost, but at Pentecost Christians began to receive the Giver of these gifts himself, the Third Person of the Trinity.[4] Such a solution (at least in its Protestant version) would appear to offer an easy way round the dilemma posed between whether the gift of the Spirit brings sonship and new covenant life, or whether it affords prophecy and missionary empowering. It could be replied that the Holy Spirit, as 'the Giving Gift', affords both: the dilemma was a false one in the first place.

Although this at first appears attractive, it nevertheless faces serious difficulties as a proposed exegesis of Luke–Acts:

1. On Adler's assumption, the Holy Spirit has (presumably) always been the third Person of the Trinity, so that it is not clear why Old Testament endowments with the Spirit should not be regarded as occasions of receiving the Holy Spirit 'himself' too. In order to maintain his contrast between the gift of the Spirit in the Old Testament and in the New, Adler would presumably have to reply that though the Holy Spirit *was* a person in the Old Testament, he was nevertheless not *experienced* as a person then. But such a response cannot really help him, because it is not obvious that all parts of the New Testament church were conscious of experiencing the Spirit *as a person* in ways beyond those already met in the Old Testament and in Judaism, nor does it seem anything but an anachronism to attribute such a fully-fledged view to Peter as early as the day of Pentecost, and there is little evidence it is a *Lukan* view either.

There seem to be several muddled issues here. Adler (and others holding the position) appears, in the first place, to have failed to observe the important distinction between saying that we receive the Spirit whose actions in us are 'personal'; and saying that we receive the Spirit *as* a person: the

---

2.   So Adler, *Pfingstfest*, pp. 74, 91; cf. also his *Taufe und Handauflegung: Eine exegetisch-theologische Untersuchung von Apg 8.14-17* (Munster: Aschendorff, 1951), p. 91.

3.   F.F. Bruce, *Commentary on the Book of Acts* (London: MMS, 1954), p. 77; F.D. Bruner, *A Theology of the Holy Spirit: The Pentecostal Experience and the New Testament Witness* (Grand Rapids: Eerdmans, 1970), p. 163; J.G. Davies, *The Spirit, the Church and the Sacraments* (London: SCM Press, 1954), ch. 1; C.B. Kaiser, 'The "Rebaptism" of the Ephesian Twelve: Exegetical Study on Acts 19.1-7', *RefR* 31 (1977–78), p. 59; J.R.W. Stott, *The Baptism and Fullness of the Holy Spirit* (Leicester: Inter-Varsity Press, 2nd edn, 1975).

4.   So Adler, *Pfingstfest*, pp. 74, 91.

Spirit *himself*. The former is much closer to a truth found elsewhere in the New Testament—and quite possibly shared by Luke—that even when the Spirit performs 'personal' functions these consist almost entirely in mediating the presence and activity of God and of his Christ. It is then the personhood of the Father (or the exalted Son) that is experienced in encounter with the Spirit, not the 'Spirit himself'. By contrast, before we could affirm Luke considered believers to receive the Spirit as a person—the Spirit 'himself' as opposed to his gracious gifting—we should wish to be sure that Luke thought the Spirit not merely to perform some 'personal' activities, but (a) actually to be a distinct person and (b) regularly to be perceived and experienced as such. This would be difficult to prove.

There are undoubtedly occasions where Luke presents the Spirit as the agent of an action, and to that extent as 'personal'. Thus the Spirit is made the subject (or semantic agent) of the following verbs: διδάσκειν ('to teach', Lk. 12.12); ἀποφθέγγεσθαι διδόναι ('to give utterance', Acts 2.4); μάρτυς εἶναι ('to be witness', Acts 5.32); λέγειν ('to say', Acts 8.29 cf. 1.16; 10.19; 11.12; 13.2; 19.1; 28.25 [λαλεῖν]); ἁρπάζειν ('to snatch away', Acts 8.39); ἐκπέμπειν ('to send', 13.4); κωλύειν ('to forbid', 16.6); ἐᾶν ('to allow', 16.7); διαμαρτύρεσθαι ('to testify', 20.23); ἐπισκόπους τιθέναι ('to appoint as overseer', 20.28). In addition, further hints of the personal nature of the Spirit are found at (1) Acts 5.3 where we find the expression ψεύσασθαι...τὸ πνεῦμα τὸ ἅγιον ('to lie...to the Holy Spirit'); which in the following verse is the apparently further defined: οὐκ ἐψεύσω ἀνθρώποις ἀλλὰ τῷ θεῷ ('you did not lie to men but to God'); (2) Acts 7.51 where the Spirit is 'resisted'; (3) Acts 10.38 where ὁ θεὸς ἦν μετ' αὐτοῦ ('*God* was with him') may define Jesus 'anointed with Holy Spirit and power'; (4) Acts 13.2 where the Spirit says 'set Barnabas and Saul apart to me...'; (5) Acts 15.28 where decisions 'seemed right...to the Holy Spirit' and to the apostolic council,[5] and finally (6) Acts 28.25-26, where a masculine participle (λέγων; 'saying') appears to have the Spirit as its antecedent.[6]

---

5. But, for a less personal explanation of this text, see Haya-Prats, *L'Esprit*, pp. 83ff.

6. J.H.E. Hull (*The Holy Spirit in the Acts of the Apostles* [London: Lutterworth, 1967], p. 155) considers this last to be conclusive; but it is far from being so: (1) the text is uncertain (A 81 and ς supporting the grammatically more correct λέγον; but would a scribe alter towards this after the emergence of the doctrine of the Trinity?) (2) The subject of λέγων may be Isaiah the prophet. In that case we would of course expect λέγοντος; but anacolouthon of case in such circumstances is almost to be anticipated. (3) In Revelation we have a number of instances of masculine being substituted for feminine or neuter participles, especially in the case of λέγων (Rev. 4.1; 9.14 and 11.15), and this was common in later Greek; not impossible, therefore, in

The important question we must ask in each case, however, concerns the intended linguistic status of such affirmations. Is the personal language intended literally (and so to imply the Spirit is a hypostasis), or is it part of the more widespread and typically Jewish tendency to personify divine attributes, or to represent the Spirit as the extension of Yahweh's own presence? Most treatments of the subject are too insensitive to the various possibilities.[7] If we bear this distinction in mind, an examination of Luke's Spirit material does not suggest he thinks Christians were any more aware of the Spirit's personhood than their Jewish contemporaries were. The 'personal' traits within his Spirit traditions rarely move beyond the types of personification of the Spirit (and of the word, the Shekinah, the name, etc.) regularly found in exclusively monotheistic Judaism.

For example, on many of the occasions in Acts the activity of the Spirit is one of *speech*; but this is common to the Old Testament (cf. particularly at 2 Sam. 23.2; 1 Kgs 22.21ff.; Zech. 7.12; Ezek. 2.2; 3.24; 11.5) and much more so to Judaism both Hellenistic and rabbinic.[8] On other occasions (Lk. 12.12, Acts 2.4 etc.) the Spirit gives the ability to speak on behalf of God, or to deliver his words, but here again the motif is shared with the Old Testament and Judaism. As in Acts, the Spirit in the Old Testament may be thought of as a *guide* or *instructor* of an individual or the nation (Neh. 9.20; Ps. 143.10; Isa. 63.11 and 14), and the same is attested in Hellenistic Judaism (e.g. Wis. 7.7, 22; 9.17 and Philo [implicitly at *Gig.* 24-28, 47, 53, 55; *Somn.* 2.252 etc.]), at Qumran (1QS 3.6-7; 4.6; 1QH 9.32; 12.11-12. etc.[9]), and in rabbinic Judaism.[10] In the Old Testament God *witnesses* to his

---

Acts. Luke was certainly able to use a masculine participle where a neuter would be expected: cf. Acts 10.37 τὸ γενόμενον ῥῆμα...ἀρξάμενος...(𝔓⁴⁵ L P correctly: ἀρξάμενον).

7.   Less sensitive treatments include K.L. Schmidt, 'Das Pneuma Hagion als Person und als Charisma', *ErJb* 13 (1965), pp. 187-236; A.W. Wainwright, *The Trinity in the New Testament* (London: SPCK, 1962) pp. 30-32, 200ff.; K.W. Baker, 'Father, Son and Holy Spirit in the Acts of the Apostles' (unpublished PhD dissertation, Marquette University, 1967), pp. 157-69. More cautious are C.F.D. Moule, 'The New Testament and the Trinity', *ExpTim* 88 (1976–77), pp. 16-20; Haya-Prats, *L'Esprit*, pp. 83-90 (following the lead of van Imschoot, *Bibellexicon* [ed. Haag; Zurich, 1951], pp. 538-39) and R. Kock (*Bibeltheologisches Wörterbuch* [ed. Bauer; Graz, 1962], pp. 451-52) and A. George, 'L'Esprit-Saint dans l'oeuvre de Luc', *RB* 85 (1978) pp. 527-33.

8.   For rabbinic references see A. Abelson, *The Immanence of God in Rabbinic Judaism* (London, 1912; New York: Hermon, 1969), chs. 18, 19; and P. Schäfer, *Die Vorstellung vom heiligen Geist in der rabbinischen Literatur* (Munich: Kösel, 1972), pp. 151, 153 and 162.

9.   See especially H.W. Kühn, *Enderwartung und gegenwärtiges Heil: Untersuchungen zu den Gemeindeliedern von Qumran mit Anhang über Eschatologie und Gegenwart in der Verkündigung Jesu* (Göttingen: Vandenhoeck & Ruprecht, 1966),

people through the Spirit in the prophets (Neh. 9.30); similarly the Spirit is a witness (or perhaps the testimony to Israel) of God's act in Christ in Acts (5.32). If the Spirit seems 'personal' because he can be *resisted* and lied to in Acts (7.51; 5.3-4), Isa. 63.10 can speak of Israel grieving the Spirit (עצבו; LXX παρώξυναν), and Philo of the Spirit being driven away by base thought and desire (*Gig.* 55). The anthropomorphic language of the Spirit seizing Philip and speaking to him (8.39, 29), too, is matched in the LXX translations of Ezek. 2.2 and 3.24. And finally, at Acts 5.3-4 and 10.38 we have what appear to be close parallels to the Old Testament presentation of the Spirit as an extension of Yahweh's presence and vitality.[11]

Our purpose here, far from attempting to give a complete list of the parallels in the Old Testament and in the writings of Judaism to alleged references to the 'personal' Spirit in Acts, is simply to show that the *kind* of evidence usually used to demonstrate the 'personality' of the Spirit in Acts is in fact matched by the Old Testament and Judaism. There is not immediately to hand, as it were, clear evidence that Luke's presentation of the Spirit marks the sort of shift in perception of the gift of the Spirit (from gifts to Giver) that Adler requires. Indeed, the personification of the Spirit in rabbinic Judaism occasionally goes *beyond* that encountered in Acts, at least in the violence of the personal language used. As Abelson points out, the Spirit not only quotes Scripture, 'It also cries. It holds dialogue with God, or some person. It pleads. It laments and weeps; it rejoices and comforts'.[12] But it would be entirely inappropriate to argue from this that rabbinic Judaism (or any other sector of Judaism for that matter) had come to think of the Spirit as an independent hypostasis distinct from Yahweh: neither the Old Testament nor Judaism were binitarian in their view of the Spirit![13]

pp. 117-75; and P. Garnet, *Salvation and Atonement in the Qumran Scrolls* (Tübingen: Mohr, 1977), pp. 154-55.

10. See the extensive examples offered by Schäfer, *Vorstellung,* pp. 151ff.

11. See especially A.R. Johnson, *The One and the Many in the Israelite Conception of God* (Cardiff: University of Wales Press, 1961), pp. 15ff., and *The Vitality of the Individual in the Thought of Ancient Israel* (Cardiff: University of Wales Press, 1964), pp. 26-39; for a major attempt to interpret the Spirit in the New Testament in similar vein see G.W.H. Lampe, *God As Spirit: The Bampton Lectures, 1976* (Oxford: Clarendon Press, 1977).

12. Abelson, *Immanence,* p. 225. Cf. Hill, *Words,* p. 223.

13. The touchiness manifest in rabbinic Judaism in the face of any suggestion of their being 'two powers in heaven' all but rules out the possibility that rabbinic personification of the Spirit (or of the Shekinah, Memra, Kabod or Torah) should be understood as anything more than literary license in describing Yahweh's immanence (so Abelson, *Immanence,* p. 224 and *passim*). A binitarian position was explicitly rejected by the rabbis on the basis of Isa. 44–47 and Deut. 32.39 (*Sifre Deut.* 379—and see A.F. Segal, *Two Powers in Heaven* [Leiden: Brill, 1977], pp. 84-89, on this passage).

Luke may indeed have thought of the Spirit as sharing fully in divine being—as John and Paul[14] probably do—and, as we shall see, the very fact that Luke understands the Spirit to mediate the presence or activity of Jesus as well as that of the Father (Acts 2.33; 16.6-7 etc.) *may* have encouraged such an understanding. But at the same time it cannot be said that Luke stresses the personality of the Spirit much beyond what can be found in the Old Testament and in the literature of Judaism; and this must throw considerable doubt on any assertion to the effect that Luke had come to think of the gift of the Spirit principally as the experience of 'the Spirit himself' as such.

The fact remains that the clearest presentation of the personal being of

But the aggressive stance of the rabbis indicates that there was lively controversy over mediators within certain sectors of Judaism, and this can be traced back at least to Philo's time if not before (Segal, *Powers, passim*). Prov. 8 and 9.1 strongly personify the figure of Wisdom (cf. Sir. 24; Wis. 10); Philo, while considering himself a monotheist, seems all but to make a divine hypostasis of the λόγος (*Somn*. 1.62-66; 230-33: cf. Segal, *Powers*, pp. 161ff.), and in the (only slightly later) apocalypses, God's chief executive angels (e.g. Jaoel in *Apoc. Abr.* 17; Eremiel in *Apoc. Zeph.* 6; and the chief angel in *Jos. and Asen.* ch. 14) can be described in exalted terms directly reminiscent of the majestic theophany in Ezek. 1. Nevertheless, Christopher Rowland concludes 'Whether we can yet speak of this angel being a second power in the heavenly world must be doubted' (C. Rowland, *The Open Heaven* [London: SPCK, 1982], p. 111), and L.W. Hurtado, *One God, One Lord* (London: SCM, 1988), gives an even more emphatically negative verdict on all claims that Judaism admitted any sort of 'second power'.

However close Judaism may have been to hypostatising an angelic being or a divine attribute, at no point does a hypostatisation of the God's Spirit come into question. At Qumran the Spirit of Truth is probably identified with the Prince of Light (1QM 13.9-12; 1QS 3.18-20; 4.21, 23; 9.33: see A.A. Anderson, 'The Use of "Ruah" in 1QS, 1QH and 1QM', *JSS* 7 [1962], pp. 298-300; and G. Johnston, "Spirit" and "Holy Spirit" in the Qumran Literature', in H.K. McArthur [ed.], *New Testament Sidelights* [Hartford: Hartford Seminary Foundation Press, 1960], pp. 39-40), and possibly with Michael (so G. Johnston, *'The Spirit-Paraclete in the Gospel of John* [Cambridge: Cambridge University Press, 1970], pp. 120-21; though cf. O. Betz, *Der Paraklet* [Leiden: Brill, 1963], pp. 113-16) and with Melchizedek (Segal, *Powers*, p. 193). The Spirit of Truth was thus 'personal'; but it is not clear whether this is the same as the Holy Spirit of 1QS 4.21 (and 9.3), and, in any case, the Spirit of Truth is part of such a strongly modified dualism with both Spirits of truth and of perversity having been created by God and acting under his sovereignty (1QS 3.16–4.20; esp. 3.25-26), that the adjective 'binitarian' would be inappropriate (cf. Segal, *Powers*, pp. 192ff.). We may concur with Johnston (in McArthur [ed.], *Sidelights*, p. 41) that at Qumran 'the Spirit like the hand, the mercy, the wisdom, and the law of God might be personified; but there is no real hypostasis, no clear theology of the Spirit of God'.

14. See G.D. Fee, *God's Empowering Presence* (Peabody: Hendrickson, 1994), pp. 827-45.

the Spirit in the New Testament comes in John 14–16, where John presents the Spirit-Paraclete as a figure set in parallel to Jesus, mediating the Father and the Son to the disciples as Jesus had mediated the Father during his ministry (Jn 14.6-11).[15] But even in these circumstances there is no suggestion made by John that Christians (after Jesus' glorification) will consciously receive the Spirit, and experience him, *as a divine Person*. Jesus as mediator of the Father revealed himself; but the Spirit precisely does not do so (16.13), revealing only Christ and the Father.[16] Appropriately, Smail entitled his chapter on the person of the Spirit, 'The Person without a Face'.[17] So the Christian is in virtually the state Adler predicates of some of the Old Testament saints who were endowed with the Spirit: he or she may have much stronger reasons than his or her Old Testament counterpart to believe the Spirit is a person, but Christian believers do not more consciously experience the Spirit as Person. Like them, he is merely aware of the Spirit's gifts (which may include revelation of the Father and of the exalted Son, or bring a sense of their presence), without being noticeably more aware of the personhood of the Giver.[18]

2. A second, and obvious, problem, related to the first, is that Adler's solution has no obvious continuity with *pre*-Lukan tradition. While Luke himself portrays the Spirit as the fulfilment of Old Testament promise, neither the Old Testament nor Judaism expected a gift of the Spirit that was the 'Spirit himself' in contrast to the extension of God's presence in charismatic activity. Nor could such a tradition readily be discerned in Mark or Q. Luke could, we may suppose, himself have developed such an idea (along the lines of John's presentation of Jesus' teaching on the Paraclete),[19] but such

---

15. See R.E. Brown, 'The Paraclete in the Fourth Gospel', *NTS* 13 (1966–67), pp. 113-32; and compare M. Turner, 'The Significance of Receiving the Spirit in John's Gospel', *VoxEv* 10 (1977), pp. 26-28. For a semi-popular but perceptive theological analysis see T. Smail, *The Giving Gift: The Holy Spirit in Person* (London: Hodder, 1988), chs. 2 and 3.

16. For a similar perspective in Paul's writings see the comments by N.Q. Hamilton, *The Holy Spirit and Eschatology in Paul* (Edinburgh: Oliver and Boyd, 1957), p. 6; and M. Turner, 'The Significance of Spirit-Endowment for Paul', *VoxEv* 9 (1975), pp. 61-65.

17. Smail, *Gift*, ch. 2.

18. W. Shepherd, *The Narrative Function of the Holy Spirit as Character in Luke–Acts* (Atlanta: Scholars Press, 1994) adds nothing material to the above discussion, as what he means by the 'character' of the Spirit pertains to literary function (and so, to some extent, the phenomenology of the Spirit) rather than ontology.

19. A strong tie between Lukan and Johannine views of the Spirit has been advocated by W.F. Lofthouse, 'The Holy Spirit in the Acts of the Apostles and in the Fourth Gospel', *ExpTim* 52 (1940–41) pp. 334-36; R.T. Stamm, 'Luke–Acts and Three Cardinal Ideas in the Gospel of John', in J.M. Myers, D. Reinherr and H.N. Bream

a hypothesis would at least require careful argument before it could be asserted, for Luke does not portray Jesus as teaching about the Spirit in that way.

3. The way Acts speaks about the 'giving' and 'receiving' of the Spirit, or of the 'gift' of the Spirit, strongly suggests that the earliest church did not use this language primarily to express the idea of 'giving' and 'receiving' of the person of the Spirit in union with believers. Such a concept would have been so strikingly new, and of such central theological importance, that it would inevitably have led to the suppression of other manners of speaking of the Spirit that could only be considered less worthy ways of referring to this profound union. Yet Acts can let Peter say 'the gift of the Spirit has been "poured out" on the Gentiles too' (Acts 10.45), without the least note of incongruity. If this gift of the Holy Spirit is supposed to express God's giving of his Spirit into a union of persons with Gentile disciples (who are said to have thus 'received the Holy Spirit' according to 10.47), then surely Luke's Peter is guilty of a strangely dissonant mixture of images! Neither 'persons' nor 'unions' are usually thought of as 'poured out' (Acts 10.45; cf. 2.33); nor, for that matter, as conveyed by laying on of hands (cf. 8.18), nor by the 'falling' of one partner on the other (Acts 10.44; 11.15[20])! Luke's typical language is simply not congruent with Adler's view of what he means by 'to receive the gift of the Spirit'. We may believe the Holy Spirit to be personal, we may accept that it is a valid way of speaking to say that Christians are brought into union with him at conversion—indeed, Luke himself may have thought so—but nevertheless, Luke quite clearly is not using the language of 'giving' or 'receiving' the Spirit primarily to express such thoughts.[21]

(eds.), *Biblical Studies in Honor of H.C. Alleman* (New York: Augustin. 1960), pp. 177-202; and M.A. Chevallier, 'Apparentements entre Luc et Jean en matière de pneumatologie', in J.N. Aletti *et al.*, *A cause de l'évangile: Etudes sur les synoptiques et les Actes* (Paris: Cerf, 1985), pp. 377-408.

20. ἐπιπίπτω may of course be used of persons; both in the regular collocation 'ἐπιπίπτω ἐπὶ τὸν τράχηλον' (meaning 'to embrace'), and (metaphorically) to denote urgent movement to someone's aid (Acts 20.10); but neither is relevant here.

21. Not surprisingly then, Bruce (*Book*, p. 77), who starts by insisting we must 'distinguish the *gift* of the Spirit from the *gifts* of the Spirit' and affirms that 'the *gift* of the Spirit is the Spirit Himself' while 'the *gifts* are [merely] the spiritual faculties which the Spirit imparts', nevertheless eventually retreats from the sort of position Adler adopts and glosses: 'but the free gift which is promised in v. 38 to those who repent and are baptized is the Holy Spirit Himself. The gift of the Spirit may comprehend a variety of gifts of the Spirit, but [quoting Stonehouse] first and foremost "the saving benefits of Christ's work as applied to the believer by the Spirit".' The purpose of the writer on this occasion is now clear; he simply wishes to avoid the impression that the gift of the Spirit designates the Spirit merely as the Spirit of prophecy, and broaden

This raises the important question of what such language *is* intended to signify. It might be possible to shed the insistence that the Spirit is received 'as Person' and fall back to less nuanced position in which the gift of the Spirit is simply God's active presence and distributor of all manner of gifts. But we have argued elsewhere that virtually all Luke's language of Spirit endowment is metaphor for different aspects of the activity of the Spirit, and accordingly that to speak of the Spirit as 'given' to a person or 'received' by someone is perhaps best explained as a metaphorical way of referring to the *inception* of a specific new activity, or coherent set of activities, believed to be initiated in and through the person concerned.[22]

This at least potentially means that the semantic content of an utterance such as 'Saul received the Spirit' (or 'the Spirit came on Saul'), in Luke (or in the mouth of one of his characters) would depend entirely on what set of activities the utterer believed the Spirit to have commenced in 'Saul' on the specific occasion concerned. Were the speaker intentionally referring to 1 Sam. 10.6, he would mean king Saul's royal authority and power as granted by God (and withdrawn at 1 Sam. 16.14); in the case of an act of reference to 1 Sam. 11.6, he will signify that vitality of God evinced in Saul's response to the news from the men of Jabesh; while if his reference were rather to Saul of Tarsus (at Acts 9.17-19), he may well mean the power by which Paul was to fulfil the commission referred to in the immediate context. Luke thus appears to means quite different things when he implies Jesus received the Spirit at the Jordan (Lk. 3.21) and when he subsequently affirms that Jesus also 'received...the Holy Spirit' on his ascension/exaltation (Acts 2.33). Here we have two 'givings' of the Spirit which are quite distinct in essential nature. Each was the beginning of a distinct nexus of activities, and I shall argue neither is quite what Luke means by saying *Christians* receive the gift of the Spirit.

We have shown it is unlikely that for Luke reception of the gift of the Spirit marked experiencing the Spirit as person—the question then is, 'to the inception of what activity, or coherent set of activities, does "the gift of the Spirit" granted to Christians refer?' The problem of trying to say it refers to both the inception of sonship and (simultaneously) to missionary empowering should now be a little more transparent. These at least potentially involve what are notionally quite different activities of the Spirit. All may require the first from the beginning of faith; but we would usually regard mission as the gift of the mature Christian, and 'missionary empowering' thus as a subsequent gifting. One might try to harmonize the ideas by positing that Luke wished to emphasize that the Spirit is active to inspire

the gift to make it the source of salvation more generally.

22. See Turner, 'Spirit Endowment', pp. 45-63.

mission through all Christians from the first day of their faith. In which case it would make sense to say they receive the Spirit as missionary empowering at conversion-initiation. But it must be shown he believes that. If he viewed the Spirit as initiating such activity only later in the Christian, and then only in *some* Christians, it would verge on semantic incoherence to say he regards the gift of the Spirit at conversion-initiation as the reception of missionary empowering.

2. *The Gift of the Spirit as New Covenant Life and Sonship*
(J.D.G. Dunn)

The publishing in 1970 of James Dunn's thesis, *Baptism in the Holy Spirit: A Re-examination of the New Testament Teaching on the Gift of the Spirit in Relation to Pentecostalism Today*, was an important milestone in the search for the meaning of the gift of the Spirit in the New Testament, and it was by no means ungenerous in the attention it devoted to the Lukan writings[23] (the canon within the canon of Pentecostal pneumatology). In many ways Dunn's work may be seen as an extension of the theses of von Baer and Büchsel. With Büchsel, Dunn sees the primary import of the descent of the Spirit at Jordan to be bound up with Jesus' 'sonship to God'—a relationship confirmed by the heavenly voice (Lk. 3.22). But while a similar conclusion left Büchsel at a loss to explain adequately how the sonship afforded by the Spirit's descent at the Jordan relates to the sonship Jesus already enjoyed (according to Luke) as the one conceived of the Spirit (cf. 1.32-35 and 2.49-50), Dunn plays out this 'sonship' along the salvation-historical baseline of von Baer's three epochs.[24] Jordan and Pentecost are the turning points of the Ages, and at each point, Jesus enters on a new and fuller phase of his messiahship and sonship. Thus, commenting on Jesus' experience at the Jordan, Dunn can insist:

> The descent of the Spirit on Jesus effects not so much a change in Jesus, his person or his status, as the beginning of a new stage in salvation-history. The thought is not so much of Jesus becoming what he was not before, but of Jesus entering where he was not before—a new epoch in God's plan of redemption...It is not so much that Jesus became what he was not before, but that history became what it was not before; and Jesus as the one who effects these changes of history from within history, is himself affected by them (pp. 28 and 29).

23. Almost half of the book is devoted to the Gospels and Acts: for Dunn's own summary of Luke's view see especially pp. 40-43, and ch. 9.

24. For explicit recognition of von Baer's structure here see *Baptism*, p. 40 n. 7, where he also points to Conzelmann—but Dunn's own division of epochs follows von Baer's not Conzelmann's.

Von Baer, it will be remembered, had not made clear whether the Spirit at Pentecost was basically an empowering parallel to that of Jesus, or whether it was associated with Christian existence at a more fundamental level. Dunn argues that Luke understood the descent of the Spirit at Jordan as *both* Jesus' own entry into the new age and covenant *and* his anointing with the Spirit as messiah, Son of God, and servant (p. 134); not merely as an empowering to effect messianic redemption, as classical Pentecostal exegesis tended to make it. How can the gift of the Spirit be both? It is because the Spirit who makes Jesus messiah, thereby makes him the representative of the eschatological Israel (for what is the king of Israel but the representative of God's son, Israel; and what king comes to Israel, but the eschatological king of the restored Israel?), and indeed the New Adam (and the temptations narrative attests both motifs). If the Spirit inaugurates Jesus into a new epoch, in which God is restoring Israel (and humanity), then (Dunn assumes) the Spirit descends as the Spirit of the new covenant. Jesus' birth thus belongs to the 'old age', the 'old covenant', and to the 'period of Israel' (p. 31); it is the Spirit's descent upon Jesus that inaugurates him into the new age, into his eschatological sonship, and into the life of the kingdom of God.

Dunn's most distinctive contribution lay in this assertion that Jesus himself is not related to the new age until the Spirit descends upon him—and in the further implication that, at Jordan, Jesus began to experience what was virtually archetypal Christian existence;[25] eschatological sonship and new covenant life (the life of the kingdom of God). Barely surprisingly, then, he insists the 'empowering for service' should not be taken as the primary purpose of Jesus' anointing: it is only a corollary to it (p. 32).

The archetypal significance of Jesus' experience is elucidated by Dunn's use (again) of von Baer's structure of epochs in Luke–Acts. Luke is said to view the second, and central epoch within the scheme—that of Jesus' ministry from John's baptism to resurrection-exaltation—as a necessary period in which Jesus is baptised with 'Spirit-and-fire', the 'fire' of which he must first quench with his own death before he may in turn then baptise the community with the 'Spirit' (alone). Only with the third epoch can the disciples enter the new age (pp. 38-54). Pentecost is not merely a continuation of what went before. For the disciples it is 'the beginning'; the inauguration of the new age, the age of the Spirit *for them*, just as Jordan had been for Jesus (p. 43). Until Pentecost, Jesus alone had experienced the life (and sonship) of the new age, and only in him was God's kingdom present.[26] Jordan was thus 'the beginning, albeit in a restricted sense, of the end-time' (p. 24) in Jesus, but Jesus' entry into the new age and covenant 'is the type of

---

25. *Baptism*, pp. 32-35, 41-42.
26. *Baptism*, p. 26; *idem*, 'Spirit and Kingdom', *ExpTim* 82 (1970–71), pp. 39-40.

every initiate's entry into the new age and covenant' (p. 32); as such this first baptism in the Spirit (at the Jordan) could well be taken as typical of all later Spirit-baptisms, the means by which God brings each to follow in Jesus' footsteps.[27]

When Dunn turns to the Pentecost account it is to draw out further the parallels with Jesus' Jordan experience. Once again we have a turning point in the ages. Peter's speech shows the gift of the Spirit is the eschatological gift promised in Isa. 32.15; 34.16; Ezek. 11.19; 36.26-27; 37.4-14 and Joel 2.28-32 as the decisive mark of the new age (p. 46). The Pentecostal gift is the Spirit of the new covenant for the disciples. This is demonstrated (i) by Luke's designation of it as 'the promise'—meaning God's *covenant* promise; the 'blessing of Abraham' (p. 47); (ii) by Peter's words 'the promise is to you and to your children' (Acts 2.38: recalling the Abrahamic covenant of Gen. 17.7-10);[28] (iii) by the inevitability of the association on Old Testament grounds (the promise of the Spirit giving inner renewal in Ezek. 36 parallels the promise of the new covenant renewal of obedience in Jer. 31.33: cf. Paul's elucidation of both themes in 2 Cor. 3.3, 6-8[29]); and (iv) by the very fact that the Spirit is granted on the *day of Pentecost*, when Jews commemorated the giving of the Sinai covenant and Law (pp. 48-49). Later sections of Dunn's thesis attempt to show that all the occasions of receiving the Spirit in Luke–Acts are concerned with conversion-initiation into the new age. If the Spirit is not inextricably linked to the water rite of baptism on most occasions in Luke–Acts, that is because the gift of the Spirit is primarily God's response to authentic faith, and only secondarily connected with baptism—i.e. merely when baptism expresses such faith.[30] Jesus' disciples only attain such authentic faith (for salvation-historical reasons) at Pentecost (pp. 38-54); the Spirit is not experienced at the baptism of the Samaritans because their 'faith' is wrongly based (being a herd response to Philip's miracles) (pp. 55-72); Cornelius receives the Spirit

27. *Baptism*, p. 32. This is not to say Jesus simply becomes the first Christian (see Dunn, *Jesus*, p. 358) even if it comes close to it for Luke–Acts.

28. *Baptism*, p. 47.

29. *Baptism*, p. 47-48.

30. *Baptism*, *passim*. In separating Spirit-baptism from water-baptism Dunn builds especially on the work of (e.g.) M. Barth, *Die Taufe ein Sakrament?* (Zollikon-Zürich: Evangelischer Verlag, 1951). His own position may be summed up in his statement: 'It is certainly not true that early Christian baptism was understood as baptism in the Spirit'; or again, 'Christian baptism remained primarily the expression of man's action (repentance/faith) towards God, whereas it was the Spirit that was recognized as the expression of God's action towards men' (*Unity and Diversity in the New Testament* [London: SCM Press, 1977], pp. 155-56; see also Dunn, 'The Birth of a Metaphor—Baptized in the Spirit', *ExpTim* 89 [1977–78], pp. 134-38, 173-75).

before baptism as God's seal on his authentic faith (pp. 79-82); the Ephesian 'disciples' were not yet true believers before they were brought to faith by Paul, and their faith was sealed in baptism (of which laying on of hands was a part) in response to which they received the Spirit (pp. 83-89).

The picture which emerges is remarkably sharp. 'Baptism in Spirit' and 'receiving the (gift of) the Spirit' are understood by Dunn almost to have been technical terms in earliest Christianity.[31] They designate that work of the Spirit in and through which a person begins to experience the new age, the kingdom of God, the new covenant, sonship resurrection 'life', and so on. In other words, according to Dunn the gift of the Spirit is the gift of the matrix of Christian life. This is how Jesus' experience of the Spirit in the second epoch is to be understood, no less than that of his disciples in the third. It is precisely, then, the Spirit on Jesus that is transferred to the disciples; and here von Baer's theory of epochs is clearly seen to undergird Dunn's concept of the meaning of the gift of the Spirit.[32] We are not surprised when we turn to a more recent publication by Dunn, *Jesus and the Spirit*, to find him answering the question posed by Gunkel ('what has the Spirit to do with the ordinary religious life of the community?')—not to mention the older and more general question: 'What has the religion of Paul to do with the religion of Jesus?'—by affirming that it is Jesus' experience of the eschatological Spirit that is the bridge between Jesus' religion and Paul's.[33]

We shall offer no detailed criticism of Dunn's thesis in this section, as the problems with it should become sufficiently clear as we present the alternative views, and we shall be reacting extensively with Dunn in the major part of this book. But his thesis certainly raises many questions. What does it mean to say Jesus first entered new age and new covenant existence at the Jordan? Would it not naturally imply that before it Jesus was considered to experience the bondage to sin that characterized 'this evil age' (i.e. Ezekiel's 'stony heart' which was to be replaced by the responsive 'heart of flesh' in and through the gift of the Spirit of the new covenant)? Is such Luke's view? Does Luke really believe Jordan was the turning point of the ages for Jesus, the beginning of the new creation—is the Spirit at his conception not already portrayed as the Spirit of the new creation? Is the

31. *Baptism, passim*; and Dunn, 'A Note on δωρεά', *ExpTim* 81 (1969-70), pp. 249-51; *idem*, 'Birth', pp. 173-75.

32. Compare E.M.B. Green, *I Believe in the Holy Spirit* (London: Hodder, 1975), p. 49, who raises Dunn's thesis virtually to the level of theological necessity. The Spirit could not be active in the disciples during the ministry 'because the Spirit was tied up with the person of Jesus. He was the funnel through whom all subsequent experience of the Spirit of God was to be mediated.'

33. *Jesus*, part 1 and pp. 357-62; *Unity*, p. 200.

limitation of the kingdom of God, and the dawning life of the new age, to Jesus' experience, and his alone, in the ministry, not entirely unconvincing—does Luke not rather portray Jesus as bringing the liberation of God's reign to others (notably at 4.18-21; 11.20 etc.)? Does Luke indeed identify the Spirit as the matrix of salvation and new covenant existence, given by God in response to authentic faith—and does he really mean the disciples only came to such belief the instant before the Spirit was poured out at Pentecost (p. 52), and that the Spirit was suspended from the baptized Samaritans precisely because they did not have such faith?[34]

All these problems (and others of the ilk) go back to one: namely, the assumption that Luke builds his picture of the Spirit first and foremost on Ezekiel 36 (and on the associated promises of the new covenant) and its fulfilment. But he does *not*: he does so neither for Jesus nor for the disciples. Jesus' experience of the Spirit, he explains chiefly in terms of Isa. 61.1-2 (Lk. 4.18-21), which looks much more like an 'empowering' to effect salvation for others, than the means of Jesus' own enjoyment of 'new covenant life' and 'sonship'. The disciples' experience of the Spirit is built rather on Joel 3.1-5 (MT; LXX; 2.28-32 [EVV]; cf Acts 2.14-18), which for Judaism was the Spirit of prophecy, not primarily the Spirit of New Creation depicted in Ezekiel 36. In short, Dunn has read Luke's pneumatology through Pauline spectacles, and especially by the light afforded in 2 Corinthians 3. This does not prevent him, by any means, from criticizing Luke; but the standard by which he judges Luke is itself a Pauline reading of the New Testament. Thus in his 1975 *Jesus and the Spirit*, Dunn claims Luke has lost the distinctive eschatological tension of the earliest community, has exalted the miraculous aspects of the Spirit's work undiscerningly, and has completely disregarded the experience of 'sonship' mediated by the Spirit—a criticism which even threatens to deconstruct his whole earlier thesis concerning Luke's pneumatology.[35] It did not seem to occur to Dunn, at this stage in his writing, that all this may mean that Luke has a different gift of the Spirit in mind (Joel's instead of Ezekiel's, and empowering rather than sonship): for him it simply indicates that Luke, the enthusiast, gives an 'inevitably lop-sided' view of the Spirit. When we come

34. So *Baptism*, ch. 5. See the criticism of E.A. Russell, '"They Believed Philip Preaching" (Acts 8.12)', *IBS* 1 (1979), pp. 169-76. Dunn's rejoinder in the same volume ('"They Believed Philip Preaching" [Acts 8.12]: A Reply', *IBS* 1 [1979], pp. 177-83)—that Luke like the rest of the New Testament writers believes it is the gift of the Spirit that makes a man a Christian, and he shared their view that the Spirit was always given to authentic faith, so the problem must have been with the Samaritans' 'faith'—amounts to *petitio principii* in virtue of its first premise, for it is widely contested Luke did so understand the gift of the Spirit.

35. *Jesus*, p. 191.

to his 1980 *Christology in the Making*, Dunn appears increasingly hesitant about appealing to Luke for the view that Jesus' experience of the Spirit is of archetypal sonship (cf. pp. 138-43), and states that the Evangelists '*understood the relation between Jesus and the Spirit in terms primarily of one inspired and empowered, a prophet like Moses*'[36]—a position we earlier found it necessary to argue against Dunn.[37] More recently still he has admitted that his division of Luke–Acts into three water-tight epochs was too sharp, and even that Luke conceives of the Spirit primarily (but certainly not exclusively) as the Spirit of prophecy (all the while rather giving the impression he never really thought otherwise).[38] But despite these interesting qualifications Dunn stands by his contention that, with greater or lesser degrees of emphasis, all New Testament writers considered 'receiving the Spirit' to inaugurate and to sustain that which Christian life distinctively is. Even for Luke the Spirit is no *donum superadditum*.[39] Others have felt bound to demur.

3. *The Spirit as the Power of Confirmation (N. Adler)*

From Adler (1938) to Menzies (1991) we have a long line of interpreters who have taken up the other side of the tension in von Baer's work and insisted Luke conceives of the Spirit primarily (not always exclusively) as some sort of empowering by the Spirit; an empowering which is at least theologically (if not always temporally) distinct from conversion-initiation.

Perhaps least exegetically nuanced with respect to Lukan concerns is the work of N. Adler: we need no more than to summarize briefly his position, as it has been chronicled and criticized sufficiently elsewhere.[40] Essentially, Adler's two volumes attempt to defend the traditional Confirmationist view[41] that the primary gift of the Spirit is imparted to the believer by laying on of apostolic hands, subsequent to conversion. But his exposition suffers serious historical and exegetical problems,[42] internal tensions,[43] and finally

---

36. *Christology in the Making* (London: SCM Press, 1980), p. 140 (Dunn's italics).

37. See Turner, 'Jesus', pp. 3-42, and 'Luke and the Spirit', ch. 2.

38. 'Baptism in Holy Spirit: A Response to Pentecostal Scholarship on Luke–Acts', *JPT* 3 (1993), pp. 3-27.

39. 'Baptism', esp. pp. 25-26. This means his revised position is a variant of the position described in , and will be discussed further there.

40. Bovon, *Luke*, pp. 220-21, 231; and Turner, 'Receiving the Spirit in Luke–Acts', pp. 142-45.

41. I use the terminology as found in Dunn, *Baptism*, pp. 3-4.

42. At first glance the thesis seems to make sense of the Samaritan incident; but Acts 8.16 would be otiose if apostolic 'confirmation' apart from baptism was the rule. And there is no further evidence in Acts of the need for the apostles to bestow the Spirit

fails at what for us is the most important point. He is unable to explain sufficiently the relationship between the Spirit's activity in baptism, and that in confirmation'[44]—a deficiency common among those who take a 'Confirmationist' view. When the confirmation gift is viewed merely as 'deepening, extending and reinforcing' the baptismal graces of justification, sonship and faith,[45] no viable criteria can be offered for distinguishing between a baptismal level, and a confirmatory level, of the Spirit's activity. How could the believer possibly distinguish which aspects of (say) his or her knowledge of 'sonship' to God belong to baptism, and which to confirmation? At best we are told that confirmation brings the recipient into a state of messianic 'fullness' of the Spirit, without being told more precisely what is conferred in this messianic 'fullness' that was not experienced before. The same theological problem is to be found in some classical

(Acts 19.6 not excepted; cf. 2.38; 9.17; 10.44): according to Luke's understanding the apostles stay for the most part in Jerusalem; he does not picture them scurrying to and fro across Asia Minor performing confirmation services: cf. J.K. Parratt, 'The Seal of the Spirit in the New Testament Teaching' (unpublished PhD dissertation, London, 1965), pp. 144ff.; and G.R. Beasley-Murray, *Baptism in the New Testament* (London: Macmillan, 1962), pp. 113-15. Nor is there evidence (whether in Acts, in the rest of the New Testament, or in the earliest church) of a second rite invariably following and making up the deficiency of baptism, whether administered by apostles or by others: see especially the probing analysis of G.W.H. Lampe, *The Seal of the Spirit* (London: SPCK, 2nd edn, 1967), ch. 5.

43. Adler criticizes H. Schlier for distinguishing a 'grundlegenden Pneuma' (received at baptism) from a 'Charismenpneuma' received when the apostles pray for the Samaritan converts with laying on of hands (*Taufe*, p. 83)—does not Luke himself say the Spirit had *not* yet come on them (8.16)?, asks Adler. But in the final analysis Adler's own position is not far from what he appears to deny to others; for he allows that baptism mediates justification and the spirit of sonship by which we cry 'abba' (cf. Gal. 4.6; Rom. 8.15), and that these graces are worked by the Holy Spirit (*Taufe*, pp. 91, 94-95; though he is not consistent in this: see Turner, 'Receiving the Spirit in Luke–Acts', p. 143). But Adler's distinction is subtly different from the Protestant one he condemns in two respects. He reverses their emphasis by affirming that the superior gift of the Spirit is the *second* 'confirming' one (*Taufe*, p. 102), and he binds it to the laying on of hands.

44. 'Confirmationists' are much more agreed *that* there was a rite of confirmation in the earliest days, than they are on the possible meaning of such a rite. For a brief history of interpretation and criticism see Lampe, *Seal*, pp. vii-xxvi; J.D.C. Fisher, *Confirmation: Then and Now* (London: SPCK, 1978), pp. 142-52. For a recent attempt to use Luke as the basis for a revised form of 'confirmation' (understood as the subjective appropriation of the fulness of the Spirit once received in Baptism), see R.M. Price, 'Confirmation and Charisma', *SLJT* 33 (1990) pp. 173-82. Against similar views see the critique of Lederle, *Treasures*, ch. 3.

45. Adler, *Taufe* p. 91; 'Confirmation', in *Sacramentum Mundi* (ed. K. Rahner), pp. 405-409.

Pentecostal exegesis.[46] Adler does seem to indicate, at least in his first volume, that what the confirmatory gift brings is the Spirit *himself* (in contrast to some mere grace or gift of the Spirit). But, as we have seen, this type of assertion, though commonplace among Confirmationist writers,[47] does not appear to be coherent.

46. See Lederle, *Treasures, passim*. In contrast, some older classical Pentecostalism (as represented by Dunn's survey, *Baptism*, cf. pp. 93, 95, 148), and the older forms of Confirmationism, both maintained that at conversion one receives the Son, while at subsequent Baptism in Holy Spirit/Confirmation one receives the Spirit. The distinction there is simultaneously admirably clear and utterly impossible: see Lampe's apostrophization of F.H. Elpis's *One Baptism* (*Seal*, p. xxii). Elpis tells us that we receive Christ in baptism, 'but as we are united to the Second Person of the Holy Trinity, who told His Church to look forward to the coming of the Paraclete, so we need also that second act or stage, commonly called Confirmation, that we may be filled with the indwelling Spirit'. But the church was *not* told to await the Paraclete after being already united with the Second Person of the Trinity, Lampe retorts; the disciples were promised the coming Paraclete as mediator of the glorified Christ: to make them Christian believers, united with the Lord (*Seal*, p. xxiii). Dunn may have exaggerated the degree to which this 'crude' theological error is found in older classical Pentecostalism, but the view does appear from time to time—even in the Elim symposium *Pentecostal Doctrine* (ed. P. Brewster [Cheltenham: Brewster, 1976], p. 28; though this is qualified by other contributors elsewhere in the volume). For an informed review of different understandings of 'Spirit Baptism' in Pentecostal and Charismatic streams see Lederle, *Treasures, passim*.

47. This is the view of, e.g., F.W. Puller (*What is the Distinctive Grace of Confirmation?* [London, 1880], p. 24), A.J. Mason (*The Relation of Confirmation to Baptism* [London: Longmans, 1891], pp. 16, 107, 171, 335, 162, 464 etc.); those cited by Adler (*Taufe*, pp. 93-97); L.S. Thornton (*Confirmation: Its Place in the Baptismal Mystery* [Westminster: Dacre 1954], *passim*, and differing from his earlier denial that baptized and unconfirmed Christians had any measure of the Spirit), and G. Dix ('Confirmation or the Laying on of Hands', *Theology Occasional Papers* 5 [1936]). Mason, Thornton and Dix distinguish between the Spirit working on us from outside in baptism and his becoming an indwelling power at confirmation; but this is probably meaningless (so A.M. Ramsey, 'The Doctrine of Confirmation', *Theol* 48 [1945], pp. 194-201; Turner, 'Spirit Endowment', pp. 47-50), and is certainly unrelated to Lukan categories. Mason and Dix differ, however, in that Mason (like Adler) subscribes to what Dix regards as the medieval view by which confirmation is merely a strengthening of graces given before. Dix (*Theology*, pp. 30ff.) holds that baptism incorporates us into Christ, but confirmation gives us the Spirit who *operates* the salvation of each Christian; but the New Testament nowhere gives evidence for a static soteriological category 'being in Christ' distinguishable from the dynamic 'Christ in you (by the Spirit)'—cf. Turner, 'The Significance of Spirit Endowment for Paul', pp. 61-66.

4. *The Gift of the Spirit Emphasized by Luke as the Spirit of Prophecy and Missionary Empowering (G.W.H. Lampe, 1950–70 Writings)*

Lampe's writings have been enormously influential. His *The Seal of the Spirit*, first published in 1951, was widely regarded as the definitive answer to the Confirmationist position, and as demonstrating that for the earliest church the 'seal of the Spirit' was not an act subsequent to baptism, but a way of describing what baptism itself meant. For Lampe this was the crucial issue, thus:

> The problem of the relation of Confirmation to Baptism cannot be solved by investigating the history of the baptismal liturgy. It must be approached by way of the theology of Baptism itself. We have to ask, not simply what sacramental sign the Church...associated with the gift of the Spirit but rather what is meant by the 'gift of the Spirit'...To receive the gift of the Spirit is to come to be, in the Pauline phrase, 'in Christ'. To be a Christian is to be indwelt by the Spirit: these are two ways of expressing one and the same reality (*Seal*, p. xxii.).

But all along Lampe was aware that his thesis was safer in the Pauline literature than it was in Luke's works, for in Acts, Luke occasionally seems to have separated baptism from receipt of the Spirit. Lampe gave two answers for this apparent divergence from the Pauline paradigm. On the one hand, he asserted that Luke typically regarded the Spirit as given to all in baptism (Acts 2.38-39), and that Acts 8, 9 and 19 were exceptional occasions which should not be regarded as paradigmatic for Luke; the Spirit is here given by laying on of hands as a kind of ordination into the apostolic ministry of preaching the Gospel at turning points in the development of mission (pp. 69-77). On the other hand, he was prepared to suggest that Luke attached *a different significance to receiving the Spirit altogether* from the one common to the earliest church[48] and witnessed in Paul. Thus, discussing the conversion of the Ethiopian eunuch, of whom it is said that he was baptized but not that the Spirit came upon him,[49] Lampe opined that perhaps 'Luke has an insufficient appreciation of the Spirit as the inner principle of the ordinary believer's life in Christ to make him interested in whether or not the average convert partakes of it'.[50] Similarly, he suggested

48. According to Lampe (*Seal*, pp. 33-37), the Spirit-baptism of John's promise was joined to water baptism in Jesus' Jordan experience, and thus became a prototype of Christian baptism from Pentecost onwards.

49. Except in Codex Z (correction by the first hand) and a handful of minor witnesses: cf. B.M. Metzger, *A Textual Commentary on the Greek Testament* (London: United Bible Societies, 1971) pp. 360-61.

50. *Seal*, p. 65; cf. 48-52.

that Luke's own understanding of the significance of baptism differed widely from St Paul's:

> For the former...the Spirit is the power which rested upon Jesus, in which He carried out his ministry and performed His mighty works, and which became as the result of Christ's death...and the climax of Pentecost, the power in which the missionary Church extended its activity to the ends of the earth. It is therefore primarily thought of as the Spirit of prophecy and of 'tongues', making its presence obvious to all and sundry. Hence, there is little appreciation of the Spirit as personal, or as other than a gift of God, something 'poured out', as Joel had foretold...whose operation often appears as a quasi-physical phenomenon (*Seal*, p. 53).

In Lampe's earliest work, then, it would seem almost as though the tension that we observed in von Baer's account of Luke's pneumatology is resolved: the Spirit (for Luke) is missionary empowering and we need not take too seriously his occasional assertions that the Spirit was given *to all*. If Luke has a different understanding of what receiving the gift of the Spirit means, from that prevailing in the early church, he can perhaps afford to alter the relationship of receiving the Spirit to baptism—though the very fact that Lampe argued so strongly that the occasions under consideration all involve exceptional circumstances suggests that he did not really think that Luke's basic concept of receiving the Spirit differed from that of the rest of the church quite as much as the above description might suggest. In reality his two 'answers' are in evident tension with each other. Lampe never truly resolved the tension, any more than did von Baer, but with him the emphasis perhaps shifted to seeing the Spirit in Luke *primarily* in terms of the Spirit of prophecy and empowering to preach—at least in his earlier works.

To elucidate the question further we must turn to his essay devoted specifically to the subject of the Holy Spirit in the Lukan writings.[51] The central theme of the essay was a demonstration of the parallels between Luke's pneumatology and that of the Old Testament. Within this framework Lampe again depicted the Spirit on Jesus in parallel to the Spirit on the disciples,[52] and, in both instances, as the Spirit of power: power to perform miracles and power to preach. This is the power of the kingdom released first

51. 'The Holy Spirit in the Writings of Saint Luke', in D.E. Nineham (ed.), *Studies in the Gospels* (Oxford: Basil Blackwell, 1955), pp. 159-200.

52. Cf. 'Spirit', p. 168: 'The suggestion that there was a twofold activity of the Spirit in relation to Jesus may indicate that the descent of the dove at the baptism denotes a messianic anointing with the particular divine power necessary for his mission, that is, with the same energy of the Spirit which his followers were to receive at Pentecost for the missionary task to which they had been appointed'.

through Jesus and then, after Pentecost, through the disciples.[53] Jesus is regarded by Luke as a prophet, and this to some extent is parallelled by the Spirit of prophecy in the Acts account.

The Spirit produced repentance, forgiveness, peace and the κοινωνία ('fellowship') into which the convert enters by baptism and receiving of the Spirit. Luke (in Acts 2.38-39, and in the citation of the Joel prophecy) clearly expects the last two to be simultaneous: indeed, Lampe added, 'the reception of the Spirit is involved in the very notion of baptism if the rite represents Christ's baptismal anointing at Jordan'[54]—and the comment is only particularly relevant, in Lampe's context of argument, if he meant that *Luke* thought so. But once again, as in Lampe's earlier work, there is a certain degree of ambiguity, for he immediately goes on to speak of the instances of the Samaritans, of Saul and of the Ephesians as involving a special gift:

> It may well be that in all three instances a special transference of the missionary power is given to converts of special importance in the development of the missionary enterprise...(We) may suppose that at three major turning-points in the history of the mission to the world new centres or foci of the Spirit are inaugurated by means of a transference of special endowments of the Spirit...These episodes will then have little bearing on the baptism and the reception of the Spirit experienced by the generality of Christian believers [according to Luke?], not all of whom were endowed with the special *charismata* of prophecy and tongues.[55]

What is not clear here is whether the three occasions spoken of were merely exceptions to the general New Testament rule or whether they were exceptions to Luke's own understanding of the Spirit (and of its relationship to baptism) too. Lampe seems to have implied the former—and this view is more consistent with Luke's own emphasis that the Spirit is the Spirit promised by Joel—but this solution encounters a formidable difficulty. How do we reconcile Lampe's restrictions (the Spirit on these occasions, and in Luke's understanding generally, is a special missionary empowering: not all had the charismata) with Luke's own emphasis in the programmatic promise of Acts 2.38-49 that the gift spoken of by Joel is universally poured out? Luke takes pains to emphasize this universality: the promise is 'to you...and *to your children* and *to all* who are far away, *everyone* whom the Lord our God may call' (2.39). In his Bampton Lectures (*God as Spirit*), Lampe resolves the difficulty by claiming that the tension is due to Luke, who himself is using two basically different concepts of the Spirit. As the

---

53. 'Spirit', pp. 170-71, 183-84, 188, 192-98.
54. 'Spirit', p. 199.
55. 'Spirit', pp. 199-200.

view he then espouses gives a much greater place to the Spirit in 'ordinary Christian living' it is better treated below (§6), along with other writers who think Luke allows soteriological functions to the gift of the Spirit.

Lampe's earlier works have highlighted three major issues: (i) the apparent Old Testament character of Luke's view of the Spirit—especially as the Spirit of prophecy; (ii) his tendency to turn the latter into 'empowering for mission'; and (iii) the somewhat tenuous nature of the connection between Luke's view of the gift of the Spirit and 'everyday Christian living'. This last raises most acutely the significance of the gift of the Spirit for Luke's soteriology. Not surprisingly, a number of writers have felt that if Luke considers the Spirit to be the Spirit of prophecy then for him the Spirit is liable to have little if any soteriological significance.

5. *The Gift of the Spirit Exclusively as the Spirit of Prophecy—Soteriological Functions of the Gift of the Spirit Denied to Luke (E. Schweizer, R. Stronstad and R.P. Menzies)*

These writers can be understood as developing to its logical conclusion Lampe's assertion that for Luke the Spirit is above all the Spirit of prophecy.

(A) *Eduard Schweizer's* main contribution came in the form of his article written for *TWNT* in 1956.[56] His section on Luke–Acts appears to be heavily influenced by Lampe's writings, though with four particularly significant differences. First, whereas von Baer and Lampe had emphasized the parallels between the gift of the Spirit to Jesus and that to the disciples, Schweizer insisted that Luke has altered the picture of Jesus' relationship to the Spirit *to distance it* from his portrayal of the disciples' relationship to the Spirit. Jesus is not thrust out into the desert by the Spirit as in Mark (1.12), but (in Luke's reformulation of Mark: 4.1, 14) he becomes rather the subject of an action performed in the Spirit. Jesus in his ministry is not portrayed as a pneumatic, but as Lord of the *Pneuma*; 'the fact that the baptism in the Jordan and the story of Pentecost were in no way assimilated to one another is a (further) possible indication that for Luke the endowment of Jesus with the Spirit lay on a different plane from that of the community'.[57]

---

56. 'πνεῦμα, κτλ', *TWNT*, VI, pp. 394ff. See also his essay 'The Spirit of Power—The Uniformity and Diversity of the Concept of the Holy Spirit in the New Testament', *Int* 6 (1952), pp. 259-78, and *The Holy Spirit* (London: SCM Press, 1981).

57. *TDNT*, VI, p. 405. Compare *Spirit*, p. 57, where he states: 'Luke deliberately seeks to emphasize Jesus' actions and to differentiate Jesus, as the unique bearer of the Spirit, from all Old Testament and other contemporary prophets who could be bounced about—almost like a ball—by some inexplicable power. The Spirit is precisely not a superhuman power, which would more or less exclude any initiative on the part of Jesus. Jesus himself, all that he says and does, is God's presence. In him the age of

Secondly, again in contrast to von Baer and Lampe, Schweizer insists the Spirit is not the source of miracles in Luke–Acts, only of speech. So while affirming that Luke is Hellenistic in his outlook insofar as he is concerned to show that pneuma manifests itself visibly and demonstrably (e.g. appearing 'bodily' as a dove in 3.22), he nevertheless holds that this Hellenism is mitigated—for 'Luke adopts the typically Jewish idea that the Spirit is the Spirit of prophecy'.[58] Luke allegedly has organized his material in accordance with this: so, for example, he shifts the saying about blasphemy against the Spirit (Lk. 12.10-11) into a context where it no longer concerns the power of God in exorcism (cf. Mk 3.28-30), but primarily concerns the Spirit as the power of God manifest in the inspired utterance of the witnesses of Jesus.[59] According to Schweizer, it is precisely Luke's adoption of the Jewish notion of the Spirit of prophecy which 'prevents him from attributing to πνεῦμα [Spirit] both the χαρίσματα ἰαμάτων [gifts of healing] on the one side and strongly ethical effects like the common life of the primitive community on the other'.[60] The only miracles he attributes to the Spirit are those of speech: tongues and prophecy (which for Schweizer includes preaching).

Thirdly, and as a corollary of Luke's view of the Spirit as the Spirit of prophecy, the Spirit does not totally shape the existence of the believer,[61] and Luke never attributes faith or salvation to the Spirit—indeed the Spirit is rather given to those who are already converted[62] and baptized. It is the

God's salvation is dawning. His life and proclamation is the event of God's presence... For this reason Luke conceives the action of the Spirit in Jesus primarily as the power behind Jesus' proclamation of the gospel (4.18, 14-15)'.

58. *TDNT*, VI, p. 407.

59. *TDNT*, VI, pp. 407-408.

60. *TWNT*, VI, p. 407. *TDNT*, VI, p. 409 actually attributes to Schweizer the opposite view: 'This does not (*sic*) prevent him from attributing to...etc.'. He goes on (*Spirit*, pp. 58-59) to say: 'The Spirit is certainly the "power from on high" (Luke 24:49; cf. also 1:17, 35; 4:14). Yet Luke consistently distinguishes between the two. In connection with miracles he always speaks of the "power" of God rather than the "Spirit" of God. He obviously does not wish to connect the activity of the Holy Spirit too closely with the working of miracles. That is why...in the Beelzebub controversy he still uses the old-fashioned phrase, "finger of God", while Matthew speaks of the Holy Spirit (Luke 11:20). Probably Luke is a little uncomfortable if the working of miracles is too closely connected with the Holy Spirit. It is true that in his action upon man the Spirit descends even to the level of the body. But he cannot be directly grasped. You cannot regard every miracle as unqestionably the work of the Spirit. The Spirit is experienced in the first place where there is a word pointing unequivocally to Christ. Miraculous healings and similar phenomena could come from entirely different "power", even powers opposed to God (10.19). That is why miracles must be done explicitly in the name of Jesus (Acts 4:30; 9:34; 16:18; 19:13).'

61. *TDNT*, VI, p. 412.

62. See *Spirit*, pp. 73-74.

power to discharge a specific task: mission.[63] The eschatological community is for Luke the community of prophets, and, in this respect unlike the Old Testament, πνεῦμα is experienced almost exclusively as prophetic action.[64] So while Lampe can be interpreted to mean that Luke merely emphasizes the prophetic role of the Spirit within a broader understanding of the Spirit's work witnessed in his writings, Schweizer identifies Luke's concept of the Spirit with the Spirit of prophecy *simpliciter.*

Fourthly, nevertheless, and this is where the tension in Schweizer's work becomes clearest, he insists that the main difference between the Old Testament concept of the Spirit and that of Luke is the fact that *all* members of the community have the Spirit and that this is mediated (usually) through baptism.[65] But why, if Luke depicts the Spirit of prophecy (understood by Schweizer primarily as the power to preach good news), does he insist that it is a universal gift, and why is it tied so tightly to conversion/initiation? Even when prophecy is extended in meaning to every kind of mission preaching the sum total of people exercising it in the church must have been considerably less than the total, and such a gift seems more appropriately received in spiritual maturity than at conversion. All Schweizer can tell us is,

> So convinced were they [the community] that God was alive, so strong was the missionary emphasis in the early church, that they give little thought to the broader work of the Spirit in the whole range of daily life, in the keeping of the commandments, and in making the right decisions in many practical questions.[66]

That does not explain much! A revised version of von Baer's dilemma appears before us: if, for Luke, receiving the Spirit is essentially (rather than incidentally) missionary empowering, does this not threaten his insistence on the universality of the gift and its connection with conversion/initiation—and vice versa? And Schweizer's claim that Luke has taken over the 'typically Jewish idea that the Spirit is the Spirit of prophecy' should also give pause. Did Jews really *typically* think of the Spirit as the power of preaching, or was it not more the means of revelation which informed oracular speech, of wisdom, and of invasive types of speech (see Chapter 3 below)?

---

63. *TDNT*, VI, p. 412. Compare *Spirit*, p. 77, where he comes very close to the traditional Pentecostal position in asserting: 'Indeed it was the Lord who opened people's hearts (3:16; 16:14). But here Luke is thinking more of Christ as he approaches a person in the preaching and calls him to turn and repent...The Spirit on the other hand is the power which enables the believers to become preachers of Jesus Christ.'

64. *TDNT*, VI, pp. 408, 412.

65. *TDNT*, VI, pp. 413-14; *Spirit*, pp. 75-78.

66. *Spirit*, pp. 78.

(B) *Roger Stronstad's* impressively suggestive short work marked the entrance of Pentecostal writers to Lukan scholarship.[67] Stronstad interpreted Luke's pneumatology against an Old Testament background of the transfer of the charismatic Spirit from leader to successors (Moses to the elders; Elijah to Elisha). He saw the Spirit on Jesus primarily as the Spirit of prophecy (Lk. 4.18-21, 24: cf. *Targ. Isa.* 61) that empowers Jesus' whole mission (including miracles), and 'the Pentecost narrative [as] the story of the transfer of the charismatic Spirit from Jesus to the disciples' (p. 49). He argued that the Septuagintal language Luke uses of the Spirit is largely drawn from the passages describing the charismatic Spirit in the earlier Old Testament narratives, and especially from Joel 3.1-5 (LXX) and the hope of restoration of prophecy. According to Stronstad, Luke's conception owes nothing to Jewish traditions of the Spirit bringing inner renewal (Ezekiel), nor does the Pentecost account draw on *Pesaḥim* 68b and the association of the Feast of Weeks with the giving of the Law. Much closer, Stronstad argued, are the parallels with Num. 11.10-30, where the Spirit on the prophet Moses comes upon the elders who burst out in prophecy. Accordingly, Acts (so ch. 4) describes the fulfilment of the wistful hopes of Num. 11.29. 'The gift of the charismatic Spirit on the day of Pentecost is paradigmatic for the experience of the eschatological people of God. In specific terms, they have become prophets—they have become a charismatic community' (p. 61). But this is not the birthday of the church. Such a false 'interpretation results from either emphasising the discontinuity between the periods of Israel, Jesus and the Church, or from attributing a soteriological rather than a charismatic significance to the gift of the Spirit' (p. 62). Pentecost is rather the church's prophetic calling and empowering for mission (see ch. 5). It follows that while Luke promises the Spirit to all, he need not attach it to baptism (so Acts 8, 9, 10 and 19 are no problem).

Stronstad's elucidation of the 'Charismatic Spirit' as 'God's gift of His Spirit to His servants, either individually or collectively, to anoint, empower, or inspire them for divine service' (p. 13) at first sounds broader in scope than Schweizer's (or Menzies') 'Spirit of prophecy'—and so one might be inclined to describe his position along with others in §7 below, but in practice he only elucidates the prophetic/witness orientated role of the gift in the church. As the majority of his arguments have been taken up and refined by Menzies, to whom we turn next, we shall offer no separate criticism of Stronstad's work.

(C) *Robert Menzies'* contribution is made in the form of his lucid, concise, thorough and hard-hitting Aberdeen dissertation, *The Development of*

---

67. R. Stronstad, *The Charismatic Theology of Saint Luke* (Peabody: Hendrickson, 1984). This originated as a Master's thesis at Regent College, 1975.

Early Christian Pneumatology with Special Reference to Luke–Acts, published in 1991.[68] It is the logical extension of Schweizer's insights, but made the more plausible both by its detailed argument of the particulars, and by its setting of the overall Lukan picture within the schema of a more general outline of development of pneumatology from Judaism to the post-Pauline Church.

In a nutshell, his position is that both Diaspora and Palestinian Judaism before the New Testament virtually ignored (or reinterpreted) Ezekiel 36, and almost always rather thought of the Spirit as the power of revelation or of inspired speech (whether on the messiah or the people of God) or (exceedingly rarely) as the power of miracles. The gift of the Spirit was thus a *donum superadditum*, not a gift required to live in right relationship with God and attain eternal life. Only in the Wisdom of Solomon and 1QH do we find the pessimistic view of humanity which makes reception of saving wisdom, imparted by the Spirit, necessary for salvation (*Development*, pp. 52-111). Correspondingly, neither John the Baptist nor Jesus conceived of the gift of the Spirit as inner ethical renewal. The 'baptism of Spirit and fire' envisaged by the former was that sifting and judging of Israel that the messiah would perform by his Spirit-inspired utterance (as in *1 En.* 49.3; 62.2; *Ps. Sol.* 17.26-37 and 1QSb 5.24-25) (pp. 135-45). For Jesus, and for the earliest church before Luke, the Spirit was the power of his preaching and of his mighty works, while for disciples after Jesus' resurrection, it was the Spirit of prophecy and power given to Christians by which they gave testimony to Jesus. Nowhere (*pace* J.S. Vos[69]) in the pre-Pauline tradition

---

68. A revised and slightly simplified version, without the chapters on Paul, but with additional theological chapters on the issues of 'Subsequence' and 'Evidential Tongues' is published in this series as *Empowered for Witness: The Spirit in Luke–Acts* (Sheffield: JSOT Press, 1994).

69. It has been relatively widely argued (though not without dissent!) the κατὰ σάρκα/κατὰ πνεῦμα ἁγιωσύνης contrast of Rom. 1.3-4 is pre-Pauline (see differently e.g. E. Schweizer, 'Röm. 1,3f, und der Gegensatz von Fleisch und Geist vor und bei Paulus', *EvT* 15 [1955], pp. 563-71; H. Schlier, 'Eine christologische Credo-Formel der römischen Gemeinde', in H. Baltensweiler and B. Reicke [eds.], *Neues Testament und Geschichte* [Zürich: Theologischer Verlag, 1972], pp. 207-18; J.D.G. Dunn, 'Jesus—Flesh and Spirit: An Exposition of Romans 1.3-4', *JTS* 24 [1973], pp. 40-68; and cf. his *Romans, ad. loc.*), and that the phrase 'according to the Spirit of holiness' is a reference to the power of Christian existence (not the power by which Jesus was raised: so Vos, *Untersuchungen*, p. 80, against e.g. Linnemann) and so implies a primarily soteriological understanding of the Spirit. Vos (*Untersuchungen*) further argued that 1 Cor. 6.9ff., Gal. 5.19-24 and 1 Cor. 15.44-50 all contain traditional catechetical baptismal formulations in which the Spirit was understood to perform soteriological functions. He explained such a view in terms of a widespread Jewish belief the Spirit would be given as the power of inner renewal: so Ps. 51; Ezek. 36; Isa. 44.1-5;

does anyone conceive of the Spirit in directly soteriologically-necessary terms. That innovation is due to Paul, who derived it from the Wisdom of Solomon, as is demonstrated by the unique parallels between Wis. 9.9-18 and 1 Cor. 2.6-16 and Gal. 4.4-6. But Paul's view was not widely influential until after the completion of Luke–Acts (making no impression whatever on the Synoptic tradition: contrast John).[70]

For his part Luke simply keeps within the lines of the pre-Pauline conception of the Spirit, but emphasizes the Spirit as the Spirit of prophecy (which he interprets almost exclusively in terms of prophetic vocation to witness to Christ) by keeping to the older Jewish view which did not attribute miracles to the Spirit. Thus Luke has carefully joined the baptismal account (3.21-22) to the preaching at Nazareth (using the redactional bridge of 4.1, 14) so that the former is interpreted as the prophetic Spirit of Isa. 61.1-2,[71] and he has removed from that latter quote the reference to healing the broken-hearted lest the Spirit be regarded as performing miracles (which Luke, in Hellenistic fashion, attributes to 'power' (δύναμις) instead (pp. 166-71). Similarly, to avoid the view the Spirit is the power of exorcism, he changes Q's saying about Jesus' exorcism 'by the Spirit of God' (Mt. 12.28) to one about casting out demons 'by the finger of God' (Lk. 11.20),[72] and alters the 'blasphemy against the Spirit' context (part of the Beelzebul controversy in Mark and Q) to reinterpret the logion's reference as failure to witness in accord with the Spirit's prompting in situations of persecution/trial.[73]

In the redactional bridge between Luke and Acts (Lk. 24.46-49 and Acts 1.4-8) the church is given Israel's prophetic role (cf. Isa. 49.6), and for this must receive 'power from on High'/'the promise of the Father', which Jesus will 'send'—all of which is then revealed to be the power to witness (1.8), the fulfilment of the Baptist's promise (1.5), and precisely the promise

---

1QS 2.25–3.12 and 3.13–4.26. Menzies (*Development*, pp. 290-94) argues against him that the flesh–Spirit antithesis in Rom. 1.3-4 is *Pauline* (this is the least convincing part of his argument); that Vos's pre-Pauline catechetical passages are not pre-Pauline (at least not in respect of the mentions of the Spirit), and that Vos has paid too little attention to how Judaism actually understood the Old Testament quotes he appeals to (while 1QS is about the renewal of anthropological 'spirit', not the granting of God's Spirit).

70. *Development*, pp. 317-18. Menzies' treatment of Paul's pneumatology (and his alleged dependence on Wisdom of Solomon for a 'soteriological' understanding of the Spirit) is a weakness in his construct. See Fee, *Presence, passim* (esp. pp. 913-15).

71. *Development*, ch. 8, developing the arguments of those from von Baer on; cf. also Turner, 'Luke and the Spirit', pp. 42-85; and 'Jesus', pp. 11-35.

72. *Development*, pp. 185-90.

73. *Development*, pp. 190-97: following but developing the arguments of Leisegang, von Baer, and George.

of Joel's 'Spirit of prophecy' (2.17ff.) identified as the promise of the Father 'sent' by Jesus at 2.33, 39 (and in Luke's redactional inclusion of 'says God' at 2.17). We are left no room to doubt that Luke interprets the gift of the Spirit in the light of Joel (3.1-5 LXX = 2.28-32), and so as the Spirit of prophecy given to the church to empower its witness. The attempt by Dunn to interpret the language of 'promise' here against the covenantal background of Genesis 17, Ezekiel 36 and Jeremiah 31, instead, simply ignores the evidence from Luke's own hand (pp. 198-204).

In the Pentecost account itself, Luke highlights the *prophetic* nature of the gift envisaged both by his addition of a second 'and they shall prophesy' to the Joel quotation (Acts 2.18), and in the evident prophetic nature of the glossolalic gift granted. By the addition of the 'list of nations' (2.9-11), he has underscored the missiological significance of the gift too (cf. Acts 2.5) (p. 211). But (*contra* most from Dupont and Dunn to Schweizer and Turner) he has not turned Pentecost into a New Sinai, nor Jesus' ascent (2.33) into a parallel to that of Moses. The claimed literary allusions to Sinai and to Psalm 68 (at 2.33) are unconvincing (being either too general, too late or simply illusory), so there is no basis for the claim the Spirit of Pentecost is the power of the new law of Christ (pp. 229-44). It is Joel's promise, the prophetic Spirit experienced in revelation, visionary phenomena and inspired speech—and so the power of mission—that Luke focuses, and this alone; both in Acts 2 and in the pages that follow. Luke nowhere ties Spirit hard and fast to baptism, and (*contra* Dunn) he plainly envisages true believers without the Spirit (Acts 8 and the Ephesian disciples in Acts 19), even though they are quickly commissioned into the same prophetic/missionary vocation by laying on of hands and reception of the Spirit (pp. 245-77).

There is much here with which I must agree, and the centrality of the Joel promise (as the Spirit of prophecy) for an understanding of both of Jewish expectation and Acts I believe to be irresistible.[74] But questions remain. First, we must ask whether Menzies has not played down the expected ethical influence of the Spirit in Judaism, and the extent to which Judaism was willing to recognize the Spirit as the source of acts of power. Secondly, we shall need to inquire what motive can possibly be offered for maintaining Luke has rejected the early Christian understanding of the Spirit as the direct source of acts of power. Menzies' view that he has simply returned to the earlier Jewish concept is not an explanation as much as a restatement of

---

74. See Turner, 'Luke and the Spirit', chs. 2, 4 and 5; also 'Spirit Endowment', pp. 57-60; 'The Spirit of Christ and Christology', in H.H. Rowdon (ed.), *Christ the Lord* (Leicester: Inter-Varsity Press, 1982), pp. 179-81, and 'Spiritual Gifts: Then and Now', *VoxEv* 15 (1985), pp. 39-41.

the question—the more so as he insists both that Luke sees the Spirit as the source (pp. 122-28) of the (Hellenistically conceived) material δύναμις[75] (which acts thus as a buffer between Spirit and miracle), and that Luke interprets the prophetic Spirit mainly in terms of power for witness. Neither of these motifs could be expected of one with a predilection for the distinctively Jewish the concept of the Spirit of prophecy! Thirdly, we must ask too whether the Spirit is so single-mindedly given for mission as to justify Menzies' verdicts that 'The soteriological dimension is entirely absent from the pneumatology of Luke' (p. 316) and that

> In Luke's perspective, the disciples receive the Spirit, not as the source of cleansing and a new ability to keep the law, nor as the essential bond by which they (each individual) are linked to God, not even as a foretaste of the salvation to come; rather, the disciples receive the Spirit as a prophetic *donum superadditum* which enables them to participate effectively in the missionary enterprise of the church. As such, *the gift is received principally for the benefit of others* (p. 279, italics mine).

It is one thing to say that the gift of the Spirit is given to the community of salvation (cf. pp. 316-17), quite another to assert it is received principally for the benefit of others rather than for the benefit of the recipient; especially when those others are chiefly understood to be outsiders. We suspect these verdicts can only be sustained by two questionable means: (a) by limiting 'salvation' in Luke to initial faith in Christ with its consequent forgiveness of sins, and admission to the community of believers, and (b) by ignoring the ecclesiastically orientated activities of the Spirit.

6. *Luke's Pneumatology as a Fusion of the Spirit of Prophecy and the Soteriological Spirit (J. Kremer, Lampe [1976], J.B. Shelton, H.S. Kim and Dunn [1994])*

It is not entirely surprising that many scholars have found the notion of the Spirit of prophecy to provide too narrow a base upon which to build the model of Luke's conception of the Spirit, especially if 'the Spirit of prophecy' is construed almost entirely in terms of 'missionary empowering'.

A variety of ways have been tried to overcome the restriction, while still giving due weight to Luke's fundamental understanding of the Spirit as the Spirit of prophecy. These attempts fall broadly into two different types. One way (which we shall examine in this section) is to argue Luke has soldered together Joel's gift with some more soteriologically fundamental gift of the Spirit (e.g. that of Ezek. 36, as typically understood), leaving the two different gifts in some tension with each other. The other (which we shall

75. *Development*, esp. p. 197 n. 1, cf. 122 n. 2 and 126 n. 1.

examine in §7) is to try to explain all the different activities attributed to the Spirit in terms of some broader conception of the Spirit of prophecy, for example, as 'Charismatic Spirit'.

Typical exponents of our first option are Kremer, Lampe (1976), J.B. Shelton, H.S. Kim and Dunn (1994).

(A) *Jacob Kremer's Pfingstbericht und Pfingstgeschehen*[76] is essentially an exegetical study of Acts 2.1-13, rather than a monograph with a specific thesis. But it nicely illustrates the difficulty experienced by modern scholarship in pinpointing the essential meaning of receiving the Spirit in Luke–Acts. Kremer can insist that the Spirit received at Pentecost is the Spirit *qua* empowering to preach Jesus throughout the world;[77] and he even goes as far as to say that the works normally associated with the Spirit in the New Testament—new creation, sanctification, sonship etc.—are *not* attributed to the Spirit in Acts.[78] But this leaves him with the problem of the universality of the promise of the Spirit (2.28-39); and, in the final analysis, he is unwilling to accept this 'cramped' concept of the Spirit of prophecy and tries to find a bridge between the Spirit as power and the Spirit as the sign and means of redemption and 'life'.[79] The only connection that he can adduce is that the verb ἐκχέω ('pour out') used in Joel 3.1 may have evoked the purifying waters of Ezek. 36.25-26, and that this may in turn have precipitated a connection between the statement that the Spirit was 'poured out' on Cornelius's household (in Acts 10.45) and the conclusion drawn from this (five chapters later) that God had 'cleansed their hearts' by faith (15.9).[80] If those connections could be established, the way would be open to argue Luke understood the Spirit not only in terms of Joel 3.1-5 but also in terms of Ezekiel's promise of the Spirit as the (theologically quite distinct) power of inner renewal.[81] But the linguistic and conceptual links are far too fragile to bear this theological crossing from Joel 3 to Ezekiel 36. In the latter passage the 'water' is not a symbol for the gift of the Spirit but for the purification which precedes it, and it is not to be 'poured out' (ἐκχέω) but 'sprinkled' (ῥαντίζω). While in Acts 10.45 the verb ἐκχέω is introduced, not to evoke Ezekiel, but to undergird Peter's declaration in 10.47 that the Gentiles received the Spirit 'just as we did' (cf. 11.15 'just as on us at the

---

76. J. Kremer, *Pfingstbericht und Pfingstgeschehen: Eine exegetische Untersuchung zu Apg 2:1-13* (Stuttgart: KBW, 197).

77. *Pfingstbericht*, pp. 180-90.

78. *Pfingstbericht*, p. 185.

79. *Pfingstbericht*, pp. 197; cf. 179, 199-202, 220.

80. *Pfingstbericht*, p. 185.

81. *Pfingstbericht*, pp. 196-97. Kremer is aware that the two concepts of the Spirit—as messianic anointing of the apostles, and as a general gift to believers—are not easily related to each other (p. 220).

beginning'):that is, to identify the Spirit that came on Cornelius as the *same* gift as the disciples received (and promised) at Pentecost: *Joel's* gift 'poured out' on all flesh.

The fact that Kremer tries so hard to establish a connection between the Spirit given at Pentecost and the Spirit of salvation, and to make them one gift, is all the more remarkable when we bear in mind that Kremer notes that perhaps different senses can be accorded to receiving the Spirit in different contexts.[82] The way therefore lay open to him to assert that the Spirit of salvation was the Spirit active at a different level from that envisaged in the use of the expression 'to receive the gift of the Spirit'; but he did not choose to explore this path. Instead, he has attempted to alloy the two fundamentally different conceptions into one gift of the Spirit. And the very attempt shows just how tenuous is the evidence Luke thought of the Spirit as fulfilling Ezekiel's promise at all.

(B) *G.W.H. Lampe's* Bampton Lectures for 1976 provide an incisive study of the relation of Christology to pneumatology, and it is within this context that he returns to the subject of Luke's view of the Spirit.[83] Luke's complex position is to be understood in the light of two factors. First, as before, Lampe insists Luke has a keen interest in the Spirit as the Spirit of prophecy. Sometimes he gives the impression that the gift is universally experienced as such, but Luke himself imposes limitations on this: closer scrutiny shows that it is only at turning points in the mission that receiving the Spirit is accompanied by prophecy and speaking in tongues, while Luke elsewhere distinguishes 'prophets' (and others who are specially inspired) from the average Christian (pp. 65-67). Secondly (and this is the new factor in Lampe's exposition of Luke), Lampe now claims Luke also recognizes the gift of the Spirit at a more fundamental level. The earliest community bears the stamp and the joy of the Spirit. The importance of the Pentecost account really lies not so much in its promise of prophecy as in its parallels to Jewish Sinai traditions, and thus in its witness to the displacing of the law by the Spirit which inspires and empowers the proclamation of the gospel (p. 68). Thus

> Luke's account of the early Church...fails to bear out his suggestion, based on Joel, that it had been constituted to be a community of prophets. It was not the gifts of prophecy and tongues in themselves which marked the

---

82. With respect to Jesus at Jordan, for example, he states, 'a saying about the reception of the Spirit (by someone) does not preclude that the one receiving already possesses this Spirit'. Then he adds, 'If Luke accords a related salvation-historical meaning to the event at the Jordan and to that at Pentecost in Jerusalem, it does not follow—despite the common terminology—that the Spirit comes in the same character on the two occasions' (p. 211).

83. *God*, pp. 64-72.

coming of the age of the Spirit. According to the wider implications of Luke's own theology, the newness of the Christian experience of the Spirit of God consists, not in the possession of special charismata, but in the fact that it is derived from the exalted Lord...and that it comes as the power and inspiration to witness to his Lordship and Messiahship (p. 69).

At this point one might suspect that Lampe has only found a more funda-mental pneumatology in Luke, from the one he first outlines, by introducing a false antithesis between the Spirit of prophecy (too narrowly conceived?) and the power to witness. But it is the next stage in the argument that seems to be crucial. The Spirit is not merely *from* Jesus but *of* Jesus: 'the Spirit comes to the believer as the Spirit of Jesus'. Lampe continues:

> They share his life which was the life of sonship, the life of man in his true relationship with God. Luke does not share Paul's profound understanding of the life in Christ which is the indwelling of the Spirit, but the striking parallels between the beginning of Acts and the beginning of the Third Gospel show that Luke means to imply a parallel *between the birth and baptism of Jesus* and the commissioning and empowering of his followers to continue his ministry (p. 70; italics mine).

It is the inclusion of the mention of a parallel with Jesus' *birth* (and its rela-tionship to the Spirit) that is suggestive of a more fundamental dimension to Luke's view of the gift of the Spirit.[84]

The problems here should be evident: first, it seems to be precisely the prophetic Spirit, based on Joel, that Peter refers to as promised to *all* (2.38-39). The force of this cannot be circumvented by pointing out that only a few Christians were actually called 'prophets'; for even in Judaism the Spirit of prophecy afforded much more than acts of prophecy. The range of charismata derived from the Spirit of prophecy included the giving of visions, revelatory dreams, wisdom, guidance, etc., and, as we shall see, this means the Spirit of prophecy was virtually the organ of communication between God and man. It is quite easy to see how Luke may have consid-ered such a gift to be universally given to Christians, especially as by the time he wrote the charismata traced to the Spirit of prophecy also included inspired speech (e.g. witness and preaching—and, possibly, the miracles attesting the kerygma). Secondly, and more important, there is no obvious parallel between Jesus' birth (and its related activity of the Spirit, Lk. 1.32-35) and the Pentecost experience of the disciples, and so Lampe has not

---

84. Lampe (*God*, p. 70) goes on to speak of the representative dimension of Christ's mission as 'son' at baptism, which he stresses rather more than Jesus' birth by the Spirit as a prefiguring of Pentecost. But it is not clear that Luke associates 'sonship' with the Spirit at Pentecost: in connection with the disciples this motif is applicable within the period of the ministry (cf. Lk. 11.2-13 and see below), or not at all.

offered any cogent evidence that Luke has fused the Spirit of prophecy and the Spirit of sonship into the one Pentecostal gift.

(C) *James Shelton's Mighty in Word and Deed*[85] is a semi-popularized revision of his Stirling PhD thesis on the role of the Holy Spirit in Luke–Acts. Written by a Pentecostal teacher at Oral Roberts University, it will not surprise us that the work emphasizes the Spirit's role in empowering witness; but Shelton is a careful critic of his own tradition too, and (*inter alia*) thinks that Luke has retained glimpses of the more general Christian position that the gift of the Spirit is given in conversion-initiation, and has some soteriological role, for example, in Acts 2.38-39 and in the threefold narrative of Cornelius's conversion. Apart from the Spirit's relation to repentance and forgiveness implicit in these and in the Baptist's promise (at Lk. 3.16-18), Shelton thinks Luke leaves the theological basis of this role unclear, and so we cannot use his research to clarify matters much further.[86]

(D) *Hee-Seong Kim's* 1992 Heidelberg doctoral dissertation, *Die Geisttaufe des Messias*,[87] interprets the prophetic-messianic empowerment of Jesus in the Jordan event as the first and prototypical Spirit-baptism (p. 93); the Spirit is thus the 'driving power' which 'unites the sending of Jesus with that of his witnesses' (p. 105). It is quite clear that Kim understands this gift primarily in terms of power for witness, and yet he can also speak of the Spirit as God's creative power in the conception of Jesus (p. 124) and, in the same context, draws a direct parallel between this and the Spirit's role in the conceiving the church (cf. pp. 133-70). But once again, as with Shelton's work, there is no explanation of how the one Spirit is simultaneously both the creative-soteriological Spirit which produces the church and the Spirit of prophecy empowering her.

(E) Forced to reinterpret his previous position in the light of his acceptance that for Luke the Spirit is primarily the Spirit of prophecy, *James Dunn's* 1994 response to his Pentecostal critics[88] offers the strongest case for the position that Luke fused prophetic and soteriological conceptions of the Spirit. The arguments essentially boil down to three. (1) While the Spirit of prophecy is central to Luke's pneumatology he will almost inevitably (as a Gentile LXX reader, rather than one steeped in Jewish intertestamental literature) have seen 'the promise of the Father' not merely in terms of Joel 3

---

85. Peabody: Hendrickson, 1991. See also his 'A Reply to James D.G. Dunn's "Baptism in the Spirit: A Response to Pentecostal Scholarship on Luke–Acts"', *JPT* 4 (1994), pp. 139-43.

86. For further detail see M. Turner, '"Empowerment for Mission"? The Pneumatology of Luke–Acts: An Appreciation and Critique of James B. Shelton's Mighty in Word and Deed', *VoxEv* 24 (1994), pp. 103-22, esp. 105-106.

87. Berlin: Lang, 1993.

88. 'Baptism', pp. 3-27.

but in terms of Isa. 32.15, 44.3-5, Ezek. 11.19-20, 36.26-27, 37.1-14 and Zech. 12.10 as well (pp. 21-22). Luke will thus hardly have identified the Spirit exclusively with tongues and witness, rather he will naturally have conceived of it as the invasion of a divine power which only gave these things among other (soteriological) benefits (cf. pp. 9-10). (2) That he thought this way should be clear from the way the promise of the Spirit is coordinated with the promise of *salvation* in 2.38-39, and in the Cornelius story (especially 11.14-18; 15.7-9) (cf. pp. 12-16). (3) Jordan and Pentecost truly initiate new eschatological stages, and do so precisely in and through the gift of the Spirit on the respective occasions—this initiatory aspect being highlighted by (*inter alia*) reference to 'baptizing' with Holy Spirit (Lk. 3.16; Acts 1.4; 11.14) (pp.16-22).

The second and third of these arguments are familiar from his earlier work, and while offered as a critique of Menzies, they ultimately fail to engage with his real position. As Menzies himself points out in a rejoinder, they beg the questions at issue.[89] Menzies (following Turner) had already argued that like the Judaisms before him, Luke saw the gift of the Spirit of prophecy as one of the great benefits promised *to* the saved/restored people of God (and so one that attested the recipient belonged to the saved community), rather than as the gift of that salvation/restoration itself.

The first of Dunn's arguments appears the most promising. Judaism or the earliest church might almost have been expected to stitch together the various individual promises of the Spirit (such as Joel 3; Ezek. 36; 37; 47 etc.) and make of them if not a seamless robe, then at least a serviceable patch-work coat with which Luke could clothe the disciples. And for that matter there was nothing to stop Luke attempting the tailoring job himself as he read his LXX. But there are two overwhelming problems facing this suggestion.

First, if Luke was a Gentile, he was nevertheless one who knew a very great deal about Judaism, and he read his LXX at least partly in the light of that knowledge. The Jews he knew did not collate the separate Old Testament promises of the Spirit and fuse them into one empowering presence that was simultaneously the Spirit of prophecy and the soteriological Spirit. If anything, they tended to reinterpret the other passages in the light of Joel 3, and see them all as 'the Spirit of prophecy'.[90] What is more, when such Jews thought of the 'Spirit of prophecy' (if Menzies is right) they meant precisely the Spirit's presence to grant revelation, wisdom and

---

89. See R.P. Menzies, 'Luke and the Spirit: A Reply to James Dunn', *JPT* 4 (1994), pp. 115-38.

90. Menzies, 'Luke', pp. 131-33. Cf. Turner, 'Luke and the Spirit', pp. 149-55, cf. 171-73.

invasive speech (all gifts related to 'prophecy' in Jewish understanding) and *not* other charismata or graces. So when Dunn asks why the Spirit should be restricted to 'the Spirit of prophecy', and why Luke cannot simultaneously think of the Spirit as a soteriological power (pp. 9-10), he appears to have misunderstood what his dialogue partner (and Judaism?) are talking about when they use the term.

Secondly, it is easy enough to surmise that Luke may have read other Old Testament references into his understanding of 'the promise of the Father'. But the fact is that while Luke's careful redaction explicitly ties this to the Joel prophecy (Lk. 24.49; Acts 1.4; 2.17-18, 33), he never formally quotes the Ezekiel or Zechariah passages, nor does he make any obvious allusion to them. And while we shall note an important allusion to Isa. 32.15 in Acts 1.8, it needs to be demonstrated that this refers to the Spirit acting in any way other than as the Spirit of prophecy.

In the final analysis, Kremer, Lampe and Dunn fail to show that Luke has indeed added another coherent 'gift of the Spirit' (i.e. the inception of some new definable nexus of activities of the Spirit) to the Joel promise, whether explicitly or implicitly, and whether within the Pentecost account or beyond it. And where they have failed it is not easy to see how others may succeed. If Luke has a broader conception of the gift of the Spirit granted to Christians than some, (for example, Schweizer and Menzies) imply, then it does not appear he has arrived at it by fusing two erstwhile different promises of the Spirit into one. Rather he must either have extended Joel's promise to include a wider range of activities than Schweizer or Menzies had admitted, or he must have considered these activities to have a wider significance for the church than the narrow missiological one that Menzies proposes. It is to these two possibilities—which are not exclusive—that we finally turn.

7. The Pentecostal Gift as a Broadened Form of the Spirit of Prophecy: The 'Charismatic Spirit' (G. Haya-Prats)

Like Lampe and Schweizer earlier, Haya-Prats focuses on Luke's concept of the Spirit as the Spirit of prophecy. In accordance with this, following Schweizer (but not Lampe), he excludes miracles from the activity of the Spirit.[91] While Haya-Prats thinks he can trace a pre-Lukan typology of the Spirit's activity, especially in the second part of Acts, in those occasions where the Spirit's action is so emphasised as entirely to eclipse the human

---

91. *L'Esprit*, pp. 37-44. Although published later than Dunn, *Baptism*, this is a translation of a 1967 dissertation, and so unfortunately was unable to interact with Dunn.

agent's role,[92] the notion that he considers to be proper to Luke is that the Spirit is a permanent endowment of the prophetic gift announced by Joel—or rather, it consists

> of a permanent offer which is realised each time the situation requires the supernatural help afforded by the Spirit. The idea of a permanent indwelling is foreign to Luke; rather it is a question of divine power which

92. These occasions (e.g. 'the Spirit snatched Philip away', Acts 8.39: cf. 13.2, 4; 16.6-7; 20.22-23; 20.28) Haya-Prats calls 'irruptions absorbantes' (see *L'Esprit*, pp. 72-82). He contrasts them with occasions of what he calls 'influx complémentaire', where the Spirit is portrayed more as an influence which leaves room for genuine human responsibility and allows the human decision to play a primary role (e.g. 'Paul resolved in the Spirit to go to Jerusalem', 19.21). All places where the Spirit is seen as a gift given to the disciples, as poured out on them, or received by them in fullness, are taken as incidents of 'influx complémentaire' (so *L'Esprit*, p. 76). This type is seen as proper to Luke, not least because he tends to convert Markan incidents of 'irruptions absorbantes' into manifestations of the 'influx complémentaire' type: contrast Mk 1.12 with Lk. 4.1b and Mk 13.11 with Lk. 12.12. On the basis of the different types of presentation he judges the first part of Acts to be the more truly Lukan (while using traditional material), the second to be mainly the addition of a redactor imitating Luke.

But neither the typologies nor the critical reconstruction of Acts is convincing. They break down at a number of points: (a) it is difficult to detect any significant conceptual difference between saying that 'the Spirit will teach you what to say' (Lk. 12.12) and e.g. 'the Spirit said to Philip, "Go and meet this chariot"' (8.29) or 'the Holy Spirit said, "Set Barnabas and Saul apart for me..." ' (13.3). In all three it is presupposed the Spirit gives revelatory 'instruction' (and in that element the human agent is entirely passive on each of the occasions), which men subsequently freely and responsibly obey (and which might as easily, in retrospect, be described as an action performed 'in the Spirit')—yet only Lk. 12.12 is regarded as 'influx complémentaire', while the latter two are alleged to be 'irruption absorbantes' instead. Such classification seems entirely artificial. It is not a matter of different *types* of activity performed by the Spirit, but a difference of narrative focus; that is all. (b) The artificiality of the distinction is particularly clear when we note that the 'influx complémentaire' type is supposed to include all those occasions where Luke reports an action performed by someone as the result of their being 'filled with the Spirit' (ἐπλήσθη/σαν πνεύματος ἁγίου), or the like; but this language, which comes closer to that of 'possession' than most else, has a greater claim to be included amongst the 'irruptions absorbantes'. Is the Paul who describes himself as going to Jerusalem 'bound in the Spirit' (δεδεμένος ἐγώ τῷ πνεύματι πορεύομαι... 19.22: a clear case of 'irruptions absorbantes' for Haya-Prats) envisaged to be significantly more 'passive' or 'deprived of human freedom and responsibility' in the process than the Paul who 'filled with Spirit' prophetically announces Elymas's doom (Acts 13.9-11)? (c) The existence side by side of descriptions that correspond to 'irruptions absorbantes' and 'influx complémentaire' can hardly be taken as an index of difference of authorship when, for example, Paul uses them side by side in the same chapter in entirely 'Pauline' material: compare, for example, the 'influx complémentaire' language of Rom. 8.13, 23, or Gal. 5.16, 18 with the 'irruption absorbante' language of 8.26b or Gal. 5.17, 22.

will exert its influence on believers without suffocating their own decisions, and will always be felt anew when they fulfil their mission of bearing witness to the ends of the earth. This repeated influx into and through the spirit of man could be thought of as a permanent indwelling of the Spirit (p. 199).

This gift of the Spirit Haya-Prats regards as 'eschatological' at least in the sense that it attests the messiahship of Jesus, and its diffusion, in accordance with the promise of Joel, inaugurates the end-time. It is universal because it is the prophetic gift promised for all flesh (and evinced most obviously in glossolalia, inspired praise to God, etc.), but it is not primarily orientated to mission as such; rather to the broader activity of 'witness' to God's salvation-historical intent (p. 100). This 'witness' may be addressed as much to the church (not least in the way prophets direct it at key points cf. 11.28, 13.1; 15.32, etc. [pp. 166-70]), and to hostile tribunals, as it is to would-be converts in evangelism[93]—and the Spirit's witness is also at times seen to be direct (e.g. 5.32), either as an external witness to God's will for the church (e.g. 15.8), or, revealed in glossolalia, joy, courage and praise, as the effect or means of an internal witness of the Spirit to Christians (pp. 110-16). Luke does not confine the Spirit's activity to witness mediated through the speech or actions of human agents to those outside the church.

An important aspect of Haya-Prats's thesis lies in his development of Gunkel's position. Haya-Prats notes the tension in von Baer's work between the Spirit as the driving force of mission, and the Spirit regarded as the source of the Christian 'life' of the community, and resolves this tension, at least in part, by denying the latter premise: that the Spirit is the source of ordinary Christian 'life'. He begins by appealing to Gunkel's position: we cannot (Gunkel affirms) assert that the actions of the Spirit have *no* religious or ethical import; there are manifestations of the Spirit which do take place at this level. But the ordinary religious functions of the Christian are not considered as gifts of the Spirit. Where moral or religious life is considered inspired by the Spirit, *it is always an intensification of what happens at the ordinary level*; and even then this activity of the Spirit as the power of the moral and religious life of the community is only of secondary interest to Luke, who rather thinks of the charismatic Spirit as evidenced more obviously in prophecy, glossolalia, powerful witness, and the like (p. 119). For Haya-Prats, to concentrate on the former could only distort the Lukan emphasis (p. 120).

Working within this framework, Haya-Prats attempts to show (1) that conversion is performed by God and forgiveness of sins given through Jesus, without being mediated by the Holy Spirit.[94] He tries further to

---

93. *L'Esprit*, pp. 94-105, 114.
94. *L'Esprit*, pp. 121-25: cf. 'La conception de Luc fait une distinction...claire

demonstrate (2) that ordinary Christian faith is always anterior to receiving the Spirit (pp. 125-30), and (3) that the Spirit is mediated by laying on of hands, not by baptism (pp. 130-38). He goes on to maintain that where faith, joy, power and wisdom are associated with the Spirit, we have to do, on each occasion, with a special charisma of these qualities (pp. 139-47), and that while the Spirit's presence undoubtedly has a vivifying effect on the community, Luke does not regard the Spirit as an agent of sanctification. An analysis of the summaries in Acts shows that Luke does not specifically relate what is said in them to the direct working of the Spirit.[95] In the final analysis, while Luke attributes the extraordinary kerygmatic dynamic of the communities to the Holy Spirit, he has not made it his business to show more precisely the exact nature of the influence of the Spirit on the religious and ethical character of the individual believer. The greatest concession Haya-Prats is willing to make towards those who want to make the Spirit the power of ethical renewal—and it is nevertheless a telling concession—is that Luke has retained a number of indications that he believes the coming of the Spirit influences the *whole* character of the charismatic. Perhaps most important of these is the way the Spirit (working as 'influx complémentaire') respects (and does not simply overwhelm) the personality of the one through whom he works (p. 147).

But does this mean that for Haya-Prats the Spirit is given primarily as the power of witness, and if so why is it offered universally? Haya-Prats overcomes this obstacle by distinguishing what he calls the 'eschatological/fruit-bearing' aspect of the Spirit's work from the historical/kerygmatic. *All* experience the prophetic Spirit promised by Joel: this is the eschatological Spirit giving us a foretaste of his end-time plenitude, and bringing forth a harvest of charismatic fruit (e.g. glossolalia, inspired praise to God, prophecies and visions, charismatic joy and faith, etc.). This is the Spirit given *to* the community of salvation to keep them *as* the people of God by shepherding them along 'the way': it is the Spirit as the power of God moulding his church, especially through prophetic intervention, and thereby exercising his sovereignty over it. All receive the Spirit so. By contrast, not *all* receive Joel's gift as an endowment to preach and bear witness to Jesus to the ends of the earth. At first the disciples alone receive this, as an 'anointing' parallel to that of Jesus at Jordan, and then gradually this historical/kerygmatic

entre l'action salvifique de Jésus et l'action de L'Esprit' (p. 206).

95. *L'Esprit*, pp. 147-56. Haya-Prats nevertheless concedes that the placing of the summaries in the structure of Acts immediately after references to the Spirit (2.42-47; 4.32-35; 5.11-16) does invite the reader to recognize the new life of the communities as some kind of outworking of the Spirit's activity through the disciples' witness. Luke has certainly not disengaged the life of the community from the work of the Spirit as definitely as he did exorcisms and miracles (p. 156).

dimension of Joel's gift is extended to other divinely chosen evangelists.[96]

All this does not mean Luke fuses together two different conceptions of the gift of the Spirit, but that he draws out two different aspects of the one gift promised by Joel: both the eschatological/charismatic and the historical/kerygmatic activities of the Spirit are plainly still part and parcel of the Spirit of prophecy. Though in making the Spirit of prophecy the author of charismatic joy, faith and worship, Haya-Prats is also somewhat extending the range of phenomena attributed to the Spirit of prophecy by Schweizer and Menzies.

Haya-Prats's thesis is impressive. In some ways it is similar to recent exegeses in Pentecostal and Charismatic sectors,[97] and also comparable with O. Mainville's work.[98] Haya-Prats, Mainville and Stronstad all do more justice to the ecclesiologically orientated aspects of the Spirit's activity than Menzies, while retaining the centrality of the Joel promise. And Haya-Prats can offer a rationale for why the Spirit is promised to all, and yet, in the

96. *L'Esprit*, pp. 173-74, 187-88, 199-200.

97. Compare also H.M. Ervin, *Conversion-Initiation and the Baptism in the Holy Spirit: A Critique of James D.G. Dunn, Baptism in the Holy Spirit* (Peabody: Hendrickson, 1984); H.D. Hunter, *Spirit-Baptism: A Pentecostal Alternative* (Lanham, MD: University Press of America, 1983); and M. Dumais, 'Ministères, charismes et Esprit dans l'oeuvre de Luc', *Eglise et Théologie* 9 (1978), pp. 413-53. My own 1980 dissertation developed a position broadly similar to that of Haya-Prats, but with much greater emphasis on the role of the Spirit as the organ of communication between the disciple and the heavenly Lord (for a summary see Menzies, *Development*, pp. 43-47).

98. O. Mainville's monograph is also a revised doctoral dissertation. She seeks to show that Acts 2.33 is the key not merely to Luke's pneumatology, but to his whole literary endeavour. The claims made by Acts 2.33-36 forge the unity not merely between the Gospel and Acts, but between the salvation-history they portray and Old Testament expectations. The Jordan event is Jesus' investiture as prophet (specifically as the servant of Isa. 42.1-2) and this is clarified as endowment also for the role of the servant figure of Isa. 61.1-2 (Lk. 4.18-21; Acts 10.38) which is probably further identified with the Mosaic prophet. His conception by the Spirit, the defeat of Satan in the wilderness with the aid of the Spirit, and the prophetic ministry of Jesus in the power of the Spirit all attest that he is ready to take the climactic role of the Davidic messiah at God's right hand (Lk. 1.32-33 is fulfilled at Acts 2.33-36) from which he pours out the same prophetic Spirit on the church (and thus continues his salvific work: pp. 321-22). This gift guarantees that the prophetic witness of Jesus himself is that of the church too. This central theme of her thesis does not leave her space for a detailed study of the nature of the gift of the Spirit to Christians, but inclines her to concentrate (rather one-sidedly in my view) on the prophetic role of the Spirit and the way the Spirit leads the church into mission. These are of course enormously important to Luke's overall schema (the subject of her investigation), but it means she does not clarify the relation of the gift of the Spirit to Luke's soteriology with the nuance she demonstrates in other areas. Nevertheless, it is clear she sees the Spirit has a significant role in the life of the church, and not merely in its mission (See esp. *L'Esprit*, pp. 277-81, 290-304, 321-22).

apostles' case, appears chiefly as an endowment for preaching. By the same token, he can explain the parallels between the Spirit on Jesus and the Spirit on the Twelve without implying all receive the Spirit from the beginning as a missionary empowering.[99] But at a number of points important problems and questions remain. The division of Acts into Lukan and post-Lukan (or traditional) contributions, on the basis of the rather artificial distinction between 'influx complémentaire' actions of the Spirit and 'irruptions absorbantes', is unlikely to commend itself. And, despite the scholarly fashion on the question, we must also question whether Luke really thought miracles to be performed by some power other than that of the Spirit (cf. Acts 10.38): Menzies is much more nuanced here. Like Menzies and Schweizer. Haya-Prats has not really offered any explanation for Luke's apparent predilection for 'the Jewish concept' of the Spirit of prophecy, nor of its relationship to developing concepts of the Spirit in the church.

But most important is the question of the relation of the Spirit to salvation. Here Haya-Prats is somewhat equivocal. On the one hand he tries (like Schweizer and Menzies) to cut von Baer's knot by denying the Spirit implements salvation: he insists that for Luke salvation is effected directly by Jesus or by the 'name' instead; neither forgiveness of sins nor ongoing purification being accredited to the Spirit.[100] What then does salvation consist in? Is it *only* forgiveness of sins, and entry into the community that shall one day be saved? Or does it still include reconciliation, sonship and ethical renewal? Haya-Prats does not say. If the latter, *how* can Jesus effect it directly—by what means can he become present to bestow these things?[101] And if, for Luke, it is precisely because Jesus is empowered by

99. In this he is not followed by Stronstad, Ervin, Hunter or Dumais mentioned above. These see the gift of the Spirit offered universally in Acts 2.38-39 simply as charismatic empowering (e.g. to preach), and so raise once again the problem of why the gift is attached to conversion-initiation.

100. *L'Esprit*, pp. 122-25. Like Menzies he can assert, 'Luke attributes to Jesus the whole work of salvation' (p. 215). Compare Stronstad, *Theology*, p. 12: 'In general terms, for Luke, the Holy Spirit is not brought into relation to salvation or to sanctification, as is commonly asserted, but is exclusively brought into relation to a third dimension of Christian life—service... Luke is found to have a charismatic rather than a soteriological theology of the Holy Spirit'.

101. For Haya-Prats, God, Jesus and the Spirit intervene in the history of the church in independent if complementary fashion. Thus, while von Baer had allowed only the appearance to Paul as a direct intervention of Jesus, and as an exception to the general rule that all visions are traced back to the work of the Spirit promised in Joel, Haya-Prats insists Luke only traces one vision to the Spirit; namely that in 7.55 (*L'Esprit*, pp. 47-49), while the editor of the second part of Acts (where Spirit and vision are frequently related) failed to carry through the Lukan distinction between interventions of God or Jesus, and actions of the Spirit. Similarly he believes that all miracles are

the Spirit (Lk. 4.16-30) that his words and actions effect messianic redemption, in the period of the ministry, why would Luke dissolve this connection between Spirit and salvation beyond the ascension?

On the other hand we have Haya-Prats's own assertions that the prophetic Spirit experienced by all brings a harvest of charismata that anticipates the eschatological fullness, and that Luke does believe these workings of the Spirit have a vivifying effect on the community (even if they are always intensifications of what happens at the ordinary level). These suggest that (despite his earlier assurances) he does after all attribute 'soteriological functions' to the Spirit. Indeed, his claim that the Spirit guides and maintains the community *as* the people of God *within* God's plan of salvation[102] certainly amounts to crediting the Spirit with soteriological activity. The Spirit must be seen as a part of the salvation bestowed on the whole person, even if not (for Haya-Prats) the author of his or her whole salvation. In Christian theology, 'salvation' is not simply a matter of forgiveness and entry to the covenant community, but also of reconciliation, restoration from the alienations (individual and community) of 'the fall', and ethical renewal and mission, all brought into being within the context of union and communion with the social Trinity to whom humankind is being restored. The charismata Haya-Prats describes are clearly individual events or processes within this broader 'salvation', and so (ultimately) any antithesis between the Spirit of prophecy and 'soteriological' Spirit is liable to be misleading. We shall need to investigate this in more detail below.

8. *Conclusion and Prospect*

We have completed our survey, and it has probably amply demonstrated there is little unity on the question of the essential nature of the gift of the Spirit Luke envisages to be granted to Christians, and its relation to Jesus' experience of the Spirit. We have seen a real problem emerge in von Baer's work: one that dominates subsequent scholarship. Is the Spirit the Spirit of sonship, and new covenant 'life', or is it empowering for mission? We have seen that the traditional answer offered by Adler and others (the Spirit

accomplished by Jesus (or the name of Jesus), and as miracles are a paradigm of man's total salvation, Jesus (or the name), are the direct source of *all* salvation (*L'Esprit*, pp. 51-52). But where did Luke come by such ideas of an independent presence and activity of Jesus on earth during his heavenly session? And whence derives the notion that 'the name' is a *means* of Christ's presence (rather than the personified metonymy it clearly is in Judaism). These 'explanations' of Luke simply lack tradition-critical credibility. And why does Luke depict Jesus' presence as mediated *by* the Spirit at Acts 16.6-7 (as Haya-Prats admits, pp. 49-50), if he can intervene 'directly'?

102. *L'Esprit*, p. 193.

'himself' is given and he gives both gifts) is both anachronistic and flies in the face of Luke's linguistic usage. The problem with Dunn's hypothesis (the Spirit is primarily new covenant life and sonship) is that it centres on fulfilment of the promise in Ezekiel 36, which Luke (unlike John and Paul) neither quotes nor alludes to, and it virtually ignores the Old Testament texts Luke offers instead: Isaiah 61 and Joel 3. Schweizer and Menzies do full justice to these latter texts, in their claim the Spirit is the Spirit of prophecy. But by making the gift of the Spirit almost exclusively endowment for mission, they fail adequately to take note of the indications Luke provides of the Spirit's role in the building up of the saints, and they can offer no explanation of why Luke thinks this gift of the Spirit should be bestowed universally and in such close proximity to conversion.

The drift of our survey barely conceals our own view that the Lukan evidence can only be explained in terms of some sort of 'mediating position' between the extremes of Dunn and Menzies. Haya-Prats, while offering some corrective here, still, in the final analysis, removes all soteriology too far from the influence of the Spirit, while the alternatives offered by Lampe and Kremer are not adequately grounded. A convincing solution will need to offer a view of the Spirit which does justice to Luke's key texts (Isa. 61 for Jesus' endowment; Joel 3 for that of the disciples), while also explaining why Luke attaches the Spirit so closely to conversion-initiation (if not to baptism as such). The proposed solution must accord fully with what is elsewhere to be discerned concerning Luke's view of salvation. And neither his pneumatology, nor his soteriology, can be presented as though it was an idiosyncrasy, a purely Lukan novelty or predilection. These must be shown to have a credible place in the developing understanding of Spirit and salvation in the church as a whole. This is not to say Luke cannot have had unique ideas or emphases; but they must be historically credible conceptions or concerns.

Part II

THE 'SPIRIT OF PROPHECY' IN JUDAISM
AND AS A BACKGROUND TO LUKE–ACTS

INTRODUCTION

In our introductory review of scholarship on Luke's view of the Spirit we noted how from Leisegang onwards the Spirit in Luke–Acts has frequently been typified as 'the Spirit of prophecy'. But the reader will have observed that we meet quite different explanations of this concept. To the 'Spirit of prophecy' on Jesus, von Baer was willing to attribute not only Jesus' powerful prophetic preaching, but also his exorcisms and healing miracles, and (presumably) his experience of new covenant 'sonship' too. At the opposite extreme, we have Schweizer's now famous assertion that Luke's adoption of the Jewish notion of the Spirit of prophecy 'prevents him from attributing to πνεῦμα ['Spirit'] both the χαρίσματα ἰαμάτων ['gifts of healing'] on the one side and strongly ethical effects like the common life of the primitive community on the other',[1] and Schweizer's position has been defended by Haya-Prats and Menzies. Of these writers, it is in fact only Menzies who has made any serious attempt to discover what the intertestamental Jewish concepts of 'the Spirit of prophecy' really were (rather than merely relying on secondary sources and surveys), and it cannot be doubted that his fresh and thorough analysis lends great authority to his substantial new defence (and revision) of Schweizer's position.

Menzies' position on the relationship of these intertestamental period views to those in Luke–Acts is essentially as follows.

1. For the Judaism of Luke's day, the Spirit was largely, if not exclusively, the 'Spirit of prophecy'.
2. The 'Spirit of prophecy' in Judaism typically affords revelation and inspired speech (e.g. preaching) and so is largely parallel to Luke's presentation of the Spirit on Jesus and his disciples. The parallels between this Jewish concept and Luke's are especially heightened by Luke's choice of Isa. 61.1-2 and Joel 3.1-5 (LXX; 2.28-32 EVV) for his programmatic texts (Lk. 4.18-19 and Acts 2.17-21).
3. In Judaism the 'Spirit of prophecy' is dissociated from divine power to perform miracles, and this aspect too is matched by Luke,

1. *TWNT*, VI, p. 407.

who (unlike Jesus, Mark and Q) is careful to attribute miracles to δύναμις ('power') rather than to the Spirit. In this, Luke leaves the path of developing Christian views of the Spirit (which regarded the Spirit as the 'charismatic Spirit', embracing not merely prophetic gifts, but also acts of power) and actually *turns back* to earlier Jewish understandings.[2]

4.   In Judaism, the eschatological gift of the 'Spirit of prophecy' is a charismatic endowment for service given *to* the repentant, restored and cleansed community (the already 'saved'); personal reception of that gift is not the means of restoration, cleansing or salvation. Luke (like the earliest Christian community) thought the same way. The circle of Jesus' disciples have already experienced restoration or salvation through Jesus' ministry, death and resurrection; so they receive 'the Spirit of prophecy' as a *donum superadditum*, specifically as empowering for mission. Only Paul (and later John) thought otherwise (and made the Spirit necessary to salvation), and his views were not at first widely influential (and, in any case, did not affect the more conservative Luke).

It should be clear that this picture of development of pneumatology depends as much on the analysis of intertestamental Jewish ideas as it does on the exegesis of Luke's, which are said to mirror them. In Chapters 3–5 I shall question some of the perceived features of the Jewish concepts which provide the alleged bridge to the pneumatology of Luke–Acts, and so enable a rather different overall picture of the development of pneumatology. We shall face a number of questions. In Chapter 3 I shall begin by asking how Menzies establishes Judaism's concept of the Spirit as 'the Spirit of prophecy'. I shall then outline a number of arguments which together put a strong question mark over his claim that 'the Spirit of prophecy' was as rigidly fixed a concept as Menzies takes it to be (one that would eliminate works of power and ethical effects from the provenance of the Spirit).[3] We shall need to review the case that in intertestamental Judaism the Spirit was largely the Spirit of prophecy, and we shall do this by establishing what types of gifts were characteristically ascribed to the Spirit,

2.   Cf. *Development*, p. 196: 'the primitive church, following in the footsteps of Jesus, broadened the perceived functions of the Spirit of God so that it was viewed not only in traditional terms as the source of prophetic power, but also as miracle-working power...Luke, on the other hand, retained the traditional understanding of the Spirit as the Spirit of prophecy'.

3.   Cf. Menzies, 'Luke', p. 12: 'Luke and the vast majority of his Jewish contemporaries present the Spirit *exclusively* as the source of esoteric wisdom and inspired speech' (Menzies' italics).

and whether Schweizer and Menzies are correct to identify 'preaching' as
characteristic of the Jewish view of the Spirit. In Chapter 4 I shall ask
whether there is sufficient evidence to justify their claims that Jews who
regarded the Spirit as the Spirit of prophecy would (for that very reason)
exclude works of power from the Spirit's activity, while in Chapter 5 I shall
investigate the assertion that Jews could not attribute direct ethical effects
to 'the Spirit of prophecy'.

Anyone wishing briefly to survey Judaism's understanding of the Spirit
of prophecy is immediately confronted with painful decisions concerning
the scope of the material to be covered, and the manner of organizing the
analysis. With respect to the first of these, Menzies (perhaps wisely) proposes limiting himself to writings from before 100 CE,[4] or, for rabbinic views,
to the Tannaitic literature (though in practice he often admits much later
evidence).[5] On consideration, however, I have decided to include any relevant Jewish material up to 200 CE,[6] and even post-Tannaitic (200 CE or
later) rabbinic material, provided there is no specific reason to suspect a profound shift in pneumatological perspectives on the question at issue. Such
material is admittedly far too late to 'explain' Christian developments (and
my argument as a whole will nowhere depend on such sources), but these
traditions still provide useful illustrations of how Jews actually understood
the Spirit—and they may hopefully subdue some of the otherwise merely *a
priori* statements frequently made about what Jews who thought of the
Spirit as the 'Spirit of prophecy' could or could not believe.

I have also included materials from the *Testaments of the Twelve
Patriarchs*, which was passed over by Menzies (because of suspected
Christian influence), though I shall only use sections where there is no
suspicion of distinctively Christian (interpolated) traits.[7] By contrast I have

4.   See *Development*, pp. 53 n. 1, 68 n. 1.
5.   *Development*, ch. 5. In practice, however, once he has established that the Spirit
is the inspiration of prophecy in *t. Soṭ* 13.2 (and parallels) and *ARN* A.34, he ranges
very widely, the majority of references coming from the post-Amoraic *Midrash
Rabbah* and *Midrash Haggadol*. Menzies' use of seventh–eighth century *ARN A*
instead of (probably third century) *ARN B*—which reads 'prophecy' instead of 'Holy
Spirit'—remains an anomaly despite the argument at *Development*, pp. 97-99.
6.   My survey will thus include the following works excluded by Menzies:
2 Baruch (early second century, though with older tradition); *2 Enoch* and *Joseph and
Aseneth* (for which dates ranging from 110 BCE to 115 CE have been seriously
proposed).
7.   The discovery of Aramaic fragments of *Testament of Levi* at Qumran favours
the Semitic origin of a *Testaments* tradition; the question then becomes how much of
our Greek *Testaments of the Twelve Patriarchs* goes back to such a source. H.C. Kee
(in J.H. Charlesworth [ed.], *Old Testament Pseudepigrapha* [2 vols.; London: Darton,
Longman & Todd, 1983], I, pp. 775-828) argues for a second-century BCE original

had to exclude references to the *Martyrdom of Isaiah* (in which virtually all references to the Spirit are part of the late Christian redaction of this document),[8] and the similarly Christian references in *Apocalypse of Moses* (43.4), *Apocalypse of Zephaniah*, and *History of the Rechabites* (16.7). Otherwise, however, I have been largely inclusive.

Restrictions of space force me to abandon a careful study of all the relevant material document by document—first for Palestinian Judaism, then for Diaspora Judaism—and I shall present the material by theme instead. Inevitably the result can only be a sketch of an area requiring more methodological and detailed study.

with relatively light Christian interpolation. Of the eight references to the Spirit (*T. Sim.* 4.4; *T. Lev.* 2.3; 18.7, 11; *T. Benj.* 8.3; 9.3*; *T. Jud.* 20.1-5; 24.2-3*), only the two asterisked occasions are clearly Christian (and at *T. Jud.* 24.2-3 this may be a Christian redaction of an earlier Spirit-saying). *T. Lev.* 18.7 is also suspect for its reference to the Spirit of understanding coming upon the messiah 'in the water', but the extent of the interpolation may be confined to this last phrase. Contrast Menzies, *Development*, p. 68 n. 1.

8.   See below, Chapter 3 §3.

Chapter 3

THE 'SPIRIT OF PROPHECY' AND ITS PROTOTYPICAL
GIFTS IN JUDAISM

1. *The Spirit as 'the Spirit of Prophecy' in Judaism*

1.1. *Terminology and Corresponding Concept*

Menzies, as we have seen, speaks of 'the traditional Jewish understanding
of the Spirit' which he identifies exclusively as 'the Spirit of prophecy', and
which he sharply contrasts with a view which also attributes miracles of
power to the Spirit (allegedly an innovative broadening out of the concept
of the Spirit introduced by Jesus himself),[1] or one which sees the Spirit as
soteriologically necessary. But how does he arrive at this alleged
'traditional' view? It is not because the Jewish literature of the pre-Christian
era regularly uses the term the 'Spirit of prophecy', for this language is only
widely used in the targums, and it seems to have been quite rare in earlier
Palestinian literature (I am only aware of *Jub.* 31.12), while an analogous
term 'the (divine and) prophetic Spirit' can be found twice in Philo (*Fug.*
186, τὸ...προφητικὸν πνεῦμα; cf. *Vit. Mos.* 1.277). So when we apply the
term 'Spirit of prophecy' to pre-Christian Jewish views we are in some
danger of anachronism.

Menzies himself arrives at this representation of Jewish views by a different route. Beginning with the Diaspora literature, he asks (a) what is characteristic of the LXX translators' views of the Spirit (and this is discerned
chiefly from the additions to Num. 23.7 and Zech. 1.6), and then (b) how
does this compare with what is said of divine πνεῦμα in the various isolated
Diaspora texts (such as Aristobulus, additions to Daniel, etc.) in Josephus,
in Wisdom of Solomon, and in Philo. He notes that in the mentioned
additions to the LXX, the issue is inspiration for prophetic speech, that there
are two similar additions in Josephus,[2] and that by and large all the

---

1.   See the summary in *Development*, pp. 196-97.
2.   Menzies (*Development*, p. 58) actually claims four such additions, but the
divine 'spirit' in *Ant.* 4.108 = Num. 22.15 is probably the angel of the MT, not the
'spirit of prophecy', and Menzies (following E. Best) himself admits Solomon's request
that God leave some portion of his Spirit in the temple (*Ant.* 8.114 = 1 Kgs 8.27-30)

remaining material is either in direct accord with this, or very closely associated with it, for example, the granting of divine wisdom or revelations. By contrast, Menzies alleges, we never find miracles of power freely ascribed to the Spirit, and when these various extra-biblical writings relate miracles these are said to be done through 'the will of God', the 'name' of God, or some means other than the Spirit. The Spirit, then, for these writers, is characteristically the author of revelations, wisdom, and prophecy, and these three things cohere together (and overlap each other) in such a transparent way that we are justified in seeing them as prime examples of a more general concept of 'prophetic phenomena'. With the exception of Wisdom of Solomon and one strand of the material in Philo (where Menzies rightly recognizes that the Spirit-wisdom given is essential to all authentic moral and religious life), the Spirit always imparts the specified divine wisdom or revelation as a *donum superadditum*, enabling the prophet or sage to fulfil some divinely ordained task. It is to the Spirit as the source of such phenomena (whether in individual texts, or as a way of generalizing 'a traditional Jewish view' or labelling the Jewish 'concept' of the Spirit) that Menzies (not inappropriately) gives the term 'the Spirit of prophecy'.

When he turns to the Palestinian literature, Menzies finds a similar distribution of data, with late parts of the Qumran material standing alongside Wisdom of Solomon, but the rest of the material largely supporting the prophetic concept of the Spirit detected in the Diaspora literature. This latter view is especially predominant in the rabbinic literature and targums where, of course, we have not only the same concept of the Spirit, but the language of the 'Spirit of prophecy' itself. While the precise terminology 'Spirit of prophecy' (רוח נבואה) is barely to be found in the rabbinic literature (though cf. *Mek. Pisha* 1 [on Exod. 12.1] and *Gen. R.* 84.19), it is regular in the targums. This is less the case in the 'standard' targum to the Pentateuch (*Targum Onqelos*), where of the ten unambiguous references to the divine Spirit only four certainly use the expression 'Spirit of prophecy',[3] but 'Spirit of prophecy' or analogous phrases are both numerically and proportionately more frequent in *Targum Jonathan* to the Former and Latter Prophets.[4] Of the (probably) later and freer Palestinian targums to the

could as easily be explained as a substitute for the Shekinah presence of God rather than as the 'Spirit of prophecy' as such. Given the content of the passage the latter is much more likely.

3.　*Targ. Onq.* Gen. 41.38; *Targ. Onq.* Num. 11.26, 29; 27.28. *Targ. Onq.* Gen. 45.27 and *Targ. Onq.* Exod. 31.3 provide the textually preferred alternatives (רוח קודשא ['Holy Spirit'] and רוח מן קדם יוי [Spirit from God], though *some* MSS have רוח נבואה). It is thus a little misleading of Menzies (*Development*, p. 101) to claim that the *Targ. Onq.* 'frequently' translates the 'Spirit of God' of the MT with 'Spirit of prophecy'.

4.　Of the 20 clear references to the divine Spirit in the Former Prophets, 9 are

Pentateuch, *Fragmentary Targum* and *Codex Neofiti* tend to prefer רוח קוּדְשָׁא
('Holy Spirit')—the latter having no instance of 'Spirit of prophecy' except
in a marginal reading of Exod. 2.12,[5] while *Targum Pseudo-Jonathan* has
both expressions (רוח נְבוּאָה at Gen. 45.27; Exod. 33.16; 35.31; 37.8; Num.
11.17, 25 [bis], 26, 28, 29; 24.2; 27.18; 'Holy Spirit' some 12[+1] times, and
'Spirit of wisdom' or the like on two other occasions).

When we press the question of what is characteristic of the targumic
'Spirit of prophecy', we find that (as with Menzies' concept bearing the
same label) the relation of 'Spirit' to 'prophecy' in the linguistic construct
'Spirit of prophecy' is not taken too exclusively to connote the Spirit as the
inspiration of prophetic/oracular speech. In eighteen occasions where the
term 'Spirit of prophecy' is used in *Targum Onqelos* and *Pseudo-Jonathan*,
only five unquestionably pertain to oracular speech.[6] But in all the other
occasions it is used for the inspiration of those charismata that fuelled
prophecy, or were traditionally closely related to it. Thus it is used inter-
changeably with 'Holy Spirit' in the targums in circumstances where the
Spirit gives charismatic *revelation* or *guidance* (whether or not this is
expressed in speech: e.g. Gen. 41.38 [*Targ. Onq.* and *Targ. Ps.-J.*], Exod.
33.16 [*Targ. Ps.-J.*]); where the Spirit *invasively* inspires charismatic
thanksgiving or worship (Gen. 45.27 [*Targ. Ps.-J.*]; Num. 11.25-29 [*Targ.
Onq.*]), and where the Spirit is given to impart charismatic *wisdom* (whether
to an artisan (Exod. 35.31; 37.8 [*Targ. Ps.-J.*]) or to leaders or elders of the
people (Num. 11.17-29 and 27.18 [*Targ. Onq.* and *Targ. Ps.-J.*]). It is the
evident congruence between the gifts characteristically attributed to the
'Spirit of prophecy' in the targumim, and those usually attributed to the
Spirit elsewhere in Judaism (even though the *term* is not used), that perhaps
especially justifies speaking of a 'traditional Jewish understanding of the
Spirit' as the 'Spirit of prophecy'.

That said, we should note the important semantic difference between
speaking of the 'concept' of the 'Spirit of prophecy' and discussing the
range of use of the *term* the 'Spirit of prophecy' in Judaism.[7] The former is

occasions of 'Spirit of Prophecy' and 9 are to a 'Spirit of power' or 'mighty Spirit'
from before the Lord.

5.   For details see Schäfer, *Vorstellung*, pp. 23-26; *idem*, 'Die Termini "Heiliger
Geist" und "Geist der Prophetie" in den Targumim und das Verhältnis der Targumim
zueinander', *VT* 20 (1970), pp. 304-14.

6.   Three of these are in *Targ.Ps.-J.* Num. 11.25-28, where the prophesying of
Eldad and Medad is no mere charismatic praise, but a specific oracle concerning
Moses' death and Joshua's succession (hence, for the targumist, Joshua's bid to have
the Spirit of prophecy withdrawn 11.28). The remaining instances concern Balaam's
prophecy Num. 24.2 (*Targ. Ps.-J.*) and Deut. 18.18 (*Targ. Ps.-J.*).

7.   On the delicate task of 'concept' studies see P. Cotterell and M. Turner,

really a modern label characterizing what is taken to be a distinct and semantically coherent cluster of pneumatological concepts (the Spirit who gives the semantically related gifts of revelation, wisdom, invasive speech, etc.) which may be said to be represented in texts even when the term the 'Spirit of prophecy' is not present. A study of the use of the *term*, by contrast, would involve a different (and narrower) distribution, and, as we shall see, a broader semantic scope. These observations inevitably raise the question we must now face.

1.2. *Was the 'Spirit of Prophecy' a Rigidly 'Fixed' Concept in Judaism?*

It is one thing to demonstrate that there was a predominant tendency in Intertestamental-Period (ITP) Judaism to associate the Spirit with wisdom, revelation, and inspired speech (Menzies has shown this, but it is relatively uncontroversial), and to use the label 'the Spirit of prophecy' as a convenient designation for this view of the Spirit. But Menzies wishes to go much further. He would have us believe that for the majority of Jews this was such a stable and well-defined idea that Jews who held it would naturally exclude gifts which fell outside these 'prophetic' categories from the provenance of the Spirit's work altogether, attributing them to other modes of divine action (power, the name, etc.) instead. For the majority of 'traditional' Judaism, the Spirit has become 'the Spirit of prophecy' *simpliciter*, and it is a relatively 'fixed' concept.

This, however, risks turning a 'tendency' into a Procrustean bed, and pushes the evidence too hard. Some of the problems such a hypothesis encounters will be reviewed briefly before making an alternative approach.

~ (A) It should be of concern to Menzies that there are so very few strictly pre-Christian uses of any *term* like the 'Spirit of prophecy' that he might point to as an indication Jews had the relatively clear-cut concept he attributes to them at this stage. To be precise, there is but one case (*Jub.* 31.12), where we are told 'And a spirit of prophecy came down upon his [Isaac's] mouth', and even in this instance the predicate 'of prophecy' may simply be descriptive after the analogy of the regular 'a spirit of wisdom/understanding', etc. Even if we extend the period to the fall of the Temple we find only two further instances, and they come from Philo (writing AD 25–40), whose view of the prophetic Spirit is quite different from what Menzies means by the 'traditional' Jewish view. Most remarkable, in contrast to the targums, is the complete absence of such terminology from the LXX and its additions. This silence may be compatible with the development of a general 'tendency' to think of the Spirit primarily in terms of revelation, wisdom and inspired speech, but it does not suggest a

Linguistics and Biblical Interpretation (London: SPCK, 1989), chs. 4–5.

clear-cut and stable concept of the 'Spirit of prophecy' at this stage, far less that the Spirit has become 'the Spirit of prophecy' almost without remainder, and a category for reinterpreting all biblical references to the Spirit. Concepts usually need to be discussed in the public forum before they become strong re-interpretive categories, and they need to be lexicalized and expounded in some way before they can even be discussed.

(B) Menzies is perhaps correct to infer that in what we may call 'neutral' contexts (i.e. contexts that did not include statements *requiring* some other understanding), a reference to Spirit might normally be taken as referring to the 'Spirit of prophecy'. However, as will be shown in more detail later, this by no means prevents either the LXX or the targums using the word 'Spirit' in contexts where the reference is quite clearly to divine power, rather than revelation, wisdom or speech, and (*contra* Menzies) there is evidence of this outside the biblical translations too. The claim that one can discern a substantial trend to distance miracles from the Spirit—because the Spirit is the Spirit of prophecy—seems to me to be misleading, and based on far too narrow a range of evidence (as we shall see in Chapter 4).

(C) A major problem I have with Menzies' approach, thorough and nuanced as it is, is that he has used what is 'characteristic' of the Spirit (or 'the predominant understanding of the Spirit in Judaism') to provide a 'rigid' concept of the 'Spirit of prophecy', which allows him to *exclude* from the domain of the Spirit activities which were earlier regularly attributed to the Spirit in the biblical tradition (such as works of power and religious/ethical renewal). This forces him to contrast the 'Spirit of prophecy' sharply with a 'charismatic pneumatology' on the one side (which includes the notion of the Spirit as the power of miracles), and a 'soteriological pneumatology' on the other (which makes the gift of the Spirit necessary for salvation).[8] Yet, for all that, Menzies' 'charismatic Spirit' (as applied to the Spirit on Jesus in Matthew and Mark) is really only his 'Spirit of prophecy' *plus* the Spirit as the power of miracles (a fusion anticipated in the Jewish messianic texts that built on Isa. 11.1-4), and his 'soteriological Spirit' (when this describes the pneumatology of Philo, Wisdom of Solomon and Qumran) is largely still the 'Spirit of prophecy', for it is the Spirit mediating the kinds of revelation and wisdom that make the gift essential for true life with God, and a basic impulse towards ethical renewal. In other words, I suggest, we have several distinguishable Jewish and Jewish Christian varieties of 'Spirit of prophecy', rather than a rigidly fixed concept of the 'Spirit of prophecy' and two other quite different types of pneumatology. The minor, though important contrasts, obscure the fundamental similarities and, to some degree, the *development* of pneumatology.

---

8.   See e.g. Menzies, *Development*, ch. 14.

The variety we encounter suggests there may have been no single 'traditional' and sharply-defined concept of the 'Spirit of prophecy', even if there was a general recognition that the Spirit was most 'characteristically' active in revelation, divine wisdom and inspired utterance.

The assertions above will, of course, need to be substantiated, and to this we shall now turn. I shall show that there is a considerable measure of continuity between most of the manifestations attributed to the Spirit in pre-Christian Judaism, and what the targumim understand by actions of the 'Spirit of prophecy'. I shall therefore accept that the latter is a useful designation to characterise much Jewish understanding of the Spirit, and we shall use the term 'the "Spirit of prophecy"' in future as a general label for a semi-stable concept that we can trace from pre-Christian Judaism through to the targums. The concept in question is that of the Divine Spirit communicating revelatory knowledge, or wisdom, or some other special enabling closely associated with one or both of these, including certain types of inspired speech.

I shall begin (§2) by outlining what the targums would generally regard as 'prototypical' gifts belonging to the concept of the 'Spirit of prophecy', and show that Judaism more widely reflects a similar understanding of what is prototypical of the Spirit's activities. The term 'prototypical' here is drawn from the discipline of Semantics, and designates the 'things' (be they objects or events) in the world which would most typically be regarded as belonging to a particular class (in this instance, the class of events regarded as actions of what we may call the 'Spirit of prophecy').[9] Having ascertained a number of gifts which are indubitably 'prototypical', in §3 we shall inquire whether 'authoritative preaching' should be counted among these (as Schweizer claims).

In Chapters 4 and 5 we shall investigate whether such divine activities as works of power and ethical renewal could be attributed to the 'Spirit of prophecy'. It cannot be shown that Jews who had a concept of the 'Spirit of prophecy' (and could perhaps identify its prototypical gifts) were unwilling to attribute other rather different divine manifestations to the Spirit as well as prophetic phenomena, even, occasionally to the Spirit called the 'Spirit of prophecy' as such. Accordingly, we need to inquire a little about the so-called semantic 'extension' of the class. The 'extension' of a class looks beyond its merely prototypical members (designating, as it were, the typical core), towards the boundaries of the class. What 'things' (objects or events) *could* (at the time) be reckoned members of the class of manifestations of the 'Spirit of prophecy' without stretching the acceptable

---

9. For the terminology 'prototypical' and 'stereotype' see Cotterell and Turner, *Linguistics*, pp. 146-54 and 170-75.

semantics of the phrase to the point where Jewish hearers/speakers would say that to attribute such a thing to the 'Spirit of prophecy' would constitute strong semantic anomaly? Schweizer, Haya-Prats and Menzies appear to believe that sentences like 'He parted the waters by the "Spirit of prophecy"' would be regarded as very strong semantic anomaly, on the grounds that the 'Spirit of prophecy' has to do (as Haya-Prats puts it) with the intelligible not with the tangible; that is, with revelation, wisdom or speech; not with physical activities. As we shall see, such statements, while they might be regarded as unusual, would not be regarded as strongly semantically anomalous. 'Works of power', while not quite prototypical of the 'Spirit of prophecy', would nevertheless be accepted as part of the extension. And in the case of messianic figures patterned on Isa. 11.1-4, we shall argue, 'works of power' might rather be regarded as 'prototypical' of the type of the 'Spirit of prophecy' that was expected to reside on that figure. Similarly (in Chapter 5) we shall find reason to question the frequent allegation that for Judaism the 'Spirit of prophecy' is not (directly) an ethical influence, and so we shall need to ask again whether it is true that the 'Spirit of prophecy' is irrelevant to restoration, cleansing and 'salvation', but only follows these.

2. *The Prototypical Gifts of the 'Spirit of Prophecy' in the Targums and of the Spirit in Early Judaism*

The following types of activities may confidently be regarded as proto-typical, and they are offered in descending order of frequency of example:[10]

2.1. *The Spirit Affording Charismatic Revelation and Guidance to an Individual*

By 'charismatic revelation' I mean to denote a certain type of event in the psyche of an individual; namely one which that individual (or some observer) conceives to be the communication of revelatory knowledge from God. For ITP Judaism the knowledge in question would prototypically be granted in a visionary experience, a dream, or in the hearing of words (or by some combination of these), and it would have as its content either fore-knowledge of the future, or revelatory insight into some aspect of the present world or of the heavenly realm. Such charismatic knowledge is explicitly attributed to the רוח נבואה ('Spirit of prophecy'), for example, at *Targ. Onq.* and *Targ. Ps.-J.* Gen. 41.38, where Joseph's ability to

---

10. The following distinctions are more fully discussed and illustrated in M. Turner, 'The Spirit of Prophecy and the Power of Authoritative Preaching in Luke–Acts: A Question of Origins', *NTS* 38 (1992), pp. 66-88.

understand Pharaoh's dream is explained in terms of charismatic revelation; in the marginal reading of *Targ. Neof.* Exod. 2.12, where Moses 'sees' by the רוח נבואה that no proselytes are due to arise from the descendents of the Egyptian taskmaster (and so Moses is free to slay him!); in *Targ. Ps.-J.* Exod. 33.16, where Moses bids God remove the Spirit of prophecy from the nations, but continue to speak to him, and to Israel, through the 'holy spirit' (effectively equating the terms). Other clear instances include: *Targ. Neb.* 2 Sam. 23.1-2; *Targ. Neb.* 2 Kgs. 5.26; *Targ.* Ezek. 8.1-3; 11.15; 37.1; 40.1-2 (and probably by implication 1.3; 3.14, 22).

When we now ask whether the targums as consistently attribute charismatic revelation to the 'Holy Spirit' we find a close match. We may note, for example, the following additions where no parallel exists in the MT of Genesis to the statement about the Spirit (all examples from *Targum Pseudo-Jonathan* except Gen. 42.1 from *Codex Neofiti*):

Gen. 27.5   And Rebekah *heard through the Holy Spirit* while Isaac spoke with Esau his son [i.e. she wasn't just spying!].

Gen. 27.42   The words of Esau, her older son who was planning to kill Jacob, *were told* to Rebekah *by the Holy Spirit*.

Gen. 30.25   When Rachel gave birth to Joseph, Jacob *said in the Holy Spirit*: 'Those of the house of Joseph are destined to be like a flame to destroy those of the house of Esau'.

Gen. 31.21   [Jacob] set his face towards the hill-country of Gilead...because *he saw in the Holy Spirit* that salvation would be wrought for his sons there in the days of Jephthah.

Gen. 35.22   [When Jacob was fearful for his sons in the light of Reuben's action in Gen. 35.22] the '*Holy Spirit answered him and said*, "Do not fear, for all (your sons) are righteous, and there is no blemish in them"'.

Gen. 37.33   He [Jacob] identified it and said, 'It is my son's cloak. It was not a wild beast that devoured him; and he was not killed by men. But *I see by the Holy Spirit* that an evil woman is standing before him' [Potiphar's wife].

Gen. 42.1   And Jacob *saw in the Holy Spirit* that corn was being sold in Egypt.

Gen. 43.14   And as for me, behold, *I have already been informed by the Holy Spirit that if* I have been bereaved of Joseph, I will be bereaved of Simeon and Benjamin.

And while, according to *Targ. Onq.* and *Targ. Ps.-J.* on Gen. 41.38, Pharaoh attributes Joseph's charismatic revelation to the 'Spirit of prophecy from before the Lord', in *Codex Neofiti* we have an almost exact parallel to the wording, but here the charisma is attributed to the Holy Spirit instead (Pharaoh said to his officers, 'Where will we find a man like this upon whom there *dwells a Holy Spirit from before the Lord*?'). A similar phenomenon (equating the 'Spirit of prophecy' and the 'Holy Spirit') is found *within* the individual targums. Thus *Targ. Ps.-J.* at Exod. 31.3 has God say to Moses (scil. Bezalel) 'I have filled him with a *spirit of holiness from before the Lord*, with wisdom and intelligence, and with knowledge in every craft' while (according to the same targum) Moses can relay the message almost verbatim to the children of Israel in 35.31, but now in terms of God having 'filled him with a *spirit of prophecy from before the Lord*, with wisdom, with intelligence, etc.' It is this sort of regular matching of evidence across and within the targums that allows us to say the targumists see the Holy Spirit (in part or in whole) as the 'Spirit of prophecy'.

But if the category 'charismatic revelation' is of transparent significance for the *targumists'* view of the Spirit as the 'Spirit of prophecy' (whether or not the latter term is used to refer to the Spirit), it should also be said that 'charismatic revelation' is the single most common gift attributed to the Holy Spirit/Spirit of God *elsewhere* in 'intertestamental' Judaism too. The many instances[11] in rabbinic Judaism of God speaking to an individual 'by the Holy Spirit', or of people 'seeing', 'hearing', 'knowing', 'foreseeing' (etc.) specific (revealed) information 'in Holy Spirit' thus provide parallel examples of the *concept* of the 'Spirit of prophecy' even where the *term* רוח נבואה is lacking. Examples of the Spirit affording charismatic revelation in the rabbinic material are very numerous indeed,[12] but charismatic revelation is also one of the two largest groupings of gifts attributed to the Spirit in the Jewish materials before and contemporary with emerging Christianity. These examples are to be found in both Palestinian Judaism (e.g. *1 En.* 91.1; *4 Ezra* 14.22; *Jub.* 31.12; *Bib. Ant.* 9.10; 28.6; 31.9; 1QS 8.16; CD 2.12; and

---

11. For lists of examples amongst the rabbis see Schäfer, *Vorstellung*, pp. 151, and 155-57.

12. Typical of the rabbinic material is *t. Pes.* 2.15 [Rabban Gamaliel was going along from Akko to Kezib. He found a loaf of cheap bread on the road. He said to his slave, Tabi, 'Take the loaf'. He saw a gentile. He said to him, 'Mabegai, take this loaf of bread'. R. Le'ii ran after him [to find out about him]...He said to him, 'What is your name?' He said to him, 'Mabegai'. He said to him, 'Now, did Rabban Gamaliel ever in your whole life meet you?' He said to him, 'No'. On the basis of this event we learn that Rabban Gamaliel divined by the Holy Spirit]. The one untypical aspect of this is that the Spirit gives charismatic revelation to a contemporary, against the consensus that the gift of the Holy Spirit was withdrawn until the eschatological age: there are three other examples of this breach *y. Šeb.* 9.1 (pertaining to R. Simeon b. Yoḥai); *y. Soṭ.* 1.4 (pertaining to R. Meir), and *Lev. R.* 21.8 (about Rabbi Akiba: died 135). For rabbinic material see (e.g.) *t. Pes.* 2.15; *y. Šeb.* 9.1; *b. Soṭ.* 11b; *b. Meg.* 14a; *b. Yom.* 73b; *Mek. Pisṣa* 13; *Mek. Shirata* 7; *Gen. R.* 37.7; 45.5; 75.8; 79.6; 84.12; 84.19; 91.6; 91.7; 93.12; 97 (bis); *Exod. R.* 1.28; *Lev. R.* 1.3; 15.2; 21.8; 32.4; *Num. R.* 9.20; 12.18; 14.5; 19.3; 21.9; *Ruth R.* 2.1; *Cant. R.* 1.1.8-9; 2.5.3 ; *Eccl. R.* 3.21.1; *Midr. Ps.* 10.6; 105.4; *'Agg. Ber.* 23.2.(47) *Pes. R.* 3.4 (4 times); Tanḥuma (Buber) וירא §12; *MHG* Gen. 442, 513, 604, 854.

Sir. 48.24) and in Hellenistic writers (e.g. Josephus, *Ant.* 4.199; Philo, *Jos.* 117; *Somn.* 2.252; *Spec. Leg.* 4.49; *Vit. Mos.* 1.175). It is worthwhile noting that it follows from our definition of charismatic revelation that this gift does not necessarily involve or lead to the subsequent giving of a prophetic oracle as such (or indeed to any kind of speech event), and many of the examples in fact do not involve a later relating of the content of the revelation by the recipient of the charisma. To say that the 'Spirit of prophecy' is primarily concerned with 'inspired speech' would thus be misleading.

2.2. *The Spirit Affording Charismatic Wisdom*

We should perhaps distinguish two terms here: 'charismatic communication of wisdom' and 'charismatic infusion of wisdom'. By the former we denote a single charismatic event (perhaps immediately consciously perceived) communicating divine wisdom; that is, an event in the psyche of an individual in which the cognition is perceived to be altered by God thereby enabling improved analysis of a particular situation or handling of a skill or problem. By 'charismatic *infusion* of wisdom', we wish to denote a series of such events—virtually a process extended over time—and not necessarily consciously perceived by the beneficiary, perhaps rather deduced by observers.

In this category we may begin with the pentateuchal tradition concerning Bezalel. In Exod. 35.30-31 (reflecting God's own words at 31.3), we are told Moses said 'See, the Lord has called by name Bezalel... and has filled him with the Spirit of God, with ability, with intelligence, and with knowledge and all craftsmanship, to devise artistic designs, to work in gold, silver and bronze, etc'. *Targum Pseudo-Jonathan*, however, renders this, 'See, the Lord has ordained with a good name Bezalel... and has filled him with *the Spirit of prophecy from before the Lord*, in wisdom, in understanding, in knowledge, and in all workmanship', etc. In addition, this targum almost gratuitously adds (at 37.8) the statement that '*by the wisdom of the Spirit of prophecy*, he [Bezalel] made the cherubim on its two sides', and generalizes the same for the craftsmen in 31.6 with the additional, 'And I have *added a spirit of* wisdom in the heart of all who are skilled'. We find similar phenomena at a number of other places: in Num. 11.17-29 God distributes the Spirit on Moses to the seventy elders, so that they may have wisdom to act as judges/leaders.[13] Both *Targum Pseudo-Jonathan* and the *Fragmentary*

---

13. It is interesting to compare the words of Philo on the same scene: 'Such a (divine) Spirit, too, is that of Moses, which visits the seventy elders that they may excel others and be brought to something better—those seventy who cannot be in real truth even elders, if they have not received a portion of that Spirit of perfect wisdom. For it is

Targum relate this to what they call the 'Spirit of prophecy'. Similarly, Joshua, who is to take the mantle of leadership from Moses, is described in the MT as a man 'in whom is the Spirit' (Num. 27.18)—that is, the Spirit who provides the appropriate gifts to match the job description. For *Targum Onqelos* and *Targum Pseudo-Jonathan* this is translated as 'a man who has within himself the Spirit of prophecy' and 'a man on whom rests the Spirit of prophecy from before the Lord' respectively. *Targum Job* 32.8 can generalize the issue, 'In truth, it is the Spirit of prophecy in a human being, and the Memra of the almighty which makes them understand'.

From this it is evident that charismatic wisdom is perceived very much as prototypical of the 'Spirit of prophecy'. The same gift is clearly equally prototypical to the Spirit in the other targumic traditions where differing terms are used as referring expressions for the Spirit—be it 'a Spirit from before the Lord for wisdom' (*Targ. Onq.* Exod. 31.3; 35.31), 'the Spirit of a prophet (?) of holiness...in wisdom' (*Targ. Neof.* Exod. 31.3), 'a Spirit of holiness from before the Lord in wisdom, (etc.)' (*Targ. Ps.-J.* Exod. 31.3; *Targ. Neof.* Exod. 35.31), 'a Spirit of wisdom' (*Targ. Ps.-J.* Exod. 31.6), 'a Spirit from before the Lord for wisdom' (*Targ. Onq.* Exod. 35.30), or 'the Spirit of wisdom' ([scil. Joshua] *Targ. Onq.* Deut. 34.9 = *Frag. Targ.* = *Targ. Ps.-J.*) And the fact that both *Targum Onqelos* and *Targum Pseudo-Jonathan* here use 'Spirit of wisdom', where earlier in Num. 27.18 they had attributed the same charisma in the same individual to the 'Spirit of prophecy', shows they were understood as co-referential expressions for the inspiration of such gifts.

The category 'charismatic wisdom' emerges as the second most frequent gift of the Spirit in the targum tradition, and once again we find a similar distribution outside the Targums (the rabbis excepted).[14] This should probably not surprise us, for the ancients appear immediately to have perceived the close connection between charismatic wisdom and charismatic revelation.[15]

written, 'I will take of the Spirit that is on you and lay it upon the seventy elders' (*Gig.* 24). See *Exod. R.* 48.4 for a similar view.

14. The only examples of which I am aware among the rabbis are *Exod. R.* 40.1; 48.4; 52.4; *Cant. R.* 1.1; *Ruth R.* Proem 7.

15. The difference between this category and that of the 'charismatic revelation' defined above is certainly not sharp, but lies in several shifts in the typology of the charisma. Charismatic 'wisdom' typically involves the heightening and moulding of a person's natural understanding and abilities, to bring them into fuller accord with God's will or to bend them to serve his purpose: in contrast to 'charismatic revelation', (i) it need not be *consciously* received; (ii) it may be incrementally imparted over a considerable period of years; (iii) it is usually associated with an on-going skill or ability to handle information (rather than being content- or information-centred), and (iv) it is typically related to and enhances natural abilities (thus Ben Sira expected the pious scholar might [under God's grace] find himself 'filled with the Spirit of

Accordingly, the *revelatory* charismata which *Targum Onqelos* attributes to the רוח נבואה in Gen. 41.38 is elsewhere described in terms of charismatic *wisdom* derived from the Spirit (*Jub.* 40.5; Philo, *Jos.* 117; and cf. *Jos. Asen.* 4.7). Indeed it would have been almost impossible for a first-century Jew to distinguish 'charismatic revelation' afforded by the 'Spirit of prophecy' from the deep revelatory wisdom and insight assumed to derive from the Spirit, for example, at *4 Ezra* 14.22, 40;[16] Josephus, *Ant.* 10.239;[17] 1QH 12.11-13 (cf. 13.18-19);[18] and Wis. 9.17-18?[19] Philo makes one of the earliest and relatively astute observations on the relation of charismatic revelation and wisdom when, commenting on what he regards as Moses' wise teaching on the Sabbath, he states, 'I need hardly say that conjectures of this kind are closely akin to prophecies. For the mind could not have made so straight an aim if there was not also the divine spirit guiding it to the truth itself' (*Vit. Mos.* 2.265).

It is this kind of understanding that assures 'charismatic wisdom' its place among the prototypical gifts of the 'Spirit of prophecy', even though many occasions of such wisdom do not issue in prophecy or other types of inspired utterance. In addition to the examples cited, see the further (and wider-ranging) expressions of an analogous type both from Palestinian (*1 En.* 49.2-3; 61.7, 11; *Pss. Sol.* 17.37; 18.7; 1QH 9.32; 14.12b-13; *Targ. Isa.* 11.1-2; Sir. 39.6; *T. Levi* 2.3) and Hellenistic writers (Aristobulus [in Eusebius, *Pr. Ev.* 8.9.38–8.10.17]; Philo, *Dec.* 175; *Gig.* 23-29; 47; 53; 55; *Rer. Div. Her.* 57; Sus. [Th] 63; Wis. 7.7, 22).

understanding' in and through his diligent study of the law [Sir. 39.6], even if he did not think the devoted student would thereby attain 'prophecy').

16. In 14.22, the speaker petitions, 'send the Holy Spirit to me, and I will write everything that has happened in the world from the beginning'. The answer is provided through the giving of a divine cup filled with water like fire (14.40)—'And I took it and drank; and when I had drunk it, my heart poured forth understanding, and wisdom increased in my breast'.

17. '...after telling him [Daniel] that he had learned of him and of his wisdom and of the divine Spirit that attended him, and how he alone was able to discover things which were not within the understanding of others, he asked him to tell him what the writing was...'

18. 1QH 12.11-13: 'I, the Master, know Thee O my God, by the Spirit which Thou has given to me, and by Thy Holy Spirit I have hearkened to Thy marvellous counsel. In the mystery of Thy wisdom Thou hast opened knowledge to me and in Thy mercies [Thou hast unlocked for me] the fountain of Thy might'.

19. Who has learned thy counsel, unless thou hast given wisdom and sent thy holy Spirit from on high? [18] And thus the paths of those on earth were set right, and men were taught what pleases thee, and were saved by wisdom'.

2.3. *The Spirit Invasively Inspiring Prophetic Speech*

By 'prophetic speech' I mean speech which is considered to be wholly or substantially a declaration addressed to a third party of the content of 'charismatic revelation' made to the speaker, that is, what Aune calls 'oracular speech'.[20] Invasive types may be conveniently distinguished from non-evasive types. The latter I have elsewhere termed 'communication of prophetic revelation',[21] that is, an event of prophetic speech which addresses a target audience with the content of some prior 'charismatic revelation' made to the speaker. A report of past revelation need not necessarily itself be a charismatic event,[22] except in a secondary sense. This type is typical of the Old Testament prophet, for example, and of the great majority of occasions of charismatic revelation in Palestinian Judaism (including incidents of 'to say' or 'to speak' 'in the Holy Spirit' which might appear at first sight to be 'invasive').[23] By contrast, 'invasive prophetic speech' may be used to denote prophetic speech conceived of as *immediately* inspired by the Spirit (and as this gift would indisputably belong to anyone's concept of the 'Spirit of prophecy' we need not divide the evidence as before). Prototypically to this concept, the Spirit is conceived of as strongly stimulating the speech event itself and granting some kind of immediate inspiration of its revelatory content, while not completely excluding the human speaker's contribution in the formulation, for example, as in the case of the Spirit 'taking hold' of Amasai and inspiring the recognition oracle in 1 Chron. 12.18. In more extreme cases the Spirit may be viewed as entirely overwhelming, eclipsing or displacing the speaker's natural faculties, such

---

20. I.e. a special type of what the ancients regarded as 'a specific form of divination that consists of intelligible verbal messages believed to originate with God and communicated through inspired human intermediaries' (D.E. Aune, *Prophecy in Early Christianity and the Ancient Mediterranean World* [Exeter: Paternoster, 1983], p. 339; cf. pp. 23ff., 35ff).

21. M. Turner, 'The Spirit and the Power of Jesus' Miracles in the Lucan Conception', *NovT* 33 (1991), pp. 124-52; *idem*, 'Spirit and Authoritative Preaching', pp. 74-75.

22. It could, however, be so if, for example, the Spirit were felt to be 'heightening' the speaker's own powers as he spoke, or somehow 'attesting' the authority of what he said: an example of this type would be 1 Kgs 21.20b-24—essentially a report of what God had already revealed to Elijah in v. 19, but, to judge by its effects (v. 27), experienced as a charismatic event.

23. The occurrences of 'to say...in the holy Spirit' or 'to speak in the holy Spirit' are relatively rare and, when context allows it to be determined, always pertain to 'communication of prophetic revelation' or (less probably) to 'invasive prophetic speech', and virtually never to 'preaching'. See e.g. *Midr. Hag.* Gen. 717 (on Gen. 41.38: praising Joseph's miraculous insight, not his charismatic speech); *y. Yom.* 73b; *Sifre Zutta* 319, and *Targ. Ps.-J.* Gen. 30.25.

that the Spirit is effectively the sole author of the words spoken, after the analogy of mantic prophecy.

Examples of invasive prophetic speech are relatively uncommon in the Palestinian literature, the targum tradition to Num. 11.26-27[24] and 2 Sam. 23.2[25] (both heavily influenced by the MT wording) together accounting for more than half the examples. Others may be found at *Jub.* 25.14; 31.12 (Rebecca and Isaac respectively bless their children by a heavenly gift of the spirit of truth and the spirit of prophecy), and *Bib. Ant.* 28.6. In each of these cases (with the possible exception of Pseudo-Philo [= *Biblical Antiquities*])[26] the invasive Spirit appears to be a relatively gentle influence.[27] The more strongly invasive form is more characteristic of the Hellenistic Jewish writings, notably in Josephus, *Ant.* 4.119 (in respect of Balaam); 6.166 (with respect to David); 6.222-23 (describing Saul as ὑπὸ τοῦ πολλοῦ πνεύματος ἐλαυνόμενος ἔκφρων γίνεται), and in Philo (*Rer. Div. Her.* 265;[28] *Spec. Leg.* 4.49; *Vit. Mos.* 1.175,[29] 277[30]), where the language of mantic prophetic possession finds its clearest echoes.

---

24. Both *Targum Onqelos* and *Targum Pseudo-Jonathan* speak of 'the Spirit of prophecy' being extended from Moses to the seventy (two?), and of the recipients beginning to prophesy as the Spirit came on them. In *Onqelos* this 'prophesying' could simply be read as invasive charismatic worship. But *Pseudo-Jonathan* specifically attributes prophetic oracles concerning Moses' death and Joshua's succession to Eldad and other oracles to Medad, so this is an indisputable case of invasive prophetic speech. There is a similar treatment in both *Codex Neofiti* and the *Fragmentary Targum*, but in these attributed to the Holy Spirit rather than to the 'Spirit of prophecy'.

25. 'David said: "By a spirit of prophecy from before the Lord I am speaking these things, and the words of his holiness in my mouth I am ordering."'

26. But here we are at the mercy of text only extant in Latin, translated from Greek, for a work that was probably originally written in Hebrew; the reference to Kenaz 'ecstasy' is thus as likely to be redactional or translational as original.

27. Among the rabbis cf. *b. Sot.* 11b; *Eccl. R.* 3.21 §1.

28. This is what regularly befalls the fellowship of prophets. The mind is evicted at the arrival of the divine Spirit (ἐξοικίζεται...ὁ νοῦς κατὰ τὴν τοῦ θείου πνεύματος ἄφιξιν), but when that departs the mind returns to its tenancy. Mortal and immortal may not share the same home. And therefore the setting of reason and the darkness which surrounds it produce ecstasy and inspired frenzy'.

29. 'After a little, he became possessed, and, filled with the spirit which was wont to visit him, uttered these oracular words of prophecy (ἔνθους γίνεται καταπνευσθεὶς ὑπὸ τοῦ εἰωθότος ἐπιφοιτᾶν αὐτῷ πνεύματος καὶ θεσπίζει προφητεύων τάδε·)'.

30. 'He [Balaam]...straightway became possessed, and there came habitually upon him the truly prophetic Spirit (ἔξω δὲ προσελθὼν ἔνθους αὐτίκα γίνεται, προφητικοῦ πνεύματος ἐπιφοιτήσαντος) which banished utterly from his soul his art of wizardry. For the craft of the sourcerer and the inspiration of the Holiest might not live together.'

2.4. *The Spirit Invasively Inspiring Charismatic Praise*

The term 'invasive charismatic praise' will be used to denote an event of doxological speech, typically (but not necessarily) addressed to God, and regarded as immediately inspired by the Spirit in a way closely related to the 'invasive prophetic speech' described above. A prime Old Testament example would be the outburst of 'prophesying' that marks the overwhelming of Saul and his messengers by the Spirit in 1 Sam. 19.20-23. As *Targum Jonathan* relates the matter:

19.20   and *a spirit of prophecy from before the Lord resided* upon the messengers of Saul, and they too were singing praise.

19.23   and *that spirit of prophecy from before the Lord resided* upon him [Saul] too, and he went about singing praise.

Similar reinterpretation of the Old Testament tradition by this Targum is visible at:

1 Sam. 10.6   'And *the spirit of prophecy from before the Lord will reside* upon you, and you will *sing praise* with them, and you will be changed into another man', and

10.10   'And behold a band of teachers met him, *and the spirit of prophecy from before the Lord resided upon him*, and he *sang praise* in their midst'.

This kind of speech event is relatively rarely referred to in intertestamental Judaism. When Enoch sees the 'Antecedent of Time' (God), he cries out 'with a great voice by the spirit of the power [= the Spirit of God?], blessing, glorifying, and extolling' (*1 En.* 71.11; cf. 61.7-11 of the eschatological congregation); Barak bids Deborah 'sing praises, and let the grace of the Holy Spirit awaken in you, and begin to praise the works of the Lord' (*Bib. Ant.* 32.14), and *t. Soṭ.* 6.2 attributes to R. Akiba (second generation Tannaim) the view that the congregation of Israel sang the Song of Moses together at the Red Sea in a unified charismatic event in response to the Holy Spirit coming upon them.[31] These (and other Jewish glosses on 1 Sam. 10.6; 19.20-23; such as Josephus, *Ant.* 6.166, 222) are the only instances of which I am aware. *T. Job* 43.2, 48.2-3 and 51.2 are sometimes cited in this connection, but do not appear truly to belong to the Jewish version of the work.[32]

---

31. Cf. the similar tradition also attributed to Akiba in *Mek. Shirata* 1. A parallel tradition exists in *Mek. Beshallaḥ* 7 attributed to R. Nehemiah (third generation Tannaim). The late *Exod. R.* 23.2 has a similar but more extensive tradition attributed to *R. Abbahu* (third generation Amoraim).

32. Eliphas's singing of a hymn by the Spirit belongs to the Paris MS of 43.2 alone; the similar theme in 51.2, and the angelic doxological tongues that Job's daughters receive in *T. Job* 48, appear to be part of a (possibly Montanist) addition to the Testament (R.P. Spittler, 'The Testament of Job' [PhD dissertation, Harvard University, 1971], pp. 58-69).

While this type of charisma is relatively rarely attested, there can be no doubt that if a Jew was asked whether such gifts were clear prototypes of the outworking of the Spirit of prophecy, the answer would be affirmative: its close relation to 'invasive prophetic speech' assured this.

Charismatic revelation, charismatic wisdom, invasive prophetic speech and invasive charismatic praise are then the four prototypical gifts of what the targum tradition calls the 'Spirit of prophecy'. This is very closely matched by what is said of 'the Holy Spirit' in the same tradition, at least 27 out of 31 references all being to phenomena falling within the range of these four gifts. Such a match suggests that in the Targum tradition 'the Holy Spirit' is effectively the 'Spirit of prophecy', though this shall soon need to be qualified. It is also striking that, even on a conservative count, more than half of the references to the divine Spirit in the extra-biblical ITP literature up to the end of the first century relate to instances of these gifts. This suggests that the concept of the 'Spirit of prophecy' which we defined earlier was prevalent in Judaism, even if it was not the whole story. It is to the rest of the story we must now turn. First we ask whether 'authoritative preaching' would be regarded as typical of the 'Spirit of prophecy' (§3); then we ask to what extent works of power (Chapter 4) and spiritual/ethical renewal (Chapter 5) might be attributed to the 'Spirit of prophecy' in Judaism.

3. *Preaching and the 'Spirit of Prophecy'*

In his influential article in *TDNT*, E. Schweizer was to claim:

> Luke adopts the typically Jewish idea that the Spirit is the Spirit of prophecy...This may be seen in Lk. 4:23-27, where the miraculous signs mentioned in the quotation in v.18 are specifically rejected as manifestations of the Spirit and only authoritative preaching is regarded as the fulfilment of the prophecy (*TDNT*, VI, p. 407).

Schweizer's contrast here is not simply between Jewish ideas and pagan ones, but more especially between what he considers to be Luke's 'new understanding' and what he regards as the more primitive position held by Mark and Matthew, who portray the Spirit as *both* the power of authoritative preaching *and* as the power of miracle.[33] This contrast has been taken up by other writers, and nowhere more forcefully than in Menzies' work. It is part of the case that Luke has turned aside from the path of development of pneumatological ideas that was taking place in Christian circles, to older Jewish ideas. How do we assess this claim? In one sense, 'preaching' has so often been partially identified with 'prophecy' in the Christian tradition, and viewed as simply another type of 'inspired speech', that the two gifts would appear to be immediately related.

33. See e.g. *TDNT*, VI, pp. 402-404.

But the issues are not quite that simple. Preaching is a specific type of what we have elsewhere called 'charismatic expository address'.[34] By this we mean to denote a type of speech event, in which the Spirit's power is perceived to be experienced by speaker, hearers, or both (hence 'charismatic'); namely one in which the speaker proclaims, expounds and applies some tradition, idea or event. The adjective 'expository' here is not used in the purely ecclesiastical sense of exposition of biblical passages, but in the broader way used in Discourse Analysis to denote any type of explanatory or argumentative discourse (from a talk on the principles of First Aid to a book on Plato's concept of justice). The most obvious examples of 'expository charismatic address' are the traditional understanding of powerful preaching or spiritual teaching. While the phrase 'charismatic expository address' might normally be expected to mean only the explanation and application of, for example, some aspect of religious *tradition*, it shall be used here to cover the elucidation of 'charismatic revelation' as well, that is, of any type of charismatic discourse where the speaker gives his own ordered reflection upon and deliberate interpretation of religious ideas, however these ideas were received. The contrasting factor with the categories of speech defined among the prototypical gifts outlined above lies in the deliberate interpretive enterprise involved when compared with the sheer divine 'givenness' of charismatic revelation or invasive prophetic speech. In a survey of Judaism we have not been able to find a single convincing and unambiguous example where the 'Spirit of prophecy' is regarded as the source of 'inspired preaching'.

Typically, within Judaism, the Spirit imparts revelation or wisdom to the charismatic; alternatively, the charismatic may be overcome by the Spirit in direct prophetic speech or doxology. The clearer the examples of the latter, the more it is stressed that the speaker's mind is *not* active in the process (so Josephus, *Ant.* 4.119; *Bib. Ant.* 62.2; and Philo, *Spec. Leg.* 4.49; *Vit. Mos.* 1.175 and 277; and compare *Rer. Div. Her.* 264-66; *Spec. Leg.* 1.65), and so a parallel with authoritative preaching becomes impossible to draw. The clearer the examples of the former, the more it is obvious the Spirit of prophecy is the power by which the charismatic *receives* his wisdom or revelation, not, as such, a power by which he *communicates* it.[35] His speech, judgments or actions may evince the charisma the man of God has received,

---

34. Turner, 'Spirit and Authoritative Preaching', pp. 75-76.

35. Even at Mic. 3.8, which is as close to Schweizer's view as the Old Testament comes, the 'power' of the Spirit is the compelling force of the prophet's conviction concerning the revelation he has received. It stands in direct contrast to the feeble dithering of the false prophets stripped of their powers and devoid of revelations (3.5-7).

but those things are not themselves the locus of the action of the Spirit of prophecy.

Two works have been claimed as the chief evidence that Judaism considered the Spirit of prophecy to be the power of charismatic discourse (rather than simply of revelatory wisdom or invasive speech); namely the *Martyrdom of Isaiah* (1.7 and 5.15) and Philo's *Virt.* (217). In the first, at 1.7 Isaiah says 'as the Spirit who speaks in me lives', and then at 5.15 we are told Isaiah 'did not cry out, or weep, but his mouth spoke with the Holy Spirit until he was sawn in two'. Taken together, these indeed probably pertain to 'charismatic discourse'—a speaking which is the direct locus of the Spirit's activity, while not simply invasive speech. But this is not Judaism: it is precisely Christianity. The language here is exactly that of the later Christian part of the book (cf. especially 6.10), and rightly regarded as a redactional addition in both places.[36] In *Virt.* 217, Philo offers the other most plausible incidence. Here Philo certainly attributes to the Spirit on Abraham his special persuasiveness of speech. But it must be observed that this is only a part of a much more general enhancement of his 'eyes, complexion, stature, carriage, movement and voice' that his possession by the Spirit brought about—and here we appear to have a view distinctive to Philo, that fuller possession by the Spirit makes one more like the heavenly spiritual Man (of *Op. Mund.* 69ff.), or like Adam before he was estranged from God and thrown out of the Garden (*Op. Mund.* 134ff., 144), and this understanding is hardly representative of Judaism.

The idea of the 'Spirit of prophecy' as the inspiration of preaching, is certainly found in Luke–Acts; but, as I have argued elsewhere, he must have got that from Christian circles, where it was common, not from Judaism (where we have no clear examples of it).[37] We need not doubt that Jewish Christians, if asked, would recognize events of charismatic preaching as a legitimate part of the extension of the phrase the 'Spirit of prophecy', and as a predictable development from earlier Jewish ideas (a development we shall need to explain later). But I do not think that any contemporary of Luke's, reading his works, would claim Luke has turned back from the usual Christian understandings and refurbished 'the typical Jewish view of the Spirit of prophecy as the power of preaching'; he or she would recognise such an idea as more pan-Christian, than typical to Judaism.

36. The Christian redactional nature of 1.7 is also evident from the words 'and as the Beloved of my LORD lives' (a referring expression for Christ).

37. See Turner, 'Spirit and Authoritative Preaching', esp. pp. 68-72, and 87-88.

4. *Conclusion*

Despite the rarity of the phrase 'the "Spirit of prophecy"' in what are provably pre-Lukan Jewish writings, we may be relatively assured that Jews of Luke's time did indeed think of the Spirit in this way: that is, chiefly as the source of charismatic revelation, wisdom, invasive prophetic speech and invasive charismatic praise. These are the prototypical gifts the targums attribute to the 'Spirit of prophecy' and they, with the rest of Judaism, consistently trace the same set of gifts to the 'Holy Spirit' (or to the Spirit of God referred to by a variety of other expressions).

Chapter 4

THE 'SPIRIT OF PROPHECY' AND MIRACULOUS 'POWER'
IN JUDAISM

Schweizer, Haya-Prats and Menzies tell us that because Luke regarded the
Spirit as 'the Spirit of prophecy', he could not attribute miracles of power
(such as healings and exorcisms) to the Spirit, so he deliberately changed his
Mark and Q traditions in order to remove such connections. Menzies goes
further, and effectively generalizes this as a comment about intertestamental
Judaism, for whom he thinks the Spirit is predominantly 'the Spirit of
prophecy'. Thus, in summing up his survey of Judaism, he tells us,

> the literature shows a general reluctance to associate the Spirit with miracu-
> lous deeds. The man or woman endowed with the Spirit may perform
> miracles, but these works of wonder are usually not attributed to the Spirit.[1]

If we ask why Jews should be reluctant to make this attribution, the
response is simply that they have increasingly come to restrict the Spirit to
'the Spirit of prophecy'. How should we evaluate this thesis?

There are important respects in which we should not doubt the validity
(and never the acuity) of Menzies' observations:[2] I would concur with him,
for example, that there was no lively interest or widespread desire to associate the Spirit with works of power in the ITP period. But that is not to say
such an interest was entirely absent. Some instances of this are hussled
over-quickly into the darkness, and others, even if late, illustrate how Jews
who subscribed to a belief in the Spirit as the 'Spirit of prophecy' could
nevertheless attribute miracles of power to the same Spirit.

Menzies excludes, for example, *2 Baruch* on the grounds that it is late;

---

1. *Development*, p. 112.
2. Menzies' book reacted in detail with my own earlier doctoral thesis on the
subject. In an article I have taken issue with both Schweizer and Menzies (Turner,
'Spirit and Power', pp. 124-52), though as Menzies had not yet published his own dissertation, I included only what I considered its major arguments. In a generous article
by way of rejoinder ('Spirit and Power in Luke–Acts: A Response to Max Turner',
JSNT 49 [1993], pp. 11-20), Menzies has probed some of my arguments, and added
some of his own that he feels I overlooked (or the force of which I minimized).

though it could be as early as 75 CE, and is regularly dated at the beginning of the second century, if not before. As Menzies makes extensive use of much later rabbinic material to elucidate his views, I do not see why *2 Baruch* is excluded. It is a Syriac translation of a Greek which ultimately seems to depend on an earlier Hebrew or Aramaic apocalypse, and there is no reason to posit Christian influence. Yet here, clearly, we have both the concept of the Spirit as author of creation (21.4), and the (related) idea of the Spirit as the author of new creation and resurrection (23.5). D. Müller was right to see this as one of the possible clues to the Pauline belief that the Spirit was the power of resurrection.[3] Similarly with *4 Ezra*, which was written before 120 CE: this work has been subjected to some Christian influence, but there is no need to posit such at 6.39-41 where Gen. 1.2 is interpreted to denote the Spirit as the power of creation.[4] Both these works subscribe to the view that the Spirit is the 'Spirit of prophecy' (*2 Bar.* 75.3-4; *4 Ezra* 14.22), but this does not prevent them from attributing creative works of power to the same Spirit. Other traditions (such as *Gen. R.* 96.5 [but only in a late MS]; *Exod. R.* 48.4; *Lev. R.* 8.2; *Cant. R.* 1.1 §9; *Pes. R.* 1.6), while they are too late to use to illustrate the sort of views circulating at the time of the earliest church, nevertheless illustrate that Jews who thought of the Holy Spirit as the 'Spirit of prophecy' had no problem with attributing resurrection and other miracles of power to the Spirit.

My main objection to Menzies' view, however, is that he minimizes the influence of the Bible 'translations'. Of course, redactional additions in the translations and interpretations of the biblical text speak strongly of 'particular interests' and 'characteristic emphases'—and these largely underscore the conclusion (which we fully accept) that it was the Spirit as the 'Spirit of prophecy' that was a predominant interest. But Menzies wishes to argue more than that. He wishes to argue the interest was so predominant that someone like Luke, who thought of the Spirit as the 'Spirit of prophecy', would (for that very reason) inevitably be inclined to *suppress* references to the Spirit in connection with miracles of power. We submit that the most obvious place to test such a hypothesis is in the textual tradition of the Hebrew Bible, and in the way the LXX and targums translate the Hebrew Old Testament. Their translations vary from the semi-literal to the very free, and if the idea of attributing miraculous deeds to the Spirit were a problem, they could easily have avoided it (or perhaps included δύναμις as a buffer between the Spirit and the miracle, to soften the association).

---

3. 'Geisterfahrung und Totenauferweckung: Untersuchungen zur Totenauferweckung bei Paulus und in den ihm vorgegebenen Überlieferungen' (PhD dissertation, Christian-Albrecht-Universität, Kiel, 1980), pp. 111-32.

4. Cf. *b. Ḥag.* 15a; *Gen. R.* 2.4; LXX Gen. 1.2, etc.

Strikingly, however, these works that had by far the widest 'readership' apparently found no problem in reasserting the Old Testament position that the Spirit was the source of both charismatic wisdom/revelation and of other types of miraculous power.

1. *The Spirit and the Power of Miracle in the LXX and Targums*

The LXX translators, who have added a couple of references to the Spirit as the author of charismatic revelation (Zech. 1.6 and Num. 23.7 [but here merely duplicating 24.2]), do not shrink from supplying πνεῦμα κυρίου in all those places where it would *have* to be understood as the power of some kind of miraculous deeds (e.g. Judg. 14.6, 19; 15.14), and the parallels in language used suggest the translators took Judg. 3.10, 6.34, 11.29, 13.25, 1 Kgdms 11.6 (= 1 Sam.), Isa. 11.4 and so on, in the same way. They could easily have supplied δύναμις κυρίου instead if there were a conceptual problem in attributing miracles to the Spirit. Similarly the translators allow that it is the πνεῦμα κυρίου that picks the prophet up, or transports him from one place to another (3 Kgdms 18.12; 4 Kgdms 2.16; Ezek. 2.2; 3.12, 14, 24; 8.3; 11.1, 5, 24; 37.1; 43.5), while at the same time (in some of the Ezekiel instances) as revealing God's message to him. These passages are perhaps particularly significant because they demonstrate that it is not a matter of two distinct and separate pneumatologies: the Spirit as the 'Spirit of prophecy' who brings Ezekiel revelation is the *same* Spirit who lifts him onto his feet, or transports him to different locations.

The LXX also seems to go beyond the MT in associating the Spirit with creative activity. The רוח of Gen. 1.2 is ambiguous in the Hebrew, and perhaps understood as 'a wind' in parts of the targum tradition,[5] but the LXX rendering πνεῦμα θεοῦ would more obviously be understood as the *divine* Spirit (compare its use at Gen. 41.38, and contrast the expressions in Gen. 8.1 or Num. 11.31 which might more readily have suggested something other than the divine Spirit). And while in Job 33.4, Ps. 103.30, 32.6 and Jdt. 16.14 the word πνεῦμα could be taken as divine 'breath' (and so as metonymy for God's word of command), these would certainly have been obvious candidates for clarificatory emendation had there been a problem with associating the Spirit with creative power.

The same sort of comments apply rather more forcefully to the targums, where the translators' 'freedom' regularly makes *The Living Bible* look stiltedly over-literal. The targums (for the tradition behind which an early dating seems increasingly attractive) emphatically and regularly identify the

---

5.   *Targ*. Job 33.4, however, reads: 'The Spirit of God has made me, and the Memra of the Almighty has sustained me'.

Spirit as the 'Spirit of prophecy' (רוח נבואה); but that does not lead them to avoid the word רוח in contexts where 'power' is meant; indeed, the connection is *firmly established* by the regular use of the expression 'Spirit of power' (רוח גבורא) amounting to half the occasions of reference to the Spirit in the whole corpus of the Former Prophets. 'Spirit of power/might' is used not only at Judg. 14.6, 19, 15.14, where we might anticipate it in relation to Samson (though even here the word רוח could so easily have been avoided altogether), but also at 6.34, 11.29, 13.25, 1 Sam. 11.6 and 16.13-14. In these the meturgeman might easily have substituted either 'Spirit of prophecy' or 'Spirit of wisdom', but did not. Of course the 'power' concerned in these cases need not have quite the same startlingly 'miraculous' quality the contexts demand for the Samson incidents; but nor is it merely charismatic wisdom and the power of revelation, either. It includes empowering of the warrior-leader to press battle against Israel's enemies. Interestingly, the targums also willingly use the term the 'Spirit of prophecy' for that mix of charismatic *wisdom* and *power* that made the judges or kings powerful protectors of Israel. Thus, according to *Targ.* Judg. 3.10, the 'Spirit of prophecy from before the Lord resided upon him [Othniel], and he judged Israel, and he went forth to wage battle' (cf. 1 Sam. 11.6; 16.13-14). Here the 'Spirit of prophecy from before the Lord' that comes upon Othniel is virtually indistinguishable from the 'Spirit of power from before the Lord' that comes upon Gideon (*Targ.* Judg. 6.34), Jephthah (*Targ.* Judg. 11.29), and, above all, upon Samson (*Targ.* Judg. 13.25; 14.6). Similarly, the 'Spirit of prophecy' promised Saul at *Targ.* 1 Sam. 10.6 is identified as the Spirit of power too at *Targ.* 1 Sam. 16.13-14 (cf. 11.6). In these cases might in battle is almost certainly intended as part of the reference.

In short, while we might surmise that the term 'Spirit of prophecy' originally connoted the operation of the Spirit in the sort of charismata associated with prophecy (dreams, visions, 'words', special wisdom, invasive speech, etc.), it appears to have become a rather more general term for the Spirit and thus a descriptive synonym for 'Holy Spirit' (and, to a lesser extent, for 'Spirit of power'). This is not, of course, to say that the qualifier נבואה 'of prophecy' has become quite as lexically empty as the qualifier קודשא in the collocation רוח קודשא ('holy Spirit'), yet nor does it have the relatively full and semantically transparent lexical force of the qualifier גבורא ('of power') in רוח גבורא ('Spirit of power'). Its use is best explained in terms of the general *tendency* within 'intertestamental' Judaism (most marked in the rabbis)[6] to understand the Spirit primarily as the organ of communication or of revelation from God to a person, while *not restricting* it to this. Discussing the typically broader understanding of 'prophecy' and the

6. See the excellent analysis of Schäfer, *Vorstellung*, p. 62 and *passim*.

implications of the range of uses of the phrase 'Spirit of prophecy' in Judaism, Hill (with particular reference to the rabbis) thus rightly comments:

> This rabbinic emphasis on the spirit of prophecy means that the term 'prophecy' is not restricted to reference to the special inspiration to foretell the future and proclaim divine judgments: it comprises the possession of deeper insight into the will of God, the infusion into man of a more than ordinary power, knowledge and discernment, enabling him to perform what is right and good more effectually than the person who lacks the gift. Thus the 'Spirit of prophecy' may be attributed to warrior and craftsman, king and messianic ruler - men whose activities would not all be included within the narrower definition of prophecy.[7]

The targums can even associate the very term 'Spirit of prophecy' quite directly with miraculous deeds. We would not expect such a connection, because the collocation 'Spirit of prophecy' semantically focuses the Spirit as the power of revelation and wisdom. Where some other activity of the Spirit is intended we might expect a different referring expression for the Spirit: for example, 'Holy Spirit', 'Spirit of the Lord', or 'Spirit of power'. However, at 2 Kgs 2.9 the targumist clarifies that the Spirit on Elijah was the 'Spirit of prophecy', and Elisha duly requests a double portion of it. And it is then precisely when Elisha divides the waters that the sons of the prophets decide the Spirit of Elijah has indeed rested on Elisha (2 Kgs 2.15). Similarly, the targums appear to have no problem with the concept of the divine Spirit lifting a man up, or transporting him from one place to another (at very least in 1 Kgs 18.12; 2 Kgs 2.16; Ezek. 8.1; 11.1, 24; 43.5, but probably in the earlier Ezekiel references too, e.g. 2.2; 3.12; 14, 24, etc.), and can occasionally even attribute this specifically to 'a spirit of prophecy from before the Lord': for example, in Ezek. 37.1, 'and He took me out by means of the spirit of prophecy, which had rested upon me from before the Lord, and He set me down in the midst of a valley' (and compare 11.24; 40.1-2), even when the MT had attributed this function to 'the hand of the Lord' and not to the Spirit at all (as at 40.1-2). It might be argued the targumist viewed some or all the occasions in Ezekiel as visionary phenomenon,[8] rather than real transportation (as must be meant in 2 Kings, and as the *Lives of the Prophets* understands Ezekiel [3.14]), but not only would such an interpretation be doubtful, it would also miss the point. One would not portray the Spirit of prophecy as lifting a man up and carrying him around even within the framework of a vision, if that notion were *conceptually* incoherent.

---

7.   D. Hill, *Greek Words with Hebrew Meanings: Studies in the Semantics of Soteriological Terms* (Cambridge: Cambridge University Press, 1967), p. 238.

8.   Cf. Menzies, 'Spirit and Power', p. 13 n. 11.

We have dealt with the LXX and the targums first because these were clearly the most influential writings in Judaism. Menzies observes, 'Virtually all of the intertestamental texts cited by Turner which associate the Spirit with miraculous deeds simply replicate OT tradition',[9] and says that compared with other relevant intertestamental references these are in any case a 'minor sampling'. I fear I cannot agree. A number of observations are pertinent. In the first instance, even on a simple count the number of references to the Spirit as the source of miraculous acts of power in the Hebrew Bible and its translations far exceeds those for the Spirit as the source of 'invasive charismatic worship', but that the Spirit was regarded as the source of the latter would not be contested. Secondly, when one turns (with Menzies) to the broader range of works of 'biblical interpetation', one would not *expect* the number of references to the Spirit as the source of miracles to be but a small fraction of those of the 'Spirit of prophecy'. In such works, manifestations of wisdom and revelation were much more common than those of miracles of power, and the question of the means of revelation in Judaism was more important than the question of the means of miracles of power.[10] Thirdly, if one excludes the numerous but somewhat eccentric references by Philo and the later rabbinic midrashim, I am not convinced that (even in purely numerical terms) the references to the Spirit as the source of miracles is such a 'minor sampling' in the works of 'biblical interpretation' compared with references to individual prophetic charismata of one kind or another. Fourthly, as I have already suggested, if it comes to *weighting*, rather than merely counting, the biblical translations and paraphrases, regularly heard by congregations, inevitably exercised far more influence than Philo, Josephus, Artapanus, Ezekiel the Tragedian *et al.*

9. 'Spirit and Power', p. 13.
10. Menzies (*Development*, pp. 75-76) finds it 'significant' that the miracles attributed to the prophets in *The Lives of the Prophets* (cf. Jeremiah [2.3-4], Ezekiel [3.8-9], Elijah [21.6] and Elisha [22.4]) are not said to be performed by the Spirit, but that work does not trace the prophets' many visions and revelations to the Spirit either. Similarly he voices surprise that Artapanus fails to attribute Moses' mighty works in Egypt to the Spirit (*Development*, p. 57), but explains them as providence or through the name of the Lord. But once again this is of very little significance, for Artapanus does not use the word Spirit at all, and for that matter the biblical tradition did not attribute Moses' mighty works to the Spirit either. Furthermore, the miracles Menzies has in mind are two: (1) the miraculous opening of prison doors by God (Eusebius, *Pr. Ev.* 9.27.21) and (2) and the king falling down speechless when Moses utters the divine name (9.27.25). I would have found them strange examples if Artapanus *had* attributed these miracles to the Spirit.

2. *The Spirit and Miracles in Other Extrabiblical ITP and Rabbinic Writings*

We have already noted the Spirit as the power of miraculous acts of creation and resurrection in *2 Baruch* and *4 Ezra*. On the remaining literature we must be brief. For the rabbis the Spirit is undoubtedly the 'Spirit of prophecy', but that does not prevent them from attributing miraculous deeds to the Spirit when the biblical context appears to require it, and even when it does not (cf. the quaint discussion in *Lev. R.* 8.2 culminating in R. Nahman's [second generation Amoraim] gratuitous proposal that when the Spirit came on Samson he clashed two mountains together as a man might pebbles in his hand). The first-century *Biblical Antiquities*, which is influenced by rabbinic exegesis, has a clear understanding of the Spirit as the Spirit of prophecy (cf. 9.10; 18.10-11; 28.6; 31.9; 32.14), and yet, according to this book, Kenaz, 'clothed with the Spirit of power' (27.10 = 'Spirit of the Lord' in 27.9), was 'changed into another man' (i.e. from judge to empowered warrior) and so struck down a host of Amorites (and similarly Gideon at 36.2[11]). The reference here (as in the targum descriptions of the judges) is to charismatic power expressed in the military sphere, in defence of Israel against her opponents; and once again the very collocation the 'Spirit of power' (where this cannot simply mean greatly wise and authoritative) should put a great question mark over any claim that Judaism is reluctant to attribute miracles of power to the Spirit.[12]

What of Josephus? Menzies argues that he is a prime example of the very practice of eliminating references to the Spirit in association with miracle, which I contest.[13] Menzies also rightly points out that I have failed to mention that Josephus 'often' *inserts* references to the Spirit in speech or revelatory contexts, while he 'regularly' *omits* references to the Spirit in contexts which feature the miraculous.[14] This would sound a telling

---

11. This latter incidence I took to have been overlooked by Menzies (*Development*, pp. 63-64); but in his response ('Spirit and Power', p. 13 n. 11) he claims it is associated rather with inspired speech. The text, however, is a reference to Judg. 7.15, 6.34 and reads: 'As soon as Gideon heard these words, he put on the Spirit of the Lord and was strengthened, and said to the three hundred men, "Rise up . . . etc."' (and they go to do battle). Surely this is a case of empowerment to liberate Israel from enemies, not merely a case of inspired speech. It may, of course, include 'wisdom' (etc.), but is not power in battle what is chiefly meant?

12. Levison's review of Menzies (*JBL* 113 [1994], pp. 340-42 [341]) observes this is a counter-tendency instance as the passage is modelled on that of the Spirit of *prophecy* coming upon Saul.

13. Menzies, 'Spirit and Power', p. 14.

14. Menzies, 'Spirit and Power', p. 14.

argument (at least for a part of the Jewish corpus) if it were not for the fact that Josephus has a total of just seven (possibly eight[15]) references to the divine Spirit in his whole writing, and this despite the fact that his histories cover the whole span of the biblical narrative![16] Of the seven, even *Ant.* 8.114 (Solomon's request that God leave a portion of his Spirit in the temple, that the people may know he is present there) may, or may not, be a reference to the 'Spirit of prophecy'; with Best, I am inclined to agree it is more probably a reference to the Shekinah.[17] So we are down to six sure mentions and just three additions. Of these three, *Ant.* 6.166 merely reduplicates a contextual reference to the Spirit, and 4.199 is strongly suggested by the context (if not its Hellenistic 'mantic' flavour). That leaves just *Ant.* 8.408, which is precisely the case in which I claim that the passage portrays the Spirit as the source of *both* prophecy *and* miracle (see below).

As for the omissions of Spirit in the context of relating miracles, on which Menzies puts so much emphasis, we had mentioned the principal cases (viz.: Judg. 14.6//*Ant.* 5.287; Judg. 14.19//*Ant.* 5.294; Judg. 15.14-15// *Ant.* 5.301),[18] but how significant are these omissions? If Josephus were translating or paraphrasing the case would be more telling. But he is retelling the stories with his own (often moralizing) emphases, and as narrator he quite regularly 'distances' his characters, especially God and the manner of his involvement in human affairs.[19] It is not surprising when he passes over these three strange irruptions of the Spirit, and glosses the last of them (in retrospect) with the comment that 'Samson, unduly proud of this feat, did not say that it was by God's assistance' (5.301). This tells us nothing, however, about the *means* by which Josephus perceived that assistance to be given. And such omission is simply of a part with his treatment of the Spirit of prophecy elsewhere, as we can see by comparing his handling of Spirit-passages with that of other Jewish interpreters. The

---

15. In *Ant.* 4.108 the reference to the approaching divine spirit may be to the angel, rather than to the 'Spirit of prophecy' (as Menzies takes it). I agree with Menzies ('Spirit and Power', p. 14) and E. Best ('The Use and Non-Use of Pneuma by Josephus', *NovT* 3 [1959], pp. 218-25, specifically p. 223), that the reference to Gen. 1.2 in *Ant.* 1.27 is possibly irrelevant to the issue, similarly *Ant.* 1.34.

16. See Best, 'Use', pp. 218-25.

17. Best, 'Use', p. 223.

18. Turner, 'Spirit and Power', p. 134.

19. This is seen even where Josephus follows the biblical narrative most closely. Compare the direct statements in the Old Testament of 1 Sam. 19.20, 23, where the Spirit is twice the *subject* of actions (the 'Spirit of God came upon...'), and Josephus's retelling of the incident in *Ant.* 6.221, which focuses the human side of the experience ('they were possessed by the divine Spirit', 'Saul losing his reason under the impulse of that mighty spirit'), and also keeps the characters at a greater narrative distance than the more direct biblical accounts.

targumists in varying degrees highlight the mention of the Spirit in (1) Pharaoh's admiring question to his court about Joseph, 'Can we find anyone else like this—one in whom is the Spirit of God?', (2) the granting of the Spirit of wisdom to Bezalel, (3) the extension of the Spirit from Moses to the seventy elders, and (4) the transfer of authority from Moses to Joshua as a man of the Spirit. Philo and the rabbis also show considerable interest in these texts. Josephus, by contrast, reshapes Pharaoh's admiration to exclude the Spirit (*Ant.* 2.87 and 2.89//Gen. 41.38), he spends a paragraph on Bezalel's great abilities in parallel to Exod. 31.3 and 35.31, yet with no comment on the source of these abilities (*Ant.* 3.200), he passes over Num. 11.17-25 in silence while dealing with adjacent material, and he relates the last incident with the words 'Moses, already advanced in years, now appointed Joshua to succeed him in both his prophetical functions and as commander-in-chief'—again with no mention of the Spirit as the *means* of this (*Ant.* 4.165). I would not deduce from these that Josephus is 'reluctant' to attribute revelatory gifts and wisdom to the Spirit: the omissions simply tell us more about his narrative technique and his implied readers than about his pneumatology—and it may be noted that Josephus has omitted a far greater number of references to the 'Spirit of prophecy' than he has to the Spirit as the source of miracles.

The disputed case between Menzies and myself is *Ant.* 8.408. I claim this unambiguously portrays the Spirit as both the Spirit of prophecy and the power of (punitive) miracle. In the context, Zedekiah, throwing doubt on Micaiah's prophecy, urges Ahab to put it to the test, saying, 'But you shall know whether he is really a true prophet and has the power of the divine Spirit (καὶ τοῦ θείου πνεύματος ἔχει τὴν δύναμιν); let him right now, when I strike him, disable my hand as Jadaos caused the right hand of King Jereboam to wither...'.[20] Menzies says this is a case when δύναμις has been inserted into the tradition as a buffer between Spirit and miracle.[21] I can only reply that I cannot see how that is the natural reading. It would appear to me that τοῦ θείου πνεύματος...τὴν δύναμιν attributes the potential miracle directly to the Spirit (regarded as 'powerful'), rather than that (even notionally) the Spirit gives rise to δύναμις which in turn affords the miracle (a view found nowhere in Judaism). But either way the prophetic Spirit remains the source of the miracle! And this is an especially telling case as Josephus has largely rewritten the scene (compare 1 Kgs 22.24; 2 Chron. 18.23) and appears himself to have created the speech (there is no sign it comes from 'tradition'!) with the proposed test of

20. Menzies (*Development*, p. 114) claims Josephus distances the miracle from the Spirit here; but I cannot see how such a claim can be substantiated.

21. Menzies, 'Spirit and Power', p. 14.

whether Micaiah has, or has not, 'the power of the divine Spirit'. If Josephus was especially 'reluctant' to attribute miracles to the Spirit, why did he not simply write, 'But you shall see whether he is really a true prophet and whether the power of God is with him' (or the like)?

Ant. 8.408 is probably not the only place where Josephus relates miraculous power to the Spirit of prophecy, for in *Ant.* 8.346 he attributes Elijah's power to run the great distance with king's chariot to his ἔνθεος γενόμενος ('becoming divinely possessed'). This is the traditional (mantic) language of prophetic possession/inspiration, and so Marcus rightly translated it, 'And the prophet...filled with the Spirit of God, ran beside the king's chariot as far as the city of Jezarēla'.[22]

Philo frequently enough emphasizes the Spirit as the power of divine revelation, and he has made the divine Spirit the power of *reason* in a striking original way (cf. *Det. Pot. Ins.* 80-84; *Leg. All.* 1.33, 37, 42; *Op. Mund.* 135, 144; *Plant.* 18, 44 etc.). This original development may explain his silence on the relation of the Spirit to miracles, and so he comes nearest to exemplifying the hypothesis under scrutiny—but even he allows that the oncoming of the divine Spirit might be attended by quasi-miraculous *physical* effects (in Abraham's case everything changes for the better, 'eyes, complexion, stature, carriage, movement, voice' [*Virt.* 217]), and it is of course only a brave person who would claim Philo as an exemplar of typical Jewish views of the Spirit.

It would appear from this all-too-brief survey that for a Jew to hold that the Spirit was received as the Spirit of prophecy did not preclude him from attributing miracles to the same Spirit. For the Jew, the two conceptions do not appear to have seemed as foreign to each other as they may look to us. But we have so far omitted an important area of evidence, that is the 'messianic' references.

3. *The Spirit and Power in the 'Messianic' Tradition*

Isa. 11.1-4 depicts a regal figure mightily endowed with the Spirit, this endowment being specified in relation to wisdom, knowledge, fear of the Lord and might. The model for this portrait of the charismatic leader is the judges of Israel, and Saul, but most especially David. The reference to 'might' apparently pertains to the power to ensure freedom from enemies, and enforce righteous rule against opposition (cf. vv. 3-4). In the targum, this reference to 'might' or 'power' in 11.2c (in the context of a gift of the Spirit that also brings wisdom, and knowledge, etc.) would be liable to

---

22. H.StJ. Thackaray and R. Marcus, *Josephus V* (LCL; London: Heinemann, 1934), p. 759.

evoke the sort of picture of Israel's mighty defenders that was characterized by joint use of the terms the 'Spirit of prophecy' and the 'Spirit of power' in relation to the Judges (and cf. *Bib. Ant.* 27.9-10; 36.2). Of more significance is the way this biblical text has been taken up and developed in various types of 'messianic' expectation. It is clear that it has moulded the picture of the Elect one of power in *1 En.* 49.2-3:

> The Elect One stands before the Lord of the Spirits; his glory is forever and ever and his power is unto all generations. In him dwells the spirit of wisdom, the spirit which gives thoughtfulness, the spirit of knowledge and strength... He shall judge the secret things. And no-one will be able to utter vain words in his presence' (cf. also 62.1-2).

as well as the depiction of the hoped for deliverer in *Psalms of Solomon*:

> And he will not weaken in his days, (relying) upon his God, for God made him powerful in the holy spirit (δυνατὸν ἐν πνεύματι ἁγίῳ) and wise in the counsel of understanding, with strength (μετὰ ἰσχύος) and righteousness (17.37; cf. 18.8-17).

With *Ps. Sol.* 17.37, the 'power' afforded by the Spirit is clearly not merely that of wisdom (and resulting authority and influence); but strength to rule with might, as the following verses also indicate. Thus (v. 38) he will not weaken because God's blessing will be with him 'in strength' (ἐν ἰσχύι); and none can oppose him for he is as 'mighty in deeds' (ἰσχυρὸς ἐν ἔργοις) as in the fear of the Lord. In short, *'powerful in the Holy Spirit' in practice means a firm grip on the righteous and a mailed fist for the opposition*; not merely prophecy or wisdom.

A similar understanding is evinced in the Qumran messianic material:

> [May you smite the peoples] with the might of your hand and ravage the earth with your sceptre; may you bring death to the ungodly with the breath [רוח] of your lips! [25] [May he shed upon you the spirit of counsel] and *everlasting might*, the spirit of knowledge and of the fear of God; may righteousness be the girdle [of your loins]...(1QSb 5.24-25).

We may be reasonably confident of the restoration of line 25, because of the clear allusion to Isa. 11.1-2, but here again it is notable that God's gift of רוח leads to 'everlasting might'. The same applies to 4QpIsa[a] Fragments 7-10 Column iii. lines 15-23, which begins with an extensive quote of Isa. 11.1-5, and glosses:

> [22] [The interpretation of the matter concerns the scion of] David, who will take his stand at the en[d of days to save] [23] [Israel and to exterminate] his [ene]mies. And God will sustain him with [a mi]ghty [spirit].[23]

---

23. The reconstruction is that of Horgan, *PESHARIM*, pp. 75-87.

The new finds from cave 4, published in preliminary form by Eisenman and Wise[24] show much more interest in this powerful Spirit-endowed Isaianic messianic Davidid than we had hitherto expected[25] (cf. 4Q215 col. 4; 4Q246 col. 2; 4Q252 [Genesis Florilegium] col. 5; 4Q285 frag. 7; 4Q286-87;[26] 4Q521 frag. 1; 4Q522 col. 2), but perhaps of greatest interest for our immediate purposes is another passage, 4Q521, which appears to describe the messiah in terms of fulfilment of both the Davidic hopes *and* Isa. 61.1-2:[27]

> Frag. 1; line 1: [...The Hea]vens and the earth will obey His Messiah (2) [...and all th]at is within them. He will not turn aside from the Commandments of the Holy Ones. (3) Take strength in His service, (you) who seek the Lord. (4) Shall you not find the Lord in this, all you who wait patiently in your hearts? (5) For the Lord will visit the Pious ones and the Righteous will He call by name. (6) Over the meek will his Spirit hover, and the faithful will he restore by his power. (7) He shall glorify the Pious ones on the throne of the eternal kingdom. (8) He shall release the captives, make the blind see, raise up the do[wntrodden.]...(11) And as for the wonders that are not the work of the Lord, when He...(12) then He will heal the sick, resurrect the dead, and to the Meek announce glad tidings (ET from Eisenman and Wise, p. 23).

Here we have a picture of 'New Exodus' hopes similar to those we already know from 11QMelchizedek,[28] but now with the first reference to (healing

---

24. R.H. Eisenman and M. Wise, *The Dead Sea Scrolls Uncovered* (Shaftesbury: Element, 1992).

25. Cf. M.L. Strauss, who argues that the available evidence suggests 'an *increase in Royal-Davidic expectation* in the sect's later years (c. 4 BC to AD 68)' (*The Davidic Messiah in Luke–Acts* [Sheffield: JSOT Press, 1995], p. 43, cf. n. 3).

26. In the latter passage, at line 13, we read, 'the Holy spirit [rest]ed upon his Messiah'; a probable allusion to Isa. 11.2 (cf. C.A. Evans' appendix, 'The Recently Published Dead Sea Scrolls and the Historical Jesus', in B. Chilton and C.A. Evans [eds.], *Studying the Historical Jesus* [Leiden: Brill, 1994], pp. 555-56).

27. So Eisenman and Wise, *Scrolls*, pp. 19-23. J.J. Collins ('The Works of the Messiah', *DSD* 1 [1994], pp. 98-112), however, argues the messianic figure in question is Elijah, on the grounds that the raising of the dead was distinctive to Elijah (pp. 99-106). This is possible, but the parallels with 11QMelchizedek do not favour an Elijianic identification, so it may be a case of a transfer of an Elijianic trait to the Davidic messiah (e.g. on the basis of Isa. 26.19). Collins finds another Elijianic trait in line 1 which he sees as echoing Elijah's prayer which shut the heavens for three and a half years; but it was God (not Elijah) who shut the heavens, and there is no biblical tradition of Elijianic universal rule. The Psalm (146) on which line 1 and the passage as a whole is based has obvious contacts with Isa. 61.1-3 (esp. in vv. 7-8), and line 1 is better explained in terms of association of the Isaianic tradition of the messiah's universal rule with the description of God in Ps. 146.6.

28. For these see Chapter 9, below.

and) 'resurrection of the dead' in the Qumran material (line 12), and one that presents it as a wonder of the messianic age (line 11), and an example of the promised 'release' of captives (line 8), and one which affords a most striking parallel to Q's inclusion of 'the dead are raised' along with the healings and other signs of 'release' fulfilling of Isa. 61.1-2 in Jesus' ministry (Mt. 11.4// Lk. 7.22). It is not quite clear whether these signs are said to be performed by the messiah or by God himself (though the contrast in line 11 rather suggests it is the messiah who performs them), but in the context we should probably not distinguish sharply. The point of the whole piece is that God is present in the messianic visitation. Our interest focuses especially on line 6: here 'Spirit' and restoring 'power' appear to be mutually interpreted by three things: (a) the structure of line 6 itself (a parallelism); (b) the context of the allusion to Isaiah 61 (there it is a Spirit-anointed figure who proclaims and effects the good news of release; cf. also 11QMelchizedek), and (c) the cotext[29] of the passage itself which clearly represents the restoration envisaged in Isaiah 61 in terms of both restoration to Israel's true calling (righteous reign!) *and* physical restoration of healing, etc.[30] Once again, it is not clear whether it is God's Spirit (independently, as it were), or whether it is more specifically God's Spirit *on and through the messiah*, which performs these works, but both the cotext of the passage and the appeal to Isaiah 61 (where God's Spirit is effective through an anointed figure) suggest the latter.[31] Either way, however, God's Spirit is strongly related to the power of restoring miracles.

In short, some of the 'messianic' passages building from Isa. 11.1-4, and associated ideas, take up the old hopes of the Spirit coming to expression in *power* (*inter alia*) through a regal deliverer. In some settings, the opposition from which God's power (through his agent) must provide salvation is sinful human structures (e.g. the sinners and the Romans in *Psalms of Solomon*). In other cases the oppressive opposition from which release must be wrought by God's Spirit/power includes the demonic and disease (esp. *Testaments of the Twelve Patriarchs*, 11QMelchizedek and 4Q521). This means that in this 'messianic' tradition the Spirit is more than simply the

29. The term 'cotext' is derived from Discourse Analysis and means the context afforded by the 'adjacent text' (including the whole work): see Cotterell and Turner, *Linguistics*, pp. 16, 39, 72.

30. Menzies argues against my association of Spirit with miracles in Luke, that the ITP literature never attributes healings or exorcisms to the Spirit ('Spirit and Power', p. 13). I suggest 4Q521 offers some of the required evidence with respect to healing, and that it was already possibly evidenced with respect to both healing and release from demonic powers in 11QMelchizedek (and in other New Exodus texts, such as *Testaments of the Twelve Patriarchs*) which I shall discuss in Chapter 9.

31. So also Collins, 'Works of the Messiah', p. 100.

'Spirit of prophecy' in Menzies' restrictive sense. The Spirit still performs some of the functions of what Menzies means by the 'Spirit of prophecy'—for the Spirit on the messiah affords him charismatic wisdom, knowledge and God's counsel, and his word of command carries power—but the messianic endowment also affords 'power' in a variety of other senses (including, it would appear, 'miraculous deeds of power'). Here the Spirit is as much God's empowering presence as his self-communicating presence. And we shall note that it is in large part within this trajectory of expectation (or a modified version of it) that Luke builds his picture of Jesus.

4. *Conclusion*

We have found remarkably little evidence that Jews who thought of the Spirit as the 'Spirit of prophecy' were thereby strongly inclined to dissociate the Spirit from works of power. The most influential works—the Hebrew Bible, its translations and various forms of biblical interpretation—largely maintained the association. The 'messianic' traditions (particularly those using and developing the hopes in Isa. 11.1-4) reasserted the expectation of a figure endowed with charismatic wisdom/righteousness and anticipated that the same Spirit would grant works of power through him to accomplish Israel's liberation and restoration. One cannot appeal to Luke's adoption of a Jewish concept of the 'Spirit of prophecy' as a basis for his excluding works of power from the activity of the Spirit.

Chapter 5

THE 'SPIRIT OF PROPHECY', ETHICAL INFLUENCE AND
'SALVATION' IN INTERTESTAMENTAL JUDAISM

Schweizer encapsulates the claims of many from Gunkel onwards when he
asserts that because Luke identifies the gift of the Spirit with the Jewish
concept of the 'Spirit of prophecy', 'this prevents him from directly attributing to the πνεῦμα...strongly ethical effects like the common life of the
primitive community'.[1] Similarly, Menzies concludes the 'Spirit of
prophecy' is of such little ethical consequence for Judaism that the gift must
rather be regarded as a *donum supperadditum*, given to those already made
righteous. I suggest this is a misleading picture with serious consequences
for the understanding both of Jewish restoration hopes and earliest
Christianity. In what follows I shall (in §1) briefly state the arguments on
which this view is based; then (in §2) analyse these and bring forward
further evidence which suggests a quite different picture, before briefly
suggesting (§3) how this relates to Jewish concepts of 'salvation'.[2]

1. *The Essentials of the Case that Judaism Envisages the Spirit of
Prophecy to Have only Secondary (if any) Ethical/Religious
Influence in Judaism*

It is easy enough to present a picture of Judaism in which the Spirit of
prophecy could be regarded as a 'supplementary gift' of little consequence
for the everyday life and religion of the believer. After all, in the past the gift
of the Spirit of prophecy was usually thought to have been given to the
privileged *few*—to the patriarchs, leaders, prophets, kings and priests, and to
only a relatively small handful beyond—and it was considered to have been
experienced typically as merely *occasional* activities of charismatic *revelation*, *wisdom* and *power*. Furthermore, there was a quite widespread

---

1. *TWNT*, VI, p. 407.
2. This chapter offers a revised (and shortened) version of M. Turner, 'The Spirit
of Prophecy and the Ethical/Religious Life of the Christian Community', in M. Wilson
(ed.), *Spirit and Renewal* (Sheffield: JSOT Press, 1994), pp. 166-90.

(though not universal) belief that the Spirit of prophecy had largely been *withdrawn* from Israel until the end, and this itself might suggest the Spirit is unlikely to have been regarded as a necessary condition of a righteous religious or ethical life. Indeed there are important elements of tradition which could be interpreted to assert that righteousness is the *prerequisite* for receiving the gift of the Spirit of prophecy rather than the *consequence* of it.[3] One could make a start with the many places which affirm (in one way or another) that the Spirit is removed either from an individual or from a community because of sin.[4] If one then combines these with those places where it is promised that God will restore the Spirit of prophecy to repentant and cleansed Israel at the eschaton,[5] one might easily conclude that the Spirit must indeed be a 'supplementary' gift; one given to those who first attain righteousness by other means. This could be further supported by appeal to the numerous places where the righteous (or particular acts of righteousness) are understood in some sense to merit the gift of the Spirit of prophecy.[6]

And finally, one could point out that in perhaps the majority of instances where a writer gives an indication of the content of revelation received through the Spirit of prophecy, it is hard at first to discern any obvious ethical significance to the charisma. A few of the more forgetful of us might indeed claim we would be better people if only the Spirit could inform us of

---

3.   This is the way Menzies, *Development*, Part I, has largely construed Judaism.

4.   E.g. Wis. 1.4-5; Philo, *Deus Imm.* 2; *Gig.* 47, 53; *t. Soṭ.* 13.2-4 (and pars.: *y. Soṭ.* 9.13-14; *b. Soṭ.* 48b; *b. Sanh.* 11a; *b. Yom.* 9b); *b. Sanh.* 65b; *Sifre Deut.* on 18.12; *Lev. R.* 37.4; *Ag. Ber.* 23.2; *Deut. R.* 6.14; *MHG Gen.* 140.

5.   E.g. *Gen. R.* 2.4; *Deut. R.* 6.14; *Tanḥuma* (Buber) Addition to חקת (on one interpretation), and cf. *Jub.* 1.23-25.

6.   The theme is rife in rabbinic Judaism; for example, the Israelites are enabled to sing in the Spirit at the Red Sea because they believed God (*t. Soṭ.* 6.2; *Mek. Beshallah* 7 [on Exod. 14.26-31]; *Mek. Shirata* 1 [on Exod. 15.1]; *Exod. R.* 23.2); the Israelite leaders are said to merit the Spirit of prophecy because they suffered for the people under the Egyptian taskmasters (*Exod. R.* 5.20); Joshua because he was a faithful servant to Moses (*Num. R.* 12.9); the sons of Samuel because they repented and changed bad deeds to good (*Num. R.* 10.5; cf. *Ruth R.* 4.3); Solomon (and any like him) because he diligently expounded Torah (*Cant. R.* 1.1.8-9); Hillel and Samuel the Small for their personal holiness (*t. Soṭ.* 13.2-4; cf. *Cant. R.* 8.9 §3, etc., and these instances are generalised in such assertions as in *Mek. Shirata* 1 on Exod. 15.1 (whoever undertakes a commandment in faith is worthy that the Holy Spirit rest on him) and *Lev. R.* 35.7 (all who study with intent of putting Torah into practice will be privileged to receive the Holy Spirit), or in the famous teaching on the 'ladder' of holiness attributed to Phinehas ben Jair (*m. Soṭ.* 9.15. Philo too thinks Moses received the prophetic Spirit for his obvious merits (*Dec.* 175), and Sir. 39.6 expresses the hope that the one who studies the law will be rewarded by being filled with the Spirit of understanding.

the names of the people we casually met, as *t. Pes.* 2.15 tells us the Holy Spirit once did for Rabban Gamiliel, but most would probably regard such a charisma as religiously and ethically inconsequential. Similarly, we might be hard put to provide significant *ethical* import to the charismata of the Spirit which afford a panorama of the future to Enoch (*1 En.* 91.1) or of the past to Ezra (*4 Ezra* 14.22), let alone for some of the more individually specific revelations allegedly granted by the Holy Spirit. Many of these seem to correspond more with what Pentecostals and Charismatics would call 'words of knowledge'.[7]

Such are the considerations which lie at the heart of the case that Spirit of prophecy was not expected to have a primary ethical impact. It should be noted that Schweizer and others who hold this position are not denying that segments of Judaism could conceive of the Spirit as having profound ethical effects. They are fully aware that a re-creating or renewing influence of the Spirit could be inferred from (e.g.) Ezekiel 36–37, *Jos. Asen.* 8.10 and the Qumran Manual of Discipline and Hymns—rather they either deny that these are significant for understanding the Spirit *qua* 'Spirit of prophecy', or they insist that such an understanding is thoroughly untypical. The first option is assumed by Schweizer's antithesis; the second is prosecuted vigorously by Menzies.[8] In our analysis of Schweizer's contention below we shall refer almost exclusively to sayings about the Spirit which involve the prototypical gifts defined above.

2. A Case that the Spirit of Prophecy Would be Expected to Have Major Ethical/Religious Consequences when Restored to Israel

A number of observations together suggest that Schweizer and Menzies may have oversimplified the portrait of 'the Spirit of prophecy' and that the Spirit of prophecy was widely anticipated as a fundamental power of ethical renewal.

2.1. Charismatic Revelation and Wisdom as Transforming Influences

We should begin by challenging the powerful assumption made by Gunkel and Schweizer that because the 'Spirit of prophecy' gives revelation and wisdom it cannot be thought of as an ethical power. Gunkel is most explicit here: commenting on extra-canonical Judaism, he polemically affirms 'Righteous conduct has nothing to do with the Spirit. Where the literature of Judaism refers to activities of the Spirit, the concern is almost always with

---

7. For a sample of these see Turner, 'Spirit of Prophecy', pp. 171-72.
8. Menzies, *Development*, Part I.

prophecy, vision, wisdom, and so on.'[9] He goes on to accept that what is revealed in the vision, prophetic oracle, or wisdom may have ethical consequences, but insists this needs to be distinguished from the Spirit having a direct ethical effect. Thus when Gunkel criticizes Pfleiderer's attempt to explain Paul's view of the Spirit–flesh antithesis in terms of the saving power of wisdom (afforded by the Spirit) in Wisdom of Solomon, the substance of his argument against Pfleiderer is simply this: wisdom merely *informs* a man, while the Spirit (in Paul) *grasps* him.[10]

I confess I find singularly unconvincing Gunkel's conviction that all 'informing' or 'teaching' of a person is of itself a merely neutral act, not a power which grips a person. This appears to be a clear instance of false antithesis. Many kinds of teaching or writing, secular as well as religious, have the power to grip us and transform us. They exercise such power when they subvert our self-understanding and give us a different view of our universe, challenging our ideals and fundamentally reshaping our motivations—for to a large extent we are shaped by the 'stories' we believe.[11] In addition, it is also undoubtedly the case that some personal encounters can themselves have similar transforming effects (most commonly at the level of falling in love), especially encounters with people of great natural charisma or 'personality'. And evidently the combination of captivating teaching, writing, politics or whatever, with strong personal charisma in the author of these may greatly reinforce the 'spell' he or she has on us.

Why then should it be thought that the impact of 'the Spirit of prophecy' would necessarily be less? One might rather expect that the Spirit who discloses God's presence and activity, reveals his nature and will, enlightens with God's wisdom and convicts of the truth of God's claim on us, would—precisely in doing these things—profoundly transform the outlook and motivations which fuel our lives. The experience of his charismata might itself thus be anticipated to carry its own compelling influence and transfiguring effect well beyond the 'event' itself, lingering like the fading glow on Moses' face. In other words, the Spirit who 'informs' and reveals and grants wisdom may *ipso facto* be the Spirit who 'grasps' the person. Indeed, for Jeremiah, it is precisely as God reveals himself (and his will) directly to human hearts (not merely through the Law or even through Spirit-anointed teachers) that Israel will be transformed (Jer. 31.33-34).

I am not, of course, claiming that every manifestation of the Spirit in Judaism would be understood to have such an effect. It is merely that at a

9.   *Influence*, p. 21.

10.   *Influence*, p. 100.

11.   For a recent statement of this see e.g. N.T. Wright, *The New Testament and the People of God* (London: SPCK, 1992), *passim*.

theoretical level Gunkel's antithesis is an unnecessary one, and so potentially a false one. We should be willing at least to risk the claim that, for many Jews, the reception of 'revelation' or charismatic wisdom (and the ongoing re-activated 'memory' of it) might itself be expected to be experienced as a religious and ethically renewing power. And when we turn from the question of theoretical possibility to examine the actual evidence of post-exilic Judaism, we soon enough encounter witnesses for an understanding of the Spirit of prophecy as the immediate impulse to, or source of, righteousness; both in the (biblical) past, and in the (writers') present.

2.2. *The Spirit of Prophecy and its Ethical Effect in the Biblical Translations (LXX and Targums)*

The targums do not make any consistent attempt to 'translate away' the connections between the Spirit and ethical transformation in the Old Testament,[12] and the LXX makes none such at all. On the whole, both traditions simply retain the ethically-orientated vision of the Spirit to be found in the MT.[13] At one point, however, *Targums Neofiti* and *Pseudo-Jonathan* move decisively to strengthen this. In 'translating' the slightly obscure words from Gen. 6.3, 'My spirit will not abide with (or contend with?) man for ever, for he is flesh', *Neofiti* renders *'Behold I have* put my spirit *in the sons of man* because they are flesh, *and their deeds are evil'* (italicized words mark departure from the MT). It would appear that for this targum God has put his own Spirit into humankind in order to counterbalance the evil tendency. Such a view is then made explicit in *Targum Pseudo-Jonathan*'s rendering, *'Did I not* put my *holy* spirit in *them that they might perform good deeds? But behold their deeds are evil.'* When we remember that for this targum 'Holy Spirit' and 'Spirit of prophecy' are virtually interchangeable terms, this provides remarkable counter-evidence to Gunkel's thesis. Nor is this unique, for *Targum Ezekiel* renders 36.27, 'And My *holy*

---

12. *Targum Isaiah* exchanges *Memra* ('Word') for Spirit at 30.1 and 63.10-11, but these do not appear to be aimed at reducing any suggestion of an ethical dimension from the Spirit's activity (and the same change is made at 34.16, 48.16 and 63.14, of which the latter two could readily be explained as 'the Spirit of prophecy' giving wisdom or revelation). In Zech. 12.10, the targum renders 'And I will pour upon the house of David and upon the inhabitants of Jerusalem the Spirit of mercy and compassion'. This is perhaps less ethically orientated than the MT and LXX ('Spirit of compassion/grace and supplication'), but only marginally so.

13. As with the MT, for example, the figure in Isa. 11.1-4 is to receive the Spirit not merely as the giver of wisdom and counsel (so 'the Spirit of prophecy') but also (as we have seen) as the giver of 'power' and as the giver of 'knowledge and fear of the Lord'. Similarly *Targ. Isa.* 44.3 promises an abundance of the Spirit as waters on dry ground, and this appears to be the natural cause of the flourishing righteousness described in 44.4-5.

spirit will I put *deep* inside of you, and I will act so that you shall walk in my statutes and keep my laws and observe them'. Here, the granting of God's Holy Spirit (= the Spirit of prophecy?) along with the creation of a 'faithful/ reverent heart' and 'faithful/reverent spirit', also 'deep inside you' (36.26), *together* assure eschatological obedience. Other relevant evidence is less dramatic, if still in the same direction.[14]

2.3. *The Spirit of Prophecy and its Ethical Influence in Philo*

Philo can say the divine Spirit, who quickly leaves the man who concentrates on the realm of the flesh and the senses, may nevertheless abide with the wise and 'leads in every right path' (or 'in every journey of righteousness' πάσης ὀρθῆς ἀφηγούμενον ὁδοῦ: *Gig.* 55). It is not always clear, when Philo is using the term πνεῦμα θεῖον ('divine Spirit'), whether this refers to the power of rational thought breathed into man at creation, by which he shares the likeness of God,[15] or whether it is truly 'prophetic Spirit' (as at *Vit. Mos.* 1.277).[16] But here in *Gig.* 55 it is the latter, for he has made the point that the Spirit given to the seventy elders was not Moses' rational spirit, but a special charismatic divine endowment (*Gig.* 26–27), like that given to Bezaleel (*Gig.* 23). It is this prophetic Spirit that only abides with the righteous, and is easily driven away (*Gig.* 28–29, 47, 53; cf. *Deus Imm.* 2), that is the referent at *Gig.* 55.[17]

Three observations may be made here. First, what Philo says discloses the peril of arguing that because sin drives away the Spirit (which returns to the righteous) it cannot be conceived as a primary ethical influence.[18] It may be

---

14. We may note, for example, that LXX Ps. 50.14 [51.12]—ἀπόδος μοι τὴν ἀγαλλίασιν τοῦ σωτηρίου σου καὶ πνεύματι ἡγεμονικῷ στήριξόν με—changes 'Restore to me the joy of thy salvation, and uphold me with a *willing* spirit' for 'establish me with your *directing* Spirit', thus simultaneously suggesting the Spirit as the Spirit of prophecy who directs, but whose direction is ethico-soteriological.

15. Cf. *Op. Mund.* 134-135; *Plant.* 18; *Det. Pot. Ins.* 83; *Spec. Leg.* 4.123.

16. On the problem of the relation between the two see, e.g. A. Laurentin, 'Le pneuma dans la doctrine de Philon', *ETL* 27 (1951), pp. 422-23; Bieder, *TDNT*, VI, pp. 374-75; M.E. Isaacs, *The Concept of Spirit* (London: Heythrop Monographs, 1976), pp. 35-64; H. Wolfson, *Philo* (Cambridge, MA: Harvard University Press, 1948), II, pp. 2-72 (esp. 24-36, 39); Hill, *Greek Words*, pp. 224-26; A.J.M. Wedderburn, *Baptism and Resurrection* (Tübingen: Mohr, 1987), pp. 272-73; M.A. Chevallier, *Souffle de Dieu* (Paris: Beauchesne, 1978), p. 72; J.A. Davis, *Wisdom and Spirit* (New York: University Press of America, 1984), pp. 54-60.

17. With Laurentin, 'Pneuma', p. 423.

18. Partly recognized by Sjöberg, *TDNT*, VI, p. 383 (with respect to Palestinian Judaism; particularly the rabbis), though put negatively: 'Possession of the Spirit is in the first instance the result of a righteous life, not the basis of such a life. Naturally the Spirit also inspires men who have this gift to continue in holiness'.

nearer the truth to affirm that on Philo's understanding the Spirit is quenched by sin because evil (and preoccupation with the tangible world) *frustrates the ethical and God-orientated intent of the Spirit's primary activity*, i.e. to impart divine wisdom: so especially *Gig.* 28–29 (cf. *Gig.* 19). A not dissimilar view is implicit in the Palestinian Judaism represented by *1 En.* 67.10, when judgment of the wicked is assured on the grounds 'they believe in the debauchery of their bodies and deny the Spirit of the Lord'.

Secondly, while recognizing the different nature and character of πνεῦμα θεῖον as (i) the divine inbreathing imparted to man in creation (a modification of Stoic beliefs in the light of Gen. 2.7, etc.)[19] and (ii) as charismatic prophetic Spirit (with overtones of Greek manticism), *both gifts share the important characteristic that they enable the (ethically and spiritually orientated) wisdom which facilitates knowledge of—and fellowship with—God.* Thus those who live according to the inbreathing of divine rational Spirit (Philo's interpretation of Gen. 2.7) distinguish themselves as bearers of the divine image from other men and women who are virtually but clods of earth (*Rer. Div. Her.* 57), and it is precisely because this divine Spirit flowed in him in full current (πολλοῦ ῥυέντος εἰς αὐτόν) that the first man formed 'earnestly endeavoured in all his words and actions to please the Father and King, following him step by step in the highways cut out by virtues' (*Op. Mund.* 144). For Philo, it would seem, experience of the divine Spirit at any level has an ethical/spiritual orientation.

Thirdly, contrary to M. Isaacs's assertion that Philo restricts the charismatic Spirit to the biblical period (and beyond it does not trace charismata to the Spirit as such),[20] his very understanding of the relation of divine Spirit to spiritual understanding and wisdom should suggest otherwise, and Philo himself specifically claims to participate in the Spirit, for example, at *Somn.* 2.251-52 (an oracle of manifestly 'spiritual/religious' orientation). It is thus not surprising to find that his descriptions about the divine (charismatic) Spirit on the wise man, in (e.g.) *Gig.* 47, 53, 55, are couched in a generalizing way that assumes their relevance to his own day.

2.4. *The Spirit of Prophecy and Ethical Influence in Wisdom Literature*
The intertestamental Wisdom literature also beyond any doubt portrays the Spirit as falling within our general stereotype of 'the Spirit of prophecy' (cf. Wis. 1.5[?]; 7.7; 9.17; Sir. 39.6;[21] 48.12, 24). Because the Spirit is the source of heavenly wisdom (supremely understanding that facilitates righteous living), the Spirit of prophecy/wisdom is guaranteed significance for the

19. See *Det. Pot. Ins.* 80-84; *Leg. All.* 1.33-42, 3.161; *Op. Mund.* 135, 144; *Plant.* 18; *Spec. Leg.* 1.171; 4.23.
20. Isaacs, *Concept*, p. 49.
21. See especially Davis, *Wisdom*, pp. 16-24, on this.

ethical and religious life of the community (though once again only those already serious about righteousness can court this wisdom [Wis. 1.5; 7.22–8.1]). Indeed it has even been claimed on the basis of Wis. 9.17-18 ('Who has learned thy counsel, unless thou hast given wisdom and sent thy holy Spirit from on high? And thus the paths of those on earth were set right, and men were taught what pleases thee, and were saved by wisdom') that the book reflects a deep pessimism about any possibility of a man or woman attaining righteousness or salvation without his or her *individually* receiving this gift of the Spirit.[22] More probably this book contains a tension (as in Philo) between the special charism of the Spirit given to Solomon (and the prophets, etc.) through which Israel is instructed in the way of salvation (Wis. 7.7; 9.17-18), and a more generally conceived 'rational spirit' (with Stoic overtones), which reflects God's wisdom, is implanted universally in creation (cf. 7.22-23; 12.1; 15.11), and is intended to serve as man's guide (1.5-7). Whichever view is nearer the truth, the point remains that on either interpretation *the Spirit of prophecy is the power of true ethical and spiritual understanding.*

2.5. *The Spirit of Prophecy and Ethical Influence in The Testaments of the Twelve Patriarchs*

In the *Testaments of the Twelve Patriarchs*, we again have a writing that knows of the Spirit as the 'Spirit of prophecy' (cf. *T. Levi* 2.3), and when *T. Sim.* 4.4 refers to Joseph as a man of the Spirit we may assume it is the Spirit of prophecy that is meant, for Joseph above all is the exemplar of one with the Spirit of prophecy in the Judaism of the day. It is noteworthy, however, that in this passage Simeon describes him as 'a good man, one who had within him the Spirit of God, and being full of compassion and mercy he did not bear ill towards me, but loved me as well as my brothers'. As the description of Joseph opens an exhortation to love with a good heart, and not to be overcome by the spirits of jealousy and envy (which play a significant role within the 'the Spirit of Error', i.e. the spiritual 'atmosphere' created by Beliar), the 'goodness' of Joseph would appear to be traced back to the influence of the Spirit of God,[23] i.e. to the Spirit of prophecy functioning as the Spirit of Truth (cf. *T. Jud.* 20.1-5).

This description of Joseph is then generalised in *T. Benj.* 8.1-3 when the one who clings to love, and to the good, is said not to fall into sexual temptation (cf. Joseph himself). This is explained: 'He has no pollution in his heart, *because upon him is resting the Spirit of God*'. Manifestly, the presence of God's Spirit is assumed to have very significant ethical import, even

---

22. Menzies, *Development*, pp. 61-63; Vos, *Untersuchungen*, pp. 64-65. *Per contra* see Turner, 'Spirit and Authoritative Preaching', p. 84 n. 36.

23. Recognized by Sjöberg, *TDNT*, VI, p. 384.

if it is difficult to tell exactly what the author(s) has in mind. Parallels with the description of Joseph suggest the Spirit of prophecy is intended; perhaps especially as the Spirit granting ethical wisdom and insight to discern evil, and prompt purity, just as the 'Spirit of understanding' that comes on Levi at *T. Levi* 2.3 (cf. the description of Joseph in *Jos. Asen.* 4.11: 'And Joseph is a man powerful in wisdom and knowledge, and the Spirit of God is upon him, and the grace of the Lord is with him').

Recently attention has been drawn to manuscript E of *Testament of Levi* which has a number of additions, including the following of immediate importance to this analysis:

> [7 Remove] far away from me, Lord, the spirit of unrighteousness and evil thought and sexual immorality, and remove arrogance from me, [8] and make known to me, Lord, the spirit of holiness (τὸ πνεῦμα τὸ ἅγιον), and give me resolution and wisdom and knowledge and strength... [14] Cleanse my heart, Lord, from all uncleanness and I will be joined to you myself' (*T. Levi* 2.3B7-8, 14).[24]

While the manuscript is late (eleventh century) the additions in other respects correspond very significantly with the fragmentary 4QTLevi ar[a], and so may well preserve very ancient material.[25] Here, the divine Spirit (for such it would appear to be) is simultaneously both the Spirit of prophecy (giving wisdom and knowledge) and an ethical power or influence affording resolution and strength, and acting against the 'spirit of unrighteousness'.

It is not clear whether the Spirit of God is regarded as an active presence with the righteous in the editor's own day,[26] or whether it is merely envisaged within the biblical period, but the part played within the Two Spirits doctrine suggests the former.

2.6. *The Spirit of Prophecy and Ethical Influence at Qumran*

Within the more eschatologically orientated thinking of the Qumran community too, the Spirit of prophecy has strong spiritual/ethical significance. This is particularly evident in 1QH, where the psalmist thanks God for the gift of his Holy Spirit by which the covenanter is 'upheld' so that he does not stumble (7.6-7), and by which he expects further purification (16.11b-12). Echoing perhaps the concepts of Ezekiel 36, the writer can bless God for sprinkling/shedding his Holy Spirit upon him (17.25-26; cf. 4Q504.5). But if we press the question of *how* the Spirit accomplishes this work, it appears to be primarily through the Spirit's *revelatory* work, especially in

---

24. Translation by R.L. Webb, *John the Baptizer and Prophet* (Sheffield: JSOT Press, 1991), p. 119.

25. See Webb, *Baptizer*, pp. 116-20.

26. Sjöberg, *TDNT*, VI, p. 385, claims it is.

bringing *wisdom*:[27] the Spirit delights the psalmist with divine truth (1QH 9.32); brings knowledge of God and his marvellous counsel (12.11-13; 14.25); assures concerning the truth and dependability of God's word (13.18-19), and brings 'understanding' which draws the psalmist closer to God (14.12b-13). What is envisaged is not primarily esoteric knowledge, but *the sort of understanding of God and of his word that elicits righteous living*. It is hardly surprising that the psalmist exclaims his intention to seek God's Spirit of knowledge, and hopes, by cleaving to the Holy Spirit, he will be able to hold fast to the truth of God's covenant (16.6-7). This accords too with the perspective of the newly published 4Q434 in which it is God-given 'understanding' of the Law which strengthens the psalmist's heart (frag. 1, line 1), or which, in the imagery of line 10, removed the psalmist's heart of stone, the evil inclination, and replaced it with a pure heart. Here the psalmist appears to celebrate the eschatological promise of Ezek. 36.25-26 and to regard it as fulfilled in and through the granting of revelatory wisdom. *In short it is the Spirit of prophecy itself which is the 'ethical influence'*.

A similar understanding appears to be involved in 1QS 4.20-23, though it is partially masked by the way the two Spirits teaching is developed. While P. Wernberg-Møller[28] and M. Treves[29] (reacting against the claim there is a hard Zoroastrian cosmic predestinatory dualism reflected in two-Spirit language of 1QS 3.18–4.26) have rightly emphasized the analogy between the universal dualism of the Manual of Discipline and rabbinic teaching on the two inclinations, this analogy should not be taken in a reductionist sense to denote merely psychological forces within a person.[30] It is more convincing to interpret the two Spirits as conflicting powers or spheres of influence at play in man, as in the *Testaments of the Twelve Patriarchs*. The Spirit of error is the totality of evil influences (seen as a unity), and *includes* the influences of the Angel of darkness (1QS 3.20-21) and the spirits of Belial (cf. CD 12.2; 11QMelch 12–13).[31] Likewise, the 'spirit of truth'[32] is

27. So M. Mansoor, *The Thanksgiving Hymns* (Leiden: Brill, 1961), p. 193.

28. 'A Reconsideration of the Two Spirits in the Rule of the Community (IQ Serek III,13—IV,26)', *ResQ* 3 (1961), pp. 413-41.

29. 'The Two Spirits of the Rule of Qumran', *ResQ* 3 (1961), pp. 449-52.

30. Treves ('Two Spirits', pp. 449-52) and Menzies (*Development*, pp. 78-80) appear to fall into this danger.

31. In the two Spirits teaching of the *Testaments of the Twelve Patriarchs* the Spirit of Error appears to be a referring expression for Beliar's activity (*T. Benj.* 6.1; *T. Jos.* 7.4; *T. Jud.* 25.3), and the 'spirits of error' which sometimes appear as human inclinations are demonic powers (against Treves who interprets them as [psychological] inclinations within man).

32. The 'holy spirit' to be 'created' (cf. Ps. 51.10-11) for Israel by God in *Jub.* 1.20-24 should probably be understood in a similar way as a sphere of God's power for righteousness set antithetically over against the 'spirit of Beliar'.

not to be conceived exclusively in anthropological terms, but includes the influence of the Prince of Lights (1QS 3.20), God, and the Angel of Truth (1QS 3.24), etc. The 'holy spirit' and 'spirit of truth' of 1QS 4.21, with which God will sprinkle his people and so purify them (again echoing Ezek. 36?), appears to include the divine Spirit[33] functioning within the framework of our stereotype of 'the Spirit of prophecy', for the result is insight in the knowledge of God and wisdom (1QS 4.22). If this is the case, 1QH and 1QM are conceptually closer than Menzies maintains,[34] and both assume that it is the Spirit of prophecy revealing God's wisdom which cleanses the covenanter. The sharpest difference between the two would then be that 1QS is framed eschatologically, while 1QH speaks (proleptically?) from the perspective of one who already enjoys the benefits of the Spirit.

2.7. The Spirit of Prophecy and Ethical Influence in Rabbinical Teaching
If the rabbis can give the impression that the Spirit of prophecy is of little ethical consequence, that is primarily in their interpretation of the historical books where they have inserted references to charismatic revelation by the Spirit in order to stress God's salvation-historical control over even minor details, for example, of the patriarchs' lives. Another side to the story is to be found in the way the Spirit of prophecy is regarded as giving charismatic revelation that is directly pertinent to ethical questions: thus, for example, the gift to Simeon ben Yoḥai enables him to expose the sinner (y. Šeb. 9.1; cf. Acts 5.1-11); that to Rabbi Meir enables him to discern the estrangement between one of his congregation and her husband, and to take action to overcome the problem (y. Soṭ. 1.4 and pars.); that to Aqiba enables him to discern that the immediate duty of one of his students is with his far-away family, not in the study, and even the gift to R. Gamiliel (t. Pes. 2.15) serves to his disciples to show that halakhah can be deduced from Gamiliel's actions because he is under the Spirit. And when the rabbis discuss Hannah's reply to Eli's unjust assumption she is drunk, they have her say, 'You are no lord, [meaning] the Shekinah and the Holy Spirit is not with you in that you take the harsher and not the more lenient view of my conduct' (b. Ber. 31b). The point here is not simply the failure of charismatic revelation (as it may be in the simpler version of the saying attributed to R. Jose b. Ḥanina), but the failure of righteous judgment evincing lack of the Spirit of prophecy. But these passages, while showing the Spirit has ethical influence in the community, still fall short of exemplifying the Spirit of

33. This is admitted even by A.E. Sekki, *The Meaning of Ruah at Qumran* (Atlanta: Scholars Press, 1989), pp. 207-208, who (excepting 1QS 4.6) otherwise regards the two spirits in 1QS 3.18–4.26 as human dispositions.
34. See Menzies, *Development*, ch. 3.

prophecy as a transforming ethical power. A passage from *Mek. Bešallaḥ* 3 (on Exod. 14.9-14) takes us a little further, for its point appears to be that the Holy Spirit's presence with all Israel is what prompts her to intercessory prayer and good deeds which in turn merit the salvation God effects.[35]

The handling of Ezek. 36.25-27 by the rabbis is of particular importance. Most of their discussion of these verses focuses on their hope for the removal of the evil *yetser* and the gift of a 'heart of flesh', and hence 36.26b is cited without reference to the Spirit. This, however, should not be taken to suggest the rabbis dissociated the gift of the Spirit from the awaited ethical renewal, or reinterpreted it in terms of the gift of a 'holy spirit' (in the anthropological sense). When the rabbis do go on to quote the relevant verse—Ezek. 36.27—they consistently take it to refer to the divine Spirit (cf. *b. Ber.* 32a [// *b. Suk.* 52b]; *Tanḥuma* [Buber] Addition to חקת;[36] *Num. R.* 9.49; and *Midr. Pss.* 73.4), and it is this understanding that is clearly maintained in the Targum. When we ask about the nature of this promise of the Spirit, and *how* the Spirit is understood to produce the new obedience, two texts which combine Ezekiel and Joel deserve special attention. *Midr. Pss.* 14.6 affirms:

> Another comment: David spoke the first time in behalf of the Master, the Holy One, blessed be He, who said: *Oh that they had such a heart as this always, to fear Me, and keep My commandments* (Deut. 5.25 [29]); and he spoke the second time in behalf of Moses who said: *Would that all the Lord's people were prophets* (Num. 11.29). Neither the words of the Master nor the words of the disciple are to be fulfilled in this world, but the words of both will be fulfilled in the world-to-come: The words of the Master, *A new heart also will I give you and ye shall keep Mine ordinances* (Ezek. 36.26), will be fulfilled; and the words of the disciple, *I will pour out My spirit upon all flesh; and your sons and daughters shall prophesy* (Joel 3.1 [2.28]), will also be fulfilled.

This has been taken to teach that God first fulfils Ezek. 36.25-27, and then consequently (even if immediately) grants the Spirit of prophecy promised in Joel 2.28 [MT 3.1].[37] This is a possible reading, but it is more natural to assume that the promise of the Spirit in Ezek. 36.27 is understood in terms of the Joel promise, and that the Spirit of prophecy is simultaneously *both*

---

35. So also W.D. Davies, 'Reflections on the Spirit in the Mekilta: A Suggestion' in D. Marcus (ed.), *The Gaster Festschrift* (New York: ANE Society, 1973), p. 101.

36. 'Concerning this the Wise say: The one who does not look at another's wife, the evil impulse has no power over him. In the world to come the Holy One, blessed be He, will take the evil impulse from us and place in us his Holy Spirit, as it is written: "I will remove the heart of stone from your flesh and I will put my Spirit in you" (Ezek. 36.26-27).'

37. Menzies, *Development*, p. 106, following Turner, 'Luke and the Spirit', p. 150.

the means of Israel's renewed existential knowledge of God's will (and this, as we have seen, naturally also constitutes the impulse to perform it) *and* the means of continuing charismatic revelation and prophetic utterance. *Deut. R.* 6.14 strongly suggests that such an interpretation existed among the rabbis.

> God said: 'In this world, because there are amongst you slanderers, I have withdrawn My Divine Presence (שכינתי) from among you,' as it is said, *Be exalted, O God, above the heavens* (Ps. 57.12 [11]). 'But in the time to come, when I will uproot the evil inclination from amongst you', as it is said, *And I will take away the stony heart out of your flesh* (Ezek. 36.26), 'I will restore My Divine Presence amongst you.' Whence this? For it is said, *And it shall come to pass afterward, that I will pour out My Spirit upon all flesh*, etc. (Joel 3.1 [2.28]); 'and because I will cause my Divine Presence to rest upon you, all of you will merit the Torah, and you will dwell in peace in the world, as it is said, *And all children shall be taught of the Lord; and great shall be the peace of my children* (Isa. 54.13)'.

At first glance, the promise of the Divine Presence seems to be quite distinct from and additional to the promise of the eradication of the evil *yetser*, grounded in the Ezekiel promise, and to be interpreted exclusively in terms of Joel 3.1, rather than in Ezek. 36.26-27. However, the affirmation that the restoration of the Divine presence will *cause Israel to merit the Torah* leads us in the opposite direction. It indicates that the Shekinah, here virtually equated with Joel's promise of the Spirit of prophecy, is a power that promotes willing submission and obedience to God. The rabbis cannot have deduced this from the text of Joel; it would appear rather to be a midrashic interpretation of the passage just cited, namely Ezek. 36.26-27! In other words, Joel's promise of the Spirit of prophecy is itself understood as the means of fulfilling Ezek. 36.26-27 (rather than something additional to it)— an interpretation which is facilitated by the sort of understanding of the Spirit of prophecy for which we have argued above.

The evidence of these two midrashim, however, is late; probably Amoraic (i.e. 200–500 CE),[38] but possibly much later. More definitely Amoraic is the tradition in *b. Ber.* 31b-32a (attributed to R. Papa [c. 350–375] claiming that the Spirit prompted and controlled the ethical content of Elijah's prayer, and this on the basis of an appeal to Ezek. 36.27. We cannot depend on such a view having been in circulation in the New Testament period. Nevertheless, the texts strongly suggest that Jews could understand the 'Spirit of prophecy' as the very power of the religious and moral life that was hoped would characterise the new covenant.

---

38. Also probably Amoraic—attributed to R. Samuel b. Nahmani (290–320 CE)— is the tradition in *Eccl. R.* 10.17 // *Gen. R.* 85.12 that the Spirit promotes justice in Israel's courts.

2.8. *The Spirit of Prophecy and Ethical Influence in 1 Enoch*

In the probably pre-Christian *Similitudes of Enoch* (*1 En.* 61.11-12), the eschatological congregation extols God charismatically 'in the spirit of faith, in the spirit of wisdom and patience, in the spirit of mercy, in the spirit of justice and peace, and in the spirit of generosity'. The picture of the congregation here is too closely modelled on the composite 'Messiah of the Spirit'[39] (on which see below) and indeed on Enoch's own invasive charismatic worship (71.11),[40] for us to explain the references to 'spirit' here as anything other than the charismatic Spirit of prophecy (as at *1 En.* 61.7) acting as an influence towards the qualities named. For these circles, at least, Gunkel's and Schweizer's antithesis got it precisely wrong.

2.9. *The Spirit of Prophecy and Ethical Influence in the 'Messianic' Traditions Based in Isaiah 11.1-4*

So far we have by-passed perhaps one of the most telling pieces of evidence in the whole case, namely the picture of the messiah held in influential circles of Judaism. As we have seen, Isa. 11.1-4 was undoubtedly one of the most significant texts in Judaism's complex and variegated messianic hopes. The description in 11.2 of the Spirit of the Lord on the messiah as the Spirit of wisdom, understanding, (divine) counsel and might, the Spirit of knowledge and the fear of the Lord, undoubtedly encouraged the understanding that this was the gift of 'the Spirit of prophecy' (explicitly in *Targ. Ps.* 45.3). But the last element is especially significant. The Spirit of prophecy bringing knowledge of the Lord *thereby* instils 'the fear of the Lord'. The passage thus envisages a strong ethical influence of the Spirit of prophecy on the messiah, and this, of course, is spelt out in the picture of the impressive righteousness of the messianic judgment with which 11.3-4 continues. The wording and ideas of Isa. 11.1-4 (sometimes combined with Isa. 4.4) can be traced clearly in *1 En.* 49.2-3; *Pss. Sol.* 17.37, 18.7; 1QSb 5.25; 4Q215 (col. 4.4-5, 9-10); 4Q252 (col. 5.1-5); 4Q285 (frag. 7.2); 4QpIsa^a 3.15-23, and *T. Levi* 18.7[41] (cf. also *Targ. Isa.* 4.2-4; 11.1-2). In each case we have an understanding of the Spirit which falls within the category of the 'Spirit of prophecy' (affording understanding, wisdom or knowledge), and yet in each case too these gifts precisely fuel the redoubtable righteousness of the messianic ruler envisaged—to the point where *1 En.* 62.1-2 can simply sum up the whole picture by saying '*the Spirit of righteousness has been*

---

39. *1 En.* 49.2-3; 62.2 (cf. 4Q215).

40. Cf. the traditions of Israel at the Red Sea; *t. Soṭ* 6.2 and pars.

41. If the words 'in the water' are bracketed off as a gloss, there is no reason to suggest what remains of 18.7 is Christian: 'And the glory of the Most High shall burst forth upon him. And the *Spirit* of understanding and sanctification shall rest upon him [in the water].'

poured upon him. The word of his mouth will destroy sinners (cf. Isa. 11.4); and all the oppressors shall be eliminated from before his face'. In pre-Christian Judaism, then, the messiah's powerful endowment with the Spirit of prophecy is not only portrayed as the source of his own outstanding righteousness, but also as the source of his immense influence for righteousness, exerted in his fiery cleansing of Zion. The same picture (as we shall see) is presented in John the Baptist's announcement of one who will baptize in the Holy Spirit and fire (Lk. 3.16//Matthew). And again we need to note that it is along this trajectory of messianic expectation that Luke has at least in part modelled his picture of Jesus. This cannot be without considerable significance.

We must conclude that Gunkel and Schweizer have seriously misled us. There are certainly instances of charismata of the Spirit of prophecy that appear to have little, if any, ethical influence or power. But that the Spirit of prophecy *could* be understood as an important ethical influence seems virtually undeniable, and the messiah expected in the circles indicated was to be an exemplar of precisely such a chrism. If we were to press the matter we might suggest that neither the Old Testament nor Judaism know of any ethically transforming or recreating gift of the Spirit that is necessarily *other* than the gift of the Spirit of prophecy which reveals God's presence, wisdom and will to the human heart in such a way as *thereby* to motivate (and so enable) the life of filial righteousness (even *Jos. Asen.* 8.10 could be understood so). The promised pouring out of the Spirit of prophecy on all Israel could only be expected to transform the nation's life before God. This in turn means the anticipated gift of the Spirit of prophecy is 'soteriological', because for 'intertestamental' Jews the language of 'forgiveness of sins' and 'salvation' is regularly used to refer precisely to such hopes for a fundamental transformation of the nation *within* history, a transformation within which the Spirit has an evidently significant role to play.

3. *The Spirit of Prophecy and 'Salvation'*

As E.P. Sanders[42] and others have shown, the general covenantal nomistic pattern of Jewish religion ensured that the large majority of practising Jews would simply assume that as the elect people, covenanted to the God of mercy, they continually received forgiveness (ritualised in the Day of Atonement, etc.), and would inevitably participate in the age to come, and the final salvation it brought. They would assume this for one of two reasons. Either they believed all Jews (excepting those who deliberately

---

42. Especially *Paul and Palestinian Judaism* (London: SCM Press, 1977); *Jesus and Judaism* (London: SCM Press, 1985).

defied the covenant) enjoyed this privilege and hope (as Sanders held was the almost universal belief), or they held some kind of remnant theology (restricting 'true Israel' to those with a more radical—even sectarian—nomistic praxis), but simultaneously believed that the group they had chosen to adhere to was itself (or would be included in) that remnant. In that sense the only 'insecure' Jews (i.e. Jews who felt unsure of their future participation in the age to come) would probably be those challenged by the more radical (or simply different) demands of some 'remnant' group they had not yet joined.

Within this covenantal 'pattern of religion', then, salvation in the age to come was relatively assured. But to what did it pertain? From the days of Weiss and Schweitzer it has regularly been assumed that it refers to the order of some quite different world, beyond this creation. More recently, however, the work of Glasson, Caird, Borg, Charlesworth, Wright[43] and others has argued persuasively that it pertains rather to God's transformation of *this* world-*order*, with a restored and liberated Israel as its centre and light. That is, from the Maccabaean period to beyond the fall of the temple, Jewish eschatology/soteriology was primarily concerned with what we may call 'the state of the nation'. The leadership was widely perceived to be corrupt, the social fabric torn apart, and the Ptolomaic, Seleucid and later Roman presences oppressive, burdensome, and, more important, a fundamental theological challenge to Israel's self-conception as a theocracy in God's land. Most Jews saw this state of affairs as temporal chastisement for the sin of the nation, like the earlier sixth-century exile. The Jews who had (partly!) returned from that, after the fall of Babylon, thus still paradoxically seemed to live 'in exile' in their own land.

What Jews in these circumstances came to hope for was a 'forgiveness of (Israel's) sins' which brought the reversal of this historical chastisement. A milder but analogous version of such hopes is well articulated from within the martyr tradition in *4 Maccabees*. With his dying breath, following brutal torture before Antiochus for refusal to eat swine's flesh, Eleazar is made to say,

> 'You know, God, that although I might save myself from fiery torments, I am dying for the Law. Be merciful to your people [who have broken the Law] and be satisfied with our sacrifice for them. Make my blood their cleansing, and receive my life as their ransom' (*4 Macc.* 6.27-29).[44]

43. For a summary of this important but developing position, and the literature related to it, see Wright, *Testament*, ch. 10.

44. Although probably written in the mid-first century in Antioch, the martyr tradition here has much older roots. LXX Dan 3.40 has Shadrach and his companions pray 'May our sacrifice be before you today, to bring about atonement with you'! This appears to be a Greek translation of a second-century BCE Hebrew Maccabean

By these words attributed to Eleazar, the narrator certainly did not signify the martyr hoped his death (and that of others to follow) would secure Israel's salvation in the world to come after the great judgment. He could be anticipated to believe Israel would enjoy that anyway unless she actually apostasized. What the words imply rather was that Israel was suffering external oppression and internal division, and lack of spiritual depth and direction, because of the nation's unrighteousness. These things were perceived as God's temporal purging wrath on her; her metaphorical slavery in 'exile'. And Eleazar was requesting God to accept his righteous death (and others to follow) as *enough* punishment for Israel. It was a plea to God to concentrate his wrath on Israel in the martyrs—and so reverse her shame and make her the righteous and free people he had always intended them to be. In short, the prayer expresses the hope that the martyrs' deaths will effect national salvation and transformation there and then, in *this* world. And the writer of *4 Maccabees* can affirm that this is indeed what God accomplished: the martyr deaths led to the successful Maccabaean uprising, and in *4 Macc.* 17.21-22 we are accordingly given a theological explanation and are told that these martyrs

> ...became...a ransom for the sin of our nation. Through the blood of these righteous ones and through the propitiation of their death the divine providence [i.e. God] rescued Israel, which had been shamefully treated.

Other traditions used sharply *eschatological* language to depict a variety of hopes for more thorough-going transformations, yet these were still largely, if not entirely, anticipated as changes to be brought about in history, and to centre on the transformation of Israel as a paradigm of authentic humanity for the world. As Wright summarizes the matter,

> The 'salvation' spoken of in the Jewish sources of this period has to do with rescue from the national enemies, restoration of the national symbols, and a state of *shalom* in which every man will sit under his vine or fig-tree...For first-century Jews it could only mean the inauguration of the age to come, liberation from Rome, the restoration of the Temple, and the free enjoyment of their own Land.
>
> Within the mainline Jewish writings of this period...*there is virtually no evidence that Jews were expecting the end of the space-time universe*... What, then, did they believe was going to happen? They believed that *the present world order* would come to an end—the world order in which pagans held power, and Jews, the covenant people of the creator god, did not.[45]

prayer—which means the martyr atonement theology of *4 Maccabees* actually rests on a much older and Palestinian understanding of the death of the righteous.

45. The first quotations come from Wright, *Testament*, p. 300; the second ones from p. 333. The italics are Wright's. See also D.L. Tiede, 'The Exaltation of Jesus and

Whether or not we agree with Wright's (thoroughly informed) analysis that salvation and eschatology refer to the historical transformation of Israel without remainder, the point stands that salvation was largely construed as the restoration, transformation and glorification of Zion from the faithful remnant.[46]

How would the gift of the Spirit of prophecy be conceived within this framework? As we have seen, in those circles which expected a messianic figure built in one way or another on Isa. 11.1-4, the Spirit on the messiah would inevitably be the *major* force in Zion's renewal—and in that sense 'soteriologically necessary'. And as the salvation concerned means the transformation of Zion, and the new order which results, the gift of the Spirit is as necessary to the messiah's experience of this 'salvation' as it is to that of his people, for the salvation involved is a corporate and social state of affairs that the messiah cannot experience on his own. In such a context, Menzies' attempt to distinguish the gift of the Spirit for oneself and the gift of the Spirit 'principally for the benefit of others'[47] tends to artificiality; as does Gunkel's between the Spirit's direct actions and the consequent ethical *effects* of the Spirit's action.

Similarly, in circles where the Spirit of prophecy is expected to be given universally (as envisaged in Joel), it is virtually impossible to believe that this would not be considered to have such a *major* transforming impact within the community as to be effectively 'soteriologically necessary'. Granted that God could be transformingly present in his Shekinah presence, his name, and so on, surely any Jew would say he became *most* clearly and transformingly active in the community in his various gifts of wisdom, revelation and inspired speech.

4. *Conclusions*

This survey shows that contrary to Schweizer's assumption, those sectors of Judaism which regarded the Spirit as the Spirit of prophecy were inclined also to think of the Spirit as exerting life-transforming or directing ethical influences: we have seen this in the LXX and targum tradition, in Philo, the Wisdom Literature, the *Testaments of the Twelve Patriarchs*, at Qumran, in

---

the Restoration of Israel in Acts 1', *HTR* 79 (1986), pp. 283-84.

46. The massive work by one of my own research students, Mark Elliott, has recently substantiated this (see 'The Survivors of Israel' [PhD dissertation, Aberdeen, 1993]). Cf. S. Talmon, 'The Concept of *Māšiaḥ* and Messianism in Early Judaism', in J.H. Charlesworth (ed.), *The Messiah* (Minneapolis: Fortress Press, 1992), pp. 79-115 (esp. 113-115)—though in my view Talmon underestimates the extent of messianic hopes.

47. *Development*, p. 279.

rabbinical teaching and in *1 Enoch*. The 'messianic' figures developed from Isa. 11.1-4 were a special case of this, the Spirit on these figures being understood as the source of his own compelling righteousness and fear of the Lord, as well as the endowment by which he would liberate, purge and restore Israel. In §3 we have seen that the kind of 'salvation' Jews awaited (and for which they used eschatological language) was largely a transformation of Israel in history. The combination of the gift of the Spirit to the messiah and the fulfilment of Joel's promise to the rest of Israel could be anticipated to provide the major means of this hoped-for 'salvation'.

CONCLUSION TO PART II

In the scope of the three chapters above I have put serious question marks over many current interpretations of Jewish concepts of the 'Spirit of prophecy'. I have provided a working definition of the 'Spirit of prophecy', and noted the charismata prototypical to it (charismatic revelation, wisdom, invasive prophetic speech and charismatic praise). However, while the 'Spirit of prophecy' was not (in Judaism) regarded as the source of charismatic preaching as such (that was a Christian development), both the Spirit, and more specifically the 'Spirit of prophecy', were accepted as the source of miracles of power and were also perceived as having the potential for spiritual/ethical renewal. This was especially the case in respect of 'messianic' traditions reflecting on Isa. 11.1-4, on which Luke builds. There is, therefore, in Judaism neither the sharp difference between the 'Spirit of prophecy' and the 'charismatic Spirit' elucidated by Menzies; nor the equally sharp one he posits between the former and the 'soteriological Spirit'. This in turn means we cannot so easily assume that the 'Spirit of prophecy' would be irrelevant to Luke's concept of salvation, and that it may safely be described as a *donum superadditum* of empowering for mission. Nor can we assume Luke disengaged the Spirit from works of power. We shall need to examine very closely how Luke takes up these strands of Jewish thinking.

Part III

THE MESSIAH OF THE SPIRIT

Chapter 6

THE COMING OF THE MESSIAH OF THE SPIRIT IN LUKE 1–2

1. *The Annunciation, Birth and Infancy Narratives as 'Previews of Salvation'*[1]

Like a blast of joyful trumpets, Lk. 1.5–2.52 sounds a theological fanfare to herald the themes which will make more measured and stately progress through the rest of Luke–Acts.[2] The origins of the material in these two chapters are disputed,[3] but four conclusions appear to be justified: (1) Luke almost certainly did not get his annunciation, birth or infancy stories from Matthew (nor vice versa).[4] (2) The agreements between Luke and Matthew

---

1.   This is the title offered for Lk. 1.5–2.40 by R.C. Tannehill, *The Narrative Unity of Luke–Acts: A Literary Interpetation.* I. *The Gospel according to Luke* (Philadelphia: Fortress Press, 1986), pp. 15-44.

2.   Compare D. Bock's comment: 'The infancy material is like an overture to a symphony. It introduces fundamental themes of Luke–Acts' (D.K. Campbell and J.L. Townsend [eds.], *A Case for Premillenialism* [Chicago: Moody, 1992], p. 183); Johnson, 35: 'By means of programmatic prophecies they [the infancy narratives] anticipate later plot developments'.

3.   Surveys of research are available readily enough, even if agreed conclusions are more difficult to find: see e.g. H.H. Oliver, 'The Lukan Birth Stories and the Purpose of Luke–Acts', *NTS* 10 [1964], pp. 202-26; R.E. Brown, *The Birth of the Messiah* (London: Chapman, 1978), especially pp. 26-38 and 235-53; Marshall, 45-50; and Fitzmyer, especially pp. 304-21).

4.   This conclusion may yet be overthrown by M.D. Goulder's vigorous attempt to demonstrate the Two Gospel Hypothesis (that Mark and Matthew were Luke's only sources of Gospel Tradition, with the LXX as an important additional resource): cf. M.D. Goulder, *Luke: A New Paradigm* (Sheffield: JSOT Press, 1989). But it has to be said, one of the least convincing parts of that hypothesis is precisely its particularly speculative account of how Lk. 1–2 was composed from the earlier Gospels. There may be passages where the agreements between Matthew and Luke against (or outside) Mark suggest Luke's use of Matthew (rather than 'Q' or some other source [see his 'A House Built on Sand' in A.E. Harvey (ed.), *Alternative Approaches to New Testament Study* (London: SPCK, 1985), pp. 1-24, esp. 7-11, also *Luke*, pp. 3-26 (11-15), and ch. 2.]), but Lk. 1–2 does not furnish convincing examples of such.

therefore strongly suggest their use of earlier traditions.[5] (3) The linguistic arguments at present favour the hypothesis that the traditions used in Luke 1–2 were substantially Hebrew or Aramaic (or a translation from these languages).[6] (4) It is probable, though less certain, that the carefully crafted parallel anunciation, birth and infancy accounts[7] that form the substance of

---

5.   There are some 12 notable points of *conceptual* (rather than linguistic) agreement between Matthew and Luke (including Jesus' virginal conception by the Spirit wthin the house of David) that suggest dependence on tradition (for lists of these see Brown, *Birth*, pp. 34-35; Fitzmyer, 307). The remarkable divergence in the way these traditions are presented does not encourage the view Luke got his material from Matthew, and somewhat taxes Goulder's ingenuity to provide plausible explanation from the LXX instead.

6.   This conclusion is justified in the light of recent study by R.A. Martin and S. Farris. It is well known there has been long and costly battle fought between those who have urged Lk. 1–2 (or parts of these chapters) reflects Semitic sources (so Burney, Winter, Laurentin), and those who have explained the same phenomena as Septuagintalisms, and as part of Luke's free imitative historiography (so Harnack, Cadbury, and Benoit). On this clash between those who follow Harnack and those who see Hebrew or Aramaic sources behind Lk. 1–2, Brown quips that the linguistic opponents have fought themselves to a draw on the issue (*Birth*, p. 246; see S. Farris, *The Hymns of Luke's Infancy Narratives* [Sheffield: JSOT Press, 1985], pp. 31-50 for a survey of the argmuents). But Farris has broken new ground. Using and developing R.A. Martin's seventeen syntactic criteria (see especially his *Syntactical Evidence of Semitic Sources in Greek Documents* [Missoula, MT: Scholars Press, 1974]), Farris is able to show Lk. 1–2 (as a whole; not merely in the 'hymns') evinces all the syntactic structure frequencies which characterize pieces of translation Greek, rather than freely composed Greek—and this more markedly than many sections of the LXX sampled, and much more so than Paul or the Apocalypse. What is more, the second half of Acts witnesses to the fact that Luke is not himself a Semiticizing writer, for here the syntactic structure frequencies are as purely Greek as Plutarch, and there are virtually no features of 'translation Greek'. Now Luke might have been able to imitate LXX vocabulary and idiom to give an archaic impression in the infancy narratives, argues Farris, but he would not have been able consistently to hit the usual translation Greek ratios of ἐν to other prepositions; of καί copulative to δέ; of preceding dependent genitives to post-substantive genitives; etc. The high incidence of 'translation Greek' features in Lk. 1–2 strongly suggests Luke is using a source (or several sources) of Semitic origin (Farris, *Hymns*, pp. 50-66. See also 'On Discerning Semitic Sources in Lk. 1–2' in R.T. France and D. Wenham [eds.], *Studies of History and Tradition in the Four Gospels* [Gospel Perspectives, 2; Sheffield: JSOT Press, 1981], pp. 201-38). This is an important argument, strangely ignored by Goulder (the apparent omission is all the more curious as he actually cites Farris at *Luke*, pp. 233, 237. Farris had himself pointed out that Goulder's earlier work had simply ignored the question of whether there was evidence indicating the use of Semitic sources in Lk. 1–2, and that a good argument for such sources would 'cause grave damage to Goulder's theory' [*Hymns*, p. 36]).

7.   The most nuanced brief account of the parallel structure is that provided by Fitzmyer, 313-15 (and cf. Brown, *Birth*, pp. 248-49).

Luke 1–2 came from a single source.[8] But while the Evangelist may have received the body of Luke 1–2 more-or-less intact, he has used it to provide the reader with a singularly appropriate 'preface'[9] to the dominating

8.   To say Luke is using originally Semitic material for his birth and infancy narratives is not, however, to say that he received it as a single source, nor to claim that what he received he left by and large unaltered. Even those who affirm his use of traditional material and written sources admit the special difficulties involved in any attempt to distinguish source and redaction in this section of Luke (cf. Schürmann, 143-44). But one further argument does incline us to accept the fourth conclusion introduced above, namely that Lk. 1–2 derives substantially from a single source. It is an argument drawn from the nature of the frequent and delicate parallelisms between the annunciation and birth of John the Baptist on the one hand and that of Jesus on the other. Of course, the fact of such parallelisms, combined with Luke's well-known predilection for forging parallel accounts, has been taken by Brown to indicate that Luke himself composed the whole parallelism from scraps of traditional material (*Birth*, p. 243; D.L. Tiede, *Prophecy and History in Luke–Acts* [Philadelphia: Fortress Press, 1980], p. 23), and by Fitzmyer to favour the view that Luke at least created the annunciation and birth of Jesus in parallel to similar stories about John the Baptist, which he inherited from a source (1.5-25, 57-66b). (*Luke*, pp. 44-45, following the lead of Dibelius, Bultmann, Leaney and Schneider.) Neither view quite squares with the linguistic observations adduced by Martin (that Lk. 1–2 as a whole shows evidence of deriving from a Semitic original), and, as Farris points out, while narrative parallelisms were commonplace in the Graeco-Roman world (and so not necessarily 'Lukan'), these particular parallels do not match Luke's handling of Jesus and John in Lk. 3–4. In Lk. 1–2 the parallels are much more extensive, and affect both form and content—thus 'annunciation matches annunciation, hymn matches hymn, old man (Zechariah) matches old man (Simeon), etc.' (Farris, *Hymns*, p. 105). In these passages too, the parallels are consistently 'tilted' to make the Jesus part transcend the John part (thus if John's parent's are described as 'upright' [1.6], Mary is addressed by the angel as the 'favoured one' of God [1.28]. If John's mother receives the miracle of a child in great age [1.7, 24-25], Mary conceives Jesus as a virgin [1.27, 34]. If John will be 'great before the Lord' [1.15], Jesus too will be great [1.32], and himself receive the designation 'Lord' along with messiah and saviour [2.11]. If John is to be a 'prophet of the Most High' [1.76], Jesus will be Son of the Most High [1.32-35], and while John is filled with the Spirit from birth [1.15], Jesus is the New Creation of the Holy Spirit [1.35], etc.). Such features are much less densely clustered in Lk. 3–4 (and, for that matter, in Luke's parallels elsewhere). This suggests that the type of parallelism in Lk. 1–2 may more easily be explained as deriving from a source than as the product of Luke's own redaction. And as most of the material within these chapters can be explained within the parallelism, it is inviting to think of a single source, rather than a plurality of them. Whether we can detect Lukan additions or changes to such material we shall have to discuss in relation to the particular passages on the Spirit to be studied below.

9.   Cf. J.P. Audet, 'Autour de la théologie de Luc I-II', *ScEccl* 11 (1959), pp. 409-18, who compares Luke's with classical and Hellenistic 'prefaces' (προοίμια), which serve to guide the reader towards the intended meaning of the body of the work (pp. 417-19).

interests of Luke–Acts, taking him or her to the very heart of the crucial issues of Israel and her promised salvation in the awaited messiah, and at least adumbrating the failure of a major part of the nation to participate in this.[10]

Recent studies informed by narrative criticism have especially highlighted the potential contribution of the various prophecies, explanatory epiphanies and hymnic celebrations of God's saving intervention, in Luke 1–2, for an overall understanding of Luke–Acts. It becomes clear that from the perspective of the narrator they are an especially important guide to God's will and plan, for (as Tannehill points out) it is a variety of entirely 'reliable spokespeople', speaking on behalf of an omniscient God, who declare the significance of the two portentous births.[11] Thus none less than the 'angel Gabriel' (1.11, 19, 26), as one of the seven great angels of the presence (1.19), first announces that of John (1.13-17) and then, in a form-critically closely parallel passage, that of Jesus (1.28-37). Later an angel announces the birth of Jesus to shepherds, and an accompanying host glorify God for the great moment of salvation it betokens (2.10-14). The other chief passages in which the significance of these two births are articulated (including the *Magnificat*, the *Benedictus* and the *Nunc Dimittis*) are all spoken by human characters, but this does not significantly lessen their reliability,[12] as the real speaker (from the narrator's point of view) is the Spirit of prophecy, and this is regularly indicated by such introductory formulae as 'Elizabeth was filled with the Holy Spirit and exclaimed...' (1.41), 'Zechariah was filled with the Holy Spirit and prophesied saying...' (1.67), and so on.[13]

---

10. Conzelmann's failure to integrate Lk. 1–2 with the rest of the Gospel was sharply and convincingly criticized by P.S. Minear, 'Luke's Use of the Birth Stories' in L.E. Keck and J.L. Martyn (eds.), *Studies in Luke–Acts* (London: SPCK, 1968) pp. 113-30. Those (e.g. Oliver, Tatum) who wished to pursue Conzelmann's theological programme had thereafter at least to demonstrate that Lk. 1–2 was consistent with it. More recently, a number (e.g. J.T. Sanders, Tannehill, Tiede, Moessner) who believe that the body of Luke–Acts emphasizes the rejection of the Gospel by 'the Jews' have recognised that this appears to subvert the main emphases of Lk. 1–2, and have fallen to quite different ways of accounting for the tension that results. Nevertheless, they recognize that the issues raised there are the ones that dominate Luke's agenda.

11. R.C. Tannehill, 'Israel in Luke-Acts: A Tragic Story', *JBL* 104 (1985), pp. 69-85. Cf. also J.T. Squires, *The Plan of God in Luke–Acts* (Cambridge: Cambridge University Press, 1993), pp. 27-32.

12. *Contra* D.P. Moessner, 'The Ironic Fulfillment of Israel's Glory', in J.B.Tyson (ed.), *Luke–Acts and the Jewish People* (Minneapolis: Augsburg, 1988), pp. 35-50 (see ch. 10 §3 below).

13. The *Magnificat* (1.46-55) is not specifically attributed to the inspiration of the Spirit, but it is barely likely that Elizabeth, Zechariah and Simeon are regarded as speaking in the Spirit while Mary (to whom Elizabeth pays homage: 1.42-45) is not.

Indeed, as Shepherd has argued, to a large extent the narrative function of the mentions of the Holy Spirit in Luke 1–2 (and throughout Luke–Acts) is precisely to legitimate the Gospel announced.[14]

The essential content of the announcements may very briefly be summed up in three moments:

1. John will fulfil the eschatological Elijianic role prescribed for him in Malachi (1.15-17; cf. Mal. 4.5-6) and prepare Israel for her salvation (1.76-77; cf. Mal. 3.1 and Lk. 7.27).
2. God will introduce Israel's long-promised (cf. 1.54-55, 70, 72-73) salvation, through Jesus (one 'born...in the city of David', 2.11) who accordingly will receive the titles, throne and redemptive functions due to the messianic Davidid (1.32-35, 69; 2.11, 26-32). This salvation will consist in 'the forgiveness of sins' (1.77) and the liberation and transformation of Israel—liberation, that is, from enemies, oppressors and social injustice (1.51-53, 74), and trans-formation as a righteous worshipping community (1.74-75) living in that eschatological freedom, harmony and evident temporal blessing of God occasionally promised in the Old Testament as 'peace' (e.g. Isa. 52.7-10; 54.10), a peace especially associated with some kind of messianic reign (e.g. Isa. 9.2-7; Ezek. 34.23-31; cf. Isa. 11.1-9 and Lk. 1.79, 2.14).
3. Israel so restored (albeit also divided, 2.34) will be a light to the nations (2.29-32), fulfilling the calling of Isa. 49.6.

These Davidic and nationalist announcements appear to cohere entirely with the narrator's perspective: it is he who makes the point of informing us that Joseph was 'of the house of David' (1.27), and that Joseph and Mary providentially went to Bethlehem, 'the city of David' (this designation would normally refer rather to Jersualem!), and it is he who explains Joseph did this 'because he was descended of the house and lineage of David' (2.4).[15] It is also the 'narrator' who informs us that Simeon was 'looking

---

The reader will be expected to deduce from the similar form of her utterance (to those of Zechariah and Simeon) that she too speaks prophetically, and it is possible the reader is intended to trace the Spirit of Lk. 1.35 in this hymn (so Menzies argues, *Development*, p. 127).

14. Thus, *contra* Moessner ('Ironic Fulfillment'), 'that Zechariah's prophecy con-cerning God's faithfulness to Israel is explicitly said to be inspired by the Holy Spirit gives it an extra degree of narrative authority' (Shepherd, *Function*, p. 119—and he draws similar conclusions throughout).

15. I am grateful to M.L. Strauss, one of my own research students, for drawing to my attention Luke's strong preference for Davidic Christology: see his *Messiah, passim*, but esp. ch. 3 (on the birth narratives).

forward to the consolation of Israel' (2.25, cf. Isa. 52.7-10), which he recognizes as fulfilled (at least in anticipation) in Jesus, and that Anna spread the news of the child of promise to all who were 'looking for Jerusalem's redemption' (2.38).[16]

What is to be inferred from all this concerning Luke's view of 'salvation' and of the Christian life and mission, which are the broader story within which his pneumatology must be explained? Insofar as he allows himself to be identified with the narrator, it suggests Luke works with an essentially Jewish soteriological paradigm of the type we have referred to in Chapter 5, that is, that God's 'forgiveness of sins' means his reversal of his temporal chastisement of Israel and issues in the Davidic messianic liberation of Zion in history.[17] As we proceed through Luke–Acts we shall need to examine how Luke sees these hopes fulfilled, modified, postponed or abandoned. But at the outset they would suggest that 'salvation' (for Luke) is not merely entry to the remnant messianic community, release from guilt, and assurance of life in some new creation beyond this one (however important these may be), but also ongoing participation in the worship, life and witness of the restored Davidic community which is increasingly cleansed and transformed in history to become 'a light to the Gentiles'. As we have seen, in the context of this view of 'salvation' we shall need to ask more carefully whether the Spirit is not indeed 'soteriologically necessary'.

2. *The Pneumatology of Luke 1–2 and its Relation to Luke's Theology*

In this section we shall survey the Spirit material in Luke 1–2, and assess its significance for the interpretation of Luke's pneumatology. Before we do so, however, it would be wise briefly to orientate ourselves to the sort of

16. This Zionist eschatological hope reflects Isa. 40.1, 49.13, 51.3, 57.18, and is the subject of the 'proclamation of good news' and the annunciation of peace in 52.7-10.

17. For a suggestive account along similar lines, but based in the overtones of the Samuel and David narratives in Lk. 1–2, see Wright, *Testament*, pp. 378-84; Tiede, *Prophecy*, pp. 23-33. T. Kaut (*Befreier und befreites Volk: Traditions- und redaktionsgeschichtliche Untersuchungen zu Magnifikat und Benediktus im Kontext der vorlukanischen Kindheitsgeschichte* [Frankfurt: Hain, 1990]) traces the view to Luke's tradition, but others are inclined to see it as fully Lukan too: K. Stalder ('Der Heilige Geist in der lukanischen Ekklesiologie', *Una Sancta* 30 [1975], pp. 287-93) argues that Luke's soteriology in the whole of Luke–Acts centres in the renewal of Zion in the Church, and cf. F.Ó. Fearghail, *The Introduction to Luke–Acts* (Rome: Pontifical Biblical Institute, 1988), pp. 7-8, 29. Most recently, L.T. Johnson has tested the hypothesis that Luke's soteriology is centred in the restoration of Israel and found confirmation for it: see 'The Social Dimensions of *Sōtēria* in Luke–Acts and Paul', in E.H. Lovering (ed.), *SBL 1993 Seminar Papers* (SBLSP, 32; Atlanta: Scholars Press, 1993), pp. 520-36.

understandings that at present dominate the critical scene, and which will be tested in the survey of the texts.

Much of the recent discussion pertinent to the interpretation of the Spirit in Luke 1–2 has been conducted in relation to the larger issue of Luke's concept of redemption history, and especially in relation to Conzelmann's thesis that Luke himself de-eschatologized the Gospel by casting the kerygmatic tradition of Christian origins history into three successive but distinct epochs. W.B. Tatum,[18] for example, has argued (in support of Conzelmann) that Luke 1–2 portrays the Spirit as the Spirit of the Old Testament, given to the exceptional few, and primarily as the occasionally active Spirit of prophecy. This is alleged to contrast on the one hand with the 'middle of time', when Jesus alone bears the Spirit (now understood as a constantly active endowment), and on the other with the period of the church (when the gift of the Spirit is given to all). Luke thus allegedly uses theologoumenon of the Spirit in Luke 1–2 to characterize that period as 'the epoch of Israel', to distinguish it clearly from the subsequent periods, and thus to support his redemptive-historical thesis. Dunn's position may be seen as another version of this view, and von Baer's as a pre-Conzelmann anticipation of it. By contrast, Menzies has argued 'distinctions between the pneumatologies of Luke 1–2 and the rest of Luke–Acts based on a rigid three epoch scheme of Luke's Heilsgeschichte must be rejected',[19] and that the return of prophecy in Luke 1–2, after the long intertestamental silence of the Spirit, marks the beginning of the new age and the eschatological renewal of prophecy. Shelton has gone beyond this to claim the language with which Luke describes the activities of the Spirit in Luke 1–2 (and in the rest of Luke) deliberately mirrors that of the post-Ascension Christian experience in Acts, and is intended to break down any distinction of epochs.[20] But while Shelton (with R.E. Brown)[21] thinks Luke interprets the pre-Pentecost pneumatologies through Christian spectacles, A. George,[22] M.A. Chevallier,[23] Mainville[24] and Stronstad (differently) argue the opposite polarization, namely that Luke portrays Christian experience in Old Testament categories.

18. 'The Epoch of Israel: Luke i-ii and the Theological Plan of Luke–Acts', *NTS* 13 (1966–67), pp. 184-95.

19. *Development,* p. 134. See pp. 131-34 for his critique of Tatum and Conzelmann.

20. Shelton, *Word,* ch. 2.

21. *Birth,* pp. 241-43, but on the grounds that Luke has composed Lk. 1–2 after the fashion of Acts 1-2, both serving as 'transitional' sections.

22. 'L'Esprit', pp. 500-42.

23. 'Luc et l'Esprit à la mémoire du P. Augustin George (1915–77)', *RSR* 56 (1982), pp. 1-16.

24. See *L'Esprit,* pp. 321-32.

With these different theses in mind we may turn to the texts. There are eight, perhaps nine, references to the divine Spirit in Luke 1–2; two pertain to the Baptist (1.15, 17 and possibly a third at 1.80),[25] one each to his parents Elizabeth and Zechariah (1.41, and 67), one to Jesus (1.35) and three to Simeon (2.25, 26, 27). With respect to the kind of activity envisaged, all but one of these (1.35) quite clearly fall within the scope of what a contemporary Jew might recognise as 'the Spirit of prophecy'.

2.1. *The References to the Spirit of Prophecy in Relation to Elizabeth (1.41) and Zechariah (1.67)*

On both these occasions the speaker is said to be 'filled' (ἐπλήσθη) with Spirit[26] and consequently to utter a prophetic oracle of recognition. The motif of charismatic revelation and/or prophetic speech afforded by the Spirit of prophecy through a relative at or approaching a rite of passage is regular in Judaism. Typical examples of the motif include the patriarchal blessings of descendants, for example, Isaac's blessing of Jacob (Gen. 27: cf. *Gen. R.* 75.8),[27] his blessing of Judah and Levi (*Jub.* 31.12, augmenting Gen. 35), and Jacob's blessing of Ephraim rather than Manasseh (*Gen. R.* 97; *Num. R.* 14.5; and *Pes. R.* 3.4 on Gen. 48).[28] Indeed the very concept of testamentary prophecy spawns a whole genre of intertestamental literature.

Prophetic speech at the *birth* of an important figure is also well enough attested: *Targ. Ps.-J.* to Gen. 30.25 depicts Jacob at the birth of Joseph prophesying through the Spirit that the house of Jacob will become a flame to devour the house of Esau, and a more widespread Jewish tradition understood Miriam to prophesy the redeemer Moses (cf. *Bib. Ant.* 9.10; *b. Soṭ.* 11b).[29] There is no necessity to believe in such cases that the one who prophesies has the Spirit of prophecy as a (semi-)permanent gift; such

25. The description of John in 1.80 (ηὔξανεν καὶ ἐκραταιοῦτο πνεύματι) should probably be taken in an anthropological sense (he 'became strong in spirit' [NRSV; REB; NJB; NIV]), rather than as a reference to growing strong in the divine Spirit (for which we would expect at least an anaphoric definite article): with Marshall, 95; Fitzmyer, 388; Nolland, 90-91 (etc.) against G.F. Hawthorne, *The Presence and the Power* (Waco, TX: Word Books, 1991), p. 54 (contradicted at p. 110 n. 3). Bovon (*Evangelium*, 110) thinks there may be a secondary reference to the divine Spirit.

26. It is not clear whether the references to being 'filled with the Holy Spirit' are redactional (so Menzies, *Development*, p. 107; Fitzmyer, 32). The exact phraseology might be (see the note on 'fill/full of Spirit' at the end of this chapter). Nolland (30) says this language is not found in LXX (ἐμπίμπλημι is frequently so used, however), but thinks the predominantly anarthrous use is Semiticizing, and sign of a source.

27. For related traditions see Schäfer, *Vorstellung*, p. 28 n. 9.

28. Compare the revelation to Jacob at the death of Rachel (*MHG Gen.* 604); and the testamentary blessing of Naphtali in respect of Deborah (*MHG Gen.* 854).

29. See Schäfer, *Vorstellung*, pp. 52-53.

instances are often rather thought of as a special gift for the specific occasion, as when 'a spirit of truth descended' upon Rebecca's mouth that she might bless Jacob (*Jub.* 25.14), and 'a spirit of prophecy came down upon' Isaac's to enable a similar charisma (*Jub.* 31.12). We might also compare the unusual account of God telling a recalcitrant Holy Spirit to 'foot it' back down to Jacob in order that the patriarch might be able to bless Ephraim (*Pes. R.* 3.4). A Jewish Christian reader would probably assume that Elizabeth and Zechariah experienced the Spirit on the reported occasions alone, rather than that they were people who (like Simeon) regularly received charismata through the Spirit.

The nature of the charisma in both 1.41 and 1.67 appears to involve what we have called 'invasive prophetic speech': this is suggested by Luke's use of 'she/he was filled with the Holy Spirit' (a clause used by Luke before verbs of speaking to designate charismatically inspired speech). In 1.67 this is specified in the clarificatory 'and prophesied', but the same is probably meant at 1.41, where Elizabeth's 'loud cry' too will denote inspired utterance. The description at this point is remarkably similar to the talmudic account of Miriam prophetically heralding the birth of Moses (*b. Sot.* 11b), where it is said 'she used to *cry out* through the Holy Spirit and say, "My mother will bear a son who will be the saviour of Israel"'.

To what extent does the portrait here reflect the attempt to accommodate these experiences to either Old Testament pneumatology, or the pneumatology of the body of Luke–Acts? The use of the verb πίμπλημι 'to fill' (with Spirit) is similar to the Old Testament, but there (with the exception of LXX Prov. 15.4) it is always rather in the form ἐμπίμπλημι, and never refers to immediate inspiration of invasive prophetic speech (or to invasive speech of any kind), but usually to the source of charismatic wisdom.[30] And while invasive charismatic praise (Acts 2.4; 10.46; 19.6) and inspired preaching (4.8) are common in Acts, the category 'invasive prophetic speech' does not appear to be found there,[31] nor is it attributed to Jesus (the nearest to it being Lk. 10.21-22). Luke's language thus establishes rather less close correspondence between these experiences and those in the period of Jesus, or of the Church, than is sometimes imagined.[32] The language and ideas are simply those of intertestamental Jewish pneumatology in general.

---

30. Cf. Exod. 28.3, 31.3, 35.31, Deut. 34.9, Isa. 11.3 and Sir. 39.6 where it is charismatic wisdom. In Sir. 48.12 it is the inception of the prophetic endowment.

31. The report that the twelve at Ephesus 'spoke with tongues and prophesied' when the Spirit came upon them, like 2.4 and 10.46, designates invasive praise, not invasive prophecy in the sense of oracular speech.

32. Cf. Shelton, *Word*, ch. 2; Laurentin, *Evangiles*, p. 216.

2.2. *The References to the Spirit of Prophecy in Relation to Simeon (2.25, 26, 27)*

A man of God with a relatively permanent endowment of the Spirit of prophecy (as the generalizing narrative introduction of 2.25 ['and the Holy Spirit was upon him'] suggests) would be rare in Judaism. But, as we have seen, there were examples of the claim even among the rabbis who otherwise tended to believe the gift was no longer available because of Israel's sin[33]—and nowhere would such an endowment be more probable than in the Temple (to which rabbinic Judaism tended to restrict the Spirit's presence) or to someone who frequented it.[34] The statement that it had been revealed by the Holy Spirit to Simeon (κεχρηματισμένον ὑπὸ τοῦ πνεύματος τοῦ ἁγίου, 2.26) that he would see the messiah before he died is a clear cut case of the prototypical gift of 'charismatic revelation'. It corresponds to the majority of intertestamental and rabbinic cases which largely pertain to foreseeing some important future salvation-historical circumstance.

The description of Simeon in 2.27 as coming into the temple 'in the Spirit' (καὶ ἦλθεν ἐν τῷ πνεύματι εἰς τὸ ἱερόν) is barely more distinctive. If it simply means Simeon entered the Temple under the prompting of the Spirit, then it is another straightforward case of 'charismatic revelation'. In the context, however, the words may be taken to imply more than that the Spirit led Simeon into the sanctuary at the right time.[35] The description may rather be intended to include that the Spirit also (i) enabled Simeon's recognition of the child as the promised messiah, and (ii) afforded the revelation that is the basis of the oracular speech in 2.29-32, 34-35.[36] But these activities are still within the traditional range of prototypical gifts of the Spirit of prophecy.[37]

---

33. *T. Pes.* 2.15 (Gamiliel); *y. Šeb.* 9.1 (Simeon ben Yoḥai; *y. Soṭ.* 1.4 (Meir); *Lev. R.* 21.8 (Akiba).

34. See especially *Mek. Pisha* 1 (on Exod. 12.1); *Num. R.* 15.10; *Pes. R.* 1.2; *Pes. R.* 32.1, and Schäfer, *Vorstellung*, on these.

35. *Contra* Creed, 40, and the many who follow him.

36. In which case the phrase 'in the Spirit' is best explained as a dative of accompaniment or attendant circumstances (cf. Lk. 1.17; 4.14; 1 Thess. 1.5): i.e. Simeon came into the temple as a man with the Spirit.

37. Menzies thinks the three references here are redactional (*Development*, pp. 120-21). (1) On 2.25 he argues the word order πνεῦμα + verb + ἅγιον, is Lukan on the basis of the same structure in Acts 1.15 (*sic.* 1.5 is meant). But the appearance of the same structure in Mt. 1.20 (and here even with the same verb) suggests rather that it is traditional. Menzies also suggests that reference to the Spirit being 'on' or 'upon' Simeon is another Lukanism, rightly pointing out that Luke uses this spatial metaphor seven times. Two, however, are quotations (4.18; Acts 2.17 as he notes), and three are interdependent, and based on the Joel citation (10.44, 45; 11.15). On the only

Once again we may note comparisons and contrasts with the Spirit in the church. The general idea of someone receiving charismatic revelation through the Spirit (as in 2.26) is commonplace in Acts as a description both of revelation given to Israel (1.16; 28.25) and of revelation given to members of the church (programmatically at 2.17-18; then 7.55; 8.29; 10.19; 11.12; 11.28; 13.2, 9[?]; 16.6-7; 19.21; 20.23; 21.4, 11), though once again it is never specifically stated of Jesus. The verb χρηματίζειν, 'to reveal', however, is used with the Spirit neither in the Old Testament nor in the body of Luke–Acts.[38] Similarly, Luke uses the preposition 'on' to denote the Spirit's relation to Christians, but he does not do so in an unqualified way, to denote a continuous state, as here.[39] Elsewhere he will speak of the Spirit 'descending upon' (Jesus, Lk. 3.22), 'coming upon' (1.8; 19.6), being 'poured out upon' (2.17; 10.45) and 'falling upon' (8.16; 10.44; 11.15) to describe the moment of reception of the Spirit. The term he would naturally use to describe Christians as people marked by notable *continuing* prophetic experience of the Spirit would be 'full of the Spirit' (as at 4.1; Acts 6.3, 5; 7.55; 11.24; 13.52). It is thus possible that his language here deliberately contrasts Simeon's experience of the Spirit as a lesser one compared with Christian experience (though it may simply be due to his source). And while Luke can allow Jesus to characterize himself with the words 'the Spirit of the Lord is *upon* me', which might suggest a deliberate parallel between Simeon and Jesus, his choice of terminology in Jesus' case is really determined by the Old Testament passage he cites (Isa. 61.1-2)—a passage that goes on to qualify what is meant by the Spirit being 'upon' Jesus in such a way as to emphasize the *unique* character of Jesus' endowment (rather than its 'typical' nature). In all, we again have no sign Luke is consciously accomodating Simeon's experience either to specifically Old Testament (rather than ITP) pneumatology or to the experience of Jesus and the Church.

occasion he notes other than Acts 1.8 (where it anticipates the Joel quote—and reflects Isa. 32.15? cf. Lk. 24.49!), 19.6 (16.6 is a misprint), the 'upon' is suggested by the immediately preceding 'laying upon' of hands. Menzies could also have included 8.16, which may have been a more telling case. In general, however, the usage is evidently based in the Old Testament, and so may be traditional rather than Lukan. And, as we shall note below, in typical Lukan usage the preposition 'upon' or 'on' is only used in expressions which denote inception/reception of the Spirit. (2) Luke may have added 'by the Holy Spirit' to a statement in his source that Simeon had been assured he would not die before he saw the messiah, but this is typically Jewish. The only candidate for Lukan redaction is 2.27 (a dative of attendant circumstances) which is unparalleled in Judaism except by the clearly Lukan 4.1.

38. Though the verb is used in Acts 10.22 of angelic revelation to Cornelius before his conversion.

39. For Luke's use of spatial metaphors in relation to the Spirit see Turner, 'Spirit Endowment', pp. 45-47, 49-50.

2.3. *The Spirit and John the Baptist (1.15, 17, [80])*

With 1.15 we have a notable new departure. John the Baptist's measure as a 'great' prophet (1.15a)[40] is seen in his being 'filled with the Holy Spirit' even from his mother's womb. While the theme of God knowing a man of God in the womb is frequent enough in the Old Testament and in Judaism,[41] to receive the Spirit of prophecy right from the womb is unparalleled. The nearest we come to it is the affirmation of Sirach (49.7) that Jeremiah was consecrated a prophet while yet in the womb (ἐν μήτρᾳ ἡγιάσθη προφήτης; cf. Jer. 1.5), that is, that God chose him and prepared him to become a prophet later. The expression ἐκ κοιλίας could mean 'from birth'; but the qualifying ἔτι suggests rather 'while yet in the womb',[42] and the description of the babe leaping in Elizabeth's womb in recognition of the messiah (1.41) is confirmation of this. The *novum* in the Baptist's case is further strengthened by the promise he will not merely be a recipient of the gift of the Spirit, he will even be 'filled with the Spirit' from the beginning. While Luke has a particular predilection for πιμπλάναι (see the appended note at the end of this chapter) with 'Holy Spirit', its presence here does not necessarily suggest it is redactional. It is part of Luke's portrayal of John in Elijianic dress (see on 1.17), and Sir. 48.12 already affirmed that on Elijah's ascent Elisha 'was filled with his Spirit' (ἐνεπλήσθη πνεύματος αὐτοῦ).

Lk. 1.17 also underscores the uniqueness of the Baptist in relation to Israel's experience of the Spirit of prophecy, by portraying this endowment as an eschatological fulfilment of hopes for the return of Elijah. The hope that a messenger figure would prepare for the eschatological visitation of God (in this sense 'go before the Lord'; 1.17)[43] was already part of the Old Testament tradition in Mal. 3.1, and the final verses of the work identified the figure with Elijah, due to reunify Israel as a covenant people (Mal. 4.5-6 [MT 3.23-24; LXX 3.22-23]). It is the wording of this final passage that is very clearly alluded to in 1.17b, thus giving John a major role in the anticipated restoration of Zion (as in Sir. 48.10).[44] As the content of 1.17 does not

---

40. That neither Luke nor his source thought John was μέγας in some more absolute way (and thus either [a] the messiah worshipped by a Baptist sect or [b] a second messiah alongside Jesus [so Shonfield, *Book*, pp. 26, 48]) has been effectively rejected by W. Wink, *John the Baptist in the Gospel Tradition* (Cambridge: Cambridge University Press, 1968), pp. 68-79.

41. For references see Marshall, 58.

42. Correctly Bovon, *Evangelium*, 56; Nolland, 31.

43. Luke's readers will perhaps see a christological sense too (cf. 1.43) thus making 'Elijah' a precursor of the messiah; so Fitzmyer, *Luke*, p. 103.

44. Curiously, Wink (*John*, p. 43) argues the Baptist is not an eschatological figure for Luke, he is merely 'like' Elijah: he claims (*inter alia*) 'John "will" not restore all things because he did not restore all things. In Luke's theology this restoration awaits

appear to be redactional,[45] we should conclude that Luke has taken over traditional material that presented John the Baptist as the eschatological Elijianic prophet.[46]

the parousia'. If Wink means that Luke has replaced the ἀποκαταστήσει καρδίαν πατρὸς πρὸς υἱόν of Mal. 3.23 (LXX) by ἐπιστρέψαι καρδίας πατέρων ἐπὶ τέκνα, and that the latter verb is non-eschatological, he has evidently ignored that Luke's wording is simply thereby closer to Sir. 48.10 which is blatantly eschatological. If Luke replaces the thought of an Elijah *redivivus* with one who serves 'in the Spirit and power of Elijah' that is not because he thinks the former is an eschatological figure and the latter not: it is because he no longer expects a literal Elijah to fulfil Mal. 3.1, 23 (EVV 3.1; 4.5-6). With the rest of the Christian tradition before him he believes John to have fulfilled it (Lk. 7.27), and there is no solid evidence Mark or Q (or Matthew) truly thought John the Baptist was literally Elijah *redivivus*. For a similar view to Wink's see Dubois, 'De Jean-Baptiste', p. 6 n. 6 and cf. pp. 15-44.

45. While the collocation of 'Spirit and power (of Elijah)' is often taken to be a sign of Lukan redaction on the basis of comparison with 1.35; 4.14 and Acts 10.38, it should be noted that 1.17 actually stands in tension with Luke's view. Elijah was especially known as a man of great power (evinced in miracles: compare the celebration of these, and the hope of Elijah's return to restore Israel, in Sir. 48.1-12). And 'power' in the Lukan collocations adduced would indeed regularly denote the power of miracles. But as Luke clearly does not believe John worked such (indeed miracles are precisely what distinguish Jesus as 'the Coming One' in response to the Baptist's doubts [7.21-22]), we must suppose the collocation here is derived from his source (with Fitzmyer, 320). It could, of course, be argued that Luke added the words πνεύματι καί to an original ἐν δυνάμει Ἡλίου, but this would not be convincing either; reference to 'the Spirit of Elijah' was already traditional (cf. Sir. 48.12; *Targ. Neb.* 2 Kgs 2.15; LXX 4 Kgdms 2.15).

46. Just how he nuanced this is disputed. Following the lead of Conzelmann, Wink argued that Luke could not think of John as the eschatological Elijah, and that he simply turned the Elijah-*redivivus* of Mark (1.2, 4-6; 9.11-13) and Matthew (11.14!) into a prophet *like* Elijah. Here clarity is obscured by two unhelpful terms. Neither Matthew nor Mark considered John the Baptist literally to be Elijah '*redivivus*' (it is Elijah who appears at the transfiguration [Mk 9.4; Mt. 17.3], not the Baptist); they imply only that John fulfils the expected Elijianic role. But, as Fitzmyer has shown, that is exactly what Luke describes John the Baptist as doing [*Luke*, pp. 102-10]. Wink's insistence that 'Luke has retained nothing of John's role as Elijah' (*John*, p. 42) is simply incomprehensible in the light not only of 1.17, but of the explicit statement in Lk. 7.27 that the promise of Mal. 3.1 is fulfilled in the Baptist. The question of whether Luke would regard such a role as 'eschatological' hangs on the sense with which the latter slippery term is used. Conzelmann (and Wink) appear to mean it in a strictly temporal sense of an event which belongs to some supposed 'End' of this cosmos itself, or to the period immediately leading up to it. In that case we may concede Luke did not think of Jesus' ministry as 'eschatological', and *a fortiori*, he could not have considered the Baptist as the 'eschatological' Elijah-figure. But if we allow that Conzelmann has perhaps misled us here, and that Luke's Jesus was 'eschatological' in the broader sense that he maintained the promised End-time salvation was already breaking in

How does the description of the Spirit on John the Baptist relate to Luke's pneumatology more generally? That it is the 'Spirit of prophecy' that John received need hardly be doubted, though Luke's portrayal of the Baptist as a unique Elijianic prophet (1.17; 7.25-27) makes it difficult to know how he would draw the lines between John's experience and that of the Church. That the Spirit afforded charismatic revelation to him is probably intended by the account of the *in utero* experience depicted in 1.41, and this motif will also account for the mention of the 'word of God' coming to John in the wilderness (3.2). On the whole, however, the Spirit-and-power of Elijah appears to be experienced primarily as the power of *preaching*. That is, John's teaching is not portrayed as oracular speech, but as charismatic expository discourse; he articulates, expands and applies the 'word of God' that came to him, and does so with charismatic and compelling power. This (and the portrayal of him as one who 'preaches good news' (εὐηγγελίζετο [3.18]) aligns him more with the description of Jesus (as we shall see) and of the church than with that of the other prophetic figures of Luke 1–2. We shall also have occasion to note that an extensive network of Elijianic features have been traced in the Lukan description of Jesus, and that John is in a variety of ways portrayed as his 'precursor'. This could suggest Luke saw the endowment of the Spirit on Jesus as in some ways similar to that on John; but, as we shall see, there are also sharp differentia. John is very much a transitional figure (as Fitzmyer has argued),[47] and this applies to Luke's conception of the Spirit upon him as much as to the more general features of the portrait.

2.4. *The Spirit in the Conception of the Messiah (1.26-38)*

The closely parallel structure and content of Lk. 1.5-25 and 1.26-38[48] shows that the annunciation story took its present form and selection of contents from analogy with what was said about John the Baptist's

within his own ministry (see Ellis, Fitzmyer, Marshall, Maddox, etc.), then the question becomes, 'Did Luke understand John as a "precursor" of Jesus, or did he (as Conzelmann avers) sharply separate the two into distinct epochs?' For Conzelmann, Luke thinks of John merely as the last and greatest prophet of the period of Israel (*Luke*, pp. 101, 159 n. 1, 161, 167 n. 1 and 185) but, as Fitzmyer has pointed out, that can barely be Luke's conception. For him, John is 'more than a prophet' (7.26), and that precisely because he fulfils the Elijah expectation (7.27) already adumbrated in 1.17 (*Luke*, p. 109). Wink too concedes that Conzelmann is quite mistaken here (*John*, pp. 51-57).

47. 'The Lucan Picture of John the Baptist as Precursor of the Lord' in *Luke*, pp. 86-116.

48. See e.g. Brown, *Birth*, pp. 292-97; Fitzmyer, 313-21; and Nolland, 40-42, for the parallels.

conception, and provides a climax to it: this requires that 1.34-35 was indeed original to the text (against Harnack) and that it was understood, from the start, to promise a divinely empowered conception (independent of and before intercourse with Joseph) to match the miraculous birth of the Baptist to aged parents.[49]

In terms of form, the passage is appropriately analysed by R.E. Brown as an 'Annunciation of Birth',[50] and there are clear parallels, not only to the annunciation of the Baptist, but to other biblical annunciations, for example, to those of Ishmael (Gen. 16), Isaac (Gen. 17), and Samson (Judg. 13). But readers with any interest whatever in messianic issues will not have missed the important signal in 1.27 (given twice) that Gabriel came to a *virgin* (παρθένος) attached to 'the house of David'. They would then be much more likely to be struck by the parallel with Isaiah 7 than with any of these other annunciations: the parallel would be highlighted not merely by the verbal parallel between Lk. 1.31 (καὶ ἰδοὺ συλλήμψῃ ἐν γαστρὶ καὶ τέξῃ υἱόν, καὶ καλέσεις τὸ ὄνομα αὐτοῦ 'Ιησοῦν) and Isa. 7.14 (ἰδοὺ ἡ παρθένος [cf. Lk. 1.27!] ἐν γαστρὶ ἕξει καὶ τέξεται υἱόν, καὶ καλέσεις τὸ ὄνομα αὐτοῦ Εμμανουηλ), but more especially by the Davidic messianic context both of 1.32-33[51] and of the remaining narrative in Luke 1–2.

While the whole of 1.26-38 raises numerous questions of exegetical inter-

---

49. G. Lohfink, *Die Sammlung Israels: Eine Untersuchung zur lukanischen Ekklesiologie* (Munich: Kösel, 1975), p. 18, thus comments: 'every attempt to reconstruct an older form of annunciation behind 1.26-38, lacking the theologumenon of Jesus' conception by the Spirit, shatters on this [observation]'. Compare Ellis, 71; Schürmann, 55; A. George, 'Le parallèle entre Jean-Baptiste et Jésus en Lc 1-2', in A. Descamps and A. de Halleux (eds.), *Mélanges bibliques en hommage au R.P. Béda Rigaux* (Gembloux: Duculot, 1970), pp. 147-71; Marshall, 62-63, and Brown, *Birth*, pp. 299-301: against A. von Harnack, 'Zu Lk 1:34-45', *ZNW* 2 (1901), pp. 53-57. Fitzmyer (338) now agrees (against his former position in 'The Virginal Conception of Jesus in the New Testament', *TS* 34 [1973], pp. 541-75) that this requires 1.35 be taken as a reference to virgin conception by the Spirit.

50. Brown, *Birth*, pp. 156 and 292-97.

51. So F. Hahn, *The Titles of Jesus in Christology* (London: Lutterworth, 1959), pp. 296-97; A. George, 'Jésus fils de dieu dans l'évangile de Saint Luc', *RB* 72 (1965), pp. 184-209; Schneider, 49; G. Voss, *Die Christologie der lukanischen Schriften in Grundzügen* (Paris: Brouwer, 1965), pp. 65-81. *Per contra*, Brown (*Birth*, p. 300, modifying but depending on Fitzmyer 'Virginal Conception'), Fitzmyer (336) and Nolland (51) all point out that the language of 1.31 is found regularly elsewhere in the 'annunication of birth' naratives, and need not point to Isa. 7.14. Brown and Fitzmyer are undoubtedly right in their fundamental argument that the description of Mary as παρθένος cannot then with any certainty be traced back to the influence of Isa. 7.14 on the passage. But once the specifically Davidic promises were added (1.32-33) the parallels with Ishmael, Isaac and Samson would largely become redundant. The Davidic focus would almost inevitably lead a first-century reader back to Isa. 7 and 9.

est, our attention must focus on the issues of the 'sonship' Christology, the part played in this by the Spirit and the eschatological or soteriological implications; effectively, on 1.32-33, and 35.

> [32] He will be great, and will be called the Son of the Most High; and the Lord God will give to him the throne of his father David
> [33] and he will reign over the house of Jacob forever; and of his kingdom there will be no end...
> [35] And the Angel said to her, 'The Holy Spirit will come upon you, and the power of the Most High will overshadow you; therefore the child to be born shall be called holy, the Son of God'.

Lk. 1.32-33 immediately takes up the parallel with the annunciation concerning John, that he would be 'great before the Lord' (1.15), and prepares for the promise of the *Benedictus* that he will be 'called prophet of the Most High' (1.76). In the stepwise parallelism, Jesus is to be 'great' (now in an unqualified way), and will be 'called son of the Most High'. This 'son' is then promised the eschatological (cf. εἰς τοὺς αἰῶνας [1.33]) Davidic rule. The themes of sonship to God and Davidic rule were of course intimately related in the Old Testament: the king represents God's 'son' Israel, and thus he becomes God's adopted 'son' on accession (Ps. 2.7); and of the Davidid especially it is said God will treat him as a son (2 Sam. 7.12-16), and he for his part will call God 'my Father' (Ps. 89.26-27; cf. also 89.19-27, expanding the 2 Sam. 7 promise). It would appear this understanding was preserved in Judaism, and we find it predicated of the expected 'branch of David' in 4QFlor 1.10-12 (and cf. 4Q246 below).[52] It follows that the assertion 'he shall be called Son of the Most High' in 1.32-33 should be understood to mean that Jesus will be (officially) recognized as the Davidic *messiah* (and *so* God's 'son'), and 1.32b could even be understood as a parallel clarifying 1.32a, rather than adding significantly to it. While from Luke's perspective this is by no means the full tale of Jesus' divine Sonship, nor of his Christology more generally, it is at least an important component within it (cf. Acts 2.30-36; 13.33), more so for being the first christological indication he provides his reader—and it would come as a clarion call to a Davidic-Zionist restoration soteriology.

Lk. 1.35 assuredly belongs form-critically (with the question in 1.34) to the annunciation story, and materially the connection is also made by the relationship of δύναμις ὑψίστου ('the power of the Most High') to the divine sonship of both 1.32 ('Son of the Most High') and 1.35 ('Son of God'). 4Q246 (an Aramaic fragment of Danielic interpretation) witnesses a similar conjunction of ideas:

---

52. Note also the use of Ps. 2 in the messianic description of *Ps. Sol.* 17.23-24.

He will be called the son of God; they will call him son of the Most High...
(5) His Kingdom will be an Eternal Kingdom, and he will be Righteous in
all his Ways. He [will jud]ge (6) the earth in Righteousness and everyone
will make peace.' (Col 2, lines 1 and 5-6).[53]

But if 1.32-33 could be read to promise divine sonship at enthronement,
1.35 traces this divine sonship to the messiah's conception by the Spirit.
This concept is strikingly unusual for Judaism (even more so for paganism)
even if much of the language finds its natural home here.[54] There are five
points of special significance for this study:

(1) Luke here equates the 'Holy Spirit' referentially with 'the Power of
the Most High' as the means of the miraculous conception. Corresponding
to the title 'Son of the Most High' in 1.32, the angel explains to Mary that
she will conceive because 'the power of the Most High' will 'overshadow'
(ἐπισκιάσει) her. Similarly, corresponding with the affirmation 'the child to
be born will be called "Holy"' (with the title 'the Son of God' being
appended in loose apposition),[55] Mary is told that πνεῦμα ἅγιον will 'come
upon' (ἐπελεύσεται) her. Both the 'overshadowing' of Mary by the
'power of the Most High' and the 'coming upon' her of 'the Holy Spirit'

53. Eisenman and Wise, *Scrolls*, pp. 70-71 (on which see pp. 68-69). As Fitzmyer
earlier cautioned ('The Contribution of Qumran Aramaic to the Study of the New
Testament', *NTS* 20 [1973–74], pp. 382-407), we cannot be sure line 1 refers to 'the
messiah', but if the figure here is the same as that in lines 5-7 it is highly probable.
Fitzmyer has repeated his caution in '4Q246: The "Son of God" Document from
Qumran', *Bib* 74 (1993), pp. 153-74, but see the criticism by C.A. Evans, 'The
Recently Published Dead Sea Scrolls and the Historical Jesus', in Chilton and Evans
(eds.), *Jesus*, pp. 549-51.

54. Against Leisegang's thesis of pagan origins of 1.32-35 see Baer, *Geist*,
pp. 125-31, and Barrett, *Spirit*, pp. 10-14. 4Q246 certainly demonstrates that we do not
require to look beyond Palestinian Judaism for the titles (and cf. P.R. Trebilco, *Jewish
Communities in Asia Minor* [Cambridge: Cambridge University Press, 1991], ch. 6, for
fresh evidence of Jewish use of ὕψιστος as a title of deity). Pagan ideas of divine
beginning are quite foreign to this context which expands concepts already present in
Isa. 7 (see Hahn, *Titles*, pp. 296-97; George, 'Jésus', pp. 184-209; though, *per contra*,
see Brown, *Birth*, p. 300, modifying but depending on Fitzmyer, 'Virginal
Conception', pp. 541-75. While Brown and Fitzmyer are not convinced that Luke has
developed Isa. 7.14, they nevertheless reject pagan influence and associated ideas of
divine procreation [see Brown, *Birth*, pp. 522-23; cf. Nolland, 51-56]. For a survey of
views see also Dubois, 'De Jean-Baptiste', pp. 69-80). G. Schneider (52) speaks of
1QSa 2.11 as referring to the begetting of the Messiah by God; but see M. Smith,
'God's Begetting the Messiah in 1QSa', *NTS* 5 (1958–59), pp. 218-24.

55. *Contra* Voss, *Christologie*, §4.4, who argues that τὸ γεννώμενον and ἅγιον are
to be taken together as the subject of κληθήσεται. Decisive against this interpretation is
the (predicative) lack of the definite article before ἅγιον. In addition καλεῖσθαι usually follows its predicate noun (Schürmann, 54): cf. υἱὸς ὑψίστου κληθήσεται at 1.32!

are thus equally tied to the conception of the child,[56] and constitute parallel co-referential expressions. The new creation power of the Most High in question, then, is (in this context) actually referentially *equated* with the Holy Spirit, even if this allows that the terms are not strictly synonymous, and that (in Luke's view) the Holy Spirit may be more than merely (re)generative power.

Menzies attempts to bring this into line with his general thesis that Luke cannot attribute miracles of power to the Spirit: he suggests Luke refers the conception principally to 'the power of the Most High' while connecting the Spirit more directly (than in the pre-Lukan tradition) to inspired speech (allegedly witnessed in Mary's prophesying of the *Magnificat* in 1.46-55).[57] Menzies' argument here is unsafe, however, (a) because (as we have seen) the contextual markers tie both Spirit and power to the nature of the child born, (b) because 1.35 is supposed to answer the question (1.34) how Mary, a virgin, will conceive, and any hint (in this context) that the Spirit will inspire speech (especially Mary's) would simply be irrelevant, and (c) because Luke does not explicitly attribute the *Magnificat* to the Spirit's inspiration (even if it is thoroughly believable that he understood the matter so).

However hard he attempts to mitigate it, even Menzies himself is finally forced to the conclusion that the Spirit is involved in the conception of Jesus, and accordingly concedes: 'Luke attributes the miraculous birth of Jesus to the activity of the Spirit because this accurately reflected early Christian tradition and it suited his structural scheme of parallelling John [filled with the Spirit from birth] with Jesus'.[58] Jesus will be υἱὸς ὑψίστου because the Spirit/Power from on High (cf. 24.49), the outpouring of which the pious of Israel awaited,[59] will attend the miraculous conception and

---

56. In the biblical tradition neither 'overshadow' nor 'come upon' has sexual connotations (see Mainville, *L'Esprit*, pp. 185-88). Mainville herself thinks the motif here is primarily on the protective presence of the Spirit though she allows that Jesus is created like Adam (cf. 3.38) by the Spirit (pp. 187-209).

57. *Development*, pp. 122-27. Following Schneider, Menzies thinks 1.34-35 is a *Lukan* reformulation of the sort of tradition in Mt. 1.18, 20, and that the addition of 'power from on high' has weakened the more direct connection between the Spirit and the conception of Jesus articulated by that tradition. This is speculative. The redactional nature of 1.34-35 is largely deduced from the parallel language in Acts 1.8. But there it is a different manner of 'coming upon', a different kind of 'power', and very different result—in short, a different (and more characteristically Lukan), pneumatology! One might more plausibly argue Luke has re-used traditional language (from Isa. 32.15 and Lk. 1.35) to formulate his own pneumatology in Acts 1.8, than that the pneumatology of Lk. 1.35 is the result of his own redaction.

58. *Development*, p. 127; cf. also 123.

59. For the tendency of apocalyptic literature to use a vertical dualism to express

penetrate to the very depths of his being. He will thus become the impress of the δύναμις ὑψίστου. Accordingly, glory will be ascribed to God ἐν ὑψίστοις, for the child so conceived will bring peace on earth to men of God's choosing (2.14).

Here, then, in Luke's opening statement about Jesus and the Spirit—the doorway as it were to everything else he will say on the subject—the Spirit is indisputably the power of a miraculous work in the physical realm, and one laden with promise for Israel's promised messianic 'peace'.

(2) The Holy Spirit/Power of the Most High here indubitably also has a profoundly 'ethical' orientation. Jesus' very existence is to reflect the vigorous action[60] of the Holy Spirit, and 'for this reason' (we are told) 'he shall be called "Holy"'.[61] By this description of the conception, Luke removes Jesus' origins from the sphere of human possibilities, and locates them in the realm of divine power and choice. Jesus is again being described in terms that are parallel to, but transcend, what is said of John the Baptist; 'Jesus is not only filled with the Spirit, like John (1.15), he owes his very existence to the divine Spirit'.[62]

The sense in which the child is to be 'Holy' is at least partly defined by the title in apposition: because of the powerful working of the Spirit in the womb of Mary, Jesus will be the messianic 'Son of God'. But this should not be played off against the religious-ethical sense of 'holy'. As we have seen (Chapter 5), it was becoming almost traditional to ascribe the total consecration and redoubtable righteousness of the expected Davidic messiah to

---

the two-aged doctrine, and to regard eschatological benefits as already existing in the heavens, which is therefore understood as a realm of power contrasting with earth, see H. Traub, *TDNT*, V, pp. 497-542, and A.T. Lincoln, *Paradise Now and Not Yet* (Cambridge: Cambridge University Press, 1981).

60. The verb ἐπέρχομαι (Luke–Acts 7×; New Testament total 9×) in Luke–Acts regularly has strong overtones of vigor, if not of violence.

61. In view of the formulation πᾶν ἄρσεν διανοῖγον μήτραν ἅγιον τῷ κυρίῳ κληθήσεται (2.23), Luke probably understood ἅγιον as 'separate to the Lord' or 'dedicated to the Lord'. The parallels to 1.35b have been explored by M. Rese, *Alttestamentliche Motive in der Christologie des Lukas* (Gütersloh: Mohn, 1969), pp. 141ff. and 185ff., but his suggestion that Lk. 2.23 was understood by Luke as the fulfilment of the annunciation promise that he will be called 'holy' (i.e. he is called 'holy' because he is a first-born Israelite) is unacceptable. Schürmann (121-22) more probably suggests that 2.23 echoes Samuel's consecration at 1 Sam. 1 (cf. παραστῆσαι τῷ κυρίῳ). This would be an acknowledgment that the child belonged in a special way to God and would perhaps explain the lack of any mention of redeeming the first-born in a context where Mary's Levitical cleansing is specified.

62. G. Schneider 53. Cf. G. Schneider, 'Jesu geistgewirkte Empfängnis (Lk 1, 34f)', *Theologisch-Praktische Quartalschrift* 119 (1971), pp. 105-16, and Kim, *Geisttaufe*, p. 39.

the Spirit (on the basis of Isa. 11.1-4, and its developments). Luke 1.35 is then only unusual in tracing the motif back to the conception itself. If Menzies is right, and if the Spirit that is to come upon Mary is also the 'Spirit of prophecy' (the inspiration of the *Magnificat*),[63] then we can only conclude that Luke is even willing to attribute such miraculous power and ethical effect to the Spirit *qua* the Spirit of prophecy.

(3) The conception of Jesus by the Holy Spirit/Power of the Most High is thematically related to the restoration of Israel. The wording of 1.35 gives further significant nuance to the angelic announcement. (a) The use of the verb ἐπισκιάζειν 'to overshadow' has called forth a variety of theological explanations,[64] but an LXX background would suggest Exod. 40.35 as the only probable allusion.[65] In which case, the divine power/Spirit of 1.35 is likened to the cloud of God's presence (cf. Lk. 9.34!), bringing God's glory into Israel's camp, and leading her through the wilderness towards the promised land. (b) The wording of the clause concerning the Spirit in 1.35a is with even greater certainty related to LXX Isa. 32.15 (ἕως ἂν ἐπέλθῃ ἐφ' ὑμᾶς πνεῦμα ἀφ' ὑψηλοῦ, 'until the Spirit come upon you from on High'). Not only is the wording of Lk. 1.35 relatively close to that of Isaiah, but the Isaianic passage in question (32.15-20) depicts the transformation of the wilderness into fruitful fields, which is a metaphor for the promised renewal/recreation of Israel.[66] The two allusions support each other in giving a strong 'New Exodus' overtone to the annunciation passage, and this in turn enriches the broader contextual expectation of Israel's messianic renewal (as we shall discover in Chapter 9, Luke has a special interest in portraying Israel's restoration in New Exodus terms).

63. Menzies, *Development*, pp. 126-27, also Shepherd, *Function*, p. 122.

64. Barrett (Spirit) detects the concept of the Spirit 'hovering' over chaos at creation, and hence, here, the Spirit of the new creation (so Schürmann, 52; cf. his essay 'Die geistgewirkte Lebensentstehung Jesu', in Ernst *et al* [eds.], *Einheit in Vielfalt* [Leipzig: St Benno, 1974], pp. 156-69). But the ἐπισκιάζειν is connected with the word δύναμις, not with πνεῦμα. And in the LXX of Gen. 1.1 the verb is ἐπεφέρετο, and is unrelated to ἐπισκιάζειν. D. Daube (*The New Testament and Rabbinic Judaism* [New York: Arno, 1973], pp. 32-36) traces a messianic typology based on Ruth 3.9 at Lk. 1.35.

65. For the view that ἐπισκιάζειν at Lk. 1.35 reflects Exod. 40.35, see Dubois, 'De Jean-Baptiste', pp. 48-82, R. Laurentin, *Structure et théologie de Luc 1-2* (Paris: Lecoffre, 1964), esp. pp. 73-79; also Fitzmyer, 351; Marshall, 70; Nolland, 54; Voss, *Christologie*, pp. 73-76; and Mainville, *L'Esprit*, pp. 186-87. On the basis of this allusion Mainville thinks the presence of the power/Spirit is to protect the messiah; but while the cloud is said to intervene protectively between the Israelites and pursuing Egyptians in Exod. 14.19-20, that is not the point in Exod. 40.34-38.

66. So Fitzmyer, 351; Marshall, 70; and (more positively) Nolland, 54.

To sum up points (1) to (3), the conception of the Davidic restorer is
directly attributed to God's Spirit experienced as his new creation, Israel-
renewing power, bringing into being that sort of sonship which most closely
reflects origins in God's gracious and transforming presence.

(4) The outcome of this messianic conception by the Spirit is portrayed in
Lk. 2.41-51, and confirms the Davidic portrait. This section is joined to the
overtly Davidic birth and epiphany narratives by the summary statement
that 'the child grew and became strong [replicating the statement about
John the Baptist in 1.80], filled with wisdom; and the grace/favour of God
was upon him'. Beyond 2.41-51 there is a similar summary (2.52), with the
same emphasis on Jesus' wisdom and God's grace. These form an *inclusio*
for 2.41-51, echoing two of the predominant features of Isa. 11.1-4, and
serving to focus the central issue of the sandwiched story, Jesus' messianic
wisdom and consecration to God's purpose.

Two features of this narrative are important for our purpose:

(a) Luke considered Jesus to recognize his special 'sonship' to God.
Thus, according to 2.49, Jesus says that his parents should have realised ὅτι
ἐν τοῖς τοῦ πατρός μου δεῖ εἶναί με. It seems probable that the ambiguous phrase ἐν τοῖς τοῦ πατρός μου is intended to mean 'about my Father's
business'[67]—even if it does not exclude the simultaneous and well-
defended[68] meaning 'in my Father's house'—and the business concerned
transcends Jesus' duty to his parents.[69] This concentrates our attention on
the expression 'my Father'. It is to be found again in Luke only at 10.22
('all things have been given to me by my Father'); 22.29 ('Just as my Father
has conferred a kingdom on me...'); and 24.49 ('I shall send the promise of
my Father')—all occasions when the highest Christology is evinced, and
where, by implication, a corresponding 'the Son' is understood in some
unique if not absolute sense:[70] so, here, at 2.49. Confirming this one need
only point to the pregnant δεῖ[71] in this verse, and to Luke's literary device
intended to underscore the hidden depths of Jesus' words—his addition of

---

67. With H.J. de Jonge, 'Sonship, Wisdom, Infancy: Luke II. 41-51a', *NTS* 24
(1977–78), pp. 331-37; cf. Brown, *Birth*, p. 490, Johnson, 58-62, and especially
M. Coleridge, *The Birth of the Lukan Narrative: Narrative as Christology in Luke 1–2*
(Sheffield: JSOT Press, 1993), pp. 201-203.

68. Cf. R. Laurentin, *Jésus au temple* (Paris: Gabalda, 1974), pp. 38-72; Fitzmyer,
443-44; Nolland, 131-32.

69. Mary's exclamation that she and ὁ πατήρ σου have been looking everywhere
for him (2.48), prepares for Jesus' transcending ὁ πατήρ μου.

70. See Marshall, 129, 430-39, and his 'The Divine Sonship of Jesus', *Int* 21
(1967), pp. 87-103: cf. de Jonge 'Sonship', pp. 351-53.

71. See de Jonge, 'Sonship', pp. 350-51; Brown, *Birth*, p. 491.

the comment 'and they did not comprehend the word which he spoke to them' (2.50).[72]

(b) The picture of Jesus at the age of twelve is designed to show that even in childhood he has the wisdom belonging to mature age; comparing favourably with Josephus's Moses whose 'wisdom did not increase with his age, but far excelled it'.[73] What Jesus demonstrates in his discussion with the teachers is religious wisdom, which with the Davidic cotext, and in the context of his implied claim to unique sonship and devotion to his Father's affairs, is to be understood against the background of messianic hopes of a ruler endowed with wisdom (cf. Isa. 11.2; *Pss. Sol.* 17.37; 18.7; *1 En.* 49.3; 1QSb 5.24-25; *T. Levi* 18.7-8) and with God's grace (cf. 2.40, 52).[74]

The overall picture of the relationship of the Spirit to Jesus' conception, birth and infancy is thus of a unique fructification which is markedly eschatological in character, in the sense that it is messianic, and has overtones both of new creation and of Israel's New Exodus restoration. Luke tells us no more about the Spirit in the life of Jesus until 3.21-22, but the reader is perhaps expected to infer that the same Spirit active in the conception of Jesus remained with him from that time on as the source of his knowledge of God and wisdom (he is unlikely to assume the Spirit played a lesser part in Jesus' life before his public ministry than in the Baptist's [cf. 1.15],[75] and the 'fit' with messianic portraits drawn from Isa. 11.1-4 would encourage such an assumption).

(5) Lk. 1.35 inevitably provides an interpretational gateway to Luke's pneumatology. It cannot be dismissed as a *novum* of earlier Jewish-Christianity which Luke merely tolerates and passes over for a more 'traditional' Jewish pneumatology. As we have seen (Chapters 4–5, and above), the concept of the Spirit being involved in creation, eschatological new creation and restorationist transformation is not as foreign to 'traditional' Judaism as many suggest.[76] So while the miraculous conception of

72. H. Schürmann, 137. This observation excludes the thesis of P. Winter ('Luc 2.49 and Targum Yerushalmi', *ZNW* 45 [1954], pp. 145ff.) that Jesus is portrayed essentially as like other pious Israelites.

73. *Ant.* 2.230. Cf. De Jonge, 'Sonship', p. 322.

74. De Jonge, 'Sonship', pp. 348-49. Laurentin (*Jésus*, pp. 135ff.) actually identifies Jesus with wisdom on the basis of Sir. 24.8-12; but see the criticism by Brown, *Birth*, p. 490.

75. So e.g. Hawthorne, *Presence*.

76. The Spirit is associated with new personal creation, resurrection and restorationist transformation quite regularly: e.g. Isa. 32.15; 44.3; Ezek. 11.19; 18.31; 36.26; 37.5; 37.6; 37.14; *Jos. Asen.* 8.9; 19.11; *Jub.* 1.20-25; *m. Soṭ.* 9.15 // *Cant. R.* 1.1; *b. ʿAbod. Zar.* 20b; *Exod. R.* 48.4; *Gen. R.* 96.5; *Pes. R.* 1.6.

the messianic Son by the Spirit is a messianological *novum*, the individual messianic and restorationist elements which make up the christo-pneumato-logical motif were already established.[77] As the very first indication of the role of the Spirit in Jesus, and in messianic drama he will initiate, Lk. 1.35 will inevitably take a place of considerable importance for the reader. If the other characters in the narrative so far have largely evinced the Spirit in the traditional 'prototypical' gifts of the Spirit of prophecy, the Spirit's action in the conception of the messiah (Lk. 1.35) moves to stage-centre activities of the Spirit which had sometimes been treated as peripheral: miraculous power in the physical realm and the ethical/religious life of Israel's restoration/new creation. For Schweizer and his followers, these activities attributed to the Spirit are merely a distraction enticing us away from a true understanding of Luke's pneumatology—a stone of stumbling for the unwary Lukan interpreter, carelessly left among the rubble of pre-Lukan traditions. But the commanding place Lk. 1.32-35 affords suggests rather he has made this a cornerstone for his building, and that we may anticipate the rest of his pneumatology takes its bearing from it. As we shall see, it is no accident that in the gateway texts to Acts the Holy Spirit/Power of the Most High of Lk. 1.35 becomes the 'Power from on High' poured out on the Church (Lk. 24.49, cf. Acts 1.8).

3. *Conclusions*

Luke 1–2 suggests an understanding of Israel's hope which consists essentially in the Davidic-Messianic restoration of Zion within history. From the narrator's perspective this has already decisively begun in the Spirit's conception of the messianic son of God (1.35)—an act of new creation power which simultaneously foreshadows Israel's New Exodus renewal (cf. the allusion to Isa. 32.15-20)—and his perspective is matched by that of the inspired characters who utter the *Magnificat*, the *Benedictus* and the *Nunc*

---

77. As R.E. Brown observes, 'the real parallel for the conglomeration of ideas in 1:35 is not an OT passage but the early Christian formulations of christology'; particularly Rom. 1.3-4, Acts. 13.32-33, and Mk 9.7 and pars. (*Birth*, p. 312. Brown's position depends heavily on L. Legrand, 'L'arrière-plan néotestamentaire de Lc 1,35', *RB* [1963], pp. 161-91). This does not mean that Luke has simply rewritten Rom. 1.3-4, nor even that he stands at the end of a tradition-historical sequence which gradually fed back language that applied supremely to Jesus' parousia (Spirit, sonship, power, reign, etc.), first of all to Jesus' resurrection (Rom. 1.3-4; Acts 13.32-33; 2.35-36), then to his transfiguration, baptism, and finally, here, to his conception (Brown, *Birth*, pp. 29-32 and *passim*, holds to such a thesis, but there is no evidence for this unilinear development: see Mainville, *L'Esprit*, pp. 201-209). But all these occasions are associated with a similar concept, viz. the one who will be glorified with power is already enjoying some ἀρραβών of that future cosmic disclosure. The same applies in Lk. 1.32-35.

Dimittis, all of which Farris correctly classifies as declarative psalms of praise (for salvation *already* wrought), not eschatological hymns (anticipating purely future salvation).[78] Any attempt to organize Luke–Acts into three (or more[79]) water-tight 'epochs',[80] with Luke 1–2 as 'the epoch of Israel' (set in sharp contrast to Luke 3–24 as that of the dawning new age of salvation in Jesus (alone), and Acts as 'the epoch of the church'), is thus doomed to failure.[81] At best these chapters could be made to support a view of successive phases of God's inbreaking salvation,[82] but as a process which commences within Luke 1–2.

At the same time we cannot quite go all the way with Menzies in summing up the activities of the Spirit in Luke 1–2 as the eschatological renewal of prophecy. 'Prophecy renewed'[83] might be an appropriate description for

---

78. *Hymns*, pp. 66-85.

79. See C.H. Talbert, *Literary Patterns, Theological Themes and the Genre of Luke–Acts* (Missoula, MT: Scholars Press, 1974) for the view Luke sees a *fourth* distinguishable period, commencing beyond the death of Paul and the horizons of Acts. C.K. Barrett sees this anticipated in an important way in Paul's speech to the Ephesian elders (Acts 20.19-35, esp. 29-30): see 'Paul's Address to the Ephesian Elders', in J. Jervell and W.A. Meeks (eds.), *God's Christ and his People: Studies in Honour of Nils Alstrup Dahl* (Oslo: Universitetsforlaget, 1977), pp. 107-21.

80. Hultgren (*Christ*, pp. 79-81) argues the term 'epoch' is quite inappropriate, signalling an unjustified historical consciousness.

81. Conzelmann's thesis in this respect is perhaps sufficiently a dead duck to spare it yet another shooting party (see Bovon, *Theologian*, for extensive reviews of *la chasse*. In fact, as E. Franklin rightly notes, Conzelmann allowed more continuities across the epochs than some of his readers perceived [see the discussion in E. Franklin, *Luke: Interpreter of Paul, Critic of Matthew* (Sheffield: JSOT Press, 1994), pp. 13-26]). Von Baer (*Geist*, p. 48) and Tatum, by allowing that Jesus' miraculous birth was an exception to the picture, should have recognized that to refer to Lk. 1–2 as the epoch of Israel was misleading: on their analysis these chapters simultaneously depict two epochs as present—and hence no 'epoch' at all! Dunn appears to recognize that his own earlier work failed fully to recognize the import of Lk. 1.35 for the characterization of Luke's salvation-history: see 'Baptism', p. 17.

82. This is the position arrived at by Fitzmyer, 181-87 (and *Luke*, pp. 57-85). Fitzmyer presents his structure as if it were a revision of Conzelmann's; but it amounts to a denial of it, for it breaks down the containing walls between the Baptist and Jesus (on one side) and between Jesus and the church (on the other), and so eliminates the special character of 'the Middle of Time' as the period of 'salvation' and 'the kingdom of God'. By allowing these waters to flow back in full measure into the church, Fitzmyer also re-eschatologizes them (for Conzelmann's only real basis for claiming Luke had de-eschatologized them was that Luke had severed the connection between 'the kingdom of God'/'salvation' and the End by interposing the period of the church in which they were substantially lacking).

83. The title Menzies gives his chapter on Lk. 1–2 is 'Prophecy Renewed'. Cf. Stronstad, *Theology*, p. 38.

what takes place at and after Pentecost, but there is rather less basis for it in Luke 1–2. The term is certainly inadequate for the single most important pneumatological context, Lk. 1.35, even if Jesus' wisdom and filial consciousness in 2.40-52 may perhaps be traced to the Spirit remaining with him (rather than simply rooted in his conception by the power/Spirit of God). For different reasons it is perhaps also not altogether satisfactory to classify the experiences of Elizabeth, Mary, Zechariah and Simeon as 'prophecy renewed': in these cases we seem to encounter the typical Jewish experience of prophecy at a turning point or crisis in the nation's history, and given to warn about, confirm or elucidate the nature of the divine intervention to come. It is only on the questionable assumption of intertestamental *cessation* of prophecy that the term 'renewal' might particularly suggest itself. But that 'dogma' was neither universally accepted, nor rigidly applied, even within the groups that held it.[84] The singular prophecies attributed to Elizabeth, Mary (?) and Zechariah are in no way to be taken to suggest they regularly prophesied, but are parallel to the merely occasional activity of a Spirit of prophecy at notable rites of passage in Jewish literature. Simeon enjoyed a more abiding charisma, but his gift too falls within the scope of possibilities envisaged by Judaism of an exemplary pious person living in or frequenting the Temple. Only John the Baptist truly breaks the mould and deserves the description 'eschatological prophet'.

We have also addressed the question of to what extent Luke has used his language of the Spirit in ways that may be said deliberately to accommodate the experiences of Luke 1–2 either to Christian experience of the Spirit (Shelton, Menzies) and/or to Old Testament pneumatology (Chevallier, Stronstad). Once again such claims seem to go beyond the evidence. As we have seen, Luke certainly has not gone out of his way to reproduce LXX expressions; his language and ideas reflect rather a more general intertestamental Jewish and Christian milieu. Similarly we have regularly noted points of distinction between what is said in Luke 1–2, and Luke's descriptions of Christian experience of the Spirit. At the point where the language is closest (Lk. 1.35//Acts 1.8) the charismata denoted are most sharply distinct (divine begetting and inspired witness). Again, Luke can say certain characters in

---

84. Cf. R. Leivestadt, 'Das Dogma von der prophetenlosen Zeit', *NTS* 19 (1973), pp. 288-300; D.E. Aune, *Prophecy in Early Christianity and the Ancient Mediterranean World* (Exeter: Paternoster, 1983), esp. pp. 103-106; R.A. Horsley, 'Popular Prophetic Movements at the Time of Jesus: Their Principal Features and Social Origins', *JSNT* 26 (1986), pp. 3-27; R. Gray, *Prophetic Figures in Late Second Temple Palestine* (London: Oxford University Press, 1993); S.L. Davies, *Jesus the Healer* (London: SCM Press, 1995), ch. 3, and ch. 5 above, for plentiful examples that prophecy was relatively widespread.

the infancy narratives were 'filled with the Spirit' and spoke, as he can of characters in the post-Pentecost period. But we have noted Luke's account also introduces differentia. I would not wish to dispute that Luke sees *some* sort of analogy between the Spirit's activity in the Old Testament, in Luke 1–2, and in the body of Luke–Acts, in the various gifts of inspired speech. But (as far as the evidence from these two chapters is concerned) it seems to be the general, phenomenological and inevitable analogy, produced by a common context; there is no evidence that he has deliberately sharpened or highlighted the analogy. The existence of this phenomenon does not serve to break down the differences in the way the Spirit was active in the successive phases of salvation; it merely permits a (somewhat uncontroversial!) common factor.[85]

Luke 1–2 does not attempt an analysis of human experience of the Spirit across the ages, nor does it provide the raw materials for one. It is concerned rather to celebrate the arrival of Zion's Davidic restorer, and to affirm that coming as a great divine intervention; one in keeping with the Old Testament promises, attested and elucidated by the Spirit of prophecy and angels, and with the Lord messiah's way duly prepared for by the awaited Elijianic prophet. The pneumatological motifs all bend to those ends. Finally, we have noted that Lk. 1.35 appears programmatically to reaffirm the Spirit of prophecy as simultaneously the power both of miraculous acts in the physical realm and of the ethical life of the eschatological age.

EXCURSUS: REFERENCES TO PEOPLE AS 'FILLED WITH' OR 'FULL OF'
THE HOLY SPIRIT OR OTHER QUALITIES IN LUKE–ACTS

The use of 'full of'/ 'fill with' language in the New Testament, in relation to *persons* said to be filled with or full of some quality, is largely confined to Luke–Acts. There is only one example in John (πλήρης, 1.14), five in Paul (πληρόω, Rom. 1.29; 15.13-14; Col. 2.10; Eph. 5.18), but twenty-seven occurrences in Luke–Acts. Of the examples outside Luke, only one (Eph. 5.18) pertains to the Spirit; whereas fourteen of the occurrences in Luke–Acts pertain to the Spirit. At least four of these occasions (marked with an asterisk below) are redactional changes to his Markan source.

There are in fact three basic forms of these metaphors in Luke–Acts:

1. a form using the passive of the verb πληρόω 'to fill': this is used of the Spirit once (Acts 13.52, joy and the Holy Spirit), while elsewhere of wisdom (at Lk. 2.40) and rejoicing (at Acts 2.28);

2. a form using its immediately related adjective πλήρης 'full of': this is used of the Spirit five times (Lk. 4.1*; Acts 6.3, 5; 7.55; 11.24), while

85. On this, see the more detailed discussion with Shelton in Turner, 'Empowerment', pp. 108-13.

elsewhere of leprosy (Lk. 5.12*); grace and power (Acts 6.8); good works and acts of charity (Acts 9.36); deceit and villainy (Acts 13.10), and rage (Acts 19.28);

3. forms using the passive of the verb πίμπλημι 'to fill (completely)': this is used eight times of the Spirit (in the aorist tense unless specified otherwise: Lk. 1.15 (future), 41, 67; Acts 2.4; 4.8, 31; 9.17 (here aorist subjunctive); 13.9, while elsewhere it is used of rage (Lk. 4.28); fear (Lk. 5.26*); fury (Lk. 6.11*); amazement (Acts 3.10), and jealousy (Acts 5.17; 13.45).

With respect to these we may note the following five points:

(1) While an analysis of the New Testament alone might suggest these are Lukanisms, a number of them are in fact traditional Septuagintalisms.[86]

a. πλήρης + subjective genitive of quality (in reference to persons) is so common in the LXX as to be a relatively standard idiom (though it is not used with divine Spirit): see e.g. Job 10.15; 14.1; 32.18; 36.17; Isa. 51.20; Sir. 1.30; 19.26; 3 Macc. 6.31, etc. and compare Philo (e.g. 'full of darkness' [*Leg. All.* 3.7]; 'full of courage' [*Ebr.* 94]).

b. πληρόω + genitive of quality (used of persons) is also well attested (though again not of divine Spirit): see e.g. 1 Kgs 7.14; Jer. 13.13; 2 Macc. 9.7; 3 Macc. 4.16; 5.1, 30 (cf. ἀναπληρόω at Sir. 24.26) etc.

c. πίμπλημι (with defining genitive) is relatively rarely used of persons (as opposed to of parts of the person, such as the 'heart' or 'soul'), though examples can be found at Dan. 3.19 and Sir. 23.11, and it is used once with 'Spirit' (at Prov. 15.4). Its cognate ἐμπίμπλημι is common, however, and seven of the occasions pertain to people filled with divine Spirit (Exod. 28.3; 31.3; 35.31; Deut. 34.9; Isa. 11.3; Sir. 39.6; 48.12—all but Isa. 11.3 and Sir. 48.12 being cases of the gift of wisdom). People are also said to be 'filled' with (*inter alia*) 'indignation' (Jer. 15.17), 'drunkeness and sorrow' (Ezek. 23.33), 'violence' (Mic. 6.12), 'fury' (Dan. 3.19), 'joy' (Sir. 4.12), 'knowledge' (Sir. 17.7) and 'iniquity' (Sir. 23.11).[87]

(2) The semantics of expressions with πλήρης + defining genitive (in relation to persons) in Luke–Acts should be relatively clear:

a. It is a spatial metaphor not a literal statement. The point is not that, for example, Tabitha (of Acts 8.36) literally had 'good works and acts of

---

86.   Most LXX occasions of πλήρης and cognates are used in the literal sense of fulness of vessels or translate שבע and cognates where these bear the meaning 'satiated', 'satisfied' or 'to be or to become satisfied', and are irrelevant to our inquiry.

87.   Cf. also Philo ('with divine Spirit, with wisdom and understanding', *Gig.* 23; 'with maladies', *Det. Pot. Ins.* 98) and Josephus ('filled with delight', *War* 7.337; 'filled with consternation', *Ant.* 16.385).

charity' inside her, but that her life was seen to be characterized by them or abound in them. Similarly, someone 'full of leprosy' (Lk. 5.12) is covered with the disease rather than containing it, and a crowd 'full of fury' (cf. Acts 19.28) is one that expresses fury, not one that bottles it up.[88]

b. To say that someone is 'full of X' is to say that *that quality clearly marks the person's life or comes to visible expression in his or her activity*, rather than merely residing in him or her as an unexpressed potential. As 'full of the Holy Spirit' (Lk. 4.1 or 'full of Spirit and wisdom' [Acts 6.3] or 'full of faith and the Holy Spirit' [Acts 6.5] etc.) is simply a variant of the more *general* metaphor, we should treat it in the same way.

c. The expression 'full of' + genitive of quality is usually used to denote a long-term state of affairs, rather than an immediate effect (for which forms of πίμπλημι are preferred), though a verbal collocation might provide the required restriction (e.g. *'becoming* full of fury' [γενόμενοι πλήρεις θυμοῦ], at Acts 19.28, is simply a stylistic variant for ἐπλήσθησαν θυμοῦ).[89]

(3) πίμπλημι is a more intensive form when compared with πληρόω, and especially appropriate (in the aorist indicative or participial forms) to denote relatively short events or immediate effects.[90] Once again we may note:

a. The metaphorical nature of the expression (in relation to persons) is evident. It would be precious to argue that either the LXX writers or Luke thought violence, drunkenness, joy, iniquity, indignation, wisdom, knowledge or fear, or whatever, were fluids literally poured into people.

b. The same applies to the collocations with a genitive of divine Spirit, which are simply specific cases of the more general metaphor.

c. In contrast to the LXX, Luke tends to use the aorist indicative or participle of πίμπλημι + genitive of divine Spirit for events or inspirations of short duration. This is usually marked by the formula 'N was filled with the Spirit and said/prophesied/cried out'. In all such instances (Lk. 1.41, 67; Acts 2.4; 4.8, 31; and possibly 13.9)[91] what is meant is that the Spirit was the immediate inspiration of the speech event specified (and no more; i.e. there is no suggestion that some more enduring endowment is semantically entailed, any more than to say that the people Luke described as

88. *Contra* Gunkel (*Influence*, pp. 42-43, 59-66), who assumes that if one can speak of people 'full of the Spirit' then the latter must be 'Stoff', and Bultmann (*Theology*, p. 155) who similarly argues we have a 'dynamistic' view of the Spirit. Such arguments would also turn 'wisdom', 'fury', 'good works' etc. into substances.

89. See Turner, 'Spirit Endowment', pp. 53-55, for fuller explanation/examples.

90. This is not to say that all such aorists necessarily denote short term punctilear events: in fact none of the Septuagintal instances with respect to the Spirit pertain to short-term endowments or inspirations.

91. Though here the charisma in question is more probably charismatic revelation (into Elymas's condition and God's impending judgement upon it) than inspired speech as such.

'filled with' 'anger', 'fear', 'amazement', etc., entered a long-term 'state of fullness' of these things).[92]

Shelton attempts to broaden this observation and to make every occasion of 'filled with' and 'full of' Spirit pertain to charismatic *speech*—that is, that the expression 'full of the Spirit' *means* 'inspired to speak by the Spirit'.[93] But this ignores the more general use of the metaphor in Luke and in the LXX (which does not mean 'speaking'); it overlooks the specific LXX use of 'filled with the Spirit' (which only once [in Sirach] entails speaking, and then not directly); it makes exceptionally heavy weather of Lk. 1.15 (John's leaping in the womb [1.41] is not speaking!), of Lk. 4.1 and of Acts 6.3, 5 and 7.55, and does not make the best sense of Acts 11.24; 13.9 or 13.52. Ultimately it is not based in sound semantics.[94]

   d.   In two cases Luke more closely follows the LXX usage and uses future or subjunctive forms of πίμπλημι to denote the inception of a lasting endowment of the Spirit in exceptional strength: Lk. 1.15 (John the Baptist) and Acts 9.17 (Paul).

(4) Once we observe that in Luke–Acts the words 'filled with Holy Spirit' usually designate short outbursts of spiritual power/inspiration, rather than the inception of long-term endowments of the Spirit, we need not agonize with, for example, J.E. Hull over the question why the disciples who were 'filled' with the Spirit at Pentecost (Acts 2.4) needed to be 'filled' again with the Spirit at 4.8, 31, etc.[95] The Lukan use of these expressions allows that a person might on many occasions be 'filled with Holy Spirit' while nevertheless remaining 'full' of the Spirit: the two types of metaphor make different but complementary assertions.

(5) The Lukan usage has been misunderstood when Acts 2.4 (with its assertion that the disciples were 'filled with Holy Spirit') has been taken to express normative Christian entry into a relatively permanent state of 'fullness' of Spirit.[96]

This sort of assertion can be found in three quite different traditions of churchmanship:

   a.   In the protestant tradition, F.D. Bruner tells us Luke teaches that all disciples receive the fullness of the Spirit at conversion, and justifies this on

---

92.   This is not to doubt that the apostles still had the gift of the Spirit beyond the speaking denoted in Acts 2.4: it is only to say that such a deduction is contextual (Peter explains they have received the gift of the Spirit), not *linguistically* entailed in the statement 'they were filled with the Spirit and began to speak in other tongues'. The phrase 'they were filled with the Spirit' here denotes only the inspiration of their glossolalia. For clarifying examples see Turner, 'Spirit Endowment', pp. 54-55.

93.   See J.B. Shelton, ' "Filled with the Holy Spirit" and "Full of the Holy Spirit": Lucan Redactional Phrases', in P. Elbert (ed.), *Faces of Renewal* (Peabody: Hendrickson, 1988), pp. 81-107.

94.   For critique, see Turner, 'Empowered', pp. 108-110.

95.   Hull, *Spirit*, pp. 121-24.

96.   Here I agree with Shelton, 'Filled', p. 99.

the wholly inadequate basis that 'the Holy Spirit is a person, and therefore where he is, he is fully, and not two-thirds or three-quarters'.[97]

b.   From the Catholic confirmationist tradition, N. Adler explains Acts 2.4 in terms of the messianic 'fullness' of Spirit normally received in Confirmation (and the power to bestow the same)—and contrasts this with the earlier absence or impoverishment of Spirit in the disciples (understood as providing an analogy for post-Pentecost Christian existence between baptism and confirmation).[98]

c.   From the classical Pentecostal position, for example, H.M. Ervin insists the ἐπλήσθησαν ('they were filled') of 2.4 is an ingressive aorist, denoting irreversible entrance into a state of 'fullness' of Spirit, understood in classical Pentecostal perspective as a second blessing of empowering to preach, etc.[99]

But all such attempts represent the importation into Luke's phenomenological metaphor of a whole conceptual structure foreign to Luke. Luke does not believe all Christians to be 'full of the Spirit': this metaphor is used precisely to distinguish those whose lives are particularly marked by the work of the Spirit from ordinary Christians (cf. Acts 6.3!). And in Lukan terms the criterion for judging whether it is appropriate to speak of someone as 'full of the Spirit' is not whether he has a baptismal or she a confirmation certificate—nor even whether the person concerned has in the past experienced some 'second blessing'—but whether the community of Christians *felt the impact of the Spirit* through that person's life and *saw the Spirit's graces and gifts regularly expressed* through him or her.

97.   *Theology*, p. 163.

98.   *Pfingstfest*, p. 91; *Taufe, passim*.

99.   *Spirit-Baptism: A Biblical Investigation* (Peabody: Hendrickson, 1987), pp. 42-61. This forces Ervin to conclude that the aorist at Acts 4.8 refers back to 2.4 (cf. also Hull, *Spirit*, p. 122), while those 'filled with the Holy Spirit' in 4.31 must be other than the 120 of Acts 2.4 (and exclude Peter and John?): i.e. the new converts made from Pentecost onwards. For a similar view see W. Wilkens, 'Wassertaufe und Geistempfang bei Lukas', *TZ* 23 (1967), pp. 26-47, pp. 26-27; *per contra* see Dunn, *Baptism*, pp. 70-71.

Chapter 7

THE PROMISE OF JOHN THE BAPTIST: 'HE SHALL BAPTIZE YOU WITH HOLY SPIRIT AND FIRE' (LUKE 3.16)

1. *The Context of the Promise*

How should the reader or hearer understand the account of the Baptist's ministry, and of his promise concerning the 'Stronger One' to come, in Lk. 3.1-19? As the decisive note of the turn of the ages has been sounded clearly enough in 1.35, he or she will not be liable to approach the narrative of John's ministry in ch. 3 as Conzelmann did, and to relegate the Baptist to the last throes of 'the period of Israel'. Amply prepared by Luke's two jubilant opening chapters, John is more likely to be perceived as part of the fulfilment of the ancient prophecies, and his Elijianic role (cf. 1.15-17, 76-79) to be understood as the beginning of God's saving action on Israel's behalf. Luke 3 reinforces such a reading:

(1) In the strongly redactional opening section (3.1-6),[1] Luke sets the Baptist's ministry in the broader context of universal history (3.1-2a), not merely for conventional historiographical reasons,[2] nor simply because he wishes to remind readers of similar synchronisms at the call of Old Testament prophetic figures,[3] but also because 'the word of God' that comes to John (3.2) has significance for 'all flesh' who soon 'shall see the salvation of God' (3.6)—a point made by Luke's own extension of the quotation of Isa. 40.3 in Mark and Q to include Isa. 40.4-5.

(2) Luke then establishes that John's preaching marks a decisive and soteriological *novum* in a number of ways:

---

1. Cf. Fitzmyer, 451-52: 'Though Luke follows Mark 1:3-4...the episode is otherwise an independent Lucan composition'. Marshall (132-37) explains the passage fundamentally in terms of redaction of Q supplemented by Mark (following T. Schramm, *Der Markus-Stoff bei Lukas* [Cambridge: Cambridge University Press, 1971], pp. 34-36; Schürmann, I, 161). On either view the passage is substantially redactional.

2. Cf. e.g. Thucydides 2.2; Polybius 1.3; and note the related synchronism of the death of Philip in Josephus, *Ant.* 18.106.

3. Cf. Isa. 6.1; Jer. 1.1; Ezek. 1.1-2, but all more exclusively centred on Israel than Lk. 3.1-2.

a. His preaching is both the return of full prophecy to Israel, and itself the *fulfilment* of Isaiah's prophecy which was taken to speak of preparation for the Lord in the form of 'a voice crying out in the wilderness' (Isa. 40.1). Thus for Luke (as for pre-Lukan tradition) the Baptist's ministry belongs not merely to the period of promise, but has at least one foot securely in the period of fulfilment.[4]

b. The mention of 'the wilderness' (3.2, 4) would itself evoke a whole Isaianic constellation of New Exodus hopes, which (as we shall see in Chapter 9) was essentially concerned with Israel's eschatological restoration.

c. The Baptist addresses all Israel[5] with a message of radical and national repentance, expressed in a unique water-rite (3.3, 7, 16) which separates remnant Israel, who are assured of divine forgiveness and may anticipate its consequent salvation, from the rest who are warned of God's wrath (3.7, 9, 17).[6]

d. If R.L. Webb is right, the wording of 3.17 implies that John viewed himself as having in large measure *effected the eschatological sifting of Israel* (through his call to repentance and baptism): all that remains for the 'stronger one' (in terms of the metaphor in 3.17) is to use the *spade* (τὸ πτύον) to 'cleanse his threshing floor' by shifting the already separated piles of grain and chaff to their separate destinations, the granary and fire respectively.[7]

---

4. See B.C. Frein, 'Narrative Predictions, Old Testament Prophecies and Luke's Sense of Fulfilment', *NTS* 40 (1994), pp. 23-24.

5. Cf. 3.3 'εἰς πᾶσαν...τοῦ Ἰορδάνου'; 3.15 'the people' = ὁ λαός; 3.18 'preaching good news to the people (= Israel)', cf. 3.21, ἄπαντα τὸν λαόν ('the *whole* people' = 'Israel'). See Kim, *Geisttaufe*, pp. 49-51.

6. For this understanding of the Baptist's ministry and water-rite, see especially the careful historical-critical case made by Webb, *Baptizer*, pp. 163-216 (and *passim*). Sanders (*Jesus*) has argued the Baptist (like nearly all Jews, including Jesus) was a covenantal nomist and so envisaged the restoration of all Israel (rather than merely that of a gathered remnant). Against this view of Judaism, see decisively Elliott, 'Survivors', *passim*, who shows the great extent to which the fierce internal struggles of Judaism from the Maccabaean period onwards spawned vigorous remnant theologies. The logion in Lk. 3.8-9 would appear deliberately to counter the sort of view Sanders thinks universal to Judaism: only those who 'gathered themselves together through baptism' (cf. Josephus, *Ant.* 18.117) as repentant and obedient Israel could anticipate salvation (see Webb, *Baptizer*, pp. 197-203).

7. *Baptizer*, pp. 295-300 (cf. also R.L. Webb, 'The Activity of John the Baptist's Expected Figure at the Threshing Floor [Matthew 3.12 = Luke 3.17]', *JSNT* 43 [1991], pp. 103-111). Webb's point hangs partly on the important observation that the coming one is said to have a *spade* to hand, not the instrument used for the winnowing process

e. The Baptist's preaching is characterized as 'proclaiming good news' (εὐαγγελίζομαι, 3.18), which evokes both the Isaianic passages concerning Zion's eschatological restoration (Isa. 40.9; 52.7; 60.6; 61.1 etc.), and (to a lesser extent) the Christian kerygma which was based in it.[8]

Given these features it is barely surprising that Luke marks John's preaching and baptising ministry as 'the beginning' of the Gospel and salvation (cf. Acts 1.22; 10.37). And if the focus of the promise in Lk. 1.17, 77-78 is that John will fulfil Elijah's function of initiating repentant reconciliation in Israel, that appears to match the focus of the ethical teaching attributed to him in Lk. 3.10-14 too, and John's Elijianic role is more generally confirmed by Jesus' own words in Lk. 7.26-27. The quest of a non-eschatological Baptist in Luke—one limited purely to the time of promise (the epoch of Israel, the law and the prophets)—is a wild goose chase. For Luke, John is a transitional figure who belongs to the dawn of salvation.[9] It is in this context that we must hear his words in 3.16-17 which contrast John's role with that of 'the stronger' to come.

2. The Form of the Baptist's Promise in Luke 3.16-17 and its Origin in Q

Luke takes over the Q version of the Baptist's promise (3.16) rather than Mark's in the context of his use of a larger section of Q (3.7-9, 16-17). This

itself, the winnowing fork (ὁ θρῖναξ). And the spade according to 3.17 was to be used 'to clear his threshing floor'. The Greek here (διακαθᾶραι τὴν ἄλωνα αὐτοῦ) could not naturally mean 'to winnow his wheat' (*contra* most commentators!). Rather it must mean 'to clear up the threshing floor (after the winnowing and threshing job is complete)'; i.e. to gather and transport the grain, etc. A similar point is made by S. Légasse, 'L'autre "baptême" (Mc 1,8; Mt 3,11; Lc 3,16; Jn 1,26,31-33)', in F. Van Segbroeck *et al.* (eds.), *The Four Gospels 1992* (Leuven: Leuven University Press, 1992), pp. 257-73, esp. p. 267 n. 38. Both Webb and Légasse depend on the more detailed work of G. Dalmann, *Arbeit und Sitte in Palästina*, III (Gütersloh: Bertelsmann, 1932).

8.   Cf. Marshall (*Luke*, p. 123), 'the primary source for the New Testament use of the word lies in Isaiah where the word is used especially of good tidings'. Against Stuhlmacher's attempt to discover a neutral meaning, and Conzelmann's (*Luke*, p. 23 n. 1) to claim such a sense in Lk. 3.18, see Marshall's fuller argument (pp. 122-25). We need not go all the way with Wink (*John*, p. 52) to say that in 3.18 'the *Christian* message of salvation is indicated' (my italics), but following a direct quotation from Isa. 40.3-5, it can barely mean less than 'to announce good news (of Zion's salvation)' to the people.

9.   See Chapter 6 nn. 41-45 above. Cf. also J.A. Darr, *On Character Building: The Reader and the Rhetoric of Characterization in Luke–Acts* (Louisville: Westminster Press, 1992), ch. 3, leading to the conclusion John the Baptist 'acts as a transition figure in that he sums up the age of the law and the prophets, but also initiates the new age of the revelation of God's salvation'.

preserved the saying about the coming one's action in the more original form:[10]

3.16 ἀπεκρίνατο λέγων πᾶσιν ὁ Ἰωάννης, Ἐγὼ μὲν ὕδατι βαπτίζω ὑμᾶς· ἔρχεται δὲ ὁ ἰσχυρότερός μου, οὗ οὐκ εἰμὶ ἱκανὸς λῦσαι τὸν ἱμάντα τῶν ὑποδημάτων αὐτοῦ· αὐτὸς ὑμᾶς βαπτίσει ἐν πνεύματι ἁγίῳ καὶ πυρί· 3.17 οὗ τὸ πτύον ἐν τῇ χειρὶ αὐτοῦ διακαθᾶραι τὴν ἅλωνα αὐτοῦ καὶ συναγαγεῖν τὸν σῖτον εἰς τὴν ἀποθήκην αὐτοῦ, τὸ δὲ ἄχυρον κατακαύσει πυρὶ ἀσβέστῳ.

3.16 John answered them all saying, "I baptize you with water; but one who is mightier than I is coming, the thong of whose sandals I am not worthy to untie; he will baptize you with the Holy Spirit and with fire. [3.17] His spade is in his hand, to clear his threshing floor, and to gather the wheat into his granary, but the chaff he will burn with unquenchable fire."

It should be admitted that some have disputed whether the words 'with Holy Spirit' belonged to Q at all, but this reading appears to make better sense of the tradition history than the suggestion that Q warned only 'He will baptize you with fire', while Matthew and Luke independently redacted the saying into its present form by merging it with Mark's 'He will baptize you with Holy Spirit' (Mk 1.8; so Catchpole[11]), or (only slightly more plausibly) that Matthew made this move first, and Luke then used him (so Goulder[12]). It is not *a priori* impossible that John the Baptist warned

---

10. In deciding whether the Q form or that in Mark is closer to the Baptist's preaching, two points have been considered decisive: (a) the form of promise met in Mk 1.8 affords a neater parallel to the statement 'I baptize with water', and should be suspect for just that reason. (b) The Markan form leaves the 'and (with) fire' of the Q version unexplained. The addition of 'with fire' can barely be a Christian pesher in the light of Pentecost (for Acts 1.5 does not speak of fire, and nor does the Pentecost event, which speaks rather of tongues like fire [2.4]); rather the 'fire' imagery belongs intrinsically with the purification and judgment theme of the Q passage (cf. Lk. 3.17). See Webb, *Baptizer*, p. 273.

11. D.R. Catchpole, *The Quest for Q* (Edinburgh: T. & T. Clark, 1993) pp. 7-12. Compare (with variations) T.W. Manson, *The Sayings of Jesus* (London: SCM Press, 1949), p. 41; S. Schulz, *Q: Die Spruchquelle der Evangelisten* (Zürich: Theologische Verlag, 1972), p. 368; and P. Hoffmann, *Studien zur Theologie der Logienquelle* (Münster: Aschendorff, 1972), pp. 28-31. That both Matthew and Luke independently produced the same unusual hendiadys with ἐν before 'Holy Spirit' (diff. Mark!), when Luke in any case prefers the Markan version that lacks the phrase 'and fire' (cf. Acts 1.5—here with ἐν πνεύματι fronted—and 11.16), seems implausible (hence the occasional suggestion the merging took place in a later version of Q known to Matthew and Luke).

12. *Luke*, I, pp. 277-78. I am not persuaded of the general thesis that Luke derived his Q material from Matthew: Luke often enough appears to have the older form and order of this strand of tradition.

merely in terms of judgment, for example, to shake the complacent (whether 'the [hostile] Pharisees and Sadducees' as in Mt. 3.7, or 'the [more neutral] people' of Lk. 3.15) into taking the only safe path which began with his water-baptism.[13] But most have recognized that the second (and connected) part of John's logion (Lk. 3.17) concentrates as much on the messianic figure gathering his grain into his granary as it does on the burning of the chaff, and suggests that the tradition spoke of *both* blessing *and* judgment (not merely the latter alone) in 3.16 too.[14] There is simply no formal grounds for the assertion that the Q original of 3.16 warned only (or even primarily) of fiery judgment: the very point of the logion is that the Stronger one will deal appropriately with the *whole* of Israel which John's baptism has divided into remnant and unrepentant rest. The 'you' addressed by Q3.16 was neither simply an opposition party[15] nor a righteous one alone, nor those on the brink of decision, but *all* 'Israel' as represented by the gathered crowds, and Luke's cotext (3.3, 15, 18, 21) simply clarifies this.[16].

Even if there were formal grounds for assuming the logion spoke of judgment alone, there would still be no substantial reason to suspect the phrase 'with Holy Spirit'. We know of no tradition in Judaism of a messianic figure baptising with fire alone. The nearest we come to this is *4 Ezra* 13.8-11, which describes something like a stream of flame and fiery *breath* from the Man-from-the-Sea's mouth, and a storm of sparks from his lips, which together consume the advancing army of the unrighteous. This expectation appears to be based in the messianic interpretation of Isa. 4.4 and 11.4,[17] and would suggest 'fire' and some sort of *pneuma* (whether 'breath' or 'Spirit') belong naturally enough together.[18] If (on formal grounds) we

13. For earlier forms of the view John the Baptist expected only a 'baptism with fire', see J.D.G. Dunn, 'Spirit and Fire Baptism', *NovT* 14 (1972), pp. 81-92, esp. p. 82, and *Baptism*, p. 8 n. 1.

14. Catchpole, *Quest*, p. 8, quite misrepresents this balance when he writes, 'the person with the winnowing-fork (*sic.*) will naturally separate off some for good, but the final and emphatic warning is the separation of others for ill, indeed for "the unquenchable fire"'. Compare the more balanced treatments of Dunn, 'Fire', pp. 82-85, 87-88, and *Baptism*, pp. 9-14, and of Légasse, 'Baptême', pp. 267-68.

15. The 'you' must include those referred to in the former part of the contrast, 'I baptize you with water' (3.16a): cf. Dunn, *Baptism*, p. 11; Webb, *Baptizer*, p. 291.

16. Correctly Webb, *Baptizer*, pp. 291-92.

17. See *Targ.* Isa. 4.4. and compare Légasse, 'Baptême', pp. 270-72.

18. Cf. G.T. Montague, *The Holy Spirit* (New York: Paulist Press, 1976), p. 239. This observation might support the oft-supported speculation that the original form of the saying promised the messiah would baptize with רוח/πνεῦμα and *fire*, and referred to *wind* and *fire*: so Best, 'Spirit-Baptism', *NovT* 4 (1960), pp. 236-43; Barrett, *Spirit*, pp. 125-26, and those cited at Dunn, *Baptism*, p. 8 n. 2. On this view it was merely subsequent Christian tradition that took the πνεῦμα to mean '(Holy) Spirit'. The

were persuaded that John's oracle was one of judgment alone then we should merely construe the whole clause 'he shall baptize in (Holy) Spirit and fire' as a hendiadys warning that the Coming One will execute fiery judgment in the power of the Holy Spirit. This would entirely cohere with the trajectory of messianic traditions built on Isa. 11.1-4 examined above[19] (even if it was only half the story that tradition wished to tell).

3. *Luke's Understanding of the Baptist's Meaning*

So far in his narrative, Luke has described Jewish hopes with considerable verisimilitude, by and large avoiding the anachronistic importation of distinctively 'Christian' ideas and ecclesial realities. Accordingly, we may relatively confidently reject the view that he expected the logion in 3.16-17 to refer more-or-less directly either to Christian water baptism understood as

arguments advanced in favour of this interpretation include: (a) neither Judaism nor the Baptist's disciples know of any messiah who bestows the *Spirit*; (b) baptism in Spirit could only refer to *Christian* baptism (about which John can have known nothing; so Bultmann); (c) taking the reference as 'wind and fire' allows the promise to fit the imagery of 3.17, where the messiah winnows the grain.

With respect to (a) Webb (*Baptizer*, pp. 273-74) counters: (i) Acts 19.2 cannot be taken to mean the disciples there had not even heard of the Spirit (and so to deny that John can have promised the messiah would bestow the Spirit), it indicates rather they had not heard the eschatological gift had now been given; (ii) 'the distance between the two key ideas—the outpouring of the spirit in the last times and a spirit-anointed messianic figure—was not great and they were bound to be bridged sooner or later' (see at §3.2 below).

With respect to (b) Webb (*Baptizer*, p. 275) points out (with Dunn) that the only places in the New Testament where a baptism of Spirit is described are the two where this is most clearly separated from water-baptism (Pentecost and Caesarea).

With respect to (c) Webb observes: (i) 'wind' was a much less common eschatological stage prop than 'Spirit'; (ii) πνεῦμα does not appear in Lk 3.17, and (decisively) the image in v. 17 is *not* of winnowing, but of activities which follow it, namely the clearing of the threshing floor. These two observations, Webb insists, make it improbable that the πνεῦμα of 3.16 means 'wind'; much more likely that it means 'Spirit' (and we might add that the mixed metaphor of a 'baptism' with 'wind' is perhaps just too incongruous to be a plausible account of John's words). Webb adds (iii) ἅγιον is not necessarily a Christian addition (though it might be), least of all if it stands for 'of holiness'—indeed the collocation with 'baptize' would positively suggest it, for (Webb claims) the messianic counterpart to John's baptism was the gift of the ethically transforming and renewing Spirit.

19. B.M.F. van Iersel ('He will Baptize you with Holy Spirit [Mark 1,8]', in J. Baarda *et al.* (eds.), *Text and Testimony: Essays on New Testament and Apocryphal Literature in Honour of A.F.J. Klijn* [Kampen: Kok, 1988], pp. 132-41) finds no problem in taking even the Markan text (which lacks the 'and with fire'), essentially as a promise of judgment at the hand of the messiah of Isa. 11.4.

mediating the Spirit[20] or to some *donum superadditum* of empowering for mission granted subsequently to Christians[21] (whether Jesus may, or may not, have been understood to re-interpret the logion in Acts 1.5 in such a direction is a quite different matter). But what did he think the Baptist meant by the promise in 3.16-17? Luke himself does not clarify, so we are forced to critical deduction and inference. There are essentially two complementary means of approach. One is orientated towards narrative criticism and reader-response interpretation. This will ask the question in the form, 'what could the implied readership (certainly not Theophilus alone) be expected to understand the promise to mean at this stage in the developing narrative? The implied readers are not limited to the text of Luke–Acts for their knowledge of Jewish matters: they already know a good deal about Judaism, its Scriptures and its hopes, even if they themselves stand just outside that Judaism in some way (most plausibly as the sort of readers Luke might anticipate amongst those he calls 'God-fearers').[22] Such readers will anticipate, from the cotext of Lk. 1.4–3.15, and from their knowledge of Jewish hopes, that the promise pertains to Israel's cleansing and restoration. Of course, readers will read not merely progressively but also retrospectively.[23] They will learn about how the promise came to be fulfilled in Acts, and that will in part effect how they understands the promise itself. But readers will not simply identify the Baptist's expectation with its fulfilment. They will know there is often a tension between the two (and they will see this narrated in terms of the Baptist's own questioning and Jesus' response in 7.18-23). Promise or expectation sometimes comes to fulfilment

20. It is quite amazing how this uncritical thesis keeps cropping up, most recently in M. Quesnel, *Baptisés dans l'Esprit* (Paris: Cerf, 1985), p. 38. One should only need to ask, 'And what does "and fire" signify?' to recognise that the utterance refers to a metaphorical baptism, not the literal water-rite. Cf. Légasse, 'Baptême', pp. 260-62, and see the criticism of the sacramentalist identification offered by Dunn, *Baptism*, pp. 18-22.

21. For similar second-blessing ideas see e.g. those cited at Dunn, *Baptism*, p. 10 n. 7.

22. See e.g. J. Neyrey, 'The Symbolic Universe of Luke–Acts: They Turn the World Upside Down', in J.H. Neyrey (ed.), *The Social World of Luke–Acts: Models for Interpretation* (Peabody: Hendrickson, 1991), pp. 271-304; V. Robbins, 'The Social Location of the Implied Author of Luke–Acts', in Neyrey (ed.), *World*, pp. 305-32; J.B. Tyson, *Images of Judaism in Luke–Acts* (Columbia: University of South Carolina Press, 1992), p. 36 and cf. pp. 181-182. Similar conclusions are reached by J.B. Chance, 'The Seed of Abraham and the People of God: A Study of Two Pauls', in E.H. Lovering (ed.), *Society of Biblical Literature 1993 Seminar Papers* (Atlanta: Scholars Press, 1993), pp. 384-411, esp. pp. 406-11.

23. A point well made by R.L. Brawley, *Centering on God: Method and Message in Luke–Acts* (Louisville: Westminster Press, 1990).

in unexpected ways, and nowhere is this more true than in the pattern of Israel's salvation as it is worked out in Luke–Acts. Luke's reader must hear the 'implied' Baptist in his own terms first.

The second means of approach to Luke's understanding of the Baptist's promise places more emphasis on the author and on the tradition history of his material. Luke wrote with a purpose, and insofar as it is discoverable, his authorial understanding and intent is important to the readers' understanding.[24] Where he uses sources we may assume that his meaning is largely the one he derives from his tradition (unless he alters the tradition or gives it a new cotextual framework). Luke will have received his gospel traditions not as anonymous written sources but as living tradition interpreted by Christian communities. What the traditions 'meant' before Luke acquired them therefore has potential significance for understanding Luke's own view, even if it may not be used as an interpretational straightjacket. In the case of the 'Q' material we probably have to do with a stream of tradition relatively well-rooted in the 'historical' Jesus (and the historical Baptist).

In what follows in this Chapter, I shall not strictly separate these complementary approaches, but will use grammatical and cotextual arguments side by side with historical and traditional considerations. I shall consider three main closely related questions of interpretation which may guide us towards an answer to Luke's understanding of the Baptist's meaning:

3.1. *Would the promise 'He will baptize you with Holy Spirit and fire' be taken to refer to a unitary event, or to separate 'baptisms' of Spirit and fire?*
J.D.G. Dunn has attacked the older view that John's warning contains two separate baptisms, one of Spirit (for the righteous) and one of fire (for the unrepentant).[25] As the single preposition ἐν ('in'/'with') governs both elements (Spirit and fire), and as this one baptism is promised to all parties assembled before John, 'the most probable interpretation is that Spirit-and-fire together describe the one purgative act of messianic judgment which both repentant and unrepentant would experience, the former as a blessing, the latter as destruction'.[26] This has been challenged recently by R.L. Webb,[27] who wishes to restrict the promise 'he will baptize you in Holy Spirit' to those who have undergone John's water baptism, because he understands the former as a gift of the Spirit of holiness given to the

---

24. Elsewhere I have argued on the basis of modern linguistics that the attempts to remove author/speaker meaning from discourse meaning is mistaken: see Cotterell and Turner, *Linguistics*, pp. 53-72.
25. Cf. Dunn, *Baptism*, pp. 8-14; 'Fire', p. 86; 'Birth', pp. 135-36, etc.
26. *Baptism*, p. 11.
27. *Baptizer*, pp. 289-95.

baptized to complete the new creation/renewal initiated in John's water-rite. But Webb's arguments are vulnerable at a number of points,[28] and

28. Webb insists the assumption of a single baptism follows only from the transformation of the singular verb into a singular noun—but (he counters) the number of the verb is determined by the subject, not by the instruments or objects. For example, the analagous sentence 'He will give an A and a B' should really be considered a transformation of something like 'he will provide gifts of an A and a B'; and these may be quite distinct. Now the ὑμᾶς of the Baptist's logion will refer not specifically to those baptized by John, but more generally to those to whom he directs his message, i.e. all Israel. The baptizing in Holy Spirit and fire probably therefore envisages *two separate* activities: the bestowal of the Spirit on the repentant, and the consuming of the wicked with fire. That is, the saying includes separate restorative and judgmental aspects (as Lk. 3.17 implies). The repentant he will 'baptize in Holy Spirit', i.e. 'with a Spirit of holiness' (cf. *Jub.* 1.23; 1QS 4.20-21) which completes the conversion/transformation initiated in repentant water baptism. The Spirit of holiness thereby creates a holy remnant. The *un*repentant he will baptize 'with fire' as the chaff are burned up and consumed; i.e. this is a purgative action which cleanses Israel by removing the wicked (so there remains a close association between the two baptizings; they both lead to the removal of evil from the land).

Whence does Webb derive his notion that the messiah will 'give' the Spirit of holiness (as a power of ethical transformation)? His thoughts here are largely dependent on his understanding of John's baptism as a repentance lustration that, while assuring forgiveness, only finds its true fulfilment in the eschatological cleansing of Israel. This, in turn, he explains on the basis of the connection between *T. Levi* 2.3B2 ('in living water I wholly bathed myself, and all my ways I made straight') and the plea, only witnessed in the (eleventh century) manuscript E of *T. Levi* 2.3, that the Lord should send upon the speaker 'the Spirit of holiness' to effect cleansing and new creation (*Baptizer*, pp. 116-20).

Two problems, then, face Webb's construction: (1) The notion that John expected the messiah to 'give' such a gift of the Spirit is difficult to believe, because (a) few if any Jews would think of the eschatological Spirit primarily as an ethically transforming power; they would think rather of the eschatological gift as the return of the Spirit of prophecy (albeit with ethical consequences beyond what is normally held to be the case: see Chapter 5 above); (b) while Qumran (with whose views of ablutions John has certain common features) certainly expected God to cleanse with a Holy Spirit—and that probably with reference to the Divine Spirit (not merely a new anthropological power, *contra* Menzies, see Chapter 5 §2.6), this action is *never* attributed to any of the messianic figures. If anything, the picture now emerging of the messiah of the Spirit at Qumran seems rather traditional (i.e. built on Isa 11.1-4: cf. 1QSb 5.24-25; 4Q215 4.4; 4Q252 5.1; 4Q285 7.2; 4QFlor 1.10-13; 4QpIsa[a] 3.15-29): i.e. with others Jews they would almost invariably think of the Spirit on the messiah as a special case of the Spirit of prophecy (largely based in reflection on Isa 11.1-4). (c) Judaism could not easily countenance a messiah who 'bestowed' or 'gave' the Spirit to all Israel, for such a 'lordship' over the Spirit would almost inevitably breech their exclusive monotheism (for reasons we shall see below). (2) The evidence of manuscript E, though admittedly shadowing the fragmentary 4QTLev ar[a] 1.8-18, is too late to provide a firm basis for

linguistically Dunn's case is the more convincing.[29]

3.2. *Would the saying imply the Messiah bestows the Spirit (or merely that he is greatly endowed with the Spirit)?*

It is common to read of this logion as promising the messiah will 'give' the Spirit to repentant Israel, or that he will 'bestow' or 'pour out' the Spirit upon her. But we should be very cautious indeed of attributing such ideas to John the Baptist, even to Q's or *Luke's* Baptist, for pre-Christian Judaism expected no such thing. Indeed, one of the main arguments regularly offered *against* the authenticity of John's saying is precisely that 'there was no expectation of the Spirit as the gift of the Messiah. The eschatological outpouring of the Spirit was not directly connected with the Messiah'.[30] Dunn and Webb both attempt to salvage the authenticity of Lk. 3.16 by suggesting that 'the step of fusing the two thoughts, of an eschatological outpouring of the Spirit and a Spirit-anointed messiah, was hardly a great one and was bound to be made sooner or later'.[31] On Dunn's understanding, Qumran brought the two ideas especially close, and John the Baptist took the 'tiny step' which remained and so 'first spoke of the Messiah's *bestowal* of the Holy Spirit under the powerful figure...of a baptism in Spirit-and-fire'.[32]

But their position is unconvincing. No Jew would easily countenance the idea of a messiah who was sovereign over God's Spirit to the extent that one might speak of such a figure 'bestowing' the Spirit on (or 'giving' the Spirit to) the whole of repentant Israel. As I have argued in some detail elsewhere, God's Spirit was God *himself* present and active, and to make the messiah 'Lord of the Spirit' in a such a way would inevitably have threatened Jewish exclusive monotheism.[33] It is for this reason, we would suggest, that Webb was unable in his earlier analysis (*Baptizer*, ch. 7) to find

the view that John's water baptism would have been regarded as incomplete and only fulfilled in a bestowal of 'the Spirit of holiness'.

29. The single ἐν governing both Spirit and fire would naturally imply something more like 'he will baptize with A-and-B' than 'he will baptize with A and he will baptize with B' (as Webb requires).

30. So Dunn, 'Fire', p. 88, summing up the consensus view he opposes.

31. Dunn, 'Fire', p. 91.

32. 'Fire', p. 92 (my italics). For Webb's very similar position, see *Baptizer*, e.g. p. 274: 'the distance between the two ideas, the outpouring of the Spirit in the last times and a spirit-anointed messianic figure, was not great and they were bound to be bridged sooner or later: the spirit-anointed figure would be the one to *bestow* the expected spirit' (my italics).

33. Turner, 'Spirit and Christology', pp. 168-90, and more fully in 'The Spirit of Christ and "Divine" Christology', in J. Green and M. Turner (eds.), *Jesus of Nazareth: Lord and Christ* (Carlisle: Paternoster, 1994) pp. 413-36.

any human figures in Judaism who matched all the various statements in Lk. 3.16-17: the decisive lack being the ability to bestow the Spirit. Webb's own conclusion was that John's picture only fully matches Yahweh himself, and that John thus depicts the 'Coming One' neither quite as a Davidid, nor yet as a new Moses, but simply as the manifestation and agent of Yahweh. There was no 'small step' between a messiah endowed with the Spirit and a messiah universally endowing with the Spirit, only a yawning chasm between such ideas. It is curious then that in ch. 8 of his study, Webb should contradict his earlier analysis by suggesting that the Judaism of *T. Levi* 18.11, *T. Jud.* 18.24, 1QIsa 52.14-15 and CD 2.12 was moving towards the idea of a messiah who would bestow the Spirit, and that John the Baptist may have taken the final 'small step'. We should rather agree with his earlier assessment that the former two of these passages should be discounted as Christian interpolations;[34] and we have argued elsewhere (against Dunn) that 1QIsa 52.14-15 does not refer to a messianic sprinkling of the nations with Spirit, and that the Spirit 'made known' by the anointed figures in CD 2.12 is not *bestowed* by such figures, but experienced through the Spirit's working in their lives.[35]

In short, Judaism was probably not able to conceive of any messianic figure *bestowing* the eschatological Spirit on Israel, and it is unlikely that John the Baptist himself (or the Palestinian Q tradition which remembered his words) took the very radical step of asserting it. It is intrinsically much more likely that his words about the Stronger One 'baptizing' Israel with Spirit and fire refer to the effect *on* Israel of the advent of her messiah mightily endowed with the Spirit, than that they anticipate his giving the Spirit *to* Israel. But we need to examine the next question before we can take this matter further.

3.3. *What does the verb 'to baptize' (with Holy Spirit and fire) connote within John's promise?*

Clearly any viable solution will need to take into account the obvious comparison and contrast intended with the statement (3.16a), 'I baptize you with water' (and we should perhaps note the lack of the preposition ἐν ['in'] here).

(1) The unmarked ('normal') meaning of βαπτίζω would be either 'to immerse', 'to dip' or 'to sink', and this accords fully with the Aramaic John almost certainly used, namely תבל, which means quite simply 'to dip, bath, wash (by immersing)'. The sense 'immerse' would make natural sense of 3.16a, for 'immersion' is almost certainly what John the Baptist practised.

---

34. See Turner, 'Luke and the Spirit', ch. 2 n. 204.
35. Turner, 'Spirit and Christology', pp. 181-83.

This latter conclusion is well supported by Webb's historical analysis of lustrations as repentance rites, for he has been able to show that when expression of repentance was the purpose of lustrations, the available evidence suggests they were conducted by immersion in running water (cf. *T. Levi* 2.3b; *Sib. Or.* 4.162-70; *Apoc. Mos.* 29.11-13).[36] What then are we to deduce from John's comparison between his own water rite (of immersion) and the future role of the messiah-of-the-Spirit? It might imply that John's metaphor deliberately depicts the messiah as 'immersing' people in a flowing river of fiery Spirit. Unfortunately, while this is not impossible, it is simply unparalleled, and so improbable. As I.H. Marshall pointed out, we find nothing in Judaism to match the idea of a messianic figure immersing people in rivers or lakes of Spirit (or fire).[37]

(2) Marshall himself (followed and developed by Turner[38]) has argued that by extension from its literal sense 'to sink' or 'to immerse', βαπτίζω came to be used as a metaphor meaning something like 'to deluge with', or 'to overwhelm with'. The Baptist's promise could then be taken to depict the messiah pouring out the eschatological flood of Spirit and fire from on high that transforms creation and the people of God and consumes all evil. This too faces problems:

a.   That the messiah might unleash an eschatological stream of *fire* is certainly within the bounds of Jewish thinking—but that he might have this degree of sovereignty over the divine *Spirit* remains improbable.

b.   We cannot be certain that John the Baptist's promise was as fully apocalyptic as this view suggests. Rather, on Webb's analysis, Lk. 3.17 assumes that the Baptist has already achieved the 'eschatological' sifting of Israel—and has achieved this in the historical activities of preaching and baptizing. The coming one might equally be expected to accomplish the cleansing destruction of the sinful and restoration of the righteous within a *historical* framework. That is, for John, the imminent judgment expected may not have been the catastrophic apocalyptic deluge of the world (as is so often held), but God's coming to Israel in history to restore her through his Spirit-endowed agent.

c.   The transition from βαπτίζω used literally to mean 'immerse' (in the case of John's baptism) to βαπτίζω used non-literally, and

36. *Baptizer*, pp. 179-83 and chs. 4–5.

37. I.H. Marshall, 'The Meaning of the Verb "to Baptize"', *EvQ* 45 (1973) pp. 130-40.

38. Turner, 'Spirit Endowment', pp. 50-53.

with the different sense 'deluge with' (for the messiah's baptism),
is awkward (though not impossible).[39]

d. While the Greek βαπτίζω may carry the sense 'overwhelm with'
    or 'deluge with' (cf. Lk. 12.50!), the almost inevitable Aramaic
    equivalent behind the Greek βαπτίζω in 3.16—טבל—is not
    attested with these senses: it means quite simply 'to dip, bath,
    wash (by immersing)'. If Lk. 3.16 retains an authentic contrast
    between John and the messiah 'baptizing', and if the Aramaic
    used was indeed טבל on both occasions, then Marshall's inter-
    pretation would appear to be excluded.

(3) Dunn has suggested that the verb βαπτίζω might at least connote
'initiate', and this raises the possibility of a contrast between John, who initiates into the remnant Israel through water-baptism, and Jesus, who initiates
into the kingdom of God/new covenant life through Spirit-baptism.[40] The
suggestion might seem particularly attractive for English speakers, for whom
the terms 'baptize' and 'baptism' are specifically religious 'initiatory' terms,
and, indeed, in semi-popular Pentecostal and Charismatic writings the
deduction has regularly been made that 'baptism in the Holy Spirit'
'initiates' into 'the things of the Spirit' as water baptism initiates into the
church. But such a sense is much less apparent for βαπτίζω, which enjoyed
widespread secular use. In the extra-biblical metaphorical usages it appears
to connote 'overwhelmed by', 'sunken deep into', not 'initiate'—thus, to
take a typical example, Gadalias βεβαπτισμένον εἰς ἀναισθησίαν καὶ
ὕπνον is not 'initiated' into unconsciousness and sleep by Ismaēlos's calcu-
lated over-generosity with the wine (he had undoubtedly known both
states before, and probably by the same cause), he is 'overwhelmed by' or
'sunken into' these (Josephus, *Ant.* 10.169; and compare Philo, *Vit. Cont.*
46). Despite a wide variety of such comparable uses,[41] I know of none

39. Marshall in fact concluded John may have practised baptism by affusion
(modelling his water-rite on his messianic expectation) rather than by immersion. In
the light of Webb's evidence and other considerations (cf. Turner, 'Spirit Endowment',
pp. 51 and 61 n. 33) this latter suggestion seems unwarranted.

40. While this way of thinking is evidently a plank in his argument against Menzies
(see 'Baptism', pp. 20-21), Dunn has not developed it formally.

41. Thus e.g. β. τίνα ὕπνῳ (*Ap.* 11.49) or ὕπνῳ βαπτίσμενος (Archig et Posidon.,
ap. Aet. 6.3) should probably be rendered 'flood(ed) by' or 'overwhelm(ed) with'
sleep, and Plato (*Symp.* 176b) uses the verb metaphorically to mean people 'soaked'
with wine (not those having their first taste of it). Cf. also Josephus, *War* 4.137 (ὁ δή
καὶ...ἐβάπτισεν τὴν πόλιν), which has been translated 'this circumstance...*wrecked*
the city'; but in view of the fact that the circumstance in question is an excessive influx
of people that strained the resources of the city, 'flooded', 'sank' or 'overwhelmed'
would provide better translations (but not 'initiated'). Philo (*Leg. All.* 3.18) offers 'καὶ

where the sense 'initiate' is plausible. It is not impossible that the Baptist deliberately coined such a live metaphor, but there is no evidence to suggest any hearer would understand his utterance so.

(4) I suggest it is more likely the intended point of comparison is not with the physical movement involved in baptizing (whether immersing in water or pouring water upon baptizands), but with the purpose for which the rite is performed. John baptized using water to wash and so to *cleanse* the repentant Israel of the contagion of sin; *mutatis mutandis*, the messiah will wash and so 'cleanse' the repentant Israel with Spirit-and-fire: he will 'cleanse it' in the fuller sense, that is, restore it as Utopian Zion. In contrast to the previous suggestion, this proposal has the clear advantage of being based both in the publicly understood meaning of John's baptism,[42] on the one hand, and the traditionally recognized function of the messiah (to purge and restore Zion), on the other.[43] As we have seen, the traditional Davidic messiah, endowed with the Spirit, was precisely so gifted in order that he might fully cleanse Zion. Need we then look any further for our explanation of John's saying than the strong traditional expectation of a messianic figure powerfully fulfilling Isa. 11.1-4 (with 4.4 and 9.2-7)—as in *1 En.* 49.2-3; 62.1-2; *Pss. Sol.* 17.37; 18.7; *4 Ezra* 13.8-11; 1QSb 5.24-25; 4QpIsa 3.15-29, and so on? The arrival of such a figure to purge and restore Israel, with his decisively authoritative Spirit-imbued command, burning righteousness, and dramatic acts of power, effecting both judgment and salvation, would *itself* be sufficient to explain the metaphor of his 'baptizing' Israel by Spirit-and-fire.[44] This view is strengthened by the probable allusion in 3.16b to

βαπτίζοντα τῇ φορᾷ τῶν παθῶν τὴν ψυχὴν...' which we should render 'overwhelms the soul with the flood of the passions', and Moulton and Milligan offer 'then we shall be overwhelmed...' at P. *Par* 47.13 (κἂν ἴδῃς ὅτι μέλλομεν, τότε βαπτιζώμεθα).

42. For the view that the historical John saw his baptism as cleansing from the contagion and guilt of sin, see Webb, *Baptizer*, ch. 6. In the Gospel tradition the same understanding is maintained in the description 'a baptism of repentance for the forgiveness of sins' (Lk. 3.3, etc.).

43. I thus come much closer to J.E. Yates, *The Spirit and the Kingdom* (London: SPCK, 1963) than my earlier dissertation allowed (see Turner, 'Luke and the Spirit', pp. 48-52, 208-10), while nevertheless still rejecting the cornerstone of Yates's thesis (that 'the word "baptize" fundamentally denotes spiritual purification': so *Spirit*, p. 2), and his major deduction from it (that Mark portrays the period of the ministry as the fulfilment of John's promise).

44. When metaphors get beyond the level of complexity of simple cases like 'Benjamin is a ravenous wolf', the task of elucidating in what way we are to see the tenor as 'like' the vector becomes increasingly difficult (on this problem see especially J.M. Soskice, *Metaphor and Religious Language* [Oxford: Clarendon Press, 1985], chs. 2 and 3). I am not suggesting this case is an easy one. Fundamentally I propose

Mal. 3.2b-3, where the 'coming one's' advent is likened to refiner's fire and fullers' soap, and its purpose is said to be to purify Levi and refine her.[45]

In further support of this understanding, it may be pointed out that a number of scholars have already noted that the salvation oracle in Isa. 4.2-6 provides one of the best clues to the collocation of 'Spirit' and 'fire' in its assertion, 'once the Lord has washed away the filth of the daughters of Zion and cleansed...Jerusalem...by a *spirit of judgment* and a *spirit of burning*'.[46] Here we have not only something approaching the Baptist's linguistic hendiadys of Spirit and fire, but also the specific connection with Zion's eschatological cleansing and restoration that we require. In addition, Menzies has drawn our attention to the way the Targum refers all this to 'the time of the messiah' (*Targ.* Isa. 4.2) and translates Isa. 4.4 as 'by a command of judgment and a command of extirpation' (performed by God most probably through his agent, the messiah). Here it would seem the messiah effects Zion's cleansing by his power of command, and (as Menzies observes) for the Targum tradition that probably means by the 'Spirit of prophecy' upon him. An interpretation which in some way refers the logion to the purging restoration of Zion undertaken by the Spirit-empowered messiah would also find strong support from 3.17 according to which the messiah comes (not to winnow the grain but) to cleanse the threshing floor.

Conclusion
To draw together the threads of our three discussions above, I propose that when John the Baptist spoke of one to come who will 'baptize you with Holy Spirit and fire' he did not mean the person concerned would *bestow* the Spirit on Israel, *give* the Spirit to Israel, *pour out* the Spirit on Israel,

---

John compares his role of cleansing Israel (through a water rite) with the messiah's cleansing of Israel (because he is mightily endowed with the Spirit). He can speak of that as a baptizing, not because the repentant are consciously envisaged as being plunged into Spirit (fiery or otherwise), but rather simply because (i) the messiah (like the Baptist) is an agent of God whose action does something for the people of God, (ii) because that 'something' is a cleansing of God's people, and (iii) a 'medium' is used in each case, water and Spirit respectively, between which there are already traditional points of comparison. With this level of explanation the metaphor is not merely viable, but fruitful enough. We need not press it further, though there may indeed be other (possibly intended) aspects of comparison; e.g. the slightly dramatic experience of being plunged under water by John may be compared with the 'engulfing' experience of encounter with the messiah and with the Spirit at work through him.

    45. See B.C. Frein, 'Predictions', p. 27.
    46. See (differently) e.g. Lampe, 'Holy Spirit', p. 162; Dunn, *Baptism*, p. 12; Légasse, 'Baptême', pp. 270-72; Menzies, *Development*, pp. 136-41; Webb, *Baptizer*, pp. 207, 224, 230; Frein, 'Predictions', p. 27.

deluge Israel with Spirit, or *immerse* Israel in fiery Spirit. He forged his metaphor to affirm the stronger one to come would *cleanse* Israel (in accordance with the Isaianic oracles as they were currently understood), and that he would be able to do this because (as those oracles promised) God would mightily endow him with Spirit-and-power to accomplish that promised restoration. The repentant would experience the Spirit's action through the messiah as a purging and vigorous transformation of Israel, the unrepentant would encounter this same Spirit-endowed messiah, but in the consuming fire of his judgments and actions taken to rout evil. One 'baptism' with Holy Spirit-and-fire, perhaps, but experienced in two quite different ways. We should not press beyond this (as Menzies does) to specify the Baptist 'had in mind [merely] Spirit-inspired oracles of judgment uttered by the Messiah, blasts of the Spirit which would separate the wheat from the chaff',[47] for we have no reason to think that anyone reading Isa. 11.1-4 and the traditions built on it would restrict the messiah's Spirit-endowment to inspired *speech* (see Chapters 4–5 above), nor did the Baptist see the Coming One's task primarily as one of winnowing. The purpose of the Baptist's promise is merely to clarify the connection between his own baptizing activity and the messianic-restoration ideology and hopes of which it was a part, not to provide a detailed programme for how the central figure will accomplish his ordained task.

It could be argued against my reading that we are not told the Baptist expected a *Davidic* messiah, nor or even a messiah at all, but rather, perhaps, the Lord himself (cf. 3.4a). Such a claim, however, is improbable even of the historical John—against it, it has been pointed out often enough that John's reference to 'a stronger one' than himself, 'whose sandal thongs I am not worthy to untie', suggests a human agent, and would verge on semi-blasphemous truism if intended to apply to God himself.[48] Webb has also shown that the traits mentioned in 3.16-17 fit the Davidic messiah better than they do any other human figure.[49] Furthermore, the description of him as ὁ Ἰσχυρότερές ηου ('the one stronger than me') might naturally evoke Isa. 11.2. But while legitimate doubt may surround the 'historical' Baptist's understanding, and the way he was 'remembered' in the circles that used Q, in Luke's setting there can be absolutely no doubt that the Baptist's words

47. *Development*, p. 140.
48. See e.g. Légasse, 'Baptême', p. 268.
49. *Baptizer*, pp. 219-60, 282-88 (and see §3 above). Webb felt one key trait of 3.16 was decisively missing from Jewish expectation concerning the Davidid. The latter was never expected to bestow the Spirit (which was God's prerogative), only to be mightily endowed with the Spirit. Having argued above that 'to baptize with Holy Spirit' need not mean 'to bestow Spirit', but could mean 'to cleanse in the power of the Spirit', we have strengthened the 'fit' between Lk. 3.16-17 and the Davidic figure.

are to be taken *to refer to the Davidic messiah and to his restoration of Israel*, both of which have been emphatically announced and celebrated throughout Luke 1–2. The light thrown by those initial chapters strengthens the case for the reading of 3.16-17 that we have proposed, for insofar as Luke characterizes John as belonging four-square with the pious David-Zion hopes articulated in Luke 1–2, his own utterance in 3.16-17 should be taken in conformity with those traditional hopes and to elucidate them. It is another matter whether Luke believes John's understanding is the whole story. To that question we shall in a moment briefly turn.

But we must first state the significance of our judgment for an understanding of the pneumatology involved. If John's words are, as we have suggested, an allusion to traditional Jewish views of the Davidic messiah—and if his point is that the messiah will be empowered to cleanse and so restore Israel through the mighty Spirit with which he is (to be) endowed—then, for the Baptist at least, *the Spirit is clearly in some sense 'soteriologically necessary'*. We need not deny the Spirit is a messianic version of the 'Spirit of prophecy' and 'empowering for mission', but that mission is first and foremost directed to Israel's 'salvation'—her cleansing, liberation and transformation. The Baptist does not (as Gunkel would) grudgingly admit the possibility of some indirect ethical consequences of the Spirit of prophecy on the messiah, but instead (passing over the means) he focuses precisely on the intended soteriological *results* of the endowment: the gifts of the Spirit of prophecy *to* the messiah will simultaneously be the effective divine power at work *through* him to accomplish Israel's purgative ethical/religious redemption.[50]

4. *Luke's Own Interpretation of the Promise in Luke 3.16*

As we have suggested above, we need at least potentially to distinguish between the views attributed to the Baptist (or other characters) within the

---

50. It is significant that Gunkel does not treat Lk. 3.16 and parallels. While Menzies speaks of the messiah's endowment to cleanse Israel, of the unrighteous consumed in fire, and the righteous remnant gathered and purified, he curiously insists 'the cleansing envisioned is not the purification or moral transformation of the individual' (*Development*, p. 139), i.e. everything is reduced to the *sifting* effect of the preaching, which separates out and gathers the believers (for Luke, if not for the Baptist too; *Development*, p. 145). Against Menzies, it should be noted the focus of John's promise is not on the operation of sifting, but on the cleansing of the threshing floor which follows it. And while Menzies does not envisage a gift of the Spirit to the individual which purges the recipient, he clearly envisages a gift of the Spirit which effects a national purging; presumably as spiritually and ethically transforming for the righteous as it is destructive for the wicked.

narrative, and those of the narrator/implied author himself. For Luke, John is *the* prophet of Israel. As such his words cannot fail. However, even though Gabriel assures the reader John is to be filled with the Spirit from birth (1.15), and Jesus lauds the Baptist as 'more than a prophet' and 'the greatest born of women' (7.26-28),[51] Luke is aware of some limitations on his understanding (cf. 7.18-21). More importantly, he is aware that the salvation historical events took a rather different 'shape' from what might have been expected by extrapolation from traditional hopes. The author takes us to the very heart of this irony perhaps when he has the disciples on the road to Emmaus explain forlornly to the risen Jesus, 'We had hoped he was the one to redeem Israel' (24.21)! Indeed, Luke himself came to see the Baptist's promise of 3.16-17 fulfilled in an unanticipated way, mainly beyond Pentecost (Acts 1.5; 11.16). But, as we shall see, he retains the central sense of the Baptist's words. Only if we understand the utterance 'he shall baptize you with Holy Spirit' as a promise concerning the Davidic cleansing of Zion through the one endowed with the Spirit, shall we be able to make sense of the conversation in Acts 1.5-8 and Peter's argument in 11.15-18, and of the significance of these for Luke's whole view of the relation of the Church to the promises made concerning Israel in Luke 1–2.

---

51. Darr (*Character Building*, p. 84) characterizes Luke's overall presentation of John in the Gospel accounts as 'the second most important character in the narrative' and as 'fully sanctioned by both the Holy Spirit and the narrator'.

Chapter 8

THE EMPOWERING OF THE MESSIANIC SON

As our introductory survey has indicated, the interpretation of Jesus' Jordan experience of the Spirit is a contentious issue. For Büchsel and Dunn (*inter alios*) it first and foremost depicts Jesus' entry into and paradigmatic experience of Christian sonship, the kingdom of God, and new covenant life in the Spirit. For others the emphasis falls primarily or exclusively on the charismatic empowering of Jesus as a paradigm for either Christian confirmation (e.g. Adler, Thornton, Dix) or for 'baptism in the Holy Spirit' understood in a more traditional Pentecostal sense of empowering for mission (e.g. Shelton,[1] Stronstad and Menzies). It is possible too that neither extreme is right—either because Luke thought there was truth in both claims (so Baer and Dunn[2]) or because he thought Jesus' experience at Jordan was a unique messianic anointing without clearly intended parallel in the disciples' experience (so Turner).[3]

We shall not be in a good position to arbitrate between these competing claims until we have examined the whole of Luke–Acts (and so we shall return to the question in Chapters 9 and 14). But the previous chapter has at least raised the possibility that Luke understood the Spirit upon Jesus primarily in rather traditional Davidic messianic terms, as the empowering of God's messianic king to accomplish the hoped-for cleansing and restoration of Zion. In this chapter we must limit ourselves to the question how Luke 3.21-22 and 4.1-14 contribute to our understanding of the Spirit on Jesus, and how this relates to developing hopes concerning Jesus and his mission in Luke's opening chapters.

1. Jesus' Baptismal Experience of the Spirit (Luke 3.21-22)

The brief narrative reads:

> 3.21 Ἐγένετο δὲ ἐν τῷ βαπτισθῆναι ἅπαντα τὸν λαὸν καὶ Ἰησοῦ βαπτισθέντος καὶ προσευχομένου ἀνεῳχθῆναι τὸν οὐρανὸν 3.22 καὶ

---

1. *Word*, pp. 46-56.
2. Especially in his later writings.
3. See especially 'Jesus', pp. 3-42. I perhaps overpressed this thesis.

καταβῆναι τὸ πνεῦμα τὸ ἅγιον σωματικῷ εἴδει ὡς περιστερὰν ἐπ᾽ αὐτόν, καὶ φωνὴν ἐξ οὐρανοῦ γενέσθαι, Σὺ εἶ ὁ υἱός μου ὁ ἀγαπητός, ἐν σοὶ εὐδόκησα.[4]

3.21 Now when all the people were baptized, and when Jesus was baptized, and while he was praying, the heaven was opened, 3.22 and the Holy Spirit descended upon him in bodily form, as a dove, and a voice came from heaven, 'Thou art my beloved Son; with thee I am well pleased'.

Luke derived his account of Jesus' baptism from tradition—substantially from Mark (though he may also have known a version in Q).[5] But what did

---

4.   A variant reading in D (also attested in most old Latin MSS, and known to Justin, Clement of Alexandria, Origen, Methodius Augustin and Hilary) offers a direct quotation from LXX Ps. 2.7: υἱός εἶ σύ, ἐγὼ σήμερον γεγέννηκά σε. To the list of those supporting this ill-attested Western reading given by Dunn (*Jesus*, II, n. 73) add Harnack, Zahn and Rese (but probably subtract Creed). Rese (*Motive*, pp. 192-5) argues that while we can explain Luke's alteration of Mark, we cannot explain why a later hand should introduce such a change. Luke tends to remove ἀγαπητός (cf. 9.35) and this reminded him of Ps. 2.7. The σήμερον of the psalm quotation would have chimed well with (e.g.) Lk. 2.11, 4.21, 23.43, while the γεγέννηκά σε would remind him of Lk. 1.35; the κληθήσεται of 1.32, 35 pointing to the future baptismal event. Schürmann's argument that Luke uses Ps. 2.7 rather of the resurrection (cf. Acts 13.33) is rejected with the assertion that in Acts 13.33 the psalm is applied to the whole of Jesus' ministry, not merely to his resurrection (and so Luke did not understand the quotation in an adoptionist sense). But Rese is not convincing. Without doubt Lk. 1.35 refers to Jesus' birth not to his baptism (with E. Schweizer, *TDNT*, VIII, p. 381). Further, Rese's own explanation does not account for the alternative and better attested reading of 3.22. If a later scribe had assimilated Luke's account to that of the other Synoptists it would have been to the *Matthean* form (οὗτός ἐστιν ὁ υἱός μου) rather than to the Markan: Matthew's Gospel dominated the early church. In addition, Schürmann (following Wellhausen) is surely right when he points out that any reading which assimilates to an Old Testament text automatically stands under grave suspicion (194); especially is this the case when the proposed reading rests on the evidence of only one Greek MS, and that an erratic one (Marshall, 155). Rese holds that if a scribe altered the Lukan towards Ps. 2.7 he would inevitably have altered Matthew and Mark as well, but this defence is hardly strong. The Lukan writings have been subjected to much greater changes in the West than either Matthew or Mark; unless Rese is willing to argue for the priority of nearly all of the D readings, his case falls to the ground. There may be some truth in H.W. Bartsch's claim that the Western text has adoptionist tendencies (*Wachet aber zu jeder Zeit* [Hamburg: Reich, 1963], p. 51), and this may explain the rise of the variant reading. Against the variant Western reading, see e.g. Fitzmyer, 485; Marshall, 154-55; Nolland, 161-62; Mainville, *L'Esprit*, p. 211, and especially D. Bock, *Proclamation from Prophecy and Pattern: Lukan Old Testament Christology* (Sheffield: JSOT Press, 1987), pp. 99-101.

5.   Luke can barely have been unaware of Mark's account of the baptism of Jesus but it has occasionally been argued, at least since Streeter's day, that he did not use it (so B.H. Streeter, *The Four Gospels* [London: MacMillan, 1927], p. 205, and, most

this enigmatic tradition mean, and, more specifically, how did *Luke* understand it?

1.1. *The Meaning of the Baptismal Account in the Pre-Lukan Tradition*
Let us review several points which have been argued elsewhere:

1.   The earliest form of the tradition was a type of Interpretation-vision with a symbolic visionary element (the Spirit descends from heaven as a dove) and heavenly voice mutually explaining each other—that is, although in the form of an address to Jesus, the voice comes not as a christological calling or recognition, but to

recently, J. Jeremias, *New Testament Theology*. I. *The Proclamation of Jesus* [London: SCM Press, 1971], p. 39). A number of minor agreements between Matthew and Luke against Mark (βαπτισθῆναι, Mt. 3.13//Lk. 3.21; aorist participle βαπτισθείς, Mt. 3.16, and βαπτισθέντος, Lk. 3.21, diff. Mk 1.9 [ἐβαπτίσθη]; ἠνεῴχθησαν [Mt. 3.16] and ἀνεῳχθῆναι [Lk. 3.21] diff. Mk 1.10 [σχιζομένους]; ἐπ᾽ αὐτόν, Mt. 3.16//Lk. 3.22, diff. Mk 1.10 [εἰς αὐτόν]), as well as the fact that Matthew and Luke share a common source for the account immediately preceding the baptism and almost immediately following it, combine to suggest that Luke had a non-Markan source dealing with Jesus' baptism (and for Streeter this was Q [*Gospels*, p. 188], for Q could not have jumped from a description of John's preaching [Lk. 3.15-18 and par.] to the temptation account [Lk. 4.1-13] without a description of Jesus' baptism [cf. Catchpole, *Quest*, p. 76; *per contra* see R. Bultmann, *The History of the Synoptic Tradition* (Oxford: Basil Blackwell, 1963), p. 251 n. 5, and Jeremias, *Theology*, p. 39]. When, however, Bultmann argues that there is no bridge between the baptismal narrative and that of the temptations to connect the accounts, his case falls to the ground: central to both is Jesus' 'sonship'). Whilst Luke's use of a non-Markan source seems indisputable, it is much less certain that Luke has abandoned Mark and is following the non-Markan source alone. Matthew, who normally follows the wording of 'Q' more closely than Luke, hardly has any significant divergence from Mark except in making the voice at the baptism speak in the third person rather than in the second—in which, in any case, he is not followed by Luke (Mt. 3.14 and 15 appear to be redactional addition: there is no reason to believe that they were part of the non-Markan source common to Matthew and Luke). Matthew, in other words, has given preference to his Markan source: with Mark (and not in Luke) we find the following features: the mention that Jesus came ἀπὸ ... τῆς Γαλιλαίας (Mt. 3.13//Mk 1.9), and that he was baptized by John (Mt. 3.13 ὑπ᾽ αὐτοῦ//Mk 1.9 ὑπὸ Ἰωάννου) in the *Jordan*. Matthew follows Mark's καὶ εὐθὺς ἀναβαίνων ἐκ τοῦ ὕδατος (1.10; cf. Mt. 3.16 εὐθὺς ἀνέβη ἀπὸ τοῦ ὕδατος), and both he and Mark have the plural of οὐρανός (Mk 1.10; Mt. 3.16), while Luke has the singular. Mt. 3.17 and Mk 1.11 agree against Luke in the wording καὶ ... φωνὴ ἐκ τῶν οὐρανῶν. The minor agreements between Matthew and Luke against Mark are thus rather to be explained in terms of their exposure to the 'Q' tradition or to coincidental redaction of Mark (so Schürmann, 188-91; Schramm, *Markus-Stoff*, p. 36, and Marshall, 150-51, among others. Contrast Schneider, 91). Luke's alterations are not in the direction of the non-Markan source of Jesus' baptismal account, but motivated by a number of concerns which we shall discuss later.

interpret the descent of the Spirit to Jesus.[6] The tradition concerning this heavenly voice was from the first a mixed citation of
which Ps. 2.7 and Isa. 42.1 were the main elements.[7]

2.   Within the structure of this parabolic vision, seeing the Spirit
        descend in the form of a dove (= a bearer of tidings: cf. Gen. 8.6-
        10; *b. Git.* 45a; *b. Sanh.* 95a; *Targ. Cant.* 2.12) to Jesus probably
        signalled that the Spirit's action through him will make him the
        bearer of 'good news' to Israel.[8]

3.   The voice, which also interprets the Spirit's descent, signalled that
        the Spirit's action through Jesus will empower him as (Davidic)
        messianic Son (cf. Ps. 2.7) and Isaianic servant-herald (cf. Isa. 42.1-
        2). Given the dove symbolism, the greater emphasis within this
        combination perhaps fell on the messenger/herald role.

4.   At the pre-literary stage the baptismal account was already con-
        nected with John's preaching (and, probably, the testing of Jesus)
        and formed an interpretive bridge between John's more sharply
        eschatological expectations and Jesus' preaching ministry.

5.   Q built on this understanding. It contained an account of John the
        Baptist's preaching (Mt. 3.1-12//Lk. 3.1-9, 15-17), of the baptism
        of Jesus (Mt. 3.13, 16-17 and pars.), and of his 'ordeal' in the
        wilderness (Mt. 4.1-11//Lk. 4.1-13).[9] These traditions, with which

---

6.   Building on, but critical of, the thesis of F. Lentzen-Deis, *Die Taufe Jesu nach
den Synoptikern* (Frankfurt: Knecht, 1970), chs. 4–6, see Turner, 'Luke and the Spirit',
pp. 43-47 and the notes on pp. 200-206.

7.   Against G. Dalman (*The Words of Jesus* [Edinburgh: T. & T. Clark, 1902],
pp. 276-80) and J. Jeremias (*TDNT*, V, pp. 701-702) who have argued the tradition
originally spoke only of the עבד/παῖς of Isa. 42.1, and that this was subsequently
rendered υἱός to bring the tradition into line with a more explicitly messianic
understanding, see Lentzen-Deis, *Taufe*, pp. 188-92; Marshall, 'Son of God or Servant
of Yahweh? A Reconsideration of Mark 1.11', *NTS* 15 (1968–69), pp. 326-36, and
Turner, 'Luke and the Spirit', pp. 44-45 and nn. 14-16. Against M.A. Chevallier
(*L'Esprit et le messie dans le bas-judaïsme et le Nouveau Testament* [Paris: Presses
Universitaires de France, 1958], pp. 62-75), who has argued the original tradition
centred purely on Davidic hopes (Ps. 2.7; Isa. 11.1-4), see Lentzen-Deis, *Taufe*,
pp. 157-58. Against P.G. Bretscher ('Exodus 4.22-23 and the Voice from Heaven',
JBL 87 [1968], pp. 301-11), who argues the tradition is based on Exod. 4.22-23 alone,
see Bock, *Proclamation*, pp. 101-102.

8.   For surveys of interpretation of the dove motif see especially L.E. Keck, 'The
Spirit and the Dove', *NTS* 17 (1970), pp. 41-68; Lentzen-Deis, *Taufe*, pp. 132-270; and
S. Gero, 'The Spirit as a Dove at the Baptism of Jesus', *NovT* 18 (1976), pp. 17-35. For
critique of the main alternatives see Turner, 'Luke and the Spirit', pp. 45-46, 203-204,
and 206 nn. 32 and 33.

9.   Lührmann (*Logienquelle*, p. 56 n. 2) disputes this on the basis that Q was not a
Gospel and did not contain narratives about Jesus of this nature. But (a) it is not wildly

Q would have opened, would have been in striking harmony with that which almost immediately followed: Mt. 11.2-19//Lk. 7.18-35.[10] In this last passage we find John the Baptist sending his disciples to ascertain whether or not Jesus is to fulfil the promise made by the Baptist concerning ὁ ἐρχόμενος (Mt. 11.3; cf 3.11). The answer Jesus gave (according to Q) was a claim that Isa. 61.1-2 was being fulfilled in his ministry—which means that Jesus' baptismal experience of the Spirit is interpreted by Q as an anointing by which Jesus is able to bring eschatological salvation to his hearers in both word and deed (Lk. 7.21-22//Mt. 11.4b-5). The theme of fulfilment of Isa. 61.1-3 in Jesus' *teaching* is nowhere more obvious than in the beatitudes (Lk. 6.20-26//Mt. 5.3-10),[11] which intervened between the 'ordeal' pericope and that concerning the messengers from John the Baptist. For the Q redactor, then, the Spirit on Jesus was a messianic anointing enabling him to preach and to act with such power that those whom he addresses participate in the fruits of the nearness of the kingdom. The themes of the baptismal pericope have been taken

---

improbable that Q should commence with some type of 'Bericht vom Anfang' different in kind from the rest, and (b) G.N. Stanton ('On the Christology of Q', in B. Lindars and S.S. Smalley [eds.], *Christ and Spirit in the New Testament* [Cambridge: Cambridge University Press, 1973], p. 35) has questioned whether these narratives are, in fact, quite so different as Lührmann supposes from the rest of the material in Q. Schulz (*Q*, pp. 177ff., 360ff.) allows both Mt. 4.1-11 and 11.2-19 to Q.

10. I assume, with V. Taylor ('The Order of Q', *JTS* 4 [1953], pp. 27-31), that the order of Q is generally better preserved by Luke than by Matthew; also that (*contra* H. Schürmann, 'Zur Traditionsgeschichte der Nazareth-Perikope Lk 4.16-30', in Descamps and de Halleux [eds.], *Mélanges bibliques*, pp. 187-205, and *Traditionsgeschichtliche Untersuchungen zu den synoptischen Evangelien* [Düsseldorf: Patmos, 1968], pp. 69-82), Lk. 4.16-30 was not originally part of Q (for details see below, Chapter 9).

11. We need not consider here the vexed question of the tradition-historical relationship of Matthew's beatitudes to those in Luke (for good accounts of which see especially R. Guelich, *The Sermon on the Mount* [Waco, TX: Word Books, 1982] ch. 1; W.D. Davies and D.C. Allison, *A Critical and Exegetical Commentary on the Gospel according to Matthew* [Edinburgh: T. & T. Clark, 1988] pp. 431-42; G.N. Stanton, 'Sermon on the Mount/Plain', in J.B. Green and S. McKnight [eds.], *Dictionary of Jesus and the Gospels* [Leicester: Inter-Varsity Press, 1992], pp. 735-44; those shared by both of them derive from Q (Schulz, *Q: Spruchquelle*, pp. 76-80; perhaps from different recensions of Q—so Marshall, 245-47) and depend on Isa. 61 (see especially Dupont, *Béatitudes*, II, pp. 123-42 and 39-44; Guelich [as above]; D.P. Seccombe, *Possessions and the Poor in Luke–Acts* [Linz: SNTU, 1982], pp. 83-92; and Catchpole, *Quest*, pp. 81-88).

up and fleshed out in terms of Isa. 61.1-2: Jesus is the messianic herald empowered to preach the good news.

6.   Mark had a similar understanding if less dependent on Isa. 61.1-2, that is, for Mark, Jesus' baptism[12] was the point at which he was anointed as preacher of the εὐαγγέλιον;[13] the herald of the kingdom of God, who also inaugurates it.[14]

1.2. Literary-Redactional Features of Luke's Account of the Jordan Event

Luke has contracted Mark's account, summing up John's baptizing ministry, Jesus' baptism, and the anointing with the Spirit in one cumbersome sentence (3.21-22). The initial ἐγένετο[15] is co-ordinated with three infinitives (and associated accusatives)—ἀνεῳχθῆναι τὸν οὐρανόν ('the heaven opened'); καὶ καταβῆναι τὸ πνεῦμα τὸ ἅγιον ('and the Holy Spirit *descended*'), καὶ φωνὴν γενέσθαι ('and a voice came')—which highlight the supernatural elements of the event:[16] other details are confined to a series of three subordinate temporal clauses using ἐν with the dative of the articular infinitive,[17] and two genitive absolutes.[18]

Lukanisms abound, not only in construction but also in vocabulary and interests: for example, ἅπας (Luke–Acts 21×; New Testament 32×);[19] λαός

12.   More strictly, as many have noted (usually in anti-sacramentalist polemic), the Spirit descends to Jesus after his baptism (1.10; ἀναβαίνων ἐκ τοῦ ὕδατος): 'The messianic endowment of Jesus does not come from the waters of John's baptism, but from Heaven' (Pesch, 90).

13.   For the redactional importance of this see W. Marxsen, *Mark the Evangelist* (Nashville: Abingdon Press, 1969), pp. 117-50; R.P. Martin, *Mark: Evangelist and Theologian* (Exeter: Paternoster, 1972), pp. 21-28; and Pesch, 103-107. It is not possible to tell whether Mark connected εὐαγγέλιον with Isa. 61 or with Isa. 42 or with the dove symbolism; he may not have connected it with any of them—the word had become a technical term in Christian circles (cf. G. Friedrich, *TDNT*, II, pp. 727ff.).

14.   Turner ('Luke and the Spirit', pp. 8-52) arguing chiefly against J.E. Yates (*The Spirit and the Kingdom* [London: SPCK, 1963]), who claims that, for Mark. John's promise of baptism in Spirit is entirely realized within the ministry of Jesus in and through this baptismal endowment of Jesus.

15.   Lukanism; see H.J. Cadbury, *The Style and Literary Method of Luke* (Cambridge, MA: Harvard University Press, 1920), pp. 106; Plummer, 45.

16.   Marshall, 152.

17.   In Luke–Acts sentences prefaced by ἐγένετο quite frequently have subordinate temporal clauses with this structure: cf. Lk. 1.8; 2.6; 3.21; 5.11-12; 9.18, 33, 51; 11.1, 27; 14.1; 17.11, 14; 18.35; 19.15; 24.4, 15, 30, 51, etc.

18.   Not infrequently in Luke–Acts sentences prefaced by ἐγένετο have subordinate temporal clauses expressed by genitive absolute or dative: cf. Lk. 3.21 (*bis*); 9.37; 11.14; Acts 16.16; 22.6 (dative), 17 (dative). Lk. 3.21 is unusual in combining two of these forms, producing three subordinate temporal clauses; but cf. 9.37 and Acts 22.17.

19.   Cf. Cadbury, *Style*, p. 195.

(Luke–Acts 84×; New Testament 141×);[20] εἶδος;[21] τὸ πνεῦμα τὸ ἅγιον (diff. Matthew and Mark).[22] There are also words such as βαπτίζειν, ἀνοίγειν (scil. heavens), and so on, that are characteristic of the writer, if not Lukanisms. Only the sure knowledge that written sources lie behind Luke's account at this point prevent us from explaining such a high incidence of Lukan vocabulary, structure and interests, as redactional creativity.

Luke is alleged to have altered his source in a number of potentially significant ways: (1) It is said that Luke has removed John the Baptist from the scene; (2) that he has separated Jesus' baptism from that of the people; (3) that he has separated the event of Jesus' baptism from that of his receiving the Spirit; (4) he has intruded a mention that Jesus was praying when he received the Spirit; (5) he has changed what was originally a story about a visionary experience into a more objective event, replacing Mark's εἶδεν by his own ἐγένετο + accusative and infinitive; (6) he has accommodated the descent of the Spirit to Hellenistic views (which present power in terms of substance) by the addition of the words σωματικῷ εἴδει ('in bodily form'); and (7) he has altered the content of the heavenly voice assimilating it more closely to Ps. 2.7.

Of these, however, the motivation for (1) is primarily literary rather than theological.[23] (2) and (3) look like misunderstandings of Greek verbal

---

20. Cf. Cadbury, *Style*, p. 189.

21. Cf. Lk. 9.29 where again he has added this to Mark.

22. Haya-Prats argues that this form of the expression is the preference of the writer of Luke–Acts (*L'Esprit*, p. 35). However, Mk 3.28 (and Q; Mt. 12.32) gave this form, and Luke has changed it to the definite form with intercalated adjective (τὸ ἅγιον πνεῦμα; Lk. 12.10); similarly at Lk. 12.12 altering Mk 13.11.

23. G.O. Williams ('The Baptism in Luke's Gospel', *JTS* 45 [1944], p. 34), Marxsen (*Mark*, p. 51), and Conzelmann (*Theology*, p. 21) argue that Luke moved the account of John's imprisonment from Mk 6.17-29 in order to create the impression that John's career was over before the Spirit descended on Jesus. In that case (with Wink, *John*, p. 38) we must take βαπτισθέντος in 3.21 as middle in force (there being no one present to baptize Jesus!), despite the obvious difficulty that βαπτισάμενου would have been more appropriate. Conzelmann believes that Luke had so to remove the Baptist from the scene, because John represents the (non-eschatological) era of Israel. But as we have seen, this view cannot be sustained. John belongs to the dawn of the new age of fulfilment (Wink, *John*, pp. 51-58), even if Jesus' ministry introduces a degree of realized eschatology with which he is not associated (7.28: *pace* R.H. Hiers, *The Kingdom of God in the Synoptic Tradition* [Gainsville: University of Florida Press, 1970], pp. 56-75). Lk. 16.16a neither definitely excludes John from the new era (*pace* Conzelmann, *Theology*, pp. 16ff.) nor from the old (*pace* Wink, *John*, p. 51); he is the bridge between the two (cf. W.G. Kümmel, '"Das Gesetz und die Propheten gehen bis Johannes"—Lukas 16.16 im Zusammenhang der heilgeschichtlichen Theologie der Lukasschriften', in O. Böcher and K. Haacker [eds.], *Verborum Veritas* [Wuppertal: Brockhaus, 1970], pp. 94ff., and cf. Fitzmyer, *Luke*, pp. 102-10). There is therefore no

aspect, and of its relationship to temporal sequencing.[24] (5) and (6) probably involve merely stylistic changes,[25] and (7), as we have seen, rests on the

salvation-historical reason to remove John from Jesus' baptism, and elsewhere it is John's baptism that marks the *terminus a quo* of Jesus' ministry (Acts 1.22, 10.37: cf. Lentzen-Deis, *Taufe*, p. 91, and E. Samain, 'La notion de APXH dans l'oeuvre lucanienne', in F. Neirynck [ed.], *L'Evangile de Luc—The Gospel of Luke* [Leuven: Leuven University Press, 1989], pp. 209-38). Here Luke has simply exercised the right of the omniscient narrator to see ahead (cf. Nolland, 155-56 for other examples in Luke): his reason for shifting the account is probably aesthetic (to avoid a clumsy parenthesis such as in Mark) and literary (further to bring out the parallel between Jesus and John in the rejection and martyrdom of the forerunner): cf. Ellis, 91; Schürmann, 184; F. Schütz, *Der leidende Christus: Die angefochtene Gemeinde und das Christuskerygma der lukanischen Schriften* (Stuttgart: Kohlhammer, 1969), p. 62, and Marshall, 148-49.

24. With respect to the first of these, Plummer (98) asserts that the clause ἐν τῷ βαπτισθῆναι ἅπαντα τὸν λαόν must mean '*after* all the people had been baptized' and not 'while' or 'when' they were baptized; cf. Burton (*Moods*, p. 51) and Blass-Debrunner (§404). As to the second, Creed (57) informs us 'the aor. part. βαπτισ-θέντος contrasted with the pres. part. προσευχομένου makes the descent of the Spirit coincident with the prayer of Jesus, not with his baptism, which has already been completed'. These statements reflect a misunderstanding of the very nature of the aorist (cf. C.F.D. Moule, *An Idiom Book of New Testament Greek* [Cambridge: Cambridge University Press, 2nd edn, 1963], p. 99; F. Stagg, 'The Abused Aorist', *JBL* 91 [1972], pp. 221-31; K.L. McKay, 'Syntax in Exegesis', *TynBul* 23 [1972], pp. 39-57, and S.E. Porter, *Verbal Aspect in the Greek New Testament: With Reference to Tense and Mood* [New York: Lang, 1989]): on both occasions the aorist participles could equally well denote baptism coincident with the action in the main verbs: e.g. 'At the time when the whole people were baptized, and when Jesus too was baptized—and while he was actually praying—heaven opened...' The remarks of Plummer and Creed deserve a place in Stagg's article, 'The Abused Aorist'. A worse error in this respect is perpetrated by H. Sahlin, *Studien zum dritten Kapitel des Lukasevangeliums* (Uppsala: Almqvist, 1949, p. 61), when he insists that baptism must have been by self-immersion because 'The aorist implies that the whole people were baptized simultaneously: it was a matter of a great collective event'! Has Sahlin not encountered the constative aorist?

25. It is regularly held that Luke's dropping of the verb εἶδεν ('he saw') and his addition of 'in bodily form' imply he no longer thinks of the event as a vision, but as an objective and observable happening in history: so e.g. U. Luck, 'Kerygma, Tradition und Geschichte Jesu bei Lukas', *ZTK* 57 (1960), p. 61, and, most recently, Fitzmyer, 481; Goulder, 281; Nolland, 161; D. Crump, *Jesus the Intercessor: Prayer and Christology in Luke–Acts* (Tübingen: Mohr, 1992), pp. 111-12; and Kim, *Geisttaufe*, pp. 54-55. Against this, however, it must be pointed out that the phrase 'the heaven(s) opened' (or the like) is *par excellence* the language of the commencement of visionary experiences (cf. Lentzen-Deis, *Taufe*, pp. 105ff.), and Luke almost certainly understands such when he uses the same language at Acts 7.56 and 10.11. In the latter case, he clearly does not think that a sheet bearing unclean animals was lowered from the skies in an observable historical event! Indeed it is the phrase 'the heaven(s) opened' in the Q tradition, not the presence or absence of the verb 'to see', which

acceptance of an unlikely textual reading. Only (4) can be accepted—Luke here, as elsewhere, has injected a reference to prayer at a turning point in redemptive history[26]—otherwise his baptismal account tells essentially the same story as Mark's. The mention of the presence of ἅπας ὁ λαός ('the whole people') to be baptized, with Jesus, by John,[27] and of Jesus praying immediately before receiving the Spirit, together are a measure of the importance of the Jordan event for Luke. But how has Luke understood the tradition?

indicates that a visionary experience is intended (after all, objective historical events can be 'seen' as well as visionary ones!) Against the view that Luke understood 3.21-22 to narrate a publicly visible event is also that there is no audience reaction (contrast Acts 9.3; 26.13ff. etc.), and that when a similar pronouncement is made by a voice from heaven in the transfiguration account (9.28-36) this is seen to be a high point of revelation, and is restricted to a smaller number of close disciples. This suggests that Luke regards 3.22 as a private revelation: corresponding to this the voice at 3.22 speaks in the second person, while that at 9.35 is in the third person. To say that Luke understood Jesus' seeing of a dove and hearing of a voice as elements of a visionary phenomenon does not mean, however, that there was no corresponding 'event' (Luke clearly believes there was a corresponding endowment which this vision interprets), nor does it preclude that John the Baptist was able to discern it.

With respect to (6), it does not appear that Luke is making any substantial change to Mark once it is allowed that Mark means that the Spirit descended in the form of a dove, not merely in dove-like manner. While L.E. Keck argues that ὡς περιστεράν in the earliest tradition was *adverbial*, not adjectival, G. Richter ('Zu den Tauferzählungen Mk 1.9-11 und Joh 1.32-4', *ZNW* 65 [1974], pp. 43-56) rightly observes: 'It is, however...hardly possible to see the Spirit and its coming unless it takes some visible form, so the ὡς περιστερά (*sic*) here must denote the (visible) form in which the Spirit descends' (i.e. in the form of a dove) (pp. 43-44). The phrase σωματικῷ εἴδει ὡς περιστεράν need mean no more than 'with the physical shape of a dove' (correctly Johnson, 69); i.e., nothing in the wording 'in the bodily form of a dove' suggests Luke has turned a visionary experience into an objective historical reality. And no Hellenist would naturally think of Spirit (a substance more refined than air!) as a flapping bird!

26. Cf. Lk. 6.12; 9.18; 9.28-29 (all additions to Mark at turning points in redemptive history). On Luke's understanding of prayer in redemptive history see e.g. M. Turner, 'Prayer in the Gospels and Acts', in D.A. Carson (ed.), *Teach Us To Pray: Prayer in the Bible and the World* (Exeter: Paternoster, 1990), pp. 58-83 and 319-25, and the literature cited there; and Crump, *Jesus*.

27. Luke's choice of the expression ἅπας ὁ λαός is theologically motivated, not merely a stylistic preference. The λαός is Israel in its character as the people of God (cf. Lohfink, *Sammlung*, chs. 2 and 3; Jervell, *Luke*, pp. 41-75; Kim, *Geisttaufe*, p. 56, and H. Strathmann, *TDNT*, IV, pp. 50ff.). It is important to Luke's ecclesiology that the whole of Israel be confronted by the redemptive-historical events out of which the church will grow (Lohfink, *Sammlung*; Jervell, *Luke*). Here, then, the Baptist's activities mark the beginning of the period of fulfillment (*contra* Conzelmann see Samain, 'ΑΡΧΗ', pp. 299-338).

1.3. *Luke's Understanding of the Theological Significance of Jesus' Jordan Experience*

We cannot know whether Luke understood the significance of the dove symbolism, but his knowledge of the Old Testament (particularly in the LXX), of Jewish messianism and of the church's Christology would have been quite sufficient for him to have detected the allusions to Ps. 2.7 and to Isa. 42.1-2. His recognition of the latter appears to be indicated by his redaction at 9.35 and 23.35. In the first of these he changes the wording of Mark's heavenly address to the disciples from οὗτός ἐστιν ὁ υἱός μου ὁ ἀγαπητός ('this is my beloved Son', Mk 9.7) to οὗτός ἐστιν ὁ υἱός μου ὁ ἐκλελεγμένος[28] ('this is my Son, my Chosen') deliberately echoing the ὁ ἐκλεκτός of Isa. 42.1. Lk. 23.35 again (redactionally) combines the Davidic and Isaianic titles in the taunt, Ἄλλους ἔσωσεν, σωσάτω ἑαυτόν, εἰ οὗτός ἐστιν ὁ Χριστὸς τοῦ θεοῦ ὁ ἐκλεκτός ('He saved others, let him save himself, if he is indeed the messiah of God, the chosen [servant]'). In view of this, the words ὁ ἀγαπητός ἐν σοὶ εὐδόκησα in the baptismal tradition would probably have been understood by Luke as a relatively free rendering of Isa. 42.1b (MT: בחירי רצתה נפשי)[29] altered to a second-person address[30] and bearing the sense '...my beloved whom I have chosen'.[31]

It is also unlikely (*contra* Mainville) that Luke missed or passed over the allusion to Ps. 2.7 in the address 'You are my Son', since he himself quotes the first two verses of the psalm to elucidate the opposition of Gentile and Jewish leaders to 'the Lord *and his messiah*' (Acts 4.25-26), and later he explicitly cites the declaration of Ps. 2.7 in full as a christological proof-text (Acts 13.33). And, while the heavenly address of Lk. 3.21 contains only part

28. See B.M. Metzger, *A Textual Commentary on the Greek Testament* (London: United Bible Societies, 1971), p. 148, for the argument: the alternative readings (ἐκλεκτός: Θ, f¹, 1365 etc. or ἀγαπητός: A C* W Δ Π f¹³ etc.) assimilate to Isa. 42.1 LXX or to Lk. 3.22 respectively.

29. Already the text of Theodotion, Aquila and Symmachus had interpreted this verse in terms of the narrower sense of 'election', rather than the broader 'good pleasure' (cf. W. Grundmann, *TDNT*, II, p. 57: G. Schrenk, *TDNT*, II, p. 739).

30. Cf. Marshall, 'Son', p. 335.

31. Similarly G. Schrenk, *TDNT*, II, p. 740. If Luke knew only the LXX of our critical editions, the link between Lk. 3.22 and Isa. 42.1 might not have been so clear, for the text reads Ἰακὼβ ὁ παῖς μου... Ἰσραὴλ ὁ ἐκλεκτός μου, προσεδέξατο αὐτὸν ἡ ψυχή μου· ἔδωκα τὸ πνεῦμά μου ἐπ' αὐτόν. But there were variations (Θ and Sym read εὐδόκησεν for προσεδέξατο) and it is possible to argue for the currency of a translation of this passage close to that provided by Mt. 12.18: ἰδοὺ ὁ παῖς μου...ὁ ἀγαπητός μου· θήσω τὸ πνεῦμά μου ἐπ' αὐτόν. Cf. R.T. France, *Jesus and the Old Testament: His Application of Old Testament Passages to himself and his Mission* (London: Tyndale Press, 1971), p. 124; M. Hooker, *Jesus and the Servant* (London: SPCK, 1959), pp. 70ff. (with corrective by Marshall, 'Son', pp. 334-35).

of Ps. 2.7, it is barely possible that Luke understood the address 'my Son' as anything less than Davidic/messianic given the explicit link between divine sonship and Davidic-restorationist hopes forged in 1.32-33, 35, and its strongly Davidic cotext.[32] Indeed, Luke 1–2 would set up the *expectation* of a Davidic messianic recognition by God (reactivated by 3.15-17)[33] and so would immediately invite such a reading of 3.21-22, and simultaneously highlight the allusion to the now well-enough known messianic Psalm.[34]

How should this experience be related to what Luke's reader already knows about Jesus? It is widely accepted that a strictly adoptionist sense is precluded by what Luke has already said in the birth narratives (1.32-35; 2.42-52).[35] But how do we evaluate the remaining possibilities?

(1) As we have seen, Dunn's earlier work proposed that 3.21-22 describes Jesus' entry into the new epoch, the kingdom of God, and archetypal Christian (eschatological) sonship. The Spirit given at the Jordan is the Spirit of Jesus' New Covenant sonship. Such assertions suggest the emphasis

32. Mainville (*L'Esprit*) argues Luke fully perceived the reference to Isa. 42.1-2 in the heavenly voice (and understood it to refer to a prophetic figure: see pp. 216-27), but interpreted the reference to 'my Son' as a mixture of 'new Adam' (on the basis of 3.38) and righteous servant/prophet motifs (pp. 227-30): hence she can affirm, 'Jesus is accorded this title [= 'my Son'] because he was the only righteous man (cf. Wis. 2.18; Ps. 73.15; Sir. 4.10), the perfect servant, as God wished Adam to be; this servant upon whom God puts his Spirit (Isa. 42.1; 61.1)' (p. 230). But such a reading is only possible when one ignores Lk. 1–2, Luke's predilection for Davidic messianic Christology more generally (see Strauss, *Messiah, passim*), and for his understanding of the Son of God title primarily in messianic terms (cf. especially 1.32-35; 4.41; Acts 13.33). Mainville (p. 212) and I. de la Potterie ('L'Onction du Christ: Etude de théologie biblique', *NRT* 80 [1958], p. 236) also believe Luke could not have recognized Ps. 2.7 in the baptismal narrative because Acts 13.33 shows that the messianic enthronement it refers to is (for Luke) the resurrection; but this fails to distinguish between an allusion to part of 2.7 addressed to Jesus (at 3.22) and a public claim that an event fulfils the whole verse (Acts 13.33).

33. See Strauss (*Messiah*, pp. 207-209) building especially on the redactional addition of 'whether he might be the messiah' in 3.15b, and on the role attributed to the figure in 3.16-17.

34. On the use of Ps. 2 in Jewish messianism see especially Chevallier, *L'Esprit*; D.C. Dulling, 'Traditions of the Promises to David and his Sons in Early Judaism and Primitive Christianity' (PhD dissertation, Chicago, 1970); Strauss, *Messiah*, ch. 2; but most fully, C.E. Wood, 'The Use of the Second Psalm in Jewish and Christian Tradition of Exegesis: A Study of Christian Origins' (PhD dissertation, St Andrews University, 1976). It is of course within Christian use that messianic interpretation of Ps. 2 becomes regular (cf. also Acts 4.25-26).

35. Cf. Marshall, 155: 'The description of Jesus as ὁ υἱός will undoubtedly have been seen by Luke in terms of 1:35; cf. 2:49; the statement is thus the declaration of an existing status, not the conferral of a new dignity'. See also especially Flender, *Luke*, pp. 135-37.

to Mark/Q which, with 4.1b, serves to connect the
ition with the baptismal narrative after the lengthy paren-
ealogy.[46] As we have seen, the description of someone as
Spirit' is a Lukanism, normally characterizing an endow-
ration (unless cotextually limited), and to mark the person
e in whose life the Spirit was regularly and powerfully felt.
nse is that the messianic endowment received at the time of
a markedly powerful presence of the Spirit that was to come
bservable) expression in and through him.[47] It is probably
narrator as a *general* characterization of Jesus' relationship
the ministry, from Jordan onwards,[48] rather than having
ce to the period of testing.[49] The more specific manner in
ness of Spirit was evinced within the period of testing itself
4.1b 'and he was led in the Spirit in the wilderness'.
b ('he was led') of 4.1b (sim. Mt. 4.1, but there in the aorist)
statement that the Spirit 'drove Jesus out',[50] though
that Luke's wording is chosen to avoid the Markan notion
npels Jesus *physically* (rather than by revelation) cannot
ed.[51]

l, 168. The particle δέ is resumptive.
ursus at the end of Chapter 6 above. Marshall (168) believes that by
ke shows more clearly than Matthew or Mark 'that the Spirit is not
lsive force upon Jesus but an inward inspiration'. While not wishing
part of what Luke wishes to affirm, we have seen that 'full of' does
ily connote *inwardness* of the genitival quality (e.g. 'works of
ely intense observable expression of the quality.
ve does not itself imply 'permanence', as Mainville claims (*L'Esprit*,
on to claim that in contrast with John, whose fullness of Spirit is
, in Jesus' case it is 'part of his being', but this misunderstands the
es interesting implications for Jesus' state before he received the

Menzies (*Development*, pp. 154-57) finds this addition 'awkward'
157), and so feels obliged to explain it as Luke's attempt to make
rience a paradigm of Christian empowering: i.e. behind πλήρης π.ά.
luce a corresponding ἐπλήσθη π.ά. at the Jordan and bringing that
with Pentecost (cf. Acts 2.4 ἐπλήσθησαν πάντες πνεύματος ἁγίου).
the motive for Luke's addition the aorist participle πλησθείς
would have been more natural at Lk. 4.1.
βάλλει need not, however, mean anything quite as strong as 'the
out into the wilderness': Palestinian shepherds do not 'thrust out'
4; cf. Lk. 10.35; Mt. 13.52).
Development, p. 157 (assuming Luke mildly rephrases Q). He means,
Spirit as the Spirit of prophecy could not be responsible for such
it on the one hand Mark's verb ἐκβάλλω is unlikely to refer to the

should fall on some (epochal) change in Jesus' religious experience of God
through the Spirit following his baptism. But the reader who has reached
Lk. 3.21-22 through a careful reading of what precedes is unlikely to consider such an option. Already in Luke 1–2 (cf. 1.35 and 2.41-52, esp. 2.49-
50) Jesus experiences a Spirit-given new creation sonship with a depth that
it would be difficult for her to envisage fundamentally changed by the
Jordan experience. This is perhaps especially the case if she understands the
Spirit-and-power through which Jesus is conceived (1.35) to remain with
him beyond the conception (as the parallel with John 'filled with the Spirit'
from the womb [1.15b] would suggest), and to be the source of the wisdom
and grace the messianic child evinces in 2.47, 49-50, 52 (which the Jewish
tradition of the messiah-of-the-Spirit would suggest should be the case).
Such a reader is more likely to interpret the Jordan event as the beginning of
a new nexus of activities of the Spirit through the messianic Son, namely the
inauguration of that restoration of Israel promised in the earlier chapters and
repeated in the immediate cotext by John the Baptist in the language of a
cleansing with Spirit and fire (3.16-17). In other words (exactly to reverse
Dunn's emphases), the reader is almost bound to interpret the Jordan experience primarily as an empowering for the messianic task of one who is
already eschatological Son (by the Spirit), and if this brings any developments in Jesus' own experience of divine sonship these are merely a corollary of that empowering and of the events wrought by Jesus through it.[36]
As Goulder sums up the matter, 'It is this gift of the Spirit, empowering him
to act out what he already is, which enables Jesus to 'begin' his ministry'.[37]
But we need to elucidate this more carefully.

(2) The reader might be tempted then to think of Lk. 3.21-22 as Jesus'
installation as Son of God,[38] king of the Israel of fulfilment. But were this the
thrust of the address the full quotation of Ps. 2.7 would have been more
appropriate (possibly in combination with Isa. 11.2-4). Besides, the New
Testament writers prefer to connect the definitive installation of Jesus as
messiah with the resurrection/ascension (if not the Parousia) and the reader
will discover Luke is no exception to this (cf. Lk. 19.12-29; 22.29-30;

36. A. Feuillet, 'Vocation et mission des prophètes, baptême et mission de Jésus.
Etude de christologie biblique', *Nova et Vetera* 54 (1979), pp. 22-40 (esp. 26-33),
notes that while the baptismal event inaugurates a whole new form of existence for
Jesus, this is not a matter of a new sort of religious experience, but the end of his
hidden life, and the beginning of his public role. Following P. Jouguelet, Feuillet
observes that we do not find any real trace of development in Jesus' inner life before
God (pp. 30-31).

37. Goulder, 282; cf. Lampe, 'Spirit', p. 168; Feuillet, 'Vocation', pp. 30-33.

38. Schweizer, *TDNT*, VIII, pp. 367-68.

23.42; Acts 2.35-36 and especially 13.33[39]). Furthermore, the banks of the Jordan provide an unlikely place for a royal enthronement, and, in any case, such rites are invariably public events whereas 3.21-22 relates a visionary experience.

(3) Scholars who have seen the problem inherent in interpreting 3.21-22 as a messianic installation have occasionally put all the weight on the allusion to Isaiah 42.1 in the latter verse, and interpreted the whole event exclusively as a prophetic calling and endowment of Jesus as God's servant. On this view, the Lukan Jesus then only becomes the Davidic king, exercising royal functions, through resurrection ascension (Acts 2.35-36; 13.33).[40] While a similar case has been argued with a degree of plausibility for a pre-Lukan community, who may have known an earlier form of the baptismal tradition alleged to read צבד ('servant') rather than 'son', we have seen that (*contra* Mainville) such a reading is virtually impossible in Lk. 3.21-22, for the connections with the Davidic divine sonship motif of Luke 1–2 would be too readily apparent, and, as Feuillet and others have pointed out, the baptismal narrative contains no calling, task or message. In addition, (a) contrary to Burger's claim,[41] Luke does not relegate the Davidic role to the post-resurrection period, rather, from 18.38 and the 'triumphal entry' (19.28-40, esp. v. 38) onwards, Luke increasingly focuses the specifically royal (Davidic) messianic character of Jesus ministry culminating in his crucifixion as *the Christ* (23.35-38; 24.26),[42] and (b) the whole hypothesis draws an oversharp distinction between royal and prophetic motifs: as is increasingly recognised, the servant of Isa. 42.1-7 himself combines prophetic (servant/herald) and kingly motifs, and some editions of the Targum to the passage even formalise this in the rendering, 'Behold my servant *the Messiah*...'[43] Accordingly, the allusion to Ps. 2.7 in Lk. 3.22

39. Against Rese (*Motive*, pp. 192-95), it is most improbable that Acts 13.33 should be applied to the whole of Jesus' ministry, rather than to the resurrection: the context demands the latter, cf. Foakes-Jackson and Lake (eds.), *Beginnings*, IV, p. 154 and Haenchen, *ad loc.*

40. So Mainville, *L'Esprit*, passim. Her whole thesis may be summarized in the quote on p. 230, 'In brief, the anointing of the Spirit, at baptism, makes the Son, Jesus, the eschatological Prophet, while the anointing of the Spirit at the resurrection [i.e. Acts 2.33] makes the Son, Jesus, the Messiah'. See also Mainville, 'Jésus', pp. 193-208.

41. C. Burger, *Jesus als Davidssohn: Eine traditionsgeschichtliche Untersuchung* (Göttingen: Vandenhoeck & Ruprecht, 1970), pp. 107-12.

42. See Strauss, *Messiah*, chs. 5–6.

43. See B. Chilton, *The Isaiah Targum* (Edinburgh: T. & T. Clark, 1987) pp. 80-81. This addition, while probably late, represents a simple deduction from the role the targum affords the figure, for here the servant appears as a figure of judgment (vv. 1, 3, 4), who cares for the '*poor*' and '*needy*' (these words being targumic additions to v. 3 (cf. 41.17) carefully matching what is said of the messiah in the *Targ.* Isa. 11.4), and

Luke's choice of the modifying phrase ἐν τῷ πνεύματι ('in the Spirit'[?]) rather than Mark's ὑπὸ τοῦ πνεύματος ('by the Spirit' 1.12// Mt. 4.1) has been perceived as a further attempt by Luke to qualify the direct subordination to the Spirit implied in saying Jesus 'was led *by* the Spirit'. This interpretation is based in the fact that Luke's phrase could be translated 'he was led in the Spirit' and taken to mean: (1) 'he was led (by God) as a man "in the Spirit"' (dative of sphere for adverb of manner) or (2) 'he was led (by God) as a man powerfully attended by the Spirit' (i.e. dative of attendant circumstances roughly equivalent to 'as a man full of the Spirit'), or the like. Conzelmann thus tells us 'It is significant that according to Luke Jesus is not "led by" the Spirit, but himself acts "in the Spirit"',[52] and Schweizer went further, claiming Luke turns the man of the Spirit of Mark's Gospel into the Lord of the Spirit by making Jesus the subject of an action performed 'in the Spirit').[53] These claims, however, are difficult to substantiate because the dative phrase in question could as readily be taken instrumentally ('he was led by the Spirit' [as in Matthew]) and so syntax alone does not settle the question of what Luke meant; we need to look at Luke's usage more widely. Recognizing this, Menzies makes his case that 'in the Spirit' is just a stylistic variant for 'by the Spirit' on the basis of a comparison of 4.1 with Lk. 2.26-27. In 2.26 Luke tells us Simeon was warned ὑπὸ τοῦ πνεύματος ('*by* the Spirit') that he would see the messiah before dying; in 2.27 Luke tells us Simeon came into the temple ἐν τῷ πνεύματι ('*in* the Spirit'). Menzies assumes the latter means '*prompted* by the Spirit' and so takes the two phrases as approximately synonymous in 2.26-27, and, by extension, in 4.1.[54] Arguing the other way, we have suggested that 2.27 envisages the Spirit not only prompting Simeon's entry, but facilitating his recognition of Jesus, and inspiring his prophecy, and so have taken the statement 'he came (into the temple) in the Spirit' to involve a dative of

Spirit transporting Jesus *physically* at all (for which αἴρω and its cognates, ἁρπάζω or [ἀναλαμβάνω, with or without ἀνάγω] were conventional: see e.g. LXX 4 Kgdms 2.16; Ezek. 2.2; 3.14; 8.3; 11.1, 24; 41.35, etc.), and on the other hand, even had Mark intended such rapture there would have been no problem in attributing such an action to the Spirit of prophecy, for the moving around of prophets was one physical effect most regularly predicated of the Spirit of prophecy (see Chapter 4 above)—cf. Acts 8.39.

52. *Theology*, p. 28. And see other views in Mainville, *L'Esprit*, pp. 236-40.

53. Schweizer, *TDNT*, VI, pp. 404-405. Similarly, Yates suggests that Luke effects the change because he himself could not conceive of the Spirit as an agent, only as an endowment (*Spirit*, pp. 33, 43, 91 and 189). But neither view is adequate. Luke elsewhere uses language which presents the Spirit as an agent (Lk. 2.26; 12.12; Acts 1.16; 2.4b; 5.3; 7.51; 8.29, 39; 10.19; 11.12; 13.2, 4; 16.6-7; 20.23, 28; 21.11; 28.25), which ruins the motive Yates attributes to Luke's change.

54. Menzies, *Development*, p. 156.

attendant circumstances. This would have a nuance that goes beyond 'he came (into the temple, prompted) by the Spirit' (even if his coming 'in the Spirit' includes the latter).[55] Comparison with 4.1b might then suggest that when Jesus is described as being 'led in the Spirit in the wilderness' this may include the idea of the Spirit as God's agent leading Jesus, but it also carries the nuance that he was led in such a way as to *manifest the Spirit*; the dative being read (as at 2.27) as a dative of attendant circumstances,[56] and as supporting what Luke already affirmed in saying that Jesus was 'full of the Holy Spirit'. In favour of this view is Luke's next summary statement: 'he returned to Galilee "in the power of the Holy Spirit"' (4.14) is certainly a dative of attendant circumstances (= 'he returned *with* the power of God's Spirit'; not 'by the power of God's Spirit').

The most important redactional change in this verse, however, comes in Luke's alteration of Mark's statement that Jesus was driven/led by the Spirit *into* (εἰς) the desert to be tested by Satan (1.12//Mt. 4.1) into an assertion that Jesus was led 'in the Spirit' *in* (ἐν) the wilderness for the forty days of his temptation. Thus while Matthew and Mark only state that the Spirit led Jesus to *where* he was tested, Luke portrays the quite different picture that Jesus was continually led (contrast Luke's imperfect ἤγετο with Matthew's aorist) 'in the Spirit' *while he was in the wilderness locked in his conflict with the devil*. These changes almost certainly focus the Spirit as some sort of 'helper' for Jesus in the fight against the evil one.[57] But what is the nature of the contest, and how does the Spirit assist?

2.2. *The Significance of the Testing Narrative for Luke*

Essentially this is a story about the beginnings of Israel's restoration, a 'New Exodus' begun in her messianic representative through an ordeal/contest with Satan (in which Jesus emerges as the victorious Isaianic servant-warrior). It is within this setting that the Spirit is active, but we shall

55. 'Luke and the Spirit', pp. 82-83.

56. Cf. Chapter 6 n. 35 above.

57. So Fitzmyer, 513 and Nolland, 182 ('strengthened by the Spirit'); Mainville, *L'Esprit*, pp. 239-40, 242. It would presumably be possible to eliminate such a reading by translating, 'He was led about (by God) by means of the Spirit in the wilderness (from one place to another) to be tempted' (Nolland, 178, argues for something like the first part of this, thus creating a parallel with Deut. 8.2, and Johnson, 73, that the participle πειραζόμενος represents a purpose clause). This would bring Luke into line with Matthew and Mark, and would remove the suggestion the Spirit was involved in the temptations themselves. But such a reading is wildly improbable: Luke would have used the infinitive πειρασθῆναι (as Mt. 4.1) to express purpose, and there is no rationale for turning Mark's scene into a roving temptations story with Jesus being led by God (by means of the Spirit), from one place to another, just to change the scene of the temptation.

need to expand on some of the significant points of this brief description before the Spirit's role can be elucidated.

(1) While the 'temptation' narrative is often portrayed as a counterpart to Adam's temptation and fall (perhaps with justification in Mark), the Q version followed by Luke does not develop such ideas, and nor does Luke himself.[58] Rather, as Strauss economically summarizes the issues:

> The scene is antitypical of the experience of Israel in the wilderness. While God's son Israel (Exod. 4.22-23) failed when tested in the wilderness, Jesus the true Son remains obedient and emerges victorious. Jesus' forty days of temptation in the wilderness are analogous to Israel's forty years, and the three OT passages Jesus cites (Deut. 8.3; 6.13, 16) are all related to Israel's failures in the wilderness. The interpretive key to the account lies in Deut. 8.2-3, where Moses recalls how 'the Lord your God led you in the wilderness these forty years, that he might humble you, testing you to know what was in your heart...' (1) Israel was tested with hunger so that she would learn dependence on God (Deut. 8.3), but failed to do so; Jesus depends wholly on God for his sustenance, quoting Deut. 8.3 (Lk. 4.4; Mt. 4.3, 4). (2) Israel was commanded to worship God alone (Deut. 6.13-15), but turned to idolatry (Deut. 9.12; Judg. 3.5-7); Jesus rejected the devil's offer of the kingdoms of the world in exchange for his worship, quoting Deut 6.13 (Lk. 4.5-7; Mt. 4.8-9). (3) Israel doubted God's power and put him to the test at Massah/Meribah (Deut. 6.16; Exod. 17.1-7); Jesus refuses to throw himself from the temple and so to test the Lord God, citing Deut. 6.16 (Lk. 4.9-12). As the messianic king and Son of God (2 Sam. 7.14; Ps. 2.7; 89.27; 4QFlor), Jesus represents the nation and fulfills the task of eschatological Israel in the wilderness.[59]

Here, then, we have Jesus (as Israel's messiah)[60] successfully 'replaying' Israel's origins, which can only signify the long-awaited renewal of Israel.

(2) Given the obvious connections with the Exodus/Deuteronomy narrative, our use of the term 'New Exodus' to describe Jesus' accomplishment

58. Luke is regularly said to be highlighting an Adamic (and so universalizing) motif by his insertion before the 'testing' of a genealogy tracing Jesus back to 'Adam, (son) of God' (3.38). But the primary purpose of his inclusion of this (probably traditional) genealogy is to establish Jesus' Davidic (and to a lesser extent Abrahamic) credentials (see Strauss, *Messiah*, pp. 209-15), and Luke shows little interest in Jesus as the 'Second/Last Adam'.

59. Strauss, *Messiah*, pp. 215-16, depending largely on the classic study by B. Gerhardsson (*The Testing of God's Son* [Lund: Gleerup, 1966]). Compare also C.A. Kimball, *Jesus' Exposition of the Old Testament in Luke's Gospel* (Sheffield: JSOT Press, 1994), pp. 80-97; J.B. Gibson, *The Temptations of Jesus in Early Christianity* (Sheffield: JSOT Press, 1995), pp. 85-87.

60. Cf. Kimball, who observes, 'Many scholars interpret the typology solely at the point of Jesus' relationship to God (i.e., at his sonship) rather than also at the point of his messiahship because they fail to see the messianic character of the temptations' (*Exposition*, p. 90).

in Lk. 4.1-13 might seem to be directly typological, and even perhaps chris-tologically confused, for it could well be asked what David, or his messianic Son, has to do with the Exodus? Our use of the term 'New Exodus', how-ever, is intended to be understood against a much broader background of Old Testament and ITP hopes, in which not only the 'Exodus' events them-selves (taken to include not merely exit from Egypt and deliverance at the Red Sea, but also the wilderness wanderings and eventual entry into the land),[61] but more especially the Deutero-Isaianic prophecies of Israel's Exodus-like release from captive exile in Babylon, and her victorious pas-sage through the wilderness to restored Zion, become the pattern for a more extensive and complex 'New Exodus' soteriological hope (on which see the section on 'New Exodus Hopes and Luke's Gospel' in the next chapter §4).

Within this Isaianic 'New Exodus' constellation of motifs, the servant passages (especially 42.1-9; 49.1-13; 50.4-11; 52.13–53.12) provide impres-sionist and enigmatic portraits of a liberator figure who appears sometimes to wear the garb of Moses,[62] sometimes that of a king echoing to the descrip-tion of the Davidic hopes in Isaiah 9 and 11[63] (cf. Isa. 55.3-5), and at other times still that of 'Israel' (whether as an individual representative [49.3, 6], or as a saving remnant). It is this mix (and the way it was developed in

61. J. Mánek ('The New Exodus in the Books of Luke', *NovT* 2 [1958], pp. 8-23) correctly notes that while 'exodos' merely meant 'going out', 'in the history of Israel, however, it became a covering concept of *the way out of Egypt to Palestine in all its phases*' (p. 13; my italics).

62. See D.C. Allison, *The New Moses: A Matthean Typology* (Edinburgh: T. & T. Clark, 1993), pp. 68-71, and the literature cited there, for a discussion of Mosaic traits in the Deutero-Isaianic servant. These include (*inter alia*) that the servant is a prophet (while Moses is regularly called God's servant); he is chosen from birth (49.1, 5, cf. Exod. 1–2), and described as God's 'elect one' (42.1, cf. Ps. 106.23); he has the Spirit upon him (42.1, cf. Moses in Num. 11.17), brings 'torah' (42.4) and teaches the words of Yahweh (50.4); he is exceedingly meek (42.2-3; 50.5-6; 53.3-4, cf. Moses as 'the meekest man upon the earth' [Num. 12.3]); he suffers for others (53.4-12, cf. Exod. 17.4; 32.30-34; Num. 11–14; Deut. 1.37-40; 3.26; 4.21-22), and acts as a mediator/ intercessor for them (53.12: cf. the list of references to Moses acting this way in Allison, *Moses*, p. 25 n. 45), and, most important, he raises up and restores the people, returning them from exile (42.7; 49.6).

63. The figure of Isa. 42.1-7(9) is the chosen servant (cf. Ps. 89.19-20 of David), endowed with the Spirit (cf. Isa. 11.2-4) to bring justice to the nations, indeed the whole earth (42.1, 4 [49.7] cf. 9.7; 11.4), his advent will be a light to the nations (42.6; 49.6, cf. 9.2) and bring release to captives (42.7), while the Davidid of 11.11-16 restores the exiles in a New Exodus which is precisely the task of the Deutero-Isaianic Servant. While it is critical orthodoxy to maintain Deutero-Isaiah replaces Davidic hopes (the kingly figure is in the first instance probably Cyrus) and democratizes them (Isa. 55), such a perspective would not be possible for later readers assuming the unity of Isaiah. See Strauss, *Messiah*, pp. 296-97.

Judaism)[64] that provides the best explanation of the Q tradition used by Luke in which the Davidic messianic Son (already identified with the servant of Isa. 42.1-7 in the baptismal account) represents *Israel* in an eschatological replay of the wilderness testing of Moses and Israel.

(3) We have deliberately used a number of different words such as 'contest', 'ordeal',[65] 'testing' and 'fight' alongside 'temptations' to describe the scene envisaged. 'Temptations' were almost certainly known to Jesus before his baptism, and according to 22.28 characterized the whole period of his ministry too (cf. 11.16); 4.2-12, however, is rather a concerted onslaught which amounts to little less than a direct contest. Its special character is brought out in 4.13 by the (redactional) addition that 'having completed every manner of testing' the devil withdrew from him 'until an opportune time'. The 'return' of Satan is then related in 22.3 and marks the beginning of his second strategy to destroy Jesus, this time through Judas's betrayal. While it may not be quite accurate with Conzelmann to speak of a Satan-free period between 4.13 and 22.3,[66] this is nevertheless a period in which the offensive lies decisively with Jesus and his disciples. The disciples receive power and authority over Satan's agents from Jesus, and their resulting ministry of exorcising and healing betokens Satan's 'fall' from power (10.17-18).[67] Jesus explains his own similar success more directly in terms of 'the stronger' (ἰσχυρότερος, cf. 3.16) having overcome the strong one (= Beelzebul/Satan cf. 11.15, 18, 19), having disarmed him, and now being able to divide his spoil (11.21-22). If one asks at what point within Luke's narrative did Jesus 'overcome' Satan, the readiest answer (as for Mark before him)[68] is in the wilderness contest: hence Fitzmyer can speak of 11.21-22 as 'recalling the vanquishing of Satan in the temptation scenes'.[69] Indeed, the wording of 11.21-22 appears to be a direct allusion to the same Isaianic New Exodus imagery, in this case from 49.24-25.

64. That the liberator and restorer would be a Davidic figure becomes widespread, even, as we have seen, decisively moulding the paraphrase of the *Targ.* Isa. 42.1-7. The roots of this connection go back to Hos. 2.14-15 + 3.5; Amos 9.7 + 9.11-12; Jer. 23.5-8; *Ps. Sol.* 11; *4 Ezra* 13 (and see Strauss, *Messiah*, pp. 292-97, on these).

65. Cf. Jeremias, *Theology*, p. 74.

66. Conzelmann, *Theology*, pp. 28-29; modifying him see S. Brown, *Apostasy and Perseverance in the Theology of Luke* (Rome: Pontifical Biblical Institute, 1969), pp. 6-11 and *passim*; Ellis, 248; and esp. Fitzmyer, *Luke*, pp. 158-64.

67. So Fitzmyer, *Luke*, pp. 164-69.

68. For the view that the temptation was already understood as a decisive victory over Satan in Mark's Gospel, see E. Best, *The Temptation and the Passion: the Markan Soteriology* (Cambridge: Cambridge University Press, 1965), pp. 3-14.

69. Fitzmyer, 919. Compare Johnson, 75 (on 4.1-13), 'The reader is to understand that by winning this most fundamental battle...the Messiah's subsequent words and deed are in effect a mopping-up operation' (there follows a quote of Lk. 11.20).

Can the prey be taken from the mighty
or the captive of a tyrant be rescued?
Surely, thus says the Lord:
'Even the captives of the mighty shall be taken, and the prey of the tyrant
      be rescued
for I will contend with those who contend with you'.

If the original passage refers to *Yahweh's* direct action, here it is performed
by Jesus as God's agent, the messianic Son/servant empowered by his Spirit.

In sum, the 'temptations' narrative is soteriological and christological in
thrust, not primarily a paradigm of how to handle every-day trials.[70] Seen in
the light of Lk. 11.20-23 it relates the beginning of Israel's New Exodus in
God's messianic Son, and the 'turning of the tide' through his victory over
the captor as the servant-warrior, God's agent, who will accomplish her liberation. If Jesus is to return to Galilee 'in the power of the Spirit' (4.14) it is
because he has achieved this potential for power in and through his success
in the contest with Israel's captor.

2.3. *The Spirit in the Temptations Narrative*
We have seen that Luke has highlighted the Spirit's role within the contest
episode itself, by (redactionally) describing Jesus as 'led "in the Spirit"'
while he was being tested in the wilderness by the devil. This strongly suggests the Spirit was viewed by Luke as affording some kind of empowering
or assistance in the trial itself. Menzies, to the contrary, maintains:

> Luke gives no indication that the Spirit enabled Jesus to overcome the
> temptation. As the repetition of γέγραπται ὅτι ['it is written'] indicates,
> Jesus was supported in his victory over the devil by Scripture... the Spirit is
> never portrayed as the direct cause of a decision to orient one's life toward
> God... Luke's redactional activity in 4.1, 14 indicates not that the Spirit is
> the source of Jesus' obedience; rather, that Jesus' obedience is the source of
> his continuing relationship with the Spirit... Because Jesus remained
> committed to his task [in the ordeal in the wilderness], he returned to Galilee
> ἐν τῇ δυνάμει τοῦ πνεύματος (*Development*, pp. 160-61).

But we suspect the real basis for this unusual claim is Menzies' assumption
that Luke, following Judaism, cannot attribute ethical effects to the Spirit
because for him the Spirit is the Spirit of prophecy. Menzies' position, however, is unconvincing at this point. He may be right to suspect any suggestion that the Spirit is conceived by Luke as an interior ethical power, irre-
sistibly generating the will and ability to obey at some subconscious level,[71]
but, as we have seen (Chapter 5), that still leaves plenty of room for ethical

---

70. J. Dupont, *Les tentations de Jésus au désert* (Paris: de Brouwer, 1968), pp. 35-
85; Schürmann, 215-16.

71. As Dupont, *Tentations*, pp. 11, 49-50?

influence through actions of the Spirit of prophecy itself. So even on his own conception of the Spirit, Menzies should have been able to admit that the Spirit might afford the divine wisdom evinced in Jesus' understanding and defensive use of the Scriptures in the context of his wrestle with Satan, for the granting of such wisdom and insight was stereotypical of 'the Spirit of prophecy'.[72] It is difficult, however, to deny that such activity of the Spirit would provide a certain direct ethical influence. While it was no doubt theoretically possible for Jesus to rebel against the direction in which the Spirit's wisdom was inclining (and so to grieve God's Holy Spirit just as Israel had in the earlier wilderness context, Isa. 63.10-11), it would surely rather be expected that such charismatic wisdom and leading in the one full of the Spirit would encourage, direct and so *strengthen* the messianic Son's filial obedience (cf. Acts 9.31, etc.). Such action of the Spirit of prophecy would therefore amount to some measure of ethical empowering.[73] Nor should this seem strange; after all, just such expectation was enshrined in the most regularly used messianic text, Isa. 11.2, where the Spirit of wisdom, understanding and counsel on the Davidid is also 'the spirit of knowledge and of the fear of the Lord' which is the power of the messiah's redoubtable righteousness.[74] Given the context of the baptismal narrative where Jesus receives the Spirit as the empowering of the Davidic messianic Son and servant, and given the servant-warrior New Exodus focus of the present passage, Menzies' absolute dissociation of the Spirit's activity from Jesus' spiritual-ethical victory (inaugurating Israel's liberation and Zion's restoration) seems quite artificial. Rather it is as the messianic Son/servant *led by the Spirit* that Jesus vanquishes Satan in the wilderness, and it is *because* this Spirit-aided victory weakens Satan's hold over Israel that Luke can immediately go on to affirm, 'Jesus returned in the power of the Spirit into Galilee' (4.14).

This does not mean we should, after all, accept Dunn's assertion that the Spirit received at Jesus' baptism is his reception of eschatological (and paradigmatic) sonship, rather Jesus' messianic endowment with the Spirit of prophecy assists and so empowers the messianic Son-and-servant in his unique task of inaugurating Israel's redemption. The Spirit's action in 4.1b thus fully resonates with both the restorationist and with the ethical-religious significance of the Spirit adumbrated in 1.35. Luke, of course, is not

72. Cf. Fitzmyer, 512-13: Jesus 'is thus portrayed as the conqueror because he is armed with "the sword of the Spirit, the word of God"'.

73. Cf. Marshall, 169 (on 4.1): 'The role of the Spirit is primarily guidance, but there is no reason to exclude the thought of his powerful inspiration which (for Luke) enabled Jesus to overcome the tempter'. I might rather have said there is a very fuzzy line between guidance and inspiration, and the one often results in the other.

74. See above Chapter 5.

concerned to tell us which part of the victory should be attributed to the Divine Spirit and which to Jesus' 'own' human filial faithfulness (few steeped in the Old Testament scriptures would attempt such a distinction, and it would be especially difficult after Lk. 1.35); his intention is simply to portray Jesus as commencing the messianic liberation in a way that would readily identify him to Jewish and Christian readers as Israel's hoped-for Spirit-anointed messianic Son/servant.

3. *Jesus' Return to Galilee 'in the Power of the Spirit' (4.14)*

Form-critically 4.14-15 is a summary unit, distinct from 4.1-13, and marking the beginning of Jesus' public ministry. It is essentially a comprehensive redaction of the summary in Mk 1.14-15,[75] but Luke's addition of the phrase ἐν τῇ δυνάμει τοῦ πνεύματος ('in the power of the Spirit'[76]) provides an important thematic link in Luke's account of Jesus and the Spirit. It serves to connect the temptation narrative with the rest of the ministry in general, and with the Nazareth pericope in particular (4.16-30), for which it prepares.

The notice that Jesus returns with the *power* of the Spirit, corresponds on the one hand with the traditional picture of the Davidic messiah as one endowed with the Spirit of might (Isa. 11.2 and dependent traditions[77]), and, on the other, more specifically to the weakening of Satan's grasp resulting from his defeat in his encounter with the Spirit-empowered servant-warrior in the wilderness (4.1-13; 11.21-22). The effects of this victory will be demonstrated in the release of Satan's victims (4.18-19; 7.21; 11.14-23; 13.16; Acts 10.38 etc.), and it is no accident that the first miracle Jesus performs in Luke's account is an exorcism at Capernaum (4.31-37) which evokes amazement at his 'power' (4.36).

This exorcism account has a triple connection with Lk. 4.14 beyond the merely thematic one of deliverance of Satan's captives: (1) the specific link established through the word 'power' (its first occurrence after 4.14), (2) the further link created by the parallel between 4.14 and 4.36-37: in both a

---

75. This has now been convincingly argued by J. Delobel, 'La rédaction de Lc., IV, 14-16a et le "Bericht vom Anfang"', in F. Neirynck (ed.), *L'Evangile*, pp. 113-33. His argument comes as a mortal blow to Schürmann's thesis that, for 3.1–4.44, Luke is largely dependant on a continuous non-Markan 'Account of the Beginnings' which was used by both Mark and Q (see Schürmann, 'Der "Bericht vom Anfang". Ein Rekonstruktionsversuch auf Grund von Lk 4.14-16', *SE*, II, pp. 242-58). See Turner, 'Luke and the Spirit', pp. 215-16 n. 100; Menzies, *Development*, pp. 158-60; Nolland, 184-86; Kim, *Geisttaufe*, pp. 57-60.

76. A further dative of attendant circumstances.

77. See Chapter 4 §3 above.

statement about the power of Jesus is immediately followed by an affirmation that report of him went out into the whole surrounding country-side (i.e. report of his power, *evidenced* in miraculous liberation), and (3) a final link provided in the challenge of 4.23 'what we have heard you did at Capernaum, do here also in your own hometown' (which confirms that the report that went out about his power concerned his liberating miracles).[78]

But the phrase 'in/with the power of the Spirit' in 4.14 is certainly not to be restricted in reference to Jesus' exorcisms and liberating miracles. Luke has a more comprehensive view of the liberation Jesus brings from Satan than that, and he will set out the programme for Jesus' ministry in Lk. 4.16-30, the passage we must examine next. In this transitional passage the sentence 'Jesus returned to Galilee in the power of the Spirit' serves (like the reference in 4.1 to Jesus as 'full of the Spirit') as a general description whose light illuminates the whole of Luke's account of Jesus' ministry, at least in Galilee, if not beyond it too. It is intended to highlight the Spirit as the empowering of Jesus' whole redemptive ministry, both of preaching and of working liberating miracles.[79]

4. *Conclusions*

The opening pictures of the ministry of Jesus in Luke's Gospel appear to correspond to and to build upon the expectations raised in Luke 1–2 and in 3.14-17. There the hopes are for a Davidic messiah, powerfully endowed with the Spirit, who will cleanse and restore Israel. Correspondingly, the Jordan event portrays the Spirit as an empowering of the messiah as king and Isaianic servant. The 'tempations' narrative follows this up with what amounts to a New Exodus renewal of the testing of God's son Israel in the wilderness (drawing largely on Deut. 6–8), the successful outcome of which portends the liberation and renewal of Israel herself. Within the context of this decisive contest with Satan, we may infer that the Spirit 'empowers' the messianic Son/Isaianic servant, at least by affording him the charismatic wisdom with which to resist the Satanic enticement (4.1b thus complements 1.35). His return 'in the power of the Spirit' then raises the expectation that

---

78. The very phrase 'in the power of the Spirit' combined with these observations reveals the impossibility of Schweizer's claim that Luke makes a clear distinction between πνεῦμα ('Spirit') and δύναμις ('power'), attributing speech to the former and miracles to the latter alone. See Turner, 'Spirit and Power', pp. 126-28, 138-42.

79. See the arguments of e.g. Baer, *Geist*, p. 15; U. Busse, *Die Wunder des Propheten Jesus: Die Rezeption, Komposition und Interpretation der Wundertradition im Evangelium des Lukas* (Stuttgart: Verlag Katholisches Bibelwerk, 1977), p. 60, and Turner, 'Spirit and Power', pp. 138-42. Compare Fitzmyer, 523; Mainville, *L'Esprit*, p. 243.

Jesus will extend the victory won there to Israel herself. It is clear that the focus of the narrative is not on any alleged archetypal new experience of the Spirit enjoyed by Jesus—some fresh dimension of spirituality introduced by an alleged turn of the epochs—but on the Spirit as the power of God with him to exercise the (unique) messianic functions involved in inaugurating Zion's redemption, the consolation of Israel.

Chapter 9

JESUS ANOINTED WITH THE SPIRIT TO ANNOUNCE
NEW EXODUS LIBERATION

Jesus himself provides the single most important clarification of the significance of his baptismal reception of the Spirit in the context of his preaching in Nazareth (Lk. 4.16-30). Luke has given this passage a place of very special importance in his whole literary enterprise,[1] and, in case the reader misses the connection with the baptismal narrative, he has laid a clearly marked track from the banks of the Jordan right up to the door of the synagogue in Nazareth through his redactional references to the Spirit in 4.1 and 4.14. In this chapter we examine Luke's understanding of Jesus' own teaching on the Spirit in 4.18-21 and related passages.

I shall begin by focusing on the Nazareth pericope (4.16-30) itself. The interest in this pericope lies largely in Jesus' claim to fulfil Isa. 61.1-2 (4.18-21). The citation of Isaiah involves some unusual features of omission,

---

1. As J.T. Sanders laconically observes, 'This scene is "programmatic" for Luke–Acts, as one grows almost tired of reading in the literature on the passage...' (*The Jews in Luke–Acts* [London: SCM Press, 1987], p. 165). All from von Baer (*Geist*, p. 63) to the most recent writers agree on the passage's import for Luke: see e.g. the list in Menzies, *Development*, p. 161 n. 8, to which one might add especially R.L. Brawley, *Luke–Acts and the Jews: Conflict, Apology and Conciliation* (Atlanta: John Knox, 1987), ch. 2; Kimball, *Exposition*, p. 97; Sanders, *Jews*, pp. 165-68; C.J. Schreck, 'The Nazareth Pericope: Luke 4,16-30 in Recent Study', in F. Neirynck (ed.), *L'Evangile de Luc—The Gospel of Luke* (Leuven: Leuven University Press, 1989), pp. 399-400; J.A. Siker, ' "First to the Gentiles": A Literary Analysis of Luke 4:16-30', *JBL* 111 (1992), pp. 73-90; and Tiede, *Prophecy*, p. 19. E. Samain's view of the significance of this section is clear in his title, 'Le discours-programme de Jésus à la synagogue de Nazareth. Luc 4,16-30', *Foi et Vie* 11 (1971), pp. 25-43. The literature on 4.16-30 is accordingly very extensive: see e.g. the bibliographies in U. Busse, *Das Nazareth-Manifest Jesu: Eine Einführung in das lukanische Jesusbild nach Lk 4.16-30* (Stuttgart: KBW, 1978), and cf. G.K. Shin, *Die Ausrufung des endgültigen Jubeljahres durch Jesus in Nazaret: Eine historisch-kritische Studie zu Lk 4,16-30* (Bern: Lang, 1989), which came to me too late for extensive use. Schreck (see above) provides a helpful review.

addition and alteration which are often attributed to Luke's distinctive view
of the Spirit—especially by those who think 4.16-30 is a creative Lukan re-
writing of Mk 6.1-6a.[2] So I shall first provide a brief literary-critical introduction (§1), indicating why I think it is more likely Luke used a parallel
account of Jesus' Nazareth preaching, rather than Mark's, and why it is
probable that account included a citation of Isa. 61.1-2 and 58.6. The Isaiah
'quotation' will then be examined in more detail, asking whether any of its
changes are likely to be Lukan (rather than deriving from his source) (§2).
Having concluded that all but one of the changes are best explained in
terms of Luke's source, I shall attempt an account of its view of Jesus and
the Spirit (§3) before investigating the implications of the citation of Isaiah
61 for Luke's own pneumatology (§4). These two sections constitute the
major part of the present chapter. The former of them will examine how Q
and the pre-Lukan source behind Lk. 4.16-28 took up New Exodus and
messianic Jubiliary hopes and saw Jesus' ministry as a fulfilment of these:
the Spirit upon him was understood as the power of God through which
Jesus proclaimed Israel's New Exodus release from captivity to Belial, and
effected it, especially (though not exclusively) in works of deliverance from
sickness and demonic affliction. Section 4 will attempt to show how Luke
made this understanding central to his own portrayal of Jesus' mission.
Through various redactional devices he identifies the Isaianic soteriological
Prophet of Isa. 61.1-3 largely with the Prophet-like-Moses who dominates
Luke's central section. But this does not require him to play down the
Davidic hopes announced in Luke 1–2, or relegate them to the period beyond
the ascension (as Burger and Mainville suggest), for as Watts and Strauss
have shown, the Isaianic New Exodus tradition he uses and develops allows
precisely for such a creative fusion of Davidic and Mosaic features. The
same background allows Luke to present the ministry as the period in which
the promises of Israel's restoration in Luke 1–2 begin to be realized, and
provides a setting in which miracles of deliverance can readily be attributed
to the Spirit on Israel's deliverer. *Contra* Schweizer, Haya-Prats and Menzies,

---

2.   So Rese, *Motive*, pp. 153-54; similarly R.C. Tannehill ('The Mission of Jesus
according to Luke IV.16-30', in W. Eltester [ed.], *Jesus in Nazareth* [Berlin: de Gruyter,
1972], pp. 52, 63-65) argues that the frequent Lukanisms in vv. 17-21, and the use of
the LXX rather than the MT, indicates the whole section as a Lukan addition to the basic
Markan (Mk 6.1-6) framework. Frequency of Lukanism does not necessarily indicate
Lukan creation, however, as we noted at Lk. 3.21-22 (the question is whether there are
also signs of pre-Lukan material), and Luke was not the only person in the Christian
community to use the LXX! At the stage when traditions passed from Aramaic to Greek
accomodation of Old Testament quotes to the LXX were to be expected.

Luke retained this latter aspect of the tradition (cf. Lk. 7.18-22 etc. and esp. Acts 10.38). Finally, in §5 we look briefly at the only other reference to Jesus and the Spirit in the Gospel, that is, his exultation in the Spirit (Lk. 10.21).

1. *Literary-Critical Introduction to Luke 4.16-30*

The scene at Nazareth is indisputably of considerable significance for Luke's work. He is going against his understanding of the chronology of Jesus' ministry (cf. 4.23)[3] in order to make this scene the first in his account of Jesus' public life and teaching. As Conzelmann observed, if it could be proved that his passage were a free adaption by Luke of Mk 6.1-6 'we should possess not only a striking illustration of his own theological outlook, but also of the degree to which he has modified his sources'.[4] But, as Conzelmann himself also notes, just this is not easy to prove.[5] On the one hand the contacts with Mark amount to no more than the story line represented in parts of 4.16, 22 and 24, and on the other hand there are clear signs of pre-Lukan tradition both in the allegedly 'Markan' story line itself and in the rest of the material. This is usually conceded at least for the logion about Elijah and Elisha in vv. 25-27,[6] but there are firm grounds for detecting non-Marcan traditional material also:

---

3. Luce, 119. Luke must also have been aware that in Mark's account a very similar story appears much later (Mk 6.1-6). Conzelmann (*Theology*, p. 34) and Tannehill ('Mission', pp. 55-56) argue that ἐρεῖτε (v. 23) prophesies a future event at Capernaum (Luke hence being aware of Mark's different order), but this interpretation is hopelessly artificial: see H. Anderson ('Broadening Horizons: The Rejection at Nazareth Pericope of Luke 4.16-30 in Light of Recent Critical Trends', *Int* 18 [1964], pp. 273-74); Schürmann, 237; Marshall, 187; and Nolland, 192. Streeter (*Gospels*, pp. 206, 209) attributes the order, however, to proto-Luke, and Schürmann thinks Luke inherited the order from a longer 'Bericht vom Anfang'—on which see n. 15 below.

4. *Theology*, p. 32. Essentially this position seems to be adopted by Creed (65) and by J. Drury (*Tradition and Design in Luke's Gospel: A Study in Early Christian Historiography* [London: Darton, Longman & Todd, 1976], p. 66), who considers Luke's only non-Markan source at this point to be the LXX.

5. *Theology*, p. 35 n. 2. L.C. Crockett, 'The Old Testament in the Gospel of Luke: With Emphasis on the Interpretation of Isa 61.1-2' (PhD dissertation, Brown University, 1966), p. 4; and L.T. Johnson, *The Literary Function of Possessions in Luke–Acts* (Missoula: Scholars Press, 1977), p. 92 n. 1, appear to think Conzelmann was less cautious. Schreck, 'Nazareth-Pericope', esp. pp. 403-27, gives a comprehensive review of source-critical analyses of the passage.

6. Cf. Bultmann, *History*, p. 31, who regarded vv. 25-27 as Aramaic tradition: cf. also Tannehill, 'Mission', pp. 52, 58; Fitzmyer, 526-27, and Siker, 'First', p. 74.

a. In 4.16, the Aramaic form Ναζαρά is used, where Luke prefers Ναζαρέθ (1.26; 2.4, 39, 51; Acts 10.38).[7]

b. In 4.18-19 itself, the 'citation' of Isa. 61.1-2 strikingly includes Isa. 58.6d, while Luke–Acts never elsewhere sandwiches one Old Testament quotation within another in this way.[8] Indeed, as this remarkable kind of embedding is not elsewhere found in the Gospels, as these Old Testament passages are not brought together in Judaism, and as such embedded citations are also rare in Judaism, Kimball argues that this feature of the citation in the tradition is most plausibly to be traced back to Jesus' own midrashic exposition (if not to his reading[9] as such).[10]

7. All agree this Ναζαρά is not Lukan. On different source-critical explantions see Schreck, 'Nazareth Pericope', pp. 417-24. Goulder, *Luke*, pp. 300-301 (and earlier writings), derives it from Matthew, against which see C.M. Tuckett, 'Luke 4,16-30, Isaiah and Q', in J. Delobel (ed.), *Logia: Les paroles de Jésus—The Sayings of Jesus* (Leuven: Leuven University Press, 1982), pp. 343-54, and W.O. Walker, '"Nazareth": A Clue to Synoptic Relationships?', in E.P. Sanders (ed.), *Jesus, the Gospels, and the Church* (Macon: Mercer University Press 1987), pp. 105-18.

8. See M. Dömer, *Das Heil Gottes: Studien zur Theologie des lukanischen Doppelwerkes* (Bonn: Hanstein, 1978), pp. 143-47; Tuckett, 'Luke 4,16-30', p. 347, and Chilton and Kimball below. Compare also Bock, *Proclamation*, p. 106, who argues more generally that Luke does not elsewhere make such extensive changes to his citations.

9. The problems of Jesus quoting Isaiah in this form in the course of his synagogue reading are well known (see Kimball, *Exposition*, p. 108; Menzies, *Development*, p. 165; and C. Perrot, 'Luc 4,16-30 et la lecture biblique de l'ancienne Synagogue', *RSR* 47 [1973], pp. 324-40), but they may perhaps be exaggerated. He could have included the equivalent of Isa. 58.6d as a gloss without searching for it if he had already come to think of it (with Isa. 61.1-2) as focusing his task, or it may even have been offered as an expanded paraphrase of the MT words ולאסורים פקח־קוח of Isa. 61.1 taken as letting prisoners see the light of freedom (cf. the targum reading, 'to those who are bound, Be revealed to light')—translation of the tradition into Greek, and accomodation to the LXX would move the citation in the direction we find in Luke.

10. See Kimball, *Exposition*, pp. 106-11. With Kimball's position we may compare B. Chilton, 'Announcement in Nazara: An Analysis of Luke 4.16-21', in R.T. France and D. Wenham (eds.), *Gospel Perspectives*, II (Sheffield: JSOT Press, 1981), pp. 147-72, esp. pp. 163-65. Menzies (*Development*, p. 165) tends to give the impression that Chilton's argument is based exclusively on concurrence of the citation with the Old Syriac Gospels, but that was an additional (if important) argument (one justifiably criticized by Bock, *Proclamation*, pp. 107-108) to his earlier conclusion that the citation form was non-Lukan, and so traditional, and to his more general conclusion (p. 164) that 'unless Jesus had expressed himself in this way, it is difficult to see why

c.   In 4.20b, the semiticizing anarthrous πάντων (οἱ ὀφθαλμοί; '[the eyes] of all') and the unnecessary repetition of 'in the synagogue' (Luke himself tends to eliminate just such redundancy) are indications of a source.[11]

d.   In 4.21, the dominical 'today' and the semiticizing '"in" your ears' are pre-Lukan.[12]

e.   In 4.22, 23, the slightly awkward transition between the positive reaction of the crowd and Jesus' negative response does not suggest free Lukan composition (similarly the 'transition' between 4.24 and 4.25-27).

f.   In 4.24, the saying about a prophet being unacceptable in his own country is preceded by 'amen, I say to you' (not in Mark) against the Lukan tendency elsewhere to eliminate 'amen' sayings from his tradition (Luke 5×; Mark 13×; Matthew 30×).

g.   In 4.29, Luke's account of the attempt to kill Jesus reflects Jewish procedure for execution by stoning (by dropping the condemned first [to stun him?]) of which Luke seems unaware elsewhere (cf. Acts 7.56-60).

Given that (1) there is actually very little verbal contact with Mark's account (it comes closest in the saying in 4.24, but even here with significant differences in wording, and only the phrase 'in his country' in common); (2) the Markan and Lukan versions end quite differently; (3) there are strong indications of pre-Lukan and *non*-Markan tradition even within the very verses of the story line said to depend on Mark (16, 22, 24); and (4) that we might have expected Luke to include something corresponding to Mk 6.3c 'and they took offence at him' (to ease the otherwise awkward passage from the seemingly positive reaction in Lk. 4.22 to Jesus' 'response' in 4.23) if he were writing with Mark in front of him, we are probably safest to assume that Luke had a parallel account to Mark of the preaching at Nazareth, and that he depended on that account largely, if not exclusively.[13] Whether that account already included vv. 23, 24ab and

any version of the New Testament would have altered the citation from the Old Testament'.

11.   See Chilton, 'Announcement', pp. 162-63.

12.   See Chilton, 'Announcement', pp. 165-66.

13.   With variations see e.g. Streeter, *Gospels*; B. Violet, 'Zum rechten Verständnis der Nazareth-Perikope', *ZNW* 37 (1938), pp. 251-71; Leaney, 50-54; Schürmann, 'Bericht', pp. 242-58 (and, by the same author, 'Nazareth-Perikope', pp. 187-205, and his commentary, 241-44, 158-59); Schramm, *Markus-Stoff*, p. 37; Marshall, 178-80; B. Chilton, 'Announcement', pp. 147-72; Seccombe, *Possesions*, pp. 45-46, Bock, *Proclamation*, pp. 106-107, 317 n. 59; Tuckett, 'Luke 4,16-30', pp. 343-54.

vv. 25-27 is less clear, but as Luke's own editing of transitions (e.g. at the beginning and ending of pericopes) tends to be relatively literary, the slight awkwardnesses in transition at 4.22, 23 and 4.24, 25-27 suggest these were already in his source, and he has passed over them.[14]

B. de Solages (*La composition des évangiles de Luc et de Matthieu et leurs sources* [Leiden: Brill, 1973], p. 84), A. Georges (*Pour lire l'évangile selon Saint Luc* [Paris: Cerf, 1973], p. 84) and Bock (*Proclamation*, p. 317 n. 59) have all argued Luke's account is a conflation of Mark with another major parallel source, but the influence of Mark (rather than of elements of tradition known to Mark) is unprovable.

14. He may not have found either 'seam' disturbing: others have found more-or-less convincing alternative explanations of them without needing to question the unity of the passage. (See Schreck, 'Nazareth Pericope', pp. 427-36, for a survey of explanations). My own reading of the first 'seam' is that the initial reaction of the crowd is positive (against J. Jeremias, *Jesus' Promise to the Nations* [London: SCM Press, 1958], p. 44) who takes the ἐμαρτύρουν αὐτῷ as a dative of disadvantage (they bore witness *against* him) and θαυμάζειν to express shock), but turns to doubt on the grounds that this local lad (= Jesus) could not fulfil the announced hopes (so the question in 4.22c—against B.J. Koet (*Five Studies in Interpretation of Scripture in Luke–Acts* [Leuven: Leuven University Press, 1989], pp. 40-41) who sees the whole of v. 22 as voicing positive reaction, and the proverb in 4.23 similarly. The proverb, however, is more probably an insulting challenge and the καί of 4.24 is then continuative, if not mildly adversative (see Nolland, 188-203, and his supporting articles; cf. Marshall, 186, and R.B. Sloan, *The Favorable Year of the Lord: A Study of Jubilary Theology in the Gospel of Luke* [Austin: Schola, 1977], pp. 83-89). The second major seam is detected at 4.24/25-26. Here the problem felt is the absence of any clear link between the proverb in 4.24 and the implicit theme of Gentile mission in vv. 25-26: so Anderson ('Horizons') calls the sermon at this point 'inchoate', and Leaney 'impossible' (52). But the problem here is exaggerated. As Fitzmyer (528) concedes, there *are* connections between 4.24 and 4.25-26. These latter verses speak of the blessing which accrued to individuals outside the πατρίς of Elijah (1 Kgs 17–18) and Elisha (2 Kgs 5) because these prophets at the time were not acceptable to their own people (Israel). *Mutatis mutandis*, if Jesus is unacceptable to his own hometown, it will not see God's blessing, but only hear of it coming to relative 'outsiders' (such as those at Capernaum; 4.23: cf. Brawley, *Luke–Acts*, pp. 23-26). Of course, Luke sees more in the story than that; but only at the level of secondary significance, and so there is no cause to speak of a problematic 'seam' here. We should be especially cautious about the oft-made claim that Luke's Jesus speaks paradigmatically of post-resurrection Jewish rejection of the Gospel and consequent 'Gentile mission' here (see Schreck, 'Nazareth Pericope', pp. 443-49, for a survey of the fierce battle on this issue). Siker's position, well captured in his title ('First to the Gentiles'), is quite unjustified: it is hard to see (as Schürmann, 237-38, admits) what the occasional blessing of two non-Israelites at a time of spiritual doldrums for Israel has to do with Gentile mission. Within the boundaries of his Gospel, the Nazareth scene prefigures rather the rejection of Jesus by the religious leaders, and the blessing of the 'outsider' 'sinners' and tax-collectors, within his ministry (cf. J.A. Sanders, 'From Isaiah 61 to

The provenance of the source is also a matter of keen dispute, but there are good reasons for thinking it came to him neither as a part of Schürmann's proposed 'Account of the Beginning',[15] nor from Q,[16] but from

Luke 4', in J. Neusner [ed.], *Christianity, Judaism and Other Greco-Roman Cults* [Leiden: Brill, 1975], pp. 98-104, esp. 101, who suggests that the point of the Elijah/Elisha parallel is that Jesus is claiming a jubilee year for those Israel considered to be outsiders to her religious hopes). Luke may have perceived such 'reversal' as in measure prefiguring the post-resurrection situation, but that is no reason for reading the church's history directly back into Lk. 4.25-27, and then using the resulting eisegesis as grounds for the complaint that Luke's sermon is anachronistic and inchoate! *Per contra* others have argued that 4.16-30 has a clear structural unity and makes quite reasonable sense as it stands (so especially J.A. Sanders and J. Bajard, 'La structure de la péricope de Nazareth en Lc. IV.16-30', *ETL* 45 [1969], pp. 165-71; and H.J.B. Combrink, 'The Structure and Significance of Luke 4.16-30', *Neot* 7 [1973], pp. 24-47). Sloan (*Year*, pp. 83-89) attributes all difficulties to Luke's telescoping or contraction of a longer account.

15. Schürmann's case ('Nazareth-Perikope', pp. 187-205) that Lk. 4.16-30 comes from a pre-Lukan source follows roughly the position above, with occasional differences of emphasis, viz. he argues that vv. 17-21 show traces of a pre-Lukan source in that (1) vv. 17-20 have a pronounced Palestinian flavour and are clearly basic to the rest of the pericope (*Lukasevangelium*, pp. 191-92); (2) Luke does not usually insert such extensive quotations into his sources, and, were it his own citation, it would conform much more to the fulfilment (cf. 7.31); (3) while Luke clearly understood the passage to refer to a messianic anointing (p. 193), the hand that first connected vv. 18-19 and 21 with 24 understood these to refer to a prophetic figure. Further, he makes a case for the view that the basic narrative in vv. 16, 22, 23b-24 (28-30) is not Markan, nor a development from it (pp. 195-200), and observes that if Luke is unlikely to have added 17-20, nor was it likely that he added 25-27 which contain material unusual for Luke (pp. 193-94) and go against his tendency in the Gospel to silence on the question of the Gentile mission (p. 194). Schürmann concludes by suggesting that the affinities with Q emphases suggest that Luke derived his account mainly therefrom: both Q and Mark depending on a more primitive 'Bericht vom Anfang' which he considers to lie behind the whole of Lk. 3.1–4.44. At three points, however, this thesis of a 'Bericht vom Anfang' must be challenged: (1) It is unlikely that such a 'Bericht' would include a forward reference to Capernaum (4.23—though it could be argued the original form of the story passed from 4.22 to 4.24; the adversative δέ with which the latter begins would then be more comprehensible); see Fitzmyer, 91 and 526-27. (2) J. Delobel ('La rédaction de Luc. IV, 14-16a et le "Bericht vom Anfang"', in Neirynck [ed.], *L'Evangile*, pp. 203-23) has demonstrated Lk. 4.14-16a to be Luke's editorial reworking of Markan material, not, as Schürmann maintained, evidence for a non-Markan source. The chain of the proposed 'Bericht vom Anfang' is thereby shattered (while allowing the pre-Lukan nature of some of its links). T. Schramm's analysis of Lk. 4.31-44 further suggests little room for confidence in Schürmann's hypothesis (*Markus-Stoff*, p. 90). (3) It is unlikely that such an account was in Q (see next note).

16. We should expect Matthew to exhibit much greater evidence of such a striking

Luke's other sources of tradition. With respect to the citation in 4.18-19, we may note it is fully integral to the story, that a citation is required by the (pre-Lukan) claim in 4.21 (cf. 4.17), and the citation form itself contains a strongly traditional feature. Accordingly Chilton claims, 'One can say not only probably but with a degree of certainty that this passage [i.e. the conflation of Isaiah 61.1-2 and 58.6] is a product neither of Luke's memory nor of his theology, but the voice of his tradition'.[17] It is to the text of the Isaiah citation which we now turn.

2. *The Citation of Isaiah 61.1-2 in Luke 4.18-19*

Isaiah	*Luke*
61.1 Πνεῦμα κυρίου ἐπ᾽ ἐμέ,	4.18 Πνεῦμα κυρίου ἐπ᾽ ἐμέ,
οὗ εἵνεκεν ἔχρισέν με·	οὗ εἵνεκεν ἔχρισέν με
εὐαγγελίσασθαι πτωχοῖς	εὐαγγελίσασθαι πτωχοῖς.
ἀπέσταλκέν με,	ἀπέσταλκέν με
ἰάσασθαι τοὺς συντετριμμένους τῇ καρδίᾳ	
κηρύξαι αἰχμαλώτοις ἄφεσιν	κηρύξαι αἰχμαλώτοις ἄφεσιν
καὶ τυφλοῖς ἀνάβλεψιν,	καὶ τυφλοῖς ἀνάβλεψιν,
[58.6 ἀπόστελλε	ἀποστεῖλαι τεθραυσμένους ἐν
τεθραυσμένους ἐν ἀφέσει].	ἀφέσει,
62.2 καλέσαι ἐνιαυτὸν κυρίου	4.19 κηρύξαι ἐνιαυτὸν κυρίου
δεκτόν καὶ ἡμέραν ἀνταποδόσεως.	δεκτόν.

The citation follows the LXX, rather than the MT, though with changes that may be summarised as follows:[18] (1) The words ἰάσασθαι τοὺς συντετριμμένους τῇ καρδίᾳ ('to heal the broken hearted') have been omitted from

tradition (so sympathetic to his emphasis on Jesus as the fulfilment of Old Testament hopes) were it indeed part of Q. Further, as Stanton points out ('Christology', pp. 33-34), it is not only Q that showed interest in Isa. 61 (cf. Acts 10.38); in any case if Q had contained the bulk of Lk. 4.16-30 early in its order, the pericope in Lk. 7.18-23 (which would follow almost immediately), with its indirect and enigmatic reply, would be somewhat hard to explain. I agree with Stanton (also Marshall, 178-81) that the material here must come from Luke's distinctive sources, not his shared ones. Criticizing Tuckett's defence of the passage as Q, see Schreck, 'Nazareth Pericope', pp. 414-20, and Turner, 'Spirit and Power', pp. 150-52.

17. 'Announcement', p. 164.

18. That Luke's source sides with LXX rather than MT is clear: 24 of his 26 words are identical to LXX; he has κυρίου in place of אדני יהוה; οὗ εἵνεκεν for יען; ἔχρισέν με for משח אתי and, most strikingly, τυφλοῖς ἀνάβλεψιν for לאסורים פקח־קוח (cf. France. *Jesus*, p. 252, who argues this translation is appropriate); cf. Rese, *Motive*, pp. 143-44.

Isa. 61.1.[19] (2) The line ἀποστεῖλαι[20] τεθραυσμένους ἐν ἀφέσει ('to set the oppressed at liberty') has been added to the end of the verse from LXX Isa. 58.6d. (3) In quoting Isa. 61.2, either Luke or his source has changed the opening word καλέσαι ('to announce') to κηρῦξαι ('to proclaim')[21] and (4) has omitted the words καὶ ἡμέραν ἀνταποδόσεως ('and the day of recompense of our God'). It is probable Luke also *read* the citation differently, putting the stop after πτωχοῖς rather than after μέ.[22]

We may represent Luke's citation as follows (curly brackets indicate an omission from Isa. 61.1-2; italicized words a minor verbal change, and underlined words an addition to the Isaiah citation):

> Lk. 4.18 The Spirit of the Lord is upon me,
> for he has anointed me
> to preach Good News to 'the poor'.
> He has sent me
> {to heal the broken hearted}
> to proclaim liberty to the captives
> and sight to the blind
> to set at liberty the oppressed (Isa. 58.6d)
> 4.19 and to *proclaim* the acceptable year of the Lord
> {and the day of vengeance of our God}.

19. The words are included in Luke's citation by A Δ Θ Ψ *pm* Ir and *MajT*, and treated as part of the text by Schürmann (226 and 229 n. 5), who argues that they prepare for v. 23b and may be echoed in 5.17. Bo Reicke ('Jesus in Nazareth—Lk 4,14-30', in H. Balz and S. Schulz [eds.], *Das Wort und die Wörter* [Stuttgart: Kohlhammer, 1973], pp. 48-49) has argued for the inclusion of the words on structural grounds, but no adequate explanation is forthcoming of why the textual tradition subsequently omitted the line. *Per contra* see Marshall, 182. When the words are omitted there is a simple chiastic structure, as noted by N.W. Lund, *Chiasmus in the New Testament* (Chapel Hill: University of North Carolina Press, 1942), pp. 236-38; L.C. Crockett, 'Old Testament', p. 179, J.N. Aletti, 'Jésus à Nazareth (Luc 4.16-30). Prophétie, écriture et typologie', in Aletti *et al.* (eds.), *A cause de l'évangile: Etudes sur les synoptiques et les Actes* (Paris: Cerf, 1985), p. 439, and Combrink, 'Structure', pp. 34-36.

20. The LXX of Isa. 58.6d reads ἀπόστελλε, but this change simply accommodates to the linguistic structure of Isa. 61.

21. France, *Jesus*, p. 243, sees this as evidence of Luke's siding with the MT against the LXX: Luke has translated both occasions of לקרא by κηρῦξαι departing from LXX Isa. 61.2. More probably Luke is simply repeating a Christian technical term.

22. With UBSGNT[3] and against Marshall, 183, and those he cites *ad loc.* Marshall argues from the parallel in 4.43 that εὐαγγελίσασθαι should be made to depend on ἀπέσταλκεν, not on ἔχρισεν. But probably more important for Luke is the consideration that Jesus is anointed *with* Spirit and power to act (Acts 10.38). Menzies (*Development*, p. 163 n. 3) argues (with Marshall) against this, but his own solution puts a second (fuller) stop after ἀπέλστακεν με, thus cutting this main verb off from its following dependant infinitives of purpose (κηρύξαι...ἀποστεῖλαι...κηρύξαι).

While we have argued that the Isaiah citation is integral to the pre-Lukan tradition, that does not exempt it from the possibility of some Lukan redactional activity. But are any of the changes to Isaiah here more likely to be attributable to Luke's redaction than to his source?

(1) It is hardly likely that Luke was first to finish the quotation short of the words 'and the day of vengeance of our God'; for the ministry of Jesus was never conceived in such a fashion. He took that 'change' from his source.

(2) Similarly it can barely be Luke who added the segment from Isa. 58.6, for reasons we have already advanced. The explanations offered for the alternative view (that Luke himself made the addition) are simply not sufficiently credible. Only one of these require mention (and perhaps only because it is so common).[23] According to this view, Luke has made the insertion of Isa. 58.6d because he understood the gift of the Spirit as 'the Spirit of prophecy'; that is, he knew that this was the 'power of preaching' (hence the change to κηρύξαι, 'to proclaim'), he knew the preaching concerned 'forgiveness of sins', and so he read the word ἄφεσις ('liberty') in Isa. 58.6d to mean (or at least to include) 'forgiveness' rather than the more literal types of release implied in the Old Testament context, and on that basis included it in the citation.[24]

This hypothesis cannot be sustained. It is perfectly true that elsewhere in Luke–Acts the word ἄφεσις is always connected with the forgiveness of sins. But Luke cannot himself have added Isa. 58.6d to the citation of 61.1-2 in order to further such a connection (e.g. to emphasize Jesus as the proclaimer of forgiveness of sins) for he must have been aware this was not the ordinary sense of ἄφεσις in Greek (its unmarked meaning was 'release', 'freedom', or the like), that it was not a LXX sense he was aware of either (it

---

23. Less credible if more ingenious is L.C. Crockett's thesis that Luke includes Isa. 58.6d as part of an extensive midrashic complex of ideas centred on the theme of the messianic banquet ('Old Testament', pp. 57-101, 277ff.). On the basis of the inclusion of Isa. 58.6d in the quotation, Crockett connects Isa. 58.7 ('share your bread with the hungry and bring the homeless poor into your house') with Isa. 61.6 (referring to 'eating the wealth of the nations'), the latter of which is construed as an allusion to the messianic feast. This is taken to mean that the anointed prophet is sent to announce the eschatological banquet at which will be included the poor, the blind, the sick and the mournful (p. 282). The point of contact between Luke's banquet midrash and the Nazareth pericope is the reference to Elijah (v. 25) who is fed by a Gentile to whom God leads him during a famine, and to Elisha who heals a Gentile in Israel. The themes of Jesus' ministry—eating, healing and forgiving—are thus all prefigured in the inaugurating sermon. Crockett has undoubtedly noted some important themes in Luke, but his central thesis is most unconvincing; the key texts on which it relies do not appear in Luke's citation, except (possibly) by association.

24. So Rese, *Motive*, pp. 145-46, 151; Tuckett, 'Luke 4,16-30', p. 348; Menzies, *Development*, pp. 171-73, and Kim, *Geisttaufe*, pp. 75-76.

was in fact never so used in the LXX; 40 of the 45 occasions pertain to literal remission from debt or release from oppressive conditions[25] and that ἄφεσις clearly could not carry the sense 'forgiveness of sins' in the immediate linguistic context of Isa. 58.6d or 61.1. Indeed, as a native Greek speaker he would have been aware that, in order for ἄφεσις to bear such a sense at all, it must be collocated with ἁμαρτιῶν (as it always is in Luke–Acts outside 4.18: cf. Lk. 1.77; 3.3; 24.47; Acts 2.38; 5.31; 10.43; 13.38; 26.18—which makes 4.18 'un-Lukan').[26] Collocated instead with αἰχμαλώτοις ('captives') as in Isa. 61.1, it could only mean the sort of 'freedom' or 'liberty' one grants to prisoners, and similarly, in the sentence ἀποστεῖλαι τεθραυσμένους ἐν ἀφέσει ('to set the oppressed at liberty') drawn from Isa. 58.6. In both cases ἄφεσις linguistically signifies that kind of 'release' that is offered to incarcerated or oppressed people—that is, liberation. In neither instance is the sense that of the idiom ἄφεσις ἁμαρτιῶν ('forgiveness of sins'), and it is unlikely a native Greek speaker would perceive any direct connection between the sort of 'release' envisaged in the Isaianic oracles and 'forgiveness of sins'—at least, not on the basis of the common word ἄφεσις.[27] The great majority of the LXX occurrences of the

---

25. Exceptions are Exod. 18.2 (scil. Moses 'releasing' Zipporah back to her father, i.e. sending her back!); 23.11 (ref. sabbatical laws that fields should be left at liberty, i.e. not farmed); Lev. 16.26 (of the scapegoat 'released' into the desert); Jdt. 11.14 (referring to 'permission' granted by elders) and Ezek. 47.3 (referring to water flowing out of the temple).

26. As Busse long ago pointed out (*Wunder*, p. 60). In every instance where ἄφεσις denotes forgiveness in the New Testament it is contextually qualified with ἁμαρτιῶν (or synonym). This applies even to those instances Abbott-Smith calls 'absolute': Mk 3.29; Heb. 9.12; 10.18a. In the first and last of these the semantic qualification is provided by the immediate cotext (Mk 3.28 and Heb. 10.18b); as for Heb. 9.12, it is the topical context which ensures no other sense of ἄφεσις could be meant (and so renders the collocation ἁμαρτιῶν redundant).

27. He or she would immediately distinguish the quite different expressions κηρύξαι αἰχμαλώτοις ἄφεσιν ('to preach liberty to the captives') and ἄφεσις ἁμαρτιῶν ('forgivness of sins') and would not relate them simply because they share the common polyseme ἄφεσις. For the semantics of this see Cotterell and Turner, *Linguistics*, ch. 5, especially pp. 135-39. We need not doubt that a New Testament writer might use the *whole clause* ἀποστεῖλαι τεθραυσμένους ἐν ἀφέσει ('to set the oppressed at liberty') metaphorically as a referring expression for forgiveness—if he viewed sin as an oppressive power from which humans needed release—but (i) it is notoriously the case that Luke does not present sin or sins as an enslaving power in the way Paul does (see especially J.-W. Taeger, *Der Mensch und sein Heil* [Gütersloh: Mohn, 1982]); (ii) he does not elsewhere use captivity or oppression metaphors in relationship to sin; and (iii) the semantic connection between the clause and its referent in such circumstances would in any case not be achieved through the lexeme ἄφεσις. We need not dispute that Luke thought the liberation Jesus brought included 'forgiveness

word ἄφεσις refer rather to various types of Jubilee 'liberation', whether to
the literal ordinances of the Jubilee legislation within Exodus, Leviticus,
Deuteronomy, Jeremiah and Ezekiel (34×), or release of Israel from oppression (whether exile, or other types of domination) echoing this same Jubilee
language (Isa. 58.6; 61.1; Dan. 12.7; cf. 1 Esd. 4.62; 1 Macc. 10.34; 13.34).
These latter (and Jewish restorationist hopes built on them) are the connotations that the inclusion of Isa. 58.6d would inevitably bring to Isa. 61.1-2,
which was already a well recognized Jubilee/New Exodus passage. Had
Luke wished to evoke the more specific (if theologically related) thought of
'release from sins' he could only have done so by adding the clarificatory
gloss ἁμαρτιῶν ('from sins') to the text from Isa. 58.6, or (as Seccombe
suggests) by turning to more suitable verses of Isaiah![28]

It follows from these last observations that whoever incorporated
Isa. 58.6 in Jesus' reading of Isa. 61.1, did so rather in order to stress the
theme of Jesus as the prophet–liberator, and possibly to clarify that he does
not merely announce messianic liberty (as the use of Isa. 61.1-2 alone might
suggest) but also *effects* it.[29] Luke, as we shall see, has an interest in such a
theme, but this interest is not so obvious as to suggest he himself made this
change, unmatched by his handling of the Old Testament anywhere else:[30] it
comes from his tradition.

(3) It is regularly held that Luke himself is responsible for dropping the
phrase 'to heal the broken hearted' from Isa. 61.1. Holtz, Rese, Haya-Prats
and Menzies all appeal to the same argument,[31] namely Schweizer's case
that for Luke the Spirit is the typically Jewish concept of 'the Spirit of
prophecy', and so the power of preaching rather than of healing miracles.
We have seen in Chapters 3 and 4, however, that Schweizer's premises are
simply incorrect. 'The Spirit of prophecy' in Judaism was not 'typically' the
power of preaching, and few Jews would have had a problem associating
the Spirit with works of power, especially in the case of a messianic figure.

---

of sins', but such a thought would find no support from the wording of Isa. 58.6d, and
cannot be used as an argument that Luke himself plucked out this unlikely verse and
transferred it to Jesus' citation in the hope that people would read it as a reference to
forgiveness.

28. Seccombe, *Possessions*, p. 47.

29. As I have argued earlier: e.g. 'Jesus', pp. 20-22.

30. Menzies contends that the addition of ἄφεσις here is part of a Lukan tendency
to repeat words in his texts (so explaining the incorporation of Isa. 58.6d as a repeat of
the ἄφεσις in Isa. 61.1: so *Development*, p. 173). This insight may well account for the
change from καλέσαι to κηρύξαι in Isa. 61.2, but hardly for the unparalleled
inclusion of a whole line from 58.6.

31. T. Holtz, *Untersuchungen über die alttestamentlichen Zitate bei Lukas* (Berlin:
Akademie Verlag, 1968), pp. 39-41; Rese, *Motive*, pp. 143-54; Haya-Prats, *L'Esprit*,
p. 40; and Menzies, *Development*, pp. 166-71.

But my real problem with such reasoning is that it is irrelevant to the issue at hand: the sort of 'healing' required by those who are 'broken-hearted' (συντετριμμένοι τῇ καρδίᾳ) is not literal bodily healing at all—*per contra*, for such as these the balm of Jesus' Spirit-anointed preaching of 'Good News' should have been considered especially appropriate! Menzies[32] tries to shore up Rese's case by arguing that for Luke ἰάομαι ('to heal') had become a technical term for *physical* healing, and so he had to excise it here in order to safeguard the Spirit as the Spirit of prophecy. But where has anyone who frequently uses a common word with its literal sense thereby become less able to distinguish (and less prone to use) its metaphorical senses? Luke must have been fully aware that no native speaker could possibly misunderstand ἰάσασθαι τοὺς συντετριμμένους τῇ καρδίᾳ as 'to (physically) heal the sick (who happen to be broken hearted [because of their illness?])' unless as a slightly mediocre joke, and indeed Luke himself plainly uses the verb metaphorically in Acts 28.27. That he also regularly uses ἰάομαι for physical healing is hardly germane to the question.[33] I assume physicians today regularly use 'to heal' and its cognates literally, but I find it quite unbelievable that any British or American doctor would as a consequence have difficulty in recognizing the metaphorical intent of the English phrase 'to heal the broken hearted'. Native language users do not make that sort of mistake. By the same token, the use of ἰάομαι in Isa. 61.1d cannot provide the motive for the deletion of the line containing it. It might be more convincing to argue the opposite case (with Busse and Goulder), namely that Luke deleted the line here because it plainly referred to merely metaphorical healing, and he intended to apply the Isaiah quotation to literal healing (cf. 7.21-22)![34]—but we should probably resist this too. It would be more plausible of his *source* (as we shall see) than of Luke himself.

(4) The only change that is plausibly attributed to Luke is the change from καλέσαι to κηρύξαι in Isa. 61.2: as Menzies points out, it might fit a Lukan pattern of reduplication of words in citations. But (as Bock notes) this change could as easily have taken place in the tradition, for it brings the citation more closely into line with the MT and with widespread Christian usage.[35]

---

32. *Development*, p. 158: *contra* Turner, 'Luke and the Spirit', pp. 60-67; *idem*, 'Jesus', pp. 16-17; Tuckett, 'Luke 4,16-30', p. 348.

33. In response to my criticism in 'Spirit and Power', p. 147, Menzies has reiterated this argument in his 'Spirit and Power', p. 17, but appears to have put much less weight on it.

34. Busse, *Wunder*, pp. 60-62, and Goulder, *Luke*, p. 302.

35. Bock, *Proclamation*, p. 106; cf. France, *Jesus*, p. 243.

Conclusion

The citation form in Lk. 4.18-19 belongs fundamentally to Luke's source, not to his own redactional activity. We must now turn to the 'message' of this pre-Lukan tradition, before asking what Luke made of it. Of course, if Luke's understanding of the passage were crystal clear we could avoid this step; but because this is not the case, a tradition-critical analysis may indicate how the community from which he derived his source understood this narrative. As I have indicated above, we should interpret Luke to stand in continuity with that understanding unless there are indications that he broke from it. In fact, as we shall see, the 'background' concerned provides vital clues to how Luke understood the passage.

3. *The Spirit-Anointed Prophet-Liberator of the Pre-Lukan Tradition in Luke 4.18-27*

We do not need to look far for the sort of background that provides the key to this text. The unprecedented embedding of Isa. 58.6d within the citation of Isa. 61.1-2, and the consequent double reference to the Jubilee language of ἄφεσις/release immediately focuses the theme of 'liberation' within the broader context of Jewish eschatological Jubilee and New Exodus hopes. Already Isa. 61.1-2 had taken up both the technical Jubilee language 'to proclaim liberty' and its associated imagery from Leviticus 25 and had re-used it as a metaphor for Israel's release from the oppressive slavery of 'exile' into which she had sold herself by her disobedience. According to the implied speaker, God had now anointed him to announce Israel's Jubilee year, that is her release from the oppressive conditions that beset her, and 'restoration' in the land. Various sectors of ITP Judaism took this hope up in a new eschatological and messianic garb,[36] and it is these hopes that form the background to Jesus' preaching.

Interest has understandably focused to a certain extent on 11QMelchizedek, which affords a fascinating parallel in its use of Isaiah 61.[37] This fragment takes up a more widespread hope in Judaism that Yahweh would soon introduce a messianic Jubilee:[38] the end-time redemptive period of release from oppression, cosmic and political alike. It offers a pesher treatment of Lev. 25.9-13, Deut. 15.2, Isa. 52.7, and Pss. 82.1-2 and

---

36. For brief surveys of the background see A. Strobel, 'Die Ausrufung des Jobeljahres in der Nazarethpredigt Jesu; zur apokalyptischen Tradition Lc 4 16-30', in W. Eltester (ed.), *Jesus in Nazareth* (Berlin: de Gruyter, 1972), pp. 42-50.

37. For other uses of Isa. 61 in Judaism see Sanders, 'From Isaiah 61', pp. 47-60.

38. For the Old Testament background of this concept see Sloan, *Year*, pp. 4-27. For Isa. 61 as already a 'midrash' of Lev. 25 and Isa. 42.7 see Sanders, 'From Isaiah 61', p. 91 n. 50.

7.8-9, all telescoped within the organizing framework of Isa. 61.1-2.[39] The writer concludes that an exalted figure (probably 'Melchizedek')[40] will appear in the tenth Jubilee (lines 7-9),[41] to 'proclaim liberty'[42] to those who are 'captives' (lines 4-6); to atone for their iniquities (lines 6[?] and 8), and to execute God's judgment on the hosts of Belial (lines 9, 11-15, 20). All of this may be described as 'the year of good favour for Melchizedek' (line 9); alternatively as Zion's announced salvation (lines 15-16, 23-24); the reign of her Elohim (cf. Isa. 52.7).

The use of Isa. 52.7 introduces the figure of a herald of good tidings (מבשר; lines 16, 18),[43] who, according to the reconstructed text of lines 18-19, is 'the Anointed by the Spirit' to bring good news of Zion's salvation.[44] If

39. See A. Van der Woude, 'Melchizedek als himmlische Erlösergestalt in den neugefundenen eschatologischen Midraschim aus Qumran Höhle XI', *OTS* 14 (1965) pp. 354-73, and M. de Jonge and A.S. Van der Woude, '11Q Melchizedek and the New Testament', *NTS* 12 (1965–66), pp. 301-26, which slightly revises the *editio princeps*. It was M. Miller ('The Function of Isa 61.1-2 in 11Q Melchizedek', *JBL* 88 [1969], pp. 467-69) who first argued that Isa. 61.1-2 provides the controlling framework, and while J.A. Fitzmyer ('Further Light on Melchizedek from Qumran Cave 11', *JBL* 86 [1967], 25-41, p. 29), and B. Chilton and C.A. Evans ('Jesus and Israel's Scriptures', in Chilton and Evans (eds.), *Studying the Historical Jesus* [Leiden: Brill, 1994], p. 323) think Lev. 25 provides the structural arrangement, they do not deny the importance of Isa. 61.1-2 in the arrangement, with allusions at lines 4, 6, 9, 13, 14, 18, 19 and 20.

40. Or someone who enjoys 'the heritage of Melchizedek': cf. Fitzmyer, 'Light', pp. 30-33.

41. For the basis of the calculation of the jubilee years at Qumran and elsewhere in Judaism see Strobel, 'Ausrufung', pp. 41-50. The years 26/27 (the beginning of the tenth Jubilee) or c. 68 CE (some ten years before the end of the tenth Jubilee) were apparently particularly associated with expectation of the messiah's appearance; but 11Q Melchizedek could not have attached much hope to the first of these dates if, as is generally assumed, it was written c. 50 CE (see F.L. Horton, *The Melchizedek Tradition* [Cambridge: Cambridge University Press, 1976], pp. 80-82).

42. I assume that the subject of the verbs in line 6 is Melchizedek, reconstructing this name at the end of line 5, and agreeing with Fitzmyer ('Light', p. 34) against de Jonge and van der Woude ('11Q Melchizedek', p. 306) that the herald of lines 16, 18-20 is not yet clearly in view.

43. For a brief account of the tradition history of the concept of the 'herald' in Judaism see Dupont, *Béatitudes*, II, pp. 124ff.; P. Stuhlmacher, *Das paulinische Evangelium: 1 Vorgeschichte* (Göttingen: Vandenhoeck & Ruprecht, 1968) pp. 142-52.

44. The *editio princeps* (van der Woude, 'Melchizedek', pp. 360-66) had read והמבשר הו[אה המ[שׁי]ח היא[ה] ('And he that brings good tidings: that is the Anointed one [about] whom...'), but this was corrected by the author and de Jonge ('11Q Melchizedek', pp. 301 and 306ff.), following Y. Yadin, 'A Note on Melchizedek and Qumran', *IEJ* 15 (1965), pp. 152-54, to read אשר [ה]הרוח מ[אה הו]ן המבשׁרוהמבשר... ('And he that bringeth good tidings: that is the Anointed by the Spirit...whom'). This is

this reconstruction is correct (as seems probable) it means the 'herald' of Isa. 52.7, who brings good news of Zion's salvation, was identified as 'the messiah' (specifically with the 'anointed prince' of Dan. 9.25 if Fitzmyer, Horton, Vermes and others are right to reconstruct the end of line 18 to read 'that is the Anointed...about whom Daniel says...').[45] The 'middle term' facilitating this identification is Isa. 61.1-2, for once the 'good tidings' of Zion's salvation (Isa. 52.7) is interpreted as the Jubilee proclamation of liberty to her (as in lines 5-9) in the language of Isa. 61.1-2, then the same passage provides the Spirit-anointed figure that will accomplish the task. In addition, this same figure appears to be identified with 'Melchizedek' who is the probable subject of the actions in lines 5-6.[46] Here, then, we would appear to have a fusion of prophetic, priestly, herald, servant and royal messianic ideas in one who is anointed with the Spirit in order that he might effectively 'proclaim liberty' to the afflicted captives of Belial and so 'set them free' (line 6). Within the context of this midrash, the Spirit is an empowering both to declare and to effect this liberation, so bringing about the state in which 'your Elohim reigns' (lines 16, 24-25 quoting Isa. 52.7 but in reference to 'Melchizedek' as God's vice regent) over a restored Israel.

While there is no suggestion that the pre-Lukan tradition in 4.18-21 is dependent on 11QMelchizedek as such,[47] and 4Q is revealing other messianic texts in which Isaiah 61 plays a notable role (especially 4Q521 and 4Q434), the important conceptual similarities should be evident. The composite Isaianic messianiology based in Isa. 61.1-2 (leaving aside the connection with Melchizedek), the eschatological programme of this figure, the

accepted by Stuhlmacher, *Evangelium*, p. 145; G. Vermes, *The Dead Sea Scrolls in English* (Sheffield: JSOT Press, 3rd edn, 1987), p. 301; and Horton, *Melchizedek* (against J.A. Fitzmyer, 'Light', p. 27); though see D. Aune, 'A Note on Jesus' Messianic Conciousness, and 11Q Melchizedek', *EvQ* 45 (1973), p. 164.

45. Though note, N.A. Dahl thinks the reference is to the expected Prophet-like-Moses: see 'Messianic Ideas and the Crucifixion of Jesus', in Charlesworth (ed.), *Messiah*, pp. 382-403, esp. pp. 386-87.

46. The text is taken this way by Fitzmyer, 'Light', p. 40; Sanders, 'From Isaiah 61', p. 91; Strauss, *Messiah*, p. 205; Chilton and Evans, *Jesus*, pp. 322-24; and Aune, 'Messianic Consciousness', pp. 161-65. The identification is a little unsure because of the fragmentary state of the text (and opposed by de Jonge and van der Woude, and Horton). The fact that Isa. 61.1-2 is so important to the framework throughout the passage supports the identification, a point overlooked by Horton (*Melchizedek*, p. 78), who argues the herald of lines 16 and 18 precedes Melchizedek, and (by the Spirit of prophecy) announces his imminent advent (so also, with added arguments, Turner, 'Luke and the Spirit', pp. 68-69). But the relation of the messiah, the Spirit, and fulfilment of Isa. 61 in 4Q521 now suggests the identification was right after all.

47. See Shin, *Ausrufung*, pp. 182-83.

focus on his liberation of 'Israel' announced in the Jubilee terminology also drawn from Isa. 61.1-2 (and understood as the manifestation of God's reign), and the connection of this text with other associated Jubilee texts, are all suggestive as much for the shape of Jesus' ministry as a whole as for the pre-Lukan tradition in 4.18-21. This is not to suggest the historical Jesus pronounced a literal Jubilee,[48] but that he too used Isa. 61.1-2 as a significant theological symbol (alongside that more dominant but complementary symbol, 'the kingdom of God') with which to articulate and explain important aspects of his mission to Israel.[49] The memory of this was preserved in the tradition, especially by Q, and most explicitly in relation to Jesus' beatitudes and in his understanding of the import of his miracles.

With respect to the first of these, it is widely recognized that the oldest strand of the beatitudes (which articulate the symbolic world from which flows Jesus' ethical teaching) is strongly shaped by Isaiah 61.[50] The terminology of these sayings reflects the Isaianic prophecy that God will bring *good news* of his liberating reign *to the poor* (that is, oppressed Israel: Isa. 61.1 // Mt. 5.3 cf. Lk. 6.20 + 24); that those who *mourn* for Zion will be *comforted* and *filled* with gladness and rejoicing (Isa. 61.2-3 // Mt. 5.4 cf. Lk. 6.21b + 25b), and that the *hungry* shall soon eat the wealth of the (oppressing) nations (61.6 // Lk. 6.21a + 25a cf. Mt. 5.6).

Jesus' understanding of the significance of his miracles too is couched in terms of Isaiah 61 in Lk. 7.18-22 // Mt. 11.2-4. These liberating miracles (including the specific mention of 'the blind now see again' = LXX Isa. 61.1e) are summed up in the words of Isa. 61.1b 'good news is preached to "the poor"' (Lk. 7.22), which suggests that those afflicted with disease are seen to epitomize oppressed Israel in her need of Jubilee release, and that the healings are to be perceived as a vivid symbol (and a concrete part) of

48. This was suggested in different forms by A. Trocmé, *Jésus-Christ et la révolution non-violente* (Geneva: Labor et Fides, 1961), and J.H. Yoder, *The Politics of Jesus* (Grand Rapids: Eerdmans, 1972). Against it, see Sloan, *Year*, pp. 166-94, Seccombe, *Possessions*, pp. 54-56, and Kimball, *Exposition*, pp. 103-104.

49. On Jesus' use of Isa. 61 see Dunn, *Jesus*, pp. 53-62. While Dunn emphasizes the significance of Isa. 61 for Jesus' own understanding, he unfortunately assigns the citation of Isa. 61.1-2 in Lk. 4.18-19 to Lukan composition on the ground that 'the *unprompted and open* claim to messianic significance at the *beginning* of Jesus' ministry is too far removed from what we know of the historical Jesus from the Synoptics themselves, and too similar to the unhistorical roll-call of christological titles in the first chapter of John's gospel to permit a contrary judgement' (p. 54). But this was not the beginning of Jesus' ministry, and it involves implicit christological claims (not open and explicit ones, far less titles). For criticism of Dunn's statement see Sloan, *Year*, pp. 77-83.

50. Davies and Allison, *Matthew*, pp. 431-42; Guelich, *Sermon*, ch. 1; Seccombe, *Possessions*, pp. 83-92. See Chapter 8 n. 11 above.

Israel's promised liberation and restoration. It has long been noted that the list of healings here is by no means arbitrary, but in addition to Isa. 61.1 also closely echoes the wording of LXX Isa. 29.18-19 and especially 35.5-6. Both of these (with Isa. 61.1-2 itself) belong to a collection of 'New Exodus' passages about the restoration of Israel and transformation in the wilderness (and so pointedly correspond to John's expectation of salvation starting with the wilderness: cf. Mk 1.2-3 and pars.) and show the broader complex of ideas in which the more specifically Jubilee language of Isaiah 61 found its place. Of the list of miracles, two have seemed out of place in this New Exodus nexus, namely 'lepers are cleansed' and 'the dead are raised' (though cf. LXX Isa. 26.19). But that the latter of these was also expected to characterise the messianic fulfilment of Isaiah 61 has now been demonstrated by 4Q521, where we are told

> [8] He shall release the captives, make the blind see, raise up the do[wntrodden]...
> [12] then He will heal the sick, resurrect the dead, and to the meek announce glad tidings.[51]

For Q, then, it would appear the Spirit on Jesus was the power to effect Israel's messianic release and transformation, through his preaching and teaching which challenged Israel to participate in the restoration God's reign was inaugurating, but also through his powerfully effective proclamation of liberty to the sick and the demonised.

Lk. 4.18-27 did not come from Q, but it is hard to believe that it came from a substantially different conceptual world.[52] Within such a context the differences from the LXX and MT are relatively easy to explain. The place of

---

51. See Chapter 4 above for the claim the subject of these actions is the messiah of the Spirit or, at least, God through him.

52. For Strobel ('Ausrufung', pp. 38-50) this was a source which reflected the calendrical conviction that the eschatological Jubilee coincided with Jesus' announcement. He sees traces of a Jubilee understanding throughout the passage: (a) the setting of the account—Jesus' return to his hometown—is said to chime with the Jubilee injunction (Lev. 25.10 LXX) καὶ ἕκαστος εἰς τὴν πατρίδα αὐτοῦ ἀπελεύσεσθε; (b) the stress on fulfilment of the prophecy 'today' (σήμερον; v. 21) corresponds on the one hand to such notices as Mk 1.15 (πεπλήρωται ὁ καιρός), and on the other to the common expectation that with 26/27 CE the last Jubilee period would dawn: the messiah being expected to appear either at the beginning of it or one week of years from its end; (c) the extension of the punishing famine from three years (as in 1 Kgs 17.1) to three and a half years (Lk. 4.25; thus, half a week of years) is said to demonstrate that the passage has been handled by those who were familiar with apocalyptic chronological calculations. None of these is especially convincing, and on the chronological difficulties associated with Strobel's theory that Jesus' ministry commenced in 26 CE see Marshall, 184 and 133. But even if Strobel were right, the affinity of such a tradition with the understanding of Jesus and the Spirit in Q would be clear.

Isa. 58.6 within the citation was assured in the tradition not simply because Jesus was believed to have brought the passages together, nor simply because of the catchword ἄφεσις in the LXX of the two passages,[53] but more especially because Isa. 58.6 belonged *thematically* to the Sabbath/Jubilee and New Exodus hopes,[54] and because the inclusion of 58.6d most sharply brought to focus the messianic Jubilee significance of the passage—that is, the repetition of the word ἄφεσις which this addition afforded inevitably made (Jubilee) 'liberation' of captive/oppressed Israel the conceptual centrepiece of the Good News to be proclaimed. For the community that circulated the tradition (as in Q) that 'liberation' was seen most dramatically to be expressed in Jesus' mighty *works* (hence the challenge in 4.23, and the response in terms of the conditions for such manifestations in 4.26-27). The association with Jesus' mighty works would have been especially apparent once ever the LXX had been adopted, for sandwiched between the statements about release of captives and setting the oppressed free would have appeared the words '(to proclaim) sight to the blind'. The dropping of Isa. 61.1c 'to heal the broken hearted' may have been due either to the desire to focus this association with Jesus' mighty works, or to give greater discourse prominence to the two affirmations concerning Jesus' mission to bring ἄφεσις, or for a combination of these two reasons.

In sum, the tradition Luke used for his programmatic sermon understood the Spirit upon Jesus in terms of contemporary (Jewish and Christian) messianic interpretations of Isa. 61.1-2, and so as the power of God through which he proclaimed Israel's New Exodus release from captivity to Belial, and effected it, especially (but not exclusively) in works of deliverance from sickness and demonic affliction. A more precise christological and soteriological picture is difficult without a further cotext and context. The passage itself certainly highlights prophetic motifs—most clearly in Jesus' saying

53. *Contra* Kimball, *Exposition*, pp. 106-107, who has then to argue Jesus preached in Greek (p. 108). While Jesus may have done so occasionally (see e.g. S. Porter, 'Jesus and the Use of Greek in Galilee', in B. Chilton and C.A. Evans [eds.], *Studying the Historical Jesus* [Leiden: Brill, 1994], pp. 123-54), it is least likely he did so in Nazareth, and the tradition bears the marks of a Semitic origin. The LXX wording was no doubt seen as providential, but there are in any case sufficient other verbal links to sustain the midrash (see Seccombe, *Possessions*, pp. 46-52; Bock, *Proclamation*, pp. 106-107), given the thematic link, and the evident partial synonymy between the דרור ('release') of Isa. 61.1 and חפש ('released') of 58.6d.

54. Cf. Sloan, *Year*, p. 40, based on M. Tannenbaum, 'Holy Year 1975 and its Origins in the Jewish Jubilee Year', *Jubilaeum* 7 (1974), pp. 63-79. Compare also C. Westermann, *ad loc.*, and P. Miller, 'Luke 4.16-21', *Int* 29 (1975), pp. 418-19, on the connection of Isa. 61.1-2 and Isa. 58.6: both scholars are quoted by Sloan.

that a prophet is not acceptable in his own hometown (4.24) and in the comparison with Elijah and Elisha (4.25-27), but also in the attempt to exe-cute Jesus (4.28-30; the fate of a false-prophet). And at least in some Jewish circles the implicit speaker of the Isaianic oracle was indeed a prophetic figure: hence the Targum translation, 'The prophet said, A spirit of prophecy before the LORD God is upon me, because the LORD has exalted me to announce good tidings...' But it will have been clear from the Jubilee nuances of the passage, and from the description of the task as not merely to proclaim but also to effect the liberation, that if this is a prophet, it is a mes-sianic prophetic figure (that is, an eschatological leader prophet). It is thus possible (given the New Exodus connections) that the tradition presented Jesus as a hoped-for 'prophet like Moses' based on Deut. 18.15-19 (cf. 1 Macc. 4.46; 14.41; *T. Benj.* 9.2; 1QS 9.10-11; 4QTest [= 4Q175]),[55] but this is uncertain and we are perhaps safer simply to speak of Jesus here as an Isaianic soteriological prophet (based in a mixture of servant and other traits).[56] It is to the Lukan understanding of the passage which we now turn.

---

55. See also Josephus, *Ant.* 2.286, 327; 20.97-99, 167-68, 188; *War* 2.261-63 for messianic pretenders emulating Moses and promising salvation beginning in the wilderness. For this hope in Judaism and earliest Christianity see the classical study of H.M. Teeple, *The Mosaic Eschatological Prophet* (Philadelphia: SBL, 1957), chs. 2–5, but also especially E. Fascher, ΠΡΟΦΗΤΗΣ (Giessen: Töpelmann, 1927); R. Meyer, *Der Prophet aus Galiläa* (Darmstadt: Wissenschaftliche Buchgesellschaft, 1970 [1940]); J. Jeremias, 'προφήτης, κτλ' *TDNT*, VI, pp. 781-861; Fuller, *Christology*, pp. 46-53; Hahn, *Titles*, pp. 352-406; W.A. Meeks, *The Prophet King: Moses Traditions and the Johannine Christology* (Leiden: Brill, 1967); J. Coppens, *Le messianisme et sa relève prophétique* (Gembloux: Duculot, 1974), pp. 172-80; and Allison, *Moses*, pp. 73-84. See, however, the cautions of R.A. Horsley, '"Like One of the Prophets of Old": Two Types of Popular Prophets at the Time of Jesus', *CBQ* 47 (1985), pp. 441-43. In my view he understates the expectation of a prophet-like-Moses because he sep-arates the evidence for this from that concerning 'prophets who led movements' (which were often typologically Mosaic/Exodus liberators; see Horsley, 'Like One of the Prophets', pp. 454-61); and he separates both from John the Baptist and Jesus by treating them as 'oracular prophets' when they better fit the category 'prophets who led movements'.

56. Compare G. Nebe, *Prophetische Züge im Bilde Jesus bei Lukas* (Stuttgart: Kohlhammer, 1989), p. 68. We may use the alternative term 'Servant-Liberator' for this figure providing it is recognized that he is not called 'Servant', but that his mission shares striking similarities with the Servant oracles of Isa. 42 and 49, leading expositors to speak of Isa. 61.1ff. as 'another servant song, a midrash on the servant idea, or the prophet (identified as Trito-Isaiah) taking on the role of the servant for himself, or for his community' (Strauss, *Messiah*, pp. 239-40).

4. *The Significance of Jesus' Citation of Isaiah for Luke*

While we are primarily concerned with the pneumatology of the passage, it will be recognized that this cannot be severed from the question of the identity and envisaged mission of the figure portrayed. If the Spirit is the power of Jesus' mission, then how he can be anticipated to experience the Spirit will evidently depend on the nature of the mission he is therewith empowered to undertake, and on the figure he is thereby to 'be' to Israel. One endowed to act as a prophet to bring God's word to Israel can be anticipated to receive an 'endowment of the Spirit' quite different in character and enabling from that envisaged on, say, Kenaz as a liberator of Israel, 'clothed with Spirit of power', and falling upon the Amorites with his magical sword (as in *Bib. Ant.* 27.9-10). Of course, those are extreme cases. The choices that lie before us with respect to Jesus' use of Isaiah 58, 61 and how Luke has understood it involve rather subtler differences—but they are not without consequence. A stress on the Isaianic figure here as the Davidic messiah might be expected to dissociate the Spirit from Jesus' miracles of exorcism and healing, and to emphasize rather the Spirit as source of his righteous restorative rule, wise judgment and power to deal with opposition. By contrast, an identification with the Mosaic prophet might enhance the connection of the Spirit with liberating miracles, and emphasize the Spirit's role as the power of Jesus' revelation and teaching. The first section of this study will discuss the Christological focus of the passage. Next we shall turn to more 'soteriological' or missiological questions. Finally, we shall examine the implications of the first two sections for an understanding of Jesus' mighty works and their relation to the Spirit.

4.1. *The Christological Focus*

As is well known, this passage provokes something of a christological mêlée among the interpreters, with different parties contending that Luke presents Jesus as 'anointed' as a prophet, as the eschatological prophet (whether Elijianic or Mosaic), as the (Davidic) messiah, as a priestly messiah, as the servant of the Lord, or as some combination of two or more of these.[57] A measure of confusion arises from the failure adequately to distinguish two questions: (1) 'what sort of figure do the specific traits of the description in 4.18-27 combine to suggest?', and (2) 'how does information elsewhere in Luke–Acts bear on the picture that emerges?' Both questions have their place, but each in its turn. Thus a consideration of the first question should put the (Davidic) messiah very much into the background: in 4.18-27, rather,

---

57. See Schreck, 'Nazareth Pericope', pp. 439-43; Kimball, *Exposition*, pp. 111-12; and Strauss, *Messiah*, pp. 226-27 for the 'lists' of contenders.

for the reasons we have indicated above (§3), it is Jesus' role as the Isaianic soteriological prophet that dominates the conceptual foreground.

Once the centrality of the Isaianic prophet is established, we may then press the second question, by asking in what ways Luke's writing uses, clarifies and extends (or even subverts) this identification.

(1) We may begin by observing that as Isaiah (LXX) was part of Luke's canon-within-the-canon[58] we need hardly doubt that he saw 4.18-19 as closely connected with the baptismal identification of Jesus as the Spirit-endowed servant of Isaiah 42 (Lk. 3.22). From the perspective of a first-century reader with what we may broadly call 'messianic' interests, the two Isaianic passages would stand thematically shoulder-to-shoulder: both speak of a liberating Spirit-endowed servant/prophet who brings release to captive Israel and opens the eyes of the blind (Isa. 42.6-7//LXX Isa. 61.1 and cf. Lk. 2.32).[59] The rest of Luke–Acts, however, evinces a rather modest 'servant' Christology compared with the prominence the use of Isaiah 42 and 61 in Luke's opening pictures of Jesus might suggest. With the exception of Acts 10.38, Luke focuses more on Isa. 52.12–53.13 or on the more general uses of the servant language.[60] It is almost as though the servant/prophet of Isaiah 42 and 61 has passed the baton on to some other christological figure.

(2) If Luke–Acts places restrained emphasis on Jesus as the Isaianic servant, the same cannot be said of his picture of Jesus as 'prophet'.[61] But

---

58. See J.A. Sanders, 'Luke and Isaiah', in Evans and Sanders, *Luke*, pp. 14-25.

59. See Chilton, 'Announcement', pp. 166-67, and Strauss, *Messiah*, pp. 239-44.

60. For the theme of Jesus as 'Servant' in Luke–Acts, see D.L. Jones, 'The Title *Pais* in Luke–Acts', in K.H. Richards (ed.), *Society of Biblical Literature 1982 Seminar Papers* (Chico, CA: Scholars Press, 1982), pp. 217-26, who in my view plays down the deutero-Isaianic contribution, and A.M. Leske, 'The Influence of Isaiah 40–66 on Christology in Matthew and Luke: A Comparison', in E.H. Lovering (ed.), *Society of Biblical Literature 1994 Seminar Papers* (Atlanta: Scholars Press, 1994), pp. 897-916, who errs in the opposite direction. For Acts see epecially E. Kränkl, *Jesus der Knecht Gottes* (Regensburg: Pustet, 1972).

61. Space does not permit me to enter into detail, in any case the basic material has been set out all too often: cf. Marshall, *Luke*, pp. 124-28; F. Schnider, *Jesus der Prophet* (Freiburg: Universitätsverlag, 1973), ch. 4.; T.R. Carruth, 'The Jesus-as-Prophet Motif' (PhD dissertation, Baylor University, 1973); E. Franklin, *Christ the Lord* (London: SPCK, 1975), pp. 67-69; Minear, *Heal*, ch. 5; Busse, *Wunder, passim*; D.P. Moessner, 'Luke 9.1-50: Luke's Preview of the Journey of the Prophet Like Moses of Deuteronomy', *JBL* 102 (1983), pp. 575-605; P.F. Feiler, 'Jesus the Prophet: The Lukan Portrayal of Jesus as the Prophet Like Moses' (PhD dissertation, Princeton Theological Seminary, 1986); D.P. Moessner, *Lord of the Banquet: The Literary and Theological Significance of the Lukan Travel Narrative* (Minneapolis: Fortress Press, 1989), Nebe, *Züge* and (with a radical new look), Davies, *Jesus*, chs. 3–4 and 10–11.

what are we to make of this figure? Luke, unlike Simon the Pharisee (7.39), certainly does not regard Jesus merely as one of the prophets, nor even (as the crowds think) a *great* prophet (7.16), one come back from the past with resurrection power (9.8, 19). For him, John the Baptist was the last and greatest in that line (7.26, 28), but now a new phase has dawned in which the kingdom is proclaimed (16.16; cf. 7.28; 10.23-24) and seen to be present in some power (11.20, cf. 10.9, 11). Luke's eschatology thus suggests he understands Jesus as *the messianic prophet*,[62] which for him means not Elijah (who is never a messianic figure in Luke, who would not be at home in the New Exodus tradition, and who is not even mentioned in Acts),[63] but

---

62. *Contra* Franklin (*Christ*, pp. 67-69), who, in the interest of his thesis that (for Luke) the ascension is the cardinal eschatological event, states that Luke knew the traditions in which Jesus was understood as the eschatological prophet, but played them down. According to Franklin, Luke preferred instead to describe Jesus as 'a prophetic person whose history is bound up with the Old Testament prophets, who is one with them, whose person is described as being like theirs and who represents the climax of God's continuing saving activity through them' (p. 67). There is an element of truth here: for Luke, Jesus is one with the prophets of old in so far as they too were God's spokesmen, adamantly rejected by Israel, and even suffering death at her hands (4.24, 25-27; 13.33; Acts 7.51-52). But this (as we shall see) is hardly the whole story.

63. We need to distinguish three types of use of Elijah material in 'messianic' contexts: (1) There was Jewish tradition based on Mal. 3.24 (LXX, 3.22; EVV, 4.5) which looked to Elijah as 'the coming one' who would 'restore' Israel in repentance ready for God's own advent at the day of the Lord (so Sir. 48.9-10, and possibly 4Q521). In this case Elijah might himself be called a messianic figure (for discussion of such traditions see Teeple, *Prophet*, pp. 4-10, and especially Collins, 'Works of the Messiah', pp. 102-106, but there is little sure evidence that Luke knew such hopes, and he nowhere explicitly identifies Jesus as the Elijah to come—at most one might speak of possible Elijah-messiah overtones in his sources (most plausibly at Acts 3.21 in the mention of χρόνων ἀποκαταστάσεως ['times of restoration']: see R.H. Zehnle, *Peter's Pentecost Discourse* [New York: Abingdon Press, 1971], p. 91, for this view; but *per contra*, Haenchen, 211. Sloan [*Year*] notes the probable 'jubilee' overtones). (2) Later in Judaism, Mal. 3.24 (EVV 4.5) was harmonized with hopes which expected some other messianic figure to play the decisive role: Elijah then simply prepares for the end-time figure. This view has not yet been demonstrated in pre-Christian Judaism, but it was certainly Mark's view (and Matthew's) of John the Baptist (cf. especially Mk 9.11-13). This is the role that Luke attributes to the Baptist at 1.17, 76 and 7.27 (*pace* Wink, *John*, pp. 44-45, who claims, 'it is, of course, only because John is *not* Elijah that Luke is free to develop the exegetical analogy between Elijah and *Jesus*' [my italics]): see Fitzmyer, *Luke*, pp. 96-99 and 102-10. For obvious reasons Luke could not follow *Targ. Ps-J.* Num. 25.12 in identifying the figure in Isa. 61.1-3 with Elijah, the forerunner of the messiah! (3) Elijah may be used as an example of the man of God, or aspects of his prophetic career may be used typologically, without any attempt formally to identify Elijah with the antitypical figure(s). This appears to be how Luke uses Elijah material with respect to Jesus, and within this framework he is also free

the prophet-like-Moses.[64] Not only does Luke explicitly identify Jesus with the promised prophet-like-Moses at Acts 3.22-23 (cf. 7.37), thereby laying something of a foundation-stone for his ecclesiology,[65] but his picture of

to develop an exegetical analogy between *Elisha* and Jesus, as well as one between Elijah and John. In the former case, the Elijah motif is connected primarily with Jesus' miracles (though in these he transcends Elijah's; compare 1 Kgs 17 with Lk. 7.11-17, where there is no beseeching of God in prayer and no prostration over the corpse, just a touch and a command), with his rejection and death (on which see A. Denaux, 'Le hypocrisie des pharisiens et le dessein de dieu. Analyse de Lc., XIII, 31-33', in F. Neirynck [ed.], *L'Evangile de Luc—The Gospel of Luke* [Leuven: Leuven University Press, 1989], pp. 155-95, 316-23, 192ff.; Hahn, *Titles*, p. 361), and, in a qualified way, with his ascension (though this is better explained in terms of other motifs, possibly even Moses' alleged ascension: see G. Lohfink, *Die Himmelfahrt Jesu* [Munich: Kösel, 1971], ch. 4 and Chapter 10 below). For other similarities between Jesus and Elijah see M. Miyoshi, *Der Anfang des Reiseberichts* (Rome: Pontifical Biblical Institute, 1974), ch. 1; Lampe, 'Spirit', pp. 176-77; and Mainville, *L'Esprit*, pp. 222-27. But Wink, who has done as much as anyone to highlight the possible parallels between Elijah and Jesus, concludes 'this "Elijah midrash" is, however, only at best a secondary motif in Luke's Gospel. It is merely one of several minor themes originating out of the desire to assimilate all exalted titles to Jesus Christ' (*John*, p. 45)—and even this may go too far, for 'Elijah' is never applied to Jesus as a title in Luke–Acts, nor is there a transparent Elijah Christology in the speeches of Acts.

64. This identification of the figure in Lk. 4.18-21 was relatively tentatively advocated by Marshall, *Luke*, pp. 124-28 (following Stuhlmacher; compare also Hahn, *Titles*, pp. 380ff.; Grundmann, 121, and Lampe, 'Spirit', p. 177). It is has became a major emphasis in (*inter alia*) P.S. Minear, *To Heal and to Reveal* (New York: Seabury, 1976), ch. 5; Busse, *Wunder, passim* (but esp. pp. 372-414), and Turner, 'Luke and the Spirit', chs. 2 and 4 (and 'Jesus and the Spirit in Lucan Perspective', *TynB* 32 [1981], pp. 25-28).

65. *Pace* Rese, *Motive*, pp. 71 and 206-207, who considers this section unimportant for the writer of Acts. As the prophet-like-Moses, Jesus can expect the obedience of the Israel of fulfilment: indeed, allegiance to him is constitutive of the latter. Luke has prepared for this in his redactional activity. He has tended to change Mark's neutral references to ὄχλος in favour of the more theologically nuanced term λαός (cf. Acts 3.23 = Lev. 23.29). This term (with phrases such as πᾶς ὁ λαός; ἐνώπιον/ἐναντίον τοῦ λαοῦ) corresponds to the LXX designation for Israel, and nowhere more richly than in Exodus. By his frequent use of these terms, Luke establishes that 'all Israel' was present at the key redemptive events (and—with exceptions that prove the rule—that 'Israel' responded positively). The pattern also emerges in Acts: 'in the period of the initial apostolic preaching, the true Israel assembles itself from among the Jewish people. And that Israel which persists in rejection of Jesus loses its entitlement to be the true people of God—it becomes mere Judaism!' (so Lohfink, *Sammlung*, p. 55, and chs. 2-3 leading up to this; cf. Jervell, *Luke*, pp. 41-74). The role of Jesus as the prophet-like-Moses cannot be limited to the post-resurrection period (see Haenchen, 209); the eschatological Moses mirrors the first in that both are rejected (cf. Acts 7.25ff., 35, 39ff.) and decisively, in the context of Acts 3.22ff., the ἀνάστασις of v. 26 is defined by the aorist ἀπέστειλεν in the same verse (Haenchen, 210).

Moses in Acts 7 is at points virtually a typology of Jesus,[66] closely modelled on the kerygma of Jesus in Acts 3,[67] and on the picture of Jesus in Luke–Acts more generally. At Lk. 24.19, the Emmaus disciples refer to him as 'a prophet powerful in deed and word before God and before the people', which is just how Stephen will describe Moses at Acts 7.22. Elsewhere, Luke's interest in Jesus as the Mosaic prophet has moulded the transfiguration account,[68] the transition to his central section (9.51-52), the sending out of the seventy (10.1-12, 17-19), and, according to Evans and Moessner, the whole presentation of Jesus' teaching ministry in chs. 9–18, which are allegedly based on Deuteronomy.[69] It is also noteworthy that, in the redaction of Lk. 7.11-35, the one who fulfils Isa. 61.1 (v. 22) is identified with the one earlier designated as 'a mighty prophet' (v. 16),[70] the

66. See especially F. Bovon, 'La figure de Moïse dans l'oeuvre de Luc' in *L'Oeuvre de Luc* (Paris: Cerf, 1987), pp. 73-96 (esp. 85-91), and compare M.D. Goulder, *Type and History in Acts* (London: SPCK, 1964), p. 164; and Hanson, 94ff.; R.C.P. Hanson, *Allegory and Event* (London: SCM Press, 1959), pp. 94-96, and 'Studies in Texts: Acts 6:13f', *Theol* 50 (1947), pp. 142-45. This speech is important for Luke, and he has not merely inherited a source which he has used verbatim (*contra*, e.g. J.C. O'Neill, *The Theology of Acts in its Historical Setting* [London: SPCK, 2nd edn, 1970], pp. 77-94); his redactional work is clear throughout; cf. the thorough stylistic study by E. Richard, *Acts 6.1–8.4: The Author's Method of Composition* (Missoula: Scholars Press, 1978), *passim*.

67. See the parallels tabulated by Zehnle, *Discourse*, pp. 78-94; 131-35: to these add that Moses, according to 7.36 performs σημεῖα which once were performed by Jesus (Acts 2.22) and which are now given in the name (4.30).

68. Luke's source, Mark (though see Schramm, *Markus-Stoff*, pp. 136ff.), already fused sonship Christology with an allusion to Jesus as the eschatological prophet: the commanding heavenly voice at 9.7 bids the disciples 'Listen to (and obey) him' (ἀκούετε αὐτοῦ), which is virtually a quotation of Deut. 18.15 and Moses' command concerning the prophet God will raise up after him. Luke's changes draw attention more powerfully to this mosaic Prophet: (1) He adds that Jesus' face became altered and reflected heavenly glory (v. 32; cf. Mt. 17.2), in parallel to Moses' experience on Mt Sinai (Exod. 34.29-35). (2) He adds a mention that Moses and Elijah (reversing Mark's order, and putting Moses in the more prominent position) discussed Jesus' ἔξοδος ('exodus'), i.e. his suffering and entry into his glory (Lk. 24.19, 26-27). (3) Luke accommodates the heavenly voice more closely to Isa. 42.1 by the replacement of ἀγαπητός with ἐκλελεγμένος (cf. on Lk. 3.22 above). The divine Son is God's Servant—a figure who has deep affinities with Moses (see Lampe, 'Spirit', pp. 177-81; A. Bentzen, *King and Messiah* [London: Lutterworth, 1955], chs. 6 and 7).

69. See below, on 'New Exodus Hopes and Luke's Gospel'.

70. It is the miracle of the raising of the widow of Nain's son in Lk. 7.11-17 which evokes the crowd's response 'a great prophet has arisen among us'. Luke understands the report of this miracle to provoke John the Baptist's question through his messengers (vv. 17 and 18), while the miracle itself prepares the way for the expansion of Isa. 35.5 and 61.1 (in 7.22) to include 'the dead are raised' in Jesus' answer to John.

description of whom closely resembles what Luke has to say about Moses (even if also manifestly echoing Elijianic traits).

EXCURSUS: THE 'GREAT PROPHET' OF 7.16—'ELIJAH OR MOSES'?

On the basis of the parallels between Lk. 7.11 and 1 Kgs 17.9-10, and between Lk. 7.15 and 1 Kgs 17.23 (amounting to the expressions: ἐπορεύθη εἰς ['he entered'], πύλῃ τῆς πόλεως ['at the gate of the city'], καὶ ἰδού ['and behold'], χήρα ['widow'], καὶ ἔδωκεν αὐτὸν τῇ μητρί ['and he gave him to his mother'], and to the fact of a raising from the dead of a widow's son, and the consequent recognition of a man of God), Gils[71] and Schnider,[72] have argued that the story is an Elijah midrash. The latter goes on to claim that its anarthrous form would have made Luke very unlikely to have recognised in the phrase μέγας προφήτης ἠγέρθη ἐν ἡμῖν ('*a* great prophet has been raised up among us') a reference to the Mosaic prophet (p.110). However, we must note three things.

First, the contacts with the Elijah story are somewhat weaker than is sometimes supposed. (1) In 1 Kings 17 the meeting at the 'gate of the city' has nothing to do with the much later restoration of the widow's son; the inclusion of the reference to the city gates in Luke, therefore, has not been derived from the LXX, but probably signals the last minute arrival of Jesus; the burial procedure was well under way. (2) The remark that Jesus 'gave him to his mother', and the following recognition of Jesus as God's powerful agent, are not distinctive to this story in Luke; both motifs are also found at 9.42-43, which is not dependent on the LXX Elijah tradition. So while there is a strongly distinctive Elijah-Elishianic trait in the story (the raising of the dead: cf. *m. Sot.* 9.15; *Cant. R.* 1.1.), and a clear Elijianic parallel (the one so raised is a widow's son)—one that Luke must have recognised (cf. 4.26)—we should not speak of a formal Elijah 'midrash'.

Secondly, within Jewish interpretation there was a tendency to assimilate Elijah to Moses, and even to portray the former as 'a New Moses' (or the promised prophet like Moses). This begins within the canon itself in 1 Kings 17–19 and 2 Kings 1–2, and continues through to the rabbis (cf. *Pes. R.* 4.2 for an extensive statement of the parallels).[73] This tendency should warn us against any sharp antithesis between recognition of someone as evincing Elijianic traits and their fitting a Moses typology. The question is rather which typology incorporates the other.

Thirdly, from a literary critical standpoint, in the broader context of Luke–Acts the wording and ideas of this account are made to evoke Moses more strongly than Elijah. Thus:

(A) For Luke it is especially Moses who is regarded in parallel to Jesus as one who performs 'signs and wonders' (Acts 7.36//Acts 2.22), and as a prophet

71. *Jesus*, p. 26.
72. *Jesus*, pp. 108-10.
73. See Allison, *Moses*, pp. 39-45, for a good brief account, and compare Horsley, 'Prophets', pp. 441-43.

'mighty' in 'word and deed' (Acts 7.22//Lk. 24.19). For the writer of the Third Gospel (as for Judaism) there is thus (*contra* Lampe)[74] certainly no antithesis between Elijah, the miracle worker and Moses, the law giver. A number of Jewish works built on the Old Testament mention of Moses as a worker of great σημεῖα καὶ τέρατα ('signs and wonders', cf. Deut. 34.10-11 LXX): most obviously Wis. 10.15-16; *Bib. Ant.* 9.7, 10; Artapanus in Eusebius, *PE* 9.27.27-37; Ezekiel the Tragedian, *Exagōgē*, 224-29; and *Jan. Jam.* (some MSS) 24 and 26. Similarly, great works in the wilderness were expected to attest messianic claimants, and this expectation clearly depends much more on a Moses typology than in hopes associated either with a Davidic king or with Elijah.[75] For Luke, then, the miracle of multiplication of loaves 'in the wilderness' (9.12) will have attested Jesus' affinity with the hoped-for prophet-like-Moses rather than either Elijah or Elisha (despite the comparable miracle by the latter in 2 Kgs 4.42-44). These examples do not include healings or raisings from the dead, but Vermes suggests Moses was already regarded as a healer before Luke's time by Artapanus (recorded in Eusebius, *Pr. Ev.* 9.27: Vermes interprets paragraph 25, 'Moses, anticipating the act of Jesus in raising the daughter of Jairus, lifted him (Pharaoh) up and revived him').[76] While Vermes build his case on slender grounds, the point remains that for Luke it is Moses who is the great miracle-working prophet. By contrast, after 4.26 (and there only allusively) the name of Elijah is never explicitly connected with the working of miracles.

(B) The recognition of the crowd that God has 'visited' his people and 'raised up a mighty prophet' (v. 16) appears to contain a subtle piece of irony.[77] While the crowd is allowed to respond in a way that typifies its perception of Jesus as Elijah ('or one of the prophets of old': cf. 9.19), the implied author suggests the inadequacy of such a Christology, partly by deliberately contrasting it with the messianic confession (9.20), and partly by careful repetition and blending of language from and in two other contexts. The exclamation of the crowd that God has 'visited' his people and 'raised up a mighty prophet among us' will thus inevitably recall 1.68-69 ('*Israel*...for God has visited and *redeemed* his people; he has raised up a horn of salvation for us' [here the Davidid]), and this language (along with that of 7.16 itself) is again taken up in 24.19 and 21 in the irony of the disciples' disappointment: Jesus, they say, was, 'a prophet, mighty in word and deed before God and before all the people...we had hoped he would be the one *to redeem Israel*'. In these last two verses, which afford a close parallel to both 1.68-69 and 7.16, we clearly hear Jesus described as the Mosaic prophet of Acts 3 and 7; the one expected to bring λύτρωσις

---

74. 'Spirit', p. 176.

75. See Jeremias, *TDNT*, IV, pp. 860-61; Meeks, *Prophet*, pp. 162-4, 212-13.

76. *Jesus*, pp. 66-67. Vermes, however, perhaps overstates the parallel.

77. Compare Nebe, *Züge*, p. 79, who requires we distinguish pre-resurrection degrees of insight into Jesus' prophetic identity in different audiences, and that these are different from Luke's own perspective as post-resurrection narrator. Alternatively, if 4Q521 witnesses an Elijah messiah connected with Isa. 61, and if 7.11-17 stood in Q alongside 7.18-22, the latter probably evoked an Elijah Christology. In that case Luke has actually subverted his tradition in favour of a Mosaic understanding.

(redemption) to Israel. The note to the effect that God has 'raised up' a great prophet (7.16) echoes Deut. 18.15, especially when the adjective μέγας underscores the prophet's uniqueness (so Wanke, *Emmauserzählung*, p.61), and the observation that the definite article is missing at 7.16 is of little consequence when we remember that it is also missing at 24.19 where there can be no doubt that Luke intends a reference to the prophet-like-Moses.

There are good reasons to suppose, then, that Luke has chosen in his programmatic passage to portray Jesus at least implicitly as the anointed Mosaic prophet, the one raised up to redeem Israel, but also fated to be rejected by her. This identification would have been facilitated in four ways: (i) the servant passages in Isaiah 42 and 61 were already to some extent modelled on Moses; (ii) the prophet of Isaiah 61 was anticipated to take a central role in a New Exodus programme of liberation, (iii) the temptation/ordeal narratives had already highlighted the New Exodus role of the one earlier endowed as (king and) servant (Lk. 3.22), and, (iv) Moses was also the archetype of the *rejected* prophet (Acts 7.35, 39, 52), a major issue in this particular context. Luke's identification of the figure in Isaiah 61 with the prophet-like-Moses might also help explain why neither Isaianic passage subsequently plays much part in Luke–Acts. It is as though for Luke the servant/prophet has emerged from the relative anonymity of Isaiah, and has stepped forward into the light as the messianic prophet-like-Moses.

(3) But is this the whole story? Bock and Strauss, while allowing some place to the eschatological prophet motif have especially emphasized the existence of more distinctively kingly motifs within the Isaiah citation in 4.18-19; most notably in the power to proclaim and effect the liberation of prisoners ('manumission is a particularly royal prerogative'),[78] but also per-haps in the very use of the word 'anointed'.[79] On this basis, 4.18-21 is seen to contain elements of Jesus' Davidic-royal messiahship in addition to the servant/prophet emphasis. Strictly speaking, however, nothing in the pas-sage itself requires this, for in Jewish tradition prophetic figures were also God's 'anointed' (cf. Isa. 61.1 itself),[80] and in any case Moses was not

---

78. Strauss, *Messiah*, p. 231 (and pp. 226-60 more generally); Bock, *Proclamation*, pp. 109-11.

79. It is claimed Luke saw Jesus' statement that God had 'anointed' (ἔχρισεν) him (with the Spirit) as the explanation of the title 'messiah' (ὁ χριστός). This is held on the basis that in Acts 4.26-27 the Davidid is spoken of in the congregational prayer as 'your holy servant, Jesus, whom you *anointed*'. So W.C. Van Unnik, 'Jesus the Christ', *NTS* 8 (1961–62), pp. 101-16, esp. 113-16, and he is followed and his argument extended by Tannehill, 'Mission', pp. 51-75 (cf. p. 69; see also Tannehill, *Unity*, I, pp. 58, 63), Schnider, *Jesus*, pp. 163-67, and Dömer, *Heil*, pp. 61-69.

80. Cf. 1 Chron. 16.22; Ps. 105.15. And while kings were anointed with oil as a

merely a prophet, but *king* and *liberator* too.[81] It is this latter tradition which is recalled by Acts 7.36-37, where Moses is described as God's appointed 'ruler and liberator/redeemer' (ἄρχων and λυτρωτής) and so the pattern for the prophet-like-Moses to come,[82] namely Jesus. In other words, *we do not need to step out of the messianic prophet tradition in order to explain any feature of 4.18-21.* That said, however, nor do we require to turn our backs on the emphatic Davidic Christology of the earlier material in Luke,[83] and Luke can describe the Davidic and the Mosaic liberators in language that draws them together: thus, as we have already noted, 1.68-69 tells us that God 'visits' and 'redeems his people' Israel by 'raising up' a Davidid, while 7.16 and 24.19, 21 use the same language of the mighty prophet. Luke, like Judaism, would probably have seen a strong congruence between Moses and David in both the former and especially in the eschatological redeemers,[84] and so perceived Mosaic and Davidic redemptive typologies as involving overlapping as well as complementary descriptions of Jesus. Indeed, he will effectively merge the figures. Nevertheless, there were differences of emphasis within the two typologies, and so of contextual appropriateness, and this is the issue here. The implicit claim to be the New Exodus prophet liberator fitted both the passage and the message Jesus intended to press from it in the envisaged context of his Nazareth ministry,

---

sign of their appointment by God, and some received the Spirit (1 Sam. 16.13 provides the closest connection), outside Luke's writings it is only prophetic figures who are anywhere actually described as anointed with the Spirit (cf. CD 2.12, 'He teaches them through those anointed by his Holy Spirit', and compare the expression '[even in the prophets...] after their anointing with the Holy Spirit [*postquam uncti sunt spiritu sancto*]' in the *Gospel of the Nazarenes* [as pointed out by de Jonge and Van der Woude, '11Q Melchizedek', p. 311 n. 2: for the text see Jerome, *Dialogi contra Pelagianos* 3.2]). In Acts 4.26-27 we have a traditional passage which hails Jesus as God's 'anointed', but here the term probably means 'God's appointed king', and there is no obvious reference to his being anointed with the Spirit. By contrast, Acts 10.38 speaks of Jesus being anointed with Spirit and power as a liberator, but in a context where there are no signs of royal motifs.

81. See especially Meeks, *Prophet King*, and Feiler, *Jesus*, pp. 208-10, for parallels. Sloan (*Year*, pp. 48-77) also sees a fusion of kingly and prophetic motifs, though not specifically Davidic ones—and he is aware of the tradition of the prophet-like-Moses as a king, at least in Samaritan expectation.

82. On Moses as redeemer and pattern for the messianic redeemer in Judaism see Allison, *Moses*, pp. 85-90.

83. Against Moessner, *Lord*, pp. 55-56, 315, 332-33, see Strauss, *Messiah*, pp. 277-78.

84. Again see Allison, *Moses*, pp. 35-39 (correctly noting that tradition comparing the former redeemers was relatively rare) and pp. 73-90 (on the eschatological redeemers) for brief accounts of the primary and secondary literature.

whereas specifically Davidic claims would simply be out of place. To some
extent that verdict is also appropriate not merely for the context of the
Nazareth pericope for the pre-Jerusalem ministry of Jesus as a whole.

We have noted that the opening chapters of Luke set up the expectation
that Jesus will emerge as messianic Son, receive the eternal kingship
promised to David's heirs (1.32-35), and so liberate and restore Israel (1.50-
55, 68-75, 79; 2.11-14; 29-32; 3.15-17, 21-22; 4.1-14). It will then come as
something of a puzzle to the reader that these hopes appear to drop out of
sight. Until ch. 18, the only one who recognizes Jesus as 'the messiah' (with
the exception of the demons who have supernatural knowledge, 4.34, 41) is
Peter (9.20), and he is immediately commanded to silence.

One explanation of this (championed in different ways by Burger and
Mainville) is that Luke connects 1.32-35 with resurrection–ascension exaltation (cf. Acts 2.22-36; 13.33), and does not think of Jesus as undertaking
specifically Davidic messianic roles during the ministry. During that period
he is more like the nobleman of 19.11-19 who must first 'depart to a distant
country' in order 'to obtain royal power for himself'. But this explanation is
at best a partial one. Luke 1–2 establishes that Jesus is already God's messiah, his endowment with the Spirit in 3.21-22 includes a Davidic focus, and
this is implicitly at the centre of the trial/ordeal narratives (4.1-14). And from
18.38 (when Bartimaus hails Jesus as 'Son of David') and the Parable of
Pounds (19.11-19) onwards, the theme of Jesus' messianic status comes to
the redactional foreground. It is thus Luke himself who makes explicit the
royal significance of the 'triumphal entry' by having the crowds of disciples
extol Jesus with the words 'Blessed is *the king* who comes in the name of
the Lord' (19.38). And Luke heightens Jesus' royal role at 20.41-44; 22.28-
30, 66-70; 23.2-3, 11, 35-38, 42; 24.26, 46, effectively turning the final part
of his Gospel into an account of 'the passion of the King'.[85] The apparent
silence on Jesus' kingship in Luke 5–17 evidently requires a quite different
explanation to that offered by Burger.

Strauss has defended the thesis that Luke's silence in these central
chapters is more 'apparent' than it is real. At the heart of his case is the
contention that 'Luke read Isaiah as a unity, and considered both the
prophet-herald of Isaiah 61 and the servant of Isaiah 40–55 to represent an
expanding Isaianic description of the Davidic messiah introduced already in
Isaiah 9, 11',[86] that is, as a first-century reader he would tend to identify
these figures (on the basis of the many shared traits) rather than contrasting
them (as modern tradition-critical scholarship does). On Strauss's reading

---

85. See Strauss, *Messiah*, ch. 6 §6, for this emphasis.
86. Strauss, *Messiah*, p. 244 (and 235-58).

there is then no 'gap' between the royal Christologies of Luke 1–4 and Luke 18–24: these chapters are bridged by traditions which refer to Jesus as 'Son' (itself a Davidic royal title in Luke's day) and Isaianic servant (a liberating prophet-king to fulfil the royal hopes of Isa. 9, 11).

There is much to commend Strauss's detailed and carefully argued thesis, though one is sometimes left wondering whether the delicate intertextuality Strauss traces was really quite so apparent to Luke as he suggests, and what prompted Luke to such a reading in the first place. Such a reading becomes more understandable if we assume that Luke's awareness of the New Exodus motif in his traditions facilitated his identification of the prophet-liberator of Isaiah 61 as the prophet-like-Moses. The kingly associations of the latter allowed him to forge the connections with the Davidic hopes that he introduced in Luke 1–2. Indeed, such Davidic hopes were already some-times associated with the New Exodus tradition (so Hos. 2.14-15 + 3.5; Amos 9.7 + 11-12; Jer. 23.5-8; *Ps. Sol.* 11; *4 Ezra* 13, etc.).

Luke's merging of prophet-like-Moses and royal Christologies poten-tially explains a number of other significant characteristics of his account, including (i) the connection between the feeding of the multitude in the wilderness (Lk. 9.12-17) and the confession Jesus is 'the Christ of God' (9.18-20, cf. Jn 6.14-15!); (ii) Luke's otherwise unexpected affirmation that the Scriptures teach 'the messiah' had to suffer and so enter his glory (24.26, 46—if for Luke this messiah is the Mosaic prophet of 24.19-24, the Scriptures certainly witness that the people kill the prophets [13.33, 34; Acts 7.51-52, cf. Lk. 4.28-30]),[87] and (iii) the striking fusion of Davidic and Mosaic motifs in Acts 2-3 (on which see Chapter 10 below).

We may conclude that Luke understood 4.16-30 to depict Jesus as the Isaianic soteriological prophet, and that he may have expected his reader to identify this figure more precisely as the Mosaic prophet-king. While it is unlikely he thought anyone would read this passage in specifically Davidic terms, he considered the Mosaic prophet and the Davidic messiah to be quite similar New Exodus redemptive figures with many overlapping traits. As such, to affirm that Jesus proclaimed and inaugurated Israel's eschatolog-ical liberation as the Mosaic prophet would automatically involve 'Davidic' functions and so simultaneously support such Davidic Christology. To that extent the Christologies were interchangeable. Different contexts, however, made either the one or the other more 'appropriate' as the primary focus. Just as the context of revelatory proclamation, liberating miracles, and potential rejection here favours a Mosaic-prophet emphasis, the same could be said of Jesus' broader ministry in Galilee and Judea. Riding up to

87. Feiler, *Jesus*, pp. 235-44.

Jerusalem on an ass and attempting the reform of the temple, however, naturally bring more distinctively Davidic motifs to the fore, and so account for
the different emphasis in Luke 19–24.

4.2. *The Missiological Focus of Luke 4.16-28*

What (for Luke) is the task for which this prophet-liberator is anointed with
the Spirit? While Luke's source may have presented Jesus as inaugurating
an Isaianic messianic Jubilee, Luke himself does not draw attention to distinctively Jubilee language or ideas in his writings. He nowhere uses the
distinctively Jubilee vocabulary (ἔτος/ἐνιαυτὸς ἀφέσεως σημασία, 'year
of Jubilee release', Lev. 25.10ff.), nor does he re-use the Isaianic absolute
ἄφεσις ('liberty/release') which might evidence his understanding of the
specifically Jubiliary background of the liberation metaphor in Isa. 61.1-2.
Sloan has attempted to argue to the contrary on the basis of Luke's regular
use of εὐαγγελίζομαι ('to preach good news') ἄφεσις ἁμαρτιῶν
('forgiveness of sins') and ἀφίημι ('to forgive'),[88] but these were the general Christian language of redemption, not specifically 'Jubilee' in overtone.
Most of Luke's closest echoes to jubiliary thoughts outside Lk. 4.18-21
simply derive from Q. In addition, Luke has virtually no positive sabbath
theology (which lay at the heart of 'Jubilee' hopes),[89] and shows no sign of
any awareness of the type of chronological calculations that were normally
associated with Jubilee hopes. The specifically Jubilee connotations of 4.18-
21 are thus simply a further indication of his use of pre-Lukan tradition.

Given that Luke has not taken up the distinctively Jubilee overtones of
the passage, we are probably safest to assume he has perceived it as part of
a more general New Exodus soteriology to which we now turn. But first we
must clarify our use of the term 'New Exodus' in relation to Luke's writing.

EXCURSUS: NEW EXODUS HOPES AND LUKE'S GOSPEL

'New Exodus' terminology has been used in at least three main ways in relation to
Luke's conception of Jesus' mission:

---

88. Sloan, *Year*, ch. 3 (and *passim*).

89. *Contra* S. Bacchiocchi, *From Sabbath to Sunday: A Historical Investigation of
the Rise of Sunday Observance in Early Christianity* (Rome: Gregorian Press, 1977),
pp. 21-22, and F. Staudinger, 'Die Sabbatkonflikte bei Lukas' (PhD dissertation, Karl-
Franzens University, Graz, 1964), *passim*; see M. Turner, 'The Sabbath, the Law, and
Sunday in Luke–Acts', in D.A. Carson (ed.), *From Sabbath to Lord's Day* (Exeter:
Paternoster, 1982), pp. 100-57.

1. *As a label for a general Mosaic typology.* J. Mánek's[90] study drew attention to the conversation with Moses and Elijah in the transfiguration account concerning Jesus' forthcoming *exodos* which he was about to 'fulfil' in Jerusalem (9.31). He identified the 'two men' in dazzling raiment of 24.4 with the same Moses and Elijah, and deduced 'the exodus in Luke's account is the leaving of the sepulchre, the realm of death, and not in any way Jesus' end, His death, His crucifixion [alone]'.[91] This became the departure point for Mánek's extensive typological comparison between the narrative about Jesus and the biblical story of Moses and Israel from the departure from Egypt to entry into the Land, with Jesus leading the new Israel from earthly Jerusalem to heavenly Jerusalem through the threatening waves of the Red Sea, his suffering and death. Mánek's account drew attention to important 'Mosaic' features of Luke's story (not least the two references to Jesus as the promised Mosaic prophet (Acts 3.22; 7.37), the fulfilment of the Passover motif in Lk. 22.15-16, the transfiguration story itself, the appointment of the seventy (Lk. 10.1//Exod. 24.1, 9), etc.) even if it was also sometimes fanciful (e.g. in making Jerusalem and its leaders the antitype of Egypt, and the fall of Jerusalem the annihilation of the Egyptians at the Red Sea).[92]

2. *As a characterization of the form and contents of the Lukan Travel Narrative seen as heavily moulded by the Deuteronomic portrait of Moses and the Exodus.* Both C.F. Evans[93] and D.P. Moessner[94] have attempted in different ways to show that Luke's transfiguration account (9.28-36) launches Luke into a prolonged Deuteronomic Mosaic typology, embracing the whole Travel Narrative. Within this central section of Luke's Gospel, Jesus is depicted as accomplishing a New Exodus (cf. 9.31), leading Israel towards the promised land. For Evans, the major argument is that the order and content of the teaching material in Lk. 10.1–18.14 roughly corresponds passage-by-passage with that of Deuteronomy 1–26.[95] Moessner recognizes the problems in Evans's position and advances the much more subtle proposal that Luke 9 presents Jesus in parallel to the Deuteronomic Moses as one called to mediate the voice of God on the mountain, yet rejected by a stubborn Israel in the journey towards the Land. The prophet's death for the sins of the people permits the

---

90. J. Mánek, 'The New Exodus in the Books of Luke', *NovT* 2 (1958), pp. 8-23.

91. 'New Exodus', p. 12.

92. 'New Exodus', pp. 17-18.

93. C.F. Evans, 'The Central Section of Saint Luke's Gospel', in D.E. Nineham (ed.), *Studies in the Gospels: Essays in Memory of R.H. Lightfoot* (Oxford: Basil Blackwell, 1955), pp. 37-53.

94. Moessner, *Lord*.

95. Unfortunately the parallels are far from convincing: see C.L. Blomberg, 'Midrash, Chiasmus, and the Outline of Luke's Central Section', in R.T. France and D. Wenham (eds.), *Gospel Perspectives*, III (Sheffield: JSOT Press, 1983), pp. 217-59, 221-28 (and pp. 228-33 against the revised version of the thesis presented by Drury [*Tradition*, pp. 138-64] and M. Goulder, *The Evangelist's Calendar* [London: SPCK, 1979]; M. Nola, 'Towards a Positive Understanding of the Structure of Luke–Acts' (PhD dissertation, Aberdeen 1987), pp. 10-54; and G.H. Wilms, 'Deuteronomic Traditions in St Luke's Gospel' (PhD dissertation, Edinburgh, 1972), pp. 17-32. W.M. Swartley (*Israel's Scripture Traditions and the Synoptic Gospels* [Peabody: Hendrickson, 1994], ch. 4) provides a modified restatement of Evans's view (but one informed by the contributions of Tiede and Moessner): see esp. pp. 130-53.

entry into the Land of those who have obeyed the prophet-like-Moses.[96] This pattern in Luke 9 provides a 'preview' which controls the central section of Luke. According to Moessner, this latter section largely articulates the Deuteronomist view of Israel's experience of prophecy, which may be summed up under four heads (following Steck's analysis)[97]: (A) Israel's history is a tale of persistent 'stiff-necked' disobedience; (B) prophets are sent by God to mediate his will, warn and promote a repentance which may avert God's judgment, but (C) a stiff-necked people reject them (persecuting or killing them), so (D) God sends judgment (especially the destruction of the Temple).[98] In taking up the Deuteronomist analysis, Luke stands in the tradition from Jeremiah to Josephus and Qumran. Like Josephus and Qumran, he has accommodated Moses to the Deuteronomist understanding, and Jesus to the Moses that results. Like Moses, the Jesus of the central section is the prophet *par excellence*. Accompanied by the manifest presence of God, he leads the people in a New Exodus from the mountain towards the central place (Jerusalem) where 'all (restored) Israel' will worship and eat and rejoice before the Lord (Deut. 16.16), while the gathering rebellious rejection of the prophet's message ensures it is a journey towards his death, which will open the way to salvation.[99] While a brief outline such as this cannot hope to do justice to the detail and subtlety of Moessner's perceptive reading (far less enter into criticism of it),[100] it will be clear enough from what we have said that what he means by 'New Exodus' is substantially what he calls a 'Moses-Exodus-Deuteronomy Typology':[101] for both Evans and Moessner 'New Exodus' means a careful replay of the narrative patterns of the Exodus, especially as this is described in Deuteronomy.

   3. *As a description of a post-Exilic constellation of hopes developed from Isaiah 40–55 and providing a framework for Luke's view of Christ and Salvation* In this instance the connection with the Exodus accounts is not direct, but mediated through Isaiah's use of Exodus typology to depict Israel's deliverance from exile. The essence of the New Exodus pattern which results includes the following:

---

   96.   Moessner, *Lord*, Part II, esp. pp. 60-70.

   97.   O.H. Steck, *Israel und das gewaltsame Geschick der Propheten* (Neukirchen–Vluyn: Neukirchener Verlag, 1967).

   98.   Moessner devotes the whole of Part III (pp. 82-257) to analysis of the central section under these four heads. A table on p. 211 conveniently lists his results: under (A) fall Lk. 11.14-54 (esp. 29-32); 17.20-37; 7.18-50; 12.54-13.9; under (B) falls every passage in Luke from 9.51 to 19.44; under (C) fall 9.51-58; 10.3, 10-11, 13, 16, 25; 11.14-26, 29-32, 47-54; 12.49-50, 54-56; 13.1-9, 14-17, 25-34; 14.1, 24; 15.1-2; 16.14-16, 27-31; 17.25-30; 18.8, 31-34; 19.7, 14, 39-44; under (D) fall 11.31-32, 50-51; 12.57-59; 13.24-30, 35; 14.24; 17.26-30; 19.27, 41-44.

   99.   See *Lord*, part IV.

   100.   Criticisms of Moessner so far have concentrated on four particular aspects: (1) the misleading statement that Moses dies for the sins of the people (Deut. 32.48-51 lays the blame for his death outside the land at 'Moses' own feet); (2) the close alignment of the disciples and the Twelve with the rebellious stiffnecked people, (3) the commencement of the new exodus with Lk. 9, and (4) the almost exclusive position accorded to 'the prophet like Moses' in the Lukan Christology (even without the central section there are others!). See Feiler, *Jesus*, pp. 196-207 (this was of course reacting to Moessner's earlier articles and his then unpublished thesis), and Strauss, *Messiah*, ch. 6 §§1-4, esp. pp. 276-84.

   101.   See *Lord*, p. 261, for this title.

a. God calls for a 'way' for the Lord to be prepared in the wilderness for his saving activity (40.3-5; 43.19).

b. His advent 'with might' as the divine warrior will defeat Israel's oppressors and release the oppressed (40.10-11; 42.13; 51.9-16; 49.9, 24-25).

c. The Lord will lead the glorious procession out of captivity along 'the way' through the wilderness, his presence before and after them (52.11-12), through water and fire (43.1-3), and he will shepherd them along the way (40.11).

d. He will sustain them in the wilderness more fully than in the Exodus, ensuring they do not hunger, and providing streams in the desert (41.17-20; 43.19-21; 49.9-10). The very wilderness will be transformed to celebrate the release of God's people (43.19; 49.10-11; 55.12-13).

e. God will pour his refreshing and restoring Spirit on his people (44.3) so that they own him as their Lord (44.5); he himself will teach them and lead them in 'the way' (54.13; 48.17), so opening the eyes of the blind and the ears of the deaf.

f. The final goal of this New Exodus is God's enthronement in a restored Zion/Jerusalem (44.26; 45.13; 54.11-12). The announcement of this 'good news' to her is her 'comfort', the occasion for her bursting into song to celebrate her salvation (40.1, 9-10; 52.1-10).

g. These things will be accomplished at least in part through a somewhat enigmatic servant figure with 'Israel', kingly and prophet-liberator traits.[102]

R.E. Watts has suggested this kind of pattern of beliefs was enriched by other related Isaianic texts (including e.g. 29.17-21; 35.1-10; 61.1-7, etc.), and New Exodus hopes from elsewhere in the Prophets, and became an important *theologoumenon* in ITP Judaism (especially in *Testaments of the Twelve Patriarchs*). He argues in detail that such a pattern provides the controlling substructure of Mark's Gospel, where it functions as an ideology. That is, it provides a whole symbolic world through which the community understands itself as 'true Israel' (e.g. over against Judaism) and rehearses its origins in Israel's founding (and refounding) moments.[103] Mark's opening quotation from Isa. 40.3 and Mal. 3.1/Exod. 23.20 would immediately evoke the New Exodus ideology, which from then on underpins and interprets the Markan account of Jesus: his baptism is the 'rending of the

---

102. For 'New Exodus' themes in Isa. 40–55 see e.g. B.W. Anderson, 'Exodus Typology on Second Isaiah', in B.W. Anderson and W. Harrelson (eds.), *Israel's Prophetic Heritage: Essays in Honor of James Muilenburg* (New York: Harper, 1962), pp. 177-95; C. Stuhlmueller, *Creative Redemption in Deutero-Isaiah* (Rome: Pontifical Biblical Institute, 1970), pp. 59-98; R.E. Watts, 'Consolation or Confrontation? Isaiah 40–55 and the Delay of the New Exodus', *TynB* 41 (1990), pp. 31-59, Strauss, *Messiah*, pp. 285-297, and the literature they cite. The enigmatic character of 'the servant' is undoubtedly at least partly the result of shifts of expectation as the hoped-for 'new exodus' under Cyrus went off like a damp squib.

103. R.E. Watts, 'The Influence of the Isaianic New Exodus on the Gospel of Mark' (PhD dissertation, Cambridge, 1990 [forthcoming Cambridge University Press]).

heavens' (cf. Isa. 64.1-2) and the anointing of the Isaianic servant, and beloved Son, Israel; his healings and exorcisms are cast as the works of the Yahweh-Warrior and liberator (cf. esp. Mk 3.22-30//Isa. 49.24-25); he provides sustenance for his people in the wilderness (Mk 6.34-44, 8.1-9) as he shepherds his people along 'the way' towards Jerusalem, opening blind eyes and deaf ears as he goes (both literally and metaphorically), and preaching the 'good news' of God's inbreaking reign, etc.

While Watts's work was on Mark, his findings have evident relevance for other Jewish and Christian writings. Although New Exodus motifs were not the central focus of his own research, Mark Strauss has been able to some extent to test Watts' paradigm in Luke.[104] He concludes (against Evans and Moessner) that it is Isaianic New Exodus motifs (rather than simply Deuteronomic Moses-Exodus typology) that prevail in Luke's work. The 'New Exodus' for Luke is not something that begins with the transfiguration account (*contra* Evans, Moessner and Ringe),[105] nor is it simply Mosaic. Rather, Luke commences this 'New Exodus' with John the Baptist's ministry in the wilderness, which, like Mark, he interprets by Isa. 40.3-5. For Luke, this Deutero-Isaianic New Exodus motif is simply another (albeit important) metaphor for the salvation which the whole of Jesus' ministry inaugurates (as his redactional extension of the Isaiah 40 quotation at Lk. 3.4-6 indicates), and in accordance with the Isaianic pattern, the goal of Jesus' 'way' is Jerusalem (whence the heavenly Zion), not the Promised Land. For Strauss's christological study, the significance of all this is that the Isaianic servant comes to the conceptual stage centre, and this figure is as much Davidic as he is Mosaic: 'it is significant,' he writes, 'that, when Isaiah is read as a unity, the eschatological deliverer may be viewed as [a] Davidic king who (like Moses) leads an eschatological new exodus of God's people through suffering as the servant of Yahweh',[106] and this he believes is how Luke construed it.

Our own application of the term 'New Exodus' as a category for describing Lukan motifs falls mainly within this third, broader, fundamentally Isaianic paradigm, while allowing it has been enriched by more specifically Mosaic typological features at certain points, especially in the Deuteronomic 'rejection of the prophet' motif, noted by Moessner, without which Luke's presentation would collapse into triumphalism.[107] With Strauss, we believe that such a motif best explains Luke's remarkable fusion of Davidic, servant and Mosaic Christologies, which otherwise might seem merely 'promiscuous',[108] if not bizarre. The same motif perhaps supplies the single most

---

104. *Messiah*, ch. 6.

105. S.H. Ringe, 'Luke 9:28-36: The Beginning of an Exodus', *Semeia* 28 (1983) pp. 83-99. Moessner in one sense should concede that the motif appears before Lk. 9, for he spends some time attempting to show that Lk. 7.18-50 parallels 11.14-54 and matches Deuteronomistic tenet A (*Lord*, pp. 98-114). Swartley (*Scripture*) sees the Travel Narrative (interpreted as Evans and Moessner) as the centrepiece of Luke's New Exodus understanding, while also finding New Exodus traits (including Isaianic and Jubilee ones) in the Galilean Narrative (see pp. 74-94), and throughout Luke–Acts.

106. *Messiah*, p. 304.

107. Cf. Tiede, *Prophecy*, pp. 45-46

108. As Conzelmann labelled it (*Theology*, p. 171).

obvious conceptual unity to the whole of Luke 1–4. We have already noticed that a 'New Exodus' emphasis marks the beginning of John's ministry in the wilderness (Lk. 3.2-6) and becomes blatant in the narrative of the testing/ordeal in wilderness (4.1-13 [14]), but we can immediately see how well the intervening baptismal 'empowering' of Jesus with the Spirit as divine son, Davidic king and Isaianic servant (Isa. 42.1 = Lk. 3.22b) would fit within such a scheme. Luke 1–2 is also replete with Deutero-Isaianic allusions (cf. esp. 1.35, 54, 76-79; 2.25, 29-32, 38) and the messianic restoration of Zion which these chapters depict is the goal towards which New Exodus imagery leads. In the context of all these allusions, Lk. 4.18-21 most probably means the Spirit-anointed Isaianic Soteriological Prophet inaugurates the 'New Exodus'.

The christological and missiological foci of Lk. 4.16-30 converge in this New Exodus motif. The Mosaic prophet announces the New Exodus good news of liberation. God is powerfully present, in his Spirit-anointed servant, to free his people from their wretched estate of 'slave-poverty', 'captive-exile', 'blindness' and 'oppression' and to shepherd them along 'the way' towards Zion's restoration. This, however, the prophet-servant can inevitably only do where his message is 'acceptable' (cf. 4.24), for it involves willing participation. When those who regard themselves as 'insider' Israelites reject him and his message (as had regularly been the case with the prophets), they will not see God at work, they will only hear of his blessing those they perceive as 'outsiders' to whom he sends the prophet instead (4.25-27). The final scene (4.28-20) reveals the darker possibility that attends any prophet, not least the Mosaic prophet.

We need not doubt that Luke considered it Jesus' mission to work for and to advance that liberating and transforming restoration of Israel that God's renewed presence in strength (i.e. the present aspect of 'the kingdom of God') was intended to accomplish. His ministry of proclamation and action, undertaken in the full power of God's Spirit, was thus to lead to her 'salvation', making her a light to the Gentiles. This aim belongs to the bedrock of authentic tradition which Luke has inherited, uniting all Jesus words and actions.[109] It explains his association with the Baptist's ministry;[110] his appointment of the twelve (i.e. as leaders of the restored twelve tribes);[111] his vigorous attempt to address all the towns and villages

---

109. See especially B.F. Meyer, *The Aims of Jesus* (London: SCM Press, 1979); *idem*, 'Jesus' Ministry and Self-Understanding', in Chilton and Evans (eds.), *Jesus*, pp. 337-52; J.K. Riches, *Jesus and the Transformation of Judaism* (London: Darton, Longman & Todd, 1980); Sanders, *Jesus*.

110. Cf. especially R.L. Webb, 'John the Baptist and his Relationship to Jesus', in Chilton and Evans (eds.), *Jesus*, pp. 179-229, esp. 211ff.

111. Cf. Sanders, *Jesus*, pp. 95-106.

of Israel with the message of God's reign, whether himself or through his commissioned representatives; the significance he attaches to liberating miracles within these missions;[112] his attempt to address all parties within Israel (Pharisees and Lawyers, as well as the common people and the outcast 'sinners');[113] his radical teaching and ethics of reconciliation, based in God's dawning reign;[114] his final journey to Jerusalem with his disciples, his 'triumphal entry', and his teaching and symbolic action in the Temple.[115] As we shall see, it is also the case that Luke thought Jesus' intention was significantly fulfilled, especially in the post-resurrection emergence of the Church. In short, Luke's understanding of the ministry of Jesus supports the New Exodus 'programme' which 4.18-21 (and indeed the whole of Lk. 1–4) suggests, even if his simultaneous use of the Deuteronomic motif of Israel's 'rejection of the prophets' (adumbrated in 4.23-30) provides the necessary complementary sober realism.

All this means the Spirit upon Jesus is a unique endowment. It is at once the Spirit on the prophet-like-Moses (on which Judaism offered no elaboration), but at the same time probably also that on the promised restoring Davidid (based in Isa. 11.1-4). Which is to say, while this is the Jewish 'Spirit of prophecy' it is, nevertheless, a specialised and powerful messianic version thereof.

4.3. *The 'Liberty' Jesus Proclaims and the Miracles of Jesus*

According to 4.18-19, Jesus is apparently anointed with the Spirit for five tasks: (1) to preach good news to 'the poor', (2) to proclaim release to the captives, (3) to proclaim sight to the blind, (4) to set at liberty the oppressed, and (5) to proclaim the acceptable year of the Lord. But the task is largely a unified one, for each of the elements in (1) to (4) involves a different Isaianic metaphor for Israel's low estate, and all five concern her impending release from such a state.[116]

---

112. See B.L. Blackburn, 'The Miracles of Jesus', in Chilton and Evans (eds.), *Jesus*, pp. 353-94 (esp. 372-92).

113. Cf. Meyer, *Aims*, Part II.

114. See esp. M.J. Borg, *Conflict, Holiness and Politics in the Teachings of Jesus* (Lewiston: Mellen Press, 1984); B. Chilton and J.I.H. McDonald, *Jesus and the Ethics of the Kingdom* (London: SPCK, 1987); A.E. Harvey, *Strenuous Commands: The Ethics of Jesus* (London: SCM Press, 1990); G. Lohfink, *Jesus and Community* (London: SPCK, 1985), Seccombe, *Possessions*, chs. 2–4.

115. Cf. Sanders, *Jesus*, pp. 63-76; C.A. Evans, 'Jesus' Action in the Temple: Cleansing or Portent of Destruction?', *CBQ* 51 (1989) pp. 237-70, and (most plausibly) R. Bauckham, 'Jesus' Demonstration in the Temple', in B. Lindars (ed.), *Law and Religion: Essays on the Place of the Law in Israel and Early Christianity* (Cambridge: Clarke, 1988), pp. 72-89.

116. Here, as in the Magnificat and in the Lukan Beatitudes, 'the poor' is simply a

The primarily metaphorical force of 4.18-19, together with the clear emphasis on Jesus being anointed with the Spirit for proclamation, have suggested to some that Luke interprets the Spirit on Jesus as the power to preach, and no more than that. On this view, while Jesus himself, Q (Mt. 12.28), Mark (3.20-30) and Matthew (Mt. 12.15-21, 22-28, 31-32) all attributed Jesus' healings and exorcisms to the Spirit upon him, Luke did not—allegedly (so Schweizer) because he returns to the Jewish concept of the Spirit as the Spirit of prophecy. Schweizer goes on to affirm Luke's debt to this Jewish concept 'may be seen in Lk. 4.23-27, where the miraculous signs mentioned in the quotation in v. 18 are specifically rejected as manifestations of the Spirit and only authoritative preaching is regarded as a fulfilment of the prophecy'.[117] Luke attributes Jesus' miracles to God's δύναμις ('power'), not to the Spirit.

We may first set aside two of the untenable arguments here to concentrate on the more plausible ones.

(1) While Lk. 4.23-27 certainly subordinates miracles to Jesus' proclamation, and allows some distance between them, Schweizer's assertion renders the debate in the synagogue incoherent. Why should Jesus suppose the Nazareth citizens might challenge him to perform for them the same works they have heard he accomplished at Capernaum if there was simply no material connection between these miracles and Jesus' New Exodus announcement? And by what logic does hesitation to perform such miracles prove they are not manifestations of the Spirit at all?

(2) As we have seen, Schweizer's position involves a double misunderstanding of the 'Spirit of prophecy'. In the first place, even for a Jew the 'Spirit of prophecy' *could* be associated with miraculous acts of power—perhaps especially in the case of the messiah bringing liberation to Israel (see Chapter 4 above). Menzies' position at this point is more subtle: he rejects the view that Luke might attribute miracles of *healing* and *exorcism* to the Spirit on Jesus, partly on the grounds that Jews never made such an association.[118] This is an important observation, for while we have shown the Spirit on the messiah could be anticipated to work deeds of power, it might be argued these would not normally include healing and exorcism. This argument, however, should not be over-pressed. (A) Within a 'New Exodus' context, healing miracles were to be anticipated (e.g. on the basis of Isa. 29.17-21; 35.1-10, etc.),[119] and we have noted that Judaism was

metaphor for oppressed Israel, not a referential term for a socio-economic group (see Seccombe, *Possessions*, pp. 21-96).

117. *TDNT*, VI, p. 407.

118. A point noted by Leisegang, *Pneuma*, p. 101; Schweizer, *TDNT*, VI, p. 398; Menzies, Development, pp. 188-89 n. 5).

119. See Watts, *Influence*, pp. 89-93.

beginning to countenance the possibility these would be worked by the messianic prophet—4Q521 links the messiah, the Spirit and miracles of healing (including specifically the blind receiving sight and resurrection of the dead) within the framework of an interpretation of Isa. 61.1-2. (B) In addition, the traditional task of the messiah of the Spirit was to liberate Israel from the oppressing enemies, and for both 11Q Melchizedek and for the *Testaments of the Twelve Patriarchs* this involved release of Israel from spiritual powers. *T. Zeb.* 8.8 anticipates a time when the Lord will 'liberate every captive of the sons of men from Beliar, and every spirit of error will be trampled down' (cf. *T. Levi* 3.2-3 and *T. Sim.* 6.6), while this task is more specifically messianic in *T. Dan* 5.10-11 and *T. Levi* 18.11-12. We cannot simply dismiss all these as due to Christian influence in the *Testaments*, and the same language and ideas are independently witnessed at Qumran (cf. 4Q525 4.11 and 5.2-5). Of course, neither Qumran nor the *Testaments* attributes exorcisms specifically to *the Spirit* upon the messiah, but it would have been very natural for Jesus (or the earliest Christian community: cf. Mk 3.22-30 and pars.) to do so, given that the Spirit was God's presence and power with the messiah to equip him for the task of releasing Israel from her 'enemies', and bringing restoration to Zion. More specifically, the language of 'liberation' of 'captives' used for the envisaged messianic programme of emancipation from spirits would make immediate connection with the Spirit for any Jew or Jewish Christian who understood Jesus' endowment in terms of Isa. 61.1-2/58.6. (C) Indeed, if Judaism found it so difficult to attribute exorcisms and healing miracles to the Spirit as Schweizer and others suggest, we must ask how it is that Jesus, Q, Mark, Matthew and Paul (cf. 1 Cor. 12.9b, 10a) ever came to assert such a connection in the first place, even though they plainly also regarded the Spirit as the 'Spirit of prophecy' (cf. *inter alia* Mk 1.12; 12.36 and pars.; 1 Cor. 12.9a, 10b-e; 14.1-33!).

Schweizer's second important misunderstanding of the 'Spirit of prophecy' lies in his claim that Luke has returned to a typically Jewish view of the Spirit as the power of authoritative preaching. As we have seen, this is factually incorrect. In pre-Christian Judaism the 'Spirit of prophecy' was not 'typically' the power of authoritative preaching at all (see Chapter 3)— the centrality within pneumatology of the idea of the Spirit as the power of preaching and of the congregation's authoritative 'witness' to the messiah was above all a Christian development, and shows that Luke (who fully embraces these two ideas) inherited his views of the 'Spirit of prophecy' not from Judaism but from the church.[120]

These two criticisms together raise the most acute problem for

---

120. See Turner, 'Spirit and Authoritative Preaching', pp. 66-88, esp. 87-88.

Schweizer's whole position. Given that Luke derived his pneumatology from this (largely Jewish influenced) church (not directly from Judaism), and given that within it the Spirit of prophecy on the messiah was simultaneously the power of Jesus' redemptive miracles (as Schweizer and Menzies fully admit), how can we possibly explain Luke's alleged denial of miracles to the Spirit? While Luke was not obliged to follow pneumatological suit, he can hardly have thought the earlier Christian view 'un-Jewish'! Nor was he aware of a different Jewish Christian tradition that held Schweizer's allegedly more 'Jewish' view of the Spirit on Jesus as the 'Spirit of prophecy'—for he does not appear to have any traditions concerning the Spirit in Jesus' ministry other than those from Mark, Q and his messianic Jubilee source (Lk. 4.16-30). If Luke really has distanced miracles from the Spirit, that cannot be because he is returning to an earlier 'Jewish' conception of the Spirit of prophecy; it must mean he is developing a later and less flexible *Christian* one. Ironically, Schweizer might have been much more convincing had he argued that Luke was so familiar with the typical Christian view of the Spirit as the power of preaching and witness (as in the Fourth Gospel?) that he forgot the older Jewish and Jewish Christian views that the Spirit of prophecy on the messiah was also the power of his liberating miracles! But, as we shall see, this is not how Luke understands matters; he is very much in touch with early Jewish Christian tradition.

We may now turn to the three more plausible arguments: (1) that Luke deliberately attributes redemptive miracles to God's 'power' instead of to the Spirit, (2) that Luke's changes to Mark and Q evidence his proclivity for the Spirit as the Jewish 'Spirit of prophecy' (unrelated to miracles) rather than the Christian 'Charismatic Spirit', and (3) that Lk. 4.18-21 pertains to the Spirit's inspiration of Jesus' proclamation of Israel's liberation, spiritual recovery of sight and restoration, not physical miracles.

Miracles, exorcisms and divine 'power' in Luke–Acts. We are regularly told Luke distances πνεῦμα from δύναμις, emphasizing the latter as the source of Jesus' miracles, and conceiving of it in a Hellenistic magical way as a *mana*-like substance, or fluid, which can flow from Jesus to heal others (5.17; 6.19; 8.46; cf. Acts 6.8).[121] This is a complex issue which threatens to take us too far from our central concerns. I have tried to show elsewhere that this claim is misleading at almost every point.[122] The following points are among the more important conclusions I have attempted to establish:

(1) The one verse of Luke which might with greatest reason be suspected

121. See esp. J.M. Hull, *Hellenistic Magic and the Synoptic Tradition* (London: SCM Press, 1974), pp. 105-109.
122. See Turner, 'Spirit and Power', pp. 124-52.

of manistic tendencies is Lk. 8.48, which (a) he derives straight from Mark, and (b) he interprets in a non-manistic way.[123]

(2) Elsewhere, Luke's view of divine 'power' (where it refers to charismatic power of one kind or another) is not of a 'substance' 'on tap', but a respectable Jewish way of saying God works *through* the person powerfully (and so, possibly, through the Spirit). This is the case too in 5.17 and 6.18-19 (often claimed as manistic), where the point is that the miracles which seem to break forth from Jesus are part and parcel of the inbreaking of God's reign and salvation through him to those who 'hear' his message.[124]

(3) While it is then natural enough for Luke to refer to miracles as expressions of God's *power* on or through Jesus, there is no convincing evidence this δύναμις is conceived as a mode of God's presence (far less a 'material') other than (and distinct from) the Spirit. For Luke, such 'power' can be a quality of the Spirit's own activity (as at 1.17; 4.14; Acts 1.8; 10.38) and so occasionally (1.35; 24.49) even a referential term for the Spirit. Of these instances, three might be argued to pertain to cases where the 'power' of the Spirit is evinced in preaching alone (1.17; 24.49; Acts 1.8). Only the first of these, however, is a convincing case (Luke does not think John the Baptist worked miracles); assertions concerning the other two involve *petitio principii*. More to the point, each of the remaining three cases (1.35; 4.14; Acts 10.38—all redactionally important) clearly connects the Spirit directly with the working of some miraculous phenomenon. Even Menzies, who perhaps fights hardest to distance miracles from the Spirit, admits this;[125] in other words, for Luke the Spirit is God's empowering presence. But if this is so, we have no reason to assume references to miracles of God's 'power' were intended to preclude the view that such miracles were brought about through the activity of God's Spirit. As we have seen, for the Old Testament and Judaism, the same Spirit of prophecy that brings God's presence in revelation, wisdom and invasive speech can also be conceived to act as a more impersonal 'power' (e.g. transporting prophets, empowering warrior-liberators, etc.).

123. For Hull's uncritical dependence on F. Preisigke's earlier work at this point, and for the resulting misapplication of manistic models to Luke, see Turner, 'Spirit and Power', pp. 126 and 136-38.

124. See e.g. A. George, 'Le miracle', in *Etudes sur l'oeuvre de Luc* (Paris: Gabalda, 1978), pp. 133-48, esp. 147; Busse, *Wunder*; H.K. Nielsen, *Heilung und Verkündigung* (Leiden: Brill, 1987); L. O'Reilly, *Word and Sign in the Acts of the Apostles* (Rome: Pontifical Biblical Institute, 1987); Turner, 'Spirit and Power', pp. 137-42.

125. In Chapter 6 we have seen how Menzies accepts that Lk. 1.35 ultimately attributes Jesus' miraculous conception to the Spirit. On 4.14 and 10.38 see Turner, 'Spirit and Power', pp. 138-42.

(4) It is incongruous to argue (as Menzies does) that Luke has a conservative Jewish view of the Spirit as 'the Spirit of prophecy' while at the same time maintaining he has fused this with a *manistic* view of δύναμις as the source of Jesus' miracles. The thesis becomes especially problematic when Menzies argues that Lk. 4.14 and Acts 10.38 imply the Spirit is the *source* of this manistic power (a view which could certainly not be attributed to any 'Jewish' view of the Spirit of prophecy).[126]

(5) If *manistic* ideas are rare in Luke (if present at all), the prevalent view (as März has argued) is that Jesus effects his liberating miracles through a word of command, a speech-act.[127] Menzies[128] counters that Luke does not always attribute Jesus' healings to a specific command (e.g. 6.19). That is true, but it remains the case he does typically so—programmatically at 4.35-36 and then regularly thereafter, for example, 4.39 (the speech-act redactionally added, as at 18.42), 5.25, 6.10, 7.7-8, 14, and so on, and these mentions are ten times more frequent than any possibly '*manistic*' alternatives. In defence of his view that the Spirit is not connected with healings and exorcisms, Menzies goes on to affirm that these words of command of Jesus are not specifically traced to the Spirit. He is of course right, but then which of Jesus' words are specifically traced to the Spirit? And will any reader really be expected to infer that Jesus' powerful words of exorcism and healing are less inspired of the Spirit than his ordinary teaching? But if Luke attributes Jesus mighty works mainly to his authoritative/powerful word of command, this could in no way threaten his understanding of the Spirit on Jesus as something like the 'Spirit of prophecy', and there is no reason to suspect that he has distanced Jesus' mighty works from the Spirit upon him, and attributed them to some other source instead[129]

Luke's changes to the Pneumatic Tradition in Mark and Q (Lk. 11.20 and 12.10). In Mk 3.22-30 (//Q = Mt. 12.22-32), Jesus explains his exorcisms in terms of his having overcome and bound 'the strong man', and so being able to plunder his house. As Watts has argued, this is a 'New Exodus' passage based in Isa. 49.24-25. Jesus, endowed with the Spirit from the rent

---

126. See e.g. *Development*, pp. 125-26.

127. C.-P. März, *Das Wort Gottes bei Lukas* (Leipzig: St Benno, 1974), p. 39; and compare Aletti, 'Jésus à Nazareth', pp. 431-52 (439).

128. *Development*, p. 160.

129. I do not hereby imply the idealism of, for example, the Health and Wealth Movement, that views spoken commands as themselves capable of producing effects in the physical realm (for a critique of such views see D. McConnell, *The Promise of Health and Wealth* [London: Hodder & Stoughton, 1990]), merely that Judaism would readily view the Spirit active in the command as the mode of God's powerful presence that effected the command.

heavens (Mk 1.10 cf. Isa. 64.ff.), thereby becomes the agent of Yahweh, the warrior-deliverer of 49.24-25, and so fulfils the sort of hopes we find in *T. Levi* 18.12 that 'Belial shall be bound by him' (the messiah), and Israel's captives consequently liberated (cf. *T. Dan* 5.10-11).[130] Towards the end of the pericope, Jesus apparently warns those who 'explain' his exorcisms in terms of involvement with Satanic powers that they are in danger of blaspheming against the Holy Spirit (3.28-30; Q = Mt. 12.31-32). This is probably an allusion to Isa. 63.10, and the point is not that they are 'blaspheming' the Spirit by calling him Beelzebul, but that their attribution of Jesus' miracles to Satan reveals the depths of their persistent rebellion against God, present in his Spirit. Just as their forefathers had rebelled and thereby 'grieved' God's Spirit in the wilderness (turning Yahweh against them), so now the leaders' malicious interpretation of Jesus' redemptive exorcisms evince an apparently total rejection of God's eschatological New Exodus 'visitation' through his Spirit-endowed servant.

Luke, however, has introduced important changes. His parallel to the warning about blasphemy against the Spirit (12.10) puts the saying in a different context, where there is no connection with exorcism. Again, Mt. 12.28 has Jesus attribute his exorcisms directly to 'the Spirit of God', while Luke has a form of the saying which attributes the exorcisms to 'the finger of God' instead (11.20). According to a line of interpreters from Schweizer to Menzies, Luke has effected both changes because he thinks of the Spirit as the Spirit of prophecy, and so cannot attribute exorcisms to the Spirit.

But is this the best explanation of Luke's changes? It may be doubted. Indeed, one hardly needs at all to 'explain' why Luke has preferred not to set the logion about blasphemy in the Spirit in its Markan/Q context. Unless we care to posit that there was a continuing and lively history of accusation against Jesus and the early church that their powers of exorcism were demonic, the saying was better freed from the particularity of the Markan and Q setting if its relevance to the church was to be perceived. By placing it where he has, Luke has indicated that the danger of blasphemy against the Spirit cannot be confined to the question of attributing Jesus' exorcisms to evil powers: it is present where the disciples encounter 'persistence in consummate and obdurate opposition to the influence of the Spirit which animates the preaching'[131]—a legitimate extension of the meaning of Jesus' logion, and one to be preferred to the main rival interpretation; namely, that

---

130. Watts, *Influence*, ch. 5.

131. So Fitzmyer, 964. Compare also E. Lövestam, *Spiritus blasphemia* (Lund: Gleerup, 1968); and I.H. Marshall, 'Hard Sayings—VII', *Theology* 67 (1964) pp. 65-67.

Luke's setting identifies failure to witness with the Spirit in times of trial as the blasphemy of the Spirit.[132]

In 11.20, Luke has altered Q's (or Matthew's) 'if I by the *Spirit* of God cast out demons...' (Mt. 12.28) to 'if I by the *finger* of God cast out demons'. Of course it has been argued that it is Luke who has the original form,[133] and that Matthew changed it; but (a) it is unlikely that Matthew would readily drop the allusion to a Mosaic Christology that δακτύλῳ θεοῦ permits (recognized since Holtzmann as an allusion to Exod. 8.15) in favour of a mention of the Spirit in which he shows little interest, (b) Matthew probably preserves the Q context of the saying, in which a reference to Jesus claiming to exorcise by the Holy Spirit would provide an explanatory preparation for the logion on 'blasphemy against the Spirit',[134] and (c) Matthew appears rather to have passed over this logion without changing it (witness the retention of 'kingdom of *God*' [12.28b] where he normally prefers 'kingdom of *heaven*').[135] Luke, by contrast, is the only New Testament writer to use the parallel anthropomorphisms the 'hand' of God (1.66; Acts 4.28, 30; 7.50; 11.21; 13.11)[136] and the 'arm' of the Lord

---

132. So von Baer, *Geist*, p. 138; Klostermann, *Lukasevangelium*, p. 134; Schweizer, *TDNT*, VI, p. 407; Menzies, *Development*, pp. 190-98. Menzies claims that only this second view adequately explains the difference between 'a word against the Son of Man' and 'blasphemy against the Spirit' (i.e. the first is committed by non-believers, the second by Christians) and that 12.8-9 demands 12.10 be taken as a warning to Christians. But 12.8-9 stresses the significance of everyday discipleship (as Mk 8.34-38); and in this setting 12.10 sharpens the issue of rejection of the Gospel. A trial scenario only first appears in 12.11-12, and a dire warning to believers not to resist the prompting of the Spirit in such circumstances could only be inferred if 12.10 followed it. Luke nowhere else suggests believers are liable to 'resist' the promptings of the Spirit and thereby fall into eternal danger, but it is a major motif of his work that unbelieving Jews do so (Acts 7.51: cf. 28.25-27): in his view their unbelief, which often turns to malicious opposition (Lk. 22.65; Acts 13.45; 18.6), threatens precisely to cut them off from the 'people of God' (Acts 3.25).

133. Barrett, *Spirit*, pp. 62-63. J. Jeremias (*Die Sprache des Lukasevangeliums* [Göttingen: Vandenhoeck & Ruprecht, 1980], p. 201) argues the Lukan form δακτύλῳ θεοῦ is original on the basis that a qualifying genitive without the definite article is 'non-Lukan', and that this is confirmed by a glance at the parallel in Matthew. But on the one hand Luke may simply have been influenced by form in Q/Matthew (if that was original), and secondly, more importantly, the phrase is an allusion to Exod 8.15 where the genitive is anarthrous.

134. Menzies, *Development*, pp. 187-88.

135. So Dunn, *Jesus*, pp. 44-46; cf. Dunn, 'Matthew 12:28/Luke 11:20—A Word of Jesus?', in W.H. Gloer (ed.), *Eschatology and the New Testament* (Peabody, MA: Hendrickson, 1988) pp. 30-49. Contrast, however, J.C. Thomas, 'The Kingdom of God in the Gospel of Mattthew', *NTS* 39 (1993), pp. 136-46, esp. 138-39.

136. So George, *Etudes*, p. 128

(1.31; Acts 13.17); and he has both a New Exodus motif and a Mosaic prophet Christology even more virile than Matthew's.[137] Not surprisingly, then, a growing number have felt it was Luke who introduced the change.[138] The major objection to this was thought to be that Luke's manifest interest in the Spirit would not allow him to change a logion that mentions the Spirit into one that does not. This, however, has been shown to be wrong by A. George who pointed out that Lk. 21.15 has rephrased the Markan logion (13.11) about help from the Spirit in time of trial and excluded any explicit reference to the Spirit (contrast Lk. 12.11-12).[139] Luke's interest in the Spirit does not mean a singular interest in the phrase 'the Holy Spirit' over other referring expressions for the same referent.

According to Menzies, Luke's Mosaic Christology (and New Exodus soteriology) is not enough to explain the change in 11.20, and the real motive for it is that Luke is trying to substitute a new *referent* as the power of exorcism because he cannot attribute this to the Spirit. But where is the evidence the change in referring expression from 'Spirit of God' to 'finger of God' implies a change of referent? In the only other place he has substituted alternative expressions for the Spirit (Lk. 21.15 = Mk 13.11), Luke clearly still believes they refer to activities performed *by* the Spirit—that is convincingly demonstrated by the way he combines the wording of the promises in Lk. 12.11-12 and 21.15 in his description of Stephen in Acts 6.10. In addition, a number of scholars have pointed out that readers would probably in any case identify 'the finger of God' as a referring expression for 'the Spirit of God', as the closely-related anthropomorphism 'the hand of the Lord' was already occasionally so understood (cf. especially the exchange of the Spirit for the hand of the Lord in *Targ.* Ezek. 1.3; 3.22; 8.1; 40.1).[140]

Of course, if we knew in advance that Luke could not associate the Spirit with exorcisms, then the shift in referring expression would naturally be taken as marking a shift in referent too. But we do not know this, and have

---

137. See George, *Etudes*, p. 129; cf. J.M. Van Cangh, '"Par l'esprit de dieu—Par le doigt de dieu" Mt 12,28 par. Lc 11.20', in J. Delobel (ed.), *Logia* (Leuven: Leuven University Press, 1982), pp. 337-42, esp. 339-41.

138. C.S. Rodd, 'Spirit or Finger', *ExpTim* 72 (1961), pp. 157-58; J.E. Yates, 'Luke's Pneumatology and Luke 11.20', in F.L. Cross (ed.), *SE*, II, pp. 295-99 (but chiefly because he thinks Luke cannot conceive of the Spirit as an agent, only as an endowment); R. Hamerton-Kelly, 'A Note on Matthew XII.28 par Luke XI.20', *NTS* 11 (1964-65), pp. 167-69; Dunn, *Jesus*, pp. 44-46.

139. *Etudes*, p. 131. George also points to Lk. 20.42 // Mk 12.36 = Mt. 22.43.

140. Barrett, *Spirit*, p. 63; Hamerton-Kelly, 'Note', pp. 168-69; G.R. Beasley-Murray, 'Jesus and the Spirit', in Descamps and de Halleux (eds.), *Mélanges bibliques*, pp. 469-70, and Dunn, *Jesus*, p. 46.

so far discovered no evidence that makes it probable Luke's understanding of the Spirit as the Spirit of prophecy required him to dissociate Spirit from miracles; rather to the contrary. Lk. 11.20 then appears itself to be the principle evidence on offer that Luke cannot associate the Spirit with exorcisms. But why should he not? There is little apparent 'incoherence' between the Spirit of prophecy and the power of exorcisms when it is allowed that the earliest Christians regarded the latter not as an encounter between bearers of different levels of *mana*-like charge or 'power', but more as an authority struggle between personal beings. For Luke, Jesus' exorcisms were accomplished by authoritative words of command (programmatically in Lk. 4.36; cf. 8.29, 31-32; 10.17, 19-20 etc.). If Jesus can be charged with exorcising 'by Beelzebul' that is because the latter is considered to be the ἄρχων ('ruler') over the demonic spirits (11.15), and so the one to whom they must give way and obey. There would surely be no problem for Luke in conceiving of the 'Spirit of prophecy' on Jesus as the source of his 'authority' and of his power of command, for that is exactly how the Spirit is perceived in the Jewish and Christian messianic tradition. It was recognition of this which led von Baer (who more than any saw the Spirit as 'the Spirit of prophecy' and the power of authoritative preaching) to believe Luke attributed exorcisms (and miracles) too to the Spirit.[141]

The case of Schweizer, George,[142] Haya-Prats[143] and Menzies that Luke effected the change to 'finger of God' in order to avoid attributing the exorcisms to the Spirit does not make sense in the context of Jewish and Early Christian pneumatology. Nor does it explain the specific form of the change to '*finger* of God'; for on their understanding Luke attributes miracles and exorcisms to God's δύναμις rather than to the Spirit, and accordingly we should expect the Lukan version of the Q saying to read 'If I by *the power* of God cast out demons...' instead. The form 'the finger of God' is much more specific to Luke's concern to portray Jesus as the Mosaic prophet-messiah and serves to bring out yet more clearly Mark's own 'New Exodus' understanding of the passage: by referring to the Spirit on Jesus as 'the finger of God', Luke clarifies that the Spirit is the power of the prophet-messiah to inaugurate the New Exodus liberation.[144]

141. *Geist*, pp. 34-38.
142. *Etudes*, pp. 130-31.
143. *L'Esprit*, p. 38.
144. Menzies gently chides me for dividing my explanations of Luke's alterations in 11.20 and 12.10 (when, according to him, it is rather a matter of Luke making two alterations to a single Q context), and for offering explanations of each that are 'unrelated to Luke's pneumatological perspective' ('Spirit and Power', p. 16). On the contrary, I argue Luke has entirely undertood Mark and Q, and both changes reflect the fusion of his pneumatology and his New Exodus soteriology. The Spirit on the

Does Luke 4.18-19 refer to metaphorical liberation by the Spirit alone?
We have implied above that the most obvious interpretation of 4.18-21 pertains to Israel's restoration, using Isaianic 'New Exodus' metaphors. It
would then be possible to argue that Luke considered Jesus to be anointed
with the Spirit to proclaim Israel's restoration, but that the Spirit was not
directly associated with the exorcisms and healings that symbolised this
(merely with Jesus' preaching). Three arguments, however, weigh heavily
against this view.

(1) Luke must have been fully aware that his sources presented matters
otherwise. As we have seen (§3 above), both Q (Lk. 7.18-22 = Mt. 11.2-6)
and Luke's messianic Jubilee source (4.16-30) most probably interpreted
Jesus' literal healings and exorcisms as the expected New Exodus miracles,
as concrete fulfilments of the words of Isa. 61.1-2/58.6, and so as direct and
exemplary expressions of the Spirit on the messianic liberator (cf. also Q =
Mt. 12.28). What then are we to make of Luke's use of this same Q tradition
in 7.18-22? The allusion to the wording of Isa. 61.1 in the clause 'good
news is proclaimed to the poor', offered as a summary (as the lack of final
conjunction implies) of the significance of the miracles in 7.22, will have
established the connection between Jesus' liberating miracles and the mission announced as inaugurated in 4.18-21. The connection would be
confirmed by the words 'the blind receive sight' with which the list of miracles commences in 7.22, and which directly corresponds to LXX Isa. 61.1.
The connections would be further reinforced by the way Jesus' redemptive
miracles become the focus of the synagogue discourse in 4.23-27.

With these clear links between the passages we cannot escape the conclusion that Luke saw the literal healing of the blind in 7.21 as a concrete
and symbolic expression of the Spirit's anointing upon Jesus to bring sight
to blind Israel (4.18), and the other healings and exorcisms as similar exemplars of his New Exodus mission to liberate oppressed Israel. It would be
only natural then to believe Luke (like Q) saw the physical healing of the
blind as empowered by the same Spirit who might bring spiritual sight to
Israel too. But Schweizer and Menzies do not allow this, suggesting instead
that Luke does not mention the Spirit in this context because he cannot
attribute such miracles to the Spirit.[145] But how could Luke have added a
mention of the Spirit to Jesus' well-formed 'reply' to the Baptist in 7.22b-
23 without literary infelicity? And why should he repeat such a reference
when most of his readers would recognize the allusion to Isa. 61.1 and see
the direct connection with Jesus' claim in 4.18-21? We can only find it

---

messiah and servant, and the 'finger of God' of the Mosaic prophet, are one and the
same—the liberating Spirit of the New Exodus.

145. Schweizer, *TDNT*, VI, p. 407 n. 484; Menzies, *Development*, p. 168 n. 5.

deeply ironic that in the one passage where Luke most clearly indicates how he thought Isaiah 61 was fulfilled, Schweizer and Menzies feel obliged to deny any influence to the Spirit! Had Luke meant so sharply to segregate the metaphorical understanding of Isaiah 61 in 4.18-19 from the more literal way it is taken to be fulfilled in 7.21-22, one can only wonder why he did not re-write his citation of Isa. 61.1 to remove the potentially confusing LXX line about 'sight for the blind' (restoring something closer to the MT, 'and release to the prisoners'), to remove Isa. 58.6, and above all to bring back those clearly metaphorical words 'to heal the broken-hearted' from Isa. 61.1c! Schweizer's position here is a piece of special pleading.

(2) We have noted that Jesus' task (according to the citation in 4.18-19) is not merely to proclaim liberty in the sense of 'to preach about it', but includes the idea of an authoritative proclamation that effects release; a performative utterance. This was probably inherent in the originally kingly language of Isa. 61.1-2, but was certainly strengthened by the inclusion of the interpretive line 'to set the captives at liberty' from Isa. 58.6d. We need not doubt that Luke understood Jesus to have fulfilled this in a variety of ways, including the remarkable way in which he was able to mediate a restorative sense of forgiveness and reconciliation with God to those commonly regarded as outsiders to Israel's hope. But it has to be admitted that the language and ideas of 'release' of 'oppressed' or 'bound' 'captives' do not feature in these contexts, but exclusively in the context of redemptive miracles and exorcisms (most notably in 13.10-17 and Acts 10.38; but cf. 10.19; 11.14-22, etc.).[146] We have also observed that Jesus' miracles and exorcisms are both regularly attributed to his authoritative/powerful word of command. It is thus perhaps not untypical of him that in the healing of blind Bartimaeus (18.35-43), while Matthew and Mark say Jesus touched the blind man's eyes, Luke does not mention this, but instead at the key moment redactionally adds the 'command' ἀνάβλεψον, 'Receive your sight!' (18.42), thus depicting Jesus as quite literally 'proclaiming sight to the blind' in accordance with 4.18. These traits suggest Luke saw Jesus' redemptive miracles and exorcisms very much as part of the Isaianic commission of 4.18-19, and so as attributable to the Spirit upon him. That is, Luke understood the Spirit as the source of Jesus' authoritative liberating utterances and as the effective and compelling power of his speech-acts.

(3) This understanding is confirmed by the speech Luke attributes to Peter in Acts 10.35-38. The wording of this short section appears to be modelled on Lk. 4.16-30 and to interpret it.[147]

---

146. See e.g. J.B. Green, 'Jesus and a Daughter of Abraham (Luke 13:10-17): Test Case for a Lucan Perspective on Jesus' Miracles', *CBQ* 51 (1989), pp. 643-54.

147. Busse, *Wunder*, p. 369, rightly speaks of a consensus on this. Whether or not

The evidence supporting this conclusion may be summarised: (i) The word δεκτός ('acceptable') makes the only appearance that it ever makes in the Lukan writings outside Lk. 4.16-30 where it occurs twice. (ii) The clause 'the message he [God] sent to...Israel...by Jesus Christ', while based on Ps. 106.20 (LXX), also echoes Jesus' 'he has sent me...' (Lk. 4.18). (iii) 'To preach good news of peace' (εὐαγγελιζόμενος εἰρήνην) derives from Isa. 52.7, but is closely associated with, and interprets the εὐαγγελίσασθαι πτωχοῖς ('to preach good news to "the poor"') of Lk. 4.18 (the same connection being made in 11QMelchizedek at lines 16-18). The εἰρήνη, 'peace', envisaged at Acts 10.36 corresponds to the Hebrew concept of 'well-being' associated particularly with the messianic age (cf. Lk. 2.14; 10.5; 19.24) and with the freedom from hostile powers, whether spiritual or temporal, that this state involves (cf. Lk. 1.78, 71). The fruits of this proclamation of 'peace' will be spelt out in Acts 10.38. (iv) While the comment 'he is Lord of all' (10.36) corresponds to Luke's post-resurrection christological stance, it should nevertheless be pointed out that he uses the title 'Lord' of Jesus in the Gospel at carefully-chosen places,[148] one of which is 7.19,[149] in a context where that 'lordship' is attested by Jesus' fulfilment of Isa. 61.1-2 (7.19-22). (v) The words 'beginning in Galilee etc.' conform to the perspective of Lk. 4.14ff. (vi) The description 'Jesus of Nazareth' (10.37) is strikingly coincidental as 'Nazareth' is not used elsewhere in Luke–Acts other than in the infancy narratives and Lk. 4.16. (vii) Both passages describe Jesus' rejection. (viii) The parallels reach their perigee in 10.38. The words 'God anointed him with Holy Spirit and power (ἔχρισεν αὐτὸν ὁ θεὸς πνεύματι ἁγίῳ καὶ δυνάμει)' echo Lk. 4.14 ('Jesus returned in the power of the Spirit to Galilee'), and are very close, in wording and in substance, to Lk. 4.18a 'The Spirit of the Lord is upon me, for he has anointed me to preach good news to the poor' (πνεῦμα κυρίου ἐπ' ἐμὲ οὗ εἵνεκεν ἔχρισέν με εὐαγγελίσασθαι πτωχοῖς).

Luke was using a source at this point is, however, not agreed: since M. Dibelius (*Studies in Luke–Acts* [London: SCM Press, 1956], pp. 110ff.) the majority of scholars have taken the view that the speech is a Lukan composition. G.N. Stanton (*Jesus of Nazareth in New Testament Preaching* [Cambridge: Cambridge University Press, 1974], pp. 70-80) has argued otherwise, pointing to the echoes of Isa. 61.1-2 and (LXX) Ps. 106.20 as evidence for a pre-Lukan tradition; but it hardly supports his case that the former is Luke's programmatic text and that the latter appears again in Paul's speech at Acts 13.26b! While I know of no good reason to doubt that the speech in essence may derive from Peter, it is quite another matter to demonstrate that the wording we have goes back to a pre-Lukan written source.

148. See I. de la Potterie, 'Le titre Κύριος appliqué à Jésus dans l'évangile du Luc', in Descamps and de Halleux (eds.), *Mélanges bibliques*, pp. 117-46.

149. With B f13 etc.; see Metzger, *Commentary*, p. 143.

What does this section tell us of Luke's view of the Spirit on Jesus? Evidently he considered the Spirit to be the chrism[150] with which Jesus was (metaphorically) anointed, rather than given in consequence of some prior act of anointing.[151] More important, it suggests Luke understood the Spirit as the power operative through Jesus' proclamation and effective in acts expressive of his kerygma. Thus, as in Acts 10.38b, immediately following the hendiadys which identifies the Spirit as the power in his ministry, Luke spells out the fruits of Jesus' proclamation of 'peace' (10.36) in terminology reminiscent of the acts of Hellenistic saviours: Jesus 'went about (διῆλθεν—Lukan)[152] performing works of beneficence (εὐεργετῶν)'.[153] It is hard to believe the hendiadys ἔχρισεν...πνεύματι ἁγίῳ καὶ δυνάμει ('anointed with Holy-Spirit-and-power') is traditional rather than Lukan,[154] harder still to believe that it is *non*-Lukan;[155] and virtually impossible to separate it from the acts which follow in Luke's description. As Luke elsewhere uses the (for the New Testament) rare and distinctive term εὐεργεσία ('deed of beneficence')[156] to describe a divine act of healing in Acts 4.9, it is probable that the words 'and healing all who were oppressed by the devil'[157]

---

150. So Barrett, *Spirit*, p. 42, and compare 1 Jn 2.20 and 27 (*bis*), and W. Grundmann, *TDNT*, IX, p. 572.

151. *Contra* R.B. Sloan, *Year*, p. 49. It would follow for Luke that the text of 4.18a should be punctuated after πτωχοῖς rather than after μέ, else the second half of v. 18a become otiose.

152. Luke 10×; Acts 21×; New Testament total 42×; for analysis see Busse, *Wunder*, p. 353 n. 2.

153. Foakes-Jackson and Lake, *Beginnings*, IV, p. 121; G. Bertram, *TDNT*, II, p. 655, and Busse, *Wunder*, pp. 354-55; again, the language is barely likely to be 'traditional', and so is probably Lukan (as are the other two occasions of εὐεργέτης-related words in Luke–Acts).

154. Other than in the Q tradition (Lk. 3.16//Matthew), there are two examples outside Luke–Acts of hendiadys involving πνεῦμα (Jn 4.23; 1 Cor 2.4); Luke has seven such expressions (1.17; 3.16; Acts 6.3, 5; 10.38; 11.24; 13.52). Of these, four (Acts 6.3, 5; 11.24; 13.52) involve genitives defining 'fill' or 'full', in other words a favourite Lukanism. It follows that these occasions of hendiadys are Lukan, and this considerably enhances the probability that 10.38 is such also (note especially the Lukan parallelism between Acts 6.5 (Stephen full of faith and of the Spirit) and 6.8 (Stephen full of grace and of power).

155. As Tuckett ('Luke 4.16-30', p. 347) and Schweizer (cf. 'The Spirit of Power', p. 266 n. 6) require.

156. εὐεργέτης ('benefactor') and related words elsewhere only appear twice in the New Testament: at Lk. 22.25 of Hellenistic 'benefactors', and at 1 Tim. 6.2. The word was very common, however, outside the New Testament in relation to literal benefaction.

157. For the view that εὐεργετῶν καὶ ἰώμενος form another hendiadys, see Busse, *Wunder*, p. 56. On the relationship of healing and exorcism in Luke, see Busse, *Wunder*, pp. 355-56; 423-50.

of 10.38 should be understood either epexegetically (i.e. explaining the intended content of 'performing works of benificence') or, at least, as providing a typical example of what was meant. The description of the healed as formerly 'oppressed by the devil' would bring Acts 10.38 into close parallel with Lk. 4.18 (and 4.31-41; 13.10-17, etc.), the whole thrust of which is that people are released from a realm of satanic affliction into a sphere of salvation.[158]

Acts 10.38, then, presents the Spirit upon Jesus as the power by which he healed those oppressed by Satan. And the addition of the phrase 'and power' within the hendiadys 'anointed... with Holy-Spirit-and-power' does not set a buffer between the Spirit and miracles (as Menzies suggests—far less, of course, does it imply Jesus was anointed with two separable modes of the presence of God, Spirit and power); it means he was endowed with the Holy-Spirit-coming-to-expression-in-power (or 'powerfully').[159]

5. Jesus' Exultation in the Spirit (Luke 10.21)

The only other direct reference to the Spirit on Jesus in Luke comes at 10.21. With the phrase 'in that hour', Luke joins the statement that Jesus ἠγαλλιάσατο (ἐν) τῷ πνεύματι τῷ ἁγίῳ ('exulted in the Holy Spirit')[160] with the return of the disciples, rejoicing because they have had a successful mission.[161] Luke almost certainly expects his readers to take this dative

158. See Busse, *Wunder*, pp. 428-46; against Stanton, *Jesus*, p. 79, and Conzelmann, *Theology*, p. 157, who regard the language of healing of the satanically oppressed as 'traditional', not Lukan.

159. For a similar view see J. Dupont, 'Dieu l'a oint d'Esprit Saint', in *Nouvelles études sur les Actes des Apôtres* (Paris: Cerf, 1984), pp. 319-28 (327-28). Dupont argues that Jesus is here portrayed as the Mosaic prophet, 'powerful in word and deeds' (cf. Acts 7.22).

160. The variety of readings demonstrates that scribes found the language either unusual or offensive from the start. ὁ Ἰησοῦς is an addition to the earliest tradition, as witnessed by the variety of positions it takes in the sentence and by its poor attestation in the majority of early texts (𝔓⁴⁵ 𝔓⁷⁵ א B D and others). Similarly the absence of τῷ ἁγίῳ should be regarded as a secondary feature (again not the mark of some of our best MSS [𝔓⁷⁵ א B D]) and can be accounted for by the desire to remove a startling reading by making the reference to πνεῦμα anthropological. The best readings are thus either ἐν τῷ πνεύματι τῷ ἁγίῳ (א D *al* it) or τῷ πνεύματι τῷ ἁγίῳ (𝔓⁷⁵ B *al*). Of these, the first is easier explained either as the influence of the LXX or as the assimilation of Lk. 4.1b and 2.27, though it is supported by the internal argument that it provides a parallel in contrast with μὴ ἐν τούτῳ (v. 20). The only pre-Christian parallel of which I am aware is 1QH 9.32: וברוח קודשכה תשעשעני; but it is not close.

161. For the redactional nature of the connection and its phraseology see Miyoshi, *Anfang*, pp. 120-22.

noun phrase as instrumental: Jesus was inspired with joy by the Holy Spirit;
cf. Acts 13.52.[162] This notice would hardly surprise a Jewish Christian
reader, for, as we have seen, the Spirit of prophecy is traditionally associated
with the inspiration of praise and doxological faith (cf. *1 En.* 61.7-11; 71.11;
Josephus, *Ant.* 6.166, 223; *Bib. Ant.* 32.14; *t. Sot.* 6.2; *Mek Beš.* 7; *Mek Šir.*
1 and 3; *Exod. R.* 23.2; *Targ. Onq.* Num. 11.25-27; *Targ. Neb.* 1 Sam. 10.6;
19.20, 23, etc.). In this instance (as often), the exultation is not the result of
the direct afflatus of the Spirit, but (as the redactional 'in that very hour'
suggests) in part or wholly evoked by the message Jesus has heard concerning the success of the mission of the disciples, and the significance he has
attached to it (10.18).[163] The Spirit is thus probably understood as the
source of charismatic wisdom which enables the joyful perception of the
significance of their report in the context of his mission,[164] and this rejoicing
is articulated in the christological and salvation-historical climax of 10.22-
24. We have here a dynamic of charismatic wisdom leading to wisdom
utterance and joyful doxology elsewhere found in, for example, Sir. 39.6.
Once again, Luke's portrait highlights Jesus as the messiah of charismatic
wisdom anticipated in Isa. 11.1-4 and the Jewish tradition which built on
this.

6. *Conclusion*

I shall draw out the theological significance of Luke's understanding of
Jesus' relationship to the Spirit in the final chapter. For the present I will
simply summarize my findings. The following points have been argued:

(1) Lk. 4.16-28 is largely, if not entirely, traditional; in particular Luke
cannot have been responsible for the significant changes to the Isaiah
citation.

---

162. Cf. Bultmann, *TDNT*, I, p. 21; Marshall, 433; P.J. Cullen, 'Euphoria, Praise and
Thanksgiving: Rejoicing in the Spirit in Luke–Acts', *JPT* 6 (1995), 13-24, esp. 15.

163. For the view that Jesus' logion concerning the casting out of Satan from heaven
is to be taken symbolically (rather than describing a visionary experience) see Danker,
128; Marshall, 428-29; Fitzmyer, *Luke*, pp. 164-69.

164. The dative noun phrase 'in the Holy Spirit' could indicate the subject of Jesus
rejoicing, contrasting with [μὴ] ἐν τούτῳ χαίρειν (v. 20). For ἀγαλλιάομαι with ἐν +
dative of subject for rejoicing cf. LXX Ps. 9.2; 12.5; 19.5, etc., and in the New
Testament, Jn 5.35 and 1 Pet. 1.6 (without ἐν, cf. Ps. 144.7). For the view that 'he
rejoiced in the Holy Spirit' means that Jesus perceived the missionary success of the
disciples to be an outworking of the Spirit upon him, shared with them, after the likeness of Num. 11.25-27 (on which Lk. 10 is based), see Turner, *Luke*, pp. 86-88, and cf.
Chapter 11 §1 below.

(2) The background that 'explains' the form of the citation is messianic Jubilee/New Exodus hopes and the way they were taken up in Q and in the separate pre-Lukan tradition in 4.16-30. These regarded the Spirit on Jesus as the power by which he initiated Israel's messianic release, epitomized in his redemptive miracles.

(3) For Luke too, 4.18-28 portrays Jesus as the Isaianic soteriological prophet, which he identifies primarily with the Mosaic prophet. The kingly functions of the latter figure, however, allow him a ready connection with his baptismal account where Jesus receives the Spirit both as Davidic king and as Isaianic soteriological prophet. Judaism had already approximated these figures to each other, and the 'new Exodus' traditions involved some fusion of them.

(4) Luke understands the mission of Jesus (as outlined in 4.18-21) not in messianic Jubilee terms but in New Exodus terms. By this is meant not a simple replay of the Deuteronomic Exodus, but a development of the primarily deutero-Isaianic New Exodus hopes. This background provides the unity for the whole of Luke 1–4 (and beyond), and explains his otherwise curious or 'promiscuous' fusion of prophet-like-Moses and Davidic Christologies. The mission of Jesus, and for which he is empowered by the Spirit, is to free Israel from her 'slave-poverty', 'exile-captive' and 'blind' estate and to lead her along the wilderness 'way' towards restored Zion. Luke thinks the aims of Jesus' actual ministry corresponds to this 'pattern' of hopes, even if he is aware they are qualified by the 'rejection of the prophet' motif.

(5) We then examined how this 'New Exodus' understanding of Jesus' mission bears on the question of understanding Jesus' miracles. At one level it clearly provides a rationale for expecting the messiah of the Spirit to work healing miracles and exorcisms, and this was becoming a part of 'messianic expectation'. But at another level it raises the possibility that Luke took 4.18-21 as metaphors for Israel's restoration, and that this allowed him to sever the connection between the Spirit and literal healings and exorcisms. We have seen, however, that all the arguments mounted in favour of this last position ultimately fail. Luke, like the Judaism and Christianity before him, saw healings and exorcism as of a piece with Israel's liberation, and regarded the Spirit as empowering the whole range of Jesus' liberating activity.

From our overall picture it must be clear that for Luke Jesus' baptismal reception of the Spirit is not for his own archetypal entry into the experience of new covenant life (*contra* Dunn), it is an empowering by which to inaugurate Israel's New Exodus liberation.

Chapter 10

PENTECOST: JESUS' ENTHRONEMENT AS ISRAEL'S MESSIAH AND THE SPIRIT AS HIS EXECUTIVE POWER IN ISRAEL'S RESTORATION

Peter's explanation of the Pentecost event in Acts 2.14-39 has perhaps greater claim than Lk. 4.16-30 to be called 'the programmatic' text of Luke–Acts. Odette Mainville even makes Acts 2.33 the interpretive key to the whole of Luke's pneumatology, and her entire monograph is arranged on that assumption.[1] What gives the Pentecost speech its central place is not simply what is said explicitly about the Spirit, but the way what is said here is reintegrated with other cardinal aspects of Luke's theology. Within the Pentecostal fire of this address Luke softens and gently reshapes the main theologoumena of the Gospel. The reader's perceptions of the kingdom of God, 'Christ', the people of God, salvation and Israel's hope will all require adjustment in its light, and, with these, his or her perception of 'the gift of the Spirit'. The significance of the changes will be spelt out by the rest of the narrative of Acts, but we must begin with the Pentecost speech itself. The task in this chapter will largely be to determine what expectations are raised by the Pentecost account.

In §1 we shall examine the Pentecost speech itself. After a brief discussion of the form in which Luke presents the text of Joel which Peter expounds (§1.1), we investigate the purpose of this extraordinarily long 'citation' (§1.2), and the stages in Peter's argument which lead up to the climactic assertions of 2.33-36, namely that, as Lord of the Spirit, Jesus now pours out Joel's gift in God's place. He is thereby revealed as the Davidic messiah and Lord upon whose name one must call for salvation, even as Joel envisaged one would call on God's name (§1.3). In §1.4 we attempt to show that (as in the Gospel) Luke combines this Davidic Christology with a prophet-like-Moses motif, which alone explains the strong Moses/Sinai parallels in 2.1-13 and the remarkable statement in 2.33. Acts 2 thus not only presents Jesus as attaining the exalted throne of David, but also as a greater Moses who ascends to God in order to grant a foundational gift to Israel. The gift of the

---

1. Mainville, 'Jésus', pp. 193-208; *idem*, *L'Esprit*, *passim* (see esp. pp. 321-22 where she claims it is also the key to Luke's composition of the two books).

Spirit would appear to be portrayed as the power of Israel's covenant renewal.

In §2 we investigate how Peter's assertions draw together the strands of Luke's teaching on the kingdom of God and Jesus' kingship. We discover (in §2.1) that in essence Acts 2.33 answers to the hopes of Lk. 1.32-33, and (*contra* Conzelmann) the kingdom of God comes in greater than hitherto experienced power and presence in Israel through Jesus' attainment of the eternal throne of David to rule over Jacob. In §2.2 we elucidate how the (redactional) ending of Luke (24.46-49) and preface of Acts (1.1-11) prepares for what we have discovered in §1 and §2.1, that is, for a deepening of the messianic cleansing, restoration and transformation of Israel through the gift of the Spirit which is now the messiah's executive power. The promise of John the Baptist (Lk. 3.16) is interpreted by Acts 1.5 to mean the Spirit will come upon the disciples not merely as the empowering by which they will witness, but as the power which cleanses and restores the messiah's Israel.

Then in §3 we shall ask whether certain cardinal aspects of the expectations raised in §§1-2 are carried through into the book of Acts as a whole: does Acts consistently represent the Spirit as the executive power of the exalted messiah for the restoration of Israel? This section introduces arguments that will be elucidated in more detail and built on in Chapter 13.

1. *The Pentecost Speech*

There can be relatively little doubt but that this speech incorporates ancient tradition,[2] for it is not likely that Luke, the Hellenist, first composed the *pesher* of Joel 3.1-5 (ET 2.28-32),[3] nor that he is responsible for the other midrashic elements in the speech,[4] even if the address as a whole expresses

2. B. Lindars, *New Testament Apologetic* (London: SCM Press, 1961), ch. 2; J. Dupont, 'Ascension du Christ et don de l'Esprit d'après Actes 2.33', in Lindars and Smalley (eds.), *Christ*, pp. 219-27. Zehnle demurs (*Discourse*, pp. 26-36; 61-70; 95-130), but see Pesch, 118-19; Turner, 'Spirit and Christology', pp. 168-90 (184-86).

3. Bock, *Proclamation*, pp. 156-87 notes that the unusually numerous and varied changes to the LXX of this passage are quite un-Lukan in character. G. Lüdemann, *Early Christianity according to the Traditions in Acts* (London: SCM Press, 1989), p. 48, accepts that the use of Joel 2.32 (LXX 3.5) is early (for it underlies 'calling on the name of the Lord [Jesus]' in Rom. 10.13 and in e.g. 1 Cor. 1.2), as is also the use of Ps. 110. But the use of Joel 2.32 christologically assumes something like the premise of Acts 2.33.

4. E.E. Ellis, 'Midrashic Features in the Speeches of Acts', in Descamps and de Halleux (eds.), *Mélanges bibliques*, pp. 306-309; J. Doeve, *Jewish Hermeneutics in the Synoptic Gospels and Acts* (Assen: van Gorcum, 1954), pp. 168ff. The 'Palestinian' reference to David as a prophet also points away from Lukan

a theology with which he fundamentally agrees.

Luke commences the account of Peter's speech with a pesher of Joel 3.1-5 [2.28-32], derived substantially from the LXX. We shall first examine its form (§1.1), then its purpose within the speech (§1.2), and the stages of Peter's argument (§1.3). Finally, within this section, we shall ask whether the Pentecost account has been moulded by the story of Moses' ascent to God to receive the Torah which he gives to Israel (§1.4).

1.1 *The Form of the Citation*

Joel	Acts
[3.1] Καὶ ἔσται μετὰ ταῦτα	[2.17] Καὶ ἔσται <u>ἐν ταῖς ἐσχάταις ἡμέραις, λέγει ὁ θεός,</u>
καὶ ἐκχεῶ ἀπὸ τοῦ πνεύματός μου ἐπὶ πᾶσαν σάρκα,	---ἐκχεῶ ἀπὸ τοῦ πνεύματός μου ἐπὶ πᾶσαν σάρκα,
καὶ προφητεύσουσιν οἱ υἱοὶ ὑμῶν καὶ αἱ θυγατέρες ὑμῶν,	καὶ προφητεύσουσιν οἱ υἱοὶ ὑμῶν καὶ αἱ θυγατέρες ὑμῶν,
καὶ οἱ πρεσβύτεροι ὑμῶν ἐνύπνια ἐνυπνιασθήσονται	καὶ οἱ <u>νεανίσκοι</u> ὑμῶν ὁράσεις ὄψονται, καὶ οἱ πρεσβύτεροι ὑμῶν <u>ἐνυπνίοις</u>
καὶ οἱ νεανίσκοι ὑμῶν ὁράσεις ὄψονται,	ἐνυπνιασθήσονται·
[3.2] καὶ ἐπὶ τοὺς δούλους καὶ ἐπὶ τὰς δούλας ἐν ταῖς ἡμέραις ἐκείναις ἐκχεῶ ἀπὸ τοῦ πνεύματός μου.	[2.18] καί <u>γε</u> ἐπὶ τοὺς δούλους <u>μου</u> καὶ ἐπὶ τὰς δούλας <u>μου</u> ἐν ταῖς ἡμέραις ἐκείναις ἐκχεῶ ἀπὸ τοῦ πνεύματός μου <u>καὶ προφητεύσουσιν.</u>
[3.3] καὶ δώσω τέρατα ἐν τῷ οὐρανῷ καὶ ἐπὶ τῆς γῆς,	[2.19] καὶ δώσω τέρατα ἐν τῷ οὐρανῷ <u>ἄνω</u> καὶ <u>σημεῖα</u> ἐπὶ τῆς γῆς <u>κάτω,</u>
αἷμα καὶ πῦρ καὶ ἀτμίδα καπνοῦ·	[2.20] ὁ ἥλιος μεταστραφήσεται εἰς σκότος καὶ ἡ σελήνη εἰς αἷμα πρὶν
[3.4] ὁ ἥλιος μεταστραφήσεται εἰς σκότος καὶ ἡ σελήνη εἰς αἷμα πρὶν ἐλθεῖν ἡμέραν κυρίου τὴν μεγάλην καὶ ἐπιφανῆ.	ἐλθεῖν ἡμέραν κυρίου τὴν μεγάλην καὶ ἐπιφανῆ.
[3.5] καὶ ἔσται πᾶς ὃς ἂν ἐπικαλέσηται τὸ ὄνομα κυρίου σωθήσεται.	[2.21] καὶ ἔσται πᾶς ὃς ἂν ἐπικαλέσηται τὸ ὄνομα κυρίου σωθήσεται.

composition: cf. J.A. Fitzmyer, 'David "Being therefore a Prophet..." (Acts 2.30)', *CBQ* 34 (1972), pp. 332-39. Of course we cannot demonstrate that the speech was actually spoken by *Peter* and on *this* occasion. Even if we could be sure that Luke had written sources for the Pentecost account, it could not be proved that they included this discourse—but at the same time there is no good reason for Lüdemann's dogmatic affirmation 'Peter did not make a speech on the first day of Pentecost in Jerusalem, certainly not with the sort of content that is reproduced in Acts' (*Christianity*, p. 48), far less to doubt that the speech may derive from the earliest church (*contra* Haenchen, *ad loc.*, who argues from the use of the LXX that the tradition cannot be ancient. Against him see Rese, *Motive*, pp. 45-55; Bock, *Proclamation*, pp. 156-87, esp. 163).

Of the changes here from the LXX, six are theologically potentially significant:[5]

a. The replacement of LXX μετὰ ταῦτα ('after these things') by ἐν ταῖς ἐσχάταις ἡμέραις ('in the last days') in 2.17, identifying the gift as the eschatological promise (which is then probably traditional rather than Lukan).

b. The addition in 2.17 of λέγει ὁ θεός. The placement here within the oracle is probably pre-Lukan,[6] though at a redactional level it serves Luke to specify the promise as that of the Father (cf. Lk. 24.49; Acts 1.4).

c. The double addition of μου after men-servants and maid-servants, which highlights the gift as one to *God's* servants, rather than to the sociological category.

d. The additional καὶ προφητεύσουσιν in 2.18 (clarifying the gift as 'the Spirit of prophecy', and emphasizing this by *inclusio* with 2.17c).

e. The addition of σημεῖα...κάτω which prepares for 2.22 while also interpreting the Pentecost event.

f. Luke omits from his source the words of Joel 3.5b 'for on Mount Zion and in Jerusalem there will be deliverance, as the Lord has said, among the survivors whom the Lord calls'. It appears to have belonged to the original citation in the source, because Peter uses its final words in 2.39 (and this section would comport well with a theophany in Jerusalem!); Luke will have dropped it partly because the citation then reaches a fitting climax about calling on the name of the lord to be saved, but partly because he knows God's salvation will not centre on Jerusalem.[7]

1.2. *The General Purpose of the Citation in the Pentecost Address*
The reason for the use of Joel 3.1-2 [2.28-29] is transparent: it explains the Pentecostal phenomenon of glossolalia. As we have seen in Chapters 3–5, Joel's promise of the Spirit would inevitably be understood in terms of the

---

5. Others are minor and stylistic: (i) ἐνυπνίοις (2.17) for accusative pl. in LXX; (ii) the omission of καί in 2.17 (but this conforms with some LXX texts); (iii) the addition of γε at 2.18, and (iv) the exchange of order of clauses concerning young men and old men in 2.17.

6. Luke does not encase such affirmations *within* citations: the phenomenon is only elsewhere found in Luke's sources (viz. 7.7, 49 in the pre-Lukan tradition of Stephen's speech).

7. J. Dupont, *Etudes sur les Actes des Apôtres* (Paris: Cerf, 1967), pp. 393-419, Rese, *Motive*, p. 50, and Lüdemann, *Christianity*, p. 45.

'Spirit of prophecy', and either Luke or his source made it the clearer by the additional 'and they shall prophesy' in 2.18. The reference to 'dreams' and 'visions' inside the *inclusio* thereby formed with 2.17d would of course entirely match Jewish expectation with respect to the 'Spirit of prophecy', for they were regular means of receiving charismatic revelation which was the prototypical gift of the 'Spirit of prophecy'. Glossolalia, as such, was not known to Judaism (as far as we are aware) and so was not specifically envisaged as a gift of the 'Spirit of prophecy' (indeed, had it been known it would probably not have required explanation). As we have seen (Chapter 3), however, invasive charismatic praise was a prototypical gift—and might be anticipated occasionally, especially in connection with either the initial reception of the Spirit or with some dramatic irruption of the Spirit on people. Within this conceptual context, glossolalia would readily enough have been regarded as a special form of doxological prophetic speech, and this is how Luke understood the gift in Acts 10.46 ('they heard them speaking in tongues and extolling God') and 19.6 ('they began to speak in tongues and to prophesy').[8]

Menzies insists the xenolalia of Acts 2 is missiological proclamation, not praise[9] on the basis that in 2.11 the Jerusalem visitors say 'we hear them in our languages uttering the mighty works (μεγαλεῖα) of God'. That Luke himself envisages the scene to involve a speech miracle (rather than a hearing miracle) is very probable; i.e. on this occasion the glossolalia is recognized xenolalia.[10] That Luke thought of it as missiological proclamation

8. Whether or not these occasions formally identify glossolalia as extolling God and prophetic speech (as Haya-Prats, *L'Esprit*, p. 4), they clearly associate them closely: see Turner, 'Luke and the Spirit', pp. 131-33, arguing glossolalia is a form of doxological prophetic speech, and cf. A.J.M. Wedderburn, 'Tradition and Redaction in Acts 2.1-13', *JSNT* 55 (1994), p. 50.

9. *Development*, p. 211, depending largely on Kremer, *Pfingstbericht*, pp. 158, 165-66. Against Kremer, see Wedderburn, 'Tradition', pp. 50-51.

10. See Turner, 'Spiritual Gifts', pp. 17-18; P. Esler, 'Glossolalia and the Admission of Gentiles into the Early Christian Community', *BTB* 22 (1992), p. 141; Wedderburn, 'Tradition', p. 49. Recently J. Everts has argued for the view that (for Luke) Pentecost involved not xenolalia, but both glossolalia and a hearing miracle, concluding from 2.4 and 2.8 that each individual in the crowd heard the entire group of disciples speaking the individual's native language ('Tongues or Languages? Contextual Consistency in the Translation of Acts 2', *JPT* 4 [1994], pp. 74-75). But this complex reconstruction (one positing a greater miracle in the audience than in the disciples, and a different sense of γλώσσαις in 2.4 and 2.11) is unlikely to commend itself: cf. W.E. Mills, *A Theological/Exegetical Approach to Glossolalia* (London: University Press of America, 1985), who comments: Luke 'does not indicate that the gift of the Spirit descended upon the crowd... Luke's emphasis was in fact upon the speaking and not the hearing' (p. 62, cf. pp. 65, 92).

rather than invasive charismatic praise, however, is unlikely: (1) Nothing in Judaism would prepare for such an understanding. (2) On the only two similar occasions (Acts 10.46 and 19.6) there are no 'outsiders' present to hear the spontaneous outbursts of prophetic praise; and neither Luke, nor any other New Testament writer witnesses knowledge of any case of glossolalia as missiological proclamation (rather Paul can assume the outsider will simply conclude the glossolaliacs rave: 1 Cor. 14.23). (3) Missiological proclamation is hardly to be implied by the noun phrase μεγαλεῖα τοῦ Θεοῦ (2.11), as Menzies claims. From the songs of Moses (Exod. 15) and Deborah (Judg. 5) onwards, extolling God's mighty acts (whether in the second or the third person) was the expected and regular feature of Jewish praise (and the *Magnificat*, *Benedictus*, and *Nunc dimittis* of Luke 1–2 evince the same focus). Had Luke wished to imply miraculous xenolalic missionary announcement of God's mighty deeds addressed to these foreigners he would probably have used a more specific verb (e.g. ἀναγγέλλω, 'announce'; διαγγέλλω, 'proclaim'; εὐαγγελίζω, 'tell the good news of'; or κηρύσσω 'preach, proclaim')—and, of course, there would have been less occasion for the crowd's insinuation of drunkenness (a charge particularly appropriate to ecstatic speech and behaviour rather than measured 'witness') and less need for Peter's own explanation and proclamation.

As Rese correctly observes, however, there is more to the Joel citation than an explanation of the Pentecostal phenomena which provide the occasion for the speech: were that the sole aim, Peter had no need of Joel 3.3-5 [2.30-32]![11] This extensive section has been incorporated because it finishes with the statement that 'all who call on the name of the Lord shall be saved' (Joel 3.5a = Acts 2.21), which the speech will finally interpret with a *christological* force. Peter is to argue that Jesus has been made 'Lord' (2.36), and closely identified with 'the Lord God' of Acts 2.39 = Joel 3.5b (and Acts 2.21 = Joel 3.5a); so closely that those who call on God in baptismal repentance undertake that rite 'in (ἐπί) the name of Jesus Christ' (2.38). This baptismal formula itself thus expresses the belief that Jesus has been identified (functionally) with the 'Lord' upon whose name one should call for salvation (Joel 3.5a).[12]

The point of Peter's speech is to provide a theological undergirding for his application of Joel 3, on the one hand to Jesus as Lord, and on the other to the hearers who are to call upon him. Peter's 'proof' depends on four points:

---

11. *Motive*, pp. 45-55.
12. See particularly Haenchen, 186; Bock, *Proclamation*, pp. 164-66 and 183-87; R. Sloan, '"Signs and Wonders": A Rhetorical Clue to the Pentecost Discourse', *EvQ* 63 (1991), p. 233; and Franklin, *Luke*, pp. 277-78 n. 2.

a.   The Joel citation has already found a measure of eschatological fulfilment in Jesus' ministry and death.

b.   Jesus is raised, and must therefore be the eschatological son of David of whom David spoke prophetically in Psalm 16 (cf. 2.25-32).

c.   As Jesus has been exalted, it is clear that the one to whom David refers as 'my Lord', and who in turn is addressed by the Lord (God) and given dominion (according to Ps. 110.1), is none other than Jesus. Jesus has been made Lord and Christ (2.33-36).

d.   The nature of the exaltation in question, and of the gift which flows from it, involves such a close identification with 'the Lord' of Joel's citation that Jesus may be presented as the redeemer upon whose name men should call for salvation (2.38-39).

The steps in this 'argument' require elucidation.

1.3. The Stages of Peter's Argument

(A) The first stage of the argument is largely secured by the inclusion of the three words ἄνω ('above'), σημεῖα ('sign') and κάτω ('below') to the Joel citation at Acts 2.19: these additions change the whole structure of the quotation, at this point, by the creation of an antithetical parallelism. This change schematically apportions 'wonders' to the realm above and 'signs' to that below,[13] interpreting the apocalyptic language of v. 19c ('blood and fire and clouds of smoke') equally (if not primarily) in terms of 'signs' on earth. The effect is twofold:

1. The Joel text now speaks of 'wonders' and 'signs', which is contrary to the usual LXX order, and unusual for Luke.[14] It evokes a number of resonances. (i) We find the same order at 2.22 where Peter refers to God working wonders and signs through Jesus in his ministry (though the connection is more allusive than exegetical, for Jesus' 'wonders' are on earth).[15] (ii) Rese observed that this order of heavenly wonder followed by earthly sign matches the way Luke has brought the rending of the veil forward and placed it directly after the darkening of the sun (Lk. 23.45),

13.   Schneider (269 n. 47) argues this is just a Lukan way of saying the signs and wonders are visible everywhere; but the disparity with Luke's view that 'signs and wonders' are worked on earth by Jesus and Moses is better explained by assuming the changes to Joel here are *pre*-Lukan.

14.   This order is found at 2.43 where a Lukan summary extends this to the apostles. Elsewhere (barring 6.8 and 7.36 where a Moses-[Stephen]-Jesus parallel is again involved), the order is reversed and follows the usual LXX formula σημεῖα καὶ τέρατα.

15.   See Sloan, 'Signs', pp. 235-37, for similar argument; indeed, he sees this as the primary reference of 2.19.

from which he deduced Luke understood the Joel citation to be entirely fulfilled in the crucifixion events.[16] While a fulfilment in the Passion is probably envisaged, it is unlikely that Luke thought that series of events entirely exhausted the language, which must at least also stretch back to the ministry. (iii) Kremer[17] has argued against Rese that the elements of v. 19c (fire, clouds of smoke) were not fulfilled at the crucifixion, and that Luke knows that σημεῖα are especially related to eschatological signs yet to come (cf. Lk. 21.11 and 25). We should probably accept each of these insights as valid, and that Luke understood the τέρατα and σημεῖα performed by Jesus, as well as those associated with the crucifixion as varying degrees of fulfilment of the Joel prophecy. The inner coherence between these (in the context of Jesus' wider ministry) and the end-events reinforces the affirmation 'the last days' have already broken in.[18] Peter has thereby gained a foothold for his christological use of the Joel passage.

2. The reader of Acts (who has not yet got to 2.22) will perceive that the changes in 2.19 also make it especially appropriate as a description of the Pentecost event as a 'wonder' given from heaven where Jesus ascended: the εἰς τὸν οὐρανόν ('into heaven') in Acts 1.9-11 corresponds to the ἐκ τοῦ οὐρανοῦ ('from heaven') of Acts 2.2, and it is 'from heaven' that the risen Lord pours out this wonder of noise and *fire* (cf. 2.3-4) onto the disciples on earth (2.33). The description of the Pentecost theophany (2.2-4) is full of Sinai allusions with which the reference to 'clouds of smoke' in the Joel citation will especially cohere.

The combined effect of these allusions is to provide a footing for Peter's claim that the Joel quotation is fulfilled in Jesus.

(B) The second stage of Peter's argument (2.25-32) is readily understandable and relies on a traditional use of Psalm 16 combined with an understanding that Jesus was a Davidic messianic claimant.[19] But the argument

---

16. *Motive*, p. 54; cf. Stanton, *Jesus*, pp. 81-82. Sloan, 'Signs', pp. 236-37 admits this is an aspect of what Luke means.

17. *Pfingstbericht*, pp. 173-74.

18. Hence the appropriateness of ἐν ταῖς ἐσχάταις ἡμέραις in 2.17. Haenchen, *ad loc.*, maintains that Luke was compelled to write μετὰ ταῦτα (with B 076 sa *al*) by his non-eschatological approach. Conzelmann (35) recognizes the weakness of the textual evidence for Haenchen's case, but claims that the words of the majority reading were not understood eschatologically by Luke. Neither option is valid. With Zehnle (*Discourse*, p. 29-30) and Rese (*Motive*, p. 52), μετὰ ταῦτα is hardly less 'eschatological' than the better attested reading and the Joel context from which it is taken (the epitome of Jewish hopes for the 'end'). Luke's expression may not delimit the period to the end chronologically, but it is eschatological in *character*. For discussion and literature, see, e.g., Bock, *Proclamation*, pp. 160-61.

19. *Contra* Rese, *Motive*, pp. 55-58, who argues that only a Hellenist could make

here only formally demonstrates that his descendant's resurrection was fore-told by David and that Jesus' identity is established by his resurrection (of which the apostles are witness) as David's eschatological heir.

(C) In the third 'stage', the logic of the argument is far less explicit. 2.33 begins with the claim, 'Being lifted up/exalted (ὑψωθείς) to the right hand of God...'. The verb ὑψόω here (as in 5.31) means 'lift to a place of status, exalt', and it refers to Jesus' ascension-exaltation to rule at God's right hand. Only such an understanding makes sense of the contrasting affirmation in 2.34-35 that it was not David who 'ascended into heaven', but that David anticipated the one he addresses as 'my Lord' would be given that position (Ps. 110.1).[20] It remains unclear, however, how the claim in 2.33a follows from what has been said before; for neither the resurrection nor the ascension into heaven which Peter can claim to have witnessed would themselves lead to the conclusion Jesus was exalted at God's right hand. There were plenty of places of exalted status in the heavenly realm below that one. So what connects 2.19-32 with the claim in 2.33? Lindars has suggested it is the continuing influence of Psalm 16 (LXX 15), and its reference in v. 11 to enjoying eternal pleasures 'in your right hand' (which could be joined by *gezerah shawah* to Ps. 110.1).[21] But as Franklin observed, Luke missed out that verse, and probably in order to make Psalm 16 apply to the resurrection rather than to the ascension. R.F. O'Toole has argued more plausibly that the connection is made by the reference in 2.30 to God's solemn promise to David that one of his descendents would sit on his throne. Psalm 110 could then be understood to describe the location of that throne (at God's right hand), and this would be taken to be in accord with Jesus' own teaching in Lk. 20.41-44 and his affirmation in 22.69. The connections between Acts 2.19-32 and 2.34-36 are thus clearly built on the promises to David,[22] and they are perhaps almost enough to explain the

such startling use of Ps. 16; but compared with much Qumran material Peter's speech is stolid. Cf. Lindars, *Apologetic*, pp. 38ff; Bock, *Proclamation*, pp. 169-81.

20. A local meaning of τῇ δεξιᾷ ('*to* the right hand of God') rather than an instrumental one ('*by* God's right hand') is thus demanded by the context: *contra* Dupont, *Etudes*, pp. 302-304; Voss, *Christologie*, p. 133, and Bruce, *Acts*, p. 126, see Lohfink, *Himmelfahrt*, pp. 226-27; D.M. Hay, *Glory at the Right Hand* (Nashville: Abingdon Press, 1973), pp. 70-73; M. Gourgues, '"Exalté à la droite de Dieu" (Ac 2:33; 5:31)', *SE* 27 (1975), pp. 303-27; *idem, A la droite de Dieu. Résurrection de Jésus et actualisation du psaume 110.1 dans le Nouveau Testament* (Paris: Gabalda, 1978), pp. 164-69; Mainville, *L'Esprit*, pp. 54-59.

21. *Apologetic*, pp. 42-44.

22. So R.F. O'Toole, 'Acts 2:30 and the Davidic Covenant of Pentecost', *JBL* 102 (1983), pp. 245-58, and Bock, *Proclamation* pp. 181-86.

affirmation that God has made this Jesus not merely 'Christ' but 'Lord and Christ' (2.36), for in *Ps. Sol.* 17.32 the title 'Lord' is messianic ('the Lord messiah'; cf. 18.7). Stage three of Peter's argument would thus be convincing enough on first-century Jewish presuppositions.

(D) The fourth stage, however, appears to require something beyond what is said so far. It is doubtful whether in a Jewish context a human figure exalted to God's right hand would readily be 'called on' for salvation in the way implied by the association of baptism 'in the name of Jesus Christ' with Joel 3.5 [2.32].[23] The presupposition which allows this surprising claim is to be found in 2.33b, c; the one exalted at God's right hand has 'received the promise of the Holy Spirit' from the Father, and himself (in God's own place, cf. 2.17b, c) *'pours out this which you see and hear'* (i.e. the Pentecostal phenomena)! This statement may in part build on Jewish expectation that the Davidic messiah would be a figure powerfully endowed with the Spirit, and that others would experience the Spirit's work *through* him, but it goes very substantially beyond such understanding.

23. This assertion is not beyond doubt. The fact is we have too little relevant evidence about what functions a Jew might expect God to delegate to a human figure exalted to God's throne as his chief executive agent. Rabbi Aqiba (died 135) debated with other rabbis whether the Davidic messiah could be seated next to God or whether such an exaltation would not simply be impossible, because blasphemous (see e.g. *b. Ḥag* 14a// *b. San* 38b and *m. Tanḥuma* [*Qedoshim* §1], and cf. Catchpole, *Trial*, pp. 140-41. Indeed D.L. Bock has argued this understanding explains why the priests perceive Jesus' claim in Lk. 22.69 and pars. as blasphemy: see Bock, 'The Son of Man Seated at God's Right Hand and the Debate over Jesus' "Blasphemy" ', in Green and Turner [eds.], *Jesus*, pp. 181-91). In *T. Abr.* 11-13, Abel sits upon a throne judging all humankind as God's appointed agent; but he is not invoked as a saving figure, and the throne is at the entrance to the heavenly city, not at God's right hand. Similarly, in *1 Enoch*, 'the Elect One' is to be given God's throne, but simply for the task of acting on God's behalf as judge over humans (45.3; 51.3), over Azaz'el and his hosts (55.4), and over the angels (61.8). The rationale (offered by *T. Abr.* 13.3) is that only a man (a creature) can appropriately judge humankind and God's other creatures. L.W. Hurtado (*One God, One Lord* [London: SCM Press, 1988], p. 59) argues that Ezekiel's *Exagōgē* (68-80) depicts Moses mounting God's throne, being given crown and sceptre, and accorded honours by a march-past of stars. But this is only a dream (as the last line shows), and Moses' father-in-law interprets it for him as his forthcoming earthly rule *over Israel*, and as the powers of revelation he will receive: i.e. there is no envisaged ascent of God's throne at all outside the universe of discourse of the dream; and too many impossible things become 'possible' in dreams. This, as far as I am aware, is the sum of the relevant ITP pre-Amoraic evidence. In the much later *3 Enoch* 9-10, Enoch is wonderfully transformed as Metatron, he is given a throne like Yahweh's, and his writ extends through the heavenly places, but even here he is not a saving figure invoked on earth.

Three subsidiary clarificatory points are required here:

1. As is widely recognized 'the promise of the Father' is a Lukan formulation already used in Lk. 24.49 and Acts 1.4 in preparation for this claim, though in those contexts the precise content of 'the promise' is left veiled.

2. Lk. 24.49 further prepares for the claim in Acts 2.33, by having Jesus mysteriously refer to this promise as a 'power from on high', which '*I* will send...upon you', and which the disciples are to receive 'in the city (= Jerusalem)'. Acts 1.5 identifies this same promise (cf. 1.4) with John the Baptist's prophecy to the effect that the Spirit-endowed messiah would cleanse/restore Israel.

3. The fulfilment of the promise envisaged in Acts 2.17-18, 33, however, takes the reader beyond anything Judaism conceived of the messiah,[24] for it relates the Spirit to Jesus in the same way as to God, the Father, himself. Thus at 2.17 Luke's tradition had specifically included the words 'God declares' (λέγει ὁ θεός) within the citation of Joel 3.1 [2.28], and immediately before the words '*I* shall pour out my Spirit'.[25] From a Jewish point of view, this addition was strictly superfluous because no being other than God could possibly be conceived as 'pouring out' God's Spirit as the universal eschatological gift of the 'Spirit of prophecy' to Israel—for, unlike God's power of eschatological judgment which he could delegate to exalted beings, God's *Spirit* (even more strongly than the *Shekinah*) *was a way of speaking of the active* (usually self-revealing) *personal presence of the transcendent God himself*. Again, to emphasize this point, while God may have many important agents of his presence and power (including principal angels, exalted patriarch, or even personifications of his own attributes, such as Wisdom and Logos), the Spirit is virtually never simply an agent, separable from God, but one of the few ways Judaism reserves for *God's own* activity *in contrast* to his activity through agents. Spirit is God's way of being, the 'breath' of his mouth, his own surging 'life', and so the unmediated extension of his personality and vitality.[26] When the audience has thus been reminded of the transcendence of God's Spirit by this emphatic inclusion of '*God* declares' before the words '*I* will pour out *my* Spirit on all flesh', it can only come as a sharp surprise to hear Peter assert that the *ascended Jesus* 'has poured out this which you see and hear' (2.33). Here Jesus does not merely mediate in the bestowing of God's Spirit as the eschatological gift; he actually also becomes the author of specific

---

24. See Chapter 7 above.

25. Luke does not elsewhere encase such assertions within a citation, except at Acts 7.4, 49 in what is plainly a pre-Lukan speech.

26. See Turner, 'The Spirit of Christ and "Divine" Christology', in Green and Turner (eds.), *Jesus*, pp. 422-24.

phenomena given to the disciples by the Spirit—he has 'poured out' the specific charismata the audience 'see' and 'hear'.

From the perspective of 'Peter's' Pentecost speech, it would appear that the Spirit of God has thus become τὸ πνεῦμα 'Inσοῦ ('the Spirit of Jesus' cf. 16.7), too. Jesus has become 'Lord of the Spirit', and the Spirit the executive power of his presence, after the analogy of God's own relationship to his Spirit (though this is only implicit in Peter's speech and brought out more fully by the narrator in the course of Acts). No such claim had ever been made in pre-Christian Judaism on behalf of a messiah or of any other exalted creature, nor could it be made without threatening Judaism's exclusive monotheism.[27] The conviction that it was Jesus who 'poured out' the eschatological Spirit in God's place would thus have been quite sufficient to guarantee that Jesus should be acknowledged as 'Lord', and that in its transcendent sense.[28] If Jesus' functions have been so aligned with Yahweh's that both can be said to pour out God's own Spirit from the throne of God,[29] then there is nothing to prevent the christological application of the Joel citation being carried through at every point. 'Jesus Christ' can barely be less than 'the name of the Lord' upon which all men should call (compare 2.36, 38-39 with 2.21 and 33);[30] a view certainly witnessed in

27. See Turner, 'Spirit and "Divine" Christology', pp. 413-36.

28. J.C. O'Neill ('The Use of KYRIOS in the Book of Acts', *SJT* 8 [1955], pp. 160-74) correctly points out that the contexts of a number of speeches in Acts, in which Jesus is referred to as 'Lord', quite clearly indicate that he stands in an absolute relationship to God in which he is the revelation of the Lord God and invested with God's title as his unique (cf. 4.12) plenipotentiary (cf. also G. Stählin, 'Tò πνεῦμα 'Inσοῦ (Apg. 16.7)', in Lindars and Smalley [eds.], *Christ*, pp. 229-52; D.L. Jones, 'The Title Kyrios in Luke–Acts', in G.W. Macrae [ed.], *SBL Seminar Papers* (Cambridge, MA: SBL, 1974), II, pp. 85-96, and compare R. Glöckner, *Die Verkündigung des Heils beim Evangelisten Lukas* [Mainz: Matthias-Grünewald, 1975], pp. 117-21; 227-40). In his article O'Neill had stated that 'Jesus was preached as the Lord whom the Jews worshipped' (p. 162), but more recently (*Theology*, p. 131) he denies that such a view could have been held by the earliest Aramaic speaking community on the basis of Ps. 110.1, for such a community could not fail to distinguish the two Lords in that verse: the first was יהוה, the second אדני. This is true for any attempt to derive Christology from Ps. 110.1 alone; but it is not clear that אדני need necessarily mean *less* than יהוה, and if the earliest community had other reasons for using God-talk of Jesus it would have read the two titles as equivalents.

29. For Luke, Jesus' act in 'pouring out' the Spirit does not replace God's; as in the Fourth Gospel (compare 14.26 with 15.26 and 16.7), Jesus 'sends' (Lk. 24.49) and 'pours out' (Acts 2.33) the Spirit at one with the Father (Acts 2.17; cf. 5.32; 11.15-17 + 15.8).

30. So Bock, *Proclamation*, pp. 184-87, though he puts much more emphasis on Jesus being exalted to God's right hand than on his bestowing the Spirit as the rationale for Peter's claim Jesus is the 'Lord' of Joel 2.28-32. Franklin (*Luke*, pp. 277-78 n. 2)

much of the remaining material in Acts.[31] If one asks on what authority such a bold claim could be made by Peter, the answer in the Lukan narrative is clear; Jesus himself had said he would 'send' the Pentecostal gift (Lk. 24.49), and he it was, too, who promised to provide inspired speech (Lk. 21.15). By Luke's own day, of course, the theology implicit in Peter's proclamation would be less exceptional.

We have seen how Peter justifies his soteriological application of the Joel oracle in terms of God's solemn promises in respect of David's eschatological heir. One can understand each of the individual arguments, but the overall pattern is puzzling. Acts 2 begins with a description of Pentecost in theophanic terms, then we hear a speech that explains matters in terms of someone having ascended to God to receive a great gift which he bestows upon God's people. The pattern does not so naturally suggest David, as it does Jewish traditions about Moses at Sinai. If Acts 2 describes the 'son of David', we have to say he appears to go to his enthronement decked out in 'Mosaic' regalia and with a Sinai chorus. That could have considerable implications for the pneumatology of Acts 2, suggesting, perhaps, the Spirit is in some way 'the Spirit of New (or, better, 'Renewed') Covenant life'.[32] Accordingly we must now examine the arguments.

1.4. *Mosaic Themes and the Spirit of the Renewed Covenant in Peter's Pentecost Speech?*

The argument in Acts 2.14-39 has so far been explored solely within the context of the Davidic promises. But is this the full story? We have seen how Luke's Gospel tended to fuse Davidic and Mosaic Christologies together in a New Exodus soteriology. And on the one occasion where Luke's Gospel anticipates Jesus being 'taken up' to heaven (9.51) the Old Testament/ITP model is either Elijah or (given the Mosaic context of the Travel Narrative and of 9.28-36; 10.1-11 in particular) more probably Moses,

argues against Bock that Jesus' exalted position as Lord 'in no way expresses identification of status' with the Lord = Yahweh. But this cannot be right: in making Jesus Lord of the Spirit, Luke does indeed in some way express such identification.

31. Cf. 4.10, 8.16; 9.28 etc.

32. So (differently) Knox, *Acts*, pp. 85-86; G. Kretschmar, 'Himmelfahrt und Pfingsten', *ZKG* 66 (1954), pp. 209-53; Dunn, *Baptism*, pp. 48-49; R. Le Déaut, 'Pentecost and Jewish Tradition', *Doctrine and Life* 20 (1970), pp. 260-62, 266; J. Dupont, 'La nouvelle Pentecôte (Ac 2, 1-11)', in *Nouvelles Etudes sur les Actes des Apôtres* (Paris: Cerf, 1984), pp. 193-95. Menzies devotes some sixteen pages (*Development*, pp. 229-44) to the task of denying Acts 2 has anything to do with Moses and Sinai largely because he does not wish to let such a thesis slip in through the back door!

and the appearance of Moses with Elijah within the transfiguration account
perhaps implies knowledge of the Jewish tradition of the 'assumption of
Moses'. The Davidic features in Acts 2 certainly do not preclude that Luke
understands Jesus' ascent and pouring out of the Spirit in Mosaic terms too.
Indeed, R.H. Zehnle has demonstrated there is an intricate network of structural parallels between the Pentecost speech and that in Acts 3, more tightly
woven that anywhere else in Acts.[33] Within Peter's speech in Acts 3 Jesus
is depicted as servant (3.13-15, 26), as the suffering, risen/ascended and
eschatological messiah at present in heaven (3.18-21), but above all as the
promised prophet-like-Moses who now confronts Israel with the 'two
ways' of her destiny (3.22-23). Does Acts 2 prepare for this emphasis? Or is
Bock nearer the truth in his assertion that a 'Mosaic background is not
significant at all for the Pentecost event'?[34] In our view, three lines of argument all converge to suggest Luke expects his reader to understand the
figure of David's Lord in 2.14-38 as Mosaic as well as Davidic.

*The Associations of the Jewish Feast of Pentecost with the Law-Giving at
Sinai.* The very mention that the Spirit descended *at Pentecost* may be
pregnant with Sinai connotations. Luke does not usually provide firm dat-
ings, and the vagueness of so many of the other details in this account
points up the significance of the relative precision of the ponderous redactional clause ἐν τῷ συμπληροῦσθαι τὴν ἡμέραν τῆς πεντεκοστῆς
('when the day of Pentecost was fully come'),[35] while the unusual rather
sonorous verb (// Lk. 9.51) might even hint at the connotation 'when the
day of Pentecost was fulfilled'.[36] 'Pentecost' (='fiftieth') is the Jewish
'feast of weeks' (*Shabuoth*), so-called after the instruction of Lev. 23.15-16
to celebrate with an offering of new grain seven weeks after the Passover
(merged with Firstfruits) Sabbath. As Passover was the middle of the first

---

33. Tabulated in Zehnle, *Discourse*, pp. 19-23.

34. *Proclamation*, pp. 182-183; similarly, but less emphatically, Strauss, *Messiah*,
pp. 135-47, esp. 145-47.

35. See E. Lohse, 'Die Bedeutung des Pfingstberichtes in Rahmen des lukanischen
Geschichtwerkes', in *Die Einheit des Neuen Testaments* (Göttingen: Vandenhoeck &
Ruprecht, 1973), pp. 187-89; Kremer, *Pfingstbericht*, pp. 92-95; J. Dupont, 'La
première Pentecôte chrétienne (Ac 2, 1-11)', in *Etudes*, pp. 482-83. συμπληροῦσθαι
would usually suggest the completion of an interval, and hence the arrival of an
expected day (cf. Lk. 9.51). But (against Haenchen, 167) it probably does not mean
something like 'when the long-awaited day of Pentecost dawned', nor, with Zerwick
(352), 'when the day of Pentecost was coming to an end' (for 2.15 establishes it is
morning, but (with Pesch, 102) 'when the day of Pentecost fully came' (i.e. the
morning of the feast, not its earlier evening).

36. Cf. C. Schedl, *Als sich der Pfingsttag erfüllte: Erklärung der Pfingstperikope
Apg 2,1-47* (Vienna: Herder, 1982), pp. 52-54; Tannehill, *Unity*, II, p. 26.

month of the Jewish calendar (= Nisan [March/April]), *Shabuoth* fell in the middle of the third month of the Jewish year. It was essentially the harvest festival. But were there further associations? 2 Chron. 15.10-12 refers to a celebration of the *renewal of the covenant* in the *third month* of Asa's fifteenth year, and some Jewish groups evidently thought Pentecost was the appropriate festival at which to celebrate the giving of the Law. Thus, for example, *Jubilees* 6 lays on Noah's descendants the duty of celebrating the renewed (Noachic) covenant at the feast of weeks, and states that after the patriarchs the meal was forgotten until renewed by God on *the mountain* (i.e. Sinai, and then as the Sinai covenant; 6.19). Menzies dismisses the connections between the feast and the giving of the Law at Sinai in this document as 'minor',[37] but this appears to overlook the fact that the whole purpose of this discourse is to summon Israel to celebrate the Sinai covenant, with which the book opens, and that *Jub.* 1.1-2 places Moses' reception of the Law at Sinai on the sixteenth day of third month, i.e. the day of the Feast of Weeks. In other words, in this book, for which proper calendrical observance of feasts is a central issue, Pentecost is the feast at which one *should* celebrate the giving of the Law at Sinai.[38] The Qumran community renewed the covenant annually (1QS 1.8–2.18), and, as they appear to have followed the Jubilees calendar, they too 'may well have done so in the third month, and hence probably at the feast of weeks'.[39] The newly published 4Q266 now confirms this as lines 17-18 require the formal coming together in the third month to curse those who depart from the Torah.[40] However, as Marshall observes, the fact that Philo and Josephus are silent about a Pentecost association with the Law (Philo associates it with the feast of Trumpets instead: *Spec. Leg.* 2.188-89) may suggest such an association was not yet fully established in official Judaism. Hard evidence for mainline views is only forthcoming from the time of R. Jose ben Ḥalafta (c. 150) who celebrated Pentecost as the day when the Law was given (*S. 'Ol. R.* 5), and this may (as Menzies and others suggest) reflect changes introduced when the fall of the Temple made the harvest festival impossible to keep fully.[41] Nevertheless, the evidence from sectarian

---

37. *Development*, p. 233.

38. So now also Wedderburn, 'Tradition', p. 34.

39. I.H. Marshall, 'The Significance of Pentecost', *SJT* 30 (1977), p. 349; cf. Le Déaut, 'Pentecost', pp. 254-56. See J.A. Fitzmyer, 'The Ascension of Christ and Pentecost', *TS* 45 (1984), pp. 432-37, for the possibility of a more complex picture. But cf. Wedderburn, 'Tradition', pp. 34-35.

40. See e.g. Eisenmann and Wise, *Scrolls*, pp. 218-19 (without accepting all their conjectures thereupon).

41. E. Lohse, *TDNT*, VI, pp. 48-50, argues for a complete lack of contact between Moses/Sinai traditions and Pentecost before the fall of Jerusalem. *Per contra*, however,

Judaism and from the Targums[42] suggests associations between Pentecost
and the giving of the Torah were very much 'in the air' in the period
covered by Acts, and that the later official connection did not just fall out of
the blue![43]

The Sinai Parallels in Acts 2.1-13. In this section we find the kind of allusions to Moses/Sinai speculation which, on the one hand forbid any strictly
literary dependence between Luke and such tradition, and on the other
hand strongly suggest that Luke's account was selected and shaped in a
milieu which had contacts with such tradition, and in which the Pentecost
account (in the form we have it) would have been especially striking.[44]
Adler, to be sure, made the point that Jewish tradition about Sinai is very
diverse, and that, anyway, the parallels between Pentecost and Sinai-
traditions are parallels shared with Jewish descriptions of other events of
redemptive historical importance.[45] This has been taken up by Menzies and
reforged as a powerful weapon against those who claim to hear echoes of
Sinai in Acts 2.1-13.[46] Menzies thinks the *differences* between the
Pentecost account and any of the alleged 'parallels' (most notably Exod.
19.16-19; Deut. 4.11-12; Num. 11.25; Philo, *Dec.* 32-36, 44-49; *Spec. Leg.*
2.188-89; *Targ. Ps.-J.* Exod. 20.2; *b. Šab.* 88b) are more striking than the
similarities. Furthermore, he claims to find at least four traditions which have
nothing to do with the giving of Law (*4 Ezra* 13; *1 En.* 14; 2 Sam. 22.8-15;
Isa. 66.15-16) and which in his view share as many theophanic features with

---

see Kretschmar, 'Himmelfahrt', pp. 223-29; B. Noack, 'The Day of Pentecost in
Jubilees, Qumran and Acts', *ASTI* 1 (1962), pp. 73-95, and J. Potin, *La fête juive de la
Pentecôte* (Paris: Cerf, 1971).

42. The date of the giving of the law is set by the Targums to Exod. 19.1 as fifty
days after Passover, and the meal in 24.11 is described in the language of the harvest
covenant meal of Deut. 16.11. See Le Déaut, 'Pentecost', pp. 258-60.

43. Cf. Potin, *Pentecôte, passim,* esp. p. 301; Le Déaut, 'Pentecost', pp. 257-58;
Kremer, *Pfingstbericht,* pp. 14-24; Haenchen, 174; Dunn, *Baptism,* p. 49 (and *NIDNTT*
II, pp. 784-85); Bovon, *Luc,* pp. 115-18, and O'Reilly, *Word,* pp. 18-20.

44. With Kremer, *Pfingstbericht,* pp. 238-52, 259 (and for detailed points of comparison see Kremer, pp. 87-166); cf. Potin, *Pentecôte,* ch. 5; R. Maddox, *The Purpose
of Luke–Acts* (Edinburgh: T. & T. Clark, 1982), p. 138; Lüdemann, *Christianity,*
pp. 38, 41-42; O'Reilly, *Word,* pp. 21-29; Kim, *Geisttaufe,* pp. 133-68. Others have
found a more-or-less direct literary influence either on Luke or at the Pre-Lukan stage:
cf. O. Betz, 'The Eschatological Interpretation of the Sinai-Tradition in Qumran and in
the New Testament', *RevQ* 6 (1967), p. 93; J. Dupont, *The Salvation of the Gentiles*
(New York: Paulist, 1979), pp. 39-45; *idem,* 'Première Pentecôte', in *Etudes,* pp. 481-
502; Wedderburn, 'Tradition', pp. 32-39.

45. *Pfingstfest,* pp. 53-58. Compare Schneider, 246-47.

46. *Development,* pp. 235-41.

Acts 2.1-11 as any of the so-called Sinai parallels. In short, the features in common between Acts and the Sinai traditions are not specific to the latter, but belong to the general currency of theophanic traditions, so the Pentecost story would not evoke comparisons with the Sinai tradition as such. Here I must confess to remain unconvinced.

With respect to the alleged parallels in Philo, *Targum Pseudo-Jonathan* and the rabbis, I think Menzies' approach certainly shows there is no direct literary dependence of Luke on any of these accounts: none provides a genetic parallel. But that is perhaps not the real question. Philo is not dependent on the Targum, nor the Targum on Philo, and they give remarkably different accounts of Sinai despite the fact that they are both actually attempting to describe that event and they have the Old Testament accounts in front of them. Luke, by contrast, is not attempting to 'describe' Sinai, but another event, so we should anticipate great differences in detail (unless Luke's account were merely a scene created in literary dependence on one of these traditions). The real question then is, would the Pentecost account strike a Jewish reader as sounding 'like' Sinai, despite the differences? Are there sufficient 'structural', linguistic and conceptual points of contact to be liable to evoke a comparison?

We may consider Philo's 'account' of the giving of the ten words at Sinai (and the Targums and Pseudo-Philo gives a complementary picture).[47] As in the perhaps later (more specific) tradition of *b. Šab.* 88b, of God's word going forth and dividing into seventy languages, Philo wishes to suggest God's Law was to be heard by all the nations. At *Dec.* 33, he states:

> I should suppose that God wrought on this occasion a miracle (θαυματουργῆσαι) [cf. Acts 2.7] of a truly holy kind [cf. Acts 2.1-13] by bidding an invisible sound (ἦχον ἀόρατον)[cf. Acts 2.4] to be created in the air more marvellous than all instruments and fitted with perfect harmonies... which giving shape and tension to the air, and changing it {?} to flaming fire [cf. Acts 2.3], sounded forth like the breath (πνεῦμα) through a

---

47. *Targ. Ps.-J.* to Exod. 20.2: 'The first word, as it came forth from the mouth of the Holy One, may his name be blessed, was like shooting stars, like lightening, and like flames of fire; a fiery torch on its right, and a fiery torch on its left, flying and floating in the air of the heavens; it returned and was seen over the camps of Israel; it circled round and was engraved on the tables of the covenant that had been given into the palms of Moses' hands'. *Targum Neofiti* provides an almost identical expansion. Compare *Bib. Ant.* ch. 11, which adds to the words of Exod. 19.16ff., 'And behold, the mountains burned like fire, and the earth quaked...and every habitable place was shaken, and the heavens were folded up, and the clouds drew up water, and flames of fire burned...and winds and storms roared, the stars gathered together...until God should establish the Law...' This does not remind us of Acts 2.1-13 so much as it does the wonders in heaven and the signs on earth, etc., of Peter's version of the Joel citation.

trumpet an articulate voice (φωνὴν...ἔναρθρον) so loud that it appeared to be equally audible to the furthest as well as the nearest...[cf. Acts 2.5-12] [35] But the new miraculous voice (φωνή) was set in action and kept in flame (ἐζωπύρε) by the power of God which breathed upon it (ἐπιπνέουσα θεοῦ δύναμις) and spread it abroad on every side and made it more illuminating in its ending than in its beginning by creating in the souls of each and all another kind of hearing far superior to the hearing of the ears...{His account of the day includes (at 44) 'the rush of heaven-sent fire' (πυρὸς οὐρανίου φορᾷ) and continues} [46] Then from the midst of the fire that streamed from heaven (ἀπ' οὐρανοῦ πυρός) [cf Acts 2.4] there sounded forth to their utter amazement [cf. Acts 2.6a] a voice, for the flame became articulate speech in the language (φλογὸς εἰς διάλεκτον) [cf. Acts 2.4] familiar to the audience [cf. Acts 2.11], and so clearly and distinctly were the words formed by it that they seemed to see rather than hear them.

In a complementary account at *Spec. Leg.* 2.189 he states:

For then the sound of the trumpet pealed from heaven and reached, we may suppose, the ends of the universe (ἄχρι τῶν τοῦ παντὸς φθάσαι περάτων), so that the event might strike terror even into those who were far from the spot and dwelling well nigh at the extremities of the earth (ἐν ἐσχατιαῖς κατοικοῦντας [cf Acts 1.8]), who would come to the natural conclusion that such mighty signs [cf. Acts 2.19, 22] portended mighty consequences (τὰ οὕτως μεγάλα μεγάλων ἀποτελεσμάτων ἐστὶ σημεῖα) [cf. Acts 2.11 τὰ μεγαλεῖα τοῦ θεοῦ].

Given that Philo and Luke are describing two different events (and given Philo's characteristic emphases and diction), one can only find the two accounts quite remarkably similar (parallel vocabulary to Luke's is underlined).[48] Both Philo and Luke (i) envisage a holy theophany before the assembled people of God; (ii) in each case we have to do with a redemptive-historical event on earth which is formative for that people of God, marking a real new beginning of some kind—a mighty 'sign' of mightier consequences, as Philo puts it; (iii) in each this sign or wonder involves a miraculous sound, and a rush of something 'like' fire from heaven descending to the people, and dividing to reach all, and (iv) in each case this results in a miraculous form of speech, spreading and so coming to be heard by a multiplicity (of Israel alone or of the far-away too?) in their own language, and destined to reach 'the ends of the earth'.[49] Given this cumulative set of

48. Wedderburn finds the parallels 'striking' ('Tradition', p. 37) and argues Luke has redacted a source which contrasted the New Covenant gift of the Spirit with the Law (p. 38) without himself implementing such a contrast.

49. On the relation of the 'table of nations' peoples who 'hear' the tongues in 2.5-11 (esp. 9-11) to Luke's envisaged programme of evangelization 'to the end of the earth' (1.8), see the important article by J.M. Scott, 'Luke's Geographical Horizon', in D.W.G. Gill and C. Gempf (eds.), *The Book of Acts in its Graeco-Roman Setting*

'correspondences', I find it difficult to see how anyone can say the Pentecost account would not 'remind' a reader of Jewish Sinai traditions. By contrast, the 'non-Sinai' parallels Menzies advances contain some similar theophanic vocabulary, but entirely lack the all-important structural features (i), (ii) and (iv), and even the similarities to (iii) are not so strong as in Philo's Sinai tradition.[50] Furthermore, we have so far made no mention of two other vitally evocative correspondences: (v) each involves an important 'gift' given to God's people and (vi) this gift comes to Israel as the consequence of Israel's leader (both Philo and Luke would add 'and king' [e.g. *Vit. Mos* 2.1-7, etc.]) ascending to God! But these two traits are better dealt with in connection with the speech itself.

Moses/Sinai parallels in Peter's Pentecost speech. (A) We may begin by noting some rather general correspondences with the Moses/Sinai traditions. The Pentecost speech opens with a quotation from Joel 3 which moves in the orbit of Moses/exodus tradition: (a) it provides the fulfilment to the wistful longing expressed in Num. 11.29, that all should receive the Spirit of prophecy (cf. *Midr. Ps.* 14.6 which also sees Joel 3.1-2 [2.28-29] as God's answer to the hope of Num. 11.29). Indeed, Kim argues the Pentecost account is partly modelled on Numbers 11, and the transfer of the Spirit from Moses to the elders.[51] (b) Its apocalyptic language is drawn from the exodus events in such a way that the 'wonders and signs' of Sinai, Pentecost and the eschaton are set in parallel. (c) The language of a heavenly wonder and sign on earth involving 'fire' and 'clouds of smoke' would especially evoke Sinai descriptions (cf. Exod. 19.16-19). In addition, (d) Luke's strong tendency to set Moses and Jesus in parallel as redemptive figures who work 'wonders and signs' (cf. 2.22//7.36 and see also 1.3 (A) above) would also evoke Moses at 2.19 and 22, and the substitution of 'in the last days' for 'after these things' may depend on Isa. 2.1 (the only place where the phrase is found in the LXX). This oracle, with its description of the Law going forth from Zion and the word of the Lord from Jerusalem, would be thoroughly appropriate to the context.[52] Finally, (e) Peter's closing appeal to his audience to save themselves from this 'crooked generation' (2.40) alludes to the wilderness generation which Moses upbraids in

(A1CS1; Carlisle: Paternoster, 1994), esp. pp. 522-44.

50. The first two (*4 Ezra* 13.1-10; *1 En.* 14), for example, pertain to visions in heaven, the third (2 Sam. 22.8-16) is a poetic celebration of David's victory over the Philistines (not really a theophany at all, but the poetic reapplication of the Sinai myth to say Sinai's God came to David's rescue), the last (Isa. 66.15-16) is an eschatological oracle, with only minor parallels to Acts 2.

51. *Geisttaufe*, pp. 164-68.

52. Cf. O'Reilly, *Word*, pp. 24-25.

Deut. 32.5, while the 'three thousand' who convert (2.41) provide a contrasting allusion to Exod. 32.28.[53]

(B) Mosaic resonances become louder and stronger, however, in 2.33-34a. No-one would wish to claim that these Mosaic features are presented in the surface structure of the argument, but they may inform the story's deep structure. For if the implicit 'story' in 2.33-34a is of Israel's ruler ascending to God where he receives a gift of great importance—which he then subsequently gives to his assembled waiting people in a theophanic context—then this whole part of the story is not essentially *Davidic* in character at all. Indeed, Luke's tradition is specific on that point; David did not ascend to God (2.34a). In this respect then, Peter admits that the one David 'foresees' as his eschatological heir is quite unlike David himself. Nor was there any tradition in Judaism that the Davidic heir might ascend to God in order to receive a gift he then grants to his people, amid such striking phenomena, far less that he might be associated with the bestowal of the Spirit of prophecy on Israel. For these reasons, it is difficult to agree with O'Toole's claim that the whole argument in 2.22-36 is built on the promise to David alone.[54] Key elements are missing, and such a gap would be unfortunate at the theological crux of Peter's argument.

But it is at this point that the Jewish (and Lukan) tendency to accommodate David to Moses and vice versa lends support to Peter's case. Based on Exod. 19.3 ('And Moses went up to God'), Judaism evinced a vital interest in Moses' 'ascent' to receive the Torah which he then gave to Israel.[55] Indeed, the closest linguistic parallel to Luke's description of a 'promise' for which Jesus ascends in 2.33, and the 'gift' he grants in 2.38, comes from what Josephus writes of Moses' ascent at Sinai: in *Ant.* 3.77-78, he tells us that the people rejoiced at the thought that Moses would soon return μετὰ τῆς ἐπαγγελίας τῶν ἀγαθῶν...παρὰ τοῦ θεοῦ ('with the promise of good things...from God'); for God was to give Moses 'a gift' (Μωυσεῖ δοῦναι δωρεάν), for which they prayed (cf. Acts 1.14).

Of more interest in the history of exegesis, however, has been the influence of this Mosaic ascent tradition on the Targum, which paraphrases Ps. 68.19 (MT; EVV 68.18) (a Pentecost Psalm): 'You have ascended to heaven, that is Moses the prophet. You have taken captivity captive, you have learned the words of the Torah, you have given them as gifts to men...'. While this targum is late, it embodies much earlier tradition, and the

---

53. Kim, *Geisttaufe*, pp. 162-63.
54. O'Toole, 'Acts 2:30', pp. 245-58.
55. See Meeks, *Prophet*, pp. 122ff. and 205ff.; W.H. Harris, 'The Descent of Christ in Ephesians 4.7-11: An Exegetical Investigation with Special Reference to the Influence of Traditions about Moses Associated with Psalm 68.19' (PhD dissertation, University of Sheffield, 1988), pp. 110-92.

'reading' here is thought to reflect first-century interpretation as it appears to have influenced the citation at Eph. 4.8 (where the one who ascends (here Christ) also receives gifts which he then gives to his people).[56] It is hardly surprising that this Pentecost Psalm (and the traditions associated with 68.18) has often been suspected as the influence behind Acts 2.33-34,[57] and the strongest case for it was made by Jacques Dupont.[58]

The essence of the case is that when τὴν ἐπαγγελίαν τοῦ πνεύματος τοῦ ἁγίου ('the promise of the Holy Spirit') and ἐξέχεεν τοῦτο ὅ...κτλ ('he has poured out this...etc.') are recognized as redactional modifications (rather than additions)[59] brought by the context, and when the phrase 'to the right hand of God' is recognised as an addition preparing the way for Ps. 110.1, what remains (ὑψωθείς...λαβὼν παρὰ τοῦ πατρός...), taken in conjunction with the assertion in v. 34 (οὐ γὰρ Δαυιδ ἀνέβη εἰς τοὺς οὐρανούς, 'David did not ascend into the heavens'—together reflecting LXX 67.19 ἀνέβης εἰς ὕψος),[60] points to a framework of thought derived from Ps. 68.18, and modified by the Moses speculations. Or to put it the other way round, 2.33-34 affirms a New Moses fulfilment of Ps. 68.18, re-contextualized in the light of Joel and the Pentecost events. One may present the conceptual substructure (entirely schematically!) as follows: (1) Peter connects Psalm 68 with the Moses/Sinai episode (as the Targum) and assumes v. 18 to mean (e.g.) 'You ascended on high...and having received the gift of God you gave gifts to men' (*scil.* 'the Torah'

56. On which see Lincoln, *ad loc.*

57. The proposal was made at least as long ago as 1902 by F.H. Chase, who noted by way of conjecture that Ps. 67.19 (LXX) had been adduced by Peter 'to express, or to confirm, his witness to the Lord's Ascension' (*The Credibility of the Book of the Acts of the Apostles* [London: Macmillan, 1902], p. 151). This position was accepted by Cadbury, *Beginnings*, V, p. 409, and explored in more detail by the apparently independent studies of Knox (*Acts*, pp. 80ff.; cf. *Paul*, pp. 194ff.), Kretschmar, 'Himmelfahrt', pp. 216, 218 and *passim* (cf. C.F.D. Moule, 'The Ascension—Acts 1:9', *ExpTim* 68 [1956–57], p. 206), and Lindars (*Apologetic*, pp. 51-59).

58. In Lindars and Smalley (eds.), *Christ*, pp. 219-28. I have defended a similar view in 'Spirit and Christology', pp. 176-79.

59. At this point the critique by Bock, *Proclamation*, pp. 181-82, fails to come to grips with what Dupont is really saying: he thinks by stripping away redactional language Dupont is cutting off the branch on which he sits (because most of the language of the verse is explicable as 'redactional'). Dupont, however, does not think this redactional language is created *ex nihilo*, and is asking the more subtle question: what wording has been transformed into the 'redactional' language?

60. O'Toole ('Acts 2:30', followed by Menzies, *Development*, p. 243) would prefer a Davidic connection, seeking to explain the ὑψωθείς by Ps. 88; but neither this psalm nor any other as neatly explains the collocation of ὑψόω and ἀνάβαιων as does Ps. 68.18.

and 'the commandments' respectively). (2) Peter saw this whole Sinai scenario as fulfilled in a new way in Jesus' ascent and the Pentecost event, and instinctively made the appropriate changes of reference: the ascent is now into the heavens, the gift Jesus receives is the Spirit promised by Joel, and the gifts he gives the Spirit's charismata. (3) Either Peter or Luke (or the tradition between) then accommodated this further to the fulfilment so that 'the gift of God' becomes more explicitly 'the promise of the Holy Spirit', and the affirmation that he 'gave gifts to men' is contextualised in the light of Joel to become 'he poured out this which you see and hear'.

It would be difficult conclusively to prove (or to disprove) whether Acts 2.33-34 reflects an intentional transformation of the actual wording of Ps. 68.18, given that Luke does not even pretend to give Peter's full argument (cf. 2.40). But the basic Moses/Sinai 'story' that such a reading of Ps. 68.18 represents—that Moses ascended on high, received the gift of God, and gave gifts to men—is in any case independent of the Psalm (indeed the targumic reading departs from the MT under its influence).[61] We may suspect this Mosaic ascent story underlies 2.23-24a for the very reason that makes the hypothesis of the use of Ps. 68.18 attractive, namely that such a hypothesis lends support where Peter's argument otherwise sounds unprecedented to Jewish ears, and coherence to the relation of the speech to the events of Pentecost. If there was no Davidic 'ascent' tradition or hope, on which to build towards 2.33, there was a flourishing Mosaic one. If the first Moses made an ascent to receive a notable gift from God to give to Israel, a Jew might not be surprised to hear that a Moses-like messiah made a more consequential ascent, to receive a yet more momentous gift for Israel. And while no-one expected *any* messianic figure to bestow God's Spirit of Prophecy on Israel, Moses was the one Jew (other than Elijah)[62] who was involved (at least passively) in the distribution of the Spirit to other Israelites. Judaism remembered how God shared the Spirit of prophecy upon him with the seventy elders—and in precisely the context in which Moses expresses the wish that the Spirit might be given to all Israel (Num. 11.26-30),[63] which Joel's promise 'fulfils'. Such a Judaism might not be quite so

61. It is a point against Dupont's thesis that the one who ascends in Ps. 68.18 receives a plurality of gifts (hence the words of the Torah in the targumic paraphrase).

62. Comparison is sometimes made with the Spirit on Elijah passing to Elisha (2 Kgs 2; Sir. 48.12). While such a motif gains some plausibility at Acts 1.1-11 (see Kim, *Geisttaufe*, pp. 98-99), in Acts 2 the Mosaic parallels are very much stronger (as Kim himself notes, *Geisttaufe*, pp. 160-62). Also against the view that Luke equates Jesus with Elijah and the disciples with Elisha is the fact that he applies both Elijah and Elisha typology to Jesus (Lk. 4.25-27; cf. Kim, *Geisttaufe*, pp. 85-86).

63. See Philo, *Fug.* 186; *Gig.* 24-27; *Exod. R.* 5.20; *Midr. Pss.* 14.6 and the Targums *ad loc.* for keen interest in this event.

surprised to hear the claim that Moses' eschatological counterpart played a greater role in a more widespread sharing of the Spirit of prophecy which he 'received' on ascent to God. The same 'Mosaic' substructure would also most readily bring together this speech which focuses on Jesus' ascent to receive a gift which he gives to Israel with the Sinai overtones of Acts 2.1-13. If the emphasis of the Pentecost speech is undeniably primarily Davidic, my claim is simply that the proclamation in 2.33 makes greatest sense (in both Jewish and Lukan contexts) on the unspoken assumption that it refers to a son of David *who is also like Moses*. David and Moses *together* fit the part played here, where the figure of David *alone* is awkward if not simply 'out of place'.

In conclusion, it appears to me there is a relatively secure case that Acts 2 deliberately evokes the fundamental Jewish story of Moses' ascent to God to receive the Torah which he then gives to Israel (and beyond) with theophanic accompaniment. It is at least a part of the explanation of the Pentecost event.[64] The parallels are not of the kind that suggest the Moses/Sinai episode has become something like an allegory for Pentecost, such that the gift of the Spirit must necessarily be seen as a direct equivalent to the Law, and so either as the power to keep the Law[65] or a superior substitute for the Law.[66] The correspondence is looser than that. But the parallels do suggest Pentecost is viewed as part of the fulfilment and *renewal* of Israel's covenant, and so ensure that the gift of the Spirit will have a vital role in Israel's restoration. And we shall need to clarify what sort of role as we proceed (see esp. Chapters 12 and 13). But in §2 we must first examine the relation of the Pentecost speech to themes already announced earlier in Luke and Acts.

---

64. This is admitted by Mainville, *L'Esprit*, p. 258.

65. Le Déaut speaks of Christ ascending to seek 'the new law, which is the Holy Spirit' ('Pentecost', p. 262, cf. pp. 266-67). Knox, *Acts*, p. 86, argues the parallels lead to the perception of the sending of the Spirit 'as the giving of the new Torah written on the tables of their hearts'; similarly Dunn (*Baptism*, p. 49) speaks of Pentecost as 'the writing of the law upon the heart by the Spirit', and compare Pesch, 113. Jervell (*Unknown Paul*, pp. 116-21) rejects any notion of the giving of a New Law, but mildly supports the view that the Spirit assists or leads to obedience of the Law, noting the Spirit leads Paul to Jerusalem for Pentecost to take a vow, etc.; cf. his conclusion, 'For the people of the Spirit the law is no longer a burden. The believing Jews, among them Paul, keep the entire law; the Gentiles part of it. There is harmony between Spirit and law' (p. 121; but see on Acts 15 below).

66. Dupont, *Salvation*, p. 40; Lampe, *God*, p. 68. O'Reilly (*Word*, p. 21) speaks of 'the new Law, the word of apostolic preaching' empowered by the Spirit. This is closer to Luke's own interests but for the phrase 'a new Law'.

2. *The Pentecost Speech and 'the Beginnings' of Jesus' Work*
(Luke 1–Acts 2)

Within this section we shall contextualize the Pentecost Speech in relation to what has gone before. In §2.1 we shall argue that Luke's Gospel looks forward to a time when the kingdom of God is expressed through Jesus' messianic rule, and that Luke believes Jesus' ascension to God's right hand realises such hopes. In §2.2 we shall argue that the form such rule is conceived to take is that of a cleansing restoration of Israel, largely in the image of Isa. 49.6-7 (as anticipated in Lk. 2). The Spirit is the power by which Jesus effects this in and through his disciples.

2.1 *The Kingdom of God and Jesus' Kingship in Relation to the Pentecost Speech*

(A) *1.32-35 The messianic reign in the infancy narratives.* The infancy and childhood narratives of Luke 1–2 set the scene for the reader. In the angelic annunciation of 1.16-17, John the Baptist was presented as one who would go before the Lord in the Spirit and power of Elijah, to prepare God's people. This makes John the messenger of God's coming in power, that is, of 'the kingdom of God'. 1.32-35 gives a parallel angelic annunciation proclaiming Jesus as the 'Son of the Most High' in whom is to be fulfilled the promise of David's eternal kingship. Within a context of Jewish hopes, this could only mean one thing: that the kingdom of God was to become present in, through and alongside the anointed king, that is, through the rule of Jesus.[67] We have noted the important part that the specifically 'Davidic' hopes have within these chapters, not least in 2.11 where the angel of the Lord declares 'to you is born this day in the city of David a saviour who is Christ, the Lord'. From this the reader will anticipate that the rest of Luke–Acts will relate the story of one born as the agent of God's rule; the anticipated Davidic vice-regent. The surprising manner in which the hopes are to be fulfilled will be spelt out in the rest of Luke's work; but these first chapters tell us *what* will be elucidated, what we are to look *for*.

(B) *God's rule and Jesus' kingship before the Passion Narrative.* The theme of God's reign is prominent in the Gospel narratives. The generations of scholarship from Weiss and Schweitzer to the end of the 70s saw the term 'the kingdom of God' as a way of denoting the end time order, whether completely future, or inaugurated in some way within Jesus' ministry.

---

67. See especially G.R. Beasley-Murray, *Jesus and the Kingdom of God* (Exeter: Paternoster, 1986), ch. 8. Just how large a section of Judaism held such a belief is in dispute: Beasley-Murray maximizes it. Contrast Wright, *Testament*, p. 307.

Perrin's last book[68] on the subject, and Chilton's first,[69] however, signalled a quite different and potentially more flexible approach. Chilton's work builds carefully on critical study of Jewish literature, especially the Targums. He sums up his position on the background (with evident polemical edge!):

> The kingdom of God was a term of reference Jesus inherited from his milieu, instanced in the *Songs* [*of the Sabbath Sacrifice*] and the Targumim, as well as in Daniel. The theologoumenon was readily understood, because it was relatively common. The phrase appears to convey the ways in which God rules—today and tomorrow, with force and immanently, righteously and in judgment, gathering the pure and yet standing alone, in Zion and everywhere.[70]

By this statement, Chilton does not suggest that Jesus' phrase 'the kingdom of God' means all these things in any one instance, but that the phrase itself was what Perrin called a 'tensive symbol', capable of multiple references (rather than simply universally meaning 'the end-time rule of God and the order it produces').[71] Any one utterance might focus but a single trait within the description above (while nevertheless potentially maintaining looser connections with the others). An important consequence of this understanding is that Jesus' use of the phrase 'the kingdom of God' in relation to events in his ministry, or in the imminent future, does not necessarily imply a chronological relationship to the End, rather the language is primarily *theocentric*.

Luke understood the phrase in a similar fashion. The sayings about the presence and 'nearness' of the kingdom of God in Jesus' ministry (e.g. 10.9, 11; 11.20; 14.15-24; 16.16; 17.20-21) are best understood to denote God's self-revealing presence or 'rule' in strength, and the consequent availability of its benefits. This is not to diminish the epochal significance of this 'presence' (cf. 10.23-24; 16.16). But it is to claim that the presence of God's reign in Luke is neither simply the *proleptic* presence of the imminent End (as in Schweitzer's and Fuller's description of Jesus' position), nor is it an 'image of the End' *replacing* the imminent End (as in Conzelmann), nor is it

---

68. N. Perrin, *Jesus and the Language of the Kingdom* (London: SCM Press, 1976).

69. B.D. Chilton, *God in Strength: Jesus' Announcement of the Kingdom* (Sheffield: JSOT Press, 1986 [1979]). His position was already indicated in his article 'Regnum Dei Deus Est', *SJT* 31 (1978), pp. 261-70, and has since been developed in his other works: for a sketch of his own work in relation to the rest of scholarship on the topic see 'The Kingdom of God in Recent Discussion', in Chilton and Evans (eds.), *Jesus*, pp. 255-80.

70. 'Kingdom', pp. 279-80.

71. Cf. Perrin, *Language*, esp. pp. 16-32, 127-31, 197-99.

(as in Franklin)[72] the 'closeness' of the transcendent kingdom which never becomes enshrined in earthly events (for Franklin these merely witness to the kingdom's metaphysical 'nearness'), nor, yet again, is it quite the *inauguration* of the End (as in Kümmel, Jeremias and Ladd), if that is taken to imply either some presence of the End *order* or the beginning of a sequence of redemptive historical events leading (eventually) to the End. Jesus' exorcisms (11.20), like other events in and alongside his ministry, are the liberating, transforming self-manifesting presence in power of the God who rules immanently and shall rule unopposed at the End. While the terminology 'the kingdom of God' is thus capable of some relatively de-eschatologized and even individualized senses (one could well envisage it used in Ps. 18.7-16, for example, where the myth of God's coming down to rule is invoked as a way of describing David's rescue from his enemies), what gives the expression its epochal connotations in Jesus' teaching is that here God's self-manifestation in strength is seen as directed towards an eschatological goal, namely the fulfilment of Old Testament hopes for Israel's New Exodus liberation, cleansing and transformation.

At first sight there is rather little evidence connecting this proclamation of *God's* rule with *Jesus'* kingship. One might be tempted to think Luke 1–2 has been forgotten. Nevertheless there are hints that Luke has not overlooked the programme he laid out there.

In the first place, God's reign is especially bound up with Jesus' activities; as 16.16 puts it, 'the law and the prophets were until John, now the kingdom of God is preached and many press violently into it'. Jesus' proclamation and associated actions provide the main locus of God's self-revelation in power. According to 11.20, his exorcisms (and those of his disciples [10.17-19], but probably not those of Jewish exorcists [11.19]) are part of the decisive victory over Satan that means *God's* reign has begun to appear for Israel; the captives are being set free because the Strong Man has been bound (11.21-22). What is more, Jesus performs his various kinds of liberating actions as one *endowed with God's Spirit* (3.21-22; 4.18-21), and for Judaism and earliest Christianity the Spirit of God was, above all, God's empowering presence, the prime (though not exclusive) means of his self-manifestation in power (cf. especially Acts 10.38).[73] These activities of the Spirit through Jesus are acts of the same Spirit with which Jesus is anointed as Davidic king (3.21-22; cf. Ps.2.7) and (Mosaic) servant-liberator (4.18-21). The baptismal and temptation narratives focus Jesus' kingly messianic identity and task. And while, in the main period of the ministry, Jesus is

---

72. *Christ*, ch. 1, and *Luke*, p. 18 and ch. 11.

73. Hence the title for G. Fee's monumental recent study on Paul's pneumatology; *God's Empowering Presence* (Peabody, MA: Hendrickson, 1994).

portrayed as servant-liberator and Mosaic prophet rather than as messianic ruler, these are figures with 'kingly' traits too; and their task is to bring New Exodus liberation to Israel, which involves the very acts that manifest God's reign as present.

Secondly, decisive evidence that Luke sees the connection between God's rule and Jesus' kingship comes at the end of the journey to Jerusalem (19.11-27). Here we find Jesus tells the disciples a parable, 'because he was near Jerusalem, and because they supposed that the kingdom of God was to appear immediately'(19.11). The parable of pounds, which is supposed to correct this understanding, is about a nobleman who goes away to a distant country to get a royal power (= kingdom) for himself, and then return (19.12, alluding perhaps to Archelaus's journey to Rome to get Herod's kingdom transferred to him as rightful descendent). The kingdom of God is not going to appear immediately when Jesus and his band arrive at the climax of their journey in Jerusalem; rather Jesus must first 'go away' in order to receive that kingship from the one with authority to delegate it to him. Here then it is anticipated that God's reign will only come more fully after Jesus ascends and receives the royal power.[74] In the very next incident (Jesus' 'triumphal entry', 19.28-40), the disciples praise *God* for all the wonders that have happened, and hail Jesus with the words, 'Blessed is the *king* who comes in the name of the Lord', thus linking the manifestations of God's reign seen in Jesus' ministry with Jesus' own messianic kingship.

(C) *The Kingdom of God and Jesus' kingship in the Passion Narrative.* This section of Gospel, which starts with the 'triumphal entry', has important references that connect Jesus' activity with God's reign, and equally obvious references to Jesus' own kingship (cf. the trial, the mocking of Jesus as king, and the titulus). Two are of especial importance: Lk. 22.29-30 and 23.42.

In 22.29-30, Jesus identifies his own kingdom simultaneously in terms of God's gift and the fulfilment of God's rule spoken of earlier in 22.16-18. Thus after speaking of the fulfilment of the Passover in the kingdom of God, and of his not eating and drinking until then (in 22.16-18), Jesus goes on to affirm, 'And I confer on you, just as my Father has conferred on me, a kingdom, so that you may eat and drink at my table in the kingdom, and you will sit on thrones judging the twelve tribes of Israel' (vv. 29-30). The implication is that the events which fulfil the Passover in the kingdom of God (a Mosaic, New Exodus function), are simultaneously the events which confer kingdom upon Jesus.[75]

---

74. With Marshall, *Luke*, pp. 90-91.
75. See Tannehill, *Narrative Unity*, I, p. 269; O'Toole, 'Acts 2:30', p. 253.

In 23.42, after a discussion about Jesus' messiahship between the two crucified criminals, one turns to him with the words: 'Jesus, remember me when you come into your kingdom', and Jesus replies with words which imply almost immediate fulfilment: 'Truly I tell you, today you will be with me in paradise'.

In sum, Luke's Gospel portrays God's reign appearing within Jesus' ministry, but looks forward to an imminent (cf. 9.27) more powerful event of the kingdom of God which will simultaneously be a revelation of Jesus' kingship. The period of the ministry merely foreshadows his fuller messianic rule.

(D) *The Kingdom of God and Jesus' kingship in Acts 1–2.* Acts 1.3-8 is part of the prologue of Acts (1.1-11),[76] which is one of the most subtle and

---

76. Marshall (55-62) distinguishes 1.1-5 as 'the Prologue' from 1.6-11 which he labels 'the Ascension of Jesus'. Haenchen, by contrast, thinks 'the Ascension' story only begins at 1.9, and so, not quite sure what to do with 1.6-8, he tags it onto 1.1-5, making 1.1-8 a single prologue unit to which he gives the heading 'Retrospect and a Farewell Speech'.

Haenchen's division has little to commend it. When we are told that the disciples were 'gathered together' (so 1.6a), that was not simply to ask the question in 1.6b, but to become witnesses of the ascension (in 1.9-11; note the importance of this in 1.22), so the wording of 1.6a ties this section with 1.9-11. The connection between the dialogue in 1.6-8 and the 'ascension proper' is further guaranteed in 1.9 ('When he had spoken these things, he was taken up as they were watching...'). Marshall is thus right to insist that on formal grounds 1.6-8 belongs with 1.9-11 as one piece; indeed an ascension story without any comment or farewell from the central character would be unusual.

But is Marshall right to separate this piece (1.6-11) from 1.1-5? Three considerations suggest such a division is also inadvisable: (i) 1.2 gives the ascension of Jesus as the *terminus ad quem* of Luke's first account of what Jesus said and did; 1.9-11 gives an account of that event which forms an *inclusio* with the opening verses. (ii) 1.6-8 is bound thematically with strong links to 1.2-5 (Jesus with the disciples; speech about the kingdom of God; specific reference to the promise of the Holy Spirit, etc.). (iii) As Marshall himself notes, a prologue which began with a statement about the content of a former book would be expected to outline the scope of the present part. Luke has actually signalled the intent to provide such information by his choice of the Greek particle μέν in 1.1; for μέν nearly always introduces a clause which is contrasted with a subsequent one introduced by δέ. It suggests Luke intended something like, 'On the one hand, in my former book...but in this book I shall relate...'. Luke, however, does not provide this second explicit and awaited contrasting statement. That can barely be because he has forgotten how he began his opening sentence; it is more likely that he has simply followed the acceptable convention of providing a programmatic narrative instead, i.e. one that would indicate the central purpose and intended scope of his second book. While 1.3-5 certainly raises some of the important issues of Luke's literary work, it is really only with the dialogue in 1.5-8 about witness expanding to the ends of the earth, with the ascension of Jesus itself (1.9: theologically pivotal for Luke), concentrated pieces of theological writing in Luke's whole enterprise. Here he cements Gospel and Acts together, parading some central themes, old and new: the Spirit-imbued instruction of the apostles (1.2),[77] the assurance of the Gospel (based in many proofs in the form of multiple appearances to the apostles, meals with them, and further private instruction [1.2-4]); the command to stay in Jerusalem; the promise of the Spirit (1.4-5); the scope of the mission that will dominate Acts (1.8), and the ascension of Jesus, taken by the cloud of God's presence into heaven like the Danielic Son of Man (1.9-11).

According to 1.3, the topic of Jesus' instruction during the forty days was principally 'the kingdom of God'. 1.3-8 demonstrates the same strong association between this 'kingdom of God' and Jesus' kingship that we have so far noted. It is thus this talk of God's reign that leads into the reminder of the *Father's* promise (1.4 = Lk. 24.49) which Luke now equates with the Baptist's in the form 'you shall be baptized with the Holy Spirit' (1.5 cf. Lk. 3.16). The connection between 'the kingdom of God' and this promise is an entirely natural one, for if the events of Jesus' Spirit-empowered ministry have involved a display of God's self-revealing presence in strength in (and for) Israel, this can only be deepened and extended when the Spirit comes to the disciples too. At the same time, while the verb here is passive, with the agent unspecified, the reader will remember that the Baptist's promise was that the *messiah* would 'baptize' Israel with Spirit and fire. So it is implicit that *Jesus* will somehow fulfil this, and that the reign of God will be manifest through his messianic rule (this in turn explains the question in 1.6, 'Lord will *you* now restore the kingdom to Israel?', on which see below).

Peter's Pentecost speech (especially 2.33-36) provides the resolution to all these expectations. This section claims Jesus has been exalted to the eternal throne of David, not in Jerusalem, but at God's right hand (2.33)—the throne promised by Ps. 110.1 for David's 'Lord' (34b-35; cf. Lk. 20.41-44). He is now in the position to rule over Jacob (in accordance with the hopes of Lk. 1.32-33). Over against MacRae (and other proponents of 'absentee Christology' in Acts), it must be emphasized that this ascent to

and with the angelic 'encouragement' in 1.10-11, that the full scope of the work is hinted at.

It is for the last of these reasons especially that Tannehill and Pesch, for example, have taken 1.1-11 as a single unit which indicates something of the purpose(s) and scope of the second volume: to outline the expansion of the Christian witness by the apostolic church under the guidance and in the power of the Spirit, and to do so in a way that would clarify the nature of the kingdom of God, including both its relationship to the ascended Lord and to the promises to Israel. Cf. Haenchen, 145-46.

77. See discussion at Chapter 11 n. 46 for justification of this reading of 1.2.

God's right hand is not the removal of Jesus from Israel, and from influence over her affairs—some kind of semi-retirement with a comfortable chair until the day of the parousia. It means quite the reverse. His throne is the place from which God exercises sovereign power, and the position at his right hand is that of his chief executive agent. Jesus' advent to this position and his action on the day of Pentecost can only mark the beginning of some fuller manifestation of God's reign on earth, for in these events the messiah pours out the gift of God's own empowering self-manifesting presence and 'life'. And, through this Lordship in respect of God's Spirit and his gifts, Jesus now also acts and speaks on earth through his witnesses (2.33; cf. Lk. 22.15; 24.49). The throne and power Jesus is given thus transcend even the expectations of the infancy narratives.[78] Jesus performs his rule over Jacob from heaven at God's right hand, acting directly as his vice-regent.[79] While we must not make the mistake of claiming the Kingdom of God and Jesus' kingdom have been strictly identified, nevertheless God's eschatological rule has come to be channelled uniquely through Jesus.

Luke regularly (and redactionally) summarizes the content of Christian preaching in Acts in terms of 'the kingdom of God' (8.12; 14.22; 19.8; 20.25; 28.23), and his very last words (forming an *inclusio* with his opening ones) are that Paul welcomed all, 'proclaiming the kingdom of God and teaching the things about the Lord Jesus Christ...' (28.31). It is significant here that 'the kingdom of God' and 'the things concerning the Lord Jesus Christ' are now so closely associated (cf. 8.12) as to be partly interchangeable: the whole subject of Christian preaching can either be said to be 'the kingdom of God' (19.8) or to be about '(the Lord) Jesus (Christ)' (5.42; 9.20; 20.21).[80] God's reign and that of his messiah have become one (functionally), at least for the period leading to the End. And while the final climactic assertion of God's reign clearly yet remains for the future (cf. 14.22), we are left in little doubt that it is the return of Jesus (cf. 1.11) which brings this.

The ascension has thereby rightly been seen as of pivotal importance for

---

78. Correctly, Strauss, *Messiah*, ch. 4; Mainville, *L'Esprit*, chs. 3 and 5. Kim (*Geisttaufe*, p. 119) and Frein ('Predictions', p. 25) miss the import of 2.25-36 when they claim the promise of the eternal throne of David in Lk. 1.33 is unfulfilled until the Parousia.

79. While God's rule is not specifically mentioned here, it is naturally presupposed, and in any case it would now be impossible to dissociate from that of the one at his right hand (especially in view of 2.35 'until I make your enemies your footstool').

80. For fuller substantiation see e.g. R.F. O'Toole, 'The Kingdom of God in Luke–Acts', in W. Willis (ed.), *The Kingdom of God in Twentieth-Century Interpretation* (Peabody: Hendrickson, 1987), pp. 147-62, and cf. E. Grässer, '*Ta peri tês basileias* (Apg 1.6; 19.8)', in Aletti *et al.* (eds.), *Cause*, pp. 707-26.

Luke.[81] This is not because it is the withdrawal of Jesus into a passive role in heaven, and so the receding of salvation, introducing a period until the End characterized by an 'absentee Christology' (as Conzelmann[82] and MacRae[83] have presented it). The truth is nearer the opposite interpretational pole (the position of Franklin):

> In the Gospel, Luke presents the life of Jesus as moving inexorably and determinedly towards this event...the whole journey to the holy city is a progression towards his ἀνάλημψις (9.51). The Ascension is not for Luke one event which brings the earthly life of Jesus to an end, but is rather the fulfilment of the whole; that which takes up, completes, and carries forward the whole to enable it to become contemporary with the church for all seasons...The life of the church as recorded in Acts proceeds from the event which enthroned Jesus, not in the sense that it describes a sequence of events moved forward by an impetus given in the past, but as a series pointing to its source in the present reality of a contemporary, exalted Christ, and moving out from him as in the manner of spokes from a wheel's hub.[84]

Jesus has been enthroned as messiah in the place of greatest possible influence over Israel, the position at God's right hand from which matters on earth are decided and effected. And Jesus exercises his rule and becomes present to the disciples in and through the Spirit (see below). We must now turn to the question of the import for Israel and her restoration.

2.2. *Pentecost and the Messianic Restoration of Israel*
John's promise in Lk. 3.16, that Jesus will 'baptize [Israel] with Spirit-and-fire, was in line with Jewish expectations for a messiah of the Spirit who would execute judgment and righteous rule in Zion. The promise of 3.16 thus coheres entirely with the perspective of the hopes of Luke 1–2. As we have seen, too, the ministry of Jesus is dominated by a 'New Exodus'

---

81. See especially E. Franklin, 'The Ascension and the Eschatology of Luke–Acts', *SJT* 23 (1970), pp. 191-200; *idem, Christ*, pp. 29-41; *idem, Luke*, pp. 249-61; Lohfink, *Himmelfahrt*; J. Maile, 'The Ascension in Luke–Acts', *TynBul* 37 (1986), pp. 29-59; M.C. Parsons, *The Departure of Jesus in Luke–Acts: The Ascension Narratives in Context* (Sheffield: JSOT Press, 1987); S.G. Wilson, 'The Ascension: A Critique and an Interpretation', *ZNW* 59 (1968), pp. 269-81; Mainville, *L'Esprit*, chs. 2–3.

82. *Theology*, pp. 16-19, and ch. 4. Speaking of the ascension, Conzelmann affirms, 'From this moment the Church needs a substitute for his "real presence", therefore it receives the Spirit, and cherishes hope' (p. 204). But from the perspective of 2.33 the Spirit is not a substitute; it brings the active presence of Christ.

83. G.W. MacRae, 'Whom Heaven Must Receive Until the Time', *Int* 27 (1973), pp. 151-65. The term 'absentee Christology', however, derives from C.F.D. Moule, 'The Christology of Acts', in Keck and Martyn (eds.), *Studies*, pp. 159-85.

84. *Luke*, pp. 249-50: cf. chs. 1 and 11. Compare Marshall, *Luke*, p. 91; Bovon, *L'oeuvre*, pp. 85-91, and Mainville, *L'Esprit*, p. 333.

pattern of hopes that has Zion's restoration as its goal. If the crucifixion of Jesus appeared to certain disciples to have terminated these hopes (cf. Lk. 24.21), the narrator's presentation of such disappointment can only be understood as irony. Anticipation of Israel's redemption springs to new life with Jesus' own resurrection, and this is highlighted at the very heart of the prologue of Acts (1.3-8).

Jesus' instruction on the kingdom of God (1.3) forms the background to the specific charge to wait in Jerusalem for the promise of the Father (1.4). The location is not determined simply by Joel's promise of the Spirit and salvation 'in Mount Zion and in Jerusalem' (2.32 EVV), nor by a cheap attempt to secure salvation-historical continuity in purely physical terms by having Christianity at least begin in the city of the religion from which it departs, but by the fact that it is a salvation that has all along concerned Zion/Jerusalem's restoration, and will spread thence to the nations (1.8).[85] Acts 1.5 supports the Zion/restoration motif with a deliberate reminder of the Baptist's promise,[86] reworded to fit the cotext. John's originally active construction concerning the messiah's activity has become a passive one so that the semantic agent of the action may now include 'the Father' (of 1.4b), and so that the whole is topicalized from the perspective of the beneficiaries ('you') who have been introduced in 1.4c, and whose story will fill the rest of Acts. There is also now no mention of 'fire', but this omission is perhaps of little significance.[87]

---

85. For Jewish expectation of salvation centring on and from the temple city, see J.B. Chance, *Jerusalem, the Temple and the New Age in Luke–Acts* (Macon: Mercer University Press, 1988), ch. 1.

86. Schneider and Pesch think 1.5 is almost redundant after 1.4, and so serves merely as a literary device to periodize salvation history: the period of the ministry which begins with Jesus' reception of the Spirit (cf. 1.22; 10.37) ends with the ascension (1.2, 22). The beginning of the period of the church is the Pentecostal outpouring on the disciples (cf. 11.15). But this fails to perceive that 1.5 serves to remind the reader of what this 'promise of the Father' is *for*, and how it relates to the hopes raised in Lk. 1–2.

87. Dunn has argued the elimination of the phrase 'and fire' is theological. For him, the gift of the Spirit is to be understood theologically as the fruit of the cross: 'Calvary without Pentecost would not be atonement *to us*' (*Baptism*, p. 44, following Moberly). Jesus must first absorb in himself the 'fire' of the Baptist's promise before the gift of the Spirit can be handed on to the church. But the first of these arguments is inconclusive: as Dunn himself points out elsewhere, it is difficult to establish that Luke attributes atoning significance to the cross (*Unity*, pp. 17-18), and while allowing that Luke may have connected atonement with the cross theologically, it is hard to believe (in the light of Jesus' proclamation of forgiveness in the ministry) that he considered atonement to be *chronologically* restricted to the period following Pentecost. The second of Dunn's arguments rests on an arbitrary connection of Lk. 3.16 with 12.49-50, and on a quite impossible interpretation of the latter. Far from saying that he

When understood as a promise of the messianic cleansing/restoration of Zion, the statement of Jesus in 1.5 leads perfectly naturally to the disciples' question in 1.6. If John's promise is about to be fulfilled in greater measure than has already been the case in Jesus' ministry, it is quite appropriate the disciples should think (a) the kingdom will soon be restored *to* Israel,[88] and (b) that *Jesus* will accomplish this. The former of these rests on the assumption that once the messiah has restored Zion, Israel will achieve supremacy amongst the nations (cf. Isa. 49.6-7, the ideas of which are echoed here more strongly than Mal. 3.23), even, perhaps, be given the rule over them (Dan. 7.14, 27, etc.)[89] The second rests on the equally reasonable assumption that if Jesus as the messiah accomplishes Israel's cleansing and redemption, it will be he who grants this exalted status to Israel.

A vigorous debate ensues as to how Jesus' answer in 1.7-8 should be construed. For Haenchen, in these verses Jesus 'forbids the asking of any questions about the hour of the Parousia', and this is because Luke 'has decisively renounced all expectation of an imminent end'.[90] But this is to

---

intends to absorb the 'fire' of the Baptist's promise *in himself* (as Dunn insists), Jesus actually claims that he has come to pour it out on earth (12.49). In Q this logion had already been interpreted as fulfilled (at least partially) in the violent division of Israel occasioned by the preaching of the kerygma (compare Mt. 10.34 where μὴ νομίσητε ὅτι ἦλθον βαλεῖν εἰρήνην ἐπὶ τὴν γῆν is explained by the expressions which follow: ἦλθον βαλεῖν... μάχαιραν. Ἦλθον γὰρ διχάσαι ἄνθρωπον κατὰ τοῦ πατρὸς αὐτοῦ (κτλ), and see R. Edwards, *The Theology of Q* (Philadelphia: Fortress Press, 1976), p. 128, and Marshall, 545-46; cf. C.P. März, '"Feuer auf die Erde zu werfen, bin ich gekommen..." Zum Verständnis und zur Entstehung von Lk 12.49', in Aletti *et al.* (eds.), *Cause*, pp. 479-512. This is also the meaning for Luke, both in the immediate context (cf. 12.51-52) and in Acts, where Spirit and fire (2.3) are experienced by the disciples at Pentecost and in the ongoing division and judgment of Israel their preaching produces. In the light of these last, the elimination of the words 'and fire', in Acts 1.5, is perhaps best explained by the topicalized focus of the promise as 'to and for the disciples'. Mainville too thinks Luke has dropped the 'and fire' because he does not think the aspect of judgment pertains to Christians (and the purificatory agent in their baptism is rather the Spirit [cf. Ezek. 36.26-27; see *L'Esprit*, p. 274]). Later, however, she suggests that for Luke the 'fire' is rather an aspect of the prophetic word (cf. Jer. 20.9), hence the linguistic association of 'tongues of fire' and glossolalic languages in the Pentecost account (p. 275, following Kremer). But the latter explanation would leave unexplained why Luke dropped 'fire' in 1.5, where (on such a hypothesis) it would be especially appropriate.

88. The noun phrase ἡ βασιλεία (τῷ Ἰσραήλ) here (as in Lk. 12.32 and 22.29) denotes Israel's kingly 'rule', not 'the kingdom of God': each of these passages echoes Dan. 7.14, 18, 27 (see Evans and Sanders, *Luke*, pp. 154-64).

89. The restorationist overtones of the whole passage have been most clearly heard by Tiede, 'Exaltation', pp. 278-86; cf. Schmitt, 'L'église'.

90. Haenchen, 143.

answer Conzelmann's question, not that of the disciples, which concerns whether or not Israel is now to be given the supremacy—an issue not necessarily tied to that of the hour of the Parousia. What the disciples cannot know, according to 1.7, are the χρόνοι or καιροί ('times or seasons') of Israel's fortunes (including that of her glorification). The reason for this will become at least partly apparent in 3.19-26; Israel's future—indeed the very question of who constitutes 'Israel'—depends on her response to the prophet-like-Moses. If she repents she will receive καιροὶ ἀναψύξεως ('seasons of refreshment and respite', 3.20)[91] and participate in the χρόνοι ἀποκαταστάσεως πάντων ('times of the restoration of all things' 3.21). But those who do not repent are cut off out of the 'people (of God)' (3.23).

Perceiving that the disciples' question is about Israel's fortunes, not the delay of the Parousia, Maddox argues 1.7-8 dramatically reinterprets the expectations voiced in 1.6.[92] For him, Luke cannot believe the kingdom will be restored to *national* Israel, which, as Acts shows us, largely rejects the Gospel; it will be given the church instead (cf. Lk. 12.32), in which at best some of national Israel will participate. Luke 1.7 therefore virtually means God has decided the 'times and seasons' not of Israel's glorification but of her doom, epitomized in the destruction of the Temple. The church is to leave behind the pious hopes for national restoration, and bend to the task of the universal proclamation of the Gospel in the power of the Spirit instead.

Maddox's reading of 1.7, however, is implausible: Jesus' reply is merely ambivalent rather than uniformly negative. And 1.8 itself reiterates the hope of Israel's restoration in its three allusions to Isaiah. The affirmation 'you will receive power when the Holy Spirit has come upon you' will remind the reader of Lk. 24.49 ('I will send the promise of the Father upon you...power from on high'). Lk. 24.49 and Acts 1.8 together evidently rest on Isa. 32.15 (LXX 'until the Spirit from on high comes upon you') which is about the New Exodus restoration of Israel and transformation of her 'wilderness' estate.[93] Similarly, the address 'you shall be my witnesses' takes up Isa. 43.10-12, where restored Israel, 'God's servant', is given this commission. And thirdly, the task of bearing witness to Jesus 'to the end of

---

91. See C.K. Barrett, 'Faith and Eschatology in Acts 3', in E. Grässer and O. Merk (eds.), *Glaube und Eschatologie* (Tübingen: Mohr, 1985), pp. 1-17 (esp. 10-13) for this understanding of the phrase (over against Zehnle, *Discourse*, pp. 71-75, who took it to denote restoration of paradisal conditions at the Parousia). Supporting Barrett see also H.F. Bayer, 'Christ-Centered Eschatology in Acts 3:17-26', in Green and Turner (eds.), *Jesus*, pp. 245-47.

92. *Purpose*, pp. 106-108.

93. Cf. C.A. Evans, 'Jesus and the Spirit: On the Origin and Ministry of the Second Son of God', in Evans and Sanders, *Luke*, p. 31.

the earth' (1.8)[94] is widely recognized to take up the closing line of Isaiah 49.6:[95]

> He [God] says:
> Is it too light a thing that you should be my servant
> to raise up the tribes of Jacob
> and to restore the preserved of Israel;
> I will give you as a light to the nations
> that my salvation may reach to the ends of the earth.

All three Isaianic allusions unequivocally point in the direction of Israel's restoration. To the circle of disciples falls the vocation of the Isaianic servant, to raise up Jacob and to restore the remnant of Israel. Their task entirely coheres with their symbolic number, 'the twelve',[96] and hence the first imperative for the group when Jesus has been taken from them is to replace Judas (1.15-26). The joining of Isa. 32.15, 43.10-12 and 49.6-7 with the Baptist's similar promise (Acts 1.5; cf. Chapter 11 §2) means *the Spirit will come upon the disciples as the power of Israel's cleansing and restoration*, and so it becomes vital first to reconstitute the group who 'will sit on thrones judging the twelve tribes of Israel' (Lk. 22.30).[97] If there is ambivalence in 1.7-8, then, it is not a denial of an important future for 'Israel', but a change of emphasis from Israel's kingship to her task as servant bringing the light of God's salvation to the nations. This deutero-Isaianic servant soteriology corresponds well with the 'shape' of Israel's salvation anticipated by Simeon in Lk. 2.31-32 (using the same Isaianic passage), and it is claimed too by Paul (albeit with a different emphasis) as his commission from the risen Lord (Acts 13.47; 26.18).[98]

---

94. The expression 'the end of the earth' here means 'all nations' (as at Lk. 24.47, and 2.32 + Acts 13.47), not Rome. *Contra* Conzelmann, Haenchen, Burchard and Dömer, see Pesch, 70 n. 18; Schneider, 203 (and n. 38); Tannehill, *Narrative Unity*, II, p. 17, and esp. van Unnik, *Sparsa Collecta*, pp. 386-401; E.E. Ellis, '"The End of the Earth" (Acts 1:8)', *BBR* 1 (1991), pp. 123-32; and J.M. Scott, 'Horizon', pp. 524-27, 539.

95. So e.g. Schneider, 203; Pesch, 70; Dömer, *Heil*, p. 117; Tiede, 'Exaltation', p. 285; Menzies, *Development*, p. 200 n. 4.

96. Cf. W. Horbury, 'The Twelve and the Phylarchs', *NTS* 32 (1986), pp. 503-27.

97. See the two perceptive essays by J. Jervell: 'Sons of the Prophets: the Holy Spirit in the Acts of the Apostles', in *Unknown Paul*, pp. 96-121 (esp. 97-98); and 'The Twelve on Israel's Thrones', in *Luke*, pp. 75-112; and cf. C.A. Evans, 'The Twelve Thrones of Israel: Scripture and Politics in Luke 22.24-30', in Evans and Sanders, *Luke*, pp. 154-70. Evans argues that Lk. 22.30 anticipates eschatological rule, rather than rule in the restored Israel of the church (as Jervell took it), but the former is the pattern for the latter (cf. Turner, 'Luke and the Spirit', p. 247 n. 61).

98. This does not imply an attempt to correct 'nationalistic' notions of Israel: *contra* e.g. D. Hill, 'The Spirit and the Church's Witness: Observations on Acts 1.6-8',

What is said in 1.3-8 thus reinforces the hopes of Luke 1–2 concerning 'Israel' rather than subverting them. We may agree substantially with Tiede.

> Jesus' response to the disciples' question is not formulated in order to correct the readers'... 'eschatology', but to introduce the whole narrative of Acts as a testimony to the deployment of the reign of God's Messiah through his twelve apostles who declare repentance and forgiveness to Israel. First the twelve are restored (Acts 1:12-26). Then the Spirit is poured out upon devout Jews 'from every nation under heaven' (Acts 2).
>
> The logic is directly from Second Isaiah: the promise of God's reign is not simply the restoration of the preserved of Israel, but the renewal of the vocation of Israel to be a light to the nations to the end of the earth. Have God's promises failed? No, the restoration which the exalted Jesus is now about to inaugurate through the Holy Spirit (the promise of the Father: Lk. 24.49) is the renewal of Israel's prophetic calling in the world.[99]

If this statement does not yet allow sufficiently for the changes of perspective introduced from Acts 7 onwards (see §3 and Chapter 13 below), it nevertheless provides an appropriate horizon for the Pentecost speech.

Conclusion to §§1-2[100]

Acts 2.33-36 stands as a climax to the previously announced promises of Israel's restoration through the messiah of the Spirit. The Spirit emerges more clearly in Lk. 24.44-49, Acts 1.4-8 and 2.14-38 as the empowering presence of God through which God's reign comes to impinge eschatologically and transformingly upon Israel—and all this takes place through the exalted Jesus who now exerts his awaited rule over Jacob through this same Spirit of God. The Baptist's promise that the messiah will baptize with Spirit and fire has been elucidated in four key ways. First, the Spirit has been clarified as the Spirit of Israel's New Exodus refreshment and transformation by the light of Isa. 32.15 and 49.6 (Lk. 24.49; Acts 1.5, 8).[101] Secondly, the Spirit has been portrayed as the ascension gift of the prophet-like-Moses, and so as the constitutive power of Israel's renewed covenant, through the Moses/Sinai allusions in Acts 2. Thirdly, it has been specified as Joel's gift of the Spirit of prophecy to be granted universally to God's people. Finally, the Spirit has been presented as the Spirit of the messiah in a new sense. The Spirit is not merely an endowment of Jesus with God's presence and power,

IBS 6 (1984), pp. 16-18, for the task of the servant in Isaiah 49 remains to and through the nation.

99. 'Exaltation', p. 286.

100. Cf. also the Conclusion at end of §1.

101. Cf. J. Kremer, 'Die Voraussagen des Pfingstgeschehens in Apg 1,4-5 und 8', in G. Bornkamm and K. Rahner (eds.), *Die Zeit Jesu* (Freiburg: Herder, 1970), pp. 145-68.

rather Jesus, like the Father, grants the Spirit to disciples, and (from the perspective of 2.33) the Spirit mediates Christ's presence and activity as much as the Father's. The Spirit of God has become the Spirit of Jesus, too.

3. *The Pentecost Speech and the Body of Acts*

The foregoing sections have raised certain expectations with respect to the rest of Acts. Does Luke think the Spirit is given to all Christians as the Spirit of prophecy promised by Joel? Does he carry through the idea of the Spirit as the executive power of the risen Christ? And does he think that Jesus pursues Israel's restoration through the Spirit? Our affirmative answer to the first of these questions will need to be postponed until Chapter 12 (§1), but here (§3.1) we shall examine whether the rest of Acts substantiates the view that the Spirit is Jesus' executive power, and (in §3.2) whether there is sufficient evidence that Acts intends to depict the messianic restoration of Israel (rather than its failure or eschatological postponement).

3.1. *Is the Spirit in Acts the Executive Power of the Exalted Christ?*

In 2.33, Jesus is presented as coming into such a relation to God's Spirit that we might reasonably speak of him as Lord of the Spirit: he 'pours out' Joel's promise of the Spirit in the diverse manifestations Peter refers to collectively as 'this which you see and hear'. The implication of this would appear to be that, for Luke, wherever God's Spirit acts as the Spirit of prophecy, there both God and the exalted Christ are actively 'present'. If for Judaism the Spirit is a way of speaking about God's own dynamic, empowering, and self-revealing presence, 2.33 implies the same for Christ too. If this perception of Christ's relation to the Spirit were genuinely representative of Luke's view, the contrast often perceived between Luke's 'absentee Christology' and the Christologies of Christ's 'presence' in Paul and John would require substantial revision.[102] Luke would be seen to stand alongside Paul and John.

For Paul and John, too, one must speak of a 'real absence' of Christ who is in heaven. For John, Jesus must depart in the ascension, and return to the

---

102. Even in his influential paper ('Whom Heaven Must Receive until the Time', *Int* 27 [1973], pp. 160-61), MacRae admits that 'absentee Christology' is 'only half the story', because Luke thinks Jesus' work of guiding his followers is carried out by the Holy Spirit (and that Jesus is 'present' in his 'name' [pp. 161-62], in the kerygma about him [pp. 162-63], and as an example that moulds discipleship [pp. 163-64]). One of my own former research students has shown that Luke's view of the relation of the Spirit to Christ is much closer to Paul's than is often envisaged: see A.D. Hui, 'The Concept of the Holy Spirit in Ephesians and its Relation to the Pneumatologies of Luke and Paul' (PhD dissertation, Aberdeen University, 1992), ch. 2.

Father (chs. 14–17; 20); for Paul, to be present in the body is to be absent from the Lord, and only death (2 Cor. 5.6-9; Phil. 1.21-24), exaltation to heaven in a vision (2 Cor. 12.1-10) or the Parousia, can overcome that distance. For John, Christ and the Father become 'present' to the disciple primarily, if not exclusively, in and through the Paraclete who comes from the Father and the Son (another Christian version of the Spirit of prophecy); for Paul the picture is similar; Christ becomes present through the Spirit of God who has become 'the Spirit of Christ' too.[103] For Paul and John, any other 'means' of the perceived presence of Christ plays a very minor role compared to his presence in the Spirit.

But to what extent may the perspective provided by 2.33 be said genuinely to be of a piece with the rest of Luke–Acts? We have already noted that Luke's interpretation of Pentecost as fulfilment of the Baptist's promise (1.5; 11.16) tends to make the Spirit Jesus' executive power, and this is underscored by the redactional closing section of Luke's Gospel, where Jesus is made to say, '*I send the promise of the Father upon you*' (24.49). Jesus' Lordship of the Spirit then also appears evident in the use of the phrase τὸ πνεῦμα Ἰησοῦ ('the Spirit of Jesus'; Acts 16.7),[104] which is created in the image of the phrase τὸ πνεῦμα κυρίου (Acts 5.9; 8.39; Lk. 4.18), and, like it, can be set in parallel to τὸ πνεῦμα τὸ ἅγιον (cf. Acts 16.6). As such it means 'the Spirit as the active, directing presence of the risen Jesus',[105] and in this context the active presence in question concerns

103. For the position in the Fourth Gospel see especially Brown, 'Paraclete', pp. 113-32; G.M. Burge, *The Anointed Community: The Holy Spirit in the Johannine Community* (Grand Rapids: Eerdmans, 1987), pp. 137-47; Turner, 'Spirit in John's Gospel', pp. 24-42; and *idem*, 'Holy Spirit', pp. 349-50. For the position in Paul see especially Dunn, 'Jesus—Flesh and Spirit', pp. 40-68; *idem*, 'Life-giving Spirit', pp. 127-42; *idem*, Jesus, pp. 318-26; G.D. Fee, 'Christology and Pneumatology in Romans 8:9-11—and Elsewhere: Some Reflections on Paul as a Trinitarian', in Green and Turner (eds.), *Jesus*, pp. 312-31; *idem*, *Presence, passim* (but especially ch. 13); and Turner, 'Spirit and "Divine" Christology', esp. pp. 424-34.

104. G. Kilpatrick's claim ('The Spirit, God and Jesus in Acts', *JTS* 15 [1964], p. 63) that this reading at 16.7 is textually unsure, and that in Acts there are no passages which integrate Spirit with Jesus, appears to make very heavy weather of the textual problems involved, and to overlook Acts 2.33 in its context. The phrase τὸ πνεῦμα Ἰησοῦ is overwhelmingly attested and explains the other readings. Because it was unique in the New Testament it was emended to the more usual κυρίου (by C* it^gig *al.*) or qualified by του ἁγίου (arm^mss, Epiphanus) or, because of the appearance of this last at 16.6, the qualifier was dropped altogether (as in HLP 81 cop^sa *al.*). The appearance of Ἰησοῦ on the basis of any other text would be virtually impossible to explain. Confidence in the majority reading is such that the commentaries by Haenchen, Foakes-Jackson and Lake (*Beginnings*, IV, p. 4) and G. Stählin do not bother to mention the variants.

105. Cf. the important study by Stählin, 'Πνεῦμα', pp. 229-52, esp. 232, 235.

revelatory guidance provided by the risen Lord to his disciples. Acts 16.7 thus matches 2.33.

That Jesus acts and reveals through the Spirit—that is, that he becomes the author of charismata afforded by the Spirit—is not confined to Acts 2.33 and 16.7. Thus, for example, Luke carefully conflates the wording of the assurance of the Holy Spirit's help in time of trial (Lk. 12.12) with that of the promise that the risen Lord will give wisdom that none can withstand (Lk. 21.15) in his redactional portrayal of Stephen's preaching in Acts 6.10. In this instance the risen Lord addresses Israel through the charismata he bestows on his witness, just as Yahweh earlier addressed Israel through the charismata he bestowed on his prophets by the same Spirit (and in both cases the Spirit is similarly resisted: 7.51). This is but one example of a far more widespread understanding that Jesus has been exalted at God's right hand 'to give repentance to Israel, and forgiveness of sins' (5.31), which he does through the Spirit God grants to his witnesses (5.32).[106] Accordingly, later, we learn that the risen Jesus himself appeared to Paul and commissioned him to open the eyes of the Gentiles and bring them into the light (26.15-18 = Isa. 42.7, 16), but Paul (filled with the Spirit to execute this task, 9.15-17) declares that it is the risen Christ himself who 'proclaims light both to the people and to the Gentiles' (22.23, cf. also 13.2–14.27): that is, it is through the Spirit on Paul that Christ himself makes the proclamation. Similarly, dreams and visions (programmatically traced to the Spirit in Acts 2.17) now regularly have the character of Christophanies in which Jesus is seen acting on behalf of the disciple (7.55, re-emphasizing the Spirit as the 'means' of such phenomena), instructing the disciple (9.10-17; cf. 16.6-7; 22.17-18, 21) or bringing encouragement (23.11) or assuring of the Lord's own protection and support (18.9-10).[107]

This last, with its promise ἐγώ εἰμι μετὰ σοῦ ('I am with you'), was formerly seen as something of a breach of Luke's (alleged) more typical 'absentee Christology', but more recently Robert O'Toole, and others, have made a convincing case that it is precisely texts such as Acts 18.10 (with e.g. Lk. 21.15; Acts 2.14-38; 5.31; 9.4-5 [22.7; 26.14], 9.34, etc.) that most truly represent Luke's Christology, which is one of soteriological omnipresence,[108] and the chief *means* of that saving presence is the Spirit as 'the

Against the different attempts by von Baer (*Geist*, p. 42), Lampe ('Spirit', pp. 193ff.), Haya-Prats (*L'Esprit*, pp. 49-50) and Dunn to read 'the Spirit of Jesus' as 'the Spirit that was upon Jesus', or 'the Spirit marked by the character of Jesus' (etc.) instead see Turner, 'Spirit and "Divine" Christology', pp. 433-34.

106. The formulation here is Theopract rather than Christopract, but Christ and the Father have already been established as together exercising Lordship in Joel's gift.

107. Cf. Hui, 'Concept', pp. 25-30.

108. R.F. O'Toole, *The Unity of Luke's Theology* (Wilmington, DE: Glazier, 1984),

Spirit of Jesus'. In Chapter 13, we shall need to discuss more fully the role of the Spirit in the restorative salvation of Israel (and whether Luke seriously envisages any other 'means' of the risen Lord's presence), but the brief sketch I have offered above appears to justify the conclusion that for Luke the Spirit is very much the executive power of the risen Jesus, a *decisive* mode of his active presence, as of the Father's (and that Luke is much closer to John and to Paul than is often allowed). We may agree with Mainville's judgment that, for Luke, 'the Spirit is the presence of Jesus when Jesus is absent'.[109]

3.2. *Does Acts Portray the Messianic Restoration of Israel?*

All readers agree Luke 1–2 sets up the expectation that God's intervention will liberate and restore Israel. In addition, we have argued that the pro-grammatic passage of the Gospel (4.18-30) reinforces such a reading by interpreting God's inbreaking rule as Isaiah's promised New Exodus libera-tion, a theme which then dominates the rest of the Gospel. Acts 1–2 again considerably intensifies these expectations, for Jesus now fully enters the promise to David, sits on the throne at God's right hand, and receives Lord-ship over the Spirit. He is thus in a better position than was ever imaginable to 'baptize' Israel with Spirit and fire (Lk. 3.16; Acts 1.5). His disciples, reconstituted as 'the twelve'—the rulers of the restored Israel—wait in prayer for his intervention from heaven. The opening event of his heavenly rule gives further pledge of Israel's renewal, with its strong echoes of Israel's foundational experience, the reception of the Law at Sinai. The readers, unaware of the actual course of historical events, might await, with bated breath, the story of a transforming glorification of Zion, and the antic-ipated streaming in of the awed Gentiles (cf. Isa.2.2-4//Mic. 4.1-3; Zeph. 3.8-10; Jer. 3.17; Isa. 56.6-7; 60.3, 14; 66.23; Tob. 13.11-12; 14.6-7; *Syb. Or.* 3.719-23; *Ps. Sol.* 17.34-36, etc.). If the same readers were then to glance at the end of the book, expecting to find there described a scene to match the description of the heavenly city in Revelation 20–21, they could only be

esp. chs. 2-3 (cf. also his essay 'Activity of the Risen Christ in Luke–Acts', *Bib* 62 [1981], pp. 471-98). D. Buckwalter has argued that the evidence on which it is nor-mally claimed Jesus is 'absent' in heaven (e.g. he is only glimpsed from earth in visions, and occasionally 'present' to his disciples by substitutes such as his 'name' or δύναμις) well matches biblical descriptions of God, and is actually part of Luke's ten-dency to portray Jesus as multifariously omnipresent (so 'The Character and Purpose of Luke's Christology' [PhD dissertation, Aberdeen, 1991], pp. 211-31).

109. *L'Esprit*, p. 333, using the very words with which R.E. Brown described the Paraclete in John (see, however, n. 17 for some distancing between the perspectives of John and Luke on this issue): cf. p. 337 for the claim the actions of the Spirit are Christ himself continuing to act.

profoundly shocked to discover instead an account of Jesus' chief missionary, in prison at Rome, apparently announcing Israel's continued blindness
and the consequent turning to the Gentiles. It is the tension between Luke
1–2 and Acts 28 that sums up the main interpretive problem of Luke–Acts;
the puzzle of the relationship of Christianity to Israel and her hopes.

Until the early 1970s the dominant position in scholarship on Luke's atti-
tude to the Jews was almost entirely negative. Major commentaries from
Loisy to Haenchen saw Luke as a Gentile writer who thought of 'the Jews'
as opponents of Christianity, which only truly becomes such when it leaves
Judaism behind. J.C. O'Neill's work *The Theology of Acts in its Historical
Setting* gave a detailed argument for the same position.[110] In 1972, however, Jervell published a collection of essays under the title *Luke and the
People of God* challenging this consensus and claiming that Luke is the
most conservative and 'Jewish' writer on the relation of Christianity to
Israel and the Law. His major contribution was his argument that Luke
thought of the earliest church as the restoration of Israel, and that he
regarded it as a great success (thousands being converted at Pentecost, five
thousand by Acts 4.4, and 'myriads' [in Jerusalem alone] by 21.20, not to
mention similar diaspora successes). But Jervell also stressed that the
kerygma *divided* empirical Israel; only 'believers' took part in the restoration, those who did not were (for Luke) to be cut off out of 'the people' (cf.
3.22-23). How does this sifting and purifying of Zion relate to the 'Gentile'
mission? Jervell took Lk. 2.32 and similar passages with utmost seriousness;
it is only *through* Israel being restored and glorified that 'light' was able to
shine out from her to the Gentiles. Through the sifting and cleansing process, 'the fallen booth of David' was 'rebuilt' (Acts 15.16) '*so that* all other
peoples may seek the Lord—even the Gentiles...' (15.17). That too, Jervell
argued, was why Luke's Paul always approached the Jews in the diaspora
mission first; in each place 'Israel' had first to be sifted and restored before

---

110. London: SPCK, 2nd edn, 1970. The same position has been maintained of late
by those who charge Luke with anti-Semitic tendencies: see e.g. J.G. Gager, 'Jews,
Gentiles, and Synagogues in the Book of Acts', *HTR* 79 (1986), pp. 91-99; L. Gaston,
'Anti-Judaism and the Passion Narrative in Luke and Acts', in P. Richardson (ed.),
Anti-Judaism and Early Christianity (Waterloo, Ont.: Wilfred Laurier University Press,
1986), pp. 127-53; and, most vociferously, Sanders, *Jews*; *idem*, 'The Jewish People in
Luke–Acts', in Tyson (ed.), *Luke–Acts*, pp. 51-75. But see the criticisms of
J.A. Weatherly, 'The Jews in Luke–Acts', *TynBul* 40 (1989), pp. 107-17; *idem, Jewish
Responsibility for the Death of Jesus in Luke–Acts* (Sheffield: Sheffield Academic Press,
1994); and C.A. Evans, 'Prophecy and Polemic: Jews in Luke's Scriptural Apologetic',
in Evans and Richards, *Luke*, pp. 171-211; and cf. the judgment of F. Bovon: 'Luke's
Gospel and the Book of Acts are the New Testament texts which are the most open to
universalism as well as being the most favourable towards Israel' ('Etudes lucaniennes:
Rétrospective et prospectives', *RTP* 125 [1993], p. 128).

Gentiles could be added. All this was the more plausible for being thoroughly in keeping with Jewish eschatological expectations, and Jervell's insights have been taken up and developed in different ways by G. Lohfink, J.B. Chance, Tiede and Moessner.[111]

I would not wish to suggest that Jervell's views have by any means commanded universal assent. But they have indicated the real possibility that Luke understood the rise of the early Jewish church as itself the locus of the fulfilment of hopes for Israel's restoration; the impact of God's reign breaking in through Jesus' ministry and (more decisively) through his ascension to the eternal throne of David and gift of the Spirit. Two key passages take us to the heart of Jervell's proposal:

(A) *Acts 3.19-25*. It has already been suggested that this part of Peter's speech is important for Luke' ecclesiology. The gist of the message appears to be contained in the following affirmations: (1) All Israel needs to repent and turn back to God that her sins may be wiped away. (2) The result of this will be καιροὶ ἀναψύξεως, 'seasons of respite or refreshment' (i.e. liberation from oppression, 'peace', God's 'blessing' etc. [cf. v. 26]), until God

---

111. Lohfink, *Sammlung*; Chance, *Jerusalem*; Tiede, 'Exaltation', pp. 278-86, cf. *idem.*, ' "Glory to Thy People Israel": Luke–Acts and the Jews', in J.B. Tyson (ed.), *Luke–Acts and the Jewish People* (Minneapolis: Augsburg Press, 1988), pp. 21-34; Moessner, 'Ironic Fulfillment', pp. 35-50. Tiede's second essay indicated here offers a quite different emphasis from the earlier one. The earlier essay anticipates Israel's restoration within the history of the church leading to the parousia. The later essay, however, is written in the light of a much greater awareness of the apparent failure of the Jewish mission (and partly in response to Tannehill's essay, 'Israel in Luke–Acts', pp. 69-85). In his 1988 essay, Tiede claims that the order 'for the falling and rising of many in Israel' (in Simeon's prophecy, Lk. 2.34) corresponds to Luke's expectation: the story in Acts is mainly about the former, but the ending of the narrative in Acts 28 is not the end of the story (p. 29)—Luke anticipates the hopes of Lk. 1–2, Acts 1.6 (etc.) will be fulfilled at the End, which will be Israel's 'rising'. This is qualified by the assertion that 'the salvation which God intends, the restoration of all . . . [is] to be attested to Israel at the beginning and at the end' (pp. 28-29), which allows that the hoped-for restoration begins in the Jerusalem Church of Acts 1–15. But the emphasis has clearly shifted towards fulfilment of the promises at the end. Moessner's essay offers a devastating critique of Tiede's. It is only by taking literally Mary's words about the powerful being brought down from their thrones, and the lowly being lifted up (1.51-53), or Zechariah's words about a powerful Davidic saviour who will rescue God's people from their enemies (1.69-71, 73), that Tiede can deduce that these promises to Israel have yet to be fulfilled. Rather, Moessner claims, these hopes have come to be fulfilled in an unexpected way; not as Mary, Elizabeth, Zechariah and the Baptist understood them (i.e. nationistically; but how does Moessner know how these characters understood the hopes?), but how Simeon and Jesus understood them, i.e. in terms of the Servant role of Isa. 49.1-7.

culminates these by sending his pre-ordained messiah, Jesus, who (3) remains in heaven until the prophesied χρόνοι ἀποκαταστάσεως, 'times of restoration of all things', reach their fulfilment (of which God's sending of his Christ provides the climax).[112] (4) This same Jesus is the promised prophet-like-Moses to whom all Israel must listen (for his teaching now transcends that of Moses). (5) Those who do not obey will be cut off from 'the people' (the language of Lev. 23.29 is incorporated here; but it perhaps only interprets the sense of Deut. 18.19 'whoever does not give heed to my words, which he will speak in my name, I myself will require it of him'). (6) All this accords with all the prophets said about 'these days' (= the period of the church), and especially with the promise (Gen. 22.18) that in Abraham's 'seed' all the families the world would be blessed (3.25), which means Israel (the 'sons of the prophets') in the first place, then, as a result, those beyond.[113]

The speech clearly identifies 'these days' of the church as a period of fulfilment of all the prophets, one of God's universal blessing, and one of 'seasons of refreshment'. It is thus inescapably envisaged as part of the 'times of restoration of all things' too, which will culminate in God's sending of Israel's messiah. Accordingly, for Jervell, Abraham's 'seed' (3.25) means Israel, and Israel's restoration ('first' 3.26) leads in turn to the blessing of 'all the families of the world' (= Gentiles).

This probably needs some exegetical adjustment, however. Had Luke meant the citation in Jervell's sense he would surely have retained the LXX wording that πάντα τὰ ἔθνη τῆς γῆς ('all the nations of the world') would be blessed, for τὰ ἔθνη was virtually a technical term for 'the Gentiles'. The change to the broader term αἱ πατριαί signals that πᾶσαι αἱ πατριαὶ τῆς γῆς denotes not merely Gentiles, but Jews, too.[114] This is further suggested by v. 26 which speaks of God raising up Jesus first to 'bless' 'you'

112. A sense of the 'times of restoration' which refers them as much to what is about to take place in the Church as to the End itself appears to be demanded by the plural form χρόνοι, which offers a clear parallel both with the καιροὶ ἀναψύξεως of 3.20, and with the statement in 3.24 that all the prophets prophesied 'these days' (subsequently clarified in 3.25-26 as the days in which all peoples are blessed in Abraham's seed). Indeed the two terms 'seasons of respite/refreshment' and 'times of restoration' evidently belong materially together, for the restoration implied in the latter is the mirror image of the liberation implied in the former. See e.g. Bayer, 'Eschatology', pp. 247-48.

113. See especially Jervell, *Luke*, ch. 2 entitled 'The Divided People of God: the Restoration of Israel and Salvation for the Gentiles', pp. 58-60.

114. See S.G. Wilson, *The Gentiles and the Gentile Mission in Luke–Acts* (Cambridge: Cambridge University Press, 1973), pp. 219-22, 227-33. Jervell is, however, aware of the potential ambiguity of αἱ πατριαὶ τῆς γῆς: at *Luke*, p. 60, he allows it may refer to 'far off' Jews as well as Gentiles.

(= as-yet-unrepentant Israel). It is not surprising that some have inferred from this that Luke understood 'the seed of Abraham' *christologically* (as Paul did in Gal. 3.16).[115] But this too probably oversimplifies. Luke–Acts more than any New Testament writing presents Israel (especially faithful Israel) as 'sons of Abraham', Lk. 1.55 and Acts 7.5-8 specifically use the expression 'his seed' (Abraham's) as a designation for Israel, and in the immediate context Peter speaks of 'your fathers... Abraham...' (3.25, cf. also 3.13).[116] It is more probable then that Abraham's 'seed' here denotes the faithful Israel gathered *with* her messiah through whom the promises to Abraham (cf Lk. 1.55; 73-75) are being met. The addressees can be called 'sons of the prophets', and of the covenant to Abraham (3.25), on the charitable assumption that they will indeed repent, and thereby show they truly belong to Israel.

This would certainly fit with what we know of the use of 'seed' motifs in sectarian Judaism, where the dualism between righteous and unrighteous Israel is explained in terms of two quite different types of 'seed' from which they have sprung, and which they embody. Thus in *Jub.* 16.15-19 the 'holy seed' of Abraham is born through the line of Isaac and Jacob (cf. chs. 19–38), but within the polemical context of the writing this seed is narrowed down to those 'who are after him' in the sense that they celebrate the feasts at their appropriate times (16.28-31), that is, the Jubilees calendar, and not that of official Judaism. The handling of Jacob and Esau in chs. 19–38 suggests they have become 'paradigms of the righteous and unrighteous seed in the author's time', that is, of that division passing through empirical Israel.[117] Within this writing the seed of Abraham is a formative spiritual influence generating true sons of the covenants, and so (by extension) a way of referring to those who genuinely keep the covenant (cf. also CD 2.11-12; 1QM 13.7-8, etc.).

Jervell's essential point remains, however, that 3.19-26 envisages the restoration of the core of Israel first, and that this leads to wider blessing. Nevertheless, these promises to Israel are only to be realized in the church; for they depend upon repentance and acceptance of the messiah's teaching. To make this point as sharply as possible, Peter invokes the prophet-like-Moses Christology. As the word of God given through Moses was

---

115. See e.g. Wilson, *Gentiles*, pp. 220-21; Bruce, 146; Pesch, 157-58; Schneider, 329-30; Schille, 130.

116. See Jervell, *Luke*, pp. 59-60. Compare J.B. Chance, 'The Seed of Abraham and the People of God: A Study of Two Pauls', in Lovering (ed.), *Society of Biblical Literature 1993 Seminar Papers*, pp. 384-411, who also insists 'seed of Abraham' in Luke designates Jews (alone).

117. See Elliott, 'Survivors', §5.2.1. Elliott points especially to 19.15-24; 21.25; 22.10-13, 15; 36.16.

constitutive for Israel of old, so now the messianic word of the prophet-like-Moses is constitutive for the 'Israel of fulfilment'—those who do not accept his teaching are cut off from 'the people (of God)'. Curiously, Rese considers this section unimportant for the writer of Acts;[118] Lohfink, however, goes straight to the heart of the matter (if polemically) when he claims: 'in the period of the initial apostolic preaching, the true Israel assembles itself from among the Jewish people. And that Israel which persists in rejection of Jesus loses its entitlement to be the true people of God—it becomes mere Judaism'![119]

As Lohfink observed, Luke has regularly changed Mark's references to Jesus teaching the ὄχλος ('crowd') into his teaching the λαός ('the people'). He has used this term, and expressions such as πᾶς ὁ λαός ('the whole people') and ἐναντίον τοῦ λαοῦ ('before (all) the people') to evoke the LXX designation for Israel. And so Jesus becomes the prophet-like-Moses addressing 'Israel'—and 'the people of God' consist precisely in those who obey this prophet (Jew, or later Gentile), while those who do not are cut off from their true heritage. Lohfink observes that after Acts 15 Jews are only rarely referred to as λαός by the narrator; while Gentile believers begin to be called God's λαός (cf. 15.14 and 18.10). Believers have become the λαός of God, because they are the ones who have listened to the eschatological Prophet.[120]

The prophet-like-Moses Christology has thus provided the lynchpin of Luke's ecclesiology, which maintains the Jewish Christian church is the 'Israel of fulfilment',[121] and suggests that there is now no longer any 'true' Israel where the claims of the Gospel are rejected. His prophet-like-Moses Christology hereby provides the ideological foundation of Luke's ecclesiology and legitimates the church as the inheritor of the promises to Israel. At the same time, it serves to diminish the 'problem' of Jewish rejection of the Gospel, by questioning the real status of those who do not repent. From the perspective of this passage there is little reason to assume Luke considered

---

118. *Motive*, pp. 71, 206-207.

119. *Sammlung*, p. 55, and chs. 2–3 preparing for this verdict.

120. *Sammlung*, chs. 2–3. This is rather overschematized however; see e.g. 21.30, 36, 40, and in speech material, 21.39, 23.5, 26.17, 28.17, 26-27.

121. I.e. that sector of Israel within which the promises come to fulfilment, and so transform Israel. Used this way the term 'Israel of fulfilment' corresponds better with Luke's theology than Lohfink's 'true Israel' (which might suggest pre-Christian Israel was 'false Israel', while Luke strives more than most to maintain the unity of the covenants), or Jervell's insistence that for Luke there is only one Israel (so the church cannot be either the 'new' Israel, nor the 'true' one), which does not allow sufficiently for the transformation Luke envisages the Gospel to bring about: against Jervell, see Turner, 'Sabbath', pp. 113-24.

the unbelief of much of contemporary Judaism to put a question mark over
the promises of Israel's restoration, or require that they be largely deferred
to the time of the parousia, when he anticipates a large-scale national
repentance. Of the last there is little trace in Luke's writings.[122]

(B) *Acts 15.12-21.* If Peter's speech in ch. 3 envisages Israel's restoration as
a process already begun, James' speech was taken by Jervell to suggest that
by Acts 15 it is largely complete. The crux is the interpretation of Amos 9.11-
12, and its place in James's argument. His point appears to be that the
Gentile converts should be accepted as 'one people' with the Israel of
fulfilment (cf. 15.14) because this accords with Amos' promise that the
rebuilding of David's fallen 'dwelling' (15.16) will cause 'the rest of
men...and/even all the Gentiles' to seek the Lord (15.17).

Following Munck,[123] Jervell claimed that the fallen dwelling of David

---

122. Cf. H. Räisänen, 'The Redemption of Israel: A Salvation-Historical Problem in
Luke–Acts', in P. Luomanen (ed.), *Luke–Acts: Scandinavian Perspectives*, (Göttingen:
Vandenhoeck & Ruprecht, 1991), pp. 94-114, who bluntly claims 'there is not a word'
of it in Luke's writings (p. 98). The main literature is incisively surveyed by Räisänen,
though since his work others have defended the view he attacks, e.g. L.R. Helyer, 'Luke
and the Restoration of Israel', *JETS* 36 (1993), pp. 317-29 and the progressive dispen-
sationalism of D. Bock, 'Evidence from Acts', in D.K. Campbell and J.L. Townsend
(eds.), *A Case for Premillenialism* (Chicago: Moody, 1992) pp. 181-98. The opinion
Luke expects a future restoration of Israel is held on the basis of five main arguments:
(1) The promises of Lk. 1–2 must be fulfilled; (2) Lk. 13.35 assumes the house of
Israel will be foresaken, for their failure to respond to Jesus, but will later welcome him
in the words of Ps. 118.26; (3) Lk. 21.28 speaks of 'your redemption' drawing near
beyond the 'times of the Gentiles' (21.24); (4) Acts 1.6-8 delays, but does not deny
Israel's ultimate rule; Acts 3.21-22 envisages Israel's messianic restoration at the end;
(5) the failure of Israel to respond to the Gospel is explained by Paul at Acts 28.26-27
in terms of Isa. 6.9-10, but the latter involves a temporary 'blindness' that God will
reverse (so V. Fusco, as yet unpublished seminar paper 'Luke–Acts and the Future of
Israel' [Edinburgh, SNTS, 1994]). Considerations of space allow only the following
brief remarks: the argument (1) above is only telling if it is assumed the prophecies are
meant literally (rather than apocalyptic language used for Israel's transformation) (see
Moessner's arguments); argument (2) allusively raises a possibility, no more, while
(3) is probably mistaken. 'The time of the Gentiles' may well be to the end itself, and
21.28 addresses believers (not all Israel). Argument (4) I have dealt with above.
Argument (5) is weak, for while Paul here probably only addresses the unrepentant
Jews at Rome as 'this people' of Isa. 6.9-10, and while Luke still leaves open the possibility of individual Jews at Rome converting (28.30—on which see especially
J. Dupont, 'La conclusion des Actes et son rapport à l'ensemble de l'ouvrage de Luc',
in Kremer [ed.], *Actes*, pp. 359-404), he makes no allusion to the Isaianic promises of
restoration beyond the 'blindness'.

123. J. Munck, *Paul and the Salvation of Mankind* (London: SCM Press, 1959),
p. 235.

here is a metaphor for Israel. Israel's restoration leads to the influx of the *// bind* Gentiles. Jervell was aware that Haenchen and others took the rebuilding of David's fallen dwelling as a metaphor for the resurrection-exaltation of Jesus to God's right hand, and that the whole citation then refers to 'the Jesus event that will cause the Gentiles to seek the Lord'.[124] Jervell countered that such was to divide v. 16 from v. 17, for the phrase 'the rest of men' (= Gentiles) implies v. 16 speaks of *Israel*. Haenchen's interpretation leaves Israel curiously unmentioned, while the whole point of the citation in context should be to explain how the large *Jewish* Christian church is to relate to the expanding group of Gentile believers.[125] If we assume the traditional Isaianic Jewish soteriology, however, Jervell urged, the quotation immediately makes sense. The restoration of Israel leads to the consequent influx and blessing of the Gentiles.[126]

Once again, the broad lines of Jervell's interpretation contain important truth, but his position requires considerable modification in significant matters of detail. Dupont and Strauss have argued the metaphor in 15.16 refers to David's fallen 'household', rebuilt through the Christ-event, and their evidence is strong enough to suggest this should at least be taken as part of the meaning.[127] The rebuilding of David's ruined 'hut' or 'booth' in 15.16 cannot simply refer to some restoration within the Jewish Christian church: we should not without further ado equate David's house with 'the house of

124. Haenchen, 448.
125. 'Divided People', pp. 52-53.
126. So also Chance, *Jerusalem*, pp. 37-39.
127. J. Dupont ('"Je rebâtirai la cabane de David qui est tombée" [Ac 15,16 = Am 9,11]', in Grässer and Merk [eds.], *Glaube*, pp. 19-32) and Strauss (*Messiah*, pp. 185-92) have supported the christological interpretation with the following arguments: (1) in the Amos context the 'fallen booth' is probably a metaphor for the weakness of the Davidic 'household' (= dynasty); (2) Judaism is aware of a messianic interpretation of the verse, for 4QFlor 1.12-13 first cites Amos 9.11 and then explains 'the fallen booth of David' is 'he that shall arise to save Israel'; (3) the change from LXX ἀνοικοδομήσω ('I shall rebuild') to ἀνορθώσω ('I will establish'), at the end of v. 16, indicates the messianic meaning is intended, for this verb is regularly used in the LXX in connection with the establishment of David's throne (cf. 2 Sam. 7.13, 16, 26; 1 Chron. 17.12, 14, 24; 22.10; compare Isa. 16.5), and (4) Luke especially emphasizes the fulfilment of 2 Sam. 7.13-14 in Jesus' life, death, and resurrection-exaltation (Acts 2.25-36; 13.23, 32-37). The view is shared by Kränkl, *Knecht Gottes*, pp. 164-66; Burger, *Jesus*, p. 149-52; Schneider, 182; and Schille, 321. The arguments of Dupont and Strauss convince me against R. Bauckham's case that the fallen hut of David is the Temple, rebuilt as the eschatological Temple = the Church (see 'James and the Jerusalem Church', in R. Bauckham [ed.], *The Book of Acts in its Palestinian Setting* [Carlisle: Paternoster, 1995], pp. 415-80, esp. 452-62). A secondary reference to the Church as the eschatological temple is certainly possible, however, for a restored messianic household would go hand in hand with a restored temple.

Israel'.[128] But a christological application to Jesus alone is equally uninviting. One can barely imagine any Jew speaking of God's re-establishment of the royal 'house of David' in glory *without* implying the Davidid's saving and restoring rule in Israel (cf. Lk. 1.68-71); for within a Jewish context to be given the throne of David *meant* to exercise rule 'over Jacob' (Lk. 1.32). Accordingly, the Targum rendered Amos 9.11, 'At that time, I will set up again the kingdom/rule of the house of David that has fallen...and I will build their cities and I shall set up their synagogues anew' (cf. *b. Sanh.* 96b). Furthermore, as Jervell himself pointed out, the purely christological explanation leaves a theological chasm between the restored dynasty of David in 15.16 and 'the rest of men', the Gentiles, in 15.17. For Luke, it is the messianic congregation, the servant of Isa. 49.6, who first provides the light to the Gentiles: the strength of Jervell's position was that it could read Amos 9.11 not merely in the light of traditional Jewish eschatological expectation, but also in the light of Luke's affirmed pattern (cf. Lk. 2.32; 24.47; Acts 1.7-8; 3.25-26; 5.31; 13.47, etc.) These considerations suggest that Luke understood the rebuilding of the fallen booth of David to mean more than that a descendent of David's line has at last been appointed as king. He means also that the Davidid's powerful restoring rule in Zion has been re-established (perhaps in and through a growing restored 'household' of faithful 'servants' [after the analogy of 4.29 in the context of 4.25-30]), so that 'the rest of men' might now seek the God of Israel in accordance with the ancient hopes (cf. 15.17c, 18a).[129] I am not convinced one can press the metaphor further,[130] but the passage strongly suggests that Zion's restoration is *well under way* as a consequence of Jesus' exaltation to David's throne.[131]

In sum, there are clear indications in the body of Acts (in what are evidently key speeches) to confirm the picture in the prologue and Acts 2. The ascended one, as Lord of the Spirit, continues the task of Israel's restorative

128. So Dupont, 'La cabane de David', pp. 23-24.

129. Cf. P.A. Paulo, *Le problème ecclésial des Actes à la lumière des deux prophéties d'Amos* (Paris: Cerf, 1985), pp. 79-85; Tannehill, *Narrative Unity*, II, p. 188; Franklin, *Luke*, p. 57.

130. Jervell takes the passage to mean the restoration of Israel is largely completed within Jewish Christianity to which the Gentiles may now be tacked on 'alongside' as an associate people of God (against this whole reconstruction see Turner, 'Sabbath', pp. 113-24). By contrast, Lohfink takes the passage to mean David's booth is restored, and Israel becomes 'true' Israel, only when the Gentiles are included within her (*Sammlung*, p. 60); but this cannot be, for within 15.16-17 the rebuilt hut is distinguished from and followed by Gentile inclusion.

131. Cf. Bock ('Evidence', pp. 194-97) arguing against the more traditional premillennial position which claims Amos 9.20 applies directly only to the eschatological order.

cleansing and transformation, which he commenced as one empowered by the Spirit.

Conclusions[132]

Throughout Luke's Gospel the hope for God's reign and Jesus' kingship have been linked with the hope for Israel's New Exodus liberation and restoration. Accordingly, the Baptist promises the coming one will 'cleanse' Israel with Spirit and fire (3.16). Within the period of the ministry, Luke depicts Jesus as partially fulfilling these hopes. But his full kingly rule (1.32-33) belongs beyond the horizon even of his arrival in Jerusalem (Lk. 9.51; 19.11-27; 23.42). Acts 2.33-36 claims that Jesus has entered on this promised rule through ascension to God's right hand as David's Lord (Ps. 110.1). He is now in a position to 'restore' Israel. But how will the Lord in heaven, at God's right hand, be able to exert his restorative rule over Israel? The answer provided by the closing section of Luke's Gospel (24.44-49), the prologue of Acts (1.3-8), and the Pentecost speech itself, is that he does so through the gift of the Spirit of which he has become Lord. The rest of Acts supports the picture of the Spirit as the executive power of the exalted messiah, and key texts imply that the restoration of Israel is indeed well under way. We shall need to nuance this general picture somewhat in Chapter 13 below.

132. See also conclusions to §§1-2 above.

Part IV

THE DISCIPLES AND THE SPIRIT

Chapter 11

THE CIRCLE OF JESUS' DISCIPLES AND THE SPIRIT FROM THE BEGINNINGS OF JESUS' MINISTRY TO HIS ASCENSION

Our understanding of the disciples' experience before Pentecost inevitably profoundly affects our perception of the gift of the Spirit to them on that day. As is well known, the traditional Pentecostal case for 'baptism in the Spirit' as a 'second' grace has been built partly on the analogy of Jesus' experience, but more especially on that of the disciples. With respect to the former, it is argued Jesus' religious life before his Jordan experience flowed from his new creation 'birth' by the Spirit (Lk. 1.35), and so he receives the Spirit at the Jordan purely as a *donum superadditum* of prophetic empowering. Similarly, the disciples receive 'salvation' in the ministry of Jesus, and in their encounters with the resurrected Lord before the ascension, and so they too now receive the Spirit at Pentecost as empowering for service and mission rather than as the presence of salvation. Dunn, by contrast, argued this denies the epochal significance of Jordan and Pentecost. Jesus' Jordan experience, as the turn of the ages, was Jesus' own first entry into the life of 'the kingdom of God' or 'salvation'; the disciples, however, only witness the realities of this in Jesus until the second epochal turning point (Pentecost) permits them to enter into the new age too. In this chapter we shall see that while both models have their strengths, neither really accords with the evidence. In §1 I shall argue that Luke regards the disciples as themselves experiencing the 'kingdom of God', 'salvation' and the Spirit within the ministry of Jesus to a far greater degree than Dunn's description suggests. In §2 we shall note (with Pentecostal writers) how Lk. 24.47-49 and Acts 1.3-8 present 'the promise' of the Spirit to the disciples very much as prophetic empowering, but (against Stronstad, Mainville and Menzies) that there is no suggestion it is this *alone* and that it is this for all. In §3 I shall use the arguments developed in §1 to suggest Luke would expect his reader to anticipate the Pentecostal gift, not merely as empowering, but also as the chief means of the disciples' on-going and deepening experience of 'salvation', when Jesus has departed.

1. *Spirit, 'the Kingdom of God' and 'Salvation' in the Ministry of Jesus*

For Dunn, Spirit-reception in Luke means receiving justification, the kingdom of God and sonship: in other words, it denotes receiving the matrix of new-creation life and new covenant relationship. The period of the ministry was one in which Jesus *alone* (and archetypally) experienced the Spirit in the sense he defines; the disciples do not participate in the same realities until Pentecost. This led Dunn to maintain that the disciples do not participate in the kingdom, or in salvation, during the ministry of Jesus. The kingdom was limited to Jesus: 'the new age and covenant had come, but only in him; only he had begun to experience them'.[1]

This, however, does not fit with the view of the Spirit on Jesus that we have discovered in Chapters 6–9 above. Luke regards Jesus as endowed with the Spirit to proclaim and to inaugurate messianic redemption, Israel's New Exodus liberation and restoration. The corollary of this would appear to be that Luke considered at least some of Jesus' hearers/disciples to have participated in the end-time 'salvation' Jesus initiated. This chapter first briefly surveys Luke's understanding of the relationship of the disciples to the kingdom of God and 'salvation' during the ministry, and then attempts to relate this discussion to the question of the disciples' experience of the Spirit before Pentecost.

1.1. *The Kingdom of God and Salvation in the Ministry of Jesus according to Luke*

In Chapter 10 it was noted that Luke envisages the period of Jesus' ministry to be one in which God's reign was proclaimed and became manifest. The parable of the Great Feast in Lk. 14.15-24 is typical, perhaps, of Luke's perspective. During table-talk, someone exclaims the blessing of those that will enjoy the messianic banquet ('eat bread in the kingdom of God'). Jesus responds with a parable that intimates the grand feast has already started, but the invited guests have offered culturally absurd excuses for not turning up which amount to flat (and insulting) rejection.[2] Accordingly their place

---

1. *Baptism*, p. 41. W.G. Kümmel, *Promise and Fulfilment* (London: SCM Press, 1961), pp. 124-55, used similar language, but with a quite different meaning. Kümmel meant that Jesus was the focus of the presence of the kingdom of God, that he was uniquely related to it, and that others only experienced the kingdom in relationship to Jesus: cf. also O. Merk, 'Das Reich Gottes in den lukanischen Schriften', in Ellis and Grässer (eds.), *Jesus*, p. 219.

2. K.E. Bailey, *Through Peasant Eyes* (Grand Rapids: Eerdmans, 1980), pp. 88-113. No Palestinian would buy a field without considerable prior inspection, nor even a single yoke of oxen without trying them. And the last excuse is more preposterous still. No-one unexpectedly marries a wife in the short interval culturally assumed between

has been taken by others who are now enjoying the feast (vv. 21-23). In short, the anticipated feast of the 'kingdom of God' has become a present reality, and is being 'enjoyed' by erstwhile 'outsiders' to its hope. Luke's point is hardly that God's reign was an experience accessible only to Jesus (until Pentecost); it is rather that Jesus' ministry made it accessible to all who accept his announcement (cf. 16.16; 8.4-15; 11.20 etc.). These assertions of the 'presence' of God's reign as his redemptive and self-revealing activity experienced by the people are matched too by sayings including parallel expressions. Thus it is no accident that Luke's first mention of the 'kingdom of God' comes in the redactional phrase 'to proclaim the good news of the kingdom of God' in Lk. 4.43.[3] Here it pertains to the working of liberating miracles at Capernaum and provides a formal parallel to Jesus' announcement in Nazareth that speaks of his being anointed 'to proclaim the good news' of (New Exodus) 'liberation' (4.18-21, cf. 4.23!). The two metaphors ('kingdom of God' and New Exodus 'liberation') interpret each other, and 4.21 emphatically and paradigmatically affirms the 'today' of the fulfilment of this hope; messianic liberation is already 'available' (cf. 7.21-22). A third important set of sayings uses the language of 'salvation' to make parallel types of claim (cf. especially 6.9; 7.50; 8.12; 19.9, 10).[4]

But what benefits does God's reign, New Exodus liberation, or 'salvation' actually bring people within Jesus' ministry? Three of the statements which most clearly point to the 'presence' of the kingdom of God (11.20; 10.9, 11) pertain to liberating miracles of healing and exorcism. Of the latter, Perrin astutely remarked 'the experience of the individual has become the arena of the eschatological conflict';[5] such 'events in the ministry of

initial invitation and the servants being sent out to say the meal is ready.

3.　　Luke alone connects the kingdom directly with verbs designating preaching, arguing, persuading, etc.; see Merk, 'Reich', pp. 204-205; M. Völkel, 'Zur Deutung des "Reiches Gottes" bei Lukas', *ZNW* 65 (1974), pp. 57-70, esp. 62-63 and 60-70. Compare Busse, *Wunder*, pp. 87-88.

4.　　On this see Marshall, *Luke*, chs. 4–6; A. George, 'L'Emploi chez Luc du vocabulaire de salut', *NTS* 23 (1976–77), pp. 307-20; R.P. Martin, 'Salvation and Discipleship in Luke's Gospel', *Int* 30 (1976), pp. 366-80; Bovon, 'Le salut dans les écrits de Luc', in *L'Oeuvre*, pp. 165-79; N. Flanagan, 'The What and How of Salvation in Luke–Acts', in D. Durken (ed.), *Sin, Salvation and the Spirit* (Collegeville, MN: Liturgical Press, 1979); Johnson, 'Social Dimensions', pp. 520-36; J.B. Green, *The Theology of the Gospel of Luke* (Cambridge: Cambridge University Press, 1995), ch. 4 (esp. pp. 94-95) and pp. 134-40; and compare C.L. Blomberg, '"Your Faith Has Made You Whole": The Evangelical Liberation Theology of Jesus', in Green and Turner (eds.), *Jesus*, pp. 75-93.

5.　　N. Perrin, *The Kingdom of God in the Teaching of Jesus* (London: SCM Press, 1963), p. 171.

Jesus are nothing less than *an experience* of the Kingdom of God'.[6] But this observation affords us little help. Certain of Jesus' followers experienced exorcism and/or healing at his hands (8.2-3), but such acts appear to have been relatively rare in the immediate circle of his disciples. They are hardly sufficient to demonstrate that Jesus' disciples experienced 'the life of the kingdom of God' before Pentecost (indeed such miracles did not necessarily involve any continuing relationship of the one exorcised to the sphere of the presence of the kingdom; cf. 11.26!), and, in any case, the disciples were not remembered as those who benefited from such deliverances, but rather as those who shared in Jesus' ministry of performing them (9.1-6; 10.1-12, 17-20, etc.). Healings and exorcisms were perhaps an important indication of the active presence of God's grace liberating men and women, but they would not be of much significance for our question unless they were simultaneously tokens of some more general manifestation of God's reign. That this was in fact the case is, however, readily suggested by e.g. Lk. 16.16 (where 'the kingdom of God' into which 'all' either 'press' or 'are pressed' can barely be expounded in such restricted terms),[7] and by the parable of the Great Feast with which we commenced. Both of these sayings come close to depicting the presence of God's reign as a sphere of God's blessing which people may enter and enjoy.

If we try to define more closely the nature of the 'benefits' afforded by this presence of God's reign, they seem to involve some measure of those very things Dunn by implication denies are available within the ministry, viz. 'justification', 'salvation', 'faith', new 'life' and 'sonship'.

With respect to 'justification', we may usefully start with Sung's claim that Jesus saw his 'forgiveness of sins' as the most significant component of his proclamation of God's reign, and of his proleptic action as the eschatological 'Son of Man'.[8] Whether or not Sung has exaggerated his case, most

6. N. Perrin, *Rediscovering the Teaching of Jesus* (London: SCM Press, 1976), p. 67.

7. βιάζεται here may be taken as middle in form and construed 'enters forcibly into' (i.e. with determination such as shown by the shrewd manager of 16.1-8); for a fuller discussion of this highly disputed logion see Marshall, 629; Nolland, 820-21; and Turner, 'Sabbath', p. 144 n. 93; against F.W. Danker, 'Luke 16.16—an Opposition Logion?', *JBL* 77 (1958), p. 235; and Ellis, 203-204. Fitzmyer, 1117-18, argues for a passive of βιάζεται with the sense 'everyone is pressed to enter it' which he explains: i.e. 'with a demanding urgent invitation (of the kingdom-preacher himself)'. This is possible (and might echo the 'compulsion' of 14.21-23). Either way, the saying implies a presence of the kingdom of God that goes well beyond healing and exorcisms.

8. Chong-Hyon Sung, *Vergebung der Sünden: Jesu Praxis der Sündenvergebung nach den Synoptikern und ihre Voraussetzungen im Alten Testament und frühen Judentum* (Tübingen: Mohr, 1993), Part C (esp. pp. 280-84).

would agree that the church's proclamation of 'justification' finds its roots and determinative shape in Jesus' ministry among the marginalized 'sinners'; this is one of the agreed 'bridges' between the 'historical Jesus' and the 'Christ' of the kerygma. Correspondingly, at the very heart of Jesus' ministry, as set out by Luke, is the extension of God's grace and forgiveness beyond the boundaries of those normally considered to be worthy of it. For Luke, the scandalous table-fellowship with 'sinners' was not merely an acted parable of a future possibility; it was an anticipatory enjoyment of the table-fellowship of the kingdom of God, firmly based in the offer and acceptance of divine forgiveness.[9] The joy associated with response to this message is characterized in a number of Luke's most striking parables and logia,[10] including those of Lk. 15.1-32. That Luke understood the eschatological overtones of this message of forgiveness and salvation is also clear in his redaction of 19.9-12, where the disciples assume that the kingdom might very soon 'be revealed' because Jesus announced that 'salvation' (probably in the form of restoring forgiveness) has come to Zacchaeus's house.

A similar phenomenon is to be observed with respect to the story of 'a sinful woman forgiven' (7.36-50), which Luke gives a key position in his redactional context,[11] using it as an illustration of the depth of response that Luke considers possible, within the ministry, to Jesus' proclamation of the kingdom. While the language of Jesus' explanation of the woman's love in 7.48 accommodates this story to that of the eschatological healing miracles ('your sins are forgiven you' // 5.20-24; 'your faith has saved you: Go in peace' // 8.48),[12] there is no question of a healing here; rather, the

---

9. See, among many others, Perrin, *Rediscovering*, pp. 102-108; J. Jeremias, 'This is my Body...', *ExpTim* 83 (1971–72), pp. 196-99; G. Bornkamm, *Jesus of Nazareth* (London: Hodder, 1960), p. 81. For the eschatological dimension of the proclamation of forgiveness of sins, particularly in apocalypticism, see H. Thyen, *Studien zur Sündenvergebung im Neuen Testament und seinen alttestamentlichen und jüdischen Voraussetzungen* (Göttingen: Vandenhoeck & Ruprecht, 1970); and Sung, *Vergebung*.

10. Perrin, *Rediscovering*, pp. 90-102.

11. This story is an extension of the themes Luke has developed from 7.1-35; it takes up the motif of Jesus' announcement of the kingdom of God and of its effects on those who respond with faith (7.10, 22-23), as well as the note of rejection of Jesus occasioned by his stance with respect to 'tax-collectors and sinners' (7.29-35, cf. 5.30-32). The pericope leads directly into a bridging summary statement (8.1-3) also concerning women 'released' by Jesus' ministry (with Fitzmyer, 695-98, against Marshall, 315, who makes 8.1-3 the beginning of a totally new section). Within the summary we are reminded once again that Jesus was 'proclaiming the good news of the kingdom of God' (8.1), and the story of the forgiveness of the sinful woman is thus in a key position to illustrate its effects.

12. U. Wilckens, 'Vergebung für die Sünderin (Lk 7.36-50)', in P. Hoffman *et al.*

story assumes a prior 'conversion' of the woman,[13] and concentrates on the wholehearted response of thankfulness and love which is a proof of the reality of the woman's *experience* of forgiveness of sins. She thus becomes a pre-Easter cameo of the response anticipated to the Church's proclamation of 'forgiveness of sins' in Jesus' name.

If this story implies a tasting of the life of God's reign in a relatively penetrating existential sense, the same may be discerned elsewhere, including within the circle of the twelve (cf. 5.1-11).[14] The significance of these occasions, however, does not lie in the psychological release from 'guilt' that such encounters may have provoked. Israel already had the covenantal mechanisms for atonement, and largely anticipated God's acquittal at the final assize: in that sense she was no stranger to 'the forgiveness of sins'. But she held these views in tension with the conviction that her national, social and spiritual doldrums were her 'exile' for her sins, and that God's intervention to save and restore Israel could only proceed from their forgiveness and cleansing, individually and corporately. It was for such intervention that John the Baptist's ministry prepared, and it is within this context that we must understand Jesus' announcement 'the Son of Man has come to seek and to save the lost' (19.10). With its clear echoes of Ezek. 34.16, Jesus here proclaims his messianic mission (Davidic too:

(eds.), *Orientierung an Jesus* (Freiburg: Herder, 1973), pp. 412-13, regards the 'formulae' given above as standard terminology in the healing miracles of the oral tradition; cf. G. Vermes, *Jesus the Jew* (London: Collins, 1973), p. 67, for a Jewish background.

13. See Wilckens, 'Vergebung', pp. 418ff., and G. Braumann, 'Die Schuldner und die Sünderin, Luk. vii, 36-50', *NTS* 10 (1963–64), p. 490.

14. Peter's own call (5.1-11) appears to assume a similar phenomenon. The redactional context in which it is found is concerned to demonstrate the appropriate response to Jesus' miracles (cf. Turner, 'Sabbath', p. 101). In Peter's case the miraculous catch of fish evokes a fitting reaction. His awareness of himself as a 'sinner', which makes Jesus' presence unbearable to him, is one side of the coin, the other side being his recognition of Jesus as a heavenly 'lord' (v. 8) (for Luke's attitude to the self-confessed 'sinner' [5.8, 32; 7.34, 37-38; 15.1ff.; 18.13; 19.7], see Glöckner, *Heils*, pp. 148ff.; W. Dietrich, *Das Petrusbild der lukanischen Schriften* [Stuttgart: Kohlhammer, 1972], p. 57. For Peter's response in this passage see Dietrich, *Petrusbild*, pp. 49, 53ff.; Brown, *Apostasy*, p. 57). The miracle itself, while unlike those which precede it, is no arbitrary demonstration of power but chosen for its integral connection with the commission to become 'fishers of men' (see e.g. Marshall, 199-200, and compare R. Pesch, 'La rédaction lucanienne du logion des pêcheurs d'hommes [Lc., V, 10c]', in Neirynck [ed.], *L'Evangile de Luc-The Gospel of Luke* (Leuven: Leuven University Press, 1989), pp. 225-44; or in Neirynck [ed.], *L'Évangile de Luc*, pp. 135-54 and 313-15). The commission to participate in the eschatological proclamation of the Kingdom of God may be presumed to involve an experience of this on Peter's part, such as would bridge the gulf between the reactions to Jesus in vv. 8 and 11.

cf. Ezek. 34.23-24) as God's agent to recover not merely a few straggling sheep, but 'lost' *Israel*. And the significance of his 'forgiveness of sins' outside the Temple/covenantal structures of sacrifice and nomistic restitution is that it betokens the hoped-for dynamic reconciling and restoring 'visitation' of God in and on behalf of Israel, and the creation of a new sphere of 'salvation' within her and for her.

If we ask what sort of 'salvation' Luke considered to be present within Jesus' ministry we again discover a rather impressionist picture. Some occasions of the use of σώζω ('to save') refer to events of exorcism and physical healing (cf. 8.36, 48, 50; 17.19; 18.42), and on such occasions the lexical sense 'rescue' or 'heal' may provide the appropriate translation. But it may be wondered whether the verb has not been deliberately chosen (in contrast to the more usual terms θεραπεύω and ἰάομαι) to express the conviction that these healings are part and parcel of some more general 'salvation' that Jesus was announcing as 'present' in his ministry. This is suggested in Lk. 6.9 (where to heal or to abstain from healing is interpreted by the pairs 'to do good' or 'to do harm' and 'to save' or 'to destroy'), and made even more probable by the way Jesus' pronouncement 'your faith has saved you: Go in peace' can be used identically of healings (8.48; cf. 17.19; 18.42) and of a case of forgiveness and personal restoration that involves no physical healing (7.50). Reciprocally, the language of physician coming 'to heal' can be used in 5.31 of the restoring of 'tax-collectors and sinners'. But little within the Gospel traditions of Jesus' ministry clarifies more precisely the content of this 'salvation'. Its use in 19.9 implies that Zacchaeus's intention to give half his wealth to the poor and to pay back fourfold any monies extorted shows he has somehow entered this sphere of salvation (or that it has come upon him),[15] and 19.10 again connects this with the mission to seek and to save 'lost' Israel, but neither context specifies in more detail the content of the salvation concerned.

15. Fitzmyer, 1218-27, follows White (and others) in arguing 19.8 describes Zacchaeus's *regular practice*, rather than his intention, and so 19.1-10 is a vindication story rather than a story of salvation, but this makes the comment 'today salvation has come to this house' even more inscrutable; what salvation does Jesus bring this Israelite? And why has this story of a tax-collector's bristling indignation against his detractors (v. 6) been used to close the Travel Narrative? J.B. Green at least offers a possible solution (building partly on the views of D. Hamm and D.A.S. Ravens): Zacchaeus is ostracized (unjustly) by the township, and Jesus' visit to his house and word of commendation 'restores' him as an Israelite with honour ('Good News to Whom? Jesus and the "Poor"', in Green and Turner [eds.], *Jesus*, pp. 69-72). The traditional understanding (for which see e.g. Marshall and Nolland) that v. 8 represents Zaccheus's change of heart, and that 9b indicates he has become a true son of Abraham rather than a nominal one (cf. 3.8; Acts 3.25), is to be preferred, however, and can accomodate Green's insight.

The reader is forced back to the opening chapters for any fuller indication of the content of the salvation Jesus announces; principally to the *Magnificat* which celebrates God as 'saviour' and to the *Benedictus* which indicates more of the terms of reference. These canticles suggest Luke understands the 'salvation' hoped for very much in continuity with the Old Testament—that is, as the special presence and blessing of God that enables a radically transformed community existence. In the *Magnificat* this hope is expressed primarily in terms of the 'reversals' that the inception of such salvation would require: the proud oppressive rich and powerful are humbled; the lowly and hungry pious are exalted (1.51-53). In the *Benedictus* the hope is spelt out more fully as entailing rescue from all oppressive enemies (1.71, 74) and consequent liberation from fear (1.74). The end of such liberation is the introduction of a state of 'peace' (1.79) in which the people of God will be able to serve God all their days in holiness and righteousness (1.75). While the hoped-for salvation is *initiated* by 'forgiveness of sins' (1.77), it consists not merely in this but also in the new state of harmony and peace to which such forgiveness leads, a state which can only be contrasted with conditions before it in terms of the terrors of darkness and night being dispelled by the coming dawn and rising sun (1.77-79). In the *Nunc Dimittis* Jesus himself is recognized as the answer to corresponding Isaianic hopes (Isa. 42.6; 49.6, 9) for salvation (2.29-32; cf. also 3.6), suggesting the salvation concerned is that renewal of Israel which is her glory and makes her a light to the nations.

How is the reader expected to be guided by the canticles of salvation in Luke 1–2? The more literally their highly charged symbolism is taken the more likely the interpreter is to decide the hopes expressed here remain unfulfilled. But we should at least question the degree to which a first-century reader would necessarily expect a one-to-one fit between the language of prophecies and the events which 'fulfilled' them. Such readers were aware of the problems of matching the often poetic and symbolic language of such oracles with their historical fulfilments, and anticipated surprise turns even in those oracles that sounded more straightforwardly literal.

Luke appears to be fully aware of the latter type of instance. In Acts 21.11 he recounts an oracle given by Agabus which was fulfilled in a quite different way from what would be suggested if the oracle were taken at face value. The Jerusalem Jews did not literally bind Paul and hand him over to the Gentiles; in the event, Luke tells us, Roman soldiery intervened to deliver Paul from a Jewish mob that would otherwise have lynched him (21.30-32). This does not necessarily mean Luke considers Agabus's prophecy to be partly mistaken (as W. Grudem has implied),[16] for he has

---

16. *The Gift of Prophecy* (Eastbourne: Kingsway, 1988), pp. 96-97.

Paul claim 'Although I have done nothing against our people...I was arrested in Jerusalem and handed over to the Romans' (28.17). Luke, then, thinks Agabus's oracle *was* fulfilled, but in an unanticipated way (perhaps interpreting the 'binding' and 'handing over' of Paul as metaphors for the Jewish actions which led to his being taken into Roman hands); or as Bovon put it, such prophecies for Luke are portraits rather than photographs.[17]

We should be wiser to ask to what extent Luke considered the salvation prophesied in Luke 1–2 to be fulfilled in the ministry of Jesus and in the Church. There can be little doubt he saw Jesus' ministry as introducing this. We have already pointed to the way Luke casts Jesus' ministry as the hoped-for Isaianic New Exodus liberation, and affirmed its programmatic 'today' in 4.18-21. The use of the language of 'salvation' for what is going on within Jesus' ministry at 6.9, 7.50, 8.12 and 19.9, 10 also points in the same direction. Within the context of the hopes announced in Luke 1–2 the connection between Jesus healings (and exorcisms) and 'salvation' becomes transparent. They are instances of messianic 'release' (cf. 4.18-21) from Satanic oppression (cf. e.g. Lk. 7.21-22; 11.20-23; 13.16; Acts 10.38) to well-being and purity. Their significance lies not merely in the physical recovery involved, but in the way in which (at least potentially) they restore the individuals concerned to their family, to the broader society of Israel, and to the worship and service of her God, from which their affliction had excluded them.[18] Seen from such a perspective, healings are then

17. F. Bovon, 'Le Saint-Esprit, l'église et les relations humaines selon Actes 20.36-21.16', in Kremer (ed.), *Actes*, pp. 339-58.

18. Johnson ('Social Dimension', pp. 524-27) notes the emphasis Luke places within the miracle stories on social and cultic 'restoration' (cf. at Lk. 4.39; 5.14; 6.9; 7.15, 8.39, 48, 56; 9.42, etc.): see esp. p. 525. J. Green ('Good News', pp. 66-69, 72-74: cf. *Theology*, pp. 79-84) sees the lame, the deaf, the leper (etc.) as the marginalized 'poor', largely or entirely excluded from society and the cultus. Their healing is always much more than mere physical cure; it is *their restoration to Israel* as community and as *God's* people (cf. *Theology*, pp. 95-96, cf. pp. 89-91). The medical conditions concerned were often relatively trivial. Thus the 'leprosy' of the lepers was not our Hansen's disease (almost unknown in the area at the time), but relatively harmless psoriasis or leukodermia; the woman of Lk. 8.42b-48 has a mild but chronic uterine haemorrhage, etc. But such diseases rendered the afflicted deeply unclean, cutting them off from the people and from the Temple. In such cases it was the alienating social and religious dimensions of the disease that were the real affliction, more than the condition itself. On the significance of Jesus' healing and its relation to salvation in Luke see J. Achtemeier, 'The Lucan Perspective on the Miracles of Jesus: A preliminary Sketch', *JBL* 94 (1975), pp. 547-62; Busse, *Wunder, passim*; J.T. Carroll, 'Jesus as Healer in Luke–Acts', in Lovering (ed.), *Society of Biblical Literature 1994 Seminar Papers*, pp. 269-85; Green, 'Daughter of Abraham', pp. 643-54; D. Hamm, 'The Freeing of

paradigmatic instances of the salvation announced in 1.74-75.

More telling, however, than the healings and acts of deliverance, is the whole 'fit' between Jesus' teaching and the picture of salvation in the canticles. I.H. Marshall and J.O. York have shown the great degree to which the 'bi-polar reversals' anticipated in the *Magnificat* are seen to be fulfilled in Jesus' ministry and teaching, and in the life of discipleship to which these point.[19] G. Lohfink, M.J. Borg and P. Stuhlmacher have demonstrated that Jesus' ethical teaching, grounded in the new possibilities created by the presence of God's reign, is a programme for a *community of reconciliation* and 'peace'.[20] This involves living out of a sense of reconciliation with the Father and extending that forgiveness, peace, and loving care to the neighbour and even to the enemy. In Borg's terms it implies a replacing of the Pharisees' paradigm of 'purity' for Israel with a paradigm of 'mercy'.

Borg's thesis is that the Pharisees perceived Roman domination as a taunt to Israel's identity as God's holy people in his holy land, and their heavy

the Bent Woman and the Restoration of Israel: Luke 13.10-17 as Narrative Theology', *JSNT* 31 (1987), pp. 23-44; W. Kirchschläger, *Jesu exorzistisches Wirken aus der Sicht des Lukas* (Klosterneuberg: KBW, 1981); J.J. Pilch, 'Sickness and Healing in Luke–Acts', in Neyrey (ed.), *Social World*, pp. 181-209.

19. I.H. Marshall, 'The Interpretation of the Magnificat: Luke 1:46-55', in C. Bussmann and W. Radl (eds.), *Der Treue Gottes trauen* (Freiburg: Herder, 1991), pp. 181-96; J.O. York, *The Last Shall Be First: The Rhetoric of Reversal in Luke* (Sheffield: JSOT Press, 1991). The 'poor' are exalted in multiple senses: the sick are healed (and rise on the shame/honour scale); the pious poor receive 'good news' that the kingdom of God is theirs; Jesus befriends the poor; the 'poor' in the sense of the excluded (see Green, 'Good News', pp 59-74); 'the sinners'—and other marginalized groups—are reintegrated; the hungry are fed (spiritually and physically); those with possessions are urged to use their riches to benefit these poor, etc. Similarly, the 'rich' are sent empty away in multiple senses too: they are warned of the woe that comes upon them (e.g. 6.24; 12.16-21; 16.13); warned that if they do not use their riches to benefit the poor they will suffer torment (16.19-31); a rich man unwilling to part with his riches departs from Jesus (18.18-23) and the rich leaders of Judaism oppose him (as do Pharisees who 'love riches' 16.14). The arrogant proud are humbled, while the lowly and marginalized become examples of the blessed (18.9-14; 7.36-50; 10.25-37; 14.15-23). In the community of the disciples, the paradigm for leadership becomes service rather than domination (22.24-27) etc.

20. Lohfink, *Jesus*; Borg, *Conflict*; P. Stuhlmacher, *Reconciliation, Law and Righteousness: Essays in Biblical Theology* (Philadelphia: Fortress Press, 1986), pp. 1-15. These works are devoted to reconstructing the views of the 'historical Jesus' rather than pressing for distinctively Lukan perspectives, but it will be observed that Luke goes further in the direction they point than the other evangelists. Also significant are L.D. Hurst's article, 'Ethics of Jesus', in Green and McKnight (eds.), *Dictionary*, pp. 210-22; A.E. Harvey, *Strenuous Commands: The Ethics of Jesus* (London, SCM Press, 1990); R.A. Horsley, *Jesus and the Spiral of Violence* (San Francisco: Harper, 1987); R.D. Kaylor, *Jesus the Prophet* (Louisville: Westminster Press, 1994).

taxation as a threat to Israel's religious institutions. They mounted a programme of semi-passive political resistance combined with a radical reassertion of Israel's status as a holy nation. With respect to the latter, they interpreted Lev. 19.1-2, 'You shall be holy, because I, Yahweh your God, am holy' in terms of separation and purity, especially emphasising the distinctives of Israel—circumcision, sabbath, festivals, tithing (to assert the importance of this was to remind Jews that dues to the Temple were more important even than the taxes for Rome, at a time when compulsory paying of the latter made it all but impossible to pay the former as well), and an attempt to imitate priestly purity in use of washings, etc. Jesus confronted this with a completely different vision, interpreting Lev. 19.1-2 in terms rather of God's merciful reconciling love; 'Be merciful, even as your Father is merciful' (Lk. 6.36). For Borg this explains the inevitable conflict with Jewish leadership that leads to Jesus' death. In their eyes Jesus threatens the very distinctives which make Israel a holy nation: thus (a) he permits acts of mercy to 'interfere' with the special status of the sabbath, thereby profaning it; (b) he subverts the high priority given to tithing and ritual purity, even eating with the religiously impure, and (c) he commends a reconciling love that reaches out to tax-collector and even to the national enemy (Lk. 6.35-36), e.g. by carrying the Roman soldier's baggage a second (legally unrequired) mile (cf. Mt. 6.40-44).

To the Pharisees, Jesus' teaching (especially the application of the 'mercy paradigm' to those outside Israel) verged on a treasonable undermining of Israel's theological identity. From the (later) perspective of his disciples, however, it was a radical reshaping of Israel's identity in the light of the deutero-Isaianic vision of Israel as God's servant, a reshaping only made possible by the transforming irruption of God's reign in Israel's affairs through the ministry of Jesus.[21] To state matters this way, however, is at the same time to highlight how inappropriate it may be to attempt to define a precise point at which one can say Jesus' followers crossed an imagined line from Old Covenant existence into 'the life of the kingdom of God' or 'salvation'. The change involved an extensive process worked in Israel over a period of time. If one must provide a Rubicon, Luke would probably set it at the banks of the Jordan in the event of John's baptism, providing the repentance and commitment this expressed were carried through into discipleship to the 'Coming One' John announced: for 'the Law and the

---

21. Borg's work was inadequate at this point; he interpreted the presence of 'the kingdom of God' largely as a static mystical realm affording a new vision (hence the title of his second book: *Jesus, A New Vision* [San Francisco, Harper & Row, 1987], rather than as God's eschatological transforming power. Similarly, Schweitzer cuts Jesus' ethics from their true power-base when he insists that for Jesus the kingdom of God was a purely future (albeit imminent) event.

prophets were until John, but from that time onwards the kingdom of God is proclaimed and all press (or are pressed) into it' (16.16; cf. Acts 1.22; 10.37).[22] The individual 'experiences' of 'salvation' within the period of Jesus' ministry (not least at 7.50; 19.9 etc.) are part and parcel of the greater restoration/transformation under way.

Do the disciples evince authentic 'faith', new 'life' and a sense of 'sonship' corresponding to this 'salvation' announced in Israel? Dunn provides a resounding 'No', arguing it is only Pentecost 'which opens the door to that realm of faith and experience which the NT calls Christian'.[23] But his assertion is strongly shaped by his reading of 2 Cor. 3.6-8, it depends on an anachronistic use of 'Christian', and, in any case, it begs the question of how such distinctively 'Christian' 'faith', 'life' and 'sonship' differ in Luke's view from those which were a response to Jesus' proclamation. Dunn appears to assume that we can know what measure or quality of these things would make them 'authentic' in Luke's perception. It is thus too easy for him to point to the greater level of understanding, commitment and quality of 'life' of the twelve after Pentecost and to use this as part of his argument that 'they became Christians' only at Pentecost.[24] But the danger is of making their post-Pentecost level of spiritual experience the paradigm for what 'Christian existence', 'authentic faith' or 'salvation' must mean, whereas Luke probably regards the twelve as somewhat exceptional, and rarely in Acts even tangentially addresses the question of what in experiential terms constitutes the base line for a genuine believer's 'life' or 'faith' or 'salvation'. Writing in the different context of conflict between Jews and Christians over christological claims, John develops a subtle set of contrasts between the sort of (post-ascension) 'believing' in Jesus that is authentic, and a variety of other stages of belief in Jesus which do not quite make the mark (or fall well short of it), but Luke offers no such distinctions. This does not itself mean he thought every expression of 'faith' was equally valid, and he is certainly aware of the disciples' developing understanding, but the very form of the Gospel traditions concerning those whose 'faith' is commended or those said to experience 'salvation' in Jesus' day suggests Luke considered these exemplary for *the church* too. That is, he does not

---

22. W.G. Kümmel, 'Luc en accusation dans la théologie contemporaire', in Neirynck (ed.), *L'Evangile*, p. 102 (with those he cites at n. 47), has pointed out that Lk. 16.16 speaks only of two epochs: that of the Law and the Prophets, and that of the preaching of the kingdom. As Acts too is depicted as a period of the preaching of the kingdom, no distinct epoch of the church is envisaged in this respect: cf. Merk, 'Reich', p. 206; Lohfink, *Himmelfahrt*, p. 255. We may agree with them that 16.16 provides a greater caesura than anything that follows.

23. *Baptism*, p. 53.

24. See below, n. 68.

draw a sharp line between the existential experience of the disciples' 'faith' or 'salvation' before and after Pentecost; rather, he draws the line between those who accept his message of salvation with faith (whether before or after Pentecost), and those who do not. For Luke, 'faith' in Jesus and his message is the distinguishing feature of those who respond to God's saving initiative. It is this which separates the world of the living dead, from that of Jesus' disciples (9.60).[25]

A clear instance of such faith is that of the sinful woman forgiven, who is told 'your faith has saved you' in parallel to the affirmation 'your sins are forgiven you' (7.48-50). The faith referred to is faith in God, specifically in the message of his reconciling love, proclaimed and in some way mediated by Jesus. Her act of service and love directed towards Jesus witnesses to her grasp of the fact that she is forgiven, and through *his* agency.[26] The corollary applies, at least to some extent, that those who serve Jesus out of love, and in response to his message (cf. the women in 8.2-3 and the disciples in general, 18.28), also manifest such 'faith'. This much appears to be assumed at 22.32 where Jesus prays for Peter lest his faith fail—here Luke probably refers to trust in Jesus as revealing God's redemption; a trust which might be shattered by the events of the passion.[27] Luke has elsewhere played down those elements in Mark which pointed to *unbelief* in the disciples' life.[28] The disciples thus stand over against those from whom Satan takes the word of the kingdom 'in order that they might not believe and be saved' (8.12, Lukan),[29] while, positively, Jesus thanks God that though his teaching has remained hidden from many who are 'wise', God has nevertheless revealed it to 'babes', the disciples (10.21). Luke gives us no reason to question the 'authenticity' of this pre-resurrection faith merely because of occasions of failure of the disciples to manifest it, or because of their failure

25. Marshall, 411; cf. M. Hengel, *Nachfolge und Charisma* (Berlin, Töpelmann, 1968), pp. 9ff.

26. S. Brown's thesis that ἡ πίστις (where it is not charismatic faith, faith for miracles or faith that Jesus is the Christ) is always *fides quae praedicatur* (the content of the faith believed, never the active faith of Christians) falls down here (as also at 8.25, 18.8 and Acts 15.9); Brown can only assert that Luke has used words that refer to the kerygma 'without reflecting that this understanding scarcely suited the context in the Age of Jesus' (*Apostasy*, p. 39).

27. Marshall, 822, however, insists that 'faithfulness' rather than 'faith' is the correct translation of πίστις (against Bultmann, Ott and Schürmann). But the faithfulness, in the circumstances, is liable to collapse precisely because Peter's faith will evaporate.

28. Brown, *Apostasy*, pp. 60-61.

29. Cf. Marshall, 325: 'Here and in 8.13 Luke adds πιστεύω to his source, thereby showing that the message of Jesus must be heard with faith; the aorist participle indicates the initial act of faith, and the present tense in 8.13 indicates that a continuing attitude is meant' (*pace* Brown, *Apostasy*, pp. 35-48).

to understand important aspects of Jesus' ministry (cf. 22.24 ff.). The church after the resurrection manifests similar phenomena.

More significant than individual cases where a person's faith is approved, or where they are said to participate in salvation, is the fact that the discipleship in which the twelve, and many others,[30] follow Jesus is itself a reflection of the vision for restored/transformed Israel. The ethics in which they are instructed are those of 'the kingdom of God' and, as Jeremias has repeatedly argued, are based on divine grace.[31] The missions of the twelve and of the seventy are highly charged with eschatological overtones,[32] and are to be understood as involving a sharing in Jesus' authority and charismatic power (10.17-20). The conditions under which the disciples travel on these occasions are themselves a reflection of the new and total trust in God's provision that is to be expected of his children (9.1-6; 10.1-12; cf. 12.29-35).[33] The disciples are to be assured on the ground of their allegiance to Jesus, and of their participation in his ministry, that they will share with him in the consummation of the kingdom (10.20; 12.32; 22.29-30),[34] and they are taught to express their whole new relationship to God in their prayer-address: 'abba' (Lk. 11.2).[35]

The evidence we have so far briefly reviewed suggests Luke thought of 'salvation' and 'the kingdom of God' as a 'sphere' of God's reconciling, liberating and transforming presence in Israel, mediated through Jesus and 'pressed into' by those who respond with faith. From the perspective of the disciples, 'the kingdom of God' was not a purely future reality that could only be entered upon at Pentecost. If Luke (as we have suggested in Chapter 10) thought Pentecost brought some new measure of God's reign in and through Jesus, it was for him *more of the same*. It was the *continuation* of

30. With Lohfink, *Sammlung*, p. 64, against J. Roloff, *Apostolat—Verkündigung—Kirche* (Gütersloh: Mohn, 1965), p. 181, Luke has not limited the circle of the disciples to the twelve: cf. 6.17!

31. J. Jeremias, *The Sermon on the Mount* (London: Athlone, 1961); *Theology*, pp. 181ff. and §§12, 15, 17 and 19.

32. Jeremias, *Theology*, §20; Hengel, *Nachfolge*.

33. Cf. Marshall, 350-51; R. Uro, *Sheep among Wolves: A Study on the Mission Instructions of Q* (Helsinki: Suomalainen Tiedeakatemia, 1987); Lohfink, *Jesus*, pp. 53-55.

34. Jeremias, *Theology*, p. 181. Dunn insists that the allusion in 10.20 to the disciples' names being written in heaven 'has to be understood in terms of the blessings of the old covenant' (*Baptism*, p. 53) (cf. Exod. 32.32-33; Dan. 12.1 etc.), because, of course, the disciples cannot receive blessings of the kingdom of God before Pentecost. But the argument fails to convince: Jesus' statement is anchored to its eschatological context and assures participation in the salvation which is breaking in through the disciples' activity (cf. Minear, *Heal*, p. 45).

35. Cf. J. Jeremias, *The Prayers of Jesus* (London: SCM Press, 1967), pp. 11-107.

what Jesus 'began' to do and to teach (cf. Acts 1.1) with greater power,[36] rather than a decisive new beginning, and the disciples' first existential experience of these things only earlier experienced by Jesus.

We have to this point, however, left the Spirit somewhat out of our discussion, and Dunn would claim such lack crucially distorts the picture. Dunn and Smalley both argue that Luke correlates Spirit and Kingdom in such a way that sayings about the disciples' imminent reception of the kingdom of God are interpreted by Luke as referring to the gift of the Spirit they are to receive at Pentecost.[37] The equation then becomes: Jesus experiences the kingdom of God through the Spirit in the ministry; the disciples experience the same through the gift of the Spirit at Pentecost. But this is a misleading construal for two reasons: first, the sayings which Dunn advances as promises of the disciples' imminent reception of the kingdom of God at Pentecost (chiefly Lk. 9.27; 12.31-32; Acts 1.3, 6)[38] evaporate on examination;[39] secondly, while few will doubt Luke correlates 'kingdom of

36. *Pace* Haenchen, 137; the ἤρξατο ('he began') of Acts 1.1 is more probably emphatic than periphrastic. Compare Marshall, *Luke*, pp. 87 n. 2, 91, 179-82; also Stählin, 11 (though note Moule [*Idiom*, p. 181] and Samain ['APXH', p. 114] have argued for a translation 'all that Jesus did, from the beginning until...')

37. Dunn, 'Spirit and Kingdom', pp. 36-40; S.S. Smalley, 'Spirit, Kingdom and Prayer in Luke–Acts', *NovT* 15 (1973), pp. 59-71.

38. To these Dunn adds the variant reading 'Let your Holy Spirit come upon us and cleanse us' at 11.2 (on which see below).

39. (1) Lk. 9.27 is not about 'receiving' the kingdom of God for the first time, but 'seeing' it powerfully manifest (and Luke has tied this even more clearly than Mark to the transfiguration [for Mark's view see Lane, 312-20; Pesch, 66-67; cf. Lk. 9.32 'they saw his glory', etc., added redactionally: see Nolland, 485-86]). While Luke may have thought Jesus' death and resurrection, Pentecost, the growth of the church, and the fall of Jerusalem (etc.), all also constituted cases of 'seeing' the kingdom of God, his removal of the Markan qualification ἐληλυθυῖαν ἐν δυνάμει ('come with power') makes it very unlikely he interpreted 9.27 primarily of Pentecost for which such language would have been especially appropriate (cf. 24.49; Acts 1.8).

(2) Lk. 12.31-32 assumes that eschatological language is already applicable to the disciples in the ministry (cf. 'little flock'; on which see J. Jeremias, *TDNT*, VI, p. 501), while the language δοῦναι ὑμῖν τὴν βασιλείαν ('to give you the kingdom') draws on Dan. 7.14, 17-18, 27, and would appear to refer to the consummation events (cf. Jeremias, *TDNT*, VI, p. 501; P. Volz, *Die Eschatologie der jüdischen Gemeinde im neutestamentlichen Zeitalter* [Hildesheim: Olms, 1934], pp. 380-81; Jeremias, *Theology*, pp. 102, 106; Kümmel, *Promise*, pp. 53-54, etc.) to be taken in the same sense as 22.29-30. While this reminder that God intends to give them the eschatological rule at the End has immediate import for the whole period from the ministry up to that point, it does not constitute a specific promise that 'the kingdom of God' would be 'given to them' at Pentecost (or at any other time). Indeed, Dunn only achieves such an interpretation by rather arbitrarily equating this saying with 11.13, where Luke asserts that the Father will give πνεῦμα ἀγαθόν to those who ask him to. From the general parallel

God' and 'Spirit', it is the nature of the correlation which is in question. As we have seen, Jesus does not receive the Spirit as his own experience of the kingdom of God, but as the power to bring it to Israel. That might suggest the terms of Dunn's 'equation' need adjustment to something like 'By the Spirit Jesus brings God's reign to Israel in the ministry; by the Spirit the disciples will bring God's reign to Israel after Pentecost'—which is, of course, much closer to what Pentecostal and Neo-Pentecostal advocates have been saying all along! While my own solution will require a modification of this, we must first examine more closely the relationship of the disciples to the Spirit before Pentecost (§1.2), and then the promise made to them concerning the gift of the Spirit (§2).

1.2. *The Disciples and the Spirit in the Ministry of Jesus*

The disciples did not receive what Luke calls 'the gift of the Spirit' until Pentecost; but before then they had come to experience the 'life' of the kingdom. A number of scholars (notably Gunkel, Lampe, Schweizer, Flender and Haya-Prats) have concluded from this that Luke does not associate the Spirit with the salvation of the individual. But this is a serious over-simplification. There is at least one important way in which Luke considers the Spirit to be active in the disciples before Pentecost: the Spirit is active through Jesus' proclamation. He may also have envisaged a second possibility, namely that the Spirit was experienced as a power shared by the disciples during the missions of the twelve and of the seventy. We shall discuss these two spheres of activity of the Spirit below.

The Spirit experienced through Jesus' proclamation. We have argued in Chapters 8 and 9 that Luke regarded the Spirit on Jesus as a power with him by which he effectively proclaimed New Exodus liberation and God's reign in Israel, in both word and deed. Earlier in this chapter we noted that the corollary of this was the presence of something like a sphere of God's reign or salvation into which hearers could 'enter'. Individuals do not have to 'receive' 'the gift of the Spirit' in order to experience this dynamic, reconciling and transforming presence of God's reign, but that hardly

between 'asking/seeking' and being 'given' in each passage, Dunn concludes 'the Kingdom and the Spirit are alternative ways of speaking about the disciples' highest good' ('Spirit and Kingdom', pp. 38-39). In fact the two sayings evidently have quite different referents (for the sense of 11.13 see below).

(3) Acts 1.3-8 undoubtedly thematically correlates 'the kingdom of God' (1.3) with the gift of the Spirit (1.4-5), but not in the form of an equation between the two (see Chapter 10). The only 'gift of the kingdom' implied in these verses is the one that will not be given to Israel 'in this time', and it is not a reference to 'the kingdom of God', but to Israel's eschatological 'rule' which 'the kingdom of God' enables.

justifies the common assertion that the Spirit is not associated with the salvation of the individual in Luke–Acts. It is rather the case that such experience of God's reign in and through Jesus is itself an experience of God's empowering, self-revealing presence *as Spirit*. Dunn himself in one sense highlights this with affirmations such as 'where the Spirit has come and cleansed, there is the Kingdom', 'the manifestation of the Spirit is the manifestation of the Kingdom',[40] and these are suitably qualified, 'It was only the unique coming of the Spirit on the unique man Jesus which brought the Kingdom among men'.[41] But he appears everywhere to shrink from the corollary that where people sense they are encountered by God's word in and through Jesus, and where they 'press into' the kingdom of God and receive 'salvation' as a result of Jesus' activity, *this too is an effect and experience of the Spirit*. It is as though, for Dunn, a person can only genuinely 'experience' the Spirit when he or she personally 'receives' 'the gift of the Spirit'. This is surprising in view of his entirely lucid account of how any one member experiences the Spirit powerfully *through the charismata of other members* in the Pauline conception of the charismatic body.[42] Such a view was, of course, not original to Paul. It was evident throughout the Old Testament and in Judaism. When CD 2.12 asserts 'He has made known His Holy Spirit to them by the hand of His anointed ones',[43] what is meant is that the Spirit is experienced by the righteous through the one endowed with the Spirit, and, as we have seen, the messiah of the Spirit was anticipated in certain circles (including those of the Baptist) to be so mightily endowed with the Spirit that his advent in Zion would be a powerful experience of Spirit and fire for all Israel. The idea that one must first personally 'receive' 'the gift of the Holy Spirit' in order at all to experience the Spirit in any strength comes closer to the Gnostic idea of redemption through the impartation of πνεῦμα as heavenly substance than it does to the Jewish concept of Spirit as God's self-revealing presence and influence extending beyond and through the charismata of the Spirit-bearer to address and affect God's people.[44] For similar reasons, I cannot understand Menzies'

40. 'Spirit and Kingdom', p. 38.
41. 'Spirit and Kingdom', p. 39.
42. See *Jesus*, part 3.
43. Vermes, *Scrolls*, p. 84. However, Crone adopts the attractive emendation from מ׳שמו to מ׳שמ׳ה, and consequently the translation 'he instructed them through the anointed ones of His holy spirit, the seers of truth' (*Prophecy*, p. 100 and 325; so also M. de Jonge, 'The Use of the Word "Anointed" in the Time of Jesus', *NovT* 8 [1966], pp. 132-48, p. 141, and *idem*, *TDNT*, IX, p. 517 n. 134.).
44. Hence Schweizer's account of Paul's pneumatology (where the gift of the Spirit becomes the matrix of all Christian life) in terms of a revision of essentially proto-Gnostic concepts: see e.g. his brief account in 'The Spirit of Power', pp. 268-72.

dismissal of the significance of this dimension of the account with the judgment that in such cases 'the Spirit is experienced only in an indirect way'.[45] For Judaism (and, I would say, Lukan Christianity) the Spirit can address or influence a person equally powerfully whether mediately or immediately.

Luke almost certainly thought along typically Jewish lines. Just as the Holy Spirit formerly confronted Israel in and through the prophets (Acts 7.51, cf. Isa. 63.10-11), so now they experience the Spirit in Jesus' proclamation and acts as a great power that they must either explain as God's presence/Spirit or explain *away* in terms of evil spirit. If in Luke's Gospel Jesus is not actually reported to say 'the words which I speak to you are Spirit and life' (Jn 6.63b) the evangelist comes quite close to such an understanding. As with John the Baptist ministering 'in the Spirit and power of Elijah', Luke thinks of the Spirit giving a numinous divine accreditation to the content of Jesus' proclamation, such that God's people feel obliged to admit his teaching is 'from heaven', not 'from men' (cf. 20.5), or that it comes with astonishing 'authority' or 'power' (4.32 etc.).[46] But the other side of this coin is that when people confess that Jesus, like Moses, was 'powerful in word' (24.19; cf. 4.32 etc.), it means that *they* felt conscious of the Spirit's power released through his teaching, and that it had a powerful effect or influence on *them*. Similarly, Acts 1.2 can speak of Jesus as instructing his followers through the Holy Spirit.[47] This can barely mean simply that

45. *Development*, p. 182 n. 3.

46. See further Turner, 'Spirit and Authoritative Preaching', pp. 70-72.

47. At Acts 1.2 we should take διὰ πνεύματος ἁγίου ('through the Holy Spirit') with ἐντειλάμενος ('having given instruction') not with ἐξελέξατο ('he chose'); but no solution is easy with respect to this clumsy sentence and there is a textual problem to complicate the issue. Ropes (in Foakes-Jackson and Lake [eds.], *Beginnings*, III, pp. 256-61) attempts to solve the difficulty by reconstructing the original text as: ἐν ἡμέρᾳ ᾗ τοὺς ἀποστόλους ἐξελέξατο διὰ πνεύματος ἁγίου καὶ ἐκέλευσεν κηρύσσειν τὸ εὐαγγέλιον (based on old Latin witnesses; chiefly codex Gigas and Augustine's commentary). The Alexandrian text is viewed as a corruption and D as conflating the two. But this reconstruction is very uninviting, and has received trenchant criticism from Lake (in Foakes-Jackson and Lake [eds.], *Beginnings*, V, p. 2); J.M. Creed, 'The Text and Interpretation of Acts 1.1-2', *JTS* 35 (1934), pp. 176-82, 180-81; and Metzger, *Commentary*, pp. 275-76. The last two have established that the original must have been at least approximately that of the Alexandrian text (so also Parsons, *Departure*, p. 129). Whether the Alexandrian or the D form (moving ἀνελήμφθη before ἐντειλάμενος and adding καὶ ἐκέλευσε [redundant] κηρύσσειν τὸ εὐαγγέλιον) be accepted, the exegetical problem of the relation of διὰ πνεύματος ἁγίου to the verbs remains the same.

Haenchen, 139 (*inter alios*), takes διὰ πνεύματος ἁγίου with the choice of the apostles: 'they represent the legitimate church in his eyes, which is why he has stressed the part played by the Spirit in their election'. Luke readily shifts stressed words forward, he contends. This is true, but elsewhere the shift makes the stress obvious, whereas here it is precisely weakened as διά is brought closer to ἐντειλάμενος: οὓς διὰ

God gave revelation *to* Jesus, through the Spirit, which he then passed on to his followers. In the first place, Luke never depicts Jesus as speaking words revealed to him by the Spirit, and secondly, the whole point of 1.2 is that the *disciples* are well prepared for their future ministry; that is that the Spirit has been active in their *reception* of Jesus' instruction. Luke, with John[48] and Paul, shares the view that to come under the influence of a man's charismatically empowered teaching is to open oneself up to the spiritual power that expresses itself therein (cf. 2 Cor. 11.4; Col. 2.8-23; [1 Tim. 4.1]; 1 Jn 4.1-2). In 2 Cor. 11.4, Paul even equates accepting the charismatic preaching of his opponents as 'receiving another πνεῦμα'.[49] Luke does not choose to say that the disciples 'received the Spirit' during Jesus' earthly sojourn (possibly to avoid confusion with what he says later concerning the Pentecostal gift). But he would readily have agreed that to accept Jesus as a powerful prophetic figure, and to receive his teaching and wisdom as the expression of God's Spirit upon him, was itself to come under the authority

πνεύματος ἁγίου ἐξελέξατο would be the way Luke would have to write the sentence if Haenchen's view of his motive were to be justified. In any case it is not clear that stress on election by the Spirit would legitimate the apostolic teaching nearly as much as stress on the apostles being instructed διὰ πνεύματος ἁγίου. Against Haechen's view, note further (1) there is no precedent for Jesus' 'choice' by the Spirit (though cf. Acts 13.2; 20.28); (2) Luke's account of the choice of the twelve does not include any allusion to his being inspired by the Spirit so to do (*pace* Foakes-Jackson and Lake [eds.], *Beginnings*, IV, p. 3); and (3) such emphasis would contrast too heavily with the choice by lot of Matthias whose position amongst the twelve is not challenged by Luke in favour of Paul (*pace* Dunn, *Baptism*, pp. 45-46; *Jesus*, p. 145. Paul does not fulfil Luke's conditions [Acts 1.21-22]. The reason why the choice is made by lot before the descent of the Spirit is that the circle of the twelve must be complete before that event: cf. Noack, 'Day', pp. 73-74, also Zehnle, *Discourse*, pp. 109-10; Jervell, *Luke*, pp. 75-112).

With Bruce, *Acts*, p. 67; Shepherd, *Function*, pp. 154-55; and Barrett, 69, we must therefore take διὰ πνεύματος ἁγίου with the participle ἐντειλάμενος, which is the most natural grammatical reading and one supported by a precedent in LXX Zech. 1.6 (ὅσα ἐγὼ ἐντέλλομαι ἐν πνεύματί μου τοῖς δούλοις μου τοῖς προφήταις). But *when* does this instruction take place? Clearly over the forty days, and ἐντειλάμενος must be a constative aorist; but if the latter, there is no reason to exclude the period of the ministry as well (*contra* Bengel, *Gnomon*, *ad loc.*, who states that Jesus 'bestowed the Spirit upon the apostles in giving them his instruction, Jn 20.22...thus before his ascension he gave them an earnest of Pentecost'). Jesus' instruction of the apostles is simultaneously an operation of the Spirit: cf. Stählin, 12.

48. Cf. Turner, 'Spirit in John's Gospel', pp. 24-35.

49. That is, he treats acquiescence to preaching as *receiving* the πνεῦμα active in the preacher (note J.J. Gunther, *Saint Paul's Opponents and their Background* [Leiden: Brill, 1973], pp. 261ff.); he means something like 'you come under the sway of some alien power expressing itself in and through the false apostles' preaching': see the commentaries *ad loc.*

and influence of the Spirit which gave the convincing power to his teaching. It was to experience that Spirit existentially as a power moulding one's life and one's beliefs. In analogous fashion after Pentecost he understands the Spirit-empowered witness of disciples to outsiders, or the inspired speech of prophetic figures addressing the church, as occasions where the Spirit exerts influence and direction on third parties. These third parties 'experience' the Spirit in and through the charismatic speaker.

We must conclude that Luke envisages the disciples to have experienced the Spirit as a divine presence addressing them, and consequently as a moulding influence upon them, long before they came to receive the Spirit themselves at Pentecost; they experienced this through Jesus' powerfully charismatic ministry and proclamation. The messiah of the Spirit was already baptizing Israel with Spirit and fire, during his earthly ministry, even if John's promise was to come to a new and more dramatic fulfilment beyond Easter.

The Spirit shared with the disciples before Pentecost? There are two further sections of Luke (the important variant reading at 11.2 excluded)[50] that imply the disciples had experienced the Spirit before Pentecost: 9.1-10.22 and 11.9-13.

The first of these, the missions of the twelve and of the seventy, has been introduced. In 9.1-6, Luke follows the Markan account of the sending of

---

50. The reading ἐλθέτω τὸ πνεῦμα σου τὸ ἅγιον ἐφ' ἡμᾶς καὶ καθαρισάτω ἡμᾶς is attested only by the late miniscules 700 and 162, but, nevertheless, supported by the words of Gregory of Nyssa and Maximus of Turin. Tertullian witnesses to Marcian's text as including this *and* the invocation ἐλθέτω ἡ βασιλεία σου; while the reading of D and d (ἁγιασθήτω ὄνομά σου ἐφ' ἡμᾶς ἐλθέτω σου ἡ βασιλεία) has been taken as demonstrating the influence of 700, 162. Since A. von Harnack (*The Sayings of Jesus* [London, 1908], pp. 63-64) the reading of 700, 162 has had considerable scholarly support: for a list see W. Ott, *Gebet und Heil: Die Bedeutung der Gebetsparänese in der lukanischen Theologie* (Munich: Kösel, 1965), pp. 113-14 (who himself supports the reading) and add R. Freudenberger ('Zum Text der zweiten Vaterunserbitte', *NTS* 15 [1968–69], pp. 419-21) who considers it to be pre-Lukan. Against these, however, it may be noted (1) that the reading of D and d is perfectly comprehensible without invoking the influence of the MSS 700, 162 (see Metzger, *Commentary*, pp. 155-56); (2) the late attestation of 700 and 162 should perhaps not be allowed to weigh too heavily against the whole of the rest of the manuscript tradition, and (3) while the tradition of this epiclesis is undoubtedly ancient (cf. *Acts of Thomas* 27), it is not clearly Lukan in content (whence Freudenberger's conviction that it must be *pre*-Lukan; 429ff.). While the idea of the cleansing of God's people through the words and actions of the messiah of the Spirit is important to Luke; there is no idea of continually calling on God for such cleansing (as would be implied if this reading were to appear in the Lord's prayer). It is perhaps more likely that the variant arose in a Lukan community that has extended his ideas than that the tradition belongs to the original text of Luke.

the twelve, though he appears to have assimilated some of the details to the Q account of the sending of the seventy.[51] He takes from Mark that Jesus gave authority to the twelve over evil spirits, and (probably) from Q that they were sent to preach the kingdom, but Luke adds the notice that they received δύναμις (9.1) and that they were expected not only to preach but also to heal (9.2).[52] The account in Luke 10 of the sending of the seventy (-two)[53] appears to be based on the incident in Num. 11.16-30, and thus interprets the power and authority (9.1; 10.19) exercised by the disciples after the analogy of the Spirit on Moses being shared with the seventy (-two) elders.[54] This would suggest Luke considered the disciples' power and authority to derive from some kind of 'extension' of the Spirit on Jesus, just as Jesus' own power and authority derived from the Spirit upon him (4.14; cf. 1.17, 35 and Acts 10.38). This would hardly justify speaking of a pre-resurrection 'gift of the Spirit' granted to the disciples (and Luke avoids such language here), but it at least points to some kind of 'fellowship' in the activity of the Spirit upon Jesus. Something of the measure of their

51. See Schürmann and Marshall *ad loc.*

52. Luke could have deduced the latter from Mark's account (6.5).

53. For the textual problems, see B. Metzger, *Historical and Literary Studies: Pagan, Jewish and Christian* (Leiden: Brill, 1968), pp. 67-76, who arrives at no definite conclusions but voices most of the possibilities. The reading ἑβδομήκοντα δύο ($\mathfrak{P}^{75}$ B D *al*) is certainly the more difficult one to explain, as there is no allusion in the context to connect the missionaries with either the 72 LXX translators (*Ep. Arist.* 40-50; though see S. Jellicoe, 'Saint Luke and the Letter of Aristeas', *JBL* 80 [1961], pp. 150-51) or the 72 nations of the world (LXX Gen. 10): the disciples are sent in *pairs* to *Israel*, not to the 70/72 nations (cf. Miyoshi, *Anfang*, pp. 78ff.). A prefiguring of the Gentile mission is thus not the explanation of the number of missionaries. For a possible explanation of the figure 72, see below.

54. We have already observed that this incident exerted a certain fascination on Jewish writers (cf. Philo, *Gig.* 24ff.; *Fug.* 186; Targums; *b. Sanh.* 17a, etc.). The view that Luke's incident mirrors the event in Num. 11 is well argued by Miyoshi, *Anfang*, ch. 3, who adds to the case already presented by Wilson (*Gentiles*, pp. 45-46) that Mk 9.38-50 (the last piece of Mark used by Luke before the great inclusion) has exerted a deep influence on the formation of Lk. 9.52–10.24. The passage from Mark was concerned with the 'strange exorcist' and contains parallels to the Num. 11 incident: especially in the words ἐπιστάτα... ἐκωλύομεν αὐτόν (cf. κύριε Μωσῆ κώλυσον αὐτούς) in a context of trying to stifle charismata when practiced outside the expected circle. As Luke regards Jesus as the eschatological Moses, the sharing of his task with the 70/72 representatives could barely have escaped his intention as an echo of the Num. 11 incident. As Jesus' task differs from that of Moses, so *mutatis mutandis* the disciples' task differs from that of the elders. A background in the Num. 11 account may also explain the textual variation between 70 and 72, the figure depending on whether Eldad and Medad were reckoned to be included within the 70 or not (see Plummer, 272; Miyoshi, *Anfang*, p. 79).

experience is witnessed at 9.6, 54 (where the disciples do not doubt that God will answer their Elijianic prayer with fire from heaven)[55] and 10.17.

Lk. 11.9-13 forms a passage on encouragement to pray. It is largely drawn from Q, though Luke has reshaped it at significant points.[56] With Matthew's account, Luke shares (v. 11) that a callous father might give his child ὄφις (a 'serpent') when the child requested ἰχθύς ('fish'). But in Matthew this is the second example of poor fatherhood (the first being to give a stone when asked for a loaf), while in Luke it is the first, and leads to a further example in which an egg is requested and a scorpion given.[57] Matthew's version is certainly the more intelligible, its point being summed up in 7.12 (redactional). For the first evangelist this is not a parable contrasting good gifts with the giving of deceitful imitations. Snakes do not resemble any of the sorts of fish a Palestinian son could have asked for; for those fish that do resemble snakes (eels) would have been levitically unclean.[58] Were any father to act in the way described it would be his emphatic 'no' to his son's request: neither less nor more. Matthew's point is then that if God does not turn down the legitimate requests of his children, so the disciples of Jesus should treat others in the same way (v. 12).[59]

But Luke's version, as W. Ott has noted, is quite different in its purpose. The exchange of ὄφις for ἰχθύς and σκόρπιος for ᾠόν reveals not merely an unwilling father, but a despicable and evil one, who sets before his child what anyone would recognize as dangerous animals. The point of the parable then becomes a most emphatic denial of the possibility that God will give evil gifts. Schulz and Marshall accept Ott's point that Luke has effected the changes, but can find no plausible motive for it. What they do not observe is the significance of the fact that in his teaching to the seventy (10.19), Jesus (according to Luke) has already used precisely this combination of 'serpent' and 'scorpion' as symbols of demonic powers.[60] Futhermore, in the section immediately following this encouragement to prayer, Jesus is accused of casting out demons by satanic power, and insists instead that he does so by the finger of God (11.20) which, as we have seen, is none other than the Spirit qua the power on Jesus to liberate the afflicted. Luke

---

55. Cf. Marshall, *ad loc.*

56. For the originality of Matthew's (Q) version see Catchpole, *Quest*, pp. 211-12, and those cited there.

57. This leads to a complex textual and tradition-historical problem; on which see especially Ott, *Gebet*, pp. 102-11; Marshall, 468-69.

58. J. Jeremias, *The Parables of Jesus* (London: SCM Press, 1963), p. 226; Ott, *Gebet, loc. cit.*

59. Ott, *Gebet*, pp. 102-11.

60. Cf. the commentaries *ad loc.*; Miyoshi, *Anfang*, pp. 102-104; Catchpole, *Quest*, p. 212.

connects 11.1-13 and 11.14ff. with the linking introduction 'and he was casting out demons...'.

The Lukan connection of thought seems, then, to be that no father worthy of that name gives his children harmful gifts, such as scorpions and snakes, when they ask for their basic needs of food. Nor when a son asks his heavenly Father will he receive demonic power when what he needs is πνεῦμα ἀγαθόν ('a good s/Spirit').[61] Thus, at one level, 11.12-13 provides part of Luke's proof that Jesus, who prayed at his baptism before receiving the Spirit (3.21-22), had indeed been given not Beelzebul's power but the Holy Spirit as the empowering presence of God by which he has bound Satan and now despoils his house. But the corollary of Luke's changes, and their connection with Lk. 10.19, is that he considers this teaching relevant not merely to the case of Jesus, but also to his followers. It is not likely that he considers it primarily applicable to the period after Pentecost, for in Acts exorcism plays a relatively inconspicuous part, and never draws the charge they are performed in collusion with evil powers. Nor does Luke depict anyone praying that he or she might receive the Spirit.[62] The *Sitz im Leben* that best explains the form of the teaching is that in which Luke has set it, namely the pre-Easter missions of Jesus and his disciples. If that is the case, however, it entails that God's Spirit (or a spirit of power from God) is portrayed as a pre-Pentecost possibility available to some of Jesus' followers. They could experience this benificent 'Spirit' from God in answer to prayer, at least as divine empowerment against the demonic.[63] There are some tensions between what Luke says here and what he affirms in 9.1-6 and

61. With 𝔓[45] L pc aur vg sy[hmg] (cf. Grundmann, 235). The readings ἀγαθὸν δῶμα (D it); δόματα ἀγαθά (Θ sy[s] arm) and πνεῦμα ἅγιον (א B etc.) can be explained most easily on the assumption of an original πνεῦμα ἀγαθόν which would invite change to the more familiar πνεῦμα ἅγιον (or removal of πνεῦμα altogether by assimilation to Mt. 7.11 or Lk. 11.13a) by anyone who had not observed the contacts between 11.12, 14 and 10.19. It is much more difficult to imagine a scribe altering a very familiar πνεῦμα ἅγιον to the somewhat unusual and superfluous πνεῦμα ἀγαθόν.

62. The prayer of Acts 1.14 is not specifically for the gift of the Spirit. The only people beyond Pentecost who clearly do not receive the Spirit within the complex of conversion and Christian baptism, and so might be expected to pray for the gift, are the Samaritans. But in their case God gives the Spirit in response to the prayers of Peter and John (8.15), and so no-one prays in accord with Lk. 11.13b. It is thus difficult to know how Luke expected his readers to contextualize this verse in their own Christian prayer, unless, perhaps, it was used to importune further fillings with the Spirit (as the need arose), such as at Acts 4.31.

63. Perhaps even also as a power at the centre of their being guarding them against the attacks of evil powers (11.24-26; cf. A.M. Farrer, 'On Dispensing with Q', in Nineham [ed.], *Studies*, pp. 70-71), though that must remain very uncertain.

10.1-12, 17-19.[64] If these tensions suggest the πνεῦμα ἀγαθόν of 11.13 is pre-Lukan, it is nevertheless the case that the passages broadly cohere in depicting the disciples as sharing in the authority and power of Jesus, and (in some derivative sense) the Spirit of God at work through him. They offer the kind of evidence that led Jeremias to speak of 'the bestowing of the Spirit on the disciples in the lifetime of Jesus'.[65] While such language goes well beyond what Luke would himself write, his toleration of the tradition here points to the vitality of the early Christian belief (also witnessed in John) that the disciples had already experienced God's Spirit in a variety of ways (however limited and indirect) before Pentecost. Even though it goes against his tendency to present Jesus as the unique bearer of the Spirit in the period of the ministry, Luke has not suppressed this older perception— perhaps because it does not involve experiencing the Spirit as the gift of the 'Spirit of prophecy', but merely as God's liberating power at work through the disciples. What then does 'the promise of the Spirit' (Lk. 24; Acts 1–2) hold out for them? It is to this we now turn.

2. The Promise of the Spirit to the Disciples (Luke 24.47-49; Acts 1.4-5, 8)

The relevant material here from the perspective of Jesus' own relation to the Spirit and the mission of the church (Chapter 10 §§2.1, 2.2 and 3.1) has been introduced, and it has been noted that these passages are of first importance, providing the transition between the Gospel and Acts: the former closes the account of Jesus' ministry, while the latter provides not merely the opening perspective from which to understand the pneumatology of Acts, but the programme for the whole book. Accordingly, we may offer just a brief summary of the contribution of these sections for our understanding of 'the promise'[66] of the Spirit to the disciples.

---

64. Notably that at 9.1 and 10.19 *Jesus* gives the power and authority, while in 11.13 it is God who grants 'a benificent Spirit'; at 9.1 and 10.19 the period of mission to Israel is one of special power against evil forces, whereas here the request is not linked specifically to the mission of the twelve or of the 70, and, above all, any reference to God's Spirit in the other passages is made relatively obliquely by expressions lacking the lexeme 'Spirit' (contrast 11.13).

65. *Theology*, p. 80, and pp. 79-80 more generally. Not all his evidence is valid, however (cf. his appeal to Lk. 6.23, 26). Wrege (*Überlieferungsgeschichte*, p. 108) also argued this was pre-Lukan on the ground that it conflicted with Luke's usual tendency to restrict the Spirit on the disciples to the period after Pentecost.

66. On the redactional nature and significance of 'the promise of the/my Father' (Lk. 24.49//Acts 1.4), see Menzies, *Development*, pp. 198-204. It undoubtedly refers (as Blass-Debrunner observe) to the content of 1.5, but it remains inexplicable why the oracle of John the Baptist about the messiah baptising with Holy Spirit should especially be called 'the promise of the Father'. Tannehill (*Narrative Unity*, II, pp. 11-12)

(1) The function of Lk. 24.44-46 and Acts 1.2-4 is to provide the reader with the assurance that the disciples fully understand the significance of the events which are about to take place, and so will be effective guarantors of the 'witness' which they are about to give. They thus have forty days of private tabletalk (1.4a)[67] and instruction 'through the Spirit' (Acts 1.2), and the risen Jesus 'opens their minds' to all the Scriptures (Lk. 24.44-46). Their question in Acts 1.6, as we have seen, is thoroughly perceptive, not a misunderstanding. In the light of this we must reject Dunn's reading, according to which the disciples have not yet attained 'Christian' faith and commitment to Jesus: such an assertion appears diametrically opposed to the Lukan intention.[68]

---

thinks the puzzled reader can only hunt backwards (into Luke's Gospel) for an explanation, and so is bound finally to alight on Lk. 11.13. This might at first make sense of the additional clause 'which you heard about from me' (1.4d) but faces an overwhelming problem: even if Lk. 11.13 were a reference to 'the Holy Spirit' (improbable: see n. 61 above), it is not really clear that this is 'the Father's promise' (but Jesus' promise about the Father). Hunting backwards offers no solution. Those scholars may be right, rather, who see 'the promise of the Father' as a simple prolepsis (anticipatory statement) which the reader will be able to fill out when he or she reads forwards and gets to Acts 2 (cf. J.H. Sieber, 'The Spirit as the "Promise of My Father" in Luke 24.49', in Durken [ed.], *Sin*, pp. 274-76). The gift of the Spirit there is precisely the gift Joel announces as the fulfilment of God's promise to pour out 'the Spirit of prophecy' (cf. Acts 2.17: 'God declares, "I will pour out my Spirit"...' [and Jesus is specifically said to receive this 'promise from the Father' and to have 'poured out' the charismata of Pentecost in 2.33], which corresponds precisely to the remarkable 'I will send the promise of my Father upon you' of Lk. 24.49). If Jesus has not referred specifically to Joel's promise in his ministry (and so explaining 'which you heard about from me'), he has nevertheless promised the Spirit as what any Jew would recognize as 'the Spirit of prophecy' (so, for example at Lk. 12.12 [cf. 21.15]), and so as Joel's (and God's) promise. Mainville may nevertheless be correct that the reference to the 'promise of my Father' in Lk. 24.49 is intentionally general, and has in view the whole promise of salvation for which the Spirit emerges as the key in Acts (*L'Esprit*, pp. 141-54, 315-16).

67. Pesch (65-66) rightly rejects the view (for which see Schneider, Bauer and Metzger) that συναλιζόμενος is an orthographic variant for συναυλιζόμενος, and takes it to mean 'eating with' (not 'dwelling with'): the point being that Luke sees the meals with the resurrected Lord as the clearest attestation that he is resurrected bodily.

68. Dunn (*Baptism*, p. 52) makes the remarkable assertion that Acts 11.17 must mean the disciples were *converted* at Pentecost (cf. 2.44; 9.42; 16.31). He claims the participial phrase πιστεύσασιν ἐπὶ τὸν κύριον qualifies ἡμῖν ('us') and should be taken as a coincidental aorist, so requiring the translation, 'when we believed in the Lord'. Further, he takes πιστεύω ἐπί to be a technical term for 'convert'. This leads him to the judgment that 'so far as Peter was concerned their belief [*scil*. that of the 120 disciples at Pentecost] in him and commitment to him as Lord and Christ did not begin until Pentecost. It was only at that moment of believing committal... that their

(2) Pentecostal scholars (especially Stronstad, Menzies and Shelton)[69] have quite rightly emphasized that from the perspective of these key Lukan sections the promise of the Spirit to the disciples is especially focused as prophetic empowering for witness. This alone makes sense of the explicit statements concerning the heavenly 'power' they will receive in Lk. 24.49 and Acts 1.8, of the undoubted reference in 'the promise of my/the Father' to Joel's promise of the 'Spirit of prophecy', and of the *mission* given the church to fulfil the role of the prophetic 'servant' of Isa. 49.6. It is then easy to understand why such scholars should make the further claim that for these disciples the promise of the Spirit comes as a *donum superadditum*. The disciples have already implicitly experienced 'forgiveness of sins', they have fully enjoyed the benefits of 'the kingdom of God' (in so far as that was present in Jesus' ministry) and of 'salvation', and they have attained the fullness of Christian faith in the crucified and risen Lord. What is left to them now is to receive the Spirit as a prophetic empowering to extend this message and its benefits to Israel and beyond. Luke here (and in Acts 2) deliberately develops an analogy with Jesus' Jordan experience. In each case people who already themselves enjoy a full and committed relationship

faith reached the level of Christian committal, only then that they became Christians in the NT sense of that word (*sic.*).' But it is surely wildly improbable that Luke would expect his reader to revise his whole understanding of the pre-Pentecost 'faith' of the disciples on the basis of this late and ambiguous comment, and so to conclude the disciples miraculously came to 'authentic' faith only in the instant immediately prior to their Pentecost reception of the Spirit. Had Luke wished to suggest such an interpretation, the Pentecost account itself would have been the obvious place to signal it, if not before.

H.A.W. Meyer (293) is probably right to correct his predecessors who construed πιστεύσασιν with αὐτοῖς It should indeed (as Dunn claims) be taken with ἡμῖν, or, more probably with both pronouns (so Bruce, *ad loc.*). But it is not a technical term (Luke has not forged technical terms in this realm; cf. πιστεύειν ἐπί, Acts 2.44; 9.42; 11.17; 16.31; 22.19; πιστεύειν εἰς, 10.43; 14.23; 19.4; πιστεύειν + dative of person 5.14; 8.12; 16.34; 18.8; 26.27; 27.35), and to insist that this must mean a punctiliar act of belief, coincident with the gift of the Spirit, is simply abuse of the aorist (cf. Stagg, 'Abused Aorist', pp. 222-31). If the aorist participle is temporal here at all it either carries a pluperfect sense (cf. Moule, *Idiom*, pp. 11 and 16), or represents a constative 'when we believed' (taken as summing up faith shown over the whole period of discipleship, or, at very least, the faith they came to through the resurrection and forty-day period). But equally it could be loosely causal (see Haya-Prats, *L'Esprit*, p. 126). Dunn's affirmation that ἀρχῇ in 11.15 demonstrates that Peter looked on Pentecost as the beginning of Christian experience is also arbitrary. In context, ἐν ἀρχῇ is the beginning of missionary enterprise, the path of which has has now led to Cornelius's door (see Samain, 'APXH', pp. 325ff.).

69. Stronstad, *Theology*, pp. 51-52; Menzies, *Development*, pp. 198-204; and Shelton, *Word*, chs. 10–11.

with God receive a *prophetic* endowment of the Spirit in the context of prayer (Lk. 3.21-22//Acts 2.1) at the beginning of a new phase in redemption history. In each case the endowment is specifically elucidated as empowering to proclaim the good news (Lk. 4.18-21//Lk. 24.47-49; Acts 1.8; 2.11), and the parties receiving the gift each preach a programmatic sermon explaining the prophetic gift that has come upon them (Lk. 4.16-28//Acts 2.14-39).[70] There can be no turning back on these insights (and, indeed, virtually all scholars from von Baer to Schweizer, Lampe, Haya-Prats and Mainville have agreed). The ending of Luke and the Prologue of Acts undoubtedly focus 'the promise' of the Spirit to the disciples especially as prophetic endowment empowering for witness, rather than, for example, as the gift of inward transformation by the Spirit (as in Ezek. 36).[71] This important parallelism helps to establish that the work of Jesus continues into the period of the church.

(3) While few Lukan scholars would wish to dispute the point just made, it is quite widely questioned whether this represents the whole picture. After all, while these transitional passages specifically highlight the promise in connection with power to act as witnesses, it is nevertheless clear from the rest of Acts that the 'Spirit of prophecy' which the disciples received at Pentecost was not confined to empowering witness. Even if we restrict ourselves to the circle of those addressed in Luke 24 and Acts 1, we find that the Spirit also gave them discernment and guidance in church matters (cf. e.g. 5.3, 9; 15.28). Beyond the circle of those disciples we could multiply such instances, the Spirit giving wisdom, direction and encouragement to the church (6.3, 5; 9.31; 11.24, 28; 13.52; 15.28; 20.28), personal guidance (20.23; 21.4, 11) and so on.[72] In other words, while empowering for mission is the aspect of the gift of the Spirit to the disciples that is most specifically

70. The parallels Luke provides between Jordan and Pentecost have long been observed: see especially von Baer, *Geist*, p. 85; Talbert, *Patterns*, p. 16; Chevallier, 'Luc', p. 5; Ervin, *Conversion-Initiation*, ch. 3 (and cf. p. 161); Stronstad, *Theology*, ch. 4; O'Reilly, *Word*, pp. 29-52; W. Russell, 'The Anointing with the Holy Spirit in Luke–Acts', *TrinJ* 7 (1986), pp. 47-63; B. Aker, 'New Directions in Lucan Theology: Reflections on Lk. 3.21-22 and Some Implications', in P. Elbert (ed.), *Faces of Renewal* (Peabody: Hendrickson, 1988), pp. 108-27; Mainville, *L'Esprit*, pp. 285-86, 291; Menzies, *Development*, pp. 201 n. 2, 206-207.

71. This point has been made powerfully by Ervin (*Conversion-Initiation*, pp. 19-21) and Menzies (*Development*, pp. 198-204, esp. p. 204) against Dunn (*Baptism*, pp. 47-49) who attempts to broaden 'the promise' to include Old Testament texts other than Joel 3, and then interprets 'the promise' principally in terms of Ezek. 36, Jer. 31 and Gen. 17. The debate has been continued in *JPT* vols. 3 and 4 (see Dunn, 'Baptism', pp. 21-22; Menzies, 'Luke', pp. 131-33).

72. See Chapter 13 §§1 and 2 below (and compare Turner, 'Empowerment', esp. pp. 113-119); *idem*, 'Spirit and Israel's Restoration', part IV.

focused in Lk. 24.49 and Acts 1.8, we cannot say the Pentecostal gift to them was 'empowering for witness' *alone*.[73] And if the promised Spirit of prophecy is envisaged to enable activities other than empowerment for witness, we cannot guarantee that Luke thought all Christians received the Spirit primarily as such empowering (as we shall see in Chapters 12 and 13).[74] There is also crucial evidence even in these very passages of a broader outlook. We have noted, for example, that to refer to the Spirit as a power 'from on high' which will 'come upon you' evokes Isa. 32.15 with its hopes for the refreshment and restoration of Israel (32.15-20). This allusion suggests the Spirit of prophecy will come as Israel's ethical/spiritual renewal. Participation in God's cleansing/restoration of Israel is implicit too in John the Baptist's promise referred to in Acts 1.5.[75] And the form of the latter semantically focuses the disciples as the beneficiaries of the action described in the verb, not as the agents of this within Israel (even if they will become this as well).

Menzies interprets Lk. 3.16 to mean the coming one will sift Israel by the Spirit of prophecy upon him (i.e. through his proclamation). He then wishes to interpret Acts 1.5 in parallel to this to mean something like 'you will be empowered by the Spirit to sift Israel through your charismatic witness'.[76] But Acts 1.5 does not say 'you shall *baptise* with Holy Spirit' (as Menzies' parallel requires) but 'you shall *be baptised* with Holy Spirit'.

These last considerations at least hint that Luke may have considered the forthcoming gift of the Spirit to be *both* prophetic empowering for witness *and* a more soteriologically related gift at the same time. One further line of

73. *Contra* Menzies' view that Luke describes 'the gift of the Spirit *exclusively* in charismatic or prophetic terms as the source of power for effective witness' ('Luke', p. 137, also p. 120—his italics).

74. At this point the logic of Menzies' criticism of Haya-Prats and Turner breaks down. Menzies (*Development*, p. 210 n. 2) argues that Haya-Prats and Turner can only escape the conclusion that the gift of the Spirit is empowering for witness by ignoring these transitional sections. In fact, neither of us ignored them. Haya-Prats argues the promise of the Spirit as empowering for witness in Acts 1.7-8 is but one concrete expression of the gift of the Spirit elsewhere understood more generally (cf. *L'Esprit*, pp. 187-88). Similarly, in the pages of my thesis that Menzies cites, the comment he quotes ('the [Pentecost] gift is not primarily an empowering for mission', p. 183) is immediately followed by the words 'such empowering is...one...sphere of activity within the [broader] nexus of the activities of the christian Spirit of prophecy' (cf. also p. 155). The comment Menzies quotes was intended as a judgment concerning the 'gift of the Holy Spirit' as seen in all believers and from the *total* perspective of Acts, while the qualification he fails to cite had the narrower focus of Lk. 24.46-49 and Acts 1.8 in mind.

75. See above, Chapter 6.

76. *Development*, p. 146; cf. 'Luke', p. 128.

argument strongly suggests this is the way the reader is expected to anticipate the Pentecostal gift, and it is to this we turn now.

3. *The Spirit as the Means of Continuation of Salvation*

There is no evidence in Luke's Gospel that 'salvation' for the disciples was something thought to begin with Pentecost. As we have seen (§1), the period of Jesus was the day of salvation. To that extent the picture in Luke fits rather more comfortably with classical Pentecostal theology than it does with Dunn's model, for example. The problem with some traditional Pentecostal theologies, however, is their tendency to conceive of 'salvation' as some status or concrete benefit that can be carried through from the period of the ministry into that after the ascension without funda- mental change. This is largely because 'salvation' is viewed in somewhat static terms as 'forgiveness of sins' (consequent on an adequate expression of faith in and commitment to Jesus and his message) and admission to the community of salvation that is assured bliss at the eschaton.[77] In the days when New Testament scholarship conceived of Judaism as a guilt-ridden religion of legalism one might understand how such a proclamation might sound like 'Good News' indeed (and would still be such to Gentiles who stood outside the covenant), but in a post-Sanders era there is little to differ- entiate it from what most Jews already believed. For Luke 'salvation' means much more than assurance of forgiveness outside the cultus; it means the inbreaking kingdom of God, God's self-revealing reconciling and redeeming presence in strength bringing to fulfilment the liberating, radical cleansing and transformation of Israel in accordance with Isaianic hopes for Israel's New Exodus. Experience of 'salvation' might *commence* in assurance of God's forgiveness, but this was understood as the beginning of an on-going experience of God's inbreaking reign. And the specific 'means' of this self- revealing transforming presence of God was primarily the Spirit at work through the ministry and teaching of Jesus (§1.2).

It would appear to be a necessary corollary of what we have just said that, from the perspective of the Gospel of Luke, *the removal of Jesus- empowered-by-the-Spirit to heaven in the ascension threatens to termi- nate the very experience of salvation that Luke has described as commencing*, or at least to reduce it to a mere shadow—a fading memory

---

77. Cf. Menzies who typically asserts that from the Samaritan experience we learn 'the Spirit is a supplementary gift given to Christians, those who have already been incorporated into the community of salvation' (*Development*, p. 258). What is this 'salvation'? It appears merely to be the forgiveness given to faith (cf. *Development*, p. 276) and assurance of ultimate salvation (cf. also p. 279). Cf Haya-Prats, *L'Esprit*, pp. 123-25.

barely kept alight by the retelling of the Jesus story in the church. This last is, of course, largely how Conzelmann viewed Luke's perception. But there has been a healthy revolt against Conzelmann's somewhat depressing picture of the 'period of the Church'. As Bovon put it, for Luke the period of the church is not just an uncomfortable waiting room, where we find consolation in admiring portraits of a Jesus who, through his life and work, prefigured the kingdom which is all too slow to arrive[78] We know from Acts that he sees the period of the church as a joyful one, marked by a stronger manifestation of God's rule—now one with the rule of the ascended Davidic messiah who sits at his right hand—and greater measure of fulfilment of promise.[79] But at the juncture of Luke and Acts that only sharpens the question of how God's self-manifesting transforming presence will be deepened in Israel (and extended beyond Israel) when the means of its presence in the ministry (Jesus empowered by the Spirit) is removed through the ascension.

The key transitional passages (Lk. 24.47-49 and Acts 1.1-8) mention only one power that Jesus will give from the Father that could possibly be expected to continue the saving/transforming momentum of Jesus' ministry, and that is the Holy Spirit.[80] Luke's reader will surely not be taken by surprise at this point, and ask what the 'Spirit of prophecy' has to do with salvation, for she will have seen that it was the Spirit's work in and through Jesus which made 'salvation' powerfully present in the period of the ministry in the first place. The outpouring of the Spirit upon the full circle of Jesus' disciples could then only be expected to deepen and further it, as well as extending it to others. If it is not yet made entirely clear to the reader by what means the Spirit will accomplish all these things, that will be elucidated by the body of Acts to which we turn next. But the transitional passages (especially Acts 1.1-8) would strongly suggest to the reader that it is the gift of the Spirit to Israel that provides the ongoing self-manifesting and transforming presence of God in strength, and so the gift of the Spirit which lies at the heart of the hope for Israel's ongoing salvation/ transformation and her mission as the Isaianic servant and light to the nations. The explicit reference to John the Baptist's promise, and the allusions to Isa. 32.15, 43.10-12 and 49.6 would reinforce this expectation.

78. *Theologian*, p. 27. See most of chapter 1 on scholarly responses to Conzelmann, also pp. 247-50, 273-77, 315-17.

79. For two important reactions to Conzelmann's position in this respect see Marshall, *Luke*, chs. 4, 7 and 8, and Franklin, *Luke*, ch. 11.

80. See Chapter 13 for consideration of the view that Jesus and/or salvation are present in the word about Jesus, or by 'the hand of the Lord', or in 'the name' (etc.). None of these plays a significant role independent of the Spirit in the Church of Acts.

Chapter 12

THE RECEPTION OF THE PENTECOSTAL GIFT
IN THE CHURCH OF ACTS

That Luke thought the circle of Jesus' own disciples received the Spirit as
something like the 'Spirit of prophecy' need hardly be disputed. This was
the gift of the Spirit Judaism most typically awaited and Jesus had himself
received a special messianic form of it. Furthermore, Lk. 24.47-49 and Acts
1.8 specify the Spirit's role as prophetic empowering to fulfil Isa. 49.1-6, the
charismata immediately manifest (2.4) clearly correspond to the 'Spirit of
prophecy', and Peter programmatically explains the Pentecostal outpouring
in terms of Joel's promise (see Chapter 10 above). But this raises two important questions. (1) Does Acts imply that the Spirit given to *all* Christians is
the 'Spirit of prophecy' promised by Joel? (2) Does Acts imply this is
always granted as a *donum superadditum* 'empowering for mission', or are
there suggestions of other functions (even 'soteriological') functions too?

The first of these questions is relatively straightforward and is addressed
in §1. Then in §2 we begin to answer the second question, by reviewing the
main passages in Acts describing *reception* of the Spirit (other evidence
being considered in Chapter 13). We note that (as Dunn argued) Acts 2.38-
39 implies a norm in which the Spirit is given at some stage within the
complex of 'conversion-initiation', and that (*contra* Menzies) Acts 8.16
portrays the separation of the Spirit from conversion-initiation as anomalous,
while 19.1-6 reaffirms the norm. Such a norm itself suggests Luke considers
the gift of the Spirit to have a more fundamental role in the life of the
Christian than Mainville, Stronstad, Shelton and Menzies allow. My review
will also show that with the exception of Paul (Acts 9) there is barely any
evidence for the view that Luke thinks the Spirit is given to converts as
empowering for mission. Some of the passages—notably Acts 2.1-13, 33-36;
11.16 and 15.6-9—also provide important clues that Luke thinks the gift of
the Spirit is the means by which the messiah continues his cleansing and
transformation of Zion, and thus to have soteriological import.

1. *Does Acts Imply that the Spirit Given to all Christians is the 'Spirit of Prophecy' Promised by Joel?*

Two lines of evidence secure an unequivocally affirmative reply to this question. First, Peter's speech guarantees *Joel's* promise of the Spirit to all who turn to the Lord, and Joel's oracle concerns the Spirit as the 'Spirit of prophecy'. Secondly, virtually every mention of the Spirit in the book of Acts concerns one of the prototypical gifts of the Spirit. I shall comment on both these lines of evidence in a little more detail.

(A) The nature of the gift of the Spirit promised to Christians in 2.38-39 is clear enough—it is Joel's gift of the Spirit of prophecy. His audience will hardly expect Peter to be speaking of any other gift of the Spirit when he has so carefully explained Pentecost in terms of fulfilment of Joel. And when Peter states that those who are baptized receive the 'gift of the Holy Spirit', what he says continues to refer back to the wording of Joel 2.28-32 (LXX 3.1-5). Thus his affirmation that this ἐπαγγελία ('promise'; cf. 2.33) is offered 'to you…and to your children' takes up and reaffirms Joel's promise that the Spirit will be poured out 'on your sons and daughters' (2.17c). When Peter then insists the promise is to 'all' called by God (cf. καὶ πᾶσιν: 2.17b), the basis for his claim again lies in Joel's assertion, 'I will pour out my Spirit on *all flesh*' (2.28a; LXX 3.1a), and the amplifying phrase τοῖς εἰς μακράν ('to all those who are far off') draws on Joel too (LXX 3.4; MT 3.8). Finally, the assertion the gift will be given to everyone 'whom the Lord our God calls to him' alludes to the last words of Joel's oracle (2.32 [3.5b]: 'whomsoever the Lord calls'), not cited earlier by Peter. In short, Peter draws on the wording of Joel's prophecy not merely for the basis of the universality spoken of, but, consequently, for the very nature of the promised gift itself. He is saying *Joel's* gift of the Spirit as the 'Spirit of prophecy' will be given universally.

(B) If we look at how the Spirit is actually portrayed in the rest of Acts, the picture we gain coheres closely with Judaism's concept of the Spirit of prophecy (for which see especially Chapter 3 above):

1.   The Spirit is thus the author of revelatory visions and dreams: pro-grammatically at 2.17, but also specifically at Acts 7.55-56. Luke would probably trace such vision/dream guidance as 9.10-18; 10.10-20; 16.9-10; 18.9-10; 22.17-18, 21; 23.11 to the Spirit (cf. the specific mention of Spirit in these contexts, 10.19; 16.6-7).[1]

---

1.   Against von Baer, Haya-Prats (*L'Esprit*, §4) curiously argues that Luke would not attribute the visions elsewhere in Acts to the Spirit except at 7.55. Luke undoubt-edly knows of heavenly dreams and visions that do not proceed from the gift of the

2. The Spirit gives revelatory words or instruction or guidance: 1.2; 1.16 (= Old Testament); 4.25 (= Old Testament); 7.51 (= Old Testament); 8.29; 10.19; 11.12, 28; 13.2, 4; 15.28; 16.6-7; 19.21; 20.22, 23; 21.4, 11; 28.25 (= Old Testament)

3. The Spirit grants charismatic wisdom or revelatory discernment: Lk. 21.15; Acts 5.3; 6.3, 5, 10; 9.31; 13.9; 16.18.

4. The Spirit inspires invasive charismatic praise, e.g. the tongues on the day of Pentecost: 2.4; 10.46; 19.6.

5. The Spirit inspires charismatic preaching or witness: Acts 1.4, 8; 4.8, 31; 5.32; 6.10; 9.17; or charismatic teaching: 9.31; 18.25(?), etc.—this is not strictly anticipated in Judaism, but it is an obvious extension of the Jewish concept of the Spirit as the Spirit of prophecy (combining some of the above), and derives from pre-Lukan Christianity.[2]

Along with the specific references to the Baptist's promise (1.5; 11.16) and references to believers receiving the gift of the Spirit (specified explicitly as Joel's gift at 2.17-18, 33, 38-39 and as 'the same Spirit' at 10.44, 45, 47; 11.15; 15.8),[3] the above include nearly all of the references to the Spirit in the book of Acts. We are left with only eight occasions that do not immediately fit the categories of gifts we would regard as prototypical of the Spirit of prophecy:

1. Acts 5.3, 9, referring to Ananias and Sapphira 'lying to' and 'testing' the Holy Spirit by their deceit;

2. Acts 6.5 and 11.24, ascribing charismatic 'faith' to the Spirit, and 13.52 similarly charismatic 'joy';

3. Acts 8.39, which speaks of the Spirit snatching Philip up and transporting him away;

Spirit granted to believers (Cornelius's pre-conversion vision [10.3] is a case in point; and Paul's Damascus road experience too), but there is little need to multiply hypotheses in the case of men of the Spirit, especially when the giving of dreams and visions was regarded as prototypical of the 'Spirit of prophecy'. Haya-Prats argues that the visions are attributed to God (16.10) or to Christ (18.9; 22.17-18; 23.11) instead, but this surely represents a false antithesis. For Luke the Spirit is the active self-revealing presence of God (and of Christ). Acts 10.10, 11.5 and 22.17 use the language of falling into a 'trance' (ἔκστασις) in connection with the inception of these visions. This not only reminds one of the decription of Stephen being *full* of the Spirit for his vision (7.55), but the language of 'trance' corresponds closely to what Philo attributes to the influx of 'the prophetic Spirit' (*Rer. Div. Her.* 265; *Spec. Leg.* 4.49; *Vit. Mos.* 1.277), and cf. *Bib. Ant.* 28.6.

2. See Turner, 'Spirit and Authoritative Preaching', especially pp. 68-72, 87-88.

3. Other reference to believers receiving the Spirit are 8.15, 16, 17, 18, 19 and 19.2, 6.

4. Acts 10.38, referring to Jesus' own anointing with Spirit and power, and

5. Acts 20.28, where the Spirit is described as appointing overseers.

These can all, nevertheless, be understood as pertaining to activities of the Spirit of prophecy. We have seen that Acts 10.38 represents Luke's view of the special messianic endowment as prophet-liberator. Acts 20.28 is readily understood after the analogy of Acts 13.2, 4. The reference to the Spirit seizing Philip away (8.39), if it genuinely belongs in the text, represents an activity traditionally associated with the Spirit on prophetic figures (Elijah and Ezekiel).[4] The special charismatic nature of the 'faith' of Stephen and Barnabas is clearly indicated by the Lukan phrase 'full of faith and the Holy Spirit' (6.5; in reverse order in 11.24); i.e. it is a faith inspired by the Spirit. But this hardly requires something different from the activity of the 'Spirit of prophecy'. Such 'faith' is a dynamic and motivating way of understanding the relation of God to one's own world, and is fuelled by God's self-revealing presence and charismatic wisdom, typically gifts of the 'Spirit of prophecy'. The same applies in the case of those 'filled with joy and the Holy Spirit' in 13.52.[5] By contrast, the hearts of Ananias and Sapphira are differently 'filled' (5.3!), but they are 'lying to' the Spirit who reveals the deceitful heart (cf. 13.9) and 'testing' the Spirit who has led the community to acts of generosity—in each case the 'Spirit of prophecy'.

Luke evidently regards the promise made to believers to be a Christianized version of Joel's promise; the gift of the Spirit of prophecy.[6] In

---

4.   Menzies (*Development*, p. 124) defends the longer minority reading of 8.39 according to which 'when he came up out of the water, the Holy Spirit fell upon the eunuch, and the Angel of the Lord snatched Philip away' (so A[c] 36 323 453 945 1739 1891 *pc* l p w sy[h**]). But this looks more like a late attempt to round out the story. The shorter and harder text is more probably the original (see Metzger, *Commentary*, p. 360), and this is supported by all the Elijah–Elisha traits within the story (see F.S. Spencer, *The Portrait of Philip in Acts* [Sheffield: JSOT Press, 1992], pp. 135-410), especially the close contacts with the story of Elijah's meeting Obadiah in the wilderness (1 Kgs 18), and it is precisely within this chapter that the possibility of Elijah being transported away by the Spirit is first mentioned (18.12).

5.   Haya-Prats, *L'Esprit*, pp. 142-44, notes this 'faith' and 'joy' are not simply the faith with which Christian life begins, and joy at the reception of messianic blessings, but charismatic faith and joy (cf. also pp. 76-79, 104, 139-41).

6.   *Contra* Jervell ('Sons of the Prophets: The Holy Spirit in the Acts of the Apostles', in *Unknown Paul*, pp. 96-97) who fails to see how the notion of the 'Spirit of prophecy' accounts for the phenomena in Acts because he has not asked what range of charismata the 'Spirit of prophecy' typically supports in a Jewish milieu. His own understanding is that this phrase may only be used of Luke's position if the 'Spirit of prophecy' is taken to mean something like 'the Spirit [which] confirms and supports prophecy, that is, the prophecy in the Holy Scriptures, which contain the gospel

that sense Acts 2.14-39 is genuinely programmatic for the pneumatology of Acts. In saying this we are simply agreeing that we cannot turn back (as Dunn attempted to) along the road so ably built by Lampe, Schweizer, Haya-Prats, Stronstad and Menzies. Luke does not spell out his pneumatology, like Paul, in terms of the fulfilment of Ezekiel 36, and new creation, but in terms of Joel 3.1-5 (EVV 2.28-32). The question now becomes, what place does this conception have in Luke's theological scheme? Is the Pentecostal gift simply a *donum superadditum* of some kind, or does it belong more fundamentally to Christian existence and life? The rest of this chapter and the one that follows address different aspects of that question, first concentrating on the passages relating to Spirit-reception, then broadening the search to other passages.

2. *The Reception of the Promise of the Spirit in Acts*

We now examine the contribution of the major Spirit-reception passages to our understanding of the nature of the promise of the Spirit in Luke–Acts. Particular, but not exclusive, attention will be paid to the question of whether Acts 2.38-39 provides a normative statement of the connection of the promise to conversion-initiation. The passages for examination are the Pentecost account of Acts 2 (§2.1), the Samaritan episode of Acts 8.4-24 (§2.2), Paul's commissioning in Acts 9.10-19 (§2.3), the conversion of the Gentiles in Acts 10.1-11.18 and 15.7-11 (§2.4), and Apollos and the Ephesian twelve (§2.5).

2.1. *The Contribution of Acts 2*
We have already considered this passage in some detail (Chapter 10), so we may confine ourselves to the following four observations:

(A) If the glossolalia of 2.4 and Peter's explanation of it perhaps typify the Pentecost experience as the 'Spirit of prophecy', and if its special nature on this occasion as xenolalia (2.6, 8, 11) possibly foreshadows the Spirit's role in witness to unbelievers, the parallels with Jewish Moses/Sinai traditions which shape the Pentecost account also imply that this same 'Spirit of prophecy' has come as some fundamental power of covenant-renewal in Israel. Like an impressionist artist, Luke appears to have included this tradition in his broader canvas for the general effect of its theological 'shape and hue' without necessarily attempting to integrate its detail and define its borders for close-up inspection. While its inclusion thus has suggested to some

---

verbatim' (p. 97), but this takes Luke right out of any convincing Jewish context. For a more nuanced view see C.A. Evans, 'The Prophetic Setting of the Pentecost Sermon', in Evans and Sanders, *Luke*, pp. 212-24, esp. 218-20.

observers that Luke considered Pentecost to be the beginning of the New Age of Salvation (at least for the disciples),[7] or, more specifically, the inauguration of the New Covenant and the replacement of the Law by the Spirit, or the granting of the Spirit as the power to keep the Law,[8] none of these explanations receives significant confirmation from elsewhere in Luke–Acts.

(1) Luke does not portray Pentecost as the *beginning* of the New Age or Salvation for the disciples because this would conflict with his view that these were initiated decisively within Jesus' ministry (see Chapters 6–9 and 11 above). The redactional phrase 'in the last days' in Peter's quotation of Joel (Acts 2.17a) means Pentecost is *part* of the promised end-time salvation (not its beginning) along with those wonders and signs, also indicated in Joel's oracle, which Luke believed already to have been partially fulfilled in the ministry, crucifixion and resurrection of Jesus.[9] Similarly, Luke's summary of Peter's preaching as 'Save yourselves from this wicked generation' (2.40) hardly makes the gift of the Spirit *itself* the gift of salvation and the matrix of Christian 'life'.[10] Peter's words exhort the Jerusalem audience to the whole complex of repentance, faith in Jesus as God's appointed Lord and Christ, and baptismal expression of this for the sake of 'the forgiveness of sins', as well as the reception of the Spirit to which these lead. 'Forgiveness of sins' is clearly part of the 'salvation' in mind (see Chapter 11 above). Similarly, while 'repentance' and 'faith' are outwardly responsible human activities (which Peter urges) they are simultaneously seen to involve divine grace and so they too are part of the 'salvation' promised by God as well (cf. especially 5.31; 11.18; 15.7). The gift of the Spirit, however important, is then but one element in this complex, not the gift of salvation simpliciter. At the same time, however, we may note that Luke's summary of Peter's exhortation in 2.40 would appear to be a poor one, missing the essence of his speech, if the gift of the Spirit is not truly part of the 'salvation' envisaged at all, but merely an 'additional gift' empowering witness to others.

(2) Luke does not use the contrasting language of 'old/new covenant' in Acts at all, preferring to portray the salvation inaugurated by Christ as the fulfilment of the one covenant made to Abraham and the fathers (Lk. 1.73 [cf. vv. 72-75]; Acts 3.25; 7.8. Indeed, with the exception of Lk. 22.20,[11]

---

7. The main protagonist is Dunn (cf. *Baptism*, pp. 91-92, etc.), but cf. N.B. Stonehouse, 'Repentance, Baptism and the Gift of the Holy Spirit', *WTJ* 13 (1950), p. 16.

8. See the conclusion to Chapter 10 §1.4.

9. See above Chapter 10 §1.3.

10. *Contra* Stonehouse, 'Repentance', p. 16; Dunn, *Baptism*, pp. 91-92.

11. In favour of the longer text of Lk. 22.19-20 see J. Jeremias, *The Eucharistic Words of Jesus* (Oxford: Basil Blackwell, 1966 [1955]), pp. 138-58; H. Schürmann,

these exhaust Luke's references to 'covenant').[12] A case can be made that
Luke thinks Jesus' proclamation of God's reign (with its associated ethical
teaching) and the presence of the Spirit in Israel have effectively displaced
the Law from its central position in the relationship between God and his
people (and so produced a set of circumstances that Paul would refer to
under the theologoumenon of 'new covenant'),[13] but this would apply as
much to the period covered by the Gospel as to that of Acts.[14]

(3) There is no adequate basis for the claims that Pentecost is either the
giving of the Spirit in place of the Law or the gift of the Spirit to enable
obedience to the Law (or to some New Law).[15] Against the former stands
the evident commitment of the early community to the Mosaic Law,[16] a
commitment which does not appear to be questioned until Acts 10 at the
earliest, and then only in part of the Church. But the (contrary) view that
the Spirit is given to further or enable obedience to the Mosaic Law cannot
be sustained either.[17] While it is true that Luke sees one of the major differences between pre-Christian Israel and messianic Israel to be that the latter
no longer *resists* the Spirit (7.51, 53)—and Jervell is right to indicate this

Der Einsetzungsbericht Lk 22.19-20 (Münster: Aschendorff, 1955), *passim*;
I.H. Marshall, *Last Supper and Lord's Supper* (Exeter: Paternoster, 1980), pp. 36-38.
Against, see M. Rese, 'Zur Problematik von Kurz- und Langtext in Luk. xxii.17ff.',
NTS 22 (1976), pp. 15-32; but for criticism of his arguments see Turner, 'Sabbath',
pp. 145-46 n. 112. The longer reading is to be preferred, but the language of 'new
covenant' is pre-Lukan, not Luke's preferred way of speaking.

12. Cf. N.A. Dahl, 'The Story of Abraham in Luke–Acts', in Keck and Martyn
(eds.), *Studies*, pp. 139-58; Jervell, 'the Law in Luke–Acts', in *Luke*, pp. 132-51.

13. I have argued such a position, against Jervell, in 'Sabbath', esp. pp. 111-13 and
113-24. Similar positions have been reached by C.L. Blomberg, 'The Law in Luke–
Acts', *JSNT* 22 (1984), pp. 53-80, and M.A. Seifrid, 'Jesus and the Law in Acts', *JSNT*
30 (1987), pp. 39-57.

14. So R.J. Banks, *Jesus and the Law in the Synoptic Tradition* (Cambridge:
Cambridge University Press, 1975), part 2, *passim*; Turner, 'Sabbath', pp. 111-13.

15. See Chapter 10 §1.4, esp. nn. 65-66. A new Law was not expected by Judaism
of its messiah(s)—so, correctly, Banks, *Jesus*, pp. 65-85; and in R.J. Banks (ed.),
Reconciliation and Hope (Grand Rapids: Eerdmans, 1974), pp. 173-85; also Schäfer,
'Termini', pp. 27-42. Hence we should suspect the claim of, e.g., O'Reilly (*Word*,
p. 21) that the Pentecost parallels with Sinai are intended to suggest 'the new Law, the
word of apostolic preaching'. It is not clear either how Luke can expect his readers to
understand the apostolic preaching as new Torah when the kerygma has so little ethical
content; the content of the kerygma bears closer analogy to the preambles to the
covenants.

16. A case made most strongly by Jervell, *Luke*, pp. 133-51, and *Unknown Paul*,
pp. 96-121 (esp. pp. 103-107, 116-21), but cf. S.G. Wilson, *Luke and the Law*
(Cambridge: Cambridge University Press, 1975), ch. 2.

17. For this view see Jervell, as at Chapter 10, n. 65.

means the Spirit directs to and inclines towards God's will[18]—God's will and the Mosaic Law are not to be simplistically identified. Luke understands the vision in Acts 10.11-16 to overturn the food purity laws (on which much of the uncleanness of the Gentiles was predicated),[19] and the Gentiles, who receive the Spirit, do *not* keep the Mosaic Law,[20] yet they are admitted as 'one people of God' with messianic Israel[21]—a view which is very difficult to reconcile with the belief that Luke thought Pentecost was the gift of the Spirit *granted to enable obedience* to the Law. In the final analysis the complex and changing relationship of the community to the Mosaic Law depicted in Acts is easier to understand if it be assumed that Luke did not consider the gift of the Spirit as a direct counterpart to Moses' gift of the Law, either establishing it or superseding it.

Thus while 'Sinai' parallels in Luke's Pentecost account forge a correspondence between Israel's history and that of the movement which will *become* the church,[22] and while they suggest that the gift of the Spirit is to

18. See Jervell, *Unknown Paul*, pp. 116-21.

19. Cf. Seifrid, 'Peter's vision unmistakably annuls Mosaic demands...Levitical food laws are overturned', 'Jesus', p. 43.

20. Jervell (*Luke*, pp. 133-51), following H. Waitz ('Das Problem des sogennanten Aposteldekretz', *ZKG* 55 [1964], p. 227), argues that Luke thinks the Gentiles did keep the Mosaic Law in so far as it was relevant to them, viz. the (cultic) code of behaviour expected of the גר תושׁב according to Lev. 17–18 and echoed in the so-called 'apostolic decree'; similarly Haenchen, 449-50; O'Neill, *Acts*, p. 82; D.R. Catchpole, 'Paul, James and the Apostolic Decree', *NTS* 23 (1977), pp. 429-30; Bauckham, 'James', pp. 459-62. Against this view see Turner, 'Sabbath', pp. 113-24, and compare Marshall, *Luke*, pp. 191-92, Wilson, *Law*, ch. 2.

21. Jervell, of course, must distinguish messianic Israel sharply from the Gentile believers whom he regards merely as an 'associate' people of God alongside Israel. Against this distinction see Turner, 'Sabbath', and J. Dupont, 'Un peuple d'entre les nations (Actes 15.14)', *NTS* 31 (1985), pp. 321-35. Franklin (*Luke*, pp. 56-57) has modified his previous position slightly in Jervell's direction, while still maintaining a critical distance from him: for Franklin, messianic Israel and the Gentile believers are one people of God, but in two interrelated, interdependent parts.

22. It is often maintained that Luke regarded Pentecost as the birthday of the church (cf. Lake, in Foakes-Jackson and Lake [eds.], *Beginnings*, I, p. 328) and this is taken to support the view that he must have considered the new covenant to have commenced then. But both the premise and the conclusion are dubious. In some respects Luke portrays the ministry of Jesus as a part of the period of the church, especially with the appointment of the Twelve (cf. Miyoshi, *Anfang, passim*). In general, however, while the group of disciples in the ministry are part of the God-given dynamic which eventually leads to 'the church', the latter term is only fully appropriate (for Luke) when a significant portion of Israel collects around the apostles and disciples—see Lohfink (*Sammlung*, ch. 3) who rightly warns against oversimplification: 'Die Kirche ist für Lukas nicht eine Grösse, die am Pfingsttag einfachhin da ist' (*Sammlung*, p. 56).

be important if not constitutive for the ongoing life and praxis of the people of God, Luke has not specified the matter further. The reader is forced to cast around for clues in the cotext, and to fit what is said here with what has already been said. There are three such clues: (a) the allusion to Isa. 32.15 (-20) in Acts 1.8 (Lk. 24.49: see Chapter 11 §2 above); (b) the reference to the Baptist's promise of messianic restorative cleansing with Spirit and fire (Acts 1.5); and (c) the related affirmation of the exaltation of Jesus to David's throne and his Lordship of and gift of the Spirit (2.33-36). Given these, the Moses/Sinai parallels in the Pentecost account would most probably suggest that *the 'Spirit of prophecy' to be given will be the effective power, not merely of Israel's witness, but also the power by which the messiah continues and deepens his New Exodus liberation and purging restoration of Israel, and so continues to fulfil to her the promises of her salvation.*

(B) In 2.4 Luke describes what was possibly the moment of the disciples' reception of the Spirit with the words 'they were all filled (ἐπλήσθησαν) with Holy Spirit and began to speak in other tongues as the Spirit gave them utterance'. A number of interpreters have taken part or all of this as paradigmatic and as a key to the understanding of Luke's pneumatology. According to these various views the period before Pentecost is either one of the absence of the Spirit in the disciples, or, at most, a period of the relatively meagre activity of the Spirit in them—both states to be contrasted with the messianic 'fullness' of the Spirit received at Pentecost and after.[23] One of the underlying assumptions here is that being 'filled with the Holy Spirit' linguistically connotes the inauguration of some *continuous state* of messianic fullness of the Spirit. But as we have seen earlier, that is to miss the import of the more general metaphor 'to be filled with (some quality)' and to misunderstand the more specific form where 'to be filled with the Spirit' is combined with a verb denoting speech.[24] The latter form (as at Acts 2.4: 'they were filled with the Holy Spirit and began to speak...') does not attempt to describe two different states of affairs (the entry into long-term messianic 'fullness' and a simultaneous speech event which

23. Compare Adler (see above Chapter 2 §3) who explains Acts 2.4 in terms of the messianic 'fullness' of Spirit normally received in confirmation (and the power to bestow the same), Bruner (*Theology*, p. 163) who equates being filled with the Spirit with reception of the Spirit at conversion (so also I.H. Marshall, cautiously, in 'Significance', p. 355), and Ervin (*Spirit-Baptism*, pp. 42-48, 49-61) who insists that ἐπλήσθησαν (in 2.4) is an ingressive aorist denoting irreversible entrance into a state of 'fullness of Spirit' understood in classical Pentecostal perspective as a 'second blessing'. But the aorist cannot possibly mean that at Lk. 1.41, 67, so what evidence is there it is meant here?

24. See the excursus at the close of Chapter 6 above.

marks it) but is a unitary metaphor specifying the (charismatic) speech event in question as one produced by the *invasive* inspiration of the Spirit (as at Lk. 1.41, 67; Acts 4.8, 31).[25] Acts 2.4 itself thus asserts little more than that within their Pentecost experience the disciples became invasively inspired to speak in tongues.

(C) Nor can we be sure that Luke thought of the Pentecost phenomenon of tongues as paradigmatic and normative. From his knowledge of Jewish background Luke may have anticipated that endowment with the 'Spirit of prophecy' would occasionally be accompanied by an event of invasive charismatic speech. But this was not usual, and it might only be anticipated on occasions of intense or epochal irruptions of the Spirit, such as here (cf. especially *Targ. Neb.* 1 Sam. 10.6, 10; 19.20, 23; *t. Soṭ* 6.2, etc.), or where there was strong reason that the Spirit-reception should be publicly attested to legitimate those concerned to the congregation of Israel (as in the case of the Spirit being granted to the seventy elders (Num. 11) that they might assist in Moses' leadership of the nation). Once again, of the charismatic phenomena that might be expected to be manifest on such occasions, invasive prophecy would be anticipated much more readily than the considerably rarer type, 'invasive charismatic praise'.[26] The specific form of charismatic doxology that we have in 'glossolalia' was entirely unknown in Judaism, and its appearance at Pentecost would be regarded as a remarkable *novum* marking an equally remarkable new phase in God's dealings with his people. But nothing in Acts 2 suggests this particular charisma of the 'Spirit of prophecy' will be widespread, let alone universal, at Spirit-reception. *Per contra*, knowledge of the tradition of Jesus' Jordan reception of the Spirit (which contains no trace of this) would argue against it. And, indeed, the specific form of glossolalia marking Pentecost—xenolalia: speech in recognized foreign languages—is found nowhere else in Acts. In short, cotextual and contextual considerations would make it very unlikely that Acts 2

25. Cf. Chapter 3 above for the category 'invasive charismatic speech'. On the relation of πνεύματος πλησθῆναι to this in the examples cited see Turner, 'Spirit Endowment', pp. 53-55. Menzies argues (against myself) that because 'to receive the Holy Spirit' and 'to be filled with the Holy Spirit' are both applied to the Pentecost experience, the expressions must mean essentially the same thing, i.e. to receive the Spirit *means* to enter into the fullness of the Spirit (*Development*, p. 212 n. 4; cf. Dunn, *Baptism*, p. 71, and Ervin, *Spirit-Baptism*, pp. 42-61), but this is a clear case of the co-referential fallacy. A similar argument at 8.16 would require that Luke thought every reception of the Spirit was a 'falling of the Spirit' (ἐπιπέπτω) on the individual, where this language is rather Luke's way of distinguishing abnormally dramatic irruptions of the Spirit, as at 10.44, 11.15 (and, by implication, at Pentecost); see Turner, 'Spirit Endowment', pp. 49-50.

26. For the few examples of the latter, see Chapter 3 §2(D) above. Of the former there are far more numerous examples—see Chapter 3 §2(C) above.

presents the Pentecostal phenomena of tongues as something that should be regularly anticipated at reception of the Spirit. On the contrary, only very strong indications in the rest of the narrative could possibly incline the reader to consider initial 'tongues' as 'regular' at all. We shall need to review the issue after our discussion of the conversion of the Ephesian twelve in Acts 19.1-6.

(D) The natural understanding of Acts 2.38-39 would be that as a rule of thumb the Spirit will from now on be given by God to those who repent and are baptized, without further conditions (for none is specified) and without delay (for none is implied).[27]

The disciples' own experience had, of course, involved a period of growing faith and knowledge of 'salvation' prior to reception of the Spirit, but only because the Spirit was not yet given. The reader will be aware that the disciples' story could not simply be repeated in the lives of others after the ascension. Beyond that event, there was no way the individual could then recapitulate the period of Jesus' ministry before entering the Pentecostal grace. In the period of the ministry, it was the presence of the Son, revealing the Father, in the power of the Spirit, that made the disciples' experience of 'faith' and 'salvation' possible (cf. e.g. Lk. 10.21-24). Beyond the ascension there was no corresponding means of the God-revealing presence of Jesus, *other than in and through the gift of the Spirit* (see Chapter 14 §3 [C]). Thus the only pre-Pentecostal part of the disciples' experience that could possibly be 'repeated' after Pentecost, without the gift of the Spirit, is the few days between ascension and Pentecost, when Jesus was absent from the disciples. Even that, however, could not strictly be the 'same' experience for someone who had not first been through some equivalent of the formative events from Jordan to ascension, and in any case Luke gives no indication whatever that he considers the ten days as some-how 'paradigmatic'! There is thus nothing in Acts 1–2 to suggest to the

---

27. With e.g. Haenchen, 184; Schneider, I, 277; Pesch, I, 125 (in '2.38 the general Christian rule is formulated'); Kremer, *Pfingstbericht*, pp. 176-79; J. Giblet, 'Baptism in the Spirit in the Acts of the Apostles', *OC* 10 (1974), pp. 162-71, esp. pp. 165-71; B. Sauvagant, 'Se repentir, être baptisé, recevoir l'Esprit, Actes 2,37ss', *Foi et Vie* 80 (1981), pp. 77-89 (esp. pp. 86-88); Quesnel, *Baptisés*, ch. 2 (but allowing Acts knows another type of conversion-initiation derived from the Pauline churches, and witnessed at Acts 8.14-17 and 19.1-6—on this see below §2.2.4; Lüdemann, *Christianity*, p. 47; and D. Jackson, 'Luke and Paul: A Theology of One Spirit from Two Perspectives', *JETS* 32 [1989], pp. 335-43, who is aware of the differences between the two but [on the basis of 2.38] asserts nevertheless that for Luke, 'There is no contemplation of a Christian without the Spirit. Such would be a contradiction in terms for both Luke and Paul' [p. 337]). The normative value of this rule would be reinforced if we could be sure the καί is a case of 'καί-consecutive' (= 'so that'), but see Haya-Prats, *L'Esprit*, pp. 136-37.

reader that those coming to faith are expected individually to recapitulate the previous stages of salvation history in their own spiritual experience, and will only receive the Spirit at some point subsequent to conversion-initiation.

Only on the assumption that 2.38-39 provides something of a 'norm' adequately explains why Luke does not feel obliged to record the reception of the Spirit by the converts who are baptized in 2.41; that is, he could assume the reader would interpret references to people being baptized in the name of Jesus (8.36-38; 16.15, 33; 18.8) as occasions when they received the Spirit unless (as in 8.16) it is explicitly stated otherwise. Similarly, when he speaks of individuals or groups coming to belief in Jesus (or turning to the Lord, being added to the Lord, etc.), Luke regularly omits to state that such converts received the Spirit (or even that they were baptized), but the norm of 2.38-39 could be taken to assure that they did indeed receive the Spirit within the process of their conversion-initiation.

If this association between repentance, baptism and the gift of the Spirit proves to be the norm anticipated by Acts, and if the exceptions are understandable special cases, then (*contra* Menzies)[28] it does indeed have implications for our understanding of the nature of the gift of the Spirit granted. It may suggest that the 'Spirit of prophecy' is not *merely* given as an empowering for *mission*, but has an important function in the spiritual life of the individual believer and in that of the community of which he or she becomes a part. It is pertinent at this point to note that Luke does not suggest that all converts were immediately impelled by the Spirit to mission (the only new convert Luke implies quickly became involved in witness and evangelism was Paul [Acts 9.20]). Rather, according to the summary which immediately follows (2.41-47), the Pentecost converts take their place in the fellowship that devote themselves to the apostolic teaching, joyfully worship God and pray together, enjoy celebratory meals together, and generously share their goods. If they have 'favour with the people' (2.47) that is because their life as a community epitomizes some of the ideals of the restored Israel, not because they have all become winsome evangelists. Had Luke wished to make the point that *all* receive the Spirit exclusively as empowering for witness he could easily have added a single clause to his lengthy summary to the effect that (e.g.) they 'all preached the word with boldness'. But that is only said of a later incident, concerning a household group of the apostles' friends, and following a *further* powerful experience of the Spirit, not an initial one (4.31). And while Luke knows that further converts were added to the community (2.47) he misses this golden opportunity to suggest it was the witness of those converted earlier that was responsible.

These observations raise the important question: if the Spirit is primarily

---

28. *Development*, p. 247.

empowering for witness, and yet does not necessarily immediately involve disciples in mission, why should we expect an especially close connection between conversion and reception of the Spirit? Would we not rather expect something like Acts 8.14-17 as the norm, with a period of Christian instruction and growth preceding reception of the Spirit? It is to the Samaritan incident that we now turn.

2.2. *Acts 8.4-24: The Samaritan Episode*

The Samaritan incident provides a clear break with the 'norm' we might expect from Acts 2.38-39, for here we are told the Samaritans believed the Christian message and were baptized (8.12), but only received the gift of the Spirit subsequently (at least days later, if not more) at the hands of the apostles (8.14-17). Those holding Confirmationist[29] and classical Pentecostal[30] models of the Spirit have argued Luke's readers will assume *this* sequence as normative. A problem with such a view is that 8.16 appears to indicate the opposite. It is difficult to see how the 'explanation' in 8.16b could be anything but redundant if Luke's readers normally anticipated a gap between baptism and reception of the Spirit. The deliberate (and emphasized) 'not yet' seems rather to indicate *contra-expectation*; i.e. although they were baptized (and the reader could have been expected from the story so far to assume they had received the Spirit, as the reader would at 2.41 etc.), nevertheless the Spirit had 'not yet' (for some marked reason) come upon them.[31] The question then becomes how we account

---

29. See especially Adler, *Taufe*, pp. 110ff; Price, 'Confirmation', pp. 174-77.

30. Most fully Menzies, *Development*, pp. 248-60.

31. Price argues the wording implies the opposite: 'Peter and John were on their way to impart the Spirit because the Samaritans did not already have it, simply because things had not progressed so far: "They had only been baptized." Luke clearly seems to imply in these words that baptism would *not* by itself impart the Spirit.' ('Confirmation', p. 176). But Luke, of course, does *not* say the apostles come to Samaria in order to impart the Spirit (as though such apostolic excursions for 'Confirmation' were regular); what they come to confirm rather is this remarkable development in which 'the word of God' had apparently been received outside 'Israel' (cf. 11.20). And if Luke's readers anticipate a Confirmationist pattern, they will not need to be told anything that 8.16 asserts. Slightly more believable is that this represents Luke's deliberate correction of any potential misunderstanding arising from 2.38; i.e. it could be argued Luke holds Acts 8 to reflect the norm, and Acts 2 to be too contracted a statement of principle to express the full reality (so Adler, *Taufe*, pp. 110ff.; cf. Menzies, *Development*), but the problems facing a Confirmationist exegesis of Acts remain insuperable (see Chapter 2, §3 above), and Luke never elsewhere portrays a reception of the Spirit separate from a conversion-initiation context (not even at Acts 19.1-6 where, whatever the previous state of the 'disciples', they are baptised by Paul as Christians). This observation rightly leads Bruner to the conclusion

for this contra-expectation. We shall review six different types of 'explanation':

(A) *Source-critical 'explanations'*. Attempts have been made to explain the departure from the 'norm' of Acts 2.38 as the artifact of a clumsy redaction of two independent sources, for example, of one which spoke of Philip bringing the gospel to Samaria, with another which either attributed the same to the apostles, instead, or simply recorded a confrontation between Peter and Simon, without the assumption of the Philip narrative that Simon was baptized.[32] This desperate thesis (as Lampe calls it)[33] does not solve the problem of how Luke understood the conflated version. Few in the redaction-critical and narrative-critical era are still prepared to argue Luke was a scissors-and-paste redactor with insufficient editorial freedom to

that Acts 2.38 is indeed the norm assumed here, though he overpresses this when he interprets the passage with the hyperbolic judgment, 'The Spirit is temporarily suspended from baptism here 'only' (*sic*) and precisely to teach...that *suspension cannot occur*' (*Theology*, p. 178; but contrast Parratt, *Seal*, chs. 3 and 4, and Dunn, *Baptism*, parts 1 and 2, who point out that in Acts there is not one single case where the Spirit is shown to be given *in* baptism). Along with interpretations of the passage which assume Acts 8.14-17 intentionally refers to a sacrament of confirmation we may also reject Käsemann's explanation (*Essays on New Testament Themes* [London: SCM Press, 1964], pp. 144-47; cf. also Haenchen, 305-308) that Luke has written matters so because he holds an early catholic view that the church is *una sancta apostolica* into which the Samaritans must be incorporated by laying on of apostolic hands in order to receive the Spirit. Against this see Dunn, *Baptism*, pp. 58-62; I.H. Marshall, '"Early Catholicism" in the New Testament', in Longenecker and Tenney (eds.), *Dimensions*, pp. 217-31 (and *Luke*, pp. 212-15), and C.K. Barrett, 'Light on the Holy Spirit from Simon Magus (Acts 8.4-25)', in Kremer (ed.), *Actes*, p. 293: 'This suggestion...takes no account of Simon, who provides the clue to Luke's fundamental conviction, which is that the Spirit does not respond to certain stimuli, such as the laying on of hands...but is given solely *ubi et quando visum est Deo*.'

32. *Contra* e.g. Bauernfeind, 124-25. Dibelius, *Studies*, p. 17, argues for Philip tradition + redactional material (cf. Haenchen, 307-308; Ehrhardt, *Acts*, p. 45; and D.A. Koch ['Geistbesitz, Geistverleihung und Wundermacht: Erwägungen zur Tradition und zur lukanischen Redaktion in Apg 8.5-25', *ZNW* 77 (1986), pp. 64-82] who argues Luke conflates a Philip source, and a Peter and Simon tradition to emphasize Philip's missionary success and unity with Jerusalem community). Dietrich (*Petrusbild*, pp. 248-51) 'explains' 8.14-17 as a traditional unit whose pneumatology differed from Luke's own (which allows even an Ananias in 9.17 to bestow the Spirit) and limits Philip's competence to bestow the Spirit without any intention to discredit him. Against such conflation theories see K. Pieper, *Die Simon-Magus-Perikope (Apg 8,5-24): Ein Beitrag zur Quellenfrage in der Apostelgeschichte* (Münster: Aschendorff, 1911), whose arguments have not yet been effectively answered, also Lampe, *Seal*, pp. 60-62; Pesch, I, 271, and above all Spencer, *Portrait*, ch. 2 (esp. pp. 26-31).

33. *Seal*, p. 69.

smooth out statements that were in contradiction to his own understanding on a key theological theme.[34] The two basic stories (Philip's mission and Peter's confrontation with Simon) could easily have been told without giving the impression that Peter was actually bestowing the Spirit on *Philip's* converts: it is only the parenthetic verses linking these stories which actually insist that the Spirit had not yet come on Philip's disciples (vv. 14-17)— and these verses are replete with characteristically *Lukan* language and themes.[35]

(B) *The Spirit suspended from baptism because of inadequate Samaritan faith?* An ingenious attempt was made by Dunn to explain the initial failure of the Samaritans to receive the Spirit in terms of the defective character of their response and commitment.[36] According to Dunn, before the arrival of the apostles from Jerusalem the Samaritans had not yet attained authentic Christian faith, partly because of Philip's failure sufficiently to distinguish his Christian proclamation from ordinary Samaritan hopes for the coming of the Taheb, and partly because the Samaritans' 'belief' was largely credulous and centred on Philip's signs.

According to Dunn, Luke will expect his readers to perceive five crucial points:

1. Philip's preaching was liable to misinterpretation. To the Samaritans, raised to fever pitch of excitement and eschatological expectation, the advent of Philip preaching the kingdom of God and 'the Christ' could only mean that the *Taheb*'s coming was imminent. Baptism would have been understood as the rite of entry into the kingdom (v. 12) and token of allegiance to Jesus as *Taheb* (prophet-like-Moses). The faith of the Samaritans was thus (accidentally) falsely directed.

2. The Samaritans were religiously credulous and indulged magical inclinations. Their response to Simon indicates that the Samaritans had very little discernment: the verbal parallels between vv. 6 and 10 suggest that their reaction to Philip was for the same reasons and of the same quality as their erstwhile response to Simon, that is, focused on his ability to perform signs, and leading to shallow 'herd' response (cf. especially the pregnant ὁμοθυμαδόν ['with one accord'] of v. 6).

---

34. So Parratt, *Seal*, pp. 144ff.; Dunn, *Baptism*, p. 60; Menzies, *Development*, pp. 249-50.

35. Turner, 'Luke and the Spirit', p. 161; Koch, 'Geistbesitz', pp. 69-71; Menzies, *Development*, p. 250, and Spencer, *Portrait*, pp. 218-19.

36. *Baptism*, pp. 63-68, and broadly followed by Montague, *Spirit*, pp. 293-94.

3. The Samaritans are described as believing in Philip, not as having faith in Christ. That is, the Samaritan πιστεύειν ('to believe') is specifically said to be directed *to Philip* (τῷ Φιλίππῳ, v. 12): Luke hereby indicates that the Samaritan response was simply an assent of the mind to the acceptability of what Philip was saying.

4. The comparison with Simon's case shows the Samaritans were not yet Christians (before 8.17); for while he, like the rest, is said to have believed and been baptized (8.13), Simon clearly emerges as one who has no part in the Christian message (8.18-24). The parting of the ways occurs when the Samaritans (except Simon) receive the Spirit. Simon himself had evidently not fulfilled the conditions for receiving the gift stipulated by Peter (Acts 2.38), viz. appropriate repentance.

5. The full flowering of the Samaritans' faith would also have been delayed by the cold winds of religious and racial animosity which blew from Jerusalem to Samaria. The Samaritans will have lacked the assurance that they were really accepted into the Christian community until the arrival of the Jerusalem apostles.

While there may be genuine historical insights in Dunn's explanation, the points he raises offer little clue to what Luke could expect his reader to understand of the incident. As most rejoinders to Dunn have pointed out, when we examine the passage from a redactional perspective everything suggests rather that Luke portrays 8.4-13 as a typical missionary success. Two points seem assured:

(1) *It is most unlikely that Luke considered Philip's preaching and ministry as either deficient or misunderstood.* Nothing in Luke's words 'he proclaimed the Christ to them' should lead the reader to believe that Philip's preaching was deficient or that the Samaritans were liable to confuse his message with their *Taheb* expectations: indeed, there is no evidence that either Luke or his readers knew of such beliefs. In Acts κηρύσσω and εὐαγγελίζομαι take a variety of objects, more dictated by style and audience than by theology,[37] and the expression concerned—parallelled elsewhere (5.42; cf. 9.22; 18.5, 28)—is to convey to the reader that Philip delivered the normal Christian message. Even had the Samaritans mistaken Jesus for the *Taheb*, soon to bring the kingdom, this would only have brought them into line with similar hopes held by a significant proportion of the early church, and close to Luke's own Christology of Jesus as the prophet-like-Moses—hardly ground for questioning the authenticity of the Samaritan faith!

37. Cf. Stanton, *Jesus*, pp. 17-30.

According to Dunn, Luke thinks that the response to Philip is shallow communal 'conversion', largely based on the evangelist's ability to perform signs,[38] but, as we have seen, Luke is far from deprecating a faith that is confirmed and undergirded by signs (indeed Luke is himself criticized by Dunn (*inter alios*) for 'credulity' in this respect),[39] so it is unlikely he considered Philip's miracles a stumbling-block to true faith in Samaria (cf. 9.35).[40] In fact, the comparison of Philip's signs with Simon's, and the account of Simon's jealousy in the face of Peter's ability to bestow the Spirit, are more probably part of a subsidiary redactional theme that Christianity transcends magic, and differs from it in character and motivation. The 'signs' worked by Christians release the afflicted and undergird the message of messianic liberation.[41] In fact, both in v. 6 and in v. 12, Samaritan response is attributed to the impact of the *message heard*, and only secondarily (and then only in v. 6) to signs seen.

Most surprisingly, if he considered Philip's preaching to have missed the mark, Luke does not take the opportunity to tell us that Peter and John corrected the misunderstanding when they arrived, nor that they added significantly to what Philip had said, nor that they needed to explain the way 'more accurately' (contrast 18.26) whether to the Samaritans or to Philip himself.

Luke's view of Philip is fairly clear. He stands out in Acts 6.3, 5 as one in whom Joel's promise is realized in full intensity, and throughout ch. 8 as a successful evangelist acting in the power of and under the guidance of the Spirit, hence the simple but eloquent recognition of him inherent in the description of 21.8, 'Philip, the evangelist'. Rather Luke describes Philip's activity and message in Samaria—and people's response—in exactly the same terms that he elsewhere describes the *apostles*' (successful) ministry,

---

38. For Dunn their response is more like herd-instinct (cf. ὁμοθυμαδόν) than true Christian commitment. But Luke's use of ὁμοθυμαδόν ('with one accord') elsewhere (cf. 1.14; 2.46; 5.12; 12.20; 15.25) does not itself suggest impulsive action (unless this nuance is specifically brought to the sentence by the verb; cf. 7.57 and 19.29), and the description of the Samaritans as 'giving heed... with one accord to what was said by Philip' (8.6) so closely matches what is said of the church in Jerusalem (1.14; 2.46) that it seems intended to emphasize Philip's *success* in Samaria, not the Samaritan failure.

39. *Jesus*, §§30 and 34.

40. Spencer (one of Dunn's own research students), after reviewing Luke's attitude to 'signs' and 'miracles' (*Portrait*, pp. 44-48) concludes, 'it is clear that Luke consistently regards signs and wonders as convincing demonstrations of authentic ministry'; cf. also O'Reilly, *Word*, pp. 216-19.

41. See e.g. Spencer, *Portrait*, pp. 93-103; S. Garrett, *The Demise of the Devil: Magic and the Demonic in Luke's Writing* (Minneapolis: Fortress Press, 1989), pp. 63-65.

and (*contra* Confirmationist explanations) there seems no intrinsic reason why, for example, Ananias (Acts 9) should be able to impart the Spirit but not Philip.

(2) Luke's attitude appears to be *that the Samaritans genuinely believed* the kerygma they heard, and that they *were thus adequately prepared for their baptism* which was properly a baptism εἰς τὸ ὄνομα τοῦ κυρίου Ἰησοῦ ('into the name of the Lord Jesus', 8.16; cf. 19.5).

Luke is most unlikely to have thought the Samaritans' bid for faith could be overshadowed by pressing fears that they might be rejected by the Jerusalem community. In the first place, Luke plays down much of the gulf that lay between Jews and Samaritans, if not quite portraying the latter as positively as Jervell's title 'the lost sheep of the house of Israel' might suggest.[42] Secondly, it is difficult to see how their potential acceptance or rejection by the Jerusalem apostolate could possibly affect their response to the kerygma (the question does not seem to have disturbed either the eunuch [8.36], or the Gentiles, who had more cause to doubt whether they could participate in Israel's blessings). In the final analysis, such considerations cannot throw light on the passage: it is thoroughly obscure why *all* should have been incapacitated by such fears and no easier to understand why *all* should have become fully assured only, but precisely, by the laying on of apostolic hands![43]

Luke chooses to tell us that the apostles heard that 'Samaria had received the Word of God' (8.14) without any suggestion that this was merely an ill-informed report, rather than a fact to be accepted. Elsewhere the same language designates true conversion: compare 11.1 with its explanation in 11.18, and similarly 2.41.

The claim that the Samaritan 'belief' was mere mental assent rather than authentic Christian commitment, and that it was directed to Philip, not to Christ himself, is at best oversubtle. Luke makes no distinction between believing an evangelist and having faith in the God he proclaims: to give heed to the former is to hear the God who speaks through him.[44] Besides,

42. See Jervell, *Luke*, pp. 113-32; but cf. Spencer, *Portrait*, pp. 55-58. If Luke can describe two model Samaritans (Lk. 10.25-37; 17.11-19), he can also describe a Samaritan village that rejects Jesus (9.51-56).

43. *Pace* Dunn, *Baptism*, p. 67. Lampe, *Seal*, p. 70, takes the laying on of hands as granting the right hand of fellowship of the Jerusalem church to Samaria. In view of the parallel at 19.6 this appears improbable, and, as Adler (*Taufe*, pp. 58-75, 81ff.) has shown, the laying on of hands follows prayer for the Spirit (vv. 15, 17) and is primarily to impart it (as Simon saw, vv. 18-19).

44. With the language of 8.12, compare Lydia's conversion (16.14) of whom we are told 'the Lord opened her heart to give heed to what was spoken by Paul' (and cf. 8.6).

Luke's participial construction (ἐπίστευσαν) τῷ Φιλίππῳ εὐαγγελι-ζομένῳ περὶ τῆς βασιλείας (v. 12) emphasizes belief in the message preached, not belief in the preacher, and nothing in Luke's wording hints at mere mental assent (cf. 1[c] and 2[a] above). While we may believe their religious credulity and erstwhile magical inclinations may initially have given the Samaritans a somewhat lopsided faith, Luke must have met similar problems frequently among Gentile converts, but nowhere does he imply the inauthenticity of the faith of those he describes as having believed (cf. Acts 19.18-20).

There is little reason to suspect that Luke doubted Simon Magus was a *bona fide* convert in the same sense as (e.g.) those on the day of Pentecost. (i) Dunn argues that Simon cannot have had true faith, because he did not receive the Spirit. But the latter assumption may well be false,[45]and, the whole argument in any case amounts to *petitio principii*. (ii) Dunn argues Simon's sin indicates he had not been truly converted. This is frequently affirmed, but remains unconvincing. Serious post-conversion sin was not unknown in the church (cf. 1 Cor. 5); indeed, Peter may consider Simon's sin so serious precisely *because* it is committed by a follower of Jesus (cf. Ananias and Sapphira). (iii) Dunn claims the wording of Peter's rebuke confirms that Simon had not moved from his pagan anchorage (8.20-23). But this inference too is unwarranted. The one sin of simony was probably sufficient to justify the strong rebuke of v. 23 that his 'heart is not right before God' and that he 'is in the bond of iniquity', but such language does not mean that he is considered still to *be* a pagan; merely that he is behaving reprehensibly like one, and deserving of God's wrath. The force of Peter's retort 'you have neither part nor lot in this matter' in v. 21a is not that Simon cannot have been (or may not remain) a Christian, but that he assuredly cannot have any part in bestowing God's Spirit,[46] and needs to pray for forgiveness for this very suggestion that such a ministry might be up for sale.[47] Nothing said elsewhere by Luke repudiates the natural force of his statements in 8.13, which are modelled on the description of the

45. Simon quite probably did receive the Spirit (with Barrett, 'Light', p. 291): he asks not for the Spirit, but for the power to bestow it (v. 19).

46. Haenchen (305) has taken v. 21a (οὐκ ἔστιν σοι μερὶς οὐδὲ κλῆρος ἐν τῷ λόγῳ τούτῳ), along with v. 20, as a formula of excommunication (similarly Pesch, I, pp. 276-77). He takes ὁ λόγος as a reference to the 'word' of Christianity. But this leaves the demonstrative adjective τούτῳ ('this') unexplained. The context requires the whole noun phrase be translated 'in this affair', and it is to be understood as referring to the apostles' authority *to bestow the Spirit*, which is specified immediately before-hand as the substance of Simon's request (v. 19).

47. See especially Barrett, 'Light', pp. 294ff. and *passim*.

conversion and discipleship of the three thousand at Pentecost (2.41-42),[48] nor does Luke show any knowledge of the later tradition that Simon was a heresiarch.[49] We are forced to conclude that Luke considered Simon's belief, baptism and initial discipleship, to be as real as anyone else's. His background of magic became the occasion of a lamentable lapse, but such phenomena cannot have been unparalleled in the ancient church—and this instance served Luke's purpose well, for it allowed him to tell a story which implies that the Christian experience of the Spirit transcends the alluring wonders of magic.

In sum, while Luke believed Simon's faith to have been shallow, at the time of his baptism, we have no warrant for thinking he considered it 'inauthentic'—far less for questioning the faith of *all* the remaining Samaritan baptizands. The whole hypothesis that Luke's readers would be expected to understand 8.4-13 as a portrait of *defective* faith in Samaria tumbles on the linguistic and contextual evidence,[50] and then shatters on the observation that it is the laying on of apostolic hands with prayer—not apostolic preaching, exhortation, or explanation—which imparts the Spirit (vv. 15, 17, 18-19). The very implication of the apostle's prayer is that they accept the Samaritan faith as authentic.[51]

48. With J.E.L. Oulton, 'The Holy Spirit and Laying on of Hands', *ExpTim* 66 (1955), p. 238.

49. Against e.g. Haenchen, 307, and C.H. Talbert, *Luke and the Gnostics* (Nashville: Abingdon Press, 1966), pp. 83-97, see e.g. J. Drane, 'Simon the Samaritan and the Lukan Concept of Salvation History', *EvQ* 47 (1975), pp. 131-37; Barrett, 'Light', p. 293; and Spencer, *Portrait*, pp. 90-92.

50. Had Luke wished to signal that there was something wrong with the Samaritans' faith he could readily have written v. 12, 'But when they heard Philip they were baptised, but they did not yet truly believe'. Instead he insists they *did* believe, and were baptised. And once again it needs to be stressed that the problem with all interpretations that rest on the alleged inadequacy of the Samaritan 'faith' is that Luke could readily clarify this e.g. by showing the apostles correcting their misunderstanding (as he does with Apollos at 18.26).

51. The above arguments were arrived at independently by Russell, 'They Believed', pp. 169-76, and Turner, 'Luke and the Spirit', pp. 161-71. They are now broadly confirmed by Menzies, *Development*, pp. 252-57, and Spencer, *Portrait*, pp. 48-53. Interestingly Dunn's response to Russell ('They Believed', pp. 177-83) makes failure to receive the Spirit the major reason for suspecting inauthentic faith in 8.12, and more recently his response to Pentecostal criticisms of his treatment of Acts 8 suggests we eschew speculation as to the reason for the delay altogether (see 'Baptism', pp. 24-25), and concentrate on Luke's main point: that where the Spirit is not given to converts the situation is abnormal and needs immediate rectification. With this last we may wholeheartedly agree.

(C) *The reception of the Spirit in 8.17 as a second gift of the Spirit?* If there was nothing essentially deficient in the Samaritans' conversion and baptism, then we still require some explanation of how Luke can tolerate the separation of conversion from reception of the Spirit in this account. One response is that there was no such separation: in accordance with the norm of Acts 2.38-39 the Samaritans received the definitive gift of the Spirit at their baptism; 8.17 merely describes a further experience they received of special charismatic endowment.[52] Perhaps the best known advocate of this position is G.R. Beasley-Murray who (tentatively) argues (1) that on the basis of the New Testament understanding of the Spirit in general, and Acts 2.38-39 in particular, the separation between water baptism and receiving of the distinctive Christian experience of the Spirit is an impossible abstraction; (2) the force of this is particularly felt when it is noted how richly blessed by the Spirit Philip's ministry is, and how the fruit of the Spirit—joy—is already widespread in Samaria (8.8); and (3) the anarthrous use of πνεῦμα ἅγιον at 8.15 may imply that what was lacking was the spiritual *gifts*, not the Spirit himself.[53]

We have seen, however, that considerable difficulties attend this last distinction,[54] and, in any case, it cannot be made to depend on the absence of the definite article.[55] Nor does the mention of 'much joy in the city' imply reception of the gift of the Spirit by the Samaritans; rather the joy of which Luke speaks he attributes to the effect of Philip's exorcisms and healings. Such joy is frequently mentioned as the response to God's various saving acts throughout Luke's two works (cf. esp. Lk. 13.17; 19.37). Beasley-Murray's first argument is no more secure. The gift apparently promised at 'conversion' in Acts 2.38-39 is the 'Spirit of prophecy' which is itself the 'charismatic Spirit', while Beasley-Murray rightly claims the Samaritans receive charismata only at 8.17, clearly subsequent to their baptism. Acts 2.38-39 can thus hardly be made the guarantee of a non-charismatic gift of the Spirit which automatically attaches to baptism. On the contrary, the evidence suggests that Luke understood the gift imparted by the laying on of

52. Varying forms of this position have been taken from the time of Chrysostom who (in his eighteenth homily on Acts) distinguished between a 'Spirit of forgiveness' bestowed by Philip's baptism and the 'Spirit of signs' which had not yet come upon them. Calvin was similarly to distinguish the common (regenerating) grace of the Spirit imparted to the Samaritans in their baptism, and 'the singular gifts... the visible presence of the Spirit' conveyed to them by the apostles.

53. *Baptism*, pp. 118-19. Similarly, Gourgues ('Esprit', pp. 376-85) with the emphasis that a Pentecost-like dramatic outpouring of the Spirit is needed to confirm and legitimate Philip's beginnings.

54. See Chapter 2 §1.

55. Dunn, *Baptism*, pp. 68-70.

hands (8.17-18) in parallel to the occasion of Pentecost, and thus he understood the promise of Acts 2.38-39 to be fulfilled only after the arrival of the apostles and not as expected (cf. οὐδέπω) at the Samaritans' baptism. As for the apostles (2.1-13), the Cornelius household and the Ephesian disciples, reception of the gift was a matter of immediate perception, corporate, plainly visible to observers, and sufficiently spectacular to provoke the lascivious response of Simon, when Philip's miracles had merely impressed him. Quite plainly Luke envisages an event as dramatic as that at Cornelius's house or Ephesus (and not surprisingly many have inferred an outburst of tongues and prophecy such as at 2.4; 10.46 and 19.6).[56] This is confirmed by Luke's terminology at 8.16, where he states that the Spirit 'had not yet fallen (ἐπιπεπτωκός) upon any of them'. This expression—the 'violence' of which Calvin, Lenski and Parratt rightly surmised as inappropriate of the more gentle and inward conversion grace—is not found outside Acts, but is very closely parallelled at 11.15 (cf. 10.44), that is, precisely in the speech Luke attributes to Peter describing Cornelius's 'Pentecost'. The promise of 2.38 is thus met at 8.17, not at the Samaritan's baptism. Neither Acts 2.38, nor any other passage in Acts, speaks of a 'gift of the Spirit' to Christians after Jesus' ascension *except* the one gift of the 'Spirit of prophecy' promised by Joel.[57] Hence Luke's unequivocal statements that the Spirit 'had *not* yet fallen on any of them' (8.16b) and that through the laying on of apostolic hands with prayer they 'received' the Spirit (8.17-19)—such statements do not suggest he considered the definitive gift of the Spirit had indeed already been granted at their baptism.

Whatever may be said for or against harmonizing Luke's pneumatology into a two-stage model at the level of biblical and systematic theology (with the Spirit received in conversion seen as bringing Johannine 'new birth' and Pauline 'new covenant life' and a second experience of the Spirit bringing Lukan 'empowering'), *Luke* does not know of two such separate 'receptions' of '(the gift) of the Spirit' in any individual (though he may well have anticipated the Spirit regularly 'filled' believers subsequent to their receiving the gift). For him, Acts 8.17 describes the Samaritans' first and only reception of 'the promise of the Spirit'.

(D) *Acts 8 as a Hellenistic-Pauline conversion-initiation pattern?* Quesnel has recently attempted to show that in Acts, Luke preserves two historically distinct initiation paradigms.[58] There was an older one modelled on a

---

56. See e.g. Menzies, *Development*, p. 258 n. 2, for a convenient list of those advancing the view.

57. With Haya-Prats, *L'Esprit*, p. 87; Menzies, *Development, passim*.

58. Quesnel, *L'Esprit, passim*. B.E. Thiering also attempts a historical explanation

Christian development of John the Baptist's: this was a baptism ἐπί (upon) or ἐν (in) 'the name of Jesus Christ', stipulated as 'for the forgiveness of sins', and understood to lead directly to receipt of the Spirit (2.38 and 10.48). But Luke was also aware of a second quite different Hellenistic-Pauline rite of baptism εἰς ('into') '(the name of) the Lord Jesus', witnessed in the epistles. Here the preposition meant something like 'into union with', and in Paul's own day this baptism was not directly associated with bestowal of the Spirit of prophecy. According to Quesnel, the Hellenists (and Paul) were actually cautious of the 'Spirit of prophecy', and it was for precisely this reason that they developed their rite centred on union with the death of Jesus, without either invocation of the Spirit or expectation of the receipt of the charismatic Spirit. These last were only added in a post-Pauline and pre-Lukan stage,[59] and it is the memory of this harmonising tradition that Luke preserves both at 8.16 and 19.6. On Quesnel's view one might 'explain' Acts 8.12-17 in terms of Luke's faithfulness (if anachronistic!) to the alternative practice which he has split between Philip and the apostles.

But while Quesnel may be right that the εἰς + personal name was originally a Hellenistic expression meaning 'into union with', there is little reason to believe anyone before Paul spoke of a baptism 'into union with' Christ's death,[60] nor that such a move was precipitated by any diminished interest in conversion-initiation as leading to the promise of the Spirit (certainly not for Paul).[61] Nor can Acts 8.12-17 easily be correlated with this allegedly Hellenistic-Pauline type of initiation as such. On Luke's view Peter and John would have been foundational representatives of the earlier Jewish paradigm signalled in Acts 2 (and, ironically, the one Quesnel believes Luke himself came to embrace). Philip, even if a Hellenist, belonged to the same mother church, and was a man richly endowed by the 'Spirit of prophecy'. Luke was thus not liable to present him as one prone to use a baptismal pattern developed out of suspicions of the charismatic Spirit, or one which deferred the Spirit from baptism by days or weeks (and there is no such delay at 19.5-6). It is more likely that Luke uses the form 'into the name of the Lord Jesus' simply as a stylistic variant for 'upon/in the name of Jesus Christ', without any awareness of differences of origin, while the other

---

based on a different baptismal paradigm (in this case drawing on Qumran parallels, see 'Inner and Outer Cleansing at Qumran as a Background to New Testament Baptism', *NTS* 26 [1980], pp. 266-77), but see the criticism by Menzies, *Development*, pp. 257-58.

59. *L'Esprit*, ch. 7 (esp. §7.6).

60. See Wedderburn, *Baptism*, pp. 54-60.

61. *Per contra*, the charismatic Spirit was central to his theology (see Fee, *Presence*, *passim*).

parallels between the Samaritan and Ephesian incidents are better explained on other hypotheses.[62]

(E) *A narrative-critical solution?* F.S. Spencer elucidates the story of Acts 8.4-24 in terms of a wider Philip-Peter forerunner-culminator (co-operative) relationship modelled on the John/Jesus relationship in Luke (and parallelled by an Apollos-Paul relationship in Acts 18-19).[63] The comparison between these tandems in Acts and the John/Jesus relationship in the Gospel is, of course, a little suspect, for the latter two stand in a promise–fulfilment relationship that straddles the division between the time of the Law and the prophets and the time of fulfilment. No such divide accounts for the relationships between Philip and Peter or between Apollos and Paul, and so there is no reason why Philip and Apollos should be confined to baptising with water.[64] And as Spencer does not press the paradigm to the point of suggesting the need for apostolic 'culminators' systematically to complete Philip's work (and Apollos') with the decisive gift of the Spirit, it becomes clear that 'forerunner-culminator' typology provides more of a literary *description* of the narrative structure than it does an *explanation* of why the Spirit is not conferred within Philip's ministry to the Samaritans.[65]

(F) *The gift of the Spirit in Acts 8.17 as donum superadditum of empowering for mission?* At this point, the explanatory power of the Pentecostal model as advocated by Stronstad, Shelton and Menzies becomes especially

---

62. See F.R. Harm, 'Structural Elements related to the Gift of the Spirit in Acts', *Concordia Journal* 14 (1988), pp. 28-41 (esp. pp. 35-38) for a consideration of these.

63. *Portrait*, pp. 211-41.

64. Kim takes Philip and Apollos as ciphers for a spreading non charismatic Markan(?) Christianity that has, but cannot convey, the Spirit. Luke seeks to bring such churches back into the power of the Spirit (*Geisttaufe*, pp. 171-86 and 208-38). But this is entirely speculative, and would be much more convincing of Apollos than of Philip, who is evidently not merely a man who has the Spirit but a remarkable charismatic in the image of the Apostles themselves.

65. Similarly, Shepherd passes by at a safe distance the attempt at explanation with the claim that Luke is not interested in providing a theology of the relation of Spirit-reception to conversion, but with other narrative interests and strategies: namely, the succession of prophetic powers, the validation of the Samaritan mission prophesied by Jesus (1.8), the linking of key steps to the apostles, and the superiority of the charismatic Spirit to magic (*Function*, pp. 178-84). While not wishing to deny these interests, the antithesis between narrative and theology is overpressed (esp. pp. 23-26: see Wright, *Testament*, esp. chs. 3, 5 and 13 for a healthy antidote), and Shepherd himself concedes that Luke 'shows' his theology rather than 'telling' it (*Function*, pp. 33-35, adopting the very position he criticizes in Fitzmyer as a wrong-headed attempt to distil systematic theology from narrative). So the question, 'What theology of conversion and Spirit-reception is "shown" here?', cannot so easily be side-stepped.

inviting. This model does not have the problem inherent in Confirmationist models of trying to distinguish what level of activity of the Spirit is granted to baptism, and which to the 'strengthening' by the Spirit that comes with confirmation (nor of explaining why the confirmation gift is treated as the single definitive gift by Luke). It posits that 'the promise/gift of the Spirit' denotes a distinct set of activities of the Spirit—the activities of the 'Spirit of prophecy' fuelling mission. If the gift of the Spirit is essentially a charismatic empowering for such a distinct nexus of activities, then there is no problem with this coming as an experience separate from conversional baptism. But the view faces three important problems.

First, nothing in the passage itself specifically connects the gift of the Spirit to mission. No unbelieving bystanders watch and ask 'What does this mean?'; nor is it said that any of the people involved went out to preach or to witness to Christ. Lampe, Coppens and Menzies have each argued that the laying on of hands (8.17, 18 and 19.6) is an 'ordination' for the missionary task,[66] and that this identifies the nature of the gift of the Spirit imparted; but this suggestion is unconvincing, for there is no evidence in the context to connect the symbolic act with the hands to any kind of commissioning (e.g. for the life of service to Christ), far less a commissioning as specific as 'ordination for *mission*'.

There are basically three different potentially relevant paradigms for laying on of hands in the New Testament period: (1) simple transfer of power (e.g. for healing; esp. also of 'touch');[67] (2) invocatory prayer (e.g. for healing [perhaps mixed with (1), cf. Acts 28.8] and/or blessing);[68] and (3) identification, representation and legal or quasi-legal transfer of authority (e.g. ordination of a student by a rabbinical school, recognizing him as a qualified representative of the school's position).[69] The notion of 'commissioning' rests on the third paradigm, and can be found in Acts at 6.6 (of the seven to oversee the charitable distribution), 13.3 (of Paul and Barnabas by the Antioch church), 14.23 (of elders by Paul). But in 8.16-19 and 19.6 there is no suggestion of transfer of legal authority or the 'right of

---

66. Lampe, *Seal*, pp. 70-78; J. Coppens, 'L'Imposition des mains dans les Actes des Apôtres', in Kremer (ed.), *Actes*, pp. 405-38; Menzies, *Development*, pp. 259-60, 276. I have noted above that Lampe also equates this laying on of hands with the granting of the right hand of fellowship; but the two symbolic acts are quite different.

67. Mt. 9.18; Mk 5.23; 6.5; 7.32; 8.23, 25; Lk. 4.40; Acts 9.12, 17.

68. Cf. Mt. 19.13, 15; Mk 10.16.

69. For the background to this see above all J. Behm, *Die Handauflegung im Urchristentum nach Verwendung, Herkunft und Bedeutung im religionsgeschichtl. Zusammenhang untersucht* (Leipzig, 1911), and J. Coppens, *L'Imposition des mains et les rites connexes dans le Nouveau Testament et dans l'église ancienne* (Paris: Cerf, 1925).

representation' from the apostles to the new converts, and so the central aspect of paradigm (3) as applied to ordination or commissioning for mission is missing. The laying on of hands which transfers the Spirit here (and 19.6) rather quite transparently conforms to paradigms (1) and (2), but not (3),[70] and Simon Magus's response confirms that he perceived the former of these as the central one.

Lampe, Stronstad and Menzies also appeals to 9.31 (Luke's summary of the growth of the church in Samaria and elsewhere) as a hint that the gift of the Spirit in 8.17 is empowerment for mission,[71] but 9.31 is a long way from 8.14-17, and hardly sufficiently specific as to demonstrate that the gift is exclusively or even primarily bound to giving witness: Luke may well have thought the Spirit, who gives many gifts for many different ends, raised up some to be evangelists (like Philip and Stephen) in Judea, Galilee and Samaria (just as the Spirit raises up overseers in 20.28); and he may have thought a charismatically endowed and holy church also naturally attracted converts—but there is no evidence he restricts the gift in 8.17 specifically to empowerment for mission, or to give spoken testimony.

Secondly, this view of the gift of the Spirit focuses too narrowly on the missiological purpose of the gift of the Spirit. While this is undoubtedly a cardinal aspect of Luke's view of the Spirit, we shall see that he thinks of the charismatic Spirit as of great significance in the life of the church too (see Chapter 13); indeed it is difficult to perceive how Luke would envisage 'salvation' as an ongoing experience in the church without this gift.

Thirdly, the view that the gift of the Spirit is primarily or exclusively missionary empowering could well explain why the gift was granted some time after initial faith expressed in baptism, for that is precisely what we should expect of such an empowering. But by the same token such an explanation fails to explain the norm of Acts 2.38-39 (and everywhere else in Acts) where Spirit-reception is tightly linked with conversion and baptism, a norm which is itself presupposed in 8.16.

(G) *Interim conclusion on the gift of the Spirit in 8.17.* From the narrator's point of view there was nothing intrinsically wrong with the 'quality' of the Samaritan baptizands' faith or baptism in 8.4-13. Yet from the writer's perspective (and in the view he implicitly attributed to the visiting apostles) they had surprisingly 'not yet' received the Spirit. If we ask *how* the apostles were expected to reach this conclusion, the answer readiest to hand is that the 'Spirit of prophecy' had not yet been manifest among the

---

70. At 19.6 the laying on of hands may also convey the notion of identification and solidarity at the admission of believers to the church, but that is only a possibility, and not one in any way suggested in 8.16-19.

71. Lampe, *Seal*, p. 72; Stronstad, *Theology*, p. 65; Menzies, *Development*, p. 260.

disciples in the kinds of charismata the writer expected to characterize possession of this gift (and which apparently did become manifest when the apostles prayed and laid their hands on the Samaritans, 8.18). If we ask *why* the Spirit was suspended from baptism, a satisfactory answer is much more difficult to obtain. The view that the gift envisaged in 8.17 is simply an empowerment for mission (and thus readily separable from conversion) finds no support in the text, and (like other forms of second grace explanation) fails to explain why even 8.16 assumes the norm of 2.38-39. In the final analysis Luke does not articulate an explanation of why the Samaritan believers did not receive the Spirit earlier. It is possible he believed God sovereignly withheld the Spirit until the leaders of the Jerusalem Church could approve and seal this first (and in principle extremely important) extension of salvation beyond Judaism (contrast the Ethiopian who was already a proselyte, but compare the next, and even more significant, leap with the Cornelius incident). The very success of Philip's ministry among the Samaritans, with God's approval indicated in the signs performed, would provide the basis for the apostles' confident expectation that God would indeed confirm the acceptance of these 'lost sheep of the house of Israel' by granting the gift of the Spirit for which they prayed.

For Beasley-Murray and for Dunn this separation of faith and baptism from the gift of the Spirit is not merely anomalous, but highly problematic; an 'impossible abstraction'. But why should such delay be considered so inconceivable to Luke? He himself knows the apostles themselves experienced 'salvation' through Jesus' Spirit-empowered ministry before the resurrection, and he also tells of a period of some 'forty' days of post-resurrection enjoyment of meals with and instruction by Jesus, yet still without their receiving the Spirit. Beyond that he recounts a further ten days between Jesus' ascension and Pentecost. For Luke, this last was not an inexplicable 'low' period of the absence of salvation for them, but one of consolidation and prayerful preparation for the next (and deepening) phase of that salvation. Luke might readily enough perceive a parallel in the Samaritan situation. Philip, empowered by the Spirit, has brought them the same 'beginnings' of salvation, and they have been united to the Israel of fulfilment by faith in Israel's messiah and by expressing this in baptism 'in the name of the Lord Jesus', the distinguishing marks of the messianic congregation (cf. 2.36, 38). And it is not as though they are without any presence of the Spirit in their congregation, for the *pneumatiker*, Philip, remains with them, and instructs them, and continues to work amazing signs among them (8.13). While the separation of baptism from their Spirit-reception may be regarded by Luke as anomalous, it is thus not necessarily seen by him as 'problematic'. At least, not while Philip remains present and the time-span involved remains relatively short. It would only have become problematic were Philip to have left these converts, and were the 'Spirit of prophecy' not to have come to them to continue and deepen that experience of salvation, so that these former lost sheep of Israel might too become part of the 'light to the nations'.

2.3. *Acts 9.10-19: Paul's Commissioning and Reception of the Spirit*

At Damascus, according to this account, Ananias was led by a vision to Paul and stated that he has been sent 'that you might receive your sight and be filled with the Holy Spirit (ὅπως ἀναβλέψῃς καὶ πλησθῇς πνεύματος ἁγίου)'. A traditional Pentecostal position (defended recently by Ervin)[72] argues 9.17 must refer to Paul's 'baptism in the Spirit', because he is already fully converted either in the Damascus Road event itself (where he acknowledges Jesus as 'Lord' [9.5]) or at least immediately after it (and so before Ananias comes to him). This, however, is an over-simplification.[73] The fact that Paul addresses the theophanic figure who appears to him on the Damascus Road with the title 'Lord' is only marginally relevant to the question of when Paul formally became a disciple. What else would a Jew call a heavenly figure who appeared to him? (The immediately preceding 'Who are you' indicates Paul's 'Lord' is no christological confession!) The point remains, however, that while we may allow (with Ervin) that Paul had probably come to christological faith through reflection on this theophanic experience before Ananias came to him, his conversional *commitment* was yet to be formalised in baptism.[74] As Dunn observes, Paul only *completes* his conversion-initiation when he submits to Ananias's direction (narrated in Acts 22.16) that he should now be baptized, wash away his sins, and call on the name of the Lord.[75] So we do not find in this narrative an instance of reception of the Spirit that is clearly subsequent to some conversion-initiation complex.

72. *Conversion-Initiation*, pp. 41-50.

73. Ervin's additional argument that Ananias assumes Paul to be a Christian when he addresses him as 'brother' (*Spirit-Baptism*, p. 76) is of little help; for so would a Jew regularly address any fellow Jew (and Christian Jews address unbelieving Jews in this way at Acts 2.29; 3.17; 7.2; 13.26; 22.1; 23.1, 6; 28.17). Aware of this (see *Conversion-Initiation*, pp. 46-48), Ervin curiously attempts to argue that these cases, which are all plural, do not inform our understanding of the use in the singular: determinative, rather, is 21.20, where James clearly means 'brother Christian' (rather than 'brother Jew') when he addresses Paul, ἀδελφέ. Ervin misses the point that such an address is simply *ambiguous*, that its sense in each case must be determined from *context*, and thus that it cannot be used to settle the question of Paul's conversion-initiation 'status' at 9.17.

74. Ervin (*Conversion-Initiation*, pp. 42-44) is right to argue the theophanic context requires for κύριε more than the sense 'sir', and that Paul's psychological 'conversion' would probably have been complete before Ananias came to him.

75. Dunn, *Baptism*, pp. 73-78.

A quite different, yet still essentially classical Pentecostal approach to the passage is made by Menzies.[76] He argues that Acts 9.1-19 (especially vv. 13-17) functions as a commissioning account, and that within it the Spirit is portrayed as an empowering for mission. This builds on much firmer ground, for Form-Critically this passage (and the related traditions in 22.4-16; 26.12-18)[77] has strong similarities with Old Testament prophetic commissionings.[78] While the Damascus Road accounts certainly relate Paul's conversion, the focus of 9.13-16 is primarily on Paul's calling as Christ's missionary representative, and this is the passage which immediately precedes mention of the gift of the Spirit.[79]

It is within the general context of this whole conversion-and-calling process that Paul's healing and reception of the Spirit is anticipated according to 9.17. But the significance of the laying on of hands and the precise timing of Paul's being filled with the Spirit remain unclear. From the perspective of 9.12, the laying on of hands is intended purely to convey the Lord's healing; that is, it is part of the regular paraphernalia of healing miracles. One would then surmise the following order of events: first Ananias lays hands on Paul for healing (9.12, 18);[80] subsequently Paul is baptized and takes food (9.18)—with the assumption that Paul receives the Spirit either at or immediately beyond the water rite (in accordance with the paradigm set forth in 2.38).[81]

But ascertaining Luke's intention is complicated by the wording of 9.17.

---

76. Menzies, *Development*, pp. 260-63.

77. On the relation of these accounts, see e.g. K. Löning, *Die Saulustradition in der Apostelgeschichte* (Münster: Aschendorff, 1973), ch. 1; G. Lohfink, *The Conversion of Saint Paul* (Chicago: Franciscan Herald Press, 1976); and C.W. Hedrick, 'Paul's Conversion/ Call: A Comparative Analysis of the Three Reports in Acts', *JBL* 100 (1981), pp. 415-32.

78. See especially Munck, *Paul*, pp. 25-35, and compare T.Y. Mullins, 'New Testament Commission Forms, Especially in Luke–Acts', *JBL* 95 (1976), pp. 603-14; B.J. Hubbard, 'Commissioning Stories in Luke–Acts: A Study of Their Antecedents, Form and Content', *Semeia* 8 (1977), pp. 103-26, and Hedrick, 'Paul's Conversion/ Call', pp. 415-32.

79. There is keen debate as to when 9.13-16 entered the tradition. Löning argues most of the material in these had already been added at the pre-Lukan stage to an earlier simple account of Paul's conversion and healing (and that Luke himself added the references to Paul's missionary activity, baptism and being filled with the Spirit in 9.17-18, 20 [*Saulustradition*, pp. 25-48, 114-15]). Burchard, *Zeuge*, Hedrick, 'Paul's Conversion/Call', pp. 415-32, and Lüdemann, *Christianity*, pp. 106-16 consider vv. 13-16 as redactional.

80. So R.F. O'Toole, 'Christian Baptism in Luke', *RevRel* 39 (1980), pp. 855-66 (esp. p. 862).

81. So Dunn, *Baptism*, p. 78.

Here, laying hands on Paul, Ananias claims 'the Lord has sent me…that you may receive your sight and be filled with the Holy Spirit'. Taken with the specific reference to Paul's calling in 9.14-16, and the immediately following account of Paul's preaching (cf. καὶ εὐθέως, 9.20), this has suggested to some that Ananias's laying on of hands constitutes a kind of ordination, or commissioning, of Paul, and was intended to impart the filling of the Spirit that would enable Paul to fulfil the call.[82]

This last suggestion, however, is improbable. We may be fairly sure the clause καὶ πλησθῇς πνεύματος ἁγίου ('that you might be filled with the Holy Spirit') is Lukan; for it is his distinctive vocabulary, even if the sense is slightly unusual.[83] But if Luke has added this to the tradition he must have been fully aware that the element of laying on of hands in the story before him was *simply for healing* (both in 9.17 and 9.12). It is difficult then to believe that he expected his readers to see in the laying on of hands some triple significance—the prayerful conveying of God's healing power + an act of ordination + the conveying of the Spirit. While the first and last of these might readily enough be combined, the notion of laying on of hands as an act of ordination remains as foreign to this context as it is in 8.17 and 19.5-6. But did Luke understand Ananias's laying on of hands to impart God's healing power and the gift of the Spirit, or the healing alone? That question is slightly more difficult to answer, but one consideration strongly favours the latter. While he actually recounts the specific phenomena of the healing itself (9.18a), Luke makes no mention of the inception of the Spirit nor of the manifestation of any of its prototypical charismata (we might have expected glossolalia here as much as anywhere else in Acts [cf. 1 Cor. 14.18]). We should probably therefore conclude that the laying on of hands in 9.17 (as at 9.12) was for healing alone, and that, with his sight restored, Paul was also baptized by Ananias and consequently received the Spirit (in accordance with the norm of Acts 2.38). In short, Ananias's words in 9.17c explain not merely his laying on of hands, but his whole commission, which will extend from this immediate restoring of his sight through to his later reception of the Spirit.

What does the passage tell us about Luke's view of Paul's conversion-initiation reception of the Spirit? The clause πλησθῇς πνεύματος ἁγίου ('so that you may be filled with the Holy Spirit') does not correspond to

---

82. So Lampe, *Seal*; Bruce, 239; Stronstad, *Theology*, pp. 65-66; Menzies, *Development*, pp. 262-63; and Shelton, *Word*, p. 131 (though Shelton allows the possibility of Lukan double-entendre, and that the Spirit is given for soteriological functions as well as for witness).

83. The aorist indicative of πίμπλημι would normally be used by Luke to denote an event of short duration, the inspiration of a specific event of charisma, while here the aorist subjunctive has ingressive and even constative value.

Luke's ordinary conversion-initiation language. He does not think all Christians are 'full of the Spirit'. As we have seen, such language (in the indicative) would usually refer to some immediate inspiration; but it would be banal to take it so here, as if Ananias were merely promising some invasive charismatic manifestation at the moment of Paul's reception of the Spirit. It seems rather that this language is intended to prepare for Luke's picture of Paul's ministry as one in which the Spirit's activity was especially strong. Like John the Baptist from his birth (Lk.1.15), and Jesus from his baptism (Lk. 4.1, 14), Paul is to experience fullness of Spirit throughout his missionary, teaching and pastoral ministry. In the context of 9.15 the expression thus designates the Spirit as the power to fulfil the commission he has just received as Christ's witness, that is, as an unusually intense presence of the Pentecostal gift of the 'Spirit of prophecy' as an empowering for mission, just as is the case with the circle of Jesus' own disciples at Lk. 24.46-49 and Acts 1.8. But as Shelton astutely observed, that does not mean the gift of the Spirit to Paul is necessarily this alone. His reception of the gift within the context of conversion-initiation suggests a broader understanding which we shall explore later.

2.4. *Acts 10.34-48, 11.11-18 and 15.7-11: Cornelius and other Gentiles Receive the Spirit*

The Cornelius episode is in a sense the crux both of the mission in Acts[84] and of its ecclesiology. The admission of Cornelius's household to baptism by one of the pillar apostles (without prior circumcision and commitment to the Torah) in principle redefines the nature of 'the people of God', who are thereby no longer simply the Torah-centred Israel of fulfilment, but some transformation of Israel.[85]

EXCURSUS: TRADITION AND REDACTION IN THE CORNELIUS NARRATIVES

There is little critical agreement on the issues of tradition and redaction.[86] The most perceptive account to date is provided by F. Bovon who distinguishes two main traditions underlying these chapters,

---

84. Cf. Wilson's verdict 'No other narrative in Acts is given quite such epic treatment as the Cornelius episode... It is the test-case *par excellence* for the admission of the Gentiles into the Church' (*Gentiles*, p. 177).

85. See Chapter 10 §3.2 above. Cf. E. Haulotte, 'Fondation d'une communauté de type universel: Actes 10,1-11,18. Etude critique sur la rédaction, la "structure" et la "tradition" du récit', *RechSR* 58 (1970), pp. 63-100.

86. For Dibelius (*Studies*, pp. 109-22) and Conzelmann, all the parts of Acts 10–11 which raise matters of principle are Lukan redaction (including all of 11.1-18); the only traditional material Luke had available was a theologically harmless story about the conversion of a pious Gentile God-

(1) An account of the conversion of a pious Roman centurion consisting of an initial vision (10.1-8); the Spirit's command to Peter to go with Cornelius's messengers (10.19b-20); Peter's arrival in Caesarea (roughly 10.24-33, but omitting the Lukan mention of Peter's vision 27-29a); the interruption of Peter's attempt to speak by the descent of the Spirit, and the consequent admission of Cornelius to baptism without further condition (10.34a, 44-48 [the content of the speech is excluded as Lukan]).[87]

(2) An etiological story about how the community came to abandon the food purity laws, and to allow mixed table-fellowship between Jewish and Gentile Christians through a vision granted to Peter, abrogating the distinction of clean and unclean foods (parts of 10.9-17a, or, in a fuller version, most of 11.2-10). Bovon thinks such a vision would explain Peter's erstwhile freedom (and that of the other Antiochene Christians) in such matters at Antioch (Gal. 2.11-12).

But this conjecture rests on the assumption that Peter's vision should be taken as having a simple literal reference, rather than being puzzling and parabolic as Luke understands it (cf. 10.17, 19a).[88] Nor, historically, does it make much sense to interpret the vision as a straightforward literal divine abrogation of the laws of purity. Had that been the clear import of Peter's vision, and had his vision become widely accepted through its incorporation in an etiological story such as Bovon suggests, it would be all the more difficult to understand the reversal of Gal. 2.11-14, and the widespread ongoing concern for matters of food-purity Jewish Christian circles reflected in both Acts and the Epistles. This is, of course, why so many commentators have found it impossible to credit such a vision and interpretation to the historical Peter. But if we once admit that the vision is enigmatic, with the intended reference of its symbolism unstated (and so unclear), then we can understand how its implications for both the literal question of food purity and for the associated question of the 'purity' of people would need to be interpreted with care, and could be subject both to dispute and to revision. In this instance, of course, there is a fairly close relationship between the elements of the vision (erstwhile unclean *foods* declared clean) and the referent the narrative supplies (erstwhile 'unclean' *people* declared 'clean'); for it was prototypically (not exclusively) their eating of unclean foods that made Gentiles and their homes 'unclean', and a threat to religiously observant Jews.[89]

fearer and a story of a vision pertaining to the question of clean and unclean foods (which nevertheless came from a different historical context). W.C. Van Unnik saw this story as an indication of a type of Christianity which existed between the earliest Jewish Christianity and the later Pauline Gentile Christianity; namely one which dispensed with the need for circumcision and the purity laws, and recognized an enlarged 'Israel' including not merely believing Jews but also pious and virtuous Gentile believers ('De achtergrond en betekenis van Handelingen 10:4 en 35', *NedThT* 3 [1948-49], pp. 260-83 and 336-54, as described in F. Bovon, 'Tradition et rédaction en Actes 10.1–11,18', *L'Oeuvre de Luc*, p. 103). Haenchen, however, has rightly questioned whether such stories could ever have been *un*controversial, if they pertained to the admission of the *un*circumcised to the church/Israel of fulfilment (cf. 11.3).

87. Though Bovon ('Tradition', pp. 113-17) thinks it contains some traditional material.

88. See Wilson, *Gentiles*, p. 174: note Lüdemann (*Christianity*, pp. 127, 130-31), is forced to argue Luke himself artificially created this enigmatic character to adapt the vision to his story. This overlooks the fact that in Judaism most (?) visions were enigmatic, and required careful interpretation.

89. Cf. Wilson, *Gentiles*, pp. 174-76; Marshall, 180-82.

This observation shows how naturally the vision fits the context Acts sets it in, where the dual problem of shared hospitality/table-fellowship with Gentiles and Gentile inclusion in God's people are both live issues (for the former see 10.20, 23, 28, 48b; 11.3, 12; for the latter see 10.47-48; 11.14, 17-18).

In Luke's view, however, it is above all God himself who impels the church to take this decisive step, and his Spirit who legitimates it at each stage (10.19-20, 44-48; 11.12, 15-18; 15.8-9), while Peter and the Jewish Christian church are in different degrees reluctant partners.[90] But what light do these passages throw on the nature of the gift of the Spirit granted to believers? On one point there is almost universal agreement: Luke describes the Cornelius event in such a way as to draw out the parallels with Acts 2, and so to depict a 'Gentile Pentecost'.[91] The important uniting factors include:

1. The common but distinctive language: 10.45 speaks of 'the gift of the Holy Spirit' (cf. 2.38-39, 11.17 and these alone) 'poured out upon' the Gentiles (cf. Joel 3.1 = Acts 2.17-18, 33, and no other instances);[92] 11.16 describes Cornelius's experience as a fulfilment of Jesus' logion 'you will be baptised with the Holy Spirit', but this description is not evoked anywhere else except at 1.5 anticipating Pentecost.

2. The common experience. Both occasions consist of a dramatic irruption of the Spirit (more so than 19.6) immediately manifest in glossolalic praise (unlike Samaria?).[93]

3. The specific comparison drawn by the apostles: cf. 10.47 '(they received the Spirit) as we did'; 11.15 '(the Spirit fell upon them) as upon us at the beginning'; 11.17 'God gave them the same gift as

90. Compare e.g. Haenchen, 362; Wilson, *Gentiles*, p. 177; Tannehill, *Narrative Unity*, II, pp. 128-45; and Squires, *Plan*, pp. 116-19.

91. See especially Kremer, *Pfingstbericht*, pp. 191-97; Haya-Prats, *L'Esprit*, pp. 180-82, 189-92 and 215-17; but also Stronstad, *Theology*, p. 67; Tannehill, *Narrative Unity*, II, p. 142; E. Richard, 'Pentecost as a Recurrent Theme in Luke–Acts', in E. Richard (ed.), *New Views on Luke and Acts* (Collegeville, MN: Liturgical Press, 1990), pp. 133-49, 181-83 (esp. 137-39); Menzies, *Development*, p. 267; D. Schneider, *Der Geist, der Geschichte macht* (Neukirchen: Aussaat, 1992), pp. 43-46, etc.

92. Two different but strongly related verbs are used (ἐκχέω and ἐκχύννομαι [a Hellenistic form of the former]).

93. Pentecost is admittedly the more dramatic, Caesarea having no corresponding noise or tongues of fire; and the Cornelius episode does not envisage *xenolalia* (it is not a matter of 'other' tongues, and so foreign languages here or at 19.6; see Menzies, *Development*, p. 265, for those who have noted this). Luke's description affords another mild linguistic parallel in that the charismatic doxology of Pentecost announces the μεγαλεῖα ('greatnesses') of God, while 10.46 uses a semantically related verb to assert they were 'magnifying' God (μεγαλυνόντων).

he gave us...'; 15.8 'God bore witness to them giving them the Holy Spirit, just as he did to us'.

It follows that the gift of the Spirit to Cornelius's household is the 'Spirit of prophecy' promised by Joel and fulfilled through the Christ-event at Pentecost. But is it then just a *donum superadditum* to enable 'the prophetic band in Caesarea' to participate effectively 'in the missionary enterprise', as Menzies maintains (while admitting there is no direct evidence for this)?[94] Or does the passage suggest that the gift of the Spirit enables these Gentiles to experience forgiveness and to enter salvation, as Dunn argues?[95] Menzies rather too easily assumes that if the Spirit is the Spirit of prophecy it cannot have soteriological import too, but this is in danger of *petitio principii*.[96]

Dunn presents essentially three points. (1) Cornelius receives the Spirit immediately after hearing Peter speak of God's forgiveness (10.43-44), and therefore, by implication, the Spirit 'was not something additional to God's acceptance and forgiveness, but constituted that acceptance and forgiveness' which Cornelius sought.[97] (2) The sentence in 11.18 ('Then God has given even to the Gentiles the repentance that leads to life') should be interpreted in the light of the 'parallel' statement in 11.17 ('God gave them the same gift that he gave us'): that is the gift of the Spirit is the gift of repentance that leads to life.[98] (3) The affirmation in 15.9, that God did not distinguish between Jews and Gentiles 'cleansing their hearts by faith' too, is equivalent to and clarifies the preceding description (15.8) that 'God, who knows the human heart, bore witness to them by giving them the Holy Spirit'.[99]

Unfortunately these arguments fall just short of proof at each stage: (1) What Cornelius received was the 'Spirit of prophecy' evinced in

94. *Development*, p. 267. The glossolalia at 10.46 are invasive charismatic praise and no unbelievers hear them. For Shelton (*Word*, p. 133), 'Spirit-inspired witness dominates [Luke's] thoughts' here; but if that is so it is only the attestation which the display of the charismatic Spirit provides to God's acceptance of these Gentiles (15.8), not any witness the Gentiles themselves present to outsiders.

95. *Baptism*, pp. 70-82; 'Baptism', pp. 12-16.

96. For Menzies, Luke's equation of the gift of the Spirit to Cornelius with the prophetic Spirit poured out at Pentecost is 'the decisive objection' to Dunn's view ('Luke', p. 136; repeating *Development*, p. 267), but as Dunn now claims the Spirit is both 'the Spirit of prophecy' and soteriological Spirit ('Baptism', pp. 3-27), Menzies' antithesis might be considered an unnecessary one.

97. *Baptism*, p. 80, cf. 'Baptism', pp. 13-14.

98. *Baptism*, p. 81; 'God gave the Spirit (11.17) means that God gave repentance unto life (11.18)', 'Baptism', p. 14.

99. *Baptism*, p. 81; 'Baptism', pp. 14-16.

charismatic speech: as this contains elements that are transparently 'additional' to forgiveness and acceptance, we have no reason to equate receiving the Spirit with God's forgiveness simpliciter. Dunn's revised statement prefers more cautiously to speak of the Spirit as the 'embodiment or transmitter of forgiveness',[100] and this is possible, but it is open to the objection that Luke elsewhere thinks of faith (and its recognition of God's forgiveness and acceptance through Jesus) as something elicited through the preacher's Spirit-empowered proclamation (as is the case throughout Luke's Gospel), rather than consequent on reception of the gift of the Spirit itself.[101] In the account of Cornelius's conversion in 10.34-48 events follow too rapidly for us to be able to tease out the respective operations of the Spirit, but 11.14 and 15.7 might naturally be taken to imply that such faith was kindled by Peter's words, and 15.8 would then mean God *attested* this operation of the Spirit in the hearers by granting them the Christian gift of the Spirit of prophecy.

(2) Both 11.17 and 11.18 speak of God's 'giving' some grace to the Gentiles, but we should not allow the mild parallelism here to force the conclusion that the gift of the Spirit (v. 17) is to be *equated* with the gift of repentance (v. 18). 11.18b is a conclusion drawn from the whole of 11.3-17, not merely a restatement of Peter's premise in v. 17. The Jerusalem Christians acknowledge that if God has given Cornelius's household the same prestigious gift of the Spirit of prophecy as Jewish Christians received at Pentecost, then he must have allowed these Gentiles the same 'repentance' previously only known to the Israel of fulfilment (cf. 5.31-32), and set them on the same path leading to 'life' (cf. 13.48; Lk. 18.30). But under no circumstances may we simply equate 'the same gift (= the Spirit)' with μετάνοιαν εἰς ζωὴν ἔδωκεν ('repentance that leads to life'): elsewhere μετάνοια is clearly the *condition* for receiving the gift of the Spirit (2.38-39) not the gift itself. And the 'life' envisaged, if not purely eschatological, at least includes resurrection life, and is thus broader in scope than the fruits of the Pentecostal gift of the Spirit.[102]

---

100. 'Baptism', p. 13.

101. See above all Haya-Prats, *L'Esprit*, pp. 121-25.

102. In his *JPT* article, Dunn attempts to sidestep Menzies' argument that the gift of repentance cannot be equated with the gift of the Spirit (the former being rather the condition for the latter) by putting all the emphasis on the qualifying 'unto life', and asserting 'the gift of the Spirit...embodies or effects the event as a whole or its climax in particular—the life brought into being or effected through the repentance expressed' ('Baptism', p. 14 n. 30). This seems to be evasion. For Luke, the emphasis falls on the quality of the repentance given: i.e., that it is of the same kind which (according to 5.31-32) God exalted Jesus to give to the Israel of fulfilment, and so assures that these Gentiles too are counted within God's people, receive forgiveness,

(3) Nor is it self-evident from the structure of 15.8-9 that the clause 'giving them the Holy Spirit' (15.8) is intended to describe the same divine action as the clause 'cleansing their hearts by faith' (15.9). The subordinate clauses in question in fact support two different (if related) main clauses ('God *bore witness* to them' and 'he did *not distinguish between* us and them' respectively), and have different roles in the overall argument. 15.9b does not function to clarify 15.8b,[103] but to provide the grounds for the conclusion in 15.10-11 (hence the inferential οὖν 'therefore' in v. 10a). The argument here is that as God cleansed the hearts of these Gentiles by faith (rather than their achieving purity within and through Torah-commitment [especially circumcision and the purity laws]), they do not need the Mosaic Law (the whole point at issue). The function of 15.8 is then to guarantee the otherwise unprovable assumption in Peter's argument, namely that God (who alone knows the human heart, hence v. 8a) has indeed cleansed the hearts of these Gentiles.[104] God's gift of the 'Spirit of prophecy' would readily 'bear witness' to the fact they were 'clean' because it was a widespread Jewish assumption that Israel's sin was the cause of God's removing the Spirit of prophecy from Israel and that the gift would only be returned when God had first restored Israel in obedience.[105] Undoubtedly the 'witness' value of the gift of the Spirit would be logically strengthened if it were believed that the 'Spirit of prophecy' was also a major influence in spiritual/ethical renewal,[106] but Peter's argument works quite adequately without that assumption (cf. 5.32).[107] Menzies' criticisms of Dunn's case

and are on the path that leads to life. God attests such people by giving them the Spirit (cf. 5.32).

103. While there can be no doubt that at Qumran cleansing of the heart was regarded as an operation of the Spirit of holiness, there is no evidence that such purification was accomplished in a (ritual) 'giving of the Spirit of Holiness' to each initiate on entry to the community (*contra* Thiering, 'Cleansing', p. 276).

104. So correctly Menzies, 'Luke', p. 136, and cf. Haya-Prats, *L'Esprit*, pp. 126-28. Dunn, 'Baptism', argues that the order of 15.8-9 should be reversed (putting cleansing of the heart before reception of the Spirit) if the classical Pentecostal model is to receive support. But the 'order' in 15.8-9 is not a chronological one. It proceeds from what can be agreed as known between the contesting parties (i.e. that the Gentiles received the gift of the 'Spirit of prophecy') to what should be inferred from that knowledge (God has not distinguished in favour of the people of the Law, but has 'cleansed' these Gentiles without it). For the place of glossolalia in the decision to admit Gentiles see e.g. the essays by Esler ('Glossolalia', pp. 136-142) and P. Borgen ('Jesus Christ, the Reception of the Spirit, and a Cross-National Community', in Green and Turner [eds.], *Jesus*, pp. 220-35).

105. See above, Chapter 3.

106. As I have argued in Chapter 5, and see below, Chapter 13.

107. One further indicator marginally supports Menzies rather than Dunn. The

has thus explored significant weaknesses in it.

Two arguments, however, imply that the Spirit has more to do with the 'salvation' of these Gentiles than Menzies is prepared to admit. *First, we need to note that once again we have returned to the 'norm' of the gift of the Spirit being immediately associated with conversional repentance and baptism,* even if the order within that complex differs from the one presupposed at Acts 2.38 (for perfectly understandable reasons: cf. 10.46-48). Cornelius is not an example of a 'Christian' without the Pentecostal gift of the Spirit.

The opposite view has been argued on the basis of the entirely positive portrait of Cornelius's piety in 10.2, 4, 22, 31, 33, and Peter's declaration that God has shown him he should call none profane or unclean (10.28), combined with his declaration of God's impartiality and that any who fear him (like Cornelius, 10.2 etc.) are 'acceptable' (δεκτός) to him (10.34-35). The language 'acceptable (to God)', and its contrasting 'profane' and 'unclean', were terms traditionally used by Jews to refer to the community of God's people and those outside of it respectively. How is it that Peter uses such language even before preaching to him? For U. Wilckens, the answer is that Peter here recognizes that Cornelius has already been converted (and for substantiation he points, for example, to the fact that Peter believes Cornelius has already heard the Gospel about Jesus: cf. 10.36, 'You know the message...'). Peter then merely becomes a witness to God's confirmation of the faith of this Gentile (in the gift of the Spirit to him), and oversees his admission (through baptism) to the Church.[108] The Cornelius incident could then be seen as roughly parallel to the Samaritan incident in Acts 8.4-24, with authentic faith preceding the gift of the Spirit. Shelton accepts something like this view of Cornelius.[109]

---

description of God as 'the one who knows the human heart' in 15.8a probably anticipates 15.9 and implies (with respect to Cornelius) that he knows this man's heart to be 'clean' (by faith), and *so* witnesses to the status by giving the Spirit. In other words, the cleansing of the heart by faith (15.9b) is already considered to precede the gift of the Spirit which attests it (15.8b). The alternative reading, that because God knows the hearts of the Gentiles he decides to cleanse their hearts by faith (through the gift of the Spirit), would leave unexplained what it is that God knows that is relevant to the case and which is parallel to the disciples' experience (cf. 15.9a).

108. *Die Missionsreden der Apostelgeschichte: Form- und traditionsgeschichtliche Untersuchungen* (Neukirchen–Vluyn: Neukirchener Verlag, 1963), pp. 46-50, 63-70.

109. *Word*, pp. 131-33. J.W. Taeger's explanation is more radical; unlike Paul, Luke does not regard the whole of humankind as fundamentally in the grip of sin and 'the flesh' as Paul does, and so universally in need of 'salvation'. For Luke there are, of course, 'sinners' who are converted and forgiven; but there are also those like Cornelius who are 'righteous' (10.22) and 'devout' (cf. 10.2, 7) people, who worship and fear the One God, give alms, and pray constantly (10.2). Such are already heard by

But this is to pay insufficient attention to the narrative development and modulation in the three accounts of the Cornelius episode.[110] Each retelling adds, subtracts, changes the order and substitutes in matters of detail, and thereby weaves a thematic unity and development of focus across the three accounts—a phenomenon of poetics referred to as 'functional redundancy'. The later retellings say nothing of Cornelius' piety and clarify that he receives salvation only through the faith elicited by Peter's preaching (cf. 11.13-14; 11.18; 15.7-9).[111] What then is the significance of the

God for their piety (10.4, 31); and so their 'conversion' and 'salvation' is an indefinite affair that brings little new (*Mensch*; J.W. Taeger, 'Paulus und Lukas über den Menschen', *ZNW* 71 [1980], pp. 96-108).

110. For a brief account see R.D. Witherup, 'Cornelius Over and Over Again: "Functional Redundancy" in the Acts of the Apostles', *JSNT* 49 (1993), pp. 45-66.

111. In the first sequence (Acts 10) the nature of Cornelius's salvation, its relation to his devotion and faith, together with his status as 'clean' and 'acceptable' before God, and the basis for his baptism and admission to the church, are all left in varying degrees unclear. But the rewording of the stories in the accounts which follow clarify matters: (1) Cornelius's 'piety', so strongly emphasized in ch. 10, and which may have seemed to provide the basis for his being treated as 'clean' in that chapter, is not mentioned at all in chs. 11 or 15, even though Peter's vision is repeated in detail in the former. (2) Rather, in 11.13-14 we learn Cornelius sent for Peter that he might hear a 'message by which you and your household will be saved' (contrast the tension-building 10.5, 22, 33 which do not yet reveal why Peter is sent for), a 'message of salvation' which involves God-given 'repentance' which 'leads to life' (11.18). And if 11.15 (like 10.44) may suggest that Peter had little opportunity to deliver such a message before the irruption of the Spirit interrupted the proceedings, 15.7 re-emphasizes that it was precisely through Peter's message that these Gentiles first became believers. In short, through his development and modulations the narrator tells us that however much Cornelius may already have heard about Jesus (10.36ff.), it was Peter's message that decisively elicited that repentant faith which (in Luke's view) leads to life and salvation (*contra* Wilckens and Shelton). (3) Similarly, we gradually receive clarification on the issue of Cornelius's 'cleanness', on the basis of this status and on the related question of God's 'impartiality'. At 10.15, 28, God's impartiality, and Peter's realization he should call none unclean, could almost be mistaken for universalism. But this is qualified in 10.34; it is those who 'fear God' and do what is 'right' who are 'acceptable' to God (cf. Dupont, 'Dieu', pp. 321-23). Even this, however, contains a measure of ambiguity that is only finally resolved in 11.16 (evoking the Baptist's promise of the messiah of the Spirit who purifies Zion: see below) and 15.9, 'he made no distinction between us and them, cleansing their hearts by faith too'. Now God's impartiality finally clearly relates to his willingness to 'accept' into the messianic congregation of the Israel of fulfilment both Jew and Gentile (without distinction) who become 'clean' through faith in the message about Christ: a position already anticipated at 10.36, where Peter's description of Jesus as 'Lord of all' draws on Joel 3.5 [2.32] (cf. J. Dupont, '"Le Seigneur de tous" [Ac 10.36; Rm 10.12]', in G.F. Hawthorne and O. Betz [eds.], *Tradition and Interpretation in the New Testament* [Tübingen: Mohr, 1987], 229-36, pp. 232-34). The contribution of Cornelius's pre-Christian piety is

eulogizing description of Cornelius's devotion in Acts 10? It is not to portray him as already essentially a 'Christian' (*contra* Wilckens and Shelton), *but as all but a pious Jew*.[112] As Esler,[113] Jervell,[114] and others have rightly seen, Cornelius is presented as a prototypical 'God-fearer' or 'semi-proselyte', and so as the most typical, and most likely kind of person to convert to the Christian faith.[115] Luke would have been aware that a significant part of the church in Paul's day did indeed come from these synagogue-attending Gentile God-fearer circles, and that on the whole they reacted much more positively to the Gospel than national Jews. Theologically this group had an importance for Luke that went well beyond their numbers. First, they represented a group (like Jewish believers) with a relatively full understanding of Judaism, and for them to accept the Gospel in part compensated for the challenge to Christian credibility created by the substantial Jewish rejection of the Gospel. Secondly, to present semi-proselytes (especially those of such piety as Cornelius) as typical converts to Christianity (as Luke certainly does) was to diminish the offence to Judaism of the church's Law-free inclusion of Gentiles. More important, this presentation, by minimizing the difference between Jewish Christianity and Gentile Christianity, also strongly supported the claim that the church was 'the messianic assembly of the Israel of fulfilment'; the true home of the sons of the covenant. It minimized the apparent break between the Old Testament expectation of eschatological 'renewal of Israel' and the Christian 'fulfilment' in the church.

The second indication that Luke attributes greater significance to the Spirit in salvation than Menzies allows lies in 11.16. The Gentile Pentecost 'reminds' Peter of Jesus' logion based in the promise of John the Baptist: 'you will be baptized in Holy Spirit' (cf. 1.5). The very fact that Peter only 'remembers' this saying (as from the semi-forgotten past) strongly argues

sharply relativized by the progressive clarifications of the complex account.

112. Cf. Wilson, *Gentiles*, p. 176, 'to show that the Gentiles were not such a bad crowd'.

113. P.F. Esler, *Community and Gospel in Luke–Acts* (Cambridge: Cambridge University Press, 1987), especially chs. 2–5.

114. J. Jervell, 'The Church of Jews and Godfearers', in Tyson (ed.), *Luke–Acts*, pp. 11-20.

115. This can hardly be because (as Esler argues) the church of Luke's day consisted mainly of Hellenistic Jewish Christians and God-fearers (there were not that many of the latter attached to the synagogues); nor can Jervell's explanation be right, that the only sort of Gentiles Luke contemplates in his (Judaic) churches are pro-Jewish God-fearers. By Luke's time we must assume there was a Gentile majority in the diaspora churches, and that many of them came from Gentile groups with no synagogue associations (for example, the Gentiles converted at Pisidian Antioch [13.48] are not merely from the synagogue, but from the whole city [13.44]), or even from entirely Gentile cities that had no synagogue, such as Lystra (Acts 14.21; and compare the numerous converts from pagan magic assumed in 20.28-29).

against the position that the terminology 'baptism in Holy Spirit' was widely current in the church of Luke's or Peter's day, and that it was used either as Dunn suggests (a term for 'initiation' through the Spirit into the Christian life)[116] or as a term for some second 'empowering'. Had such terminology been commonplace Peter could no doubt simply have affirmed, for example, 'they received the same baptism in the Holy Spirit as we did/we all do' (cf 11.17; 15.8). For lack of such common terminology Peter recalls Jesus' logion. But that raises the further question why Peter 'remembers' Jesus' words precisely here and here alone? What is there about this situation which makes John's promise especially apposite when it was not generally applied to the frequent (no doubt sometimes dramatic) experiences of Spirit-reception? The answer is probably that Luke understood the logion to imply *the messiah cleanses and restores his Israel through the executive power of the Holy Spirit which he pours out*. Not only have we seen that this is the most likely explanation of Lk. 3.16-17 and Acts 1.5, but it has immediate and double relevance to the context in 11.1-18, and so explains Peter's remembering it here. (a) It justifies Peter's association with those the circumcision party reckon to be 'unclean' (11.2-3), by resolving the significance of Peter's enigmatic vision about clean and unclean entities. The implicit argument here is that Gentiles who believe and receive the Spirit may most assuredly be considered 'clean', because the Spirit manifest in them is the very power by which the messiah purges 'Israel'. (b) It simultaneously justifies Peter's incorporation of the Gentile converts into the Church, the Israel of fulfilment by baptism, for all those upon whom the messiah bestows his Spirit are thereby identified as having a part in his restoration of Zion. The charismata manifest through Cornelius's believing household and friends show that *these Gentiles too have a place in the messianic cleansing and transformation of Israel being performed through the Spirit poured out by the ascended and glorified Christ*.

These two lines of argument are then combined decisively in Acts 15.8-9; 'God bore witness to them, *giving them the Holy Spirit just as he did us*; and he made no distinction between us and them, but *cleansed* their hearts by faith'. Jesus' baptizing the Cornelius household with the Spirit here is interpreted in terms of his cleansing a people for his name (cf. 15.14). In other words, while above we found no semantic *structural* grounds for identifying 15.8b with 15.9b, 11.16 provides an important background *conceptual* clue that suggests Dunn's reading was actually along the right lines: the Spirit of prophecy is simultaneously the soteriological Spirit in so far as it is the power of Zion's cleansing/restoration.

---

116. See Chapter 7 §3.3 for the view that 'to baptize' used as a metaphor did not have initiatory connotations.

2.5. Acts 18.24-28 and 19.1-6: Apollos and the Ephesian Twelve

Once again, in the case of the Ephesian twelve we have an alleged incident of believing Christian disciples who only receive the Spirit as a distinct second gift. The very use of the unqualified τινες μαθηταί ('certain disciples' 19.1; as opposed to 'disciples of John' or whatever) might strongly suggest they are presented as Christians, for οἱ μαθηταί in Luke is virtually a technical term for believers.[117] Furthermore, the fact that these 'disciples' are said only to have received John's baptism (19.4) may suggest Luke thinks they were Apollos's disciples (for the same is said of him in 18.25c)—and Luke evidently portrays Apollos as a Christian missionary who is merely slightly corrected on some issue (Christian baptism?) by Paul's co-workers in Ephesus (18.26).[118]

E. Käsemann argues the Ephesian twelve are portrayed by Luke as anomalous semi-Christians,[119] so that Luke can have them rebaptised and granted the Spirit through apostolic laying on of hands in order to submit them to the *una sancta apostolica*.[120] In short, the anomaly is explained by

117. As Dunn, *Baptism*, p. 84, admits. Cf. Aker, 'Directions', §D(4), who argues that John's disciples are true believers who simply have not received appropriate empowering for Christian ministry.

118. So e.g. Menzies, *Development*, pp. 268-77 (also Kim, *Geisttaufe*, pp. 268-77, and Shepherd, *Function*, pp. 224-30). The suggestion that Luke added the words 'he had been instructed...things concerning Jesus' (18.25a,b) to his source to make a Baptist Apollos into a Christian appears to founder on 18.26; similarly that he added 18.25c, 26bc ('he knew only the baptism of John...expounded to him the way of God more accurately') to make a Christian Apollos into a not-yet-Christian hardly does justice either to v. 26c or to vv. 27-28. So, rightly, C.K. Barrett, 'Apollos and the Twelve Disciples of Ephesus', in W.C. Weinrich (ed.), *The New Testament Age: Essays in Honor of Bo Reicke* (Macon: Mercer University Press, 1984), 1, p. 31

119. 'The Disciples of John the Baptist in Ephesus', in *Essays on New Testament Themes* (London: SCM Press, 1964) pp. 136-48. Even this, Käsemann thinks, is Luke's creation; historically such disciples would not be awaiting another. And Baptist groups would have been a competing group with the church. C.B. Kaiser points out, however, that any group that had not heard of the Spirit would barely have had much contact with Christian churches ('Rebaptism', pp. 57-61).

120. Similar motives are said to account for the subordination of the otherwise fully Christian powerful Apollos. But would that not rather require his teaching (and rebaptism?) at the hands of Paul rather than Pauline associates? By contrast, E. Schweizer ('Die Bekehrung des Apollos, Apg 18, 24-26', in *Beiträge zur Theologie des Neuen Testaments: Neutestamentliche Aufsätze (1955–1970)* [Zürich: Zwingli Verlag, 1970], pp. 71-79) argues Apollos was a Jew, and powerful synagogue preacher, converted by Priscilla and Aquila; Luke has misunderstood 'the way of the Lord' to mean 'the things of Jesus', and taken πνεύματι as a reference to the Holy Spirit, thus turning him into a Christian who does not need baptism because he has the gift it brings. For criticism of this hypothesis see Menzies, *Development*, pp. 268-70.

Luke's alleged early catholic *Tendenz*. His explanation in terms of Luke's 'early catholicism', however, finds too little support in Luke–Acts.[121] F.S. Spencer[122] rejects the positions of Käsemann and Wolter[123] and detects a forerunner-culminator (mutually co-operative, but like John and Jesus; Philip and Peter) relation between Apollos and Paul in respect of the twelve—but the thesis must rest on the dubious assumption (see below) that the twelve are Apollos's disciples. And there is certainly no global suggestion that Apollos requires a culminator to be effective.

But the view that the twelve were converts of Apollos is not without its difficulties. Rather than connecting the 'disciples' with Apollos, Luke appears to be *contrasting* them with him. Apollos is described as a man zealous in the Spirit (18.25),[124] but the 'disciples' do not even know the Spirit has been given (19.2)—which makes it most improbable they are actually Apollos's disciples.[125] And most significantly the 'disciples' are rebaptised, Apollos was not.[126]

121. For those accepting Käsemann's position see Coppens, 'Mains', p. 426. Against Käsemann's proposal see on 8.14-17, and e.g. Marshall, 'Early Catholicism', pp. 217-31; Schweizer (as above); Barrett, 'Apollos', pp. 32-36; and Menzies, *Development*, pp. 268-70.

122. *Portrait*, pp. 232-39.

123. M. Wolter ('Apollos und die ephesinischen Johannesjünger [Act 18.24-19.7]', *ZNW* 78 [1987], pp. 49-73) too rejects Käsemann's early catholic view; but replaces it with a similar understanding in which (against a background of trouble in the Pauline churches with pneumatic disciples of Apollos) Luke is determined to portray Paul as the superior, deliberately and ironically making Paul the more accomplished pneumatic.

124. The description of Apollos as ζέων τῷ πνεύματι (18.25), sandwiched between 'he was instructed in the way of the Lord' and 'he taught accurately the things of Jesus', is most naturally understood as a reference to *God's* Spirit; not human spirit ('burning with zeal' or the like; cf. Rom. 12.11, and see the arguments of Käsemann, 'Disciples', p. 143; Dunn, *Baptism*, pp. 88-89; and Haenchen, 491 n. 10). Kim also notes that Luke's use of παρρησιάζεσθαι (8.26) virtually confirms Apollos as a man of the Spirit (for in Luke this is virtually an expression for preaching in the power of the Spirit) (*Geisttaufe*, pp. 217-18). Had Apollos not received the Spirit, Priscilla and Aquila would have had more to give him than additional precision on an unspecified theological issue.

125. Menzies, *Development*, p. 272, argues Apollos's experience of the Spirit does not presuppose an awareness of Pentecost and adds a surprising '(cf. Lk. 1–2)'. But does this not minimize the problem of disciples of Apollos who are not aware of the availability of the Spirit? It is very difficult to believe Luke is thinking of some pre-Pentecostal gift to a Christian Apollos; and it is almost as difficult to understand how the disciples would not have heard of the Spirit with which their preacher was 'fervent': cf. the criticisms of Atkinson, 'Responses', pp. 113-14.

126. Barrett thus rightly notes Luke makes 'Apollos more and the twelve disciples less Christian' ('Apollos', p. 38).

When we now look at these 'disciples' more closely, it may be questioned whether Luke regards them as Christians at all.[127] According to 19.5, once the disciples have 'heard' Paul, they are baptised 'into the name of the Lord Jesus'. But what is it Luke believes they have 'heard' from Paul which justifies this step. It cannot simply be that they hear the Spirit is now given,[128] for were that the case Paul could simply have laid hands on them and prayed they receive the Spirit as in 8.15-17; there would be no need for rebaptism. According to 19.4, Paul reminds them that John's baptism was of repentance, and faith in the Coming One. This much they must have known to be John's disciples at all, and to explain how Paul initially assumed they were baptized as *messianic* disciples and so would have the Spirit. The only candidate for significant new information,[129] on the basis of which one might be rebaptized, is in the identification of the messianic Coming One to whom the Baptist had pointed: τοῦτ' ἔστιν εἰς τὸν Ἰησοῦν ('that is, in Jesus'). But if that is the *novum*, then these 'disciples' were formerly not *Christians* at all; and we may certainly understand why they were rebaptized, and Apollos not![130]

I think this is a little more probable than D.A. Carson's explanation whereby the 'disciples' are assumed to know quite fully about Jesus (like Apollos), and only somehow to have missed out on Pentecost and subsequent developments.[131] Why then does Luke's Paul simply rehearse what *ex hypothesi* they already fully know? At the other end of the interpretational spectrum, Pesch (II, 165) thinks Luke characterizes the twelve as ignorant of John's preaching of a coming messiah.[132] But if these 'disciples'

127. Correctly Pesch, 163-66.

128. *Contra* Webb, *Baptizer*, pp. 273-74.

129. Spencer, *Portrait*, p. 236, says Paul is simply reminding the disciples of the theological content of John's baptism, already fully known to them (for they are Apollos' Christian disciples), and that it is not stated that they repented or believed. But in that case, why does Luke bother to mention the reminder (which serves no purpose), and why are the 'disciples' submitted to water-baptism at all (Apollos was not; Spencer [p. 240] can only suggest that Paul does not command this baptism, the disciples merely proceed to it [of their own initiative?]). That Luke does not specify they repented and believed is surely explicable as avoiding redundancy with 19.4.

130. Shelton (*Word*, pp. 134-35) has no real explanation for this. After admitting that John's baptism for repentance and forgiveness continues to be valid in the church, he must explain baptism in the name of the Lord Jesus as being associated with the empowering for witness (the only thing, on his view, these disciples as yet lack). But one cannot appeal to the promise of Jesus as baptizer in the Holy Spirit for this view of water baptism as such.

131. *Showing the Spirit: A Theological Exposition of 1 Corinthians 12–14* (Grand Rapids: Baker, 1987), pp. 148-50.

132. Similarly, J.K. Parratt ('The Rebaptism of the Ephesian Disciples', *ExpTim* 79

did not understand their baptism as related to a specifically *messianic* hope, how did Paul come to mistake them for Christians in the first place?

If we are right, Luke thinks of these 'disciples' as people baptized by John and awaiting the messiah he promised. Paul identifies this hope as fulfilled in Jesus, and the 'disciples'[133] 'hear' in the sense of accepting Paul's proclamation. Their submission to baptism completes their conversion-initiation, and in the context of this they receive the Spirit of prophecy when Paul lays his hands on them.[134]

We may make four further observations on the passage: (A) Paul's question in 19.2—'Did you receive the Spirit when you believed?'—appears to assume that for Luke there is a possibility of some sort of 'believing' without receiving the Spirit (as 8.12-17).[135] But this instance differs from the

---

[1967–68], pp. 182-83) who posits the twelve had merely heard a confused account of John's preaching including his baptism of repentence, but not John's messianic preaching. According to Parratt they are rebaptized, not because John's baptism is deficient over against Christian baptism, but because their defective faith means they have not really even had the former; their baptism amounts to no more than a lustration.

133. I must assume with Dunn that τινες μαθηταί does not *necessarily* refer to Christians (as the absolute μαθηταί would), even if it may (as at 9.10; 16.1): see *Baptism*, p. 85 (and his older argument softened in 'Baptism', p. 24; so also Pesch, II, 165—against Schneider, II, 263). Barrett ('Apollos', pp. 36-38) offers a half-way house. He posits that in earliest Christianity John's disciples would be regarded as near-Christians. Some would say they had received all the baptism that Jesus had, and, with acceptance of Jesus' lordship, should need no more. Others would see baptism in the name of Jesus, conveying the Spirit, as the distinctive rite of entry to full Christian existence. K. Haacker ('Einige Fälle von "erlebter Rede" im Neuen Testament', *NovT* 12 [1970], pp. 70-77) offers an alternative explanation, namely that this is a case in which Luke's formulation as narrator deliberately echoes Paul's initial belief (not Luke's own understanding), a possibility which need not rest on Haacker's assumption that Luke himself could not tolerate the idea of believers who had not received the Spirit (as Menzies, *Development*, p. 273, infers).

134. No separation of receiving the Spirit from their Christian baptism is necessarily to be deduced from the statement that the Spirit was conferred in the laying on of hands (v. 5), for the latter may well have been part of Paul's baptismal procedure. When Coppens ('Mains', p. 426) admits that laying on of hands normally accompanied baptism, but insists that the former is nevertheless a distinct 'post-baptismal' act of benediction bestowing the Spirit in confirming power, he draws a scarcely legitimate distinction between the act of dipping in (or affusion of) water, and 'baptism' understood in a wider sense as the rite of initiation. In the latter case, the water-rite and epiclesis of the Spirit would be complementary aspects of Christian 'baptism'. Luke certainly does not encourage the view that laying on of hands is a necessary condition of receiving the Spirit: see particularly Barrett, 'Apollos'.

135. Stronstad, *Theology*, p. 68, argues the question must be understood in the light of the outcome in the narrative: i.e. the question is whether they have received the gift

Samaritan episode, in that the narrative development in 19.3-5 reveals Paul'
initial assumption of Christian belief is questionable. Paul leads the twelve *to*
belief in Jesus as the hoped-for messiah, and corresponding commitment
expressed in re-baptism. One might surmise that for Luke those who have
submitted to John's baptism and become disciples of Jesus (like the apostles
and Apollos) do not require Christian baptism. It is those who are confronted with the kerygma and brought to conversion that are baptised (or
rebaptized) in the name of Jesus.

(B) For whatever reason Luke has portrayed the Ephesian 'twelve' as
'almost' Christians up to 19.4, the point remains that the Spirit is then
granted as usual as part of their conversion-initiation package—no
significant 'delay' is implied between 19.5 and 19.6. Furthermore, *contra*
the claims of Ervin (that the laying on of hands and gift of the Spirit are not
especially tied [temporally] with baptism here),[136] the very fact that Paul,
having ascertained the 'disciples' do not know of the gift of the Spirit,
immediately asked 'Into what, then, were you baptized?' (19.3) suggests a
usual association between baptism and reception of the Spirit. Once again
the norm of Acts 2.38-39 is assumed to hold.[137]

(C) When we turn more specifically to the nature of the gift envisaged
here, it is immediately obvious that Luke portrays it in parallel to the
Pentecost event (compare 'the Holy Spirit came upon them' [19.6] with
Acts 1.8 'when the Holy Spirit comes upon you', and in each case this
'coming' is manifest in tongues): it is therefore the Christian Spirit of
prophecy that Luke has in mind.[138] This also coheres with the fact that
Luke expects this matter of having received the Spirit *to be a matter of
immediate perception:*[139] the Ephesians are expected to know whether or
not they did in fact receive the Spirit when they 'believed' (19.2), whether

of the Spirit of prophecy. Dunn (*Baptism*, pp. 86-87) rightly criticizes the uninformed
assumption of some popular writings that the participle πιστεύσαντες *must* refer to an
action which precedes the verb ἐλάβετε (*because* the participle is aorist). It is probably
a typical case of coincident aorists, though it should be admitted (*contra* Haya-Prats,
L'Esprit, p. 128) that the classical Pentecostal interpretation ('Did you receive the Spirit
after you came to belief?') is not as such ruled out by the syntax.

136. *Conversion-Initiation*, pp. 63-66.

137. This is admitted by Haya-Prats, *L'Esprit*, p. 135, and by Menzies, *Development*,
p. 274 n. 2, though he softens the admission with the qualification 'the Spirit is not
inextricably bound to the rite of baptism (cf. Acts 8.17; 10.44)' (so 'Luke', p. 123).
But this last is not really a counter-example (except against sacramentalism); for reception of the Spirit becomes the grounds for arguing immediate admission to baptism.
Acts 10.44 thus supports rather than weakens the normative value of 2.38.

138. So also Stronstad, *Theology*, p. 68.

139. We do not, with Shelton, *Word*, p. 134, need to suppose this implies it is a matter
of receiving empowering for mission rather than 'internal working' of the Spirit.

from 'initial' charismata or following experience. We have no need here, with Lampe,[140] to invoke a special missionary endowment separate from an alleged baptismal gift of the Spirit; nor is there any sure grounds for Menzies' conclusion that 'through the laying on of hands, Paul commissions the Ephesians as fellow-workers in the mission of the church and the twelve are thus endowed with the prophetic gift'.[141] While it is entirely believable that 'the twelve' became fully involved with Paul's evangelism, there is no specific evidence for it (and nothing whatever to suggest that the gift of the Spirit was considered to be empowerment for mission alone). Menzies points to references to 'disciples' associated with Paul's mission at 19.9, 30 and 20.1, but the 'disciples' of these references are the increasing band of believers, not merely the twelve. And none of the texts associates them directly with witness.[142]

(D) One final question is forced on us by the description of events at Ephesus. It is the question whether Luke considered the gift of tongues to be 'normative' to reception of the Spirit. We have already seen that in Judaism reception of the Spirit would only be anticipated to be accompanied by some kind of initial outburst of charisma when either the illapse of the Spirit was a dramatic one, or when public attestation to the transfer of the Spirit was necessary to legitimate the recipients in some way to Israel (cf. §2.1[C] above). On all other occasions in Acts where the advent of the Spirit of prophecy was marked by an immediate illapse of charismata, the circumstances suggest a certain appropriateness of this. Pentecost was of unique salvation-historical importance, and the xenolalia that attended it,

---

140. *Seal*, 76: Lampe's argument is that (according to Luke) a special missionary empowering is given at each point when the gospel crosses an important boundary (Acts 8, to the Samaritans; Acts 10, to the Gentiles), and at Acts 19 as the church is founded from which the mission extends to Asia minor and even to Europe. But Luke does *not* regard 19.1-6 as the founding of the Ephesian church (cf. 18.24-25; 19.1ff.).

141. *Development*, p. 271 (and see pp. 275-77); compare F. Pereira, *Ephesus: Climax of Universalism in Luke–Acts: A Redaction-Critical Study of Paul's Ephesian Ministry (Acts 18.23–20.1)* (Anand: GSP, 1983) pp. 106-108. O'Toole (noted by Menzies, *Development*, p. 271 n. 2) describes this in parallel to Samaria, 'Paul puts the finishing touches to Apollos' work in Ephesus much as Peter and John did to Philip's work in Samaria'. But we have seen there are problems with the assumption that the twelve are Apollos's disciples. There are also problems with Menzies' speculative contention that the twelve were amongst the elders addressed at Miletus (on the basis of 20.18), and that 20.28 ('Give heed...to the Holy Spirit who made you overseers') suggests the Spirit came upon the Ephesian twelve in order to equip them to sustain the work of mission in the region (pp. 276-77).

142. In 19.9 the singular of the participle διαλεγόμενος means *Paul* was the one arguing in the hall of Tyrannus, not the disciples he took with him from the synagogue.

and were understood by people from all over the known world, symbolize the extension of the Gospel in the power of the Spirit to the end(s) of the earth (cf. 1.8). In Acts 8.17-19 charismata mark the end of an anomalous delay, and ratify the Spirit has come upon a group whose status with respect to the Israel of fulfilment was uncertain; they indicate that a new stage in the programme of Acts 1.8 has been reached. At Acts 10.46, the irruption of the Spirit in a manner so closely reminiscent of Pentecost assures Peter and the Jewish Christian church that the gift of the Spirit could be bestowed even on Gentiles. At each of these important turning points we would be surprised if there had been no immediate attestation provided of the Spirit's inception; all were strikingly powerful experiences, and questions of legitimation were especially important in the latter two cases. These instances would not, however, suggest that Spirit-reception should universally or even normally be attested by initial charismata amongst uncontroversial classes of converts (e.g. Jewish converts after Pentecost; Samaritan ones after Acts 8; Gentiles after Acts 10 [or Acts 15]). Within such groups there would be no need for 'initial evidence', but merely for ongoing experience of the Spirit of prophecy.

Acts 19.6 then becomes a case of special interest precisely because it relates the Spirit-reception of a relatively uncontroversial class of convert, a 'normal' group. On this occasion there is no immediately obvious reason why any initial manifestation should take place, yet we are told 'the Holy Spirit came upon them; and they began to speak with tongues and to prophesy'.[143] This instance could be taken to suggest that Luke considered such manifestations, particularly tongues, normally to attend the instant of receiving the Spirit, and might even be pressed (taken with other arguments) to imply the more contentious view that Luke considered 'initial tongues' *normative* for the Church.[144]

---

143. I take the imperfect tenses following the aorist ἦλθε to be inceptive.

144. The arguments against a normative association between Spirit-reception and glossolalia have been stated by the Pentecostal scholar G.D. Fee (*Gospel and Spirit: Issues in New Testament Hermeneutics* [Peabody, MA: Hendrickson, 1991], chs. 6 and 7), and by those otherwise sympathetic to the Pentecostal Church (e.g. L.W. Hurtado, 'Normal, but Not a Norm: Initial Evidence and the New Testament', in G.B. McGee [ed.], *Initial Evidence: Historical and Biblical Perspectives on the Pentecostal Doctrine of Spirit Baptism* [Peabody, MA: Hendrickson, 1991], pp. 189-201; J.R. Michaels, 'Evidences of the Spirit, or the Spirit as Evidence? Some Non-Pentecostal Reflections', in McGee [ed.], *Evidence*, pp. 202-18). The same volume naturally presents the more traditional Pentecostal position(s), for which see especially the historical essays by J.R. Goff and C.M. Robeck, and the more theological-methodologically orientated contribution by D.A. Johns ('Some New Directions in the Hermeneutics of Classical Pentecostalism's Doctrine of Initial Evidence', in McGee [ed.], *Evidence*, pp. 145-67). The most informed defence of the traditional position is provided by Menzies,

The latter claim, however, goes well beyond the evidence. Luke does not say that *each* of the twelve began to speak in tongues and to prophesy, but that the group as a whole manifested these diverse gifts (similarly at 10.46). Even if this means that each experienced some charismatic phenomenon (which is probable, but not certain), the description does not imply that each spoke in tongues. Several may have experienced glossolalia while others experienced invasive prophecy/praise (cf. 10.46). Either gift would function as 'initial evidence' of the presence of the Spirit of prophecy. But, as we have seen, a first-century reader with Luke's knowledge of Judaism would anticipate more of the latter and less of the former.[145] If Luke wished his readers to understand that each and every convert receiving the Spirit spoke in tongues (rather than, or in addition to, manifesting some other charisma of the Spirit of prophecy, or none), he would have needed to make this more explicit in order to counter the presumption in favour of invasive prophecy or of charismatic praise in the speakers' own native languages. The addition of ἕκαστος ('each') at the relevant points would have established the issue, but Luke makes no attempt to offer such clarification; indeed, he even fails to mention tongues at Samaria at all when it is clear there were charismatic manifestations of some kind (8.17-19), and recounts a number of significant individual conversion-initiations without any mention of tongues (or other charismata) becoming manifest (8.39; 9.17-18; 16.15, 33-34, etc). Noting these, Harm perhaps rightly deduced that, for Luke, tongues 'appeared [only] spasmodically; *it was not the general rule*'.[146]

Can, then, an argument for 'normativity' be based on what amounts to the single otherwise unexplained case of 19.6? Could there not be other reasons why Luke chose to record that the inception of the Spirit on this occasion was marked by a display of charismata? Might he not have

---

Empowered, ch. 13 (J.K. Parratt came very close to arguing the same position, before ultimately modifying it [*Seal*, pp. 182ff.]; cf. Dunn, *Jesus*, §34). Admiring Menzies' case as I do, I have to admit strong reservations. His basic argument has two aspects: (1) As the Spirit of which Luke speaks is the 'Spirit of prophecy' we may expect the gift of glossolalia with which it first came to expression (2.4), and which is so demonstrably prototypical to it, to be evinced regularly; (2) tongues is so distinctive as to provide the most appropriate form of 'initial evidence' of this gift (as opposed to the less evidential gifts of charismatic revelation or other forms of inspired speech), and hence did actually serve as the 'initial evidence' in the conversion of the Gentiles. But the question is surely whether for *ordinary* Christian conversions 'initial evidence' was a question at all: there is no reason to assume such evidence was expected of *every* conversion within the *otherwise accepted* classes of converts.

145. Even the 'all' of Acts 2.4 does not necessarily mean 'all without exception' were filled with the Spirit and spoke in tongues, πᾶς ('all') is often a generalization meaning 'most', 'as a group', 'a representative proportion', or the like.

146. Harm, 'Elements', p. 38.

considered this instance 'extraordinary', or merely 'ordinary', rather than 'normative'? While the incident certainly shows that Luke considered it in some way 'fitting' that the Ephesian twelve experienced invasive charismatic praise of different kinds at the moment the Spirit came upon them, this is hardly strong evidence he thought it should always be so. Various literary and historical factors may as easily account for his narrative choice. Luke's account of Ephesus stands at the end of the fourth division of Acts, and before Paul's 'passion' (19.21ff.). The picture beyond this point is more of Paul as pastor and prisoner: only at Rome does he begin again to preach the gospel (though his apologetic speeches are partly evangelistic). In 18.18–19.20, Luke thus gives his final picture of mission as a crescendo to the theme which has dominated the earlier four parts. He depicts Ephesus as a place in which God's Spirit was particularly strikingly active: tremendous inroads are made against magic; the 'word' is repeatedly depicted as flourishing richly (19.8, 10, 12, 16, 17, 18 and finally 19.20—repeating the redactional summary of 6.7), and it is here that Luke stresses that God worked 'out of the ordinary miracles...through the hands of Paul' (19.11). In this setting it is barely surprising that when Paul lays those same hands on the Ephesian 'disciples', the effect is immediate and dramatic. And these disciples are also a slightly special case in several other respects. In the first place, as Shepherd points out,[147] their story provides Luke with a closure to one of his major sub-plots. John the Baptist, one of the main figures of Luke's Gospel, looked forward to the coming of the messiah who would baptize mightily with Holy Spirit (3.16-17; Acts 1.8; 11.16). Here, in 19.1-6, disciples taught by him at last come into the community established by Jesus and his disciples through the Spirit. Luke may have considered it a particularly fitting closure to the plot to recount that they experienced the Spirit in 'out of the ordinary' power and manifestation. He may have anticipated that as it was precisely the *lack* of the Spirit which had raised questions concerning their baptism, and its focus, God would legitimate their new step by granting the Spirit in this very evident way. Furthermore, Paul had previously been forbidden by the Spirit to speak the word in Asia (16.6), and his consequent uncertainty as to whether he may yet evangelize in this area is expressed in 18.21: 'I will return to you *if God wills*'. On his return to the city, the Ephesian twelve represent his first converts. So Luke may well have considered the initial outburst of charismata to be a form of attestation and sign of encouragement to Paul that it was now the appropriate time for the important ministry based in Ephesus that was to follow. In addition, one of Luke's major literary purposes in Acts is to present Paul as at one with Peter (and the Jerusalem apostles). To accomplish this he uses the literary

147. *Function*, p. 229.

convention of drawing numerous parallels between Peter's speech and actions and those of Paul.[148] The account of the 19.1-6 is cast partly as a parallel to the Samaritan incident, with 19.6 complementing the granting of the Spirit through the hands of Peter and John in 8.17.[149] The manifestation of the distinctively Pentecostal tongues here, alongside prophecy, in this first account in Acts of Paul's own conversion-initiation procedures, serves to underline that the same Spirit that works through Peter and John works through Paul too. I would not suggest any one of these considerations (or the combination of them) is provably 'the explanation' of Luke's choice of this incident. But such considerations serve to indicate how difficult it is to be sure he understood the incident to be paradigmatic for *all* Spirit-reception, in the church. The account may suggest Luke considered 'tongues' to be 'regular' where God was working with special power, but it does not show he thought them normative. We may perhaps venture as far as the verdict offered by Montague: for Luke, 'some external expression of its [scil. the Spirit] reception is normal. Among these expressions, tongues and prophecy have a privileged place', but 'it would be a mistake to make the charismatic expectation into a rigid law',[150] rather Luke sees initial charismatic expression as the specially gracious confirmation of God.

3. *Conclusions*

In §1 we saw there is ample evidence that it is the gift of the Spirit as the 'Spirit of prophecy' that Peter promises all believers, and that the phenomena attributed to the Spirit in the rest of Acts conforms with this understanding. Our review of the Spirit-reception passages in §2 has confirmed this conclusion. In the latter section we have also observed that all the passages we have surveyed (including 8.16) assume the norm of 2.38-39, that is, that conversion, baptism and reception of the 'Spirit of prophecy' formed a single 'conversion-initiation' unit of closely related *theologoumena*. Within it, baptism was the central rite through which the person who repented and came to faith expressed and crystallised these:[151] baptism was not temporally

---

148. See Talbert, *Patterns*; A.J. Mattill, 'The Purpose of Acts: Schneckenburger Reconsidered', in W.W. Gasque and R.P. Martin (eds.), *Apostolic History and the Gospel* (Exeter: Paternoster, 1970), pp. 108-22; S.M. Praeder, 'Jesus-Paul, Peter-Paul, and Jesus-Peter Parallelisms in Luke–Acts: A History of Reader Response', in E. Richards (ed.), *Society of Biblical Literature 1984 Seminar Papers* (Chico, CA: Scholars Press, 1984), pp. 23-49.

149. See Harm, 'Elements', pp. 35-38.

150. G.T. Montague, 'Pentecostal Fire: Spirit-Baptism in Luke–Acts', in McDonnell and Montague, *Initiation*, p. 40.

151. See Dunn, *Baptism*, pp. 91-102 and *passim* (and *Unity*, §39, as a summary of his views).

separated from conversion (e.g. as in the later church by a prolonged period of catechumenate), but integrally connected with it (cf. 2.41, and throughout Acts [cf. 8.12-13; 36-38]; 9.18; 10.47-48; 16.15, 33; 18.8, 19.5). Similarly, it is assumed that the Spirit is immediately given to those who believe and are baptized. As Dunn and others have so persuasively argued, this does not mean the water rite actually conveys the Spirit,[152] rather the Spirit is given to conversional faith, expressed in baptism, but may precede the water rite itself (as with Cornelius) or be granted immediately after the water rite proper, e.g. through laying on of hands (19.5-6). But this separation of the gift of the Spirit from the water rite itself does not imply any sharp theological dissociation from it:[153] the gift of the Spirit is always assumed to be part-and-parcel of the broader complex of 'conversion-initiation' even where there is modulation within the ordering of the constitutive elements. Faith and baptism which does *not* lead to the gift of the Spirit is regarded as an *anomalous* state of affairs to be corrected (8.14-17; 19.1-6).[154]

But if 2.38-39 represents a norm in which the gift of the Spirit is expected to be granted along with conversion and baptism, this would suggest the 'Spirit of prophecy' was not merely an endowment for mission/witness, but a more wide-ranging gift with fundamental significance for Christian existence and the experience of God's salvation in the church.

In the review of the passages concerned with Spirit-reception, we have noted that, with the exception of Pentecost (Acts 1.8; 2.4, 11), there is only one occasion where there is any suggestion that the initial gift of the Spirit is given directly as an empowerment for preaching and witness (Acts 9.17, 20). This conforms with the picture that may be obtained elsewhere in Acts. While the Spirit's empowerment to witness is a very important aspect of Luke's pneumatology, on the whole Luke does not portray the majority of Christians as actively involved in evangelism. By and large, in Jerusalem it is not the company of believers in general but the apostles who preach, work

152. Dunn, *Baptism*, pp. 98-102. See p. 98 n. 17 for a list of those who *per contra* think with Richardson that 'All Christian baptism is baptism in the Holy Spirit'.

153. The exceptions, of course, are those baptised with John's baptism who become disciples of Jesus before Pentecost (and cf. Apollos).

154. So Dunn, 'Baptism', p. 25; more tellingly, because they are from the Pentecostal sector, D. Petts, 'The Baptism in the Holy Spirit in relation to Christian Initiation' (MTh dissertation, Nottingham University, 1987), e.g. p. 65; Montague, 'Fire', pp. 39-41; and Atkinson, 'Responses', esp. pp. 128-29. Reaching similar conclusions on very different grounds see Quesnel, *Baptisés*, chs. 1–2 and 7 (and see his trenchant criticisms of W. Wilkens's attempt ('Wassertaufe', pp. 26-47) to maintain Luke usually separates water and Spirit baptism because for him the former corresponds to the Law and the prophets, the latter to the age of the Spirit (Quesnel, *Baptisés*, pp. 20-23).

signs, and have 'the ministry of the word of God' (6.2: cf. 4.33). Evangelism he sees primarily as the task of the Twelve, of Paul, and of specially endowed people like Stephen (6.8, 10), Philip (8.5-40), Barnabas, John Mark, Silas, Timothy, Apollos etc.; that is, of evangelists and their co-workers (cf. 19.22; 20.4), of whom, no doubt, Luke knew far more than he has named, as 8.4,[155] 11.19-20 (etc.) indicate. On the remarkable occasion of the 'Little Pentecost' in 4.31, the Spirit even comes upon a whole group in one house, and fills them afresh, giving them 'all' courage to proclaim the gospel boldly. But this is precisely not an initial reception of the gift of the Spirit by those involved (certainly not for Peter and John), and those concerned were probably a group of Peter and John's 'friends' (cf. πρὸς τοὺς ἰδίους, 4.23);[156] in any case a group of household size, not the Jerusalem church in general. It is not obvious that Luke considered this occasion typical, far less that he thought it typical of the initial reception of the gift of the Spirit. Most telling against either view is the fact that Luke's key 'summary passages' (2.42-47; 4.32-37; 5.12-16),[157] which speak of a variety of aspects of church life, and of the witness and signs of the *apostles*, are nevertheless entirely silent on the matter of congregational witness or evangelism by the rank and file of the church; similarly the briefer 'progress reports' at 6.7; 9.31; 12.24; 16.5 and 19.20. These observations too should set a question mark over the claim that for Luke the gift of the Spirit is primarily (Shelton) or even exclusively (Menzies) empowerment for mission.

The gateway texts into Acts certainly put missionary proclamation high on the Spirit's agenda (Lk. 24.49; Acts 1.8), but it is probably a mistake to read these as statements pertaining directly to each individual believer (rather than to the disciples in particular, and to the church in general). And before the reader meets the Spirit as the power of witness in Acts 1.8, he or she encounters the Spirit first and foremost as the power of Israel's cleansing, restoration and transformation, in 1.4-8. Taking up the hopes expressed here, Acts 2 portrays the Pentecostal Spirit as the power of Israel's covenant

155. Acts 8.1 generalizes that 'all' were scattered, and 8.4 that 'those who were scattered went about preaching the word', but the latter does not repeat the 'all' of 8.1, and in no way suggests that 'each' preached the word; merely that as a result of their going out, the word was spread (by some).

156. With Marshall, 104: 'to their close circle of *friends* and supporters—obviously a smaller group than the whole Christian community of 4:4'; cf. also Bruce (1990), 156; Pesch, 175.

157. For critical introduction to these see Haenchen, Schneider and Pesch *ad loc.*, also S.E. Pattison, 'A Study of the Apologetic Function of the Summaries of Acts' (PhD dissertation, Emory University, 1990), and M.A. Co, 'The Major Summaries in Acts: Acts 2,42-47; 4,32-35; 5,12-16. Linguistic and Literary Relationship', *ETL* 68 (1992), pp. 49-85.

renewal and the fulfilment of the Baptist's promise of the messianic cleansing and restoration of Israel. This last is also taken up in 11.16 to justify the inclusion of Gentiles, and free association with them, on the grounds that they too are seen to have a part in the Israel of fulfilment that the messiah is cleansing and restoring.

We must now press the enquiry beyond the narrow confines of the passages concerned with reception of the Spirit. Does the remaining material in Acts support the view that the gift of the 'Spirit of prophecy' is necessary for the ongoing experience of 'salvation' among the people of God?

Chapter 13

THE EFFECTS OF THE PENTECOSTAL GIFT IN THE LIFE OF THE CHURCH AND 'SALVATION' IN ACTS

In the previous chapter we have found ample evidence to support the view that Luke understands the gift of the Spirit promised to Christians as the 'Spirit of prophecy'. Among those who have argued most persuasively that Luke thinks of the Spirit this way, however, there has been a strong tendency to conclude that the Pentecostal gift granted to all (2.38-39) is theologically a 'supplementary gift'. Some of the most significant of the studies pressing for this conclusion have, however, based their argument on a rather lop-sided presentation of Luke's pneumatology, concentrating too narrowly on but part of the evidence. Mainville and Stronstad thus relate the Pentecostal Spirit to prophecy or prophetic vocation alone.[1] And Menzies has boldly described the Spirit of prophecy as 'exclusively' 'the source of power for effective witness'.[2] Each indubitably brings out an important aspect of Luke's understanding, but at the expense of over-looking other significant elements. Haya-Prats gave a more balanced picture when he described the Charismatic Spirit of Acts as the 'Strength of the Church', and saw there were ways in which the Spirit contributed directly to the life of the Church itself as much as empowering its mission to

---

1. *L'Esprit*, pp. 285-317 (this includes, however, inspired preaching). Stronstad (*Theology*) uses broader categories when he says 'Luke relates the gift of the Spirit to service and witness; that is, to vocation' (p. 81), but in practice only discusses 'prophetic' (including missionary) vocation (while including within this the power to work miracles, p. 51).

2. 'Luke', pp. 119 and 138-39—he even italicizes the 'exclusively'. I have pointed to evidence in his earlier writing which suggests he does not quite mean this (see 'Empowerment', p. 122 n. 32). Occasionally Menzies admits a wider reference: thus, for example (when drawing parallels from Lk. 1-2, and the Spirit on Jesus), he speaks of the Spirit as 'empowering to carry out a task' (*Development*, pp. 212, 278), and he relates the Spirit directly to the task of the seven in Acts 6.6 (though even here he refers to it as 'commissioning of believers for service in the church's mission', p. 259). See also *Development*, pp. 224-25, and the long footnote 2 there; and his Appendix to *Empowered* (pp. 258-59).

outsiders.[3] In §§1-2 we shall survey the scope of the charismata attributed to the Spirit of prophecy; the former briefly treats the Spirit as empowerment for mission, while in we examine the relationship of the charismata of the Spirit of prophecy to the spiritual 'life' of the community in Acts. Then in §3 we examine the relationship of the Spirit to salvation in Acts, arguing that Luke sees the Spirit as the principal means of God's saving/transforming presence for Israel (and through her to the nations), and that receiving the gift of the Spirit enables participation in this.

1. *The Spirit as the Empowerment of Mission/Witness to Unbelievers*

Since Hans von Baer, no contribution of significance to Lukan pneumatology has been able to escape the conclusion that Luke considers the gift of the Spirit to be 'the driving force of mission'. The gateway texts into Acts (Lk. 24.49; Acts 1.5-8) ensure this for the Pentecostal gift, portraying it as the empowering of servant Israel (cf. Isa. 49.6) to restore the rest of Israel and to bring light to the nations. That the Spirit initiates, empowers and directs 'witness' (in the sense of advocacy of Christ to unbelievers), and so is directly missiologically orientated, is then clear from a whole series of further texts, notably 4.8, 31; 6.10; 8.29, 39; 9.17-20, 31; 10.19; 11.12; 13.2, 4; 16.6-7; 18.25-28(?). The Spirit also plays an important part in confirming or attesting the people of God, their witness and their mission (cf. 5.32; 15.8), but also all places where signs and wonders attest the apostolic witness (4.30-33; 5.12-16; 13.9-12; 19.11-20), for Luke would attribute these to the Spirit[4].[5] For Menzies, these texts are the essence of Luke's pneumatology, and where the Spirit brings visions, revelation, wisdom, joy, comfort or faith to Christians it is but to fuel that witness. So under the same head he can include 2.4, 17-18, 33, 38-39; 6.5; 7.55; 11.24; 13.9, 52; 15.28, and all the references to reception of the Spirit which he brackets with 1.8 as receiving prophetic empowerment for mission.

Once it is granted that Acts is dominated by the account of the expansion of the Church it is hardly surprising that a majority of the references to the Spirit occur in the context of mission, and in some way or other serve, direct

---

3. See *L'Esprit*, chs. 6–7, though as we shall see he always gives the former a missiological 'spin' too.

4. See Chapters 4 and 9 (§4.3) above. Having attributed Jesus' miracles to the Spirit upon him, it is unlikely Luke envisaged a different source for the miracles of the apostles and other witnesses. See also below, and for more detailed argument Turner, 'Luke and the Spirit', §4.4.3.

5. For a brief treatment of this theme see e.g. H.C. Kee, *Good News to the Ends of the Earth: The Theology of Acts* (London: SCM Press, 1990), pp. 30-39 (esp. 35-36); Mainville, *L'Esprit*, ch. 6 (§§2.1.2 and 2.2).

or empower it. This is uncontroversial, and as we have examined the area elsewhere we shall not develop this line of thought further here.[6] But there is something unsatisfyingly one-sided about such an emphasis. As astute an observer of Acts as Jervell has even claimed the Spirit is connected directly with preaching surprisingly rarely in Acts.[7] There are equally many texts that have little or nothing to do with 'mission' unless this is construed sufficiently widely as to mean any kind of service for God's people or outsiders, or unless each activity which is for God's people is seen as enhancing the church, and so making it more missiologically effective. The first of these ploys is in danger of rendering the term 'mission' vacuous, and seriously obscures the possibility that many of the 'services' rendered to the church may have soteriological import for the church, for example, by having transforming impact on the community. The second always amounts to a 'reading' of events from an arbitrarily chosen missiological perspective, rather than a discernment of the author's intention: one simply has no grounds to maintain that Luke thinks of (say) Agabus's prophecy of famine (11.28) and the response to it, as primarily 'missiological' because, somehow, indirectly, the church may have been strengthened, and outsiders challenged.[8]

Most notable among the many texts that have virtually no direct evangelistic significance, and, rather, evidently speak of actions of the Spirit for the benefit of the church herself, are 5.3, 9 (Ananias and Sapphira's sin is a lying to the Spirit; implying the Spirit promotes and monitors the holiness of the church); 6.3 (spiritually wise are to serve tables in the context of a dispute); 11.28 (Agabus's prophecy of famine, allowing the Antioch church to arrange relief) and 20.28 (appointment of leaders by the Spirit to the

---

6. See Turner, 'Spirit and Authoritative Preaching', esp. pp. 68-72 for a brief account of the different ways the charismata of the 'Spirit of prophecy' empower the preaching and witness in Luke–Acts.

7. Jervell claims there are only five places in Acts where the Spirit is connected with the preaching of the gospel (1.8; 2.4; 4.8, 31; 5.32), and that it is the 'boldness' with which the preacher's speak (rather than the content of the message) which is attributed to the Spirit (*Unknown Paul*, pp. 110-12). As one-sided as this is, it provides an important reminder of how easy it is to overstate the case that in Acts the Spirit is 'empowering for mission'.

8. In a private letter to me (7 May 1995), Menzies acknowledges that prophetic phenomena in Luke–Acts are occasionally directed toward the community and thus are not always directed toward non-believers in the form of witness. Nevertheless, he maintains this sort of Spirit-inspired 'encouragement' cannot be separated from the Christian mission to the world (e.g. Acts 9.31) as Luke's larger focus suggests (e.g. Lk. 24.49; Acts 1.8; 4.31). For this reason, Menzies prefers 'empowerment for witness' to the more general 'charismatic' as a descriptive term for the Spirit in Acts. In taking this line Menzies comes uncomfortably close to the second of the above strategies.

church). A number of other texts relate to purely personal prophecies (e.g. those of warning to Paul in 20.23; 21.4, 11). Admittedly, some charismata that benefit or direct the church also have secondary missiological significance. As well as clarifying relations between Jews and Gentiles *within* the church, the decision prompted by the Spirit in Acts 15.28 probably made mission to the Gentiles easier; similarly, churches that live in the fear of the Lord, and the comfort of the Spirit, may expect to attract converts (9.31), just as churches encouraged and challenged by men like Barnabas (11.24) would. And missionaries who by God's grace become 'filled with joy and the Holy Spirit' even when they are rejected (13.52) are undoubtedly thereby refreshed for the next bout of mission. But these are secondary missiological effects, sometimes suggested by the connections in Luke's narrative; they are not evidently the primary purposes of the charismata in question. It is to the significance of such charismata for God's people that we now turn.

2. *The Spirit of Prophecy as the Transforming Self-Manifesting Presence of God in and for the Community*

When von Baer described the Spirit as the driving force of mission he did not simply mean the Spirit empowered witness to unbelievers; he saw this theologoumenon as the unifying factor in the period of Israel (Lk. 1–3) and in the period of Jesus, as well as in that of the church. He was acutely aware of the Spirit's role in the mission *to* and *for* (faithful) Israel as well as through her to as-yet unbelieving Israel and those beyond. In this he was surely on firm ground.

(1) Nothing in the Jewish background would suggest the expectation of a gift of the Spirit on Israel that was exclusively orientated to witness addressed to unbelieving Israel or to the Gentiles; everything rather suggests the expectation is of an eschatological gift to Israel (Isa. 11.1-9, 32.15-20; Ezek. 36-37; Joel 3.1-5 etc., and all the ITP traditions dependent on them)[9] which will restore *Israel*, and enable her to walk in close communion with her God, and so perhaps make her a light to the nations (cf. Isa. 2.1-4; 42.1-9; 49.1-6). We need not doubt the awaited eschatological outpouring thus had very important missiological consequences both for alienated Jews and for Gentiles, but mission is only part of the gift.

(2) Little, if any, of the material in Luke 1–2 would suggest the 'Spirit of prophecy' is primarily empowering for witness to unbelievers in or beyond Israel.[10] The angelic word concerning the Spirit in 1.32-35 is about

---

9.   See Chapters 4 and 5 above.
10. Lk. 1.35 and 2.26 evidently have nothing to do with such witness.

fulfilment of Israel's hopes in her promised Davidid, and directed to a pious Israelite; the prophetic words of the other characters are either recognition oracles (mixed with characteristics of announcement of salvation oracles) (1.42-45; 1.68-79; 2.29-32) or charismatic thanksgiving (1.46-55), and are again directed to God's people or to God himself.[11] John the Baptist's ministry to be undertaken in the 'Spirit and power of Elijah' (1.17) evidently comes closest to the notion of prophetic 'empowering for mission', but it should be noted his task is not exclusively or even primarily to address 'unbelievers'. He is sent to initiate Israel's restoration by addressing 'the people' of God and calling them to radical repentance (1.76-79), and he executes this task by teaching the faithful (3.10-14) as well as by challenging the complacent (3.7-9). It should be noted, too, he is a man of the Spirit for some thirty years before ever he begins this task (1.15; 3.2), so we must envisage this a period in which the Spirit of prophecy primarily shapes the Baptist's own life before God (cf. 1.80), rather than acting through him towards others. No doubt, too, he himself was addressed by the word of the Lord when that came to him (3.2), and was affected by it, as directly as was the Israel to which he relayed it.

(3) We have seen that Jesus' endowment with the Spirit was very much an empowering for mission (3.21-22; 4.18-21)—to liberate others and extend God's reign to them. But this does not mean either that the Spirit was irrelevant to his own experience of sonship to God (4.1; 10.21; cf. also 2.40-52), nor that the mission in question was addressed solely to unbelievers to elicit initial faith and repentance. The mission for which he was empowered of the Spirit was to accomplish Israel's New Exodus liberation and transformation, to purge and to restore Zion, and much of what he did was directed to the already repentant, to instruct, guide and strengthen them.

(4) If the messianic Spirit of prophecy upon Jesus was largely the means of the presence of salvation to Israel, then when the messiah is established on David's throne at God's side, and pours out an analogous gift upon the whole church (2.33-36), we should expect the soteriological impact to be the greater, not the less. Accordingly Luke has kept the fulfilment of the Baptist' promise that the messiah would cleanse his Israel with Spirit-and-fire largely for the period of the church (Acts 1.5; 11.16; 15.9), and he has portrayed Pentecost in terms that also evoke Moses' ascent for the Law at

11. It is misleading, in my view, to characterize these speeches as instances of 'bearing witness' (*contra* e.g. Shelton, *Word*, pp. 15-32), not least because the vector of that metaphor is the advocacy of God's case in the cosmic trial against unbelief (which is not the issue in these oracles): see A.A. Trites, *The New Testament Concept of Witness* (Cambridge: Cambridge University Press, 1977).

Sinai and his gift of it to the people. All this should suggest the Spirit's presence in the church is of vital significance for its ongoing 'life' before God, as
well as for its spoken witness. Corresponding to this expectation, we find
that for Luke the church is very much a community the quality of whose life
is profoundly shaped by the presence of God (and of Christ) in the charismatic Spirit. We have pointed to a number of specific instances of this (see
§1 above), and shall now clarify some of the more important cases of these
in 2.1-4.

2.1. *The Church as a Community of the Spirit in Acts 5.1-11*

A clear (if also perplexing) case is found in the account of Ananias and
Sapphira (5.1-11). The church is here portrayed as a community of the Spirit,
for in the attempted deceit over the extent of their generosity to the community, the pair are said to 'lie to the Spirit' (5.3; = 'to God', 5.4), not
merely to 'men'. The contrast between the united community becoming
'filled with the Spirit' in 4.31 and the heart of Ananias being 'filled by
Satan' to lie to the Spirit (5.3) is evidently intentional, and indicates quite
clearly that the Spirit's role in the community is seen as part of a cosmic and
soteriological dualism: the Spirit versus Satan; salvation versus judgment.[12]
Similarly, according to 5.9, the pair have also 'put the Spirit to the test' (5.9),
which appears to mean 'go against the direction the Spirit has already
clearly indicated' (cf. 15.10).[13] The latter suggests that Luke considers the
loving and united generosity of the community reported earlier (2.44-45;
4.32, 34-37) to be *prompted by the Spirit* (whether through prophecy, or
through apostolic teaching of the Jesus tradition on riches, or whatever).
The hapless pair evidently felt that in the eyes of the community they
should have been more generous than they were prepared to be
(presumably having volunteered whatever the sale of the land would
fetch),[14] whence the lie. Marguerat is probably correct that this represents
a retreat from the restored Paradisal unity of the new congregation into
the alienated individualism of 'the fall'.[15] As such, it is an affront to the

---

12. Cf. D. Marguerat, 'La mort d'Ananias et Saphira (Ac 5.1-11) dans la stratégie
narrative de Luc', *NTS* 39 (1993), pp. 209-26, esp. 218-19.

13. See Haya-Prats, *L'Esprit*, pp. 158-59. For the Old Testament overtones
of putting God to the test in the wilderness (and so rebelling against his Spirit [cf.
Isa. 63.10]), see e.g. Seccombe, *Possessions*, p. 213.

14. With Seccombe, *Possessions*, p. 212. Less likely (in view of 5.4b) is
B.J. Capper's thesis that the pair have withheld what had been formally committed to
the community as part of their initiation procedure as at Qumran (cf. 'The Interpretation of Acts 5.4', *JSNT* 19 [1983], pp. 117-31). For parallels with the Achan story see
Haenchen, 240-41 (but cf. Dunn, *Jesus*, p. 166).

15. Marguerat, 'Mort', pp. 219-23. On 'salvation' as fundamentally the overcoming

soteriological direction of God's restoration of Israel, being fostered and promoted by the Spirit, and hence a 'a putting of the Spirit to the test', as Israel had in the wilderness generation (Isa. 63.10). Accordingly the fateful discovery of their deceit—presumably through revelatory discernment granted by the Spirit (as at 13.9)—brings dramatic divine judgment. Whether or not the Spirit is seen as the presence of God which effected that judgment (in which case, as at 13.9-11, we are seeing some of the purgative fire of the Spirit which the Baptist expected),[16] the Spirit has afforded charismata that profoundly shaped the life of the community, and guarded its 'holiness'.[17]

2.2. *The Church Strengthened by the Spirit through Charismata of the Spirit of Prophecy*

In a revealing incidental aside in Acts 15.32, Luke tells us that Judas and Silas exhorted (παρεκάλεσαν) the brethren in Antioch and 'strengthened them' 'being themselves prophets'. E.E. Ellis rightly perceived that what Luke means is that Judas and Silas were able to have this effect because they were especially charismatically endowed,[18] that is, the Spirit 'strengthened' the congregation through them. Similarly, the summary in 9.31 attributes the increase in numbers of the church throughout Judea, Galilee and Samaria (along with its the peace, upbuilding) to their walking in the 'fear of the Lord' and in comparable 'encouragement (παράκλησις)[19] of the Holy Spirit' (and cf. 11.24). In these instances the Spirit is seen to have a transforming or enhancing influence on the congregation, and the increase

---

alienation, and restoration of paradisal unity with God and between humankind, see S. Hanson, *The Unity of the Church in the New Testament* (Uppsala: Almqvist, 1946); and M. Turner, 'Mission and Meaning in Terms of "Unity" in Ephesians', in A. Billington, A. Lane and M. Turner (eds.), *Mission and Meaning* (Carlisle: Paternoster, 1995), pp. 138-66.

16. See Shepherd, *Function*, p. 211.

17. Cf. 'This community has been brought into being by God's Spirit and is jealously guarded by him' (Seccombe, *Possessions*, p. 212). Haya-Prats (*L'Esprit*, pp. 157-60) is forced to admit this, and, after consideration, resists the temptation to by-pass the narrative as unassimilated pre-Lukan tradition. The language of the Spirit sections is Lukan. For the Qumran community as a congregation of the Spirit of holiness, see Chapter 5 §2.6 above; F.F. Bruce draws attention to the parallel of CD 7.3-4 in which the covenanter must 'not defile his holy Spirit' ('The Holy Spirit in the Acts of the Apostles', *Int* 27 [1973], pp. 166-83).

18. Ellis, *Prophecy and Hermeneutic in Early Christianity* (Tübingen: Mohr, 1978), p. 132.

19. Whether the noun is translated 'comfort/consolation' as at Lk. 2.25, 6.24, or 'encouragement' as at 4.36 (?) and 15.31, or exhortation as at 13.15, it is the church that is the semantic beneficiary of the action.

in the church mentioned at 9.31 and 11.24 could more readily be explained
as the effect of the church thereby *becoming* a witness than as the effect of
direct evangelism (of which there is no hint). While these mentions are
infrequent, they may presumably be generalized—at least to the extent of
including other prophetic teachers such as the apostles and above all Paul,
who for Luke is 'the [charismatic] teacher of Israel'[20] *par excellence*, and
who is regularly described as 'strengthening' the disciples by his
exhortation and teaching (14.22; 15.41; 18.23). This suggests that (for
Luke) just as the charismatic witness of the apostles and others *elicits* faith,
Spirit-empowered exhortation and teaching informs, extends and *strengthens* faith. This should not surprise us, for it is entirely in accord with what
we might expect of the 'Spirit of prophecy' affording 'wisdom' to the
people of God, for example, kindling the sort of understanding of the Gospel
that flows into confident faith and/or joyful praise (by analogy with e.g.
Sir. 39.6).

2.3. *The Spirit of Prophecy and the Christian Wisdom, Faith, and Joy of the Individual*

If so far we have commented on the impact on the congregation of charismata *through* individuals, we should also note that Luke envisages the
Christian life of believers might be considerably deepened and strengthened
by the gift of the Spirit they themselves receive. This perhaps should not
need to be argued in detail, because it has already in a sense been strongly
affirmed by Gunkel and Haya-Prats: both pointed in this respect to such
passages as 6.3, 5, 11.24 and 13.52. On each of these occasions, as they
rightly maintain, we have a (redactional) statement to the effect that individuals were 'filled with' or 'full of' the Holy Spirit, and this is coupled with
some second quality (6.3 = wisdom; 6.5 and 11.24 = faith; 13.52 = joy) in
such a way that the quality in question is seen to derive from the Spirit.[21]
Haya-Prats would also include the goodness/holiness of Barnabas mentioned along with his faith (in 11.24) as due to the effect of the Spirit, and
we are inclined to concur.[22] It is not difficult to see how the Spirit as the
Spirit of prophecy could be responsible for these qualities, and it should be

---

20. See Jervell's essay by this title, *Luke*, pp. 153-83.

21. Gunkel, *Influence*, pp. 16-20; Haya-Prats, *L'Esprit*, pp. 139-47. That 6.3
involves a means–result relation (the Spirit is the means, the wisdom the result) is clear
from the parallel in 6.10 which represents a fusion of Lk. 12.12 and 21.15. The same
may be inferred at 6.5, 11.24 and 13.52.

22. Haya-Prats, *L'Esprit*, p. 143; compare the examples from Judaism in Chapter 5,
esp. Philo, *Gig.* 55; *T. Sim.* 4.4; *T. Benj.* 8.1-3; *T. Levi* 2.3B; 1QH 7.6-7; *Targ. Ps.-J.*
Gen. 6.3; and the 'messianic' figures based in Isa. 11.1-4, esp. *1 En.* 49.2-3; 62.1-2;
Pss. Sol. 17.37; 18.7; 1QSb 5.25; 4QpIsa 3.15-23.

noted that in each case (13.52 excepted) we are dealing not with a single brief charisma, but a longer-term characteristic imprinted on the life of the person in question; i.e. what Paul would refer to as the fruit of the Spirit (cf. Gal. 5.22-23). Gunkel and Haya-Prats, however, tended to regard these instances as marginal for Luke's pneumatology and his view of the 'normal Christian life' on the grounds that they are infrequent, that they concern special giftings to marked individuals (not the common experience), and that Luke is more interested in them for their pastoral and evangelistic impact than in what they show of the Spirit's work in the life of the individual believer.[23] Admittedly, there is valid insight in these last three observations, but each needs qualification.

While we should not be surprised at the relative paucity of such references (given the scope and topic of Luke's work), the fact that they are *redactional* gives them greater significance, and Luke undoubtedly understands them as typical at least in the sense that he would expect the reader to extend what is said of Steven, the Seven and Barnabas to (*inter alios*) the apostles and Paul, whom he regards as equal if not greater exemplars of charismatic wisdom and faith.

Gunkel and Haya-Prats took 6.3, 5; 11.24 and 13.52 to denote special charismatic gifts, sharply distinguished from 'ordinary' Christian faith and wisdom (etc.) Their line of thinking is relatively clear. In Acts 'faith' and repentance precede the gift of the Spirit, and this (allegedly) shows that ordinary Christian 'faith' is a human ability independent of the Spirit. Faith derived *from the Spirit*, by contrast, must then denote occasions where the Spirit intensifies faith beyond the realm of ordinary human possibility, for example, supernaturally making it specific to some situation such as the granting of faith for miracles or enabling persistent joyful faith in circumstances of persecution that would normally be expected to quench it (as 13.52).[24]

Accordingly, Haya-Prats understands the expressions 'full of' the Holy Spirit and faith (or wisdom, etc.) to denote extraordinary and specialized intensifications by the Spirit of the latter otherwise merely human qualities: he appears to explain the 'wisdom' of 6.3 primarily (though not exclusively) as the charismatic grasp of God's plan and ability to communicate it evidenced in 6.10, and the 'faith' of 6.5 as the expectation of God's miraculous intervention as in 6.8.[25] This analysis, however, appears to distort the evidence at significant points. First, Luke does not think of

23. See especially Haya-Prats, *L'Esprit*, pp. 138-47.
24. Gunkel, *Influence*, pp. 16-17; Haya-Prats, *L'Esprit*, §19, esp. p. 129.
25. *L'Esprit*, pp. 142-43.

faith and repentance as purely human abilities.[26]

As Gunkel himself observed, in the ordinary sequence of conversion 'faith comes through the preaching', and the gift of the Spirit is received only subsequently. But that should not have led him to the conclusion that 'faith...is not derived from the Spirit':[27] Luke would hardly devote so much effort to assuring us the Spirit is the empowering of the proclamation if at the end of the day he thought the 'faith' of those who respond was simply a purely human potentiality, attained without divine aid! It would almost be truer of him to say that for Luke faith, repentance and obedience are a matter of *not resisting* the Spirit (cf. 7.51).

Secondly, Haya-Prats tends to misrepresent Luke's usage in so far as he effectively takes the expression 'men full of the Spirit and wisdom' (6.3), and analogous statements, to mean 'men who have wisdom from the Spirit, as opposed to believers whose religious wisdom is merely the expression of human ability'. This makes the metaphor 'full of' a vehicle for making distinctions of kind rather than of degree, whereas in Lukan usage it is the other way around—as at 6.8 where the description of Stephen as 'full of grace and power' differentiates him only in degree from the 'all' upon whom there was 'great grace' according to 4.33.[28] When the Jerusalem church are enjoined to choose seven who are 'full of the Spirit and wisdom', they are not being asked to discern who has spiritual wisdom as opposed to merely human wisdom, but to select seven men who stand out for their spiritual wisdom (with the inference that others have it in less remarkable degree).[29] In short, the infrequent uses of the expression 'full of the Spirit and wisdom (faith, etc.)', far from suggesting a relationship between the Spirit and these qualities is unusual, permits rather that the Spirit regularly enables such qualities, but that some people were more marked by them than others. At this point we need to remember once again that, for a Christianity that grew out of Judaism, a life-transforming 'spirit of understanding', 'insight' or 'wisdom' would be prototypical to the 'Spirit of prophecy'—these are the very activities of the Spirit which would be

---

26. Cf. 5.31 (Jesus is exalted to give repentance to Israel); 11.18 (God grants even to the Gentiles the repentance that leads to life); 13.48 (as many believed as were destined to eternal life); 14.27 (God opened the door of faith to the Gentiles); 16.14 (God opened the heart of Lydia to give heed to Paul's words), etc.

27. *Influence*, p. 17; similarly Haya-Prats, *L'Esprit*, §19.

28. See the excursus at the end of Chapter 6 above.

29. If Luke thought the Jerusalem congregation could choose at least seven who fitted the description from amongst the Hellenists alone (to judge by the names in 6.5), the circle of those who might have been chosen was presumably quite extensive; and by implication there would be an even wider circle of those with 'the Spirit and wisdom' who were less outstanding in respect of this quality.

most readily *expected* in anyone who had received the fulfilment of Joel's promise (cf. Chapter 3 §2.2 above).

Thirdly, the spiritual wisdom sought in 6.3 is not the power to communicate the Gospel to unbelievers, but a wisdom that facilitates the application of the Gospel pastorally to the day-to-day praxis of the church (in a situation of potential division). It would appear to be a more general gift of wisdom, of which the evangelistic skill and adroitness evinced in 6.10 is a more specialized instance. Similarly, we have no reason to restrict the Spirit-given 'faith' of 6.5 to the expectation of God's miraculous intervention in the sort of miracles envisaged in 6.8, though such expectation may exemplify an aspect of the former. Both 6.3 and 6.5 (along with 11.24) refer to spiritual qualities with wide ranging application to the Christian life, not merely to more specialized gifts such as empowering to preach and faith for miracles.[30] If this is so, then (taken with the second point above) we must conclude that for Luke the Spirit is of considerably greater relevance to the development of the Christian life than even Haya-Prats allows.

Similarly, though we may agree that 13.52 marks a particularly striking charisma of joy, we should anticipate from our knowledge of the Jewish background that the Spirit of prophecy would inspire praise (see Chapter 3 §2.4 above), and that the same Spirit would give the wisdom/faith that fuelled joy at a less invasive level (cf. also Sir. 39.6). What Luke understands of those 'filled with joy and the Holy Spirit' at 13.52 we should expect to be commonplace to those with the Spirit of prophecy at less remarkable levels. And certainly we find joy, praise, magnifying of God etc. regularly associated with the Spirit's activity, and in a way that defies the artificial distinction between the 'activity of the Spirit proper', and the 'merely human response' of joy, which Haya-Prats attempts to articulate: in this connection one thinks especially of Elizabeth's joyful exclamation by the Spirit (Lk. 1.41-42), the Baptist 'full of the Spirit' leaping in the womb for joy (1.44), the praises of Zechariah (1.68-79) and Simeon (2.29-32), Jesus' own 'rejoicing in the Holy Spirit' (10.21), the ecstatic semi-inebriation of Pentecost (Acts 2.4-13, 15), and the outbursts of invasive praise at 10.46 and 19.6. These all appear to assume a close and regular association between the Spirit of prophecy and the joy.[31]

We may allow that Luke's engagement in providing an account of the

---

30. At certain points Haya-Prats quite clearly accepts this broader understanding (see especially *L'Esprit*, pp. 142, 147), and he agrees that Luke 'leaves some indications' attesting the fact that the Spirit inspires the general *attitudes* of these charismatics (p. 147). But the implication of his statements are that these amount to incidental corollaries in which Luke shows no interest, and manifestations only significant in exemplary charismatics.

31. Cf. Cullen, 'Euphoria', pp. 13-24.

expansion of Christianity makes him more interested in the Spirit's impact through key figures in its development than on the Spirit's place in the individual lives of the Christians concerned. That does not, however, mean we should minimize the importance of those places where he gives some indication of his view of the latter, as though we are pursuing an effect of the Spirit he merely concedes rather than one he affirms (as Haya-Prats suggests), or (worse) one swimming *against* the current of his theology (as Schweizer protests). A pneumatology of Luke must attempt to organize his concepts in a way that makes due allowance for emphases that his literary purposes prevent him from developing.

2.4. The Spirit of Prophecy and the Summary Passages of Acts (2.42-47 and 4.32-37, and 5.12-16)

Perhaps one of the most significant indications of the impact of the Spirit in the life of believers as individuals and as community is afforded by the so-called 'summary passages'. As is well known, Gunkel has contested the relevance of these passages, asserting (with respect to 2.42-47 in particular), 'there is not one syllable to indicate that the ideal state of the community described derives from the Spirit'.[32] In the literal sense of his statement, he is, of course, right (and the more detailed study of Haya-Prats has partly confirmed his results).[33] The Spirit is not mentioned in this passage, and it could be argued that none of the activities described is *necessarily* attributed to the Spirit: not the unity and devotion to prayer (cf. 1.14), nor the common meals, nor the communal generosity, nor even perhaps the praise (2.47; cf. Lk. 24.53) and exultation (2.46). But Gunkel's verdict rests more particularly on his assumption that it is exclusively the otherwise inexplicable supernatural activities—those *beyond* 'natural human possibilities'—that would be attributed to the Spirit. This must be challenged at two points. (a) Jews did not think that every activity of the Spirit of prophecy was manifest in an unambiguous way (clearly differentiated from related merely human possibilities), least of all when it came to the giving of wisdom and its associated phenomena (understanding of God's ways, faith, joy etc.). The spectrum between the faith of the Samaritans in 8.12 and that of Stephen or Barnabas in (6.5; 11.24) offered no sharp dividing line between what was possible before reception of the gift of the Spirit and what was possible to one 'full of the Spirit and faith', and even the former was aided by the Spirit (through Philip's preaching and teaching). (b) Gunkel himself made a very clear distinction between how the earliest Christians might have come to 'diagnose' an event to be one inspired by the Spirit (in which

---

32. Gunkel, *Influence*, p. 10.
33. See Haya-Prats, *L'Esprit*, pp. 147-56.

case a certain 'immediacy' of the Spirit's manifestation might have been necessary) and how a later religious writer might construe the same events, where this factor might be less important in arriving at a decision.[34] So the question becomes, would Luke (with hindsight) attribute the life of the congregations depicted in the summaries to the presence of the Spirit within community? To this question Haya-Prats himself gives a cautious affirmative.[35] If anything, the evidence suggests he could have been more positive.

(A) The summary passages provide a picture of an unexpectedly 'enthusiastic' congregation, and it is this total picture, rather than each individual element, that requires explanation. The disciples are now for the first time regarded as a 'fellowship' (κοινωνία, 2.42) which is portrayed as generous community of 'friends' who have all things in common (κοινά, 2.44; 4.32), and a united brotherhood of reconciliation (cf. 'of one heart and soul', 4.32; 'one together' 2.44, 46; 5.12),[36] enjoying table-fellowship (2.42, 46), joyfully worshipping God (2.47), and being held in high esteem by the rest of the people (2.47; 5.13). In this community there are no poor left in need, nor hungry to mourn, nor rich who oppress, and they are freed from the fear of their enemies to serve God (cf. 4.29-31, in context). The description corresponds in considerable measure to the 'salvation' envisaged in Lk. 1.71-76,[37] and to the aims of Jesus' ministry for Israel's transformation that we noted earlier (cf. Chapter 11 §1.1 above). But if that is the case, the readiest explanation of the change is that the messiah is now baptising his people with Spirit (1.5) or that the 'Spirit of prophecy' has been given to his

34. See *Influence*, pp. 22-23.

35. See esp. *L'Esprit*, p. 156, where he admits that the context of the first two summaries 'probably' indicates that Luke attributes the dynamic 'life' of the community to the Spirit, even if this is but a minor incidental theme in his narrative. He adds, 'Luke does not intend to speak [directly] of ethical consequences of the gift of the Spirit, but he knows the dynamism of the Spirit also inspires the religious and moral outlook which the believers have adopted since they accepted the message about Jesus. The renunciation of worldly goods and the communal prayer are ways of life which find their origin in the teaching of Jesus, but one gets the impression that the experience of the gift of the Spirit intensifies these practices and spreads them forth to the point where they become a sort of witness to the holiness of the community.' Cf. also p. 163.

36. Cf. D.L. Mealand, 'Community of Goods and Utopian Allusions in Acts II–IV', *JTS* 28 (1977), pp. 96-99, who argues Luke's statements more closely echo Greek utopianism than the ideals of friendship, but *per contra* see Seccombe, *Possessions*, pp. 200-209. For a more nuanced position see B. Capper, 'The Golden Age, Reciprocity, and the Ethics of Acts', forthcoming in I.H. Marshall and D. Petersen (eds.), *The Book of Acts in its First Century Setting* (Grand Rapids: Eerdmans; Carlisle: Paternoster Press, forthcoming), VI.

37. See Seccombe, *Possessions*, pp. 200-209; York, *Last*, p. 62. On deliverance 'from enemies' anticipated in Lk. 1.71, 74, see below.

people by the ascended prophet-like-Moses as the Pentecost Spirit of Israel's covenant renewal (2.1-11, 33), the transforming Spirit of Israel's restoration promised in Isa. 32.15 (cf. Acts 1.8).

(B) The cotext of the first two summaries supports this view. Commenting on the promise of the Spirit in 2.38-39, Giblet notes that contrary to the expectations raised by 2.4 and 2.17-18, 'the immediate context leads one to think [rather] that the sharing in the messianic community... of the Holy Spirit experiences itself [not in tongues and prophecy but] in the style of life described in Acts 2:42ff.'[38] One can see his point. Acts 2.42-47 follows so immediately (with 2.41) upon Peter's promise, that the reader naturally assumes the state of affairs described there is a measure of the impact of the promised Spirit on the community. The lack of any specific comment about the Spirit in 2.42-47, to earth the tense expectation built up from 2.1-11 through to 2.38-39, serves only to strengthen the reader's assumption. If one does not presume that the Spirit underlies the overall picture of the community here (and/or individual elements of it), then the silence on the Spirit in 2.42-47 becomes astonishingly incongruous, a sharp dissonance in the narrative and thematic development. The second summary (4.32-37) follows almost equally hard on the account of the 'Little Pentecost' in 4.31, though here there is at least a change of subject between 4.31 and 4.32. Once again there is literally 'not a syllable' to indicate that the Spirit is behind the life of the community depicted there, though in this case the Spirit would evidently be *presumed* to be the source of the 'great power' with which the apostles gave their testimony (4.33; cf. Lk. 24.49; Acts 1.8), and so might equally plausibly be supposed, while unmentioned, behind other aspects of the community life, especially its communal generosity (cf. what is said on 5.3, 9 above).

(C) Certain elements in the summaries suggest or require explanation in terms of the Spirit. The powerful preaching of 4.33 falls into the latter category, the communal care into the former. The 'apostolic teaching' of 2.43 would too almost certainly be imagined to be charismatic in character and to have considerable spiritual impact on the community after the stunning success of Peter's preaching—the apostles will not be supposed to lag behind Barnabas (11.24), Judas and Silas (15.32) in this respect. Other evident candidates for consideration are the 'exultation (ἀγαλλίασις) of heart' (2.46) and the praise (αἰνεῖν, 2.47) of the community. Of course Gunkel and Haya-Prats are right to caution us that the words used here can apply to 'merely human' responses to God's salvation.[39] But is there any reason to

38. 'Baptism', p. 166.
39. For the first see Acts 16.34, for the second see Lk. 2.20; 19.37; Acts 3.8, 9 (and compare e.g. Lk. 24.53 [εὐλογεῖν]).

think that such alone is meant? If we may presume the *Magnificat* is a prophetic utterance then both occasions of ἀγαλλίασις in Luke's Gospel refer to an 'exulting' *in the Spirit* (1.49; 10.21), and so this must be a very distinct possibility in 2.46.[40] The verb αἰνεῖν ('to praise [God]') itself tells us nothing about whether the action concerned is performed as an unaided human response, as an influenced human response, or as invasive charismatic speech. But we would suggest that given the invasive doxological phenomenon of the 'other tongues' in the immediately preceding scene of Pentecost (2.4, 11), the reader will anticipate that at least some of the exultation and praise of 2.46-47 resulted from a variety of levels of inspiration by the Spirit, from a praise articulating joyous charismatic faith to occasions of full-blooded invasive charismatic speech.

Given the understanding of the 'Spirit of prophecy' and its prototypical gifts in Judaism, and given that it is this very Spirit that is promised in the passage immediately before the first summary (2.38-39), what is said in 2.42-47 (and in similar summaries) should most naturally be taken to imply that the actions of the Spirit of prophecy significantly influenced and shaped the development of (at least significant aspects of) the religious and ethical/moral life of the community, and gave it its general 'enthusiastic' tenor.[41] In short, it is only by treating the summaries as isolated units, patched in by a scissors-and-paste editor, that one can maintain Gunkel's radical distance between the promise of the Spirit and the life of the community. But from a narrative critical perspective, *the theme of Acts 2.42–5.41 is how the Pentecostal Spirit takes hold of this first Christian community, and shapes it and strengthens it as a community of salvation, in its growing conflict with the religious authorities.*[42]

2.5. *Conclusions to §2 and Implications for Lukan Pneumatology*

Our brief survey in (§1 and) §2 has indicated that far from being an empowering for mission alone, the Spirit in Acts has a vital place in and for the life of the people of God. If the Spirit brings prophetic empowering to address outsiders (1.8; 2.4; 4.8, 32; 9.17) and to call them into saving faith, the same Spirit of prophecy addresses the church in teaching and encouragement which strengthens her (9.31; 11.24; 15.32 and cf. the summary passages) and provides guidance of her councils (15.28) and revelations of import to her (11.28). If the Spirit calls certain men to the task of evangelistic mission

---

40. Haya-Prats admits as much, *L'Esprit*, p. 149.

41. As Haya-Prats admits, *L'Esprit*, p. 163.

42. Correctly, Marguerat, 'Mort', p. 215. Cf. E. Haulotte, 'La vie en communion, phase ultime de la Pentecôte, Acts 2,42-47', *Foi et Vie* 80 (1981), pp. 69-75; Shepherd, *Function*, pp. 166-67 ('the Spirit is pictured as initiating an ideal community'); Johnson, *Acts*, p. 62.

(13.2, 4), the same Spirit appoints elders to oversee God's flock, protect it and nurture it (20.28, cf. 18-35), a provision laden with import for the church of Luke's day.[43] If the Spirit guides the day to day moves of the missionaries (cf. 16.6-7, 9), Luke also knows of visions and guidances to Christians who are not engaged in mission (9.10-16), and about matters other than the mission (19.21; 20.22, 23; 21.4; 21.11). On this point there can be no doubt, the Spirit is an empowering to serve the church as much as it is to serve its mission to outsiders, even if Luke's account of the expansion of Christianity inevitably gives more space to the latter.

This survey also suggests that the Spirit is related to the development of the Christian life both of the individual and of the church corporate. This has been noted as happening in two ways: (a) the Spirit may influence, strengthen and guide through the teaching, direction, and inspired actions of other charismatic members of the church, and the corporate 'atmosphere' of faith, expectation, and worship which this inspires, but also (b) the Spirit is noted as more immediately involved in the lives of at least some Christians enabling unusual depths of wisdom and faith, with the probable implication that others too experienced the same if in lesser degree,[44] a probability which becomes virtually a certainty when it is remembered that spiritual 'wisdom' or 'understanding' were prototypical effects anticipated of the 'Spirit of prophecy' in Judaism. The 'summary passages' in their context (especially the first) are most naturally taken to imply that the actions of the Spirit of prophecy significantly influenced and shaped the development of the religious and ethical/moral life of the community. Nor should this surprise us, for, as we have seen, the Spirit of prophecy in Judaism was anticipated to have such an effect.

It would appear, then, that for Luke the Spirit provides the charismatic dimension of the Christian life which brings the believer (individually and corporately) God's directing, transforming and strengthening presence, supporting a wide variety of Christian activity, including witness. This may provide a large part of the explanation for why he considers receiving the gift of the Spirit something that should normally take place at conversion-initiation. It is of fundamental importance for the ongoing experience of God and of Jesus' kingship in the community.

This might still leave unexplained why he should expect *all* normally to

43. C.K. Barrett describes this passage as the most important paragraph in Acts, for here 'Luke makes explicit the relation between the period about which he writes and the period in which he writes' ('Paul's Address', p. 107).

44. It is not without significance that the only believers in Acts said to be 'full of faith (or wisdom)' receive this from the Spirit, and with the exception of 16.5 ([?] but cf. the evident parallel with 15.30-32) none are described as growing in these qualities by any other means.

receive the gift at conversion-initiation, for one could envisage converts entering the community of the Spirit and to some extent being built up in their faith and discipleship by the Spirit active through others, without themselves needing to receive the gift (as was perhaps the case in Samaria, through Philip, before the arrival of Peter and John). Though my view goes much further to explaining the 'norm' of Acts 2.38 than does the hypothesis that the Spirit is a 'supplementary gift' merely empowering witness, there is admittedly still a gap in the evidence here. But it is perhaps legitimate at this point to draw out some implications of what we have learned so far, and ask whether these do not at least partially bridge the gap in the explicit evidence.

Granted that the Spirit is the Spirit of prophecy giving various forms of revelation, wisdom and invasive speech and praise for the benefit of the church herself as well as for her mission, it is very probable that Luke envisaged the same Spirit performing similar functions within the individual, shaping and deepening his or her Christian life and commitment. In the interests of his thesis that the gift of the Spirit is a *donum superadditum*, Menzies has denied this, asserting instead:

> the Spirit comes upon the disciples to equip them for their prophetic vocation (i.e. for their role as 'witnesses'). The disciples receive the Spirit...as the essential bond by which they (each individual) are linked to God; indeed, *not primarily for themselves*. Rather, as the driving force behind their witness to Christ, the disciples receive the Spirit for others.[45]

But this position that the gift is 'essentially for the benefit of others (not for the recipient of the gift)', while making a valid point, is surely wrong in what it denies. No-one with Luke's knowledge of Judaism would be liable to have viewed the gift in such a way. The large majority of examples of charismatic revelation, wisdom and invasive charismatic praise in the ITP literature benefited the recipient either exclusively or along with others. The Old Testament/ITP figure most clearly endowed with the Spirit for the benefit of others is perhaps the 'messianic' Davidid of Isa. 11.1-4, but one can hardly deny that the charismata of wisdom, understanding, knowledge and 'the fear of the Lord' which these verses describe were thought to be as important for his own life and standing before God as for the task he was to undertake. It would similarly be quite artificial to invoke Menzies' distinction for, for example, Lk. 1.15 (the Baptist is filled with Spirit for thirty years [cf. 1.80; 3.2] before he undertakes any task for the benefit of Israel), 2.26 (Simeon knows the messiah will come before he dies), 2.40-52, 4.1, 10.21 (Jesus' wisdom and knowledge of God, his ability to overcome the tempter, and his exultation are all derived from the Spirit) and so on. And it

---

45. *Development*, p. 207 (my italics).

would be equally perilous to argue in Acts that the Spirit only gave invasive praise, joy, wisdom, encouragement, assurance and faith for the benefit of the mission, or for the benefit of others in the church, not for the benefit of the *pneumatiker* himself. Even when Luke's narrative hints at the missiological and ecclesial pertinence of such charismata, he would barely wish to play down the strengthening these would bring to the life of the charismatic himself. And while Luke's account inevitably focuses largely on the Spirit's contribution to the expansion and strengthening of the church, are we really to assume he thought the Spirit worked in these dimensions alone, and not in the individual life of faith? No Judaism, nor any other Christianity thought thus, so we should not infer it from Luke's silences. It would be far safer to conclude that Luke expected his reader to fill in his silences from the common Jewish and Christian presupposition pool concerning the Spirit. That is, the reader is expected to assume that the same Spirit of prophecy whose charismata fuelled the mission and strengthened and directed the life of the church would by the same means strengthen the individual too: (a) as the revelatory gift that made him or her aware of God's presence and leading;[46] (b) as the source of spiritual wisdom facilitating the sort of inner dynamic and motivating comprehension of the Good News which fuelled active personal discipleship, prayer and doxology;[47] and (c) as the combination of these, enabling him or her to take active part in the communal life and witness of the church.

3. *The Spirit of Prophecy as the Primary Means of the Restoration/Salvation of Israel in Acts*

In this section it shall be argued (A) that Luke considers Israel's promised restoration/salvation to be largely complete in the church; (B) that he regards the Spirit of prophecy as the primary if not only means of this, and

---

46. Elsewhere I have referred to the 'Spirit of prophecy' in Judaism, Luke–Acts and John as 'the organ of communication between God and a man' ('Spiritual Gifts', p. 40), and so as an essential means by which the disciple becomes aware of God and the risen Lord, and at the same time the means by which Jesus may continue to exercise his lordship over his disciples beyond the ascension (cf. 2.33). As this (without the christological focus) is so evidently in keeping with Jewish understanding of the 'Spirit of prophecy', I cannot see why Menzies attempts to deny its importance in Luke's pneumatology (as at *Development*, pp. 206, 279).

47. We have seen how what Menzies describes as the 'soteriological Spirit' at Qumran is the Spirit of prophecy affording knowledge, wisdom and insight that inspires righteous living (Chapter 5 §2.6); such an understanding would provide an analogy for what is suggested here. We have also seen parallels in the 'messianic' traditions based in or echoing Isa. 11.1-4 (see Chapter 5 §2.9).

(C) that he does not indicate any other 'means' of the presence of salvation independent of the Spirit. Limitations of space allow only a sketch of relevant arguments here.

(A) Israel's restoration or salvation is a cardinal theme of Luke–Acts. Three converging arguments suggest Luke thought of this as largely complete by Acts 15 (rather than e.g. that he deferred the major thrust of this hope to the Parousia).

(1) As we have seen, the hopes announced in Luke 1–2 came to partial fulfilment in the ministry of Jesus, where they were largely articulated in Isaianic New Exodus symbolism. These same hopes reach a new climax of expectation with the transition from Luke to Acts. Jesus' ascent to the 'throne of David' at God's right hand may be anticipated to commence his messianic rule over Israel (cf. Lk. 1.32-33; Acts 2.34-36).

(2) Answering to these hopes, as we just observed in §2.4, the 'summary passages' of Acts depict a new sort of community that approximates more fully to the hopes of salvation announced in Luke 1–2 than anything which has preceded.[48] What lay at the heart of the hoped for restoration/salvation has largely been fulfilled through the Christ-event and the inauguration of the messianic community and fellowship. If Lk. 1.68-76 is one of Luke's clearest statements about the content of her hoped-for salvation, it is fundamentally a *community* hope. It centres on the forgiveness of sins that redeems Israel from her beleaguered estate, a Davidic ruler liberating her from her enemies, a renewal/fulfilment of the covenant God promised Abraham (cf. Acts 3.25-26), and a freedom to serve God in righteousness and without fear. To this, Simeon's song (2.29-32) adds the hope that Israel's salvation will make her a light to the Gentiles in accord with Isa. 42.6/49.6-9. It is not difficult to see how Luke may have thought the Jerusalem leaders in Acts 15 came to perceive those hopes as substantially fulfilled in the messianic community of reconciliation and 'peace' he has described in Acts! As Stalder claimed, 'For Luke the existence of the church is *the* visible *soteriological* consequence of the mission of Jesus';[49] that is, the aims of the mission of Jesus (cf. Chapter 11 §1.1 above) find their major soteriological fulfilment in the type of community Luke depicts.

(3) That Israel's restoration is thereby *in principle* complete by Acts 15, seems to be the inference to be drawn from James' use of Amos 9.11-12 in 15.16-17, and of the conclusion of the conference. The passage is used to support the claim that because the fallen booth of David has been restored,

---

48. The same is true in other 'reports' in Acts, e.g. 9.31, which portrays the church in the blessing of God's peace.

49. 'Heilige Geist', p. 290 (my italics).

the Gentiles may now be added. The restored 'booth' in question, as we have seen, is probably the Davidic household and the messiah's powerful rule in Israel, and the assumption of James's argument is that 'Israel' has been 'restored' in an unexpected way (i.e. around the Twelve in the messianic Jewish church), and so has become the eschatological 'light to the nations' to which the Gentiles may now be added.[50]

If the earlier chapters of Acts, especially 3.17-26 (on which see Chapter 10 §3.2), still look largely to the future for Israel's restoration, the events which followed may well explain the different emphasis in Acts 15. By the time of the Apostolic Council, the Jewish church had reached its zenith, not merely in Jerusalem but in parts of the diaspora too. Far more important, the whole understanding of the nature of the Israel of fulfilment and of the relationship of the people of God to empirical Israel has been fundamentally revised in the light of the three great surprises of the Cornelius episode: (i) Peter's vision throwing a question over the applicability of the purity laws; (ii) the evidence that Gentiles too are part of the 'Israel' the messiah cleanses with his Spirit, and (iii) their inclusion in the people of God without circumcision and Torah-commitment. One may anticipate that Peter's view of Israel and what her restoration meant would have been fundamentally revised by these events, and the revisions they portend would be away from a strongly nomistic and nationalist restoration. While we cannot exclude the possibility that Luke may have envisaged a future landslide of unbelieving Jews into the faith, as some have discerned Paul to teach in Rom. 11.25-27,[51] he nevertheless has very little to say about such hopes, and absolutely nothing beyond the all-important watershed of the inclusion of the Gentiles. It is difficult to believe he would have thought the restored Zion so expanded would differ sharply in kind from the Israel of fulfilment he already knew in the church.

(B) If Acts, then, is largely an account of Zion's messianic 'restoration' around the twelve, and her consequent mission to be a light to the Gentiles,

---

50. See Chapter 10 §3.2 above, and compare Kee, who aptly comments, 'Omitted by the author of Acts from his quotation of Amos' prophecy is the phrase found in both the Hebrew text and in the LXX which declares that the kingdom will be restored "just like the days of old" (Amos 9:11). *What is happening is seen as transformation rather than merely restoration of the Israelite monarchy*' (*News*, p. 59, my italics). Cf. Schmitt, 'L'Eglise', pp. 209-18.

51. The most coherent case for this traditional view of Rom. 11.25-27 is presented by G. Wagner, 'The Future of Israel: Reflections on Romans 9–11', in W.H. Gloer (ed.), *Eschatology and the New Testament: Essays in Honor of George Raymond Beasley-Murray* (Peabody, MA: Hendrickson, 1988), pp. 77-112. The case against, however, is more compellingly presented by N.T. Wright, *The Climax of the Covenant: Christ and the Law in Pauline Theology* (Edinburgh: T. & T. Clark, 1991), ch. 13.

we must ask by what divine *means* this was accomplished. In the ministry of Jesus it was through the empowering of the Spirit that he brought the beginnings of this salvation to Israel. By what means was messianic salvation to continue and be strengthened in Israel by the messiah now enthroned at God's right hand? *The most obvious means of such restorative rule from heaven is the gift of the Spirit of prophecy, of which Jesus now becomes Lord, and which he pours out as the Spirit of Jesus* (2.33; 16.7). Four lines of evidence clearly point in that direction:

1. That the Spirit of prophecy is understood as the means of the messiah's restorative rule corresponds well with the promise of the Baptist that the messiah will cleanse Israel with Spirit and fire (Lk. 3.16; Acts 1.5; 11.16). Here the Spirit is portrayed as divine power by which the messiah completes the soteriological task, and this motif comports with Luke's more general understanding of the Spirit of prophecy as the executive power of the risen Lord (Acts 2.33; 16.7, and see Chapter 10 §3.1 above).
2. That the Spirit of prophecy is the means of the messiah's restoration of Israel corresponds with the key transitional passages (Lk. 24.44-49 and Acts 1.1-11) which present the Spirit which Jesus will grant (Lk. 24.49) not only as the endowment of the Church for its prophetic vocation as the servant of Isaiah 49, but also as the fulfilment of Isa. 32.15-20, which depicts the Spirit as the renewing power of the community.
3. That the Spirit of prophecy is the means of the messiah's saving restoration of Israel also comports well with the Moses/Sinai allusions of the Pentecost account. These last suggest the Spirit of prophecy from the ascended one is a gift of foundational importance for the life of the Israel of fulfilment (as the Law was for Israel, but more); not merely an endowment to extend its borders.
4. In §2 above we have seen how the charismata of the Spirit of prophecy poured out by the heavenly Lord could be thought to effect this programme of renewal *within* the Israel of fulfilment as much as providing the endowment to witness to those outside it.

    Some further aspects of the hopes raised in Luke 1–2 might be accounted for by the gift of the Spirit. If the church still has some powerful enemies (leaving the hopes of Lk. 1.71, 74 apparently unfulfilled), she knows God can intervene dramatically on her behalf (4.23-30; 5.19; 9.1-31; 12.1-11 [and vv. 18-23]; 14.19-20; 16.25-26 etc.), that her life is lived in parallel with the rejected and crucified Prophet, and, more important (in line with Lk. 1.74), *the Spirit frees the church from the fear of these enemies*, whether directly inspiring her courage (4.32), or granting comforting visions (7.55-56; 9.13-16; 18.9), or by revealing that the way ahead leads to suffering (with the implication that this is in God's hands and serves his purposes; cf. 9.16; 20.22-23; 21.4, 11).

The evidence is sufficient to justify the verdict that for Luke the Spirit is at least a principal means of God's saving restoration and transformation of Israel.

In the light of this one can only be a little surprised by the attempts in some quarters to claim that for Luke salvation is made present chiefly by *other* means, and that the Spirit is a 'second gift' beyond salvation.[52] Where this kind of claim is made, what is usually meant in the first place is simply that repentance, faith and baptism (for forgiveness of sins and as entry to the community of salvation) normally precede the gift of the Spirit.[53] But this is to confuse initial entry to salvation with the salvation itself. For Luke the experience of 'salvation' to which men and women are called before the eschaton *commences* with the forgiveness of sins (and assurance of eschatological justification), but it is *experienced* in participation in the ongoing life, witness and worship of the new community, the people of God among whom the promises of Israel's transformation are being fulfilled. In other words, 'salvation' consists in a new way of being in the world—one which consists in existential knowledge of the reconciling love of the Father (cf. esp. Lk. 15) and the response of joyful worship, one which submits to the heavenly Lordship, rule and direction of Israel's messiah and saviour, and one which lives by the 'paradigm of mercy' that Jesus exemplified and taught. In all of this the gift of the Spirit of prophecy plays a decisive part; not merely in promoting the witness which first draws people into the people of God, but also in the shaping of the community's spiritual and corporate life as the light of salvation to both Jew and Gentile.[54]

(C) The question then arises whether the Spirit of prophecy is regarded as an *indispensable* means of ongoing experience of salvation, or whether

---

52. The most blatant form of this is undoubtedly that of Flender who maintains, 'the exalted Christ is present to the community in virtue of his name. The name has the power to save (Acts 2.21). But...the Holy Spirit...fills the community with courage and comfort, thus equipping it for its divine mission in the world...hence there is a clear distinction of function between Christ and the Spirit' (*Luke*, p. 139.)

53. This is the form the argument takes in Haya-Prats, *L'Esprit*, §§18-19, and Menzies, *Development*, pp. 258-60, 275-76, 279.

54. In so far as Haya-Prats (*L'Esprit*, chs. 6 and 7) agrees the Spirit performs these functions, he permits the Spirit has what Menzies would term a soteriological function. Menzies' denial of the latter to the Spirit in Acts, and his assertion of an 'exclusively' missiological function, unfortunately fails to consider the relevant detail.

Luke regarded the Spirit as one among many such means. One might concede the gift of the Spirit was a 'supplementary' gift for him, only if there were sufficient evidence that alternative or parallel 'means' existed for the continued experience of salvation.

'Means' other than the Spirit, by which God's presence and assistance might savingly be made known to believers in Acts, have certainly been mooted.[55] One might include among the possibilities for discussion here:

a. the angel of the Lord (5.19; 8.26; 12.7-11[?]);
b. other angels (27.23);
c. Christophanies (i) on the Damascus Road (9.1-9; 22.6-11; 26.13-18) or (ii) other visions or hearings of Christ (7.55; 9.10; 18.9-10; 22.17-18; 23.11);
d. the 'hand of the Lord' (4.30; 11.21; 13.11);
e. 'power' (3.12; 4.7, 33; 6.8; 10.38);
f. the 'name of Jesus';
g. the scriptures and the Jesus tradition.

But of these only the last two are strictly pertinent. The rest are either special cases (c [i]), or empowerments for mission, or derive from or refer to the Spirit.[56]

---

55. We await a detailed research of these (but cf. Haya-Prats, *L'Esprit*, pp. 37-52). What follows is but a scanty sketch of areas that need discussion in detail, but constraints of space forbid more.

56. (a) and (b) may be dismissed as of marginal relevance to Luke's picture of Christian 'salvation'. References to 'the angel of the Lord' denote the extension of God's own presence (rather than an intermediary) and may even be an alternative way of speaking of the Spirit (cf. 8.29, 39): see Baer, *Geist*, pp. 43 and 199-201, and Haya-Prats, *L'Esprit*, pp. 44-47. (As Bruce [*Acts*, p. 225] notes, the Elijah parallels of the story of Philip and the eunuch especially highlight the parallelism between the angel here and the Spirit of the Lord who moved Elijah from place to place [1 Kgs 18.12; 2 Kgs 1.3; 2.16]). In any case, these are rare, and probably traditional rather than Lukan. And Luke does not imagine any believer being sustained in 'salvation' by a succession of angelophanies; if one were obliged to categorize their function it would come under 'empowerment for mission' and 'liberation' rather than soteriology. The Christophanies (c [i]) are potentially more interesting, though with Baer and Haya-Prats we should exclude the Damascus road appearances which Luke regards as exceptional direct actions of Christ. In the case of the other visions (c [ii]), however, it is not at all clear that Luke envisages a divine 'means' independent of the Spirit, for he programatically attributes visions and dreams to the Spirit of prophecy; where it concerns men of the Spirit, the dream/visions should be attributed to the Spirit (cf. 7.55) unless there are indications to the contrary (see Chapter 12 §1 above, esp. n. 1). (d) and (e) are evidently also cases of empowering for mission, and in both we appear to have special locutions for the Spirit's own activity, rather than some means strictly independent of the Spirit. This is relatively clear for the use of 'power' in Acts. Despite the claims

First, with respect to the Scriptures and teaching/proclamation about Christ. It has been noted that Conzelmann, Flender, Wilckens and others have spoken of salvation being present to the community (initially) in the kerygma and (beyond conversion) in the word about Jesus (with which we may bracket both the Scriptures which point to him and the Lord's Supper which articulated the redemptive meaning of his death).[57] The important place of these in the community need not be doubted, even if there is less evidence than we might expect of their centrality in the day-to-day life of Christians.[58] But it is doubtful whether Luke envisages these as the dynamic behind the new communities' life, or even being effective at all as

made that in the Gospel God's δύναμις can denote his miracle-working manistic power, distinct from the Spirit, this is not a serious possibility in Acts, where the hendiadys in 10.38 specifies Jesus' power to heal as derived directly from the Spirit (see Chapter 9, §4.3 above). It is then difficult to avoid the conclusion that 6.8 (Stephen 'full of grace and power' working miracles) refers to similar enablement by the Spirit, as Stephen is a remarkable *pneumatiker* (6.3, 5, 10; 7.55) and the working of 'wonders and signs' is widely recognized as part of a set of intentional Jesus–Stephen parallels (cf. 2.22). At 4.7 (cf. 3.12) the question is 'by what "enabling" or "potency"?', not 'by what (manistic) "substance"?' That only leaves 4.33 which (like 1.8) refers to enablement to give powerful spoken witness. The same probably applies for the 'hand of the Lord'. This is an anthropomorphism for God's effective power in creation and history (cf. Philo, *Plant.* 50), and does not strictly identify any one separate 'means' of that powerful presence. In Ezek. 3.14, 8.3, 37.1, the term is used in parallel with the Spirit of the Lord and as a co-referential expression, especially where the action of the Spirit in question concerns or includes e.g. works of power, such as the transportation of the prophet, rather than purely revelatory acts (cf. 3.22, 8.1, etc. where it is used for what Ezekiel elsewhere attributes to the Spirit); accordingly the rabbis tend to translate the anthropomorphism with *either* בוּרה or רוּח (cf. E. Lohse, *TDNT*, IX, p. 428). The use of 'the hand of the Lord' at Acts 4.30 and 13.11 is contextually immediately associated with the Spirit, and so, like the 'finger of God' at Lk. 11.20, probably refers to the Spirit's activity evinced in miraculous power (whether of healing and blessing or in judgment) (cf. Rodd, 'Spirit or Finger', pp. 157-58; Hamerton-Kelly, 'Note', pp. 167-69). Ockham's razor should be wielded against the proposition that we have two independent 'means' of God's action in the same place and at the same time, when we already know Luke is willing to attribute Jesus' miracles to the empowering of the Spirit (for more detailed substantiation see Turner, 'Luke and the Spirit', pp. 143-44). The general and missiological role assigned to 'the hand of the Lord' in 11.21 strongly suggests that here it is a Septuagintalism for activities performed largely (if not exclusively) through the Spirit.

57. On the first see e.g. J. Jervell, 'The Center of Scripture in Luke', in *Unknown Paul*, pp. 122-37. On the second, Marshall, *Supper*, pp. 101-106.

58. In Acts those who study the scriptures avidly are the eunuch (8.32) and synagogue Jews, like the Beroeans (17.11)—i.e. those not yet believers—and the evangelists who use the scriptures to persuade them to faith (8.35; 17.11; 18.24, 28; cf. 15.21). Some form of the Lord's Supper may be inferred only at 2.42, 46 and 20.7-11.

'means' of the presence of salvation, without assuming a correlative work of the Spirit (if only through other believers who have received the gift of the Spirit). We have already had cause to consider the degree to which the kerygma is effective when empowered by the wisdom provided by the Spirit (cf. 6.10) and by other associated gifts of the Spirit (including signs and wonders), and have noted that it is precisely charismatic teachers (Jesus, the twelve, Paul, Barnabas *et al.*) who mould and strengthen the congregation. This entirely accords with a Jewish background which sees the gift of the Spirit of prophecy as providing the wisdom, revelation and illumination that vividly contextualizes the Scripture to the community and so transforms it into a congregation of salvation, as, for example at Qumran (cf. 1QH 9.32; 12.11-13; 13.18-19; 14.12-13, 25 etc.). Of the saving function of the word of the Jesus tradition on its own, devoid of the Spirit, Luke says not a word.

Secondly, Jesus (and with him 'salvation') is frequently said to be present in the 'name' of Jesus. Flender ventures the challenge, 'We must at all costs free ourselves from the popular dogma that Christ is present in the community through the Spirit', arguing he is present in 'the name' instead.[59] A brief glance indicates something of the scope of Luke's usage:

> The 'name' is (a) preached, taught, or carried to people (4.17-18; 5.28, 40; 8.12; 9.15, and possibly 9.27-28[60]), (b) opposed (26.9); (c) believed in (as an act of conversion: 8.12); (d) called upon for salvation (2.21; 4.12; 9.14; 22.16); (e) the focus of the baptismal rite (2.38; 8.16; 10.48; 19.5; 22.16); (f) suffered for (5.41; 9.16; 21.13); or life is risked for it (15.26; 21.13). In addition, (g) miracles and exorcisms are worked 'in the name' of Jesus (3.6, 16[?]; 4.7, 30; 16.18; 19.13 [cf. 17]).

Flender's view builds from, for example, 3.16, where the 'name' might be understood as the active healing presence of Jesus himself, after the analogy of 9.34, 'Aeneas, Jesus heals you'. It is clear from the range of uses indicated that Luke does not think of the 'name' here as a quasi-magical power,[61] nor as an *independent* hypostasis active on earth while Jesus is himself inactive in heaven,[62] and so it has been taken as a way in which Jesus is himself present,[63] and with him 'salvation'.

---

59. *Luke*, p. 135.

60. Though here the dative construction 'in the name of Jesus' may mean with his authority or on his behalf.

61. *Contra* J. Ziesler, 'The Name of Jesus in the Acts of the Apostles', *JSNT* 4 (1979), p. 33 (uncritically following Hull), see O'Toole, *Unity*, pp. 50-53. The nearest Luke comes to magical understanding of the name is 19.13-19, which is intended to subvert such an understanding (see Garrett, *Demise*).

62. See Marshall, *Luke*, p. 179.

63. For the name as a mode of Christ's presence see Kränkl, *Knecht Gottes*, pp. 177-80; Marshall, *Luke*, p. 179.

Closer examination suggests this is misleading. (1) It will be evident that with the possible exception of 3.16 'the name' of Jesus is never the subject of an activity, always an object, benefactor or instrument in an event performed by others.[64] The 'name' of Jesus does not act to effect or present salvation, nor does it take any other form of initiative, nor is anyone 'full of the name', or whatever.

(2) Excepting dative/instrumental constructions (which carry the varied senses 'by the authority of', 'on behalf of', etc.), 'the name' appears to be a circumlocution for Jesus himself, used (like 'the name of the Lord') to guard the transcendence of an exalted heavenly figure. That is, the 'name' of the Lord is not strictly a 'means' of God's or Jesus' presence, but simply a reverential way of referring to God or to Jesus himself: *mutatis mutandis*, 'to preach or teach about "the name" of Jesus' is neither to offer a course on the christological titles nor to discourse on the mystical means of the presence of the transcendent, but to preach about *Jesus himself* (essentially about his death, resurrection and present Lordship at God's right hand).

(3) It follows from (1) and (2) that it would misrepresent Luke to say Jesus is present *by means* of his name. Rather, the passages using the expression 'the name' variously state Jesus is present (a) in the sense that his authority is exercised by his representatives in miracles and exorcisms performed 'in his name'; (b) where he (= his name) is preached or taught (in the sense that he is the topic of such discourse); and/or (c) where he (= his name) or the word about him is believed in and honoured (in the sense that he is the one to whom such faith and service is directed). None of these, however, amounts to his presence independent of the Spirit, through 'the name' instead.[65] Flender himself articulated the presence of Jesus in his name

64. The syntax of v. 16 is difficult: τὸ ὄνομα αὐτοῦ is subject of the verb ἐστερέωσεν. It is difficult either to repunctuate (so Burkitt: see Bruce, *Acts*, p. 110) or to believe (as Bruce [1951] did, following Torrey) that we have a misunderstanding of an original Aramaic which should have been translated 'and by faith in his name He has made whole this man whom you see and know'—for the verb ἐστερέωσεν deliberately recapitulates 3.7 (rightly Haenchen). The awkwardness must then be explained in terms of the speaker's attempt to qualify the basic idea 'Jesus' name made the man strong'. In itself that would be susceptible of an almost magical interpretation; so it is qualified 'on the grounds of faith in his name' and elucidated 'the faith which came through it (i.e. through the name—meaning Peter's proclamation of it?) gave him this "soundness"'. Not Luke at his most rhetorical; is it a source? See Barrett, 'Faith', pp. 1-17.

65. The implicit argument that the use of different terms such as 'Spirit', 'hand of the Lord', 'the name', or 'power' implies reference to different entities and divine means is linguistically naive (overlooking the frequent use of differently nuanced but co-referential expressions). The same argument applied to e.g. 4.30 should demonstrate that 'your hand' (*scil.* God) and 'the name of Jesus' are separate 'means' giving

largely in terms of (b) the proclamation *about* Jesus—but in that case we are back to salvation present in 'the word' concerning Jesus by a different route, and it is not independent of the Spirit, but made effective precisely by Spirit-inspired preachers and teachers. And *Christians* who exercise active faith in him and honour him may do so through the Spirit of prophecy.

In order to avoid misunderstanding, let us clarify that we are not denying that Luke thought Jesus himself became present to his disciples. I have already argued he became present through the Spirit in preaching, prophetic utterance, wisdom, visions, healings and the other charismata. I am simply arguing that the *theologoumenon* 'the name (of Jesus)' is not some independent means of salvation alongside or prior to the activity and the gift of the Spirit.

In the final analysis, we may adjust our earlier formulation that the Spirit was a principal means in the continuation and deepening of Israel's salvation beyond the ascension of Jesus. It has become increasingly clear that claims on behalf of other 'means' are difficult to substantiate. There is little evidence Luke thought there was any form of divine power at work in tandem with the Spirit to which 'salvation' might be attributed, leaving the gift of the Spirit as a second 'supplementary' gift. We may thus safely claim he thought the Spirit was *the principal* divine power maintaining, developing and extending Israel's salvation/transformation, and that without the gift of the charismatic Spirit of prophecy the sort of 'salvation' he had in mind would simply evaporate from Israel like the departure of the cloud of God's glory and presence.

As Bovon concluded, Luke does not provide us with a treatise on the nature of salvation, but shows us how God takes the initiative in it and the church lives in it. 'Everything seems to comes down to a presence of the Holy Spirit in the person and the life of the local congregation. That is not many words, but for Luke it was a great deal of joy.'[66]

---

rise perhaps to a parallel series of healings from God and signs and wonders from 'the name' independently.

66. Bovon, 'Salut', p. 173.

Chapter 14

CONCLUSIONS

The major findings of this study have been summarized at the end of
chapters and at various other points in the preceding argument. Here (in
§§1-4) I shall attempt to draw together the threads of the discussion, and
relate it to the agenda provided by previous scholarship as outlined in our
first two chapters. In §5 I shall venture brief remarks on the relationship of
our findings to the present debate between traditional Protestant and
Pentecostal/Charismatic positions.

1. *Jesus and the Spirit*

Luke's portrait is dominated by his broader intention to portray the ministry
of Jesus, and the Church which results, as the fulfilment of God's promises
savingly to restore his people Israel and make her a light to the nations. It is
this ideological purpose which largely explains both his emphases and his
comparative silences.[1] Accordingly, Luke 1–2 presents the dawn of God's
eschatological reign which will restore Israel, and focuses especially on the
epochal births of the Elijianic prophet (John the Baptist) and of the
promised Davidid (the embodiment of Israel and royal Son of God) who will
bring the hoped for transformation through his rule (1.32-35). Within this
context, Luke presents Jesus as the anticipated messiah of the Spirit. He
uses traditional material which traced Jesus' conception as the Son of God
to the Spirit and combines this with an allusion to Isa. 32.15, and hence to
the Spirit as the power of Israel's renewal. In 2.40-52 he uses a further messianic tradition to depict Jesus as full of wisdom and aware of his unique
sonship and consecration to God's purposes. In the light of these chapters,
Jesus' reception of the Spirit on the occasion of his baptism (3.21-22) must

---

1.   That is, Luke is attempting to explain and so to legitimate the Church in the
light of her founding moments. The term 'ideological' here is used to denote a
construal of the community's symbolic universe intended to justify the community
over against some other group. For this usage in social sciences, and its perceptive
application to Mark's Gospel, see Watts, *Influence*, pp. 243-46.

be understood as bringing Jesus a new nexus of activities—not (*contra* Dunn) 'eschatological sonship', which has been more than fully assured by 1.35 (and displayed in 2.40-52), but empowering for the messianic task. The voice from heaven alludes to Ps. 2.7 and Isa. 42.1-2, and so interprets the coming of the Spirit upon him as the enabling to fulfil the task of the royal messiah and of the prophetic Isaianic servant-herald (and, as we have seen, Luke builds heavily on both christological motifs). It is as the messianic Son and Isaianic servant-warrior (cf. Isa. 49.24-25//Lk.11.20-22) that he represents Israel in a replay of the Exodus/wilderness testing of the nation. With the Spirit's aid (as 4.1 redactionally asserts), Jesus overcomes Satan in the contest situation, and returns to Galilee 'in the power of the Spirit' (4.14) to proclaim and effect Israel's release in terms of fulfilment of the hopes then associated with Isaiah 61 (Lk. 4.18-21). Luke's main source in 4.16-30 had already presented Jesus as the Isaianic soteriological prophet announcing Israel's messianic Jubilee and New Exodus, and Luke used this (and the obvious thematic connections with Isa. 42.1-7) to fuse his royal and Mosaic/prophetic/servant Christologies. From the perspective of this passage and its associated hopes, Jesus is empowered by the Spirit to free Israel from her 'slave-poverty', 'exile-captive' and 'blind' estate and lead her along the wilderness way towards restored Zion, and similar hopes are echoed in Luke's one description of Jesus' ministry in Acts (10.36-39).

The main emphasis in Luke's portrait of Jesus and the Spirit in the Gospel narrative thus supports the views of Schweizer, Stronstad, Menzies and others, who have seen Jesus' Jordan experience almost exclusively in terms of empowering for mission, rather than as bringing him 'new covenant life' or 'eschatological sonship'. Indeed, Luke shows rather little interest in how the Spirit affected Jesus' own religious life before God. Perhaps most surprisingly, he fails to make explicit whether the Spirit by which Jesus was conceived remained as a divine guiding and revealing presence with him (he lacks any parallel to what is said of the Baptist at 1.15, 80). A reader noting the way the parallelism between John and Jesus in Luke 1–2 always favours the latter may *surmise* the Spirit remains with him, and, if she knew the Jewish messianic traditions building on Isa. 11.1-4, she would probably assume the Spirit was the source of the wisdom and knowledge of his special sonship evinced in 2.40-52. The fact remains, however, that Luke does not explicitly state this. Nor does he explain in what ways Jesus experienced the leading of the Spirit in the wilderness. Lk. 10.21 alone speaks of a psychological effect of the Spirit on Jesus, and even here the description 'he exulted in the Holy Spirit and said' serves more to designate the content of the speech event which follows as charismatic and revelatory than to highlight a benefit to Jesus' own religious life and perception. We would be unwise to build too many theological conclusions from these silences, but it will be apparent that he is more interested in assuring his reader *that* Jesus was the expected messiah of the Spirit and *that* he was so empowered for his mission, than he was in explaining what Jesus' endowment at the Jordan contributed to his own life before God. This interest may also explain why Luke shows no real reserve about connecting the Spirit on Jesus with works of power (*pace* Schweizer *et al.*; cf. 1.35; 4.18-25; 7.21-22; Acts 10.38). The traditions of the messiah of the Spirit expected the one endowed to be empowered by the Spirit to liberate Israel (see Chapter 4), and within the context of Isaianic New Exodus hopes this 'liberation' was readily extended to miracles of healing and deliverance (see Chapter 9). Equally (again *contra* Schweizer and others), the traditions of the messiah of the Spirit expected the one so endowed to exhibit a robust righteousness through the Spirit of wisdom, knowledge, and fear of the Lord upon him (he was to purge Israel by it), and Lk. 4.1b echoes this. This emphasis on the Spirit as the *messiah's* endowment should also warn us against too quickly assuming Luke presents Jesus as a pattern for all other Christians' experience of the Spirit. Both the timing of his reception of the Spirit and the nature of his endowment with the Spirit might be anticipated to have unique elements corresponding to his unique mission. We shall return to that subject later.

Certainly unique to Jesus' experience of the Spirit is the dramatic post-ascension development according to which he now 'receives' the gift of the Spirit anew, this time as his executive power (2.33). As the Mosaic prophet and Davidic messiah, he pours out the divine Spirit promised by Joel in God's place (Acts 2.33; cf. Lk. 24.49), and becomes 'the Lord of all' (Acts 10.36), that is, functionally one with the Lord God of Israel upon whose name the repentant are to call for salvation (Acts 2.21//2.36, 38; cf. Joel 3.5 and Rom. 10.12). The Spirit of God has become the Spirit of Jesus too (Acts 16.7) in the sense of extending his presence in the communicating of his gifts (as those of the Father), and so enabling the continuation from God's right hand of what he began in his ministry. Thus Jesus 'pours out' the individual charismata ('this which you see and hear') of the day of Pentecost, and he becomes the subject of visions and dreams that direct and assure his people (cf. Chapter 10 §3.1). While Luke has not developed this line of thought to the extent we discover in Paul and John (where the Spirit becomes the means of an overtly [and reciprocal] personal unity between the disciple and the Father-and-Son), his sketch nonetheless has important elements of their more developed portrait. Jesus is not significantly more 'absent' than the Father, both being presented as transcendent beings whose activities shape, energize and direct human affairs: indeed, it is he who baptizes Israel with Holy Spirit, cleansing, purging, and so restoring her, and taking her forth as a light to the world. But in Acts the indwelling Spirit brings gifts from, and reveals, the Father and the Son *from heaven*, while for Paul and John the union of the Father and the Son with the Spirit is emphasized to the point that the indwelling Spirit means the indwelling of the Father and the Son too. Whether this amounts to a significant theological difference is unclear; it may simply be the product of Luke's narrative perspective. For Luke, the whole salvation-historical plan 'to the end(s) of the earth' is initiated by God and mediated through Israel's messiah and exalted Lord. The story of the unfolding of this plan, however, is told from the perspective of an earthly narrator who is mainly alongside the 'witnesses' whose life and mission extended the church over the known world, and who were as often as not taken by surprise by the divine developments. Luke therefore tends to portray the Father and the messianic Son in the position of power over the *oikoumenē* (God's throne in heaven) and *intervening* in its affairs, a factor which in measure inevitably somewhat 'distances' them from the disciples, and may account for the different emphasis in his pneumatology (comparable in this respect with that in Revelation).

2. *The Nature of the Gift of the Spirit to the Disciples*

This study has confirmed the position of those from Lampe onwards who have insisted the Pentecostal Spirit in Acts is the 'Spirit of prophecy'; that is, that Joel's promise of the Spirit is what Peter programatically extends to all believers in Acts 2.28-39. We have noted how all the activities of the Spirit mentioned in Acts can be traced to this one (albeit complex) concept, and Luke has not extended the concept of the gift of the Spirit by making it include other Old Testament promises of the Spirit *in addition* to the 'Spirit of prophecy' (*contra* Dunn and Kremer). While others have already asserted something like this position, they have usually then tended to give a one-sided if not reductionist account of the Spirit in Acts because they have failed adequately to elucidate the scope of the gifts attributed to the 'Spirit of prophecy'. This is most markedly the case with Mainville (who reduces it to prophetism, including inspired witness), Schweizer (who reduces it to inspired speech, especially preaching), and Stronstad and Menzies (who reduce it to empowering for mission). Each of these studies (especially that of Menzies) makes an important contribution, but overlooks significant pieces of evidence.

The 'Spirit of prophecy' anticipated in Judaism prototypically afforded revelation, wisdom and invasive prophetic and doxological speech. The Spirit as 'the power of preaching' was a Christian understanding which involved the combination of one or more of these enhancing the speaker's argument/exhortation, and/or providing signs that corroborated the speaker's discourse, and/or a numinous convincing power sensed in the speaker or his speech giving his message special 'impact' for the hearer.[2] It is thus easy to see how the Spirit was 'empowering for mission' in the sense of inspiring witness to Jesus. Luke has given a special place to this through Lk. 24.46-49 and Acts 1.8, because it was above all the witness to Jesus which initially called men and women into the messianic people of God and so brought salvation to them, and this same witness extended the church towards 'the end(s) of the earth' in accordance with the programme in 1.8. But Luke does not in fact portray the whole church as actively involved in witness (see Chapter 12), and he was well aware that the same gifts could as readily fuel the preaching and teaching which built up and directed the Christian church in its walk with God (9.31; 11.24; 15.32; cf. Chapter 13 §2.2 and §2.4). Thus the Spirit was either more than simply 'empowering for mission', or this last must at least be taken sufficiently broadly to include the building up of God's people. Furthermore, Luke is aware of the church being served by the spiritual gifts of wisdom (e.g. 6.3, 5) and revelation (e.g. 5.1-10; 11.28; 15.28[?]; 20.28[?]), outside the context of witness, preaching or teaching. If Luke's account gives less space to these activities they are nonetheless indisputably important aspects of his understanding of the Spirit's work, and natural to any Jewish or Jewish-Christian understanding of the eschatological 'Spirit of prophecy'. In this respect, Haya-Prats gave a much more balanced account of the gift of the Spirit than Mainville, Stronstad or Menzies.

Haya-Prats allowed the Spirit of prophecy at least some place too in the individual believer's own religious life. Instances of this vary from cases of prophecies directed to an individual (20.23; 21.4, 11) to the potentially more significant mentions of the deepening of spiritual faith, wisdom and joy of individuals (6.3, 5; 11.24; 13.52). Menzies admits these last only as examples of the Spirit empowering mission, but any advantage for mission in these cases is at best a secondary consequence of the charismata in question, and Menzies' case that the Spirit is given to the individual only to benefit others (not the one who receives the gift) is unprecedented, unparalleled and ultimately artificial. Haya-Prats himself tended to marginalize the theological significance of these instances by claiming they were untypical charismata granted only to certain prominent Christians. But his case rests on Gunkel's oversharp distinction between natural and charismatic expressions of faith, joy and wisdom, and makes insufficient allowance for a normal Jewish understanding that the Spirit of prophecy enhances wisdom and understanding (not merely invasively and intensely, but also in ways not immediately perceptible to the recipient's consciousness) and naturally leads to joy

---

2.   See Turner, 'Spirit and Authoritative Preaching', pp. 68-72, 87-88.

and doxology. The same Spirit which grants these gifts in the more remarkable cases signalled in 6.3, 5, 11.24 and 13.52 (and the occasions of charismatic praise) would be assumed to provide analogous gifts at less intensive levels in the congregation more generally. Such activities are indigenous to the very concept of the 'Spirit of prophecy' in much of Judaism (and this understanding appears to have been taken over, for example, in Paul's exposition of the 'fruits' of the Spirit). Similarly, we have argued (Chapter 5) that Judaism expected the Spirit of prophecy to bring about individual and corporate ethical renewal in a variety of ways—from individual promptings of the Spirit and the giving of life-transforming wisdom and revelation, to prophetic challenges and wisdom-imbued teaching, and the renewed corporate atmosphere these created. A special case of this expectation was the 'messianic' figure(s) derived from Isa. 11.1-4 who, mightily endowed with the Spirit, would bring about the restoration of Zion through the wisdom and power the Spirit afforded him. In Chapter 13 we have also argued Luke presupposed and built upon such an understanding both in the Ananias and Sapphira episode and in the way he relates the renewed community life structurally to the promise of the gift of the Spirit in the Pentecost account.

The Spirit's involvement in these various dimensions of Christian life and witness throws a question mark over the widely-held thesis that for Luke the gift of the Spirit is a *donum superadditum*. The Spirit appears to afford a charismatic dimension that is as vital to on going Christian existence and transformation (corporate and individual) as to the witness of the Church. How, then, is the Spirit related to salvation in Luke–Acts?

3. *The Spirit and Salvation in Luke–Acts*

Schweizer, Haya-Prats, Stronstad and Menzies argue that the gift of the Spirit is a *donum superadditum* on essentially three grounds: (1) the Spirit of prophecy is by its very nature a vocational gift for service (which Luke stresses as empowering for witness); (2) it is given to those who have already repented, believed and been baptized, and so have entered on salvation; and (3) this pattern is confirmed by the experience of the twelve (and other disciples) who had clearly experienced faith and salvation well before they received the Spirit (at Pentecost) as empowering to preach in parallel with Jesus' Jordan experience. Each of these arguments represents a serious over-simplification of Luke's position.

(A) The complex pattern of parallels between Jesus and the disciples are a marked feature of Luke–Acts, and certainly express the unity between Jesus' mission and that of the Church. Thus the Jesus-Stephen-Paul parallels may help us understand that the theology of Acts is a theology of suffering as much if not more than a theology of glory,[3] but we cannot press the many evident parallels between Jesus' journey to suffering in Jerusalem (Lk. 19–24) and Paul's in Acts (19–28) to equate them theologically. The parallels highlight significant common elements, not identity of meaning. Those between Jordan and Pentecost suggest the Spirit will be granted as empowering for mission to the disciples (and this is highlighted by Lk. 24.49; Acts 1.8), but that cannot be forced to mean the apostles and other Christians receive the Spirit of prophecy in exactly the same character as Jesus did. His experience of the gift was as an anointing as messiah, servant-liberator and prophet-like-Moses to inaugurate the emancipation and transformation of Israel; the apostles and others in varying degrees participate in that ongoing task through the Spirit, but they are also the *beneficiaries* of it—they are part of the Israel of fulfilment that continues to undergo transformation through the activities of the Spirit of prophecy shed forth by the heavenly Lord in varied gifts distributed through the congregation. Again, the parallels between Jordan and Pentecost do not necessarily imply the apostles experience the gift of the Spirit as empowering *alone*, for Jesus had already received the Spirit in some fundamental way in Lk. 1.35 before his Jordan experience, and this was so far unparalleled in the disciples' case. One might then as easily take the Jesus/disciples parallels to argue that Pentecost involves elements of Israel's new creation or new birth through the Spirit (// Lk. 1.35) *as well as empowering*—and indeed this may well be intended by Luke's use of Isa. 32.15 both in relation to Jesus' conception by the Spirit (Lk. 1.35) and in relation to the anticipated Pentecostal gift (Acts 1.8). The observation of parallels between Jordan and Pentecost thus does not provide knock-down arguments for any of the main contending interpretations of Luke's pneumatology. Interpretations which depend on them also all too easily fall into the trap of reading the story of Jesus and the disciples up to Pentecost

---

3. See D.P. Moessner, '"The Christ Must Suffer": New Light on the Jesus-Peter, Stephen, Paul Parallels in Luke–Acts', *NovT* 28 (1986), pp. 220-56; C.K. Barrett, 'Theologia Crucis—In Acts', in C. Andresen and G. Klein (eds.), *Theologia Crucis— Signum Crucis* (Tübingen: Mohr, 1979), pp. 73-84; and more generally e.g. R. Pesch, 'Der Christ als Nachahmer Christi: Der Tod des Stefanus (Apg 7) im Vergleich mit dem Tod Christi', *Bibel und Kirche* 24 (1969), pp. 10-11; Talbert, *Patterns*; A.J. Mattill, 'The Jesus-Paul parallels and the purpose of Luke–Acts', *NovT* 17 (1975), pp. 15-46; R.F. O'Toole, 'Parallels between Jesus and His Disciples in Luke–Acts: A Further Study', *BZ* 27 (1983), pp. 195-212; W. Radl, *Paulus und Jesus im lukanischen Doppelwerk: Untersuchungen zu Parallelmotiven im Lukasevangelium und in der Apostelgeschichte* (Bern: Lang, 1975); Praeder, 'Jesus-Paul', pp. 23-49.

as a thinly disguised allegory of the individual pilgrimage to faith and power beyond it. Luke 1–Acts 1 is Israel's story more than our story.

(B) In Chapter 11 we argued (*contra* Dunn) that the disciples had experienced 'faith', 'forgiveness', 'the kingdom of God' and 'salvation' before Pentecost. This could (and has) been taken to support the view that the gift of the Spirit at Pentecost is purely a *donum superadditum*, and my argument there that Luke is aware of ways in which the disciples had already experienced the Spirit, even before Pentecost, could be taken as additional support for this position. But this too would result in a misleading oversimplification of Luke's picture. Salvation and its benefits are made present in the ministry only through Jesus-empowered-by-the-Spirit. This raises most acutely how 'salvation' can continue to be experienced after the withdrawal of Jesus to the right hand of God through the ascension. As everyone knows, Conzelmann's answer was that it could not—or rather that salvation was largely only present in the memory of the life of Jesus and in the understanding of its soteriological implications. We have seen, *per contra* (with e.g. Franklin), that Luke regarded the ascent of Jesus to God's right hand as the fulfilment of the hopes in Lk. 1.32-33, and as potentially deepening the messianic rule and the disciples' experience of the kingdom of God (cf. Chapter 10). But *how* was this continuation of Jesus' saving actions to be experienced? The key transitional passages (Lk. 24.46-49 and Acts 1.4-8) mention only *one* means by which the risen Lord will be actively present to and through the disciples, and that is the same means by which Jesus inaugurated salvation, namely the Spirit. This suggests that (for Luke) beyond the ascension of Jesus the gift of the Spirit *becomes soteriologically necessary*—even for Jesus' band of disciples.

(C) The argument that faith, repentance and baptism securing the forgiveness of sins (salvation) all *precede* the gift of the Spirit has been widely used to justify the claim that reception of the Spirit is not soteriologically necessary but a supplementary gift. Once again we must suspect this as an oversimplification of Luke. If all 'salvation' means is forgiveness of sins, entry into the people of God, and assurance of future justification at the day of the Lord, then one might indeed be prepared to accept that receiving the gift of the Spirit is not necessary for these. However, we must make the following caveats.

(1) I have suggested that for Luke the Spirit plays an important role leading up to 'conversion' and entry into the people of God as a divine power active through the messenger (in a variety of ways) giving conviction to the message, and so prompting repentance and belief even if not mechanistically ensuring it (Chapter 11).

(2) I have proposed that the conception of 'salvation' involved in this argument is inadequate, and would barely constitute much 'Good News' for most Jewish hearers (who already believed they had these benefits as God's covenant people), even if it was far more significant for non-Jews. For Luke, the Old Testament promises of salvation/the kingdom of God largely concern the end of the current world-order in which Israel is alienated from God, and enslaved and oppressed by spiritual and temporal forces. Salvation means her cleansing and restoration as a community of reconciliation, worship, and fearless service, and so as a glorious light to the nations. These are the hopes he announced in Luke 1–2, and portrayed as inaugurated in Jesus' message and ministry (see Chapters 6–9), even if the ideals for which Jesus worked (Israel's corporate repentance and new life lived in the mercy paradigm) were largely unfulfilled. Jesus' ascent to the position of power at God's right hand gives new impetus to these hopes and Luke portrays the church of Acts very much as the restoration and radical transformation of Israel hoped for. It is a community in which the ideals of the *Magnificat*, *Benedictus* and Beatitudes are met, 'a community in which there are no poor, hungry, or weeping people because the community's lifestyle overcomes such needs'.[4] God's people serve without fear, enjoy the active presence of God and his Christ, know their direction and intervention, and joyfully worship (cf. Lk. 1.71-76). From the perspective of Acts 3.21-25, unbelieving Jews simply cut themselves off from the messianic people of God, while Acts 15 sees the church under Christ's rule as the restored Israel to whom the Gentiles are now added in accordance with all the ancient promises. Luke does not think *all* eschatology has been swallowed up in Israel's transformation as the Church (he anticipates judgment on unbelieving Jerusalem in the form of its destruction, the extension of the Gospel to the ends of the known earth, and finally, perhaps far off, the End), but the decisive moves have been made in the events of the Gospel and in the first fifteen chapters of Acts. He would not look back to Luke 1–2 and lament the failure of promise (*contra* Tiede and Tannehill), but rejoice that it had been fulfilled in a remarkable and unexpected way. Salvation for him is largely new life, worship and joyful service to God in the messianic community of grace and peace, the brotherhood and New Exodus 'way' leading to ultimate salvation. We then need to ask whether Luke regards the Spirit as playing an important role in the shaping of this new awareness of God (and the heavenly Christ) and consequent way of life—and the answer must be a strong affirmative (see Chapter 13). The Spirit acts to support this both in the charismata afforded the individual him-/herself and through the charismata that address him/her through the community of charismatics. In so far

---

4. York, *Last*, p. 62.

as this is the case, the Spirit is soteriologically 'necessary'.

(3) It has been shown (with Dunn, and against his critics) that Luke regards Acts 2.38 as providing a 'norm' in which the Spirit is granted immediately to all who evince repentant faith (usually expressed in baptism), and that Acts 8, 10 and 19 *assume* such a norm, Acts 8 being regarded as anomalous by the narrator himself (see Chapter 12). It remains to be explained why the gift of the Spirit should be given universally to converts if it is a second grace of empowering. The close connection with conversion-initiation suggests rather that the Spirit is regarded as of soteriological import (to equip the believer for the Christian life in the variety of ways indicated in Chapter 13).

(4) We have seen that the allusion to Isa. 32.15 in Acts 1.8 suggests the Pentecostal Spirit is the power of Israel's renewal, and that this reading is apparently supported by the relatively clear (*pace* Bock and Menzies) parallels between Acts 2 and Jewish Moses/Sinai traditions. I have further argued that the same understanding is supported by Lk. 3.16, Acts 1.5, 11.16 and 15.9, where the Spirit is portrayed as the power by which the Davidic messiah cleanses (restores, transforms) his Zion. In this respect we again find the evidence partially supporting Dunn's position, even if we have arrived there by different arguments. And it should be noted that my claim does not involve the attempt to argue that Luke has 'added' the other Old Testament promises of the Spirit to Joel's promise in order to achieve a soteriological dimension for the Spirit, rather he has interpreted the activities of the 'Spirit of prophecy' itself as bringing about the renewal of Israel envisaged in Isa. 32.15 (just as, it has been argued, some rabbis expected Joel's promise to bring about the transformation described in Ezek. 36–37).

(D) We have seen that the Spirit of prophecy in Judaism is not merely a *donum superadditum*. At least for the Qumran community the eschatological gift of the Spirit as the Spirit of prophecy was soteriologically necessary because its revelation and wisdom decisively moulded the community of salvation and inspired its commitment to 'the way'. It has been argued that some Rabbis understood Ezekiel 36 in a similar way. What is more, Luke's hero, Paul, developed the concept of the Spirit of prophecy in a clearly soteriological direction: for Paul the revelatory/wisdom granting function of the Spirit becomes the power of new creation, renewal and spiritual transformation (1 Cor. 2.6-16; 2 Cor. 3.12-18; cf. Eph. 3.14-19) and 'leads' the Christian in the life of sonship and in the battle against 'the flesh' (Rom. 8.13-15; Gal. 5.13-18, 25; 6.8).[5] And for John (with whose

5. See Turner in Wilson (ed.), *Spirit*, pp. 188-90.

pneumatological tradition Luke has striking features in common)[6] the same 'Spirit of prophecy' (a) grants the revelatory wisdom through Jesus which is necessary for 'life' (Jn 3.34-36; 4.10, 13-14; 6.63); (b) becomes the power of God that brings about new birth/creation by revealing the significance of the cross in such a way as to enable authentic transforming belief (Jn 3.5-16); (c) becomes the sole means (after Jesus' ascension) by which the disciple is made aware of the presence and direction of the Father and the Son (whom to know is life); and (d) by becoming their revealer-teacher and guide simultaneously becomes the Spirit-Advocate through them to the World.[7] In short, there is nothing inherent in the notion of the Spirit of prophecy that requires it be interpreted as a vocational *donum super-additum*, and the one other New Testament writer who most forcefully presents the Spirit of prophecy as 'empowering for mission'—John—is also the author who most adamantly insists the wisdom-granting revealing Spirit is simultaneously soteriologically necessary (both for the inception and for the continuation of Christian life). The question then is rather whether Luke's presentation of the activities of the Spirit of prophecy suggests he thought the Spirit performed soteriologically significant functions in the believer, and I have argued that this is indeed the case, even if Luke has made less of it than he might have.

4. The Spirit and 'Sonship' in Luke–Acts

Büchsel, von Baer and Dunn have in different ways argued that for the New Testament writers (including Luke) the Spirit was essentially the Spirit of (eschatological) 'sonship'. There was some tension between this assertion and the claim in Baer that the Spirit was also essentially 'empowerment for mission'. The analysis in this book overcomes the problem here, for the concept of the Spirit as the 'Spirit of prophecy' affording charismatic revelation and wisdom provides the natural basis for both statements. The Spirit who reveals the Father and the Son, brings their direction, and provides charismatic wisdom (invasive and infused) to understand the Gospel, God's will, and how to walk in it, might inevitably be expected to enable a fuller, more obedient, more joyful and more effective Christian discipleship (as with Jesus at e.g. Lk. 4.1b; cf. 1.35). The same Spirit (granting analogous gifts along with invasive prophetic and doxological speech) would also 'empower' service to the Church and witness to those outside it.

---

6. See M.A. Chevallier, 'Apparentements entre Luc et Jean en matière de pneuma-tologie', in Aletti *et al.*, *Cause*, pp. 377-408.

7. See Turner, 'The Spirit and Ethical Religious Life', pp. 188-90 and the further literature cited there.

5. *The Implications of this Thesis for the Pentecostal/Charismatic Debate*

As the questions involved here are to be treated in a parallel volume, which permits fuller discussion of contemporary issues,[8] I confine myself to brief remarks. In §5.2, I will address the challenge of understanding of Luke's pneumatology for some classical Pentecostal views, and argue for the need of a new pneumatological paradigm. But first, in §5.1 I elucidate what is perhaps the more fundamental challenge posed by this study to those sectors of the traditional Churches which have rejected Pentecostal/Charismatic spirituality.

5.1. *Lukan Pneumatology as a Challenge to Non-Pentecostal/Non-Charismatic Sectors of the Church*

(A) *The challenge of the Spirit's transcendence in respect to the church.* This is undoubtedly the most radical challenge. It is endemic in fallen humankind to assert its autonomy over against God, and (among Christians) to over-formalize and over-institutionalize the divine presence and modes of address. In sacramentalism we may guarantee the presence and activity of the Spirit we may not otherwise be aware of; in preaching Scripture we may seek to guarantee the voice of the Spirit that we do not otherwise hear. In ordination we may guarantee the gifting and authority of the Spirit, which is not otherwise apparent, and in the corporate worship of the church we may claim we partake in the responsive theocentric doxological inspiration of the Spirit without necessarily feeling moved. Of course, where such 'formalizing' of the relation of human actions to the divine presence and activity is a way of expressing a genuine awareness that the Spirit of God makes himself present in our actions, then it is entirely appropriate. But when it becomes a substitute for any significant immediate awareness of God, then we risk reducing the Spirit to the immanence of God in the church. At times we may then even suspect that our language of the Spirit is merely mythological language for purely human actions.

Acts, by contrast, represents the Spirit as the transcendence of God, over, to, and through the church. The Spirit is the God who cannot be gagged. The Lord, 'grace', 'the word', or 'the Name' may be ways of speaking of the immanence of God in Acts, but for Luke the Spirit is not the immanence of God in the church: the Spirit is virtually always rather the self-*manifesting* presence of God. The Spirit comes with the noise of wind, the likeness of tongues of fire (Acts 2.2-3), or the shaking of the house (4.31). The Spirit plucks up and transports the evangelist (8.39). When the Spirit 'fills' a

---

8. *The Spirit and Spiritual Gifts: Then and Now* (Exeter: Paternoster, 1996).

person, it is compulsively, invasively, and with immediately-perceived effects (whether speech, or vision, or charismatic faith, or joy, or the like),[9] overcoming human weakness or breaking through merely human ability (for different types of this see e.g. 2.4; 4.31; 6.10; 9.17; 13.52 etc.). It is notable that a magician of some prowess even offers money to purchase the ability to convey the power of the Spirit he sees brought by the laying on of hands (8.17-19). It is an interesting and sobering question whether Simon Magus would be tempted in the same way by what he saw (or did not see) in many of our churches today. In this respect, the 'feel' of the Spirit in Acts is much closer to the revivalist phenomena of the Great Awakening, Pentecostalism, the Charismatic movement, Toronto, and so on, than it is to the measured solemnity of many other churches. We may point to just three different dimensions of this 'transcendence' of the Spirit:

(1) For Luke, 'Holy Spirit' is not a *theologoumenon* for retrospectively rubber-stamping merely human or ecclesial decisions (even at 15.28). For him, the Spirit takes the initiative—often startlingly—and the Church follows. The movement to the Gentiles provides the most startling series of instances, commencing with the puzzling vision to Peter, and the instructions of the Spirit to accompany Cornelius' messengers (10.19; 11.12), moving to the remarkable outpouring of the Spirit in 10.44, which commits the Church to accepting this Gentile household without Judaizing (10.45, 47; 11.15-18), but then also following through, in the dramatic call of Barnabas and Saul (13.2, 4), to a mission which brings more Gentiles to faith. All this stands behind James's assertion 'it seems good to the Spirit and to us...', that is, the will of the Spirit had been made manifest. Not only in the major theological moves, but also in the more mundane or individual matters of the mission and life of the church, the Spirit takes the initiative and directs: cf. 8.29; 16.6, 7; 19.21; 20.28. The Pentecostal and Charismatic churches regularly witness to this same kind of remarkably 'intrusive' action of the Spirit—not merely as retrospective hagiographical judgments on 'how matters turned out', but as profound experiences of the churches that shaped the events to follow. They listen to their brothers and sisters in other parts of the Church to hear similar testimony, and, where it fails, conclude that the Pentecostal Spirit is absent. As we shall see (§5.2 [E]), this judgment may largely be premature, but we can see how it represents a genuine and significant element of the Lukan challenge to today.

(2) For Luke, the Spirit is God's *power made manifest* in and through the Church. Not only does the Spirit give charismatic wisdom that empowers the witness (Lk. 12.12; 22.15; 24.49; Acts 1.8; 6.10, etc.), but, through the Spirit (cf. Lk. 4.18-20; Acts 10.38), God performs liberating 'signs and

9. See pp. 161-65 [this manuscript] above.

wonders' (2.43; 4.16, 22, 30; 5.12; 6.5-8; 8.6, 13; 14.3; 15.12; 19.10-12) which embody the message of Israel's restoration and which further attest the divine presence with the messenger and in the message. As the cotexts of these examples show, Luke evidently believed such miraculous healings (etc.) were an important aspect of the convincing power of the Gospel (to the point where he has been accused of credulity). For him, the promised Holy Spirit is so palpably 'present' in the Church, and in her witness, that that presence can itself be appealed to as a witness: 'we are witnesses of these things', Peter declares to the Council, 'and so is the Holy Spirit whom God has given to those who obey him' (5.32). In other words, even unbelieving Jews with a knowledge of the Scripture are expected to be able to recognize the presence of God's Spirit with the Church, and to draw deductions from it.

(3) The Spirit's transcendence is felt too in the worship, praise and thanksgiving of the Church. It is inevitably most sharply (and, to some degree, paradigmatically) felt in the invasive charismatic praise and glossolalia of, for example, 2.4, 11, 10.46, and 19.6, but also in the more general rejoicing of the community of the Spirit (e.g. 2.42-47), and on particular occasions of irruption of joy through the Spirit (e.g. 13.52).[10] (Luke does not seem particularly aware of the problem of formal, bland, dutiful but wearisome 'worship'). Of these, it is the distinctively new Christian phenomenon of invasive glossolalia which most strongly marks the transcendence of the Spirit. In this gift, the Spirit is the theophanic presence of the redeeming God, which inspires joyful doxology.[11] At the same time, however, invasive glossolalia paradoxically underlines the remaining sharp distance between humankind and God (the 'tongue' inspired is incomprehensible!), while perhaps pointing forward to the eschatological renewal of language in the final reconciliation.[12] It is this understanding of invasive glossolalia as a sacramental sign of deep and joyful encounter with the *mysterium* of God, and its paradigmatic nature for Pentecostalism, that prompted Malony and Lovekin to speak of the movement in terms of Troeltsch's *third* sociological class of religious movements—not 'Church', nor 'Sect', but 'Mysticism'.[13] In making this observation they were pointing to the fact that Pentecostalism is marked out less by the pattern of its relationships to

10. See Cullen, 'Euphoria', pp. 13-24.

11. L. Cerfaux, 'Le symbolisme attaché au miracle des langues', in *Receuil L. Cerfaux II* (Gembloux: Duculot, 1954), pp. 183-87; J.M. Ford, 'Toward a Theology of Speaking in Tongues', *TS* 32 (1971), pp. 3-29; F.D. Macchia, 'Sighs too Deep for Words: Towards a Theology of Glossolalia', *JPT* 1 (1992), pp. 47-73.

12. Cf. J.G. Davies, 'Pentecost and Glossolalia', *JTS* 3 (1952), pp. 228-31.

13. H.N. Malony and A.A. Lovekin, *Glossolalia: Behavioural Science Perspectives on Speaking in Tongues* (Oxford: Oxford University Press, 1985), pp. 260-62.

(or withdrawal from) society, and more by the way its institutions and activities as a group are primarily shaped by the drive for *encounter* with God. While this does not give adequate account of the mission orientation within Pentecostalism, it is a good measure of the degree to which the Spirit is perceived as the transcendence of God in the worshipping community. When Pentecostals or Charismatics attend the Sunday services of traditional Protestant churches, they may (or may not!) feel something of the Spirit's voice in the preaching, but other aspects of the worship (even creative, and well performed ones) may not appear to them to evince the activity of the Spirit in any direct way. When allowance is made for the Christofocal character of the remaining elements, they may feel such worship differs little in this respect from the sort of devotions they might also find in a good synagogue.

The central challenge of Lukan pneumatology to the churches outside the Pentecostal/Charismatic streams (and even to those in them) is to recover and maintain the evident and refreshing (but challenging) transcendence of the Spirit. Luke grounds this not merely in a single reception of the Spirit and initial evidence, but primarily in the continuing expectant prayer of the community, and in the divine response of fresh comings or 'fillings' with the Spirit (e.g. as at 4.23-31).[14]

(B) *The challenge of the Spirit's universality and gifting in the church.* This is the challenge to allow the Lukan (and Pauline) 'democratization' of the Spirit, and perhaps should be seen as but another aspect of the challenge to recover and maintain the transcendence of the Spirit. Without the latter, formalization of the Spirit tends to an institionalization, and to a clericalism, where those performing the activities of preaching, leading of worship, teaching and evangelism become a small (often professional) elite, depending on learned skills, while the rest are largely passive observers. The pneumatology of Acts (and, to an even greater extent that of Paul in 1 Cor. 12-14; Rom. 12) challenges to a quite different expectation.[15] With the Spirit of prophecy poured out on all, potentially any individual might (e.g.) receive the word from God to address the congregation, or the charismatic wisdom and empowering (like Stephen in Acts 6.5, 10) to articulate powerful witness. These points are asserted strongly by M.E. Evans, who elucidates Joel 2.28-32 in terms of what she calls 'the prophethood of all

14. On the way Luke, as redactor, highlights the importance of prayer importuning God, as the gateway to experience of God, see P.T. O'Brien, 'Prayer in Luke–Acts', *TynBul* 24 (1973), pp. 111-27; Smalley, 'Spirit'; Turner, 'Prayer'; cf. S.F. Plymale, 'Luke's Theology of Prayer', in D.J. Lull (ed.), *Society of Biblical Literature 1990 Seminar Papers* (Atlanta, Scholars Press, 1990), pp. 529-51.

15. Compare Dunn, *Jesus*, parts II and III; Turner, 'Spiritual Gifts'.

believers',[16] and by Stronstad, Shelton and Menzies, who consider the essence of the Spirit given to all to be empowering for mission. It will be clear from what was said in Chapters 12 and 13, that I believe they have overstated their respective cases. The Spirit of prophecy affords a far wider range of activities than these, but correspondingly no one person is necessarily involved in all. Luke's position is closer to Paul's view, that the one charismatic Spirit creates a community with different gifts and ministries, than is usually perceived.[17] But the challenge remains. From the shape of Luke's pneumatology the reader anticipates a large number of the congregation will receive charismata from the Spirit to make different contributions, both spontaneously, and in more long-term ministries of the Spirit in the Church and in her mission. Pentecostal and Charismatic churches have led the way in promoting the expectation that each believer will actively experience the Spirit working through him or her for the benefit of the Church. This has often lead to rejuvenation of the congregation and a warm 'passion for the Kingdom',[18] as individuals learn that God can even speak to them and use them, weak and inadequate as they may have felt.[19]

(C) *The challenge to the recovery of tongues, prophecy and healing.* As we have seen, according to Acts 2.38-39, Peter extends Joel's promise of the Spirit of prophecy to *all* believers. It is evident from the rest of Acts that much of Christian life is a charismatic existence. Traditional Protestant interpretation has tended to limit this charismatic dimension to spiritual illumination and preaching, and then to turn to Paul or John for the rest of its (selectively non-charismatic) biblical spirituality. This position has little coherence. If the Spirit makes Christ present to believers, and illumines Scripture to them, and guides them in the decisions of discipleship, then such actions can only derive from what Luke means by the 'Spirit of prophecy', and the same Spirit, by the same *means* (i.e. charismatic revelation and wisdom), affords prophecy, and should also be anticipated to

16. See her essay by this title in Billington, Lane and Turner (eds.), *Mission*, pp. 31-40 (she does not, of course, mean that all are what the New Testament would call 'prophets'; but uses her terminology in parallel to 'the priesthood of all believers').

17. See Hui, 'Concept', ch. 5 (and note especially his argument against Käsemann's view that Luke has institutionalized charisma as 'office').

18. S. Land sees this as the essence of Pentecostal spirituality; see his 'A Passion for the Kingdom: Revisioning Pentecostal Spirituality', *JPT* 1 (1992), pp. 19-46, and, at greater length, *Pentecostal Spirituality: A Passion for the Kingdom* (Sheffield: JSOT Press, 1993).

19. For the pneumatological ecclesiology of the so-called New Church Movement, see M. Turner, 'Ecclesiology in the Major "Apostolic" Restorationist Churches in the United Kingdom', *VoxEv* 19 (1989), pp. 83-108.

provide gifts of invasive prophetic speech and charismatic praise (including glossolalia[20]). As we have seen, these four—charismatic revelation, wisdom, invasive prophecy and praise—are the prototypical gifts of the 'Spirit of prophecy' promised by Peter to *all* believers. *They belong to the very essence of what is meant by the 'Spirit of prophecy'*. It is then a strange logic which argues that we should expect wisdom to continue (in illumination and preaching), and the others to fall into disuse. Only a fundamental misunderstanding of the nature and purpose of glossolalia along purely evidentialist lines, and of prophecy as given essentially to provide the necessary infallible revelation for the completion of the canon of Scripture, could possibly lead to such a position. This, I would argue, is patently not Luke's view of either of these gifts.

With respect to 'prophecy', for example, F.D. Farnell finds it necessary to argue that the gift of Joel 2.28-32 in Peter's Pentecost speech refers to the return of the full infallible Old Testament gift of prophecy accorded the canonical prophets, and it is granted to provide infallible New Testament Scripture.[21] But this represents a complete failure to understand the nature of the 'Spirit of prophecy' in Judaism and in Acts, and (*ex hypothesi*) implies that Peter's promise in 2.38-39 means *all* believers receive this! The fact is, however, that *none* of the occasions of prophecy in Acts pertain to the granting or elucidation of dogma, rather the 'Spirit of prophecy' guided the church in matters of detail (e.g. 11.28, a warning of famine in Judea), or provided particularistic personal revelations (16.6-13; 18.10; 20.23; 21.4, 11).

Similarly, as we have seen, Luke views healings not as evidentialist proofs to guarantee the content of apostolic proclamation and teaching, which may be dispensed with when the church is adequately 'founded' and the canon of Scripture complete, but as works of the Spirit which are part and parcel of the restorative salvation announced, and belong intrinsically with it. They would be expected to continue as signs of the presence of God's eschatological reign.[22] There are undoubtedly problems involved in the responsible appropriation of these various gifts today. Unfortunately, an adequate discussion of the issues here is impossible, and we shall need to explore them elsewhere.[23] Even if the Pentecostal and Charismatic sectors of the Church

20. Paul may also refer to a type of 'oracular' tongues, which addresses the congregation, and, when interpreted, functions like prophecy; but Luke does not depict this (cf. 1 Cor. 12.28, 30; 14.4-5).

21. F.D. Farnell, 'The Gift of Prophecy in the Old and New Testaments, Is the Gift of Prophecy for Today?', *BSac* 149 (1992), pp. 388-93.

22. See Chapter 11 §1.1, above, and W.J. Bittner, *Heilung: Zeichen der Herrschaft Gottes* (Neukirchen–Vluyn: Aussaat Verlag, 1984).

23. For current critiques of varying types of cessationism see e.g. Turner, 'Spiritual Gifts'; *idem*, *Spirit*; J. Ruthven, *On the Cessation of the Charismata: The Protestant*

have sometimes handled the issues involved uncritically, however, their witness nevertheless points, in enthusiastic fashion, to the ongoing challenge of Luke's pneumatology. We should not pretend, however, that this same pneumatology is without challenge for the classical Pentecostal position too.

5.2 *Lukan Pneumatology as a Challenge to Classical Pentecostalism*
(A) *The challenge to the Doctrine of Subsequence*. It will be clear that we have felt the evidence of Luke–Acts does not support the classical Pentecostal view of 'subsequence', that is, that the gift of the Spirit in Luke–Acts is simply a *donum superadditum*, for example, empowering for mission. In the first place, Luke is much closer to the Paul of 1 Corinthians 12–14 than is often imagined. He sees the charismatic 'Spirit of prophecy' as serving the church and empowering its pastoral ministries (of those who serve tables in Acts 6.3, 5, as well as that of prophets (Acts 11.28; 21.4, 11 etc.), of teachers (Acts 9.31; 11.24; 15.32 etc.) and of elders/overseers (Acts 20.28), as well as its evangelism. This much would not be disputed too heavily among writers from the Pentecostal and Charismatic sectors.[24] But, we would argue, Luke is also more like the Paul of 1 Cor. 2.6-16 and 2 Cor. 3.12-18 who regards the Spirit who reveals and grants wisdom as essential for that real Christian understanding of the Gospel which transforms human existence and leads to the life of sonship. For him (as for Paul and John, though differently) the Spirit of prophecy affords the whole charismatic dimension of revelation and spiritual wisdom which makes the difference between the vibrant, joyful, worshipping and generously supportive messianic community and what went before. His enthusiasm for this new community allows him to see it as the Israel of fulfilment, and to some extent to fill in the rifts that emerge from a critical examination of the epistles with eirenic and partially idealizing summaries. The radical holiness and corporate unity of this community is actively promoted and vigilantly preserved by the Spirit (cf. Acts 5.1-10) and her disputes are settled in appropriately reconcilatory fashion and under the Spirit's influence (15.28).[25] All this is 'salvation' and the Spirit is necessary to it.

That is not to deny that Luke thinks the circle of Jesus' disciples experienced the beginnings of salvation before Pentecost, nor to deny he thought

Polemic on Postbiblical Miracles (Sheffield: JSOT Press, 1993); and W. Grudem, *Systematic Theology: An Introduction to Biblical Doctrine* (Leicester: Inter-Varsity Press, 1994), chs. 52-53.

24. See e.g. Lederle, *Treasures*, chs. 1 and 2, but also especially Land, *Pentecostal Spirituality*.

25. Cf. P.J. Achtemeier, *The Quest for Unity in the New Testament Church: A Study in Paul and Acts* (Philadelphia: Fortress Press, 1987).

Samaria tasted salvation before the advent of the apostles in Acts 8.14. But on the one hand the Spirit was not *absent* from these situations (being powerfully at work through the charismata of Jesus and Philip respectively), and on the other, Luke could not envisage how the experience of salvation and discipleship could be maintained, deepened and extended without the gift of the Spirit granted to the disciples, and in the absence of any *pneumatikers*. That is why Pentecost must follow ascension, and why the anomaly of the Samaritans' failure to receive the Spirit must be corrected.

The Pentecostal Spirit is thus not simply 'the gift of power upon the sanctified life',[26] but the charismatic Spirit of prophecy as a 'power from on high' which both transforms and shapes ('sanctifies') the community and drives and empowers her mission. The position advocated here is thus very close to that of Gordon Fee's writings on Paul and Acts, and Lederle's more theological analysis.[27] For Luke the convert should receive the Spirit without delay, because the gift of the Spirit of prophecy is the only means by which the heavenly Lord can communicate with his people, guide them, assure them of his love, renew the sense of forgiveness after failings, prompt obedience, grant them the wisdom and understanding to enable the transformed life, and empower their service and witness. For the writer of Acts one cannot have a community of reconciliation, walking in the knowledge of God, and serving him joyfully, without the Spirit of prophecy, and those 'full of the Spirit' are the beacons that illuminate what the Spirit does in less intense fashion throughout the congregation. It is not, then, surprising that Luke considers the Spirit normally to be given in the broader complex of conversion-initiation (while, nevertheless, preserving to some degree the divine sovereignty and the freedom of the Spirit in this). The challenge here is to provide a coherent doctrine of the relationship of the Spirit to conversional baptism, such as is already being developed by many writers in the broader Charismatic tradition.[28]

(B) *The challenge to the rule of Evidential Tongues*. The majority of traditional Pentecostals[29] consider that Acts makes initial glossolalia normative to Spirit-reception, and required evidence of it. Luke certainly anticipated that glossolalia might quite regularly attend Spirit-reception, particularly

26. Contrast *The Apostolic Faith* (1906), p. 2.

27. Fee, *Presence, passim*; *idem, Gospel*, chs. 6–7; Lederle, *Treasures*, chs. 4–5. See Lederle, *Treasures*, pp. 29-32, for key Pentecostal leaders who have rejected the doctrine of subsequence.

28. See Lederle, *Treasures*, chs. (3), 4 and 5 for some more or less convincing attempts.

29. See V. Synan, 'The Role of Tongues as Initial Evidence', in Wilson (ed.), *Spirit*, pp. 67-82.

when the Spirit came in an especially powerful way (e.g. at epochal events), or where questions of legitimation (or demonstration of unity with the Pentecost initiative) were at issue. The evidence does not suggest, however, that 'tongues' was the only such manifestation: outbursts of charismatic praise or invasive prophesy (10.46; 19.6) would provide natural alternative attestation to the presence of the Spirit of prophecy among groups where these gifts were mixed together. In such instances (as we have seen) there is no evidence that Luke envisaged that *each* believer manifested *both* gifts, and first-century readers would be predisposed to understand the verses otherwise. In Jesus' case, Spirit-reception was marked neither by tongues, nor by prophesy, but by a vision (Lk. 3.21-22), another prototypical gift of the Spirit of prophecy. It thus cannot be convincingly demonstrated exegetically that Luke considered *tongues* (as opposed to some other regular gift of the Spirit of prophecy) to attest *every* reception of the Spirit. To avoid misunderstanding, I should clarify that I am not claiming the evidence of Acts 'absolutely refutes' the majority traditional Pentecostal view on initial tongues (even less am I attempting to diminish the theological significance of glossolalia, when and where it occurs).[30] I am merely saying the evidence to support it is weak and fragmentary, and so the case for the view is very largely inferential. The alternative reading (that tongues is merely one of several charismata that might attest initial reception of the Spirit) is more plausible because it accounts for slightly more evidence and reads it more contextually. It is the fragmentary nature of the evidence which ensures that any attempt to make evidential tongues normative will remain controversial and divisive, even within Pentecostal and Charismatic circles.[31] Luke–Acts does not provide adequate support to make such a rigid 'rule' a 'safe' verdict.[32]

30. I agree considerably with F.D. Macchia ('The Question of Tongues as Initial Evidence', *JPT* 2 [1992], pp. 117-27) that glossolalia may function as a sacramental sign of the Spirit (and, I further agree substantially, with his theological account of the significance of ongoing experiences of glossolalia in the church: cf. 'Sighs too Deep for Words', pp. 47-73). But then, (1) each occurrence of glossolalia may be such a sacramental sign, (2) other expressions of the christologically orientated 'Spirit of prophecy' (prophecy, vision, charismatic doxology) may also be such a sacramental sign, and (3) there is no reason to assume that glossolalia will necessarily mark the inception of the Spirit (any more than that glossolalia will mark any other single subsequent 'coming' of the Spirit).

31. For the disputes and different evaluations, see Synan, 'Role', Menzies, *Empowered*, ch. 13, and the different contributors in McGee (ed.), *Evidence*.

32. On whether such relatively insecure verdicts should be enshrined in Confessions, and so be allowed to divide churches, see Turner, 'Mission', pp. 157-66, esp. 164-65.

(C) *The challenge to the rule of Initial Evidence.* The case that Luke expected at least some charisma of the Spirit of prophecy to become manifest at each believer's initial reception of the Spirit is clearly stronger than the case that tongues alone served such a purpose. But we have noted that the Judaism from which earliest Christianity sprang did not anticipate that Spirit-reception would always (or even usually) be accompanied by some 'initial manifestation'. 'Initial evidence' was only truly pertinent when some sort of divine confirmation or legitimation was an issue (e.g. of Saul at 1 Sam. 10; of those appointed as elders at Num. 11, etc.) That the Spirit's advent upon the Samaritans and upon the first Gentiles converts at Caesarea might be evidenced by an initial outburst of charismata would be entirely predictable. Similar initial manifestation among the firstfruits of the Pauline mission in Ephesus (19.1-6) need hardly surprise us (even if it is less clearly predictable), especially as Paul had previously been forbidden by the Spirit to minister in Asia, and guided to Macedonia instead. Besides, whether or not the twelve had received the Spirit in their baptism was the very issue raised by Paul, and, when the underlying reasons for its failure had been dealt with (19.4-5), it might be anticipated that the Spirit would be given in an *evident* way; to legitimate their last step and as a signal that the Baptist's promise had finally indeed been fulfilled among them.

But why should one expect 'initial evidence' for the generality of uncontroversial cases? If, of course, 'baptism in Holy Spirit' were some definite 'subsequent' crisis experience beyond conversion-initiation (by weeks, months or years), initial evidence might be an issue.[33] But for Luke the Spirit performs important soteriological functions and so Spirit-reception normally attaches to the complex of conversion-initiation itself. In that case, however, the believer's responsive faith to the message, and submission to baptism, would generally be more than enough 'initial evidence' that the convert had joined the Israel of fulfilment, the people of the Spirit. Or, to put it another way, one might anticipate that for many, if not most, the actual moment of Spirit-reception passed relatively unnoticed as one in the whole series of experiences involved in the titanic upheaval of conversion-initiation. Would the converts on the day of Pentecost (2.41), for example, necessarily have been able to distinguish the very moment of their own Spirit-reception within the powerful train of events which led from their seeing and hearing the Spirit's power in the disciples, and their being struck to the heart by Peter's Spirit-inspired words (2.37), to their own response of

---

33. And so it *became* an issue in the late nineteenth and early twentieth centuries, when different movements were seeking a separate and superior level of Holy Spirit empowerment, and anticipated a distinguishing mark of having attained this: see Hurtado, 'Normal', pp. 191-92.

baptismal commitment to the Lord of the Spirit revealed? In their minds it may all have seemed one flowing liquid 'event' of the Spirit, which continued on into charismatic expressions in the church. Perhaps for this reason, Luke does not mention that the Pentecost converts received the Spirit with charismatic 'initial evidence'. And he regularly describes conversion-initiations (even in some detail) yet without mentioning the moment of reception of the Spirit or any initial charismata (cf. 8.36-39; 9.1-19; 16.14-15; 16.30-34, etc.) In such instances, the following rejoicing of the Eunuch (8.39), the vigorous preaching of Paul (9.20-22), or the joy of the Philippian household (different from 8.8 where the 'great joy' in the city is simply response to miracles of deliverance) will be taken as adequate ongoing evidence of the Spirit earlier received, even if not mentioned. In short, for the uncontroversial types of convert, 'initial evidence' (beyond conversional baptism itself and e.g. joy in the gospel) would not have been an issue. It would only *become* an issue were there no *ongoing* evidence of the Spirit's presence and manifestation (as, apparently, at 8.15-16). Luke–Acts thus falls short of suggesting there was *always* (or even 'usually') some specific charismatic manifestation at the moment of reception of the Spirit. Does this not imply that the concentration on 'initial evidence' in some Pentecostal and Charismatic circles is a misplaced emphasis? This leads us to our next challenge.

(D) *The challenge to ensure the dynamic of the Lukan 'spirituality'.* One of the great strengths of classical Pentecostalism lies precisely in its attempt to meet such a challenge. However, explicit statements in several key works suggest there is a major concern that unless the twin doctrines of 'subsequence' and 'initial evidence' are staunchly defended, the Lukan dynamic cannot be maintained. Thus, for example, Menzies argues that Gordon Fee's denial of the doctrine of subsequence will cut to the heart of true Pentecostal spirituality by confusing the Pentecost promise of the Spirit with conversion, and so cutting it off from mission, and diminishing one's sense of expectation. For then

> ... it is always possible to argue, as most non-Pentecostals do, that while all experience the soteriological dimension of the Pentecostal gift at conversion, only a select few receive gifts of missiological power... The doctrine of Spirit-baptism, in the Pentecostal sense, is distinct from... conversion. This conviction, I would add, is integral to Pentecostalism's continued sense of expectation and effectiveness in mission.[34]

The 'rule' of initial evidence, indeed initial glossolalia, then gives this its distinctive bite. Until one receives glossolalia, the distinctive Pentecostal gift of

---

34. *Empowered*, p. 236.

the Spirit still lies ahead; something to aspire to and to strive for. Synan's argument too ultimately boils down to this: Dennis Bennett was right—if we do not emphasize the essentially subsequent experience of baptism in the Holy Spirit, with the accompanying sign of tongues, 'every pastor in town will relax and cease to seek for a full Pentecostal experience'.[35]

While sharing the pastoral concern, I must confess amazement at the line of argument. By Menzies' own admission Paul spoke only of *one* gift of the Spirit, given in conversion-initiation, which was simultaneously soteriological, charismatic and missiological. Thus, for example, in possibly his earliest letter, the Spirit is clearly the Spirit of prophecy whose prophetic charismata must not be quenched (1 Thess. 5.19), but it is at the same time the missiologically orientated Spirit that brought Paul's gospel to the Thessalonians 'not merely in word, but also in power and in the Holy Spirit with conviction' (1.5). The Thessalonian converts received his gospel 'with joy inspired by the Holy Spirit' (1.6), and this gift of the Spirit which they received turns out, in 4.8, to be none other than the promise of Ezekiel 36 (the clause 'who gives his Holy Spirit εἰς ὑμᾶς [lit. 'into you']' can only be explained as an allusion to the language of Ezek. 37.6, 14, 26-27).[36] It is the Spirit which sanctifies and transforms 'Israel' as an obedient and responsive people of God and guards the holiness of the community (cf. v. 7). All this sounds like the narrative theology of Acts transformed into pastoral teaching. Yet neither here, nor elsewhere, does Paul teach, let alone emphasize, a doctrine of subsequence and initial tongues. To judge from his letters, however, this did not lead to spiritual apathy (as Synan fears). Nor did his clear emphasis on the soteriological import of the Spirit cut the Spirit off from mission, and reduce expectation (as Menzies fears). Nor could anyone who has read through Fee's comprehensive account of Paul's pneumatology[37] fairly deduce that either Paul's or Fee's own insistence on the soteriological necessity of the Spirit would be inclined to collapse the charismatic and missiological dimensions of the Spirit into conversion. The essential point is this. It is not the doctrines of subsequence and initial evidence that safeguard the spiritual dynamic of the church (these can lead to the complacency of having arrived and consequent formalism that is not entirely unknown in Pentecostal churches); the only safeguard for the spiritual dynamic of the church is to ensure that the gifts and pneumatological emphases of Acts (and Paul) are *in fact* continually implemented in the church. This involves careful comparison of what is actually happening in

---

35. Synan, 'Role', p. 68 (quoting Bennett).

36. Fee, *Presence*, pp. 50-53; Horn, *Angeld*; *idem*, 'Holy Spirit', in D.N. Freedman (ed.), *The Anchor Bible Dictionary* (New York: Doubleday, 1992), III, esp. pp. 271-76.

37. Fee, *Presence*.

our churches with the picture in Acts, and appropriate teaching, exhortations and pastoral modelling, to raise prayerful expectations in areas that are lacking (as, e.g., in 1 Cor. 12–14). The relevant test is not 'initial evidence', but *ongoing* evidence. In this context we can understand Lederle's claim that the Charismatic churches usually preserve the 'pearl' of Pentecostal 'life in the Spirit' without the packaged 'rule' of 'initial tongues'.[38]

(E) *The challenge to a broader recognition of the Pentecostal gift.* The effect of the twin doctrines of subsequentism and initial evidence has been a tendency to deny the presence of the Pentecostal gift in the majority of the traditional Protestant denominations (outside the specifically Charismatic streams). Writers in the classical Pentecostal tradition have regularly pointed to Acts 8.12 as offering an analogy for the state of non-Pentecostal/non-Charismatic[39] Christians. The Samaritan episode thus serves as a justification for dividing Christians into two classes, those who are 'baptised with the Spirit' (in the classical Pentecostal sense) and those who are not yet so. But we must question whether the analogy with the Samaritan experience is being used appropriately. I would argue that in most cases it is used incorrectly.

(1) As we have seen, Luke's promise that the messiah will baptize in the Holy Spirit refers to the purging/cleansing effect on 'Israel' of the charismatic Spirit, as well as her empowering as servant. The Pentecostal 'Spirit of prophecy' is the restoring, transforming power and life of the people of God, as much as the missiological power at work *through* the people of God. The Samaritans, before they receive this, have but a toe-hold in the comprehensive 'salvation' of which Luke speaks. And they only have the little they have by virtue of the fact that the Spirit is present to them and addresses them through Philip, who himself has the Pentecostal gift.

(2) Those who apply the analogy of the Samaritan converts to traditional Protestantism are usually sufficiently charitable to recognize renowned spiritual leaders and pastors, powerful preachers and expositors, effective missionaries, and great men and women of prayer and of obedient discipleship in those other traditions (people who nevertheless disagree with classical Pentecostal or other 'Charismatic' expositions of the Spirit). But is it coherent to claim such men and women of God do these things *without* what

38. H.I. Lederle, 'Initial Evidence and the Charismatic Movement: An Ecumenical Appraisal', in McGee (ed.), *Initial Evidence*, pp. 131-41.

39. It will be clear we do not think that any authentic Christians are 'non-charismatic' in the sense of totally devoid of the gifts of the Spirit of prophecy; here the term is used to denote those who do not belong to what Lederle calls 'the Charismatic Renewal Movement' nor share its understanding of the Spirit and spiritual gifts.

Luke means by the Pentecostal gift of the Spirit? I would suggest their lives
and ministries imply rather that in *Lukan* terms they are people 'full of the
Spirit', in at least one dimension of the Spirit-of-prophecy's activity. For in
their case the work of the Spirit is manifest especially in spiritual
wisdom/insight bringing illumination of the Scriptures and the Gospel to
them, enabling convincing, upbuilding and liberating communication of it,
and promoting faithful obedience to what they have understood. *Just such
wisdom and insight is prototypical to the 'Spirit of prophecy'.* It does not
make Lukan sense to claim that the effective spiritual preachers, missionaries
and evangelists outside the Pentecostal/Charismatic stream have yet to
receive the Pentecostal 'Spirit of prophecy' if, as so many have affirmed, the
Pentecostal Spirit in Luke is above all 'empowering for witness'.

Again, much of the non-Charismatic and non-Pentecostal Evangelical
tradition has promoted a spirituality of 'personal relationship with the Lord
Jesus'. This includes the expectation of a warm sense of Christ's presence
by the Spirit, the 'opening up' of Scriptures by the Spirit, and a strong
spiritually-granted assurance of forgiveness of sin and of the controlling
hand of God on the disciple's life. Often also there is an expectation that
God would 'speak' and 'guide' during prayer on matters touching
Christian life and vocation. Within these traditions the call to ministry would
regularly be expected to involve a pronounced spiritual awareness of God's
leading in the matter, and the preaching/teaching would occasionally be felt
to be specially assisted by God and might typically be introduced by such
assertions as 'the Lord laid on my heart...etc.' In these various elements of
traditional Evangelical and pietist spirituality there is a common assumption
that the Spirit acts as the organ of communication between the Father (or
the risen Lord) and the Christian disciple. Can the Pentecostal or
Charismatic Christian logically deny that such activities are derived from
what Luke means by the 'Spirit of prophecy'?[40] If the Samaritan converts
had witnessed boldly and effectively to their neighbours, prayed with
fervour and with a sense of joyful communion with God, and had taught the
Scriptures in a way that gripped and motivated the church and moved it

---

40. This is, I think, a decisive flaw in David Pawson's neo-Pentecostal exposition
under the title *The Normal Christian Birth* (London: Hodder, 1989). He argues that
most non-Pentecostal/non-Charismatic Evangelicalism has repented, believed, been
baptized, but has not received the Spirit. But to achieve this (see esp. ch. 35) he must
interpret all non-Pentecostal Evangelical mature spirituality, and faith-relationship with
God, as mere 'belief' and thus collapse it into the quite different Lukan conversional
'coming to belief'. He has, in other words, ignored the yawning semantic chasm
between 'faith[1]' as conversional conviction concerning the kerygma, and 'faith[2]' as
faithful life in relationship to God (which, from a New Testament perspective, requires
the gift of the Spirit).

forward with God, we can be perfectly sure Luke would not have concluded, 'The Spirit had not yet fallen upon any of them'.[41] For all these are
the work of the Spirit of prophecy.

Given this, where are the parallels to the Samaritan converts today? The
closest analogies will be found in those individuals and even congregations
where the gospel is 'believed', but where it does not kindle personal active
faith, where there is no sense of meeting with and being led by God, no
'heart for God', no dynamic awareness of God's grace, no joy in the gospel,
that is, where, in experiential terms, God is effectively the remote transcendent God of the deist, or the totally immanent God, who is the ground of our
being (but never breaks through that being or confronts it), or the God who
is always perceived to be active in the other, but never in the self. There are
indeed such people (and congregations), but I venture it would be untrue
(and offensive) to suggest this situation pertains *generally* in the non-
Pentecostal/non-Charismatic sector. For example, in those broadly 'evangelical' and pietist circles that have a strong tradition of warm relational and
missionary spirituality, the issue is not the *absence* of the Pentecostal gift of
the 'Spirit of prophecy', but both the *degree* (or 'depth') of the Spirit's
'presence' and the limits and constraints imposed on the ways in which the
Spirit is sought to act.

(F) *The challenge to a new pneumatological paradigm.* The challenge of
Luke's pneumatology to the Pentecostal Churches lies in part to their
ability to adjust their theological statements in the light of widespread and
responsible exegetical and theological criticisms. In this, scholarship in the
Charismatic sectors of the Church has made great progress, and this has
been well charted by the later chapters of Lederle's, *Treasures Old and
New*. With him I agree we need a paradigm which accepts that the large
majority of converts receive the Pentecostal 'Spirit of prophecy' in their
conversion-initiation experience. This is not only the norm Luke states (Acts
2.38-39), but, (a) the remaining conversion-initiation accounts (including
8.16) assume it, and (b) the broad range of the functions of the 'Spirit of
prophecy' in the life of the church undergirds it. The Spirit of prophecy is
the charismatic dimension of *all* Christian life, worship and service, and as
such the power of 'Israel's' restoration, the messiah's baptism with Holy
Spirit and fire.

This said, a new pneumatological paradigm built from Luke–Acts would
not assume that all (in conversion-initiation) receive the Spirit *in power
and fullness*; nor that each who receives the Spirit necessarily thereafter

---

41. We must endorse the judgment of Atkinson: 'Luke knows of *no ongoing*
[active] *Christian life without the reception of the Spirit*' ('Reponses', p. 130).

experiences the broad range of the charismata Luke (or Paul) describes. Rather, the Spirit becomes present as the *potential* of these things, but that potential is only realized in obedient discipleship and expectant prayer. Those whom Acts describes as 'full of the Holy Spirit' are not people who have simply had some crisis experience of the Spirit, accompanied by initial charismata. They are people in whom the potential of the Spirit of prophecy has become realized in a *greater than normal measure*. Further, the actual flowering of this potential may take different forms. One may not assume all, even ideally, become a Paul: the shape and power of his ministry were partly a matter of divine choices (cf. 9.15).

Luke's phenomenological use of 'fullness' terminology poses a challenge to all believers. Pentecostal or Charismatic believers cannot afford to rest on the laurals of some past experience of 'initial tongues': the question Luke's description poses to them is whether or not the Pentecostal Spirit of prophecy is *regularly* manifest through them now. Is he or she realizing the particular form of its range of expressions that is God's will for him or for her? Only people in and through whose lives the Spirit of prophecy is regularly and deeply 'felt', by the person himself, and/or by the congregations, and/or by outsiders, would be described by Luke as 'full of the Holy Spirit'. The pathway to this may depend on several repeated 'crisis' experiences of the Spirit 'coming upon' them afresh, or might come about by a gradual flowering of the conversion-initiation potential.

By the same token, traditional Protestant believers are faced with the question whether they evince the workings of the Pentecostal Spirit in their lives, and whether they have not 'closed themselves off' to some of the expected gifts of the 'Spirit of prophecy', by doctrinal assumptions or by other means. An over-emphasis on personal piety and developing the 'fruits' of the Spirit, for example, may blind them to the corporate dimension of the church, and the need to look to God for enablements of the Spirit to serve the church in bringing words of comfort, direction or congregational challenge as God's spokesperson. Or they may, even through mere shyness, quench any movement of the Spirit in them to articulate the kinds of inspired praise to God that might bring fresh life and joy to the congregation. Luke's description should challenge them, if they are willing to hear it, to recognize that the dynamic interplay of the charismata of the Spirit of prophecy through individuals was the powerful instrument the risen Lord used to cleanse and transform his church. Equally, reading Luke's account in Acts, she may perceive the need for the aid of the charismatic Spirit in witnessing to others. Understanding these things by the illumination of the Spirit, such a person does not need to 'receive' the Pentecostal Spirit. But they may need teaching and prayer, and their progress into these other dimensions of the Spirit's activities may come either as a crisis of release (or a series of them) as they are prayed for by others, or through quiet and gradual development. The diversity of 'rules' within the Pentecostal and Charismatic churches indicates that the 'way' is not so important. What is important, however, is the progress towards the goal of living in the fullness of the Spirit.

The final challenge to all 'sides' must be to maintain the tension expressed in the title of this work. The Spirit as the 'Power from on High' is the transcendence of God. As the 'Spirit of prophecy' promised in the Old Testament Scriptures, this Spirit is the power of 'Israel's' restoration, cleansing and purging her as the messianic people of God, through the variety of charismata afforded, and through the way they impact on the community and on the individual. As this Israel is 'restored', however, she finds herself transformed to be the servant of Isaiah 49, and thus a light to 'the nations' outside the doors of the church. Her new way of life as a community of reconciliation and unity, promoted and guarded by the Spirit, makes her a witness; and the Spirit also fills different individuals to articulate this witness with power to those outside the community, to draw them in. Both restoration and mission thus lie at the heart of Lukan pneumatology: the 'Power from on High' may not be truly felt unless we are willing to be committed to both. For Luke, the Spirit is the charismatic dimension of all Christian life and mission, not merely of the one or of the other.

SELECT BIBLIOGRAPHY

This bibliography has been kept to a minimum. It consists largely of items that are referred to more than once in this work, and so must be included because in subsequent references only a brief title is given. A residual number of items, that are only quoted once in the text, are included here because they are key works pertinent to the interpretation of Luke's pneumatology. In addition, a small handful of works on pneumatology are included in the Bibliography that have not been formally referenced in the text, but have been influential in my research.

Abelson, A., *The Immanence of God in Rabbinic Judaism* (London: Hermon, 1969 [1912]).

Achtemeier, J., 'The Lucan Perspective on the Miracles of Jesus: A Preliminary Sketch', *JBL* 94 (1975), pp. 547-62.

Achtemeier, P.J., *The Quest for Unity in the New Testament Church: A Study in Paul and Acts* (Philadelphia: Fortress Press, 1987).

Adler, N., *Das erste christliche Pfingstfest. Sinn und Bedeutung des Pfingstberichtes Apg 2:1-13* (Münster: Aschendorff, 1938).

—*Taufe und Handauflegung: Eine exegetisch-theologische Untersuchung von Apg 8:14-17* (Münster: Aschendorff, 1951).

Aker, B., 'New Directions in Lucan Theology: Reflections on Luke 3.21-22 and Some Implications', in P. Elbert (ed.), *Faces of Renewal* (Peabody, MA: Hendrickson, 1988), pp. 108-27.

Aletti, J.N., 'Jésus à Nazareth (Luc 4.16-30). Prophétie, écriture et typologie', in Aletti *et al.*, *Cause*, pp. 431-52.

Aletti, J.N., *et al.*, *A cause de l'évangile: Etudes sur les synoptiques et les Actes* (Paris: Cerf, 1985).

Anderson, A.A., 'The Use of "Ruah" in 1QS, 1QH and 1QM', *JSS* 7 (1962), pp. 293-303.

Anderson, H., 'Broadening Horizons: The Rejection at Nazareth Pericope of Luke 4.16-30 in Light of Recent Critical Trends', *Int* 18 (1964), pp. 259-75.

Atkinson, W., 'Pentecostal Responses to Dunn's Baptism in the Holy Spirit: Luke–Acts', *JPT* 6 (1995), pp. 87-131.

Aune, D.E., *Prophecy in Early Christianity and the Ancient Mediterranean World* (Exeter: Paternoster, 1983).

Bacchiocchi, S., *From Sabbath to Sunday: A Historical Investigation of the Rise of Sunday Observance in Early Christianity* (Rome: Gregorian Press, 1977).

Baer, H., von., *Der Heilige Geist in den Lukasschriften* (Stuttgart: Kohlhammer, 1926).

Baker, K.W., 'Father, Son and Holy Spirit in the Acts of the Apostles' (PhD dissertation, Marquette University, 1967).

Banks, R.J., *Jesus and the Law in the Synoptic Tradition* (Cambridge: Cambridge University Press, 1975).

Barrett, C.K., *The Acts of the Apostles* (Edinburgh: T. & T. Clark, 1994).

—'Apollos and the Twelve Disciples of Ephesus', in W.C. Weinrich (ed.), *The New Testament Age: Essays in Honor of Bo Reicke* (Macon, GA: Mercer University Press, 1984), I, pp. 29-39.

—'Faith and Eschatology in Acts 3', in Grässer and Merk (eds.), *Glaube*, pp. 1-17.

—*The Holy Spirit and the Gospel Tradition* (London: SPCK, 2nd edn, 1966).

—'Light on the Holy Spirit from Simon Magus (Acts 8.4-25)', in Kremer (ed.), *Les Actes*, pp. 281-95.

—'Paul's Address to the Ephesian Elders', in J. Jervell and W.A. Meeks (eds.), *God's Christ and his People: Studies in Honour of Nils Alstrup Dahl* (Oslo: Universitetsforlaget, 1977), pp. 107-21.

Bayer, H.F., 'Christ-Centered Eschatology in Acts 3.17-26', in Green and Turner (eds.), *Jesus*, pp. 236-50.

Beasley-Murray, G.R., *Jesus and the Kingdom of God* (Exeter: Paternoster, 1986).

—*Baptism in the New Testament* (London: Macmillan, 1962).

—'Jesus and the Spirit', in Descamps and de Halleux (eds.), *Mélanges Bibliques*, pp. 463-78.

Behm, J., *Die Handauflegung im Urchristentum nach Verwendung, Herkunft und Bedeutung im religionsgeschichtl. Zusammenhang untersucht* (Leipzig, 1911).

Best, E., 'Spirit-Baptism', *NovT* 4 (1960), pp. 236-43.

—'The Use and Non-Use of Pneuma by Josephus', *NovT* 3 (1959), pp. 218-25.

Betz, O., *Der Paraklet* (Leiden: Brill, 1963).

—'The Eschatological Interpretation of the Sinai-Tradition in Qumran and in the New Testament', *RevQ* 6 (1967), pp. 89-107.

Billington, A., T. Lane and M. Turner (eds.), *Mission and Meaning: Essays Presented to Peter Cotterell* (Carlisle: Paternoster, 1995).

Blomberg, C.L., 'The Law in Luke–Acts', *JSNT* 22 (1984), pp. 53-80.

Bock, D.L., *Proclamation from Prophecy and Pattern: Lucan Old Testament Christology* (Sheffield: JSOT Press, 1987).

Borg, M.J., *Conflict, Holiness and Politics in the Teachings of Jesus* (Lewiston, NY: Mellen, 1984).

Borgen, P., 'Jesus Christ, the Reception of the Spirit, and a Cross-National Community', in Green and Turner (eds.), *Jesus*, pp. 220-35.

Bornkamm, G., and K. Rahner (eds.), *Die Zeit Jesu* (Freiburg: Herder, 1970).

Bovon, F., *Das Evangelium nach Lukas. I. Lk 1,1–9,50* (Zürich: Benziger Verlag, 1989).

—*L'Evangile selon Saint Luc 1–9* (Geneva: Labor et Fides, 1991).

—'La figure de Moïse dans l'oeuvre de Luc', in *L'Oeuvre de Luc* (Paris: Cerf, 1987) 73-96.

—*Luc le théologien: Vingt-cinq ans de recherches (1950–1975)* (Paris: Delachaux, 1978).

—*Luke the Theologian: Thirty-three Years of Research (1950–1983)* (Allison Park: Pickwick, 1987).

—*L'Oeuvre de Luc* (Paris: Cerf, 1987).

—'Le Saint-Esprit, l'église et les relations humaines selon Actes 20.36–21.16', in Kremer (ed.), *Les Actes*, pp. 339-58.

—'Le salut dans les écrits de Luc', *RTP* 3 (1973), pp. 296-307.

—'Tradition et rédaction en Acts 10,1–11,18', in *L'Oeuvre de Luc*, pp. 97-120.

Brandenburger, E., *Fleisch und Geist: Paulus und die dualistische Weisheit* (Neukirchen–Vluyn: Neukirchener Verlag, 1968).

Braumann, G., 'Die Schuldner und die Sünderin, Luk. vii, 36-50', *NTS* 10 (1964–65), pp. 487-93.

Brawley, R.L., 'The Blessing of All the Families of the Earth: Jesus and the Covenant Traditions in Luke–Acts', in E.H. Lovering (ed.), *Society of Biblical Literature 1994 Seminar Papers* (Atlanta: Scholars Press, 1994), pp. 252-68.

—*Luke–Acts and the Jews: Conflict, Apology and Conciliation* (Atlanta: John Knox, 1987).

—*Centering on God: Method and Message in Luke–Acts* (Louisville, KY: Westminster Press, 1990).

Broer, I., 'Der Geist und die Gemeinde. Zur Auslegung der Lukanischen Pfingstgeschichte (Apg 2.1-13)', *BibLeb* 13 (1972), pp. 261-83.

Brown, R.E., *The Birth of the Messiah* (London: Geoffrey Chapman, 1978).

—'The Paraclete in the Fourth Gospel', *NTS* 13 (1966–67), pp. 113-32.

Brown, S., *Apostasy and Perseverance in the Theology of Luke* (Rome: Pontifical Biblical Institute, 1969).

—' "Water Baptism" and "Spirit-Baptism" in Luke–Acts', *ATR* 59 (1977), pp. 135-51.

Bruce, F.F., *The Acts of the Apostles: The Greek Text with Introduction and Commentary* (Leicester: Apollos, 3rd edn, 1990 [1951]).

—*The Book of Acts* (Grand Rapids: Eerdmans, 1988).

—*Commentary on the Book of Acts* (London: Marshall, Morgan & Scott, 1954).

—'The Holy Spirit in the Acts of the Apostles', *Int* 27 (1973), pp. 166-83.

Bruner, F.D., *A Theology of the Holy Spirit: The Pentecostal Experience and the New Testament Witness* (Grand Rapids: Eerdmans, 1970).

Büchsel, F., *Der Geist Gottes im Neuen Testament* (Gütersloh: Bertelsmann, 1926).

Buckwalter, D., 'The Character and Purpose of Luke's Christology' (PhD dissertation, Aberdeen, 1991).

Bultmann, R., *The History of the Synoptic Tradition* (Oxford: Basil Blackwell, 1963).

Burchard, C., *Der dreizehnte Zeuge: Traditions- und kompositionsgeschichtliche Untersuchungen zu Lukas' Darstellung der Frühzeit des Paulus* (Göttingen: Vandenhoeck & Ruprecht, 1970).

Burge, G.M., *The Anointed Community: The Holy Spirit in the Johannine Community* (Grand Rapids: Eerdmans, 1987).

Burger, C., *Jesus als Davidssohn: Eine traditionsgeschichtliche Untersuchung* (Göttingen: Vandenhoeck & Ruprecht, 1970).

Busse, U., *Die Wunder des Propheten Jesus: Die Rezeption, Komposition und Interpretation der Wundertradition im Evangelium des Lukas* (Stuttgart: VKB, 1977).

—*Das Nazareth-Manifest Jesu: Eine Einführung in das lukanische Jesusbild nach Lk 4.16-30* (Stuttgart: KBW, 1978).

Cadbury, H.J., *The Style and Literary Method of Luke* (Cambridge, MA: Harvard University Press, 1920).

Cangh, J.M. van, ' "Par l'Esprit de Dieu—par le doigt de Dieu" Mt 12,28 par. Lc 11.20', in Delobel (ed.), *Logia*, pp. 337-42.

Capper, B.J., 'The Intepretation of Acts 5.4', *JSNT* 19 (1983), pp. 117-31.

Carroll, J.T., 'Jesus as Healer in Luke–Acts', in E.H. Lovering (ed.), *Society of Biblical Literature 1994 Seminar Papers* (Atlanta: Scholars Press, 1994), pp. 269-85.

Carruth, T.R., 'The Jesus-as-Prophet Motif' (PhD dissertation, Baylor University, 1973).

Carson, D.A., *Showing the Spirit: A Theological Exposition of 1 Corinthians 12–14* (Grand Rapids: Baker, 1987).

Catchpole, D.R., *The Quest for Q* (Edinburgh: T. & T. Clark, 1993).

Chance, J.B., *Jerusalem, the Temple and the New Age in Luke–Acts* (Macon, GA: Mercer University Press, 1988).

—'The Seed of Abraham and the People of God: A Study of Two Pauls', in E.H. Lovering (ed.), *Society of Biblical Literature 1993 Seminar Papers* (Atlanta: Scholars Press, 1993), pp. 384-411.

Charlesworth, J.H. (ed.), *The Messiah* (Minneapolis: Fortress Press, 1992).

Chevallier, M.-A., '"Pentecôtes" lucaniennes et "Pentecôtes" johanniques', in J. Delorme and J. Duplacy (eds.), *La parole de grâce: Etudes lucaniennes à la mémoire d'Augustin George* (Paris: Recherches de Science Religieuse, 1981), pp. 301-14.

—'Apparentements entre Luc et Jean en matière de pneumatologie', in Aletti *et al.*, *Cause*, pp. 377-408.

—*L'Esprit et le Messie dans le bas-judaïsme et le Nouveau Testament* (Paris: Presses Universitaires de France, 1958).

—'Luc et l'Esprit, à la mémoire du P. Augustin George (1915–77)', *RSR* 56 (1982), pp. 1-16.

—*Souffle de Dieu: Le Saint-Esprit dans le Nouveau Testament* (Paris: Beauchesne, 1978).

Chilton, B., 'Announcement in Nazara: An Analysis of Luke 4.16-21', in R.T. France and D. Wenham (eds.), *Studies of History and Tradition in the Four Gospels*, II (Sheffield: JSOT Press, 1981), pp. 147-72.

—*God in Strength: Jesus' Announcement of the Kingdom* (Sheffield: JSOT Press, 1986 [1979]).

—'Regnum Dei Deus Est', *SJT* 31 (1978), pp. 261-70.

—'The Kingdom of God in Recent Discussion', in Chilton and Evans (eds.), *Studying*, pp. 255-80.

—*The Isaiah Targum* (Edinburgh: T. & T. Clark, 1987).

Chilton, B., and C.A. Evans (eds.), *Studying the Historical Jesus* (Leiden: Brill, 1994).

Co, M.A., 'The Major Summaries in Acts: Acts 2,42-47; 4,32-35; 5,12-16. Linguistic and Literary Relationship', *ETL* 68 (1992), pp. 49-85.

Coleridge, M., *The Birth of the Lukan Narrative: Narrative as Christology in Luke 1–2* (Sheffield: JSOT Press, 1993).

Collins, J.J., 'The Works of the Messiah', *DSD* 1 (1994), pp. 98-112.

Combrink, H.J.B., 'The Structure and Significance of Luke 4.16-30', *Neot* 7 (1973), pp. 27-47.

Conzelmann, H., *Die Apostelgeschichte* (Tübingen: Mohr, 1972).

—'Luke's Place in the Development of Early Christianity', in Keck and Martyn (eds.), *Studies*, pp. 298-316.

—*The Theology of Saint Luke* (London: Faber, 1960).

Coppens, J., *Le messianisme et sa relève prophétique* (Gembloux: Duculot, 1974).

—*L'Imposition des mains et les rites connexes dans le Nouveau Testament et dans l'église ancienne* (Paris: Cerf, 1925).

—'L'Imposition des mains dans les Actes des Apôtres', in Kremer (ed.), *Les Actes*, pp. 405-38.

Cotterell, P., and M. Turner, *Linguistics and Biblical Interpretation* (London: SPCK, 1989).

Creed, J.M., *The Gospel according to Saint Luke* (London: Macmillan, 1930).

Crockett, L.C., 'Luke 4.25-27 and Jewish–Gentile Relations in Luke–Acts', *JBL* 88 (1969), pp. 177-83.

—'The Old Testament in the Gospel of Luke: With Emphasis on the Interpretation of Isa. 61.1-2' (PhD dissertation, Brown University, 1966).

Crone, T.M., *Early Christian Prophecy* (Baltimore: St Mary's University Press, 1973).

Cullen, P.J., 'Euphoria, Praise and Thanksgiving: Rejoicing in the Spirit in Luke–Acts', *JPT* 6 (1995), pp. 13-24.

Danker, F.W., *Jesus and the New Age: According to Saint Luke: A New Commentary on the Third Gospel* (St Louis: Clayton, 1972).

Darr, J.A., *On Character Building: The Reader and the Rhetoric of Characterization in Luke–Acts* (Louisville, KY: Westminster Press, 1992).

Davies, J.G., 'Pentecost and Glossolalia', *JTS* 3 (1952), pp. 228-31.

Davies, S.L., *Jesus the Healer: Possession, Trance and the Origins of Christianity* (London: SCM Press, 1995).

Davies, W.D., 'Reflections on the Spirit in the Mekilta: A Suggestion', *JANES* 5 (1973), pp. 95-105.

Davis, J.A., *Wisdom and Spirit: An Investigation of 1 Corinthians 1.18–3.20 against the Background of Jewish Sapiential Tradition in the Greco-Roman Period* (New York: University Press of America, 1984).

Delobel, J., 'La rédaction de Lc., IV,14-16a et le "Bericht Vom Anfang"', in Neirynck (ed.), *L'Evangile*, pp. 113-33 and 306-12.

Descamps, A, and A. de Halleux (eds.), *Mélanges bibliques en hommage au R.P. Béda Rigaux* (Gembloux: Duculot, 1970).

Dibelius, M., *Studies in Luke–Acts* (London: SCM Press, 1956).

Dietrich, W., *Das Petrusbild der lukanischen Schriften* (Stuttgart: Kohlhammer, 1972).

Dix, G., 'Confirmation or the Laying on of Hands', *Theology Occasional Papers* 5 (1936).

—*The Theology of Confirmation in Relation to Baptism* (Westminster: Dacre, 1946).

Drury, J., *Tradition and Design in Luke's Gospel: A Study in Early Christian Historiography* (London: Darton, Longman & Todd, 1976).

Dubois, J.D., 'De Jean-Baptiste à Jésus: Essai sur la conception lucanienne de l'Esprit à partir des premiers chapîtres de l'Evangile' (DTh dissertation, Strasbourg, 1977).

Dumais, M., 'Ministères, charismes et Esprit dans l'oeuvre de Luc', *Eglise et Théologie* 9 (1978), pp. 413-53.

Dunn, J.D.G., '1 Corinthians 15.45—Last Adam, Life-giving Spirit', in Lindars and Smalley (eds.), *Christ*, pp. 127-42.

—*Baptism in the Holy Spirit: A Re-examination of the New Testament Teaching on the Gift of the Spirit in Relation to Pentecostalism Today* (London: SCM Press, 1970).

—*Christology in the Making* (London: SCM Press, 1980).

—'The Birth of a Metaphor—Baptized in Spirit', *ExpTim* 89 (1977), pp. 134-38, 173-75.

—*Jesus and the Spirit* (London: SCM Press, 1975).

—'Jesus—Flesh and Spirit: An Exposition of Romans I.3-4', *JTS* 24 (1973), pp. 40-68.

—'Matthew 12.28/Luke 11.20—A Word of Jesus?', in W. Gloer (ed.), *Eschatology and the New Testament: Essays in Honor of George Raymond Beasley-Murray* (Peabody, MA: Hendrickson, 1988), pp. 30-49.

—'A Note on δωρεά', *ExpTim* 81 (1969–70), pp. 249-51.

—'Spirit and Fire Baptism', *NovT* 14 (1972), pp. 81-92.

—'Spirit and Kingdom', *ExpTim* 82 (1970–71), pp. 36-40.

—'Spirit-Baptism and Pentecostalism', *SJT* 23 (1970), pp. 397-407.

—' "They Believed Philip Preaching" (Acts 8.12): A Reply', *IBS* 1 (1979), pp. 177-83.

—'Baptism in the Spirit: A Response to Pentecostal Scholarship on Luke–Acts', *JPT* 3 (1993), pp. 3-27.

—*Unity and Diversity in the New Testament: An Enquiry into the Character of Earliest Christianity* (London: SCM Press, 1977).

Dupont, J., 'Ascension du Christ et don de l'Esprit d'après Actes 2.33', in Lindars and Smalley (eds.), *Christ*, pp. 219-28.

—'La conclusion des Actes et son rapport à l'ensemble de l'ouvrage de Luc', in Kremer (ed.), *Les Actes*, pp. 359-404.

—'Dieu l'a oint d'Esprit Saint', in *Nouvelles études*, pp. 319-28.

—*Etudes sur les Actes des Apôtres* (Paris: Cerf, 1967).

—'"Je rebâtirai la cabane de David qui est tombée" (Ac 15,16 = Am 9,11)', in Grässer and Merk (eds.), *Glaube*, pp. 19-32.

—'La nouvelle Pentecôte (Ac 2, 1-11)', in *Nouvelles études*, pp. 193-98.

—*Nouvelles études sur les Actes des Apôtres* (Paris: Cerf, 1984).

—'Un peuple d'entre les nations (Actes 15.14)', *NTS* 31 (1985), pp. 321-35.

—'La première Pentecôte chrétienne', in *Etudes*, pp. 481-502.

—*The Salvation of the Gentiles* (New York: Paulist Press, 1979).

—' "Le seigneur de tous" (Ac 10.36; Rm 10.12)', in G.F. Hawthorne and O. Betz (eds.), *Tradition and Interpretation in the New Testament* (Tübingen: Mohr, 1987), pp. 229-36.

—*The Sources of Acts* (London: Darton, Longman & Todd, 1964).

—*Les tentations de Jésus au désert* (Paris: Brouwer, 1968).

Durken, D. (ed.), *Sin, Salvation and the Spirit* (Collegeville, MN: Liturgical Press, 1979).

Edwards, R., *The Theology of Q* (Philadelphia: Fortress Press, 1976).

Ellis, E.E., *The Gospel of Luke* (London: Marshall, Morgan & Scott, 1974 [1964]).

—'Midrashic Features in the Speeches of Acts', in Descamps and de Halleux (eds.), *Mélanges bibliques*, pp. 303-12.

—'The Role of the Christian Prophet in Acts', in *Prophecy and Hermeneutic in Early Christianity: New Testament Essays* (Tübingen: Mohr, 1978) pp. 46-57.

Ervin, H.M., *Conversion-Initiation and the Baptism in the Holy Spirit: A Critique of James D.G. Dunn, Baptism in the Holy Spirit* (Peabody, MA: Hendrickson, 1984).

—*Spirit-Baptism: A Biblical Investigation* (Peabody, MA: Hendrickson, 1987).

Esler, P.F., *Community and Gospel in Luke–Acts: The Social and Political Motivations of Lucan Theology* (Cambridge: Cambridge University Press, 1987).

—'Glossolalia and the Admission of Gentiles into the Early Christian Community', *BTB* 22 (1992), pp. 136-42.

Evans, C.A., 'Jesus and the Spirit: On the Origin and Ministry of the Second Son of God', in Evans and Sanders, *Luke*, pp. 26-45.

—'The Twelve Thrones of Israel: Scripture and Politics in Luke 22.24-30', in Evans and Sanders, *Luke*, pp. 154-70.

Evans, C.A., and J.A. Sanders., *Luke and Scripture: The Function of Sacred Tradition in Luke–Acts* (Minneapolis: Fortress Press, 1993).

Evans, C.F., 'The Central Section of Saint Luke's Gospel', in Nineham (ed.), *Studies*, pp. 37-53.

—*Saint Luke* (London: SCM Press, 1990).

Everts, J., 'Tongues or Languages? Contextual Consistency in the Translation of Acts 2', *JPT* 4 (1994), pp. 71-80.

Farnell, F.D., 'The Gift of Prophecy in the Old and New Testaments', *BSac* 149 (1992), pp. 387-410.

Farris, S., *The Hymns of Luke's Infancy Narratives* (Sheffield: JSOT Press, 1985).

Fascher, E., ΠΡΟΦΗΤΗΣ (Giessen: Töpelmann, 1927).

Fee, G.D., 'Christology and Pneumatology in Romans 8.9-11—and Elsewhere: Some Reflections on Paul as a Trinitarian', in Green and Turner (eds.), *Jesus*, pp. 312-31.

—*God's Empowering Presence: The Holy Spirit in the Letters of Paul* (Peabody, MA: Hendrickson, 1994).

—*Gospel and Spirit: Issues in New Testament Hermeneutics* (Peabody, MA: Hendrickson, 1991).

Feuillet, A., 'Vocation et mission des prophêtes, baptême et mission de Jésus. Etude de christologie biblique', *Nova et Vetera* 54 (1979), pp. 22-40.

Fisher, J.D.C., *Confirmation: Then and Now* (London: SPCK, 1978).

Fitzmyer, J.A., 'Further Light on Melchizedek from Qumran Cave 11', *JBL* 86 (1967), pp. 25-41.

—*The Gospel according to Luke (I–IX)* (New York: Doubleday, 1981).

—*The Gospel according to Luke (X–XXIV)* (New York: Doubleday, 1985).

—*Luke the Theologian* (London: Geoffrey Chapman, 1989).

—'The Ascension of Christ and Pentecost', *TS* 45 (1984), pp. 409-40.

Flanagan, N., 'The What and How of Salvation in Luke–Acts', in Durken (ed.), *Sin*, pp. 203-13.

Flender, H., *Saint Luke: Theologian of Redemptive History* (London: SPCK, 1967).

Foakes-Jackson, F.J., and K. Lake (eds.), *The Beginnings of Christianity*, I (5 vols.; London: Macmillan, 1920–33).

Foerster, W., 'Der Heilige Geist im Spätjudentum', *NTS* 8 (1961–62), pp. 117-34.

Ford, J.M., 'Toward a Theology of Speaking in Tongues', *TS* 32 (1971), pp. 3-29.

France, R.T., *Jesus and the Old Testament: His Application of Old Testament Passages to himself and his Mission* (London: Tyndale Press, 1971).

Franklin, E., 'The Ascension and the Eschatology of Luke–Acts', *SJT* 23 (1970), pp. 191-200.

—*Christ the Lord* (London: SPCK, 1975).

—*Luke: Interpreter of Paul, Critic of Matthew* (Sheffield: JSOT Press, 1994).

Frein, B.C., 'Narrative Predictions, Old Testament Prophecies and Luke's Sense of Fulfilment', *NTS* 40 (1994), pp. 22-37.

Gaffin, R.B., *Perspectives on Pentecost: Studies in New Testament Teaching on the Gifts of the Holy Spirit* (Phillipsburg: Presbyterian and Reformed, 1979).

Garrett, S., *The Demise of the Devil: Magic and the Demonic in Luke's Writing* (Minneapolis: Fortress Press, 1989).

Gasque, W.W., *A History of the Criticism of the Acts of the Apostles* (Tübingen: Mohr, 1975).

Geldenhuys, J.N., *Commentary on the Gospel of Luke* (London: Marshall, Morgan & Scott, 1950).

Gelin, A., 'L'Annonce de la Pentecôte (Joël 3,1-5)', *BVC* 27 (1959), pp. 15-19.

George, A., 'L'Emploi chez Luc du vocabulaire de salut', *NTS* 23 (1976–77), pp. 308-20.

—'L'Esprit-Saint dans l'oeuvre de Luc', *RB* 85 (1978), pp. 500-42.

—*Etudes sur l'oeuvre de Luc* (Paris: Gabalda, 1978).

—'Israël dans l'oeuvre de Luc', *RB* 75 (1968), pp. 481-25.

—'Le miracle', in *Etudes*, pp. 133-48.

—'Note sur quelques traits lucaniens de l'expression "par le doigt de Dieu" (Lc XI.20)', *ScEccl* 18 (1966), pp. 461-66.

Gero, S., 'The Spirit as a Dove at the Baptism of Jesus', *NovT* 18 (1976), pp. 17-35.

Giblet, J., 'Baptism in the Spirit in the Acts of the Apostles', *OC* 10 (1974), pp. 162-71.

Gill, D.W.G., and C. Gempf (eds.), *The Book of Acts in its Graeco-Roman Setting* (Carlisle: Paternoster, 1994).

Gils, F., *Jésus prophète d'après les évangiles synoptiques* (Leuven: Leuven University Press, 1957).

Glöckner, R., *Die Verkündigung des Heils beim Evangelisten Lukas* (Mainz: Matthias-Grünewald, 1975).

Gloël, J., *Der Heilige Geist in der Heilsverkündigung des Paulus* (Halle: Niemeyer, 1888).

Goulder, M.D., *Luke: A New Paradigm* (Sheffield: JSOT Press, 1989).

Gourgues, M., *A la droite de Dieu: Résurrection de Jésus et actualisation du psaume 110:1 dans le Nouveau Testament* (Paris: Gabalda, 1978).

—'Esprit des commencements et esprit des prolongements dans les Actes: Note sur la "Pentecôte des samaritains" (Act., VIII, 5-25)', *RB* 93 (1986), pp. 376-85.

—'"Exalté à la droite de Dieu" (Ac 2:33; 5:31)', *SE* 27 (1975), pp. 303-27.

Grässer, E., 'Die Parusieerwartung in der Apostelgeschichte', in Kremer (ed.), *Les Actes*, pp. 99-127.

—'Ta peri tês basileias (Apg 1.6; 19.8)', in Aletti *et al.*, *Cause*, pp. 707-26.

Grässer, E., and O. Merk (eds.), *Glaube und Eschatologie: Festschrift für Werner Georg Kümmel zum 80. Geburtstag* (Tübingen: Mohr, 1985).

Green, E.M.B., *I Believe in the Holy Spirit* (London: Hodder, 1975).

Green, J.B., *The Death of Jesus: Tradition and Interpretation in the Passion Narrative* (Tübingen: Mohr, 1988).

—'Good News to Whom? Jesus and the "Poor"', in Green and Turner (eds.), *Jesus*, pp. 59-74.

—'Jesus and a Daughter of Abraham (Luke 13.10-17): Test Case for a Lucan Perspective on Jesus', Miracles', *CBQ* 51 (1989), pp. 643-54.

—*The Theology of the Gospel of Luke* (Cambridge: Cambridge University Press, 1995).

Green, J.B., and M. Turner (eds.), *Jesus of Nazareth: Lord and Christ. Essays on the Historical Jesus and New Testament Christology* (Carlisle: Paternoster, 1994).

Greenspahn, F.E., 'Why Prophecy Ceased', *JBL* 108 (1989) pp. 37-49.

Grudem, W., *The Gift of Prophecy in the New Testament and Today* (Eastbourne: Kingsway, 1988).

Grundmann, W., *Das Evangelium nach Lukas* (Berlin: Evangelische Verlagsanstalt, 2nd edn, 1961).

—'Der Pfingstbericht der Apostelgeschichte in seinem theologischen Sinn', in F.L. Cross (ed.), *Studia Evangelica*, II (Berlin: Akademie Verlag, 1964) pp. 584-94.

Gundry, R.H., '"Ecstatic Utterance" (NEB)?', *JTS* 17 (1966), pp. 299-307.

Gunkel, H., *The Influence of the Holy Spirit: The Popular View of the Apostolic Age and the Teaching of the Apostle Paul* (Philadelphia: Fortress Press, 1979).

—*Die Wirkungen des Heiligen Geistes nach der populären Anschauung der apostolischen Zeit und der Lehre des Apostels Paulus* (Göttingen: Vandenhoeck & Ruprecht, 1888).

Haacker, K., 'Einige Fälle von "erlebter Rede" im Neuen Testament', *NovT* 12 (1970), pp. 70-77.

—'Das Pfingstwunder als exegetisches Problem', in O. Böcher and K. Haacker (eds.), *Verborum Veritas* (Wuppertal: Brockhaus, 1970), pp. 125-31.

Haenchen, E., *The Acts of the Apostles* (Oxford: Basil Blackwell, 1971).

Hahn, F., *The Titles of Jesus in Christology: Their History in Early Christianity* (London: Lutterworth, 1959).

Hamerton-Kelly, R., 'A Note on Matthew XII.28 par Luke XI.20', *NTS* 11 (1964–65), pp. 167-69.

Hamm, D., 'Acts 3.1-10: The Healing of the Temple Beggar as Lucan Theology', *Bib* 67 (1986), pp. 305-19.

Hanson, R.C.P., *The Acts in the Revised Standard Version* (Oxford: Oxford University Press, 1967).

Harm, F.R., 'Structural Elements related to the Gift of the Spirit in Acts', *Concordia Journal* 14 (1988), pp. 28-41.

Harnack, A. von., 'Zu Lk 1:34-35', *ZNW* 2 (1901), pp. 53-57.

Harrington, W. (ed.), *Witness to the Spirit* (Dublin: Koinonia Press, 1979).

Hartman, L., 'Taufe, Geist und Sohnschaft: Traditionsgeschichtliche Erwägungen zu Mk 1.9-11 Par', in *Jesus in der Verkündigung der Kirche* (Linz: SNTU, 1976), pp. 89-110.

Haufe, G., 'Taufe und Heiliger Geist in Urchristentum', *TL* 101 (1976), pp. 561-71.

Haulotte, E., 'Fondation d'une communauté de type universel: Actes 10,1–11,18. Etude critique sur la rédaction, la "structure" et la "tradition" du récit', *RechSR* 58 (1970), pp. 63-100.

—'La vie en communion, phase ultime de la Pentecôte, Acts 2,42-47', *Foi et Vie* 80 (1981), pp. 69-75.

Hawthorne, G.F., *The Presence and the Power* (Waco, TX: Word Books, 1991).

Hay, D.M., *Glory at the Right Hand: Psalm 110 in Early Christianity* (Nashville: Abingdon Press, 1973).

Haya-Prats, G., *L'Esprit force de l'église* (Paris: Cerf, 1975).

Hedrick, C.W., 'Paul's Conversion/Call: A Comparative Analysis of the Three Reports in Acts', *JBL* 100 (1981), pp. 415-32.

Helyer, L.R., 'Luke and the Restoration of Israel', *JETS* 36 (1993), pp. 317-29.

Hemer, C.J., *The Book of Acts in the Setting of Hellenistic History* (Tübingen: Mohr, 1989).

Hengel, M., *Nachfolge und Charisma* (Berlin: Töpelmann, 1968).

Hill, D., *Greek Words with Hebrew Meanings: Studies in the Semantics of Soteriological Terms* (Cambridge: Cambridge University Press, 1967).

—'The Rejection of Jesus at Nazareth (Luke iv.16-30)', *NovT* 13 (1971), pp. 161-80.

—'The Spirit and the Church's Witness: Observations on Acts 1.6-8', *IBS* 6 (1984), pp. 16-26.

Horn, F.W., *Das Angeld des Geistes: Studien zur paulinischen Pneumatologie* (Göttingen: Vandenhoeck & Ruprecht, 1992).

Horsely, R.A., ' "Like One of the Prophets of Old": Two Types of Popular Prophets at the Time of Jesus', *CBQ* 47 (1985), pp. 435-63.

Horton, F.L., *The Melchizedek Tradition* (Cambridge: Cambridge University Press, 1976).

Horton, H., *The Gifts of the Spirit* (Nottingham: Assemblies of God, 1968).

Hubbard, B.J., 'Commissioning Stories in Luke–Acts: A Study of their Antecedents, Form and Content', *Semeia* 8 (1977), pp. 103-26.

Hui, A.W.D., 'The Concept of the Holy Spirit in Ephesians and its Relation to the Pneumatologies of Luke and Paul' (PhD Dissertation, Aberdeen, 1992).

Hull, J.H.E., *The Holy Spirit in the Acts of the Apostles* (London: Lutterworth, 1967).

Hultgren, A.J., *Christ and his Benefits* (Philadelphia: Fortress Press, 1987).

Hunter, H.D., *Spirit-Baptism: A Pentecostal Alternative* (Lanham, MD: University Press of America, 1983).

Hurtado, L.W., 'Normal, but not a Norm: Initial Evidence and the New Testament', in McGee (ed.), *Initial Evidence*, pp. 189-201.

—*One God, One Lord* (London: SCM Press, 1988).

Imschoot, P. van, 'L'Action de L'Esprit de Jahvé dans l'Ancien Testament', *RScPhilT* 23 (1934), pp. 553-87.

—'Baptême d'eau et baptême d'Esprit', *ETL* 13 (1936), pp. 653-66.

—'L'Esprit de Jahvé et l'alliance nouvelle dans l'Ancien Testament', *ETL* 22 (1936), pp. 201-26.

—'L'Esprit de Jahvé, source de vie dans l'Ancien Testament', *RB* 44 (1935), pp. 481-501.

—'Sagesse et Esprit dans l'Ancien Testament', *RB* 47 (1938), pp. 23-49.

Isaacs, M.E., *The Concept of Spirit* (London: Heythrop Monographs, 1976).

Jackson, D., 'Luke and Paul: A Theology of One Spirit from Two Perspectives', *JETS* 32 (1989), pp. 335-43.

Jeremias, J., *New Testament Theology. I. The Proclamation of Jesus* (London: SCM Press, 1971).

—*Die Sprache des Lukasevangeliums* (Göttingen: Vandenhoeck and Ruprecht, 1980).

Jervell, J., 'The Church of Jews and Godfearers', in Tyson (ed.), *Luke–Acts*, pp. 11-20.

—'The Divided People of God: The Restoration of Israel and Salvation for the Gentiles', in *Luke*, pp. 41-74.

—'The Law in Luke–Acts', in *Luke*, pp. 133-51.

—'The Lost Sheep of the House of Israel: The Understanding of the Samaritans in Luke–Acts', in *Luke*, pp. 113-32.

—*Luke and the People of God* (Minneapolis: Augsburg, 1972).

—'Sons of the Prophets: The Holy Spirit in the Acts of the Apostles', in *Unknown Paul*, pp. 96-121, 172-79.

—'The Twelve on Israel's Thrones', in *Luke*, pp. 75-112.

—*The Unknown Paul: Essays on Luke–Acts and Early Christian History* (Minneapolis: Augsburg, 1984).

—'Das Volk des Geistes', in J. Jervell and W.A. Meeks (eds.), *God's Christ and his People: Studies in Honour of Nils Alstrup Dahl* (Oslo: Universitetsforlaget, 1977), pp. 87-106.

—'Die Zeichen des Apostels: Die Wunder beim lukanischen und paulinischen Paulus', in E. Fuchs (ed.), *Studien zum Neuen Testament und seiner Umwelt 4* (Linz: SNTU, 1979), pp. 54-75.

Johnson, L.T., *The Literary Function of Possessions in Luke–Acts* (Missoula: Scholars Press, 1977).

—*The Gospel of Luke* (Collegeville, MN: Liturgical Press, 1991).

—'The Social Dimensions of *Sōtēria* in Luke–Acts and Paul', in E.H. Lovering (ed.), *Society of Biblical Literature 1993 Seminar Papers* (Atlanta: Scholars Press, 1993), pp. 520-36.

Johnston, G., *The Spirit-Paraclete in the Gospel of John* (Cambridge: Cambridge University Press, 1970).

Jones, D.L., 'The Title Kyrios in Luke–Acts', in G.W. MacRae (ed.), *SBL Seminar Papers*, II (Cambridge, MA: SBL, 1974), pp. 85-101.

Jonge, H.J., de., 'Sonship, Wisdom, Infancy: Luke II. 41-51a', *NTS* 24 (1977–78), pp. 317-54.

Jonge, M. de, and A.S. Van der Woude, '11Q Melchizedek and the New Testament', *NTS* 12 (1965–66), pp. 301-26

Käsemann, E., *Essays on New Testament Themes* (London: SCM Press, 1964).

Kaiser, C.B., 'The "Rebaptism" of the Ephesian Twelve: Exegetical Study on Acts 19.1-7', *RefR* 31 (1977–78), pp. 57-61.

Keck, L.E., 'The Spirit and the Dove', *NTS* 17 (1970), pp. 41-68.

Keck, L.E., and J.L. Martyn (eds.), *Studies in Luke–Acts: Essays Presented in Honour of P. Schubert* (London: SPCK, 1968).

Kee, H.C., *Good News to the Ends of the Earth: The Theology of Acts* (London: SCM Press, 1990).

Kerrigan, A., 'The "Sensus Plenior" of Joel III,1-5', in *Sacra Pagina II* (Paris: Gabalda, 1959).

Kilpatrick, G., 'The Spirit, God and Jesus in Acts', *JTS* 15 (1964), p. 63.

Kim, H.-S., *Die Geisttaufe des Messias: Eine kompositionsgeschichtliche Untersuchung zu einem Leitmotiv des lukanischen Doppelwerks* (Berlin: Lang, 1993).

Kimball, C.A., *Jesus' Exposition of the Old Testament in Luke's Gospel* (Sheffield: JSOT Press, 1994).

Kjeseth, P.L., 'The Spirit of Power: A Study of the Holy Spirit in Luke–Acts' (PhD dissertation, Chicago, 1966).

Knox, J., *Chapters in a Life of Paul* (Nashville: Abingdon Press, 1950).

Knox, W.L., *The Acts of the Apostles* (Cambridge: Cambridge University Press, 1948).

Koch, D.-A., 'Geistbesitz, Geistverleihung und Wundermacht: Erwägungen zur Tradition und zur lukanischen Redaktion in Apg 8.5-25', *ZNW* 77 (1986), pp. 64-82.

Koch, R., *Geist und Messias* (Vienna: Herder, 1950).

Koet, B.J., *Five Studies in Interpretation of Scripture in Luke–Acts* (Leuven: Leuven University Press, 1989).

Kolasny, J., 'An Example of Rhetorical Criticism: Luke 4.16-30', in Richard (ed.), *New Views*, pp. 67-77, 171-72.

Kränkl, E., *Jesus der Knecht Gottes* (Regensburg: Pustet, 1972).

Kremer, J. (ed.), *Les Actes des Apôtres* (Gembloux: Duculot, 1979).

—*Pfingstbericht und Pfingstgeschehen: Eine exegetische Untersuchung zu Apg 2:1-13* (Stuttgart: KBW, 1973).

—'Die Voraussagen des Pfingstgeschehens in Apg 1,4-5 und 8', in Bornkamm and Rahner (eds.), *Die Zeit Jesu*, pp. 145-68.

—'Was geschah Pfingsten? Zur Historizität des Apg in 2,1-13 berichteten Pfingstereignisses', *WW* 3 (1973), pp. 195-207.

Kretschmar, G., 'Himmelfahrt und Pfingsten', *ZKG* 66 (1954), pp. 209-53

Kümmel, W.G., 'Luc en accusation dans la théologie contemporaire', in Neirynck (ed.), *L'Evangile*, pp. 3-19 and 295.

Lagrange, M.-J., 'La conception surnaturelle du Christ d'après Saint Luc', *RB* 11 (14), pp. 60-71 and 188-208.

Lampe, G.W.H., *God as Spirit: The Bampton Lectures* (Oxford: Clarendon Press, 1976, 1977).

—' "Grievous Wolves" (Acts 20:29)', in B. Lindars and S.S. Smalley (eds.), *Christ and Spirit in the New Testament* (Cambridge: Cambridge University Press, 1973), pp. 253-68.

—'The Holy Spirit and the Person of Christ', in S. Sykes and J. Clayton (eds.), *Christ, Faith and History: Cambridge Studies in Christology* (Cambridge: Cambridge University Press, 1972), pp. 112-30.

—'The Holy Spirit in the Writings of Saint Luke', in Nineham *(ed.)*, *Studies*, pp. 159-200.

—'Miracles in the Acts of the Apostles', in C.F.D. Moule (ed.), *Miracles: Cambridge Studies in their Philosophy and History* (London: Mowbray, 1965), pp. 163-78.

—*The Seal of the Spirit* (London: SPCK, 2nd edn, 1967).

Land, S.J., *Pentecostal Spirituality: A Passion for the Kingdom* (Sheffield: JSOT Press, 1993).

Laurentin, A., 'Le pneuma dans la doctrine de Philon', *ETL* 27 (1951), pp. 391-404.

Laurentin, R., *Jésus au Temple* (Paris: Gabalda, 1974).

—*Structure et théologie de Luc 1–2* (Paris: Lecoffre, 1964).

Le Déaut, R., 'Pentecost and Jewish Tradition', *Doctrine and Life* 20 (1970), pp. 250-67.

Leaney, A.R.C., *The Gospel according to Saint Luke* (London: A. & C. Black, 1966).

Lederle, H.I., 'Initial Evidence and the Charismatic Movement: An Ecumenical Appraisal', in McGee (ed.), *Initial Evidence*, pp. 131-41.

—*Treasures Old and New: Interpretations of 'Spirit-Baptism' in the Charismatic Renewal Movement* (Peabody, MA: Hendrickson, 1988).

Leenhardt, J., *Le baptême chrétien, son origine, sa signification* (Neuchâtel: Delachaux, 1946).

Légasse, S., 'L'autre "baptême", (Mc 1,8; Mt 3,11; Lc 3,16; Jn 1,26,31-33)', in F. Van Segbroeck, C.M. Tuckett, G. Van Belle, and J. Verheyden (eds.), *The Four Gospels 1992* (Leuven: Leuven University Press, 1992), pp. 257-73.

Leisegang, H., *Der Heilige Geist: Das Wesen und Werden der Mystisch-Intuitiven Erkenntnis in der Philosophie und Religion der Griechen* (Berlin: Teubner, 1919).

—*Pneuma Hagion: Der Ursprung des Geistesbegriffs der synoptischen Evangelien aus der griechischen Mystik* (Leipzig: Hinrichs, 1922).

Leivestadt, R., 'Das Dogma von der Prophetenlosen Zeit', *NTS* 19 (1973), pp. 288-300.

Lincoln, A.T., 'Theology and History in the Interpetation of Luke's Pentecost', *ExpTim* 96 (1984–85), pp. 204-209.

Lindars, B., *New Testament Apologetic: The Doctrinal Significance of the Old Testament Quotations* (London: SCM Press, 1961).

Lindars, B., and S.S. Smalley (eds.), *Christ and Spirit in the New Testament* (Cambridge: Cambridge University Press, 1973).

Loader, W.R.G., 'Christ at the Right Hand—Ps CX.1 in the New Testament', *NTS* 24 (1977–78), pp. 199-217.

Lofthouse, W.F., 'The Holy Spirit in the Acts of the Apostles and in the Fourth Gospel', *ExpTim* 52 (1940–41), pp. 334-36.

Lohfink, G., *The Conversion of Saint Paul* (Chicago: Franciscan Herald Press, 1976).

—*Die Himmelfahrt Jesu* (Munich: Kösel, 1971).

—*Jesus and Community* (London: SPCK, 1985).

—*Die Sammlung Israels: Eine Untersuchung zur lukanischen Ekklesiologie* (Munich: Kösel, 1975).

Lohse, E., *Die Einheit des Neuen Testaments: Exegetische Studien zur Theologie des Neuen Testaments* (Göttingen: Vandenhoeck and Ruprecht, 1973).

Loisy, A., *Les Actes des Apôtres* (Paris, 1920).

Löning, K., *Die Saulustradition in der Apostelgeschichte* (Münster: Aschendorff, 1973).

Lövestam E., *Spiritus Blasphemia: Eine Studie zu Mk 3,28f par Mt 12,31f, Lk 12,10* (Lund: Gleerup, 1968).

Luck, U., 'Kerygma, Tradition und Geschichte Jesu bei Lukas', *ZTK* 57 (1960), pp. 51-66.

Lüdemann, G., *Early Christianity according to the Traditions in Acts* (London: SCM Press, 1989).

Luomanen, P. (ed.), *Luke–Acts: Scandinavian Perspectives* (Göttingen: Vandenhoeck & Ruprecht, 1991).

Macchia, F.D., 'The Question of Tongues as Initial Evidence: A Review of Initial Evidence, Edited by Gary B. McGee', *JPT* 2 (1992), pp. 117-27.

—'Sighs too Deep for Words: Towards a Theology of Glossolalia', *JPT* 1 (1992), pp. 47-73.

MacRae, G. W., 'Whom Heaven Must Receive until the Time', *Int* 27 (1973), pp. 151-65.

Maddox, R., *The Purpose of Luke–Acts* (Edinburgh: T. & T. Clark, 1982).

Maile, J., 'The Ascension in Luke–Acts', *TynBul* 37 (1986), pp. 29-59.

Mainville, O., *L'Esprit dans l'oeuvre de Luc* (Montreal: Fides, 1991).

—'Jésus et l'esprit dans l'oeuvre de Luc: Eclairage à partir d'Ac 2,33', *Science et Esprit* 42.2 (1990), pp. 193-208.

Mánek, J., 'The New Exodus in the Books of Luke', *NovT* 2 (1958), pp. 8-23.

Manns, F., *Le symbole eau-esprit dans le judaïsme ancien* (Jerusalem: Franciscan Press, 1983).

Marguerat, D., 'La mort d'Ananias et Saphira (Ac 5.1-11) dans la stratégie narrative de Luc', *NTS* 39 (1993), pp. 209-26.

Marin, L., 'Essai d'analyse structurale d'Actes 10,1-11,18', *RechSR* 58 (1970), pp. 39-61.

Marsh, T., 'The Holy Spirit in Early Christian Teaching', *ITQ* 45 (1978), pp. 101-16.

Marshall, I.H., 'Acts and the "Former Treatise"', in B.W. Winter and A.D. Clarke (eds.), *The Book of Acts in its Ancient Literary Setting* (Carlisle: Paternoster, 1993), pp. 163-82

—*The Acts of the Apostles: An Introduction and Commentary* (Leicester: Inter-Varsity Press, 1980).

—'"Early Catholicism" in the New Testament', in R.N. Longenecker and M.C. Tenney (eds.), *New Dimensions in New Testament Study* (Grand Rapids: Zondervan, 1974) pp. 217-31.

—*The Gospel of Luke: A Commentary on the Greek Text* (Exeter: Paternoster, 1978).

—'Hard Sayings—VII', *Theology* 67 (1964) pp. 65-67

—'The Interpretation of the Magnificat: Luke 1.46-55', in C. Bussmann, and W. Radl (eds.), *Der Treue Gottes trauen* (Freiburg: Herder, 1991), pp. 181-96.

—*Last Supper and Lord's Supper* (Exeter: Paternoster, 1980).

—*Luke: Historian and Theologian* (Exeter: Paternoster, 1970).

—'The Meaning of the Verb "to Baptize"', *EvQ* 45 (1973), pp. 130-40.

—'The Significance of Pentecost', *SJT* 30 (1977), pp. 347-69.

—'Son of God or Servant of Yahweh? A Reconsideration of Mark 1.11', *NTS* 15 (1968–69), pp. 326-36

Martin, Fr, 'Le baptême dans l'Esprit: Tradition du Nouveau Testament et vie de l'église', *NRT* 106 (1984), pp. 23-58.

Martin, R.P., 'Salvation and Discipleship in Luke's Gospel', *Int* 30 (1976), pp. 366-80.

März, C.P., *Das Wort Gottes bei Lukas: Die lukanische Worttheologie als Frage an die neuere Lukasforschung* (Leipzig: St Benno, 1974).

Mattill, A.J., 'The Jesus–Paul Parallels and the Purpose of Luke–Acts', *NovT* 17 (1975), pp. 15-46.

McDonnell, K., and G.T. Montague, *Christian Initiation and Baptism in the Holy Spirit: Evidence from the First Eight Centuries* (Collegeville, MN: Liturgical Press, 1991).

McGee, G.B. (ed.), 'Early Pentecostal Hermeneutics: Tongues as Evidence in the Book of Acts', in McGee (ed.), *Initial Evidence*, pp. 96-118.

—*Initial Evidence: Historical and Biblical Perspectives on the Pentecostal Doctrine of Spirit Baptism* (Peabody, MA: Hendrickson, 1991).

—'Popular Expositions of Initial Evidence in Pentecostalism', in McGee (ed.), *Initial Evidence*, pp. 119-30.

McPolin, J., 'Holy Spirit in Luke and John', *ITQ* 45 (1978), pp. 117-31.

Meeks, W., *The Prophet King: Moses Traditions and the Johannine Christology* (Leiden: Brill, 1967).

Menoud, P., 'Pendant quarante jours', in W.C. van Unnik (ed.), *Neotestamentica et Patristica* (Leiden: Brill, 1962), pp. 148-56.

—'La Pentecôte lucanienne et l'histoire', *RHPR* 42 (1962), pp. 141-47.

—'Remarques sur les textes de l'ascension dans Luc–Actes', in W. Eltester (ed.), *Neutestamentliche Studien für Rudolf Bultmann* (Berlin: Töpelmann, 2nd edn, 1957), pp. 148-56.

Menzies, R.P., 'The Distinctive Character of Luke's Pneumatology', *Paraclete* 25 (1991), pp. 17-30.

—*The Development of Early Christian Pneumatology with Special Reference to Luke–Acts* (Sheffield: JSOT Press, 1991).

—*Empowered for Witness: The Spirit in Luke–Acts* (Sheffield: JSOT Press, 1994).

—'James Shelton's *Mighty in Word and Deed*: A Review Article', *JPT* 2 (1993), pp. 105-15.

—'Luke and the Spirit: A Reply to James Dunn', *JPT* 4 (1994), pp. 115-38.

—'Spirit and Power in Luke–Acts: A Response to Max Turner', *JSNT* 49 (1993), pp. 11-20.

Merk, O., 'Das Reich Gottes in den lukanischen Schriften', in E.E. Ellis and E. Grässer (eds.), *Jesus und Paulus* (Göttingen: Vandenhoeck & Ruprecht, 1975), pp. 201-20.

Merkel, H., 'Israel im lukanischen Werk', *NTS* 40 (1990), pp. 371-98.

Metzger, B.M., 'The Ascension of Jesus Christ', in *Historical and Literary Studies: Pagan, Jewish and Christian* (Leiden: Brill, 1968), pp. 77-81.

—*A Textual Commentary on the Greek Testament* (London: United Bible Societies, 1971).

Meyer, H.A.W., *Critical and Exegetical Handbook to the Acts of the Apostles* (Edinburgh: T. & T. Clark, 1883).

Meyer, R., *Der Prophet aus Galiläa* (Darmstadt: Wissenschaftliche Buchgesellschaft, 1970 [1940]).

Michaels, J.R., 'Evidences of the Spirit, or the Spirit as Evidence? Some Non-Pentecostal Reflections', in McGee (ed.) *Initial Evidence*, pp. 202-18.

Miller, M., 'The Function of Isa 61:1-2 in 11Q Melchizedek', *JBL* 88 (1969), pp. 467-69.

Miller, P.D., 'Luke 4.16-21', *Int* 29 (1975), pp. 417-21.

Miller, R.J., 'Elijah, John, and Jesus in the Gospel of Luke', *NTS* 34 (1988), pp. 611-22.

Mills, W.E., *A Theological/Exegetical Approach to Glossolalia* (London: University Press of America, 1985).

Minear, P.S., 'Luke's Use of the Birth Stories', in Keck and Martyn (eds.), *Studies*, pp. 113-30.

—*To Heal and to Reveal: The Prophetic Vocation according to Luke* (New York: Seabury, 1976).

Miyoshi, M., *Der Anfang des Reiseberichts: Lk 9.51–10.24* (Rome: Pontifical Biblical Institute, 1974).

Moessner, D.P., '"The Christ Must Suffer": New Light on the Jesus-Peter, Stephen, Paul Parallels in Luke–Acts', *NovT* 28 (1986), pp. 220-56.

—'The Ironic Fulfillment of Israel's Glory', in Tyson (ed.), *Luke–Acts*, pp. 35-50.

—'Luke 9.1-50: Luke's Preview of the Journey of the Prophet Like Moses of Deuteronomy', *JBL* 102 (1983), pp. 575-605.

—'Paul and the Pattern of the Prophet Like Moses in Acts', in K.H. Richard (ed.), *Society of Biblical Literature 1983 Seminar Papers* (Chico: Scholars, 1983), pp. 203-12.

Montague, G.T., *The Holy Spirit: Growth of a Biblical Tradition* (New York: Paulist Press, 1976).

Moule, C.F.D., 'The Ascension—Acts 1.9', *ExpTim* 68 (1956–57), pp. 205-209.

—'Baptism with Water and with Holy Spirit', *Theology* 48 (1945), pp. 246-49.

—*The Holy Spirit* (London: Mowbrays, 1978).

—*An Idiom Book of New Testament* Greek (Cambridge: Cambridge University Press, 2nd edn, 1963).

Müller, D., 'Geisterfahrung und Totenauferweckung: Untersuchungen zur Totenauferweckung bei Paulus und in den ihm vorgegebenen Überlieferungen' (PhD dissertation, Christian-Albrecht-Universität, Kiel, 1980).

Mullins, T.Y., 'New Testament Commission Forms, Especially in Luke–Acts', *JBL* 95 (1976), pp. 603-14.

Mussner, F., 'In den letzten Tagen (Apg 2.17a)', *BZ* 5 (1965), pp. 263-65.

Navone, J., *Themes of Saint Luke* (Rome: Gregorian University Press, 1970).

Neale, D.A., *None but the Sinners: Religious Categories in the Gospel of Luke* (Sheffield: JSOT Press, 1991).

Neirynck, F. (ed.), 'Acts 10,36a τὸν λόγον ὧν', *ETL* 60 (1984), pp. 118-23.

—*L'Evangile de Luc—The Gospel of Luke: Revised and Enlarged Edition of L'Evangile de Luc: Problèmes littéraires et théologiques* (Leuven: Leuven University Press, 1989).

—'Le livre des Actes: 6. Ac 10, 36-43 et l'évangile', *ETL* 60 (1984), pp. 109-17.

—'The Miracle Stories in the Acts of the Apostles. An Introduction', in Kremer (ed.), *Les Actes*, pp. 169-213.

Nellessen, E., *Zeugnis für Jesus und das Wort: Exegetische Untersuchungen zum lukanischen Zeugnisbegriff* (Cologne: Hanstein, 1976).

Nielsen, H.K., *Heilung und Verkündigung* (Leiden: Brill, 1987).

Nineham, D.E. (ed.), *Studies in the Gospels: Essays in Memory of R.H. Lightfoot* (Oxford: Basil Blackwell, 1955).

Noack, B., 'The Day of Pentecost in Jubilees, Qumran and Acts', *ASTI* 1 (1962), pp. 73-95.

Nolland, J., *Luke 1–9.20* (WBC, 35a; Dallas: Word Books, 1989).

—*Luke 9.21–18.34* (WBC, 35b; Dallas: Word Books, 1993).

Noorda, S.J., 'Scene and Summary: A Proposal for Reading Acts 4,32–5,16', in Kremer (ed.), *Les Actes*, pp. 475-83.

O'Brien, P.T., 'Prayer in Luke–Acts', *TynBul* 24 (1973), pp. 111-27.

O'Collins, G., and G. Marconi (eds.), *Luke and Acts* (New York: Paulist Press, 1993).

Oliver, H.H., 'The Lukan Birth Stories and the Purpose of Luke–Acts', *NTS* 10 (1964), pp. 202-26.

O'Neill, J.C., *The Theology of Acts in its Historical Setting* (London: SPCK, 1961, 1970)

O'Reilly, L., *Word and Sign in the Acts of the Apostles* (Rome: Pontifical Biblical Institute, 1987).

O'Toole, R.F., 'Activity of the Risen Christ in Luke–Acts', *Bib* 62 (1981), pp. 471-98.

—'Acts 2.30 and the Davidic Covenant of Pentecost', *JBL* 102 (1983), pp. 245-58.

—'Christian Baptism in Luke', *RevRel* 39 (1980), pp. 855-66.

—'The Kingdom of God in Luke–Acts', in W. Willis (ed.), *The Kingdom of God in Twentieth-Century Interpretation* (Peabody, MA: Hendrickson, 1987), pp. 147-62.

—'Luke's Understanding of Jesus' Resurrection-Ascension-Exaltation', *BTB* 9 (1979), pp. 106-14.

—'Parallels between Jesus and his Disciples in Luke–Acts: A Further Study', *BZ* 27 (1983), pp. 195-212.

—*The Unity of Luke's Theology* (Wilmington, DE: Glazier, 1984).

Oulton, J.E.L., 'The Holy Spirit and Laying on of Hands', *ExpTim* 66 (1955), pp. 236-40.

Parratt, J.K., 'The Holy Spirit and Baptism. I. The Gospels and Acts of the Apostles', *ExpTim* 78 (1966–67), pp. 231-35.

—'The Rebaptism of the Ephesian Disciples', *ExpTim* 79 (1967–68), pp. 182-83.

—'The Seal of the Spirit in the New Testament Teaching' (PhD dissertation, London, 1965).

Parsons, M.C., *The Departure of Jesus in Luke–Acts: The Ascension Narratives in Context* (Sheffield: JSOT Press, 1987).

—'The Text of Acts 1:2 Reconsidered', *CBQ* 50 (1988), pp. 58-71.

Perrin, N., *Jesus and the Language of the Kingdom* (London: SCM Press, 1976).

Pesch, R., *Die Apostelgeschichte*, I, II (Neukirchen–Vluyn: Neukirchener Verlag, 1986).

—'La rédaction lucanienne du logion des pêcheurs d'hommes (Lc., V, 10c)', in Neirynck (ed.), *L'Evangile*, pp. 135-54 and 313-15.

Pfitzner, V.C., '"Pneumatic" Apostleship? Apostle and Spirit in the Acts of the Apostles', in W. Haubeck and M. Bachmann (eds.), *Wort in der Zeit: Festgabe für Karl Heinrich Rengstorf* (Leiden: Brill, 1980), pp. 210-35.

Pieper, K., *Die Simon-Magus-Perikope (Apg 8, 5-24): Ein Beitrag zur Quellenfrage in der Apostelgeschichte* (Münster: Aschendorff, 1911).

Plümacher, E., *Lukas als hellenistischer Schriftsteller: Studien zur Apostelgeschichte* (Göttingen: Vandenhoeck & Ruprecht, 1972).

Plummer, A., *A Critical and Exegetical Commentary on the Gospel according to Saint Luke* (Edinburgh: T. & T. Clark, 1922).

Potin, J., *La fête juive de la Pentecôte* (Paris: Cerf, 1971).

Potterie, I. de la, 'L'Onction du Christ: Etude de théologie biblique', *NRT* 80 (1958), pp. 225-52.

Praeder, S.M., 'Jesus-Paul, Peter-Paul, and Jesus-Peter Parallelisms in Luke–Acts: A History of Reader Response', in H.K. Richards (ed.), *Society of Biblical Literature 1984 Seminar Papers* (Chico, CA: Scholars, 1984), pp. 23-49.

Price, R.M., 'Confirmation and Charisma', *SLJT* 33 (1990), pp. 173-82.

Puller, F.W., *What is the Distinctive Grace of Confirmation?* (London, 1880).

Quesnel, M., *Baptisés dans l'Esprit* (Paris: Cerf, 1985).

Radl, W., *Paulus und Jesus im lukanischen Doppelwerk: Untersuchung zu Parallelmotiven im Lukasevangelium und in der Apostelgeschichte* (Bern: Lang, 1975).

Räisänen, H., 'The Redemption of Israel: A Salvation-Historical Problem in Luke–Acts', in Luomanen (ed.), *Luke–Acts*, pp. 94-114.

Rese, M., *Alttestamentliche Motive in der Christologie des Lukas* (Gütersloh: Mohn, 1969).

Richard, E. (ed.), *Acts 6.1–8.4: The Author's Method of Composition* (Missoula: Scholars Press, 1978).

—*New Views on Luke and Acts* (Collegeville, MN: Glazier, 1990).

—'Pentecost as a Recurrent Theme in Luke–Acts', in Richard (ed.), *New Views*, pp. 133-49, 181-83.

Rodd, C.S., 'Spirit or Finger', *ExpTim* 72 (1961), pp. 157-58.

Roloff, J., *Die Apostelgeschichte* (Göttingen: Vandenhoeck & Ruprecht, 1981).

Russell, E.A., '"They Believed Philip Preaching" (Acts 8.12)', *IBS* 1 (1979), pp. 169-76.

Russell, W., 'The Anointing with the Holy Spirit in Luke–Acts', *TrinJ* 7 (1986), pp. 47-63.

Sabbe, M., 'Le baptême de Jésus', in I. de la Potterie (ed.), *De Jésus aux évangiles* (Gembloux: Duculot, 1967) pp. 184-211.

Sala, H.J., 'An Investigation of the Baptizing and Filling Work of the Holy Spirit in the New Testament Related to the Pentecostal Doctrine of "Initial Evidence"' (PhD dissertation, Bob Jones University, 1966).

Samain, E., 'Le discours-programme de Jésus à la synagogue de Nazareth. Luc 4,16-30', *Foi et Vie* 11 (1971), pp. 25-43.

—'La notion de ΑΡΧΗ dans l'oeuvre lucanienne', in Neirynck (ed.), *L'Evangile*, pp. 209-38, 327.

—'Le récit de la Pentecôte, Ac 2,1-13', *La Foi et le Temps* 1 (1971), pp. 227-56.

Sanders, E.P., *Jesus and Judaism* (London: SCM Press, 1985).

—*Paul and Palestinian Judaism: A Comparison of Patterns of Religion* (London: SCM Press, 1977).

Sanders, J.A., 'From Isaiah 61 to Luke 4', in *Christianity, Judaism and Other Greco-Roman Cults* (Leiden: Brill, 1975), pp. 75-106.

—'From Isaiah 61 to Luke 4', in Evans and Sanders, *Luke*, pp. 46-69.

—'Isaiah in Luke', in Evans and Sanders, *Luke*, pp. 14-25.

Sanders, J.T., 'The Jewish People in Luke–Acts', in Tyson (ed.), *Luke–Acts*, pp. 51-75.

—*The Jews in Luke–Acts* (London: SCM Press, 1987).

Sauvagnat, B., 'Se repentir, être baptisé, recevoir l'Esprit. Actes 2,37ss', *Foi et Vie* 80 (1981), pp. 77-89.

Schäfer, P., 'Die Termini "Heiligen Geist", und "Geist der Prophetie", in den Targumim und das Verhältnis der Targumim zueinander', *VT* 20 (1970), pp. 304-14.

—*Die Vorstellung vom Heiligen Geist in der rabbinischen Literatur* (Munich: Kösel, 1972).

Schedl, C., *Als sich der Pfingsttag erfüllte: Erklärung der Pfingstperikope Apg 2,1-47* (Vienna: Herder, 1982).

Schille, G., *Die Apostelgeschichte des Lukas* (Berlin: Evangelische Verlagsanstalt, 2nd edn, 1984).

Schmidt, K.L., *Die Pfingsterzählung und das Pfingstereignis* (Leipzig: Hinrichs, 1919).

Schmitt, J., 'L'Eglise de Jérusalem ou la "restauration" d'Israël d'après les cinq premiers chapitres des Actes', *RevSR* 27 (1953), pp. 209-18.

Schneider, D., *Der Geist, der Geschichte macht* (Neukirchen: Aussaat, 1992).

Schneider, G., *Die Apostelgeschichte*, I, II (Freiburg: Herder, 1980, 1982).

—'Die Bitte um das Kommen des Geistes im lukanischen Vaterunser (Lk 11,2 V.l)', in W. Schrage (ed.), *Studien zum Text und zur Ethik des Neuen Testaments* (Berlin: de Gruyter, 1986), pp. 344-76.

—'Jesu geistgewirkte Empfängnis (Lk 1, 34f)', *Theologisch-Praktische Quartalschrift* 119 (1971), pp. 105-16.

Schnider, F., *Jesus der Prophet* (Freiburg: Universitätsverlag, 1973).

Schreck, C.J., 'The Nazareth Pericope: Luke 4.16-30 in Recent Study', in Neirynck (ed.), *L'Evangile*, pp. 399-471.

Schreiner, J., 'Geistbegabung in der Gemeinde von Qumran', *BZ* 8, pp. 161-80.

Schürmann, H., 'Die geistgewirkte Lebensentstehung Jesu', in W. Ernst and K. Feiereis (eds.), *Einheit in Vielfalt* (Leipzig: St Benno, 1974), pp. 156-69.

—*Traditionsgeschichtliche Untersuchungen zu den synoptischen Evangelien* (Düsseldorf: Patmos, 1968).

—'Zur Traditionsgeschichte der Nazareth-Perikope Lk 4.16-30', in Descamps and de Halleux (eds.), *Mélanges bibliques*, pp. 187-205

Schütz, F., *Der leidende Christus: Die angefochtene Gemeinde und das Christus kerygma der lukanischen Schriften* (Stuttgart: Kohlammer, 1969).

Schwagen, R., 'Wassertaufe, ein Gebet um die Geisttaufe?', *ZKT* 100 (1978), pp. 36-61.

Schweizer, E., 'Die Bekehrung des Apollos, Apg 18, 24-26', *Beiträge zur Theologie des Neuen Testaments: Neutestamentliche Aufsätze (1955–1970)* (Zürich: Zwingli Verlag, 1970), pp. 71-79.

—*The Good News according to Luke* (London: SPCK, 1984).

—*The Holy Spirit* (London: SCM Press, 1981).

—'πνεῦμα, κτλ', *TDNT*, VI, pp. 389-455.

—'The Spirit of Power—The Uniformity and Diversity of the Concept of the Holy Spirit in the New Testament', *Int* 6 (1952), pp. 259-78.

Seccombe, D., 'Luke and Isaiah', *NTS* 27 (1981), pp. 252-59.

—*Possessions and the Poor in Luke–Acts* (Linz: SNTU, 1982).

Seifrid, M.A., 'Jesus and the Law in Acts', *JSNT* 30 (1987), pp. 39-57.

Sekki, A.E., *The Meaning of Ruah at Qumran* (Atlanta: Scholars Press, 1989).

Shelton, J.B., ' "Filled with the Holy Spirit" and "Full of the Holy Spirit": Lucan Redactional Phrases', in P. Elbert (ed.), *Faces of Renewal* (Peabody, MA: Hendrickson, 1988), pp. 81-107.

—*Mighty in Word and Deed: The Role of the Holy Spirit in Luke–Acts* (Peabody, MA: Hendrickson, 1991).

—'A Reply to James D.G. Dunn's "Baptism in the Spirit: A Response to Pentecostal Scholarship on Luke–Acts" ', *JPT* 4 (1994), pp. 139-43.

Shepherd, W., *The Narrative Function of the Holy Spirit as Character in Luke–Acts* (Atlanta: Scholars Press, 1994).

Sieber, J.H., 'The Spirit as the "Promise of my Father" ', in Luke 24.49', in Durken (ed.), *Sin*, pp. 271-78.

Sloan, R.B., *The Favorable Year of the Lord: A Study of Jubilary Theology in the Gospel of Luke* (Austin: Schola, 1977).

—' "Signs and Wonders": A Rhetorical Clue to the Pentecost Discourse', *EvQ* 63 (1991), pp. 225-40.

Smail, T., *The Giving Gift: The Holy Spirit in Person* (London: Hodder, 1988).

—*Reflected Glory: The Spirit in Christ and Christians* (London: Hodder, 1975).

Smalley, S.S. 'Spirit, Kingdom and Prayer in Luke–Acts', *NovT* 15 (1973), pp. 59-71.

Smith, M.D., 'Glossolalia and Other Spiritual Gifts in a New Testament Perspective', *Int* 28 (1974), pp. 307-20.

Spencer, F.S., *The Portrait of Philip in Acts* (Sheffield: JSOT Press, 1992).

Squires, J.T., *The Plan of God in Luke–Acts* (Cambridge: Cambridge University Press, 1993).

Stählin, G., 'τὸ πνεῦμα ᾽Ιησοῦ (Apg. 16.7)', in Lindars and Smalley (eds.), *Christ*, pp. 229-52.

—*Die Apostelgeschichte* (Göttingen: Vandenhoeck & Ruprecht, 1970).

Stalder, K., 'Der Heilige Geist in der lukanischen Ekklesiologie', *Una Sancta* 30 (1975), pp. 287-93.

Staley, J.L., ' "With the Power of the Spirit": Plotting the Program and Parallels of Luke 4.14-37', in E.H. Lovering (ed.), *Society of Biblical Literature 1993 Seminar Papers* (Atlanta: Scholars Press, 1993), pp. 281-302.

Stanton, G.N., *Jesus of Nazareth in New Testament Preaching* (Cambridge: Cambridge University Press, 1974).

—'On the Christology of Q', in Lindars and Smalley (eds.), *Christ*, pp. 27-42.

Stolle, V., *Der Zeuge als Angeklagter. Untersuchungen zum Paulusbild des Lukas* (Stuttgart: Kohlhammer, 1973).

Stonehouse, N.B., 'Repentance, Baptism and the Gift of the Holy Spirit', *WTJ* 13 (1950), pp. 1-18.

Stott, J.R.W., *The Baptism and Fullness of the Holy Spirit* (Leicester: Inter-Varsity Press, 2nd edn, 1975).

Strauss, M.L., *The Davidic Messiah in Luke–Acts: The Promise and its Fulfillment in Lukan Christology* (Sheffield: JSOT Press, 1995).

Stravinskas, P.M.J., 'The Role of the Spirit in Acts 1 and 2', *BibTod* 18 (1980), pp. 263-69.

Strobel, A., 'Die Ausrufung des Jobeljahres in der Nazareth-predigt Jesu; zur apokalyptischen Tradition Lc 4 16-30', in W. Eltester (ed.), *Jesus in Nazareth* (Berlin: de Gruyter, 1972), pp. 38-50.

Stronstad, R., *The Charismatic Theology of Saint Luke* (Peabody, MA: Hendrickson, 1984).

Stuhlmacher, P., *Reconciliation, Law and Righteousness: Essays in Biblical Theology* (Philadelphia: Fortress Press, 1986).

Suurmond, J.J., 'The Ethical Influence of the Spirit of God: An Exegetical and Theological Study with Special Reference to 1 Corinthians, Romans 7.14-8.30, and the Johannine Literature' (PhD dissertation, Fuller Theological Seminary, 1983).

Synan, V., 'The Role of Tongues as Initial Evidence', in Wilson (ed.), *Spirit*, pp. 67-82.

Tachau, P., 'Die Pfingstgeschichte nach Lukas: Exegetische Überlegungen zu Apg 2.1-13', *Der evangelische Erzieher* 29 (1977), pp. 86-102.

Taeger, J.W., *Der Mensch und sein Heil: Studien zum Bild des Menschen und zur Sicht der Bekehrung bei Lukas* (Gütersloh: Mohn, 1982).

Talbert, C.H., *Literary Patterns, Theological Themes and the Genre of Luke–Acts* (Missoula: Scholars Press, 1974).

Tannehill, R.C., 'Israel in Luke–Acts: A Tragic Story', *JBL* 104 (1985), pp. 69-85.

—'The Mission of Jesus according to Luke IV.16-30', in W. Eltester (ed.), *Jesus in Nazareth* (Berlin: de Gruyter, 1972), pp. 51-75.

—*The Narrative Unity of Luke–Acts: A Literary Interpetation*. I. *The Gospel according to Luke* (Philadelphia: Fortress Press, 1986).

—*The Narrative Unity of Luke–Acts: A Literary Interpetation*. II. *The Acts of the Apostles* (Philadelphia: Fortress Press, 1990).

Tatum, B., 'The Epoch of Israel: Luke i–ii and the Theological Plan of Luke–Acts', *NTS* 13 (1966-67), pp. 184-95.

Taylor, V., 'The Order of Q', *JTS* 4 (1953), pp. 27-31

Teeple, H.M., *The Mosaic Eschatological Prophet* (Philadelphia: SBL, 1957).

Thiering, B.E., 'Inner and Outer Cleansing at Qumran as a Background to New Testament Baptism', *NTS* 26 (1980), pp. 266-77

Thornton, L.S., *Confirmation: Its Place in the Baptismal Mystery* (Westminster: Dacre, 1954).

Tiede, D.L., 'The Exaltation of Jesus and the Restoration of Israel in Acts 1', *HTR* 79 (1986), pp. 278-86.

—'"Glory to thy People Israel": Luke–Acts and the Jews', in Tyson (ed.), *Luke–Acts*, pp. 21-34.

—*Prophecy and History in Luke–Acts* (Philadelphia: Fortress Press, 1980).

Treves, M., 'The Two Spirits of the Rule of Qumran', *RQ* 3 (1961), pp. 449-52.

Trites, A.A., *The New Testament Concept of Witness* (Cambridge: Cambridge University Press, 1977).

Tuckett, C.M., 'Luke 4.16-30, Isaiah and Q', in J. Delobel (ed.), *Logia: Les paroles de Jésus—The Sayings of Jesus* (Leuven: Leuven University Press, 1982), pp. 343-54.

Turner, M.M.B., '"Empowerment for Mission"? The Pneumatology of Luke–Acts: An Appreciation and Critique of James B. Shelton's *Mighty in Word and Deed*', *VoxEv* 24 (1994), pp. 103-22.

—'Holy Spirit', in J.B. Green and S. McKnight (eds.), *Dictionary of Jesus and the Gospels* (Leicester: Inter-Varsity Press, 1992), pp. 341-51.

—'Jesus and the Spirit in Lucan Perspective', *TynB* 32 (1981), pp. 3-42.

—'Luke and the Spirit: Studies in the Significance of Receiving the Spirit in Luke–Acts' (PhD dissertation, Cambridge, 1980).

—'Prayer in the Gospels and Acts', in D.A. Carson (ed.), *Teach Us To Pray: Prayer in the Bible and the World* (Exeter: Paternoster, 1990), pp. 58-83, 319-25.

—'The Sabbath, the Law, and Sunday in Luke–Acts', in D.A. Carson (ed.), *From Sabbath to Lord's Day* (Grand Rapids: Zondervan, 1982), pp. 100-57.

—'The Significance of Receiving the Spirit in John's Gospel', *VoxEv* 10 (1977), pp. 24-42.

—'The Significance of Receiving the Spirit in Luke–Acts: A Survey of Modern Scholarship', *TrinJ* 2 (1981), pp. 131-58.

—'The Significance of Spirit-Endowment for Paul', *VoxEv* 9 (1975), pp. 56-69.

—'The Spirit and the Power of Jesus' Miracles in the Lucan Conception', *NovT* 33 (1991), pp. 124-52.

—'Spirit Endowment in Luke–Acts: Some Linguistic Considerations', *VoxEv* 12 (1981), pp. 45-63.

—'The Spirit of Christ and Christology', in H.H. Rowdon (ed.), *Christ the Lord* (Leicester: Inter-Varsity Press, 1982), pp. 168-90.

—'The Spirit of Christ and 'Divine', Christology', in Green and Turner (eds.), *Jesus*, pp. 413-36.

—'The Spirit of Prophecy and the Ethical/Religious Life of the Christian Community', in Wilson (ed.), *Spirit*, pp. 166-90.

—'The Spirit of Prophecy and the Power of Authoritative Preaching in Luke–Acts: A Question of Origins', *NTS* 38 (1992), pp. 66-88.

—'Spiritual Gifts: Then and Now', *VoxEv* 15 (1985), pp. 7-64.

Turner, M.M.B., and G.M. Burge., 'The Anointed Community: A Review and Response', *EvQ* 62 (1990), pp. 253-64.

Tyson, J.B., 'The Problem of Jewish Rejection in Acts', in Tyson (ed.), *Luke–Acts*, pp. 124-37.

Tyson, J.B. (ed.), *Luke–Acts and the Jewish People* (Minneapolis: Augsburg, 1988).

Unnik, W.C. van, 'Jesus the Christ', *NTS* 8 (1961–62), pp. 101-16.

Verbeke, G., *L'Evolution de la doctrine du pneuma du stoicisme à S. Augustin* (Paris: Brower, 1945).

Vermes, G., *Jesus the Jew* (London: Collins, 1973).

—*The Dead Sea Scrolls in English* (Sheffield: JSOT Press, 3rd edn, 1987).

Vigne, D., *Christ au Jourdain: Le baptême de Jésus dans la tradition judéo-chrétienne* (Paris: Gabalda, 1992).

Völkel, M., 'Zur Deutung des "Reich Gottes" bei Lukas', *ZNW* 65 (1974), pp. 57-70.

Volz, P., *Der Geist Gottes und die verwandten Erscheinungen im Alten Testament und im anschliessenden Judentum* (Tübingen: Mohr, 1910).

Vos, J., *Traditionsgeschichtliche Untersuchungen zur paulinischen Pneumatologie* (Assen: Van Gorcum, 1973).

Voss, G., *Die Christologie der lukanischen Schriften in Grundzügen* (Paris: Brouwer, 1965).

Weatherly, J.A., 'The Jews in Luke–Acts', *TynBul* 40 (1989), pp. 107-17.

Webb, R.L., 'The Activity of John the Baptist's Expected Figure at the Threshing Floor (Matthew 3.12 = Luke 3.17)', *JSNT* 43 (1991), pp. 103-11.

—'John the Baptist and his Relationship to Jesus', in Chilton and Evans (eds.), *Jesus*, pp. 179-229

—*John the Baptizer and Prophet* (Sheffield: JSOT Press, 1991).

Wedderburn, A.J.M., 'Traditions and Redaction in Acts 2.1-13', *JSNT* 55 (1994), pp. 27-54.

Weiser, A., 'Tradition und lukanische Komposition in Apg 10.36-43', in Aletti *et al.*, *Cause*, pp. 757-68.

Wendt, H.H., *Die Begriffe Fleish und Geist im biblischen Sprachgebrauch* (Gotha, 1878).

Wernberg-Møller, P., 'A Reconsideration of the Two Spirits in the Rule of the Community (I Q Serek III,13–IV,26)', *ResQ* 3 (1961), pp. 413-41.

Wilckens, U., 'Interpreting Luke–Acts in a Period of Existentialist Theology', in Keck and Martyn (eds.), *Studies*, pp. 60-83.

—*Die Missionsreden der Apostelgeschichte: Form- und Traditionsgeschichtliche Untersuchungen* (Neukirchen–Vluyn: Neukirchener Verlag, 1963).

Wilkens, W., 'Wassertaufe und Geistempfang bei Lukas', *TZ* 23 (1967), pp. 26-47.

Wilkinson, T.L., 'Two-Stage Christianity: Baptism with the Holy Spirit', *Vox Reformata* 21 (1973), pp. 1-21.

Williams, G.O., 'The Baptism in Luke's Gospel', *JTS* 45 (1944), pp. 31-38.

Wilson, M.W. (ed.), *Spirit and Renewal: Essays in Honor of J. Rodman Williams* (Sheffield: JSOT Press, 1994).

Wilson, S.G., 'The Ascension: A Critique and an Interpretation', *ZNW* 59 (1968), pp. 269-81.

—*The Gentiles and the Gentile Mission in Luke–Acts* (Cambridge: Cambridge University Press, 1973).

—*Luke and the Law* (Cambridge: Cambridge University Press, 1975).

Windisch, H., 'Jesus und der Geist nach synoptischer Überlieferung', in S.J. Case (ed.), *Studies in Early Christianity* (New York: Century, 1928), pp. 209-36.

Wink, W., *John the Baptist in the Gospel Tradition* (Cambridge: Cambridge University Press, 1968).

Winn, A.C., 'Pneuma and Kerygma: A New Approach to the New Testament Doctrine of the Holy Spirit' (PhD dissertation, Union Theological Seminary, 1956).

Winter, B.W., and A.D. Clarke (eds.), *The Book of Acts in its Ancient Literary Setting: The Book of Acts in its First-Century Setting* (Carlisle: Paternoster, 1993).

Witherup, R.D., 'Cornelius Over and Over Again: "Functional Redundancy" in the Acts of the Apostles', *JSNT* 49 (1993), pp. 45-66.

Wolter, M., 'Apollos und die ephesinischen Johannesjünger (Act 18.24–19.7)', *ZNW* 78 (1987). pp. 49-73.

Woude, A. van der, 'Melchizedek als himmlische Erlösergestalt in den neugefundenen eschatologischen Midraschim aus Qumran Höhle XI', *OTS* 14 (1965), pp. 354-73.

Wright, N.T., *The Climax of the Covenant: Christ and the Law in Pauline Theology* (Edinburgh: T. & T. Clark, 1991).

—*The New Testament and the People of God: Christian Origins and the Question of God: Part I* (London: SPCK, 1992).

Yates, J.E., 'Luke's Pneumatology and Luke 11.20', in F.L. Cross (ed.), *Studia Evangelica*, II (Berlin: Akademie Verlag, 1964), pp. 295-99.

—*The Spirit and the Kingdom* (London: SPCK, 1963).

York, J.O., *The Last Shall Be First: The Rhetoric of Reversal in Luke* (Sheffield: JSOT Press, 1991).

Zehnle, R.H., *Peter's Pentecost Discourse* (New York: Abingdon Press, 1971).

—'The Salvific Character of Jesus' Death in Lukan Soteriology', *TS* 30 (1969), pp. 420-44.

Ziesler, J.A., 'The Name of Jesus in the Acts of the Apostles', *JSNT* 4 (1979), pp. 28-41.

INDEXES

INDEX OF REFERENCES

OLD TESTAMENT

Power from on High

24.47-49	318, 344, 348
24.47	223, 301, 314
24.49	36, 60, 72, 150, 157, 160, 162, 254, 270, 277-79, 295, 296, 300, 302, 304, 332, 341-43, 345, 356, 399, 402, 403, 414, 421, 430, 434, 440
24.51	193
24.53	412, 414
28.23	296
28.31	296
29.30	332
47.1-13	190

John

1.14	165
3.5-16	438
3.34-36	438
4.10	438
4.13-14	438
4.23	263
5.35	265
6.14-15	243
6.63	335, 438
10.4	202
14–17	304
14–16	45
14.6-11	45
14.26	278
16.7	278
16.13	45
20	304
20.22	336
51.26	278

Acts

| 1–15 | 308 |

1–2	306, 341, 358
1	344
1.1-11	268, 288, 294, 421
1.1-8	294
1.1-5	294
1.1	332
1.2-5	294
1.2-4	295, 342
1.2	294, 295, 298, 335, 336, 342, 350
1.3-8	294, 298, 302, 315, 318, 333
1.3-5	294
1.3	285, 295, 298, 332, 333
1.4-8	64, 302, 399, 435
1.4-5	36, 295, 333
1.4	71, 72, 270, 277, 298, 341, 342, 350
1.5-8	187, 294, 402
1.5	64, 149, 173, 176, 187, 201, 268, 277, 295, 298, 299, 301, 302, 304, 306, 341, 345, 350, 380, 386, 387, 405, 413, 421, 437
1.6-11	294
1.6-8	294, 312
1.6	294, 295, 299, 300, 308, 332, 342
1.7-8	299-301, 314, 345
1.7	300
1.8	36, 37, 64, 72, 150, 157, 162, 254, 284, 295, 298, 300-302, 332, 343-45, 348, 350, 356, 371, 378, 392, 394, 396, 398, 399, 402, 403, 414, 415, 424, 432, 434, 437-40
1.9-11	274, 294, 295
1.9	294
1.10-11	295
1.11	296
1.12-26	33, 302
1.14	33, 286, 364, 412
1.15-26	301
1.15	149
1.16	41, 150, 203, 304, 350, 336
1.21-22	172, 195
1.22	294, 298, 329
1.49	415
2–3	243
2	22, 38, 65, 267, 271, 279, 280, 285, 288, 289, 302, 314, 342, 343, 352,

PSEUDEPIGRAPHA

QUMRAN

TARGUMS

RABBINIC WRITINGS

OTHER ANCIENT REFERENCES

INDEX OF AUTHORS